剑桥“英语在用”（English in Use

MW01709459

剑桥中级英语语法

（第四版中文版）

ENGLISH GRAMMAR IN USE

（Fourth Edition）

（英）Raymond Murphy 著

外语教学与研究出版社
FOREIGN LANGUAGE TEACHING AND RESEARCH PRESS
北京 BEIJING
剑桥大学出版社
CAMBRIDGE UNIVERSITY PRESS

京权图字：01-2015-4135

This is a China reprint edition of the following title published by Cambridge University Press:

English Grammar in Use Students Book Intermediate with Answers 4th Edition (ISBN: 9780521189064)

图书在版编目（CIP）数据

剑桥中级英语语法：第四版中文版 /（英）墨菲（Murphy, R.）著. -- 北京：外语教学与研究出版社，2016.3（2019.3 重印）
（剑桥“英语在用”丛书）
ISBN 978-7-5135-7305-4

Ⅰ. ①剑… Ⅱ. ①墨… Ⅲ. ①英语－语法－自学参考资料 Ⅳ. ①H314

中国版本图书馆CIP数据核字（2016）第068279号

出 版 人　蔡剑峰
责任编辑　张红岩
执行编辑　宣婧雅
封面设计　平　原
出版发行　外语教学与研究出版社
社　　址　北京市西三环北路 19 号（100089）
网　　址　http://www.fltrp.com
印　　刷　保定市中画美凯印刷有限公司
开　　本　787×1092　1/16
印　　张　25
版　　次　2016 年 4 月第 1 版 2019 年 3 月第 11 次印刷
书　　号　ISBN 978-7-5135-7305-4
定　　价　49.90 元

购书咨询：（010）88819926　电子邮箱：club@fltrp.com
外研书店：https://waiyants.tmall.com
凡印刷、装订质量问题，请联系我社印制部
联系电话：（010）61207896　电子邮箱：zhijian@fltrp.com
凡侵权、盗版书籍线索，请联系我社法律事务部
举报电话：（010）88817519　电子邮箱：banquan@fltrp.com
物料号：273050001

记载人类文明
沟通世界文化
www.fltrp.com

出版说明

剑桥“英语在用”（English in Use）丛书原由剑桥大学出版社出版，是一套享誉全球的英语学习用书，主要包括英语词汇、短语、习语、惯用搭配和语法等系列，自出版以来，全球销量已逾千万册，既可用于读者自学，也可用于课堂教学，是许多学习者手边必备的参考书。

剑桥“英语在用”丛书专为非英语国家的学习者编写，作者均为剑桥大学出版社卓有经验的权威，内容实例取材于剑桥国际英语语料库，在编排结构上条理明晰，形式简约，重点突出，注重实用；并采取版面左手页讲解、右手页练习，书后附参考答案的方式，达到即学即练的巩固效果。

自2001年以来，外语教学与研究出版社从剑桥大学出版社陆续引进了“英语在用”丛书的词汇、语法系列的学习用书及练习册，深受英语学习者和一些培训学校的青睐和好评。近来剑桥大学出版社重新修订、扩充了丛书内容，并推出了新的版本。鉴于“英语在用”丛书在学习者中的口碑和良好的学习效果，外语教学与研究出版社新引进了“英语在用”丛书的词汇、语法系列的修订新版以及此前未引进的系列（短语、习语等），特此推介给广大的读者，同时稍微更改了纸型和版式，使之更便于阅读。希望读者朋友们通过这套高品质的学习丛书，真正提高自己的英语水平。

剑桥“英语在用”丛书新出版书目：

词汇：

《剑桥入门级英语词汇》（第二版中文版）
《剑桥入门级英语词汇练习》（第二版中文版）
《剑桥初级英语词汇》（第二版中文版）
《剑桥初级英语词汇练习》（第二版中文版）
《剑桥中级英语词汇》（第二版中文版）
《剑桥中级英语词汇练习》（中文版）
《剑桥高级英语词汇》（新中文版）
《剑桥高级英语词汇练习》（新中文版）

短语、习语、惯用搭配：

《剑桥中级英语习语》（中文版）
《剑桥高级英语习语》（中文版）
《剑桥中级英语惯用搭配》（中文版）
《剑桥高级英语惯用搭配》（中文版）
《剑桥中级英语短语动词》（中文版）
《剑桥高级英语短语动词》（中文版）

语法：

《剑桥初级英语语法》（第三版中文版）
《剑桥初级英语语法练习》（第三版中文版）
《剑桥中级英语语法》（第四版中文版）
《剑桥中级英语语法练习》（第四版中文版）
《剑桥高级英语语法》（第二版中文版）

附剑桥“英语在用”丛书原出版书目：

词汇：

《剑桥初级英语词汇》（中文版）
《剑桥中级英语词汇》（中文版）
《剑桥中级英语词汇练习》（中文版）
《剑桥高级英语词汇》（中文版）

《剑桥初级英语词汇》（英文版）
《剑桥中级英语词汇》（英文版）
《剑桥高级英语词汇》（英文版）

语法：

《剑桥初级英语语法》（中文版）
《剑桥初级英语语法练习》（中文版）
《剑桥中级英语语法》（中文版）
《剑桥中级英语语法练习》（中文版）
《剑桥高级英语语法》（中文版）

《剑桥初级英语语法》（英文版）
《剑桥初级英语语法练习》（英文版）
《剑桥中级英语语法》（英文版）
《剑桥中级英语语法练习》（英文版）
《剑桥高级英语语法》（英文版）

目录

如不确定从哪一个单元开始学习，可参考第326页的“学习指导”。

如不确定从哪一个单元开始学习，可参考第326页的“学习指导”。

冠词与名词

代词与限定词

定语从句

如不确定从哪一个单元开始学习，可参考第326页的“学习指导”。

如不确定从哪一个单元开始学习，可参考第326页的“学习指导”。

如不确定从哪一个单元开始学习，可参考第326页的“学习指导”。

Thanks

This is the fourth edition of *English Grammar in Use*. I wrote the original edition when I was a teacher at the Swan School of English, Oxford. I would like to repeat my thanks to my colleagues and students at the school for their help, encouragement and interest at that time.

Regarding the production of this fourth edition, I am grateful to Nóirín Burke, Annabel Marriott, Matthew Duffy, Liz Driscoll, Jane Walsh, Jeanette Alfoldi and Kamae Design. I would like to thank Cambridge University Press for permission to access the Cambridge International Corpus.

Thank you also to the following illustrators: Humberto Blanco, Paul Fellows, Sophie Joyce, Katie Mac, Ian Mitchell, Gillian Martin, Sandy Nicholls, Roger Penwill, Lisa Smith, Dave Whamond and Simon Williams.

致学生

本书主要为英语语法学习者自学使用，也可作为教师的课堂教材。

如果你不确定下列问题的答案是什么，那么这本书将使你获益良多。

- I did 与 I have done 有什么区别？
- 什么情况下用 will 来表示将来？
- I wish 之后用什么句子结构？
- 什么情况下用 used to do，什么情况下用 used to doing？
- 什么情况下用 the？
- like 与 as 有什么区别？

本书将对包括这些内容的语法项目进行详细讲解，并配备了相应的练习。

读者对象

本书主要为已学过基本英语语法知识的中级英语学习者编写，集中讲解那些他们想要使用但感到有些吃力的语法项目。本书也可供高级英语学习者参考使用。

本书结构

本书包括 145 个单元，每个单元着重讲解一个特定的语法项目。有些较难的语法项目（如现在完成时或 the 的用法）需要两个或更多的单元。每个单元的具体内容请参见目录。

每个单元包括两页，左手页是对语法项目的讲解和例句，右手页是相应的练习。书后附有练习答案（第 336 页）。

书后还有 7 个附录（第 292—301 页），列出了不规则动词、动词的各种形式、拼写法和美国英语等。

书的最后部分是索引（第 373 页）。

如何使用本书

本书不是按照从易到难的顺序编写的，因为本书的目的不在于让学习者从头到尾学习一遍各个语法项目，而是让不同的学习者针对自己的语法难点，选择学习。

学习本书可以分为以下 6 个步骤：

- 通过目录和 / 或索引找出自己感兴趣的单元；
- 如果不确定需要学习哪个单元，可以利用第 326 页的“学习指导”进行自测；
- 学习所选单元左手页对语法项目的讲解和例句；

- 做所选单元右手页的练习；
- 对照书后练习答案，检查正误；
- 如果发现答案不正确，重新学习相关的语法项目。

当然，学习者也可以不做练习，仅把本书当作语法学习的参考书使用。

补充练习

本书书后设有补充练习（第 302—325 页）。这些练习帮助学生集中复习巩固书中所讲解过的语法知识。例如，练习 16 是根据第 26—36 单元所讲述的语法项目设计的。

致老师

《剑桥中级英语语法》是一本用于自学的语法书，但老师也可以把它用作课堂教学的补充材料。

本书适合具有中级或中高级英语水平的学习者，帮助他们复习巩固已有的语法知识并学习新的语法结构。本书同样适用于水平更高一些的学习者。

本书内容按语法范畴分类（如现在时与过去时、冠词与名词、介词等）。各单元并不按从易到难的顺序排列，因此无须逐单元学习。老师可以根据教学大纲和学生的学习难点，让学生有选择地灵活使用。

本书既可以在课后练习中使用，也可以用来复习或补习英语语法知识；既可以让全班学生一起使用，也可以让不同的学生针对自己的弱点单独使用。每单元左手页的讲解和例句是为学生自学准备的，但也可以用作老师的教学资料；右手页的练习可以让学生独自完成，也可以课上完成或布置为家庭作业。此外，如果部分学生而非全班学生对某些语法项目存在困难，也可以指导他们自学相关的单元。别忘了使用书后的补充练习（参见“致学生”）。

《剑桥中级英语语法》（第四版）进行了修订和更新。书中没有增加新的单元，但一些练习进行了重新设计或替换。

我们还编写了《剑桥中级英语语法》课堂版，但是没有答案，也许有些老师更喜欢在课堂上使用这本书。

剑桥中级
英语语法

ENGLISH GRAMMAR IN USE

Unit 1

现在进行时 (I am doing)

A 请看下列例句：

Sarah is in her car. She is on her way to work.

She **is driving** to work.

在说话时，她正驾车行驶。驾驶动作还没有完成。

am/is/are + -ing 是现在进行时的构成形式：

I	**am**	(= I'm)	**driving**
he/she/it	**is**	(= he's 等)	**working**
we/you/they	**are**	(= we're 等)	**doing** 等

B **I am doing** something 表示"我正在做某事，我已开始做某事，但尚未完成"。通常在说话时动作仍在进行：

- Please don't make so much noise. **I'm trying** to work. (而不用 I try)
- 'Where's Mark?' 'He**'s having** a shower.' (而不用 He has a shower)
- Let's go out now. It **isn't raining** any more. (而不用 It doesn't rain)
- (*at a party*) Hi, Jane. **Are** you **enjoying** the party? (而不用 Do you enjoy)
- What's all that noise? What'**s going** on? (= What's happening?)

但有时在说话的当下，动作并不是正在进行，例如：

Steve is talking to a friend on the phone. He says:

在说话时，汤姆并不是正在读书。他的意思是这本书他已经开始读了，但还没有读完。

再看一些例句：

- Kate wants to work in Italy, so she**'s learning** Italian. (但在说话的当时她可能并没有在学意大利语)
- Some friends of mine **are building** their own house. They hope to finish it next summer.

C 现在进行时可以与**today / this week / this year** 等连用，表示现在这一阶段正在发生的动作或行为：

- A: You**'re working hard today**. (而不用 You work hard today)
  B: Yes, I have a lot to do.
- The company I work for **isn't doing** so well **this year**.

D 现在进行时常与下列动词连用，表示现在一段时间内正在发生的变化：

get change become increase rise fall grow improve begin start

- **Is** your English **getting** better? (而不用 Does your English get better)
- The population of the world **is increasing** very fast. (而不用 increases)
- At first I didn't like my job, but **I'm beginning** to enjoy it now. (而不用 I begin)

现在进行时与一般现在时比较 ➜ Units 3–4　现在时表示将来 ➜ Unit 19

Exercises

1.1 正确搭配左右两栏的句子。

1 Please don't make so much noise.	a It's getting late.
2 I need to eat something soon.	b They're lying.
3 I don't have anywhere to live right now.	c It's starting to rain.
4 We need to leave soon.	d They're trying to sell it.
5 They don't need their car any more.	e I'm getting hungry.
6 Things are not so good at work.	f ~~I'm trying to work.~~
7 It isn't true what they said.	g I'm looking for an apartment.
8 We're going to get wet.	h The company is losing money.

1 f
2 ....
3 ....
4 ....
5 ....
6 ....
7 ....
8 ....

1.2 用括号中的词完成下列对话。

1 A: I saw Brian a few days ago.
B: Oh, did you? What's he doing these days? (what / he / do)
A: He's at university.
B: ....? (what / he / study)
A: Psychology.
B: .... it? (he / enjoy)
A: Yes, he says it's a very good course.

2 A: Hi, Nicola. How ....? (your new job / go)
B: Not bad. It wasn't so good at first, but .... better now. (it / get)
A: What about Daniel? Is he OK?
B: Yes, but .... his work right now. (he / not / enjoy)
He's been in the same job for a long time and .... to get bored with it. (he / begin)

1.3 用动词的适当形式填空。有时需用否定形式（**I'm not doing** 等）。

1 Please don't make so much noise. I'm trying (I / try) to work.
2 Let's go out now. It isn't raining (it / rain) any more.
3 You can turn off the radio. .... (I / listen) to it.
4 Kate phoned me last night. She's on holiday in France. .... (she / have) a great time and doesn't want to come back.
5 I want to lose weight, so this week .... (I / eat) lunch.
6 Andrew has just started evening classes. .... (he / learn) Japanese.
7 Paul and Sally have had an argument. .... (they / speak) to each other.
8 .... (I / get) tired. I need a rest.
9 Tim .... (work) today. He's taken the day off.
10 .... (I / look) for Sophie. Do you know where she is?

1.4 用下列动词完成句子。

start get ~~increase~~ change rise

1 The population of the world is increasing very fast.
2 The world .... Things never stay the same.
3 The situation is already bad and it .... worse.
4 The cost of living .... Every year things are more expensive.
5 The weather .... to improve. The rain has stopped, and the wind isn't as strong.

Unit 2

一般现在时 (I do)

A

请看下列例句：

Alex is a bus driver, but now he is in bed asleep.
因此：He is not driving a bus. (He is asleep.)

但是：He **drives** a bus. (He is a bus driver.)

drive(s)/**work**(s)/**do**(es) 等是一般现在时的构成形式：

I/we/you/they	**drive/work/do** 等
he/she/it	**drives/works/does** 等

B

一般现在时用来谈论现时的情况或状态，它用来表示一直发生的动作或行为，或是重复发生的动作或行为，或是普遍的真理，而动作是否发生在说话的当时并不重要：

- Nurses **look** after patients in hospitals.
- I usually **go** away at weekends.
- The earth **goes** round the sun.
- The café **opens** at 7.30 in the morning.

注意，用 **he/she/it** 作主语时，动词原形后要加 **-s**，**-es** 或变为其他形式：

I **work** … 但用 He **works** … They **teach** … 但用 My sister **teaches** …

有关一般现在时动词第三人称单数的拼写法，参见附录6。

C

我们用 **do/does** 来构成一般现在时的疑问句和否定句：

do **does**	I/we/you/they he/she/it	**work**? **drive**? **do**?

I/we/you/they he/she/it	**don't** **doesn't**	**work** **drive** **do**

- I come from Canada. Where **do** you **come** from?
- I **don't go** away very often.
- What **does** this word **mean**? (而不用 What means this word?)
- Rice **doesn't grow** in cold climates.

在下列例句中，**do**和**doesn't**后的**do**是主要动词：

- 'What **do** you **do**?' 'I work in a shop.'
- He's always so lazy. He **doesn't do** anything to help.

D

一般现在时用来表示经常发生的动作或行为：

- I **get** up at 8 o'clock **every morning**.
- **How often** do you **go** to the dentist?
- Julie **doesn't drink** tea **very often**.
- Robert usually **goes** away **two or three times a year**.

E

I promise / I apologise 等

有些行为是靠说话完成的。如作出允诺，可以说**I promise** …；提建议，可以说**I suggest** …。在这类句子中使用一般现在时：

- **I promise** I won't be late. (而不用 I'm promising)
- 'What do you **suggest** I do?' '**I suggest** that you …'

同样也可以说：**I apologise** … / **I advise** … / **I insist** … / **I agree** … / **I refuse** … 等。

现在进行时与一般现在时比较 → Units 3–4 现在时表示将来 → Unit 19

Exercises

2.1 用下列动词完成句子。

cause(s) **connect(s)** **drink(s)** **live(s)** **open(s)** ~~**speak(s)**~~ **take(s)**

1 Tanya ...speaks... German very well.
2 I don't often .... coffee.
3 The swimming pool .... at 7.30 every morning.
4 Bad driving .... many accidents.
5 My parents .... in a very small flat.
6 The Olympic Games .... place every four years.
7 The Panama Canal .... the Atlantic and Pacific oceans.

2.2 用括号内动词的适当形式填空。

1 Julie ...doesn't drink... (not / drink) tea very often.
2 What time .... (the banks / close) here?
3 I've got a car, but I .... (not / use) it much.
4 'Where .... (Ricardo / come) from?' 'From Cuba.'
5 'What .... (you / do)?' 'I'm an electrician.'
6 It .... (take) me an hour to get to work. How long .... (it / take) you?
7 Look at this sentence. What .... (this word / mean)?
8 David isn't very fit. He .... (not / do) any sport.

2.3 用下列动词的适当形式填空，有时需用否定形式。

believe **eat** **flow** ~~**go**~~ ~~**grow**~~ **make** **rise** **tell** **translate**

1 The earth ...goes... round the sun.
2 Rice ...doesn't grow... in Britain.
3 The sun .... in the east.
4 Bees .... honey.
5 Vegetarians .... meat.
6 An atheist .... in God.
7 An interpreter .... from one language into another.
8 Liars are people who .... the truth.
9 The River Amazon .... into the Atlantic Ocean.

2.4 根据莉萨与她家庭的情况提问。

1 You know that Lisa plays tennis. You want to know how often. Ask her.
How often ...do you play tennis... ?
2 Perhaps Lisa's sister plays tennis too. You want to know. Ask Lisa.
.... your sister .... ?
3 You know that Lisa reads a newspaper every day. You want to know which one. Ask her.
.... ?
4 You know that Lisa's brother works. You want to know what he does. Ask Lisa.
.... ?
5 You know that Lisa goes to the cinema a lot. You want to know how often. Ask her.
.... ?
6 You don't know where Lisa's grandparents live. You want to know. Ask Lisa.
.... ?

2.5 用下列短语完成句子。

I apologise **I insist** **I promise** **I recommend** ~~**I suggest**~~

1 Mr Evans is not in the office today. ...I suggest... you try calling him tomorrow.
2 I won't tell anybody what you said. ....
3 (*in a restaurant*) You must let me pay for the meal. ....
4 .... for what I did. It won't happen again.
5 The new restaurant in Hill Street is very good. .... it.

现在进行时 (I am doing) 与一般现在时 (I do) 比较 (1)

A

请看下列例句：

现在进行时 (I am doing)

现在进行时表示说话时正在发生的行为，动作还没有完成。

I am doing

过去 现在 将来

- The water **is boiling**. Can you turn it off?
- Listen to those people. What language **are** they **speaking**?
- Let's go out. It **isn't raining** now.
- 'I'm busy.' 'What **are** you **doing**?'
- **I'm getting** hungry. Let's go and eat.
- Kate wants to work in Italy, so she**'s learning** Italian.
- The population of the world **is increasing** very fast.

现在进行时表示暂时的情况：

- **I'm living** with some friends until I find a place of my own.
- A: You**'re working** hard today.
  B: Yes, I have a lot to do.

更多信息参见Unit 1。

一般现在时 (I do)

一般现在时表示一般性的或经常性的行为。

I do

过去 现在 将来

- Water **boils** at 100 degrees Celsius.
- Excuse me, **do** you **speak** English?
- It **doesn't rain** very much in summer.
- What **do** you usually **do** at weekends?
- I always **get** hungry in the afternoon.
- Most people **learn** to swim when they are children.
- Every day the population of the world **increases** by about 200,000 people.

一般现在时表示永久的情况：

- My parents **live** in London. They have lived there all their lives.
- Joe isn't lazy. He **works** hard most of the time.

更多信息参见Unit 2。

B

I always do 与 **I'm always doing**比较

I always do (something) 表示"我总是做（某事）"：

- I **always go** to work by car. (而不用 I'm always going)

还可以说 **I'm always doing** something，但表达的意思不同。例如：

I'm always losing things 表示经常丢东西，到了不正常的程度。

再看一些例句：

- You**'re always playing** computer games. You should do something more active. (= You play computer games too often)
- Tim is never satisfied. He**'s always complaining**. (= He complains too much)

现在进行时与一般现在时比较 (2) ➜ Unit 4　　现在时表示将来 ➜ Unit 19

Exercises

3.1 下列句子中画线部分的动词是否正确？如有错误，请改正。

1 Water <u>boils</u> at 100 degrees Celsius. 对
2 The water <u>boils</u>. Can you turn it off? 错：is boiling
3 Look! That man <u>tries</u> to open the door of your car. ……
4 Can you hear those people? What <u>do they talk</u> about? ……
5 The moon <u>goes</u> round the earth in about 27 days. ……
6 I must go now. <u>It gets</u> late. ……
7 <u>I usually go</u> to work by car. ……
8 'Hurry up! It's time to leave.' 'OK, <u>I come</u>.' ……
9 I hear you've got a new job. How <u>do you get</u> on? ……
10 Paul is never late. <u>He's always getting</u> to work on time. ……
11 They don't get on well. <u>They're always arguing</u>. ……

3.2 用动词的现在进行时或一般现在时形式填空。

1 Let's go out. It isn't raining (it / not / rain) now.
2 Julia is very good at languages. She speaks (she / speak) four languages very well.
3 Hurry up! …… (everybody / wait) for you.
4 '…… (you / listen) to the radio?' 'No, you can turn it off.'
5 '…… (you / listen) to the radio every day?' 'No, just occasionally.'
6 The River Nile …… (flow) into the Mediterranean.
7 The river …… (flow) very fast today – much faster than usual.
8 …… (we / usually / grow) vegetables in our garden, but this year …… (we / not / grow) any.
9 A: How's your English?
B: Not bad. I think …… (it / improve) slowly.
10 Rachel is in New York right now. …… (she / stay) at the Park Hotel. …… (she / always / stay) there when she's in New York.
11 Can we stop walking soon? …… (I / start) to feel tired.
12 A: Can you drive?
B: …… (I / learn). My father …… (teach) me.
13 Normally …… (I / finish) work at five, but this week …… (I / work) until six to earn a little more money.
14 My parents …… (live) in Manchester. They were born there and have never lived anywhere else. Where …… (your parents / live)?
15 Sonia …… (look) for a place to live. …… (she / stay) with her sister until she finds somewhere.
16 A: What …… (your brother / do)?
B: He's an architect, but …… (he / not / work) at the moment.
17 (*at a party*) …… (I / usually enjoy) parties, but …… (I /not / enjoy) this one very much.

3.3 用 **always + -ing** 完成下列对话。

1 A: I've lost my phone again.
B: Not again! You're always losing your phone.
2 A: The car has broken down again.
B: That car is useless. It …… .
3 A: Look! You've made the same mistake again.
B: Oh no, not again! I …… .
4 A: Oh, I've forgotten my glasses again.
B: Typical! …… .

Unit 4

现在进行时 (I am doing) 与一般现在时 (I do) 比较 (2)

A

进行时用来表示已经开始但尚未结束的动作或行为（they **are eating** / it **is raining** 等）。有些动词（如 **know** 和 **like**）通常不用于进行时，因此不能说 I am knowing 或 they are liking，而要说 I **know** 或 they **like**。

下列动词通常不用于现在进行时：

like	**want**	**need**	**prefer**			
know	**realise**	**suppose**	**mean**	**understand**	**believe**	**remember**
belong	**fit**	**contain**	**consist**	**seem**		

- I'm hungry. I **want** something to eat. (而不用 I'm wanting)
- **Do** you **understand** what I **mean**?
- Anna **doesn't seem** very happy at the moment.

B

think

当 **think** 意为"认为"时，不用于进行时：

- I **think** Mary is Canadian, but I'm not sure. (而不用 I'm thinking)
- What **do** you **think** of my plan? (= What is your opinion?)

当 **think** 意为"考虑"时，可以用于进行时：

- **I'm thinking** about what happened. I often **think** about it.
- Nicky **is thinking** of giving up her job. (= she is considering it)

C

see hear smell taste

上述动词通常用于一般现在时，而不用于进行时：

- **Do** you **see** that man over there? (而不用 Are you seeing)
- This room **smells**. Let's open a window.

经常用 **can** + **see/hear/smell/taste**：

- **I can hear** a strange noise. **Can** you **hear** it?

D

look feel

look 和 **feel** 可以用于一般现在时或现在进行时来表示某人现在的表情或感觉：

- You **look** well today. 或 You**'re looking** well today.
- How **do** you **feel** now? 或 How **are** you **feeling** now?

但是

- I usually **feel** tired in the morning. (而不用 I'm usually feeling)

E

He is selfish 与 **He is being selfish** 比较

He**'s being** 表示"行为举止/动作表现"，相当于 he is behaving/he's acting。请比较：

- I can't understand why he**'s being** so selfish. He isn't usually like that.
  (**being** selfish 表示此时此刻的行为自私)
- He never thinks about other people. He **is** very selfish. (而不用 He is being)
  (他平常都很自私，不仅仅表现在此时此刻)

用 **am/is/are being** 来表示某人的行为，通常不用于其他句子中：

- It**'s** hot today. (而不用 It is being hot)
- Sarah **is** very tired. (而不用 is being tired)

现在进行时与一般现在时比较 (1) ➜ Unit 3 **have** ➜ Unit 17 现在时表示将来 ➜ Unit 19

Exercises

4.1 用动词的现在进行时或一般现在时形式填空。

1 Are you hungry? ....Do you want.... (you / want) something to eat?
2 Don't put the dictionary away. .... (I / use) it.
3 Don't put the dictionary away. .... (I / need) it.
4 Who is that man? What .... (he / want)?
5 Who is that man? Why .... (he / look) at us?
6 Alan says he's 80 years old, but nobody .... (believe) him.
7 She told me her name, but .... (I / not / remember) it now.
8 .... (I / think) of selling my car. Would you be interested in buying it?
9 .... (I / think) you should sell your car. .... (you / not / use) it very often.
10 Air .... (consist) mainly of nitrogen and oxygen.

4.2 看下列几幅图，用括号内的词造句。（在做这个练习前应先复习一遍 Unit 3。）

4.3 画线部分的动词是否正确？如有错误，请改正。

1 Nicky <u>is thinking</u> of giving up her job. ....对....
2 <u>Are</u> you <u>believing</u> in God? ....
3 <u>I'm feeling</u> hungry. Is there anything to eat? ....
4 This sauce is great. It<u>'s tasting</u> really good. ....
5 <u>I'm thinking</u> this is your key. Am I right? ....

4.4 用动词 **be** 的一般现在时（**am / is / are**）或现在进行时（**am / is / are / being**）形式完成句子。

1 I can't understand why ....he's being.... so selfish. He isn't usually like that.
2 Sarah .... very nice to me at the moment. I wonder why.
3 You'll like Sophie when you meet her. She .... very nice.
4 You're usually very patient, so why .... so unreasonable about waiting ten more minutes?
5 Why isn't Steve at work today? .... ill?

一般过去时 (I did)

A

请看下列例句：

Wolfgang Amadeus Mozart **was** an Austrian musician and composer. He **lived** from 1756 to 1791. He **started** composing at the age of five and **wrote** more than 600 pieces of music. He **was** only 35 years old when he **died**.

lived/started/wrote/was/died 都是一般过去时的构成形式。

B

动词的一般过去式是将动词原形变成以 **-ed** 结尾（规则动词）：

- I work in a travel agency now. Before that I **worked** in a department store.
- We **invited** them to our party, but they **decided** not to come.
- The police **stopped** me on my way home last night.
- Laura **passed** her exam because she **studied** very hard.

有关拼写法（sto**pp**ed，stud**ied** 等），参见附录6。

但许多动词的过去式是不规则的，并非是以 **-ed** 结尾，例如：

write → **wrote**		Mozart **wrote** more than 600 pieces of music.
see → **saw**		We **saw** Tanya in town a few days ago.
go → **went**		I **went** to the cinema three times last week.
shut → **shut**		It was cold, so I **shut** the window.

不规则动词表参见附录1。

C

我们用 **did/didn't** + 动词原形来构成一般过去时的疑问句和否定句：

I she they	**enjoyed** **saw** **went**

did	you she they	**enjoy**? **see**? **go**?

I she they	**didn't**	**enjoy** **see** **go**

- A: **Did** you **go** out last night?
  B: Yes, I **went** to the cinema, but I **didn't enjoy** the film much.
- 'When **did** Mr Thomas **die**?' 'About ten years ago.'
- They **didn't invite** us to the party, so we **didn't go**.
- '**Did** you **have** time to do the shopping?' 'No, I **didn't**.'

在下列例句中，**did** 和 **didn't** 后的 **do** 是主要动词：

- What **did** you **do** at the weekend? （而不用 What did you at the weekend?）
- I **didn't do** anything. （而不用 I didn't anything）

D

动词 **be (am/is/are)** 的过去式是 **was/were**：

I/he/she/it	**was/wasn't**
we/you/they	**were/weren't**

was	I/he/she/it?
were	we/you/they?

注意，在有 **was/were** 的句子中，不使用 **did** 来构成否定句和疑问句：

- I **was** angry because they **were** late.
- **Was** the weather good when you **were** on holiday?
- They **weren't** able to come because they **were** so busy.
- Did you go out last night or **were** you too tired?

一般过去时与过去进行时比较 ➜ Unit 6　　一般过去时与现在完成时比较 ➜ Units 12–14

Exercises

5.1 读下列劳拉所讲的通常一个工作日的情况：

I usually get up at 7 o'clock and have a big breakfast. I walk to work, which takes me about half an hour. I start work at 8.45. I never have lunch. I finish work at 5 o'clock. I'm always tired when I get home. I usually cook a meal in the evening. I don't usually go out. I go to bed at about 11 o'clock, and I always sleep well.

Laura

昨天是劳拉的一个典型的工作日。写出她做了什么或没做什么。

1 She got up at 7 o'clock.
2 She ...... a big breakfast.
3 She ....
4 It ...... to get to work.
5 ...... at 8.45.
6 ...... lunch.
7 ...... at 5 o'clock.
8 ...... tired when ...... home.
9 ...... a meal yesterday evening.
10 ...... out yesterday evening.
11 ...... at 11 o'clock.
12 ...... well last night.

5.2 用下列动词的正确形式完成句子。

buy catch cost fall hurt sell spend teach throw ~~write~~

1 Mozart wrote more than 600 pieces of music.
2 'How did you learn to drive?' 'My father ...... me.'
3 We couldn't afford to keep our car, so we ...... it.
4 Dave ...... down the stairs this morning and ...... his leg.
5 Joe ...... the ball to Sue, who ...... it.
6 Ann ...... a lot of money yesterday. She ...... a dress which ...... £100.

5.3 詹姆斯刚刚度假归来，你向他询问情况。写出你的问题。

Hi. How are things?

Fine, thanks. I've just had a great holiday.

1 Where did you go ?

To the U.S. We went on a trip from San Francisco to Denver.

2 How ...... ? By car?

Yes, we hired a car in San Francisco.

3 It's a long way to drive. How long ...... to get to Denver?

Two weeks.

4 Where ...... ? In hotels?

Yes, small hotels or motels.

5 ...... good?

Yes, but it was very hot – sometimes too hot.

6 ...... the Grand Canyon?

Of course. It was wonderful.

5.4 用括号内动词的正确形式完成下列句子，有时需用否定形式。

1 It was warm, so I took off my coat. (take)
2 The film wasn't very good. I didn't enjoy it much. (enjoy)
3 I knew Sarah was busy, so I ...... her. (disturb)
4 We were very tired, so we ...... the party early. (leave)
5 The bed was very uncomfortable. I ...... well. (sleep)
6 The window was open and a bird ...... into the room. (fly)
7 The hotel wasn't very expensive. It ...... much to stay there. (cost)
8 I was in a hurry, so I ...... time to phone you. (have)
9 It was hard carrying the bags. They ...... very heavy. (be)

Unit 6

过去进行时 (I was doing)

A

请看下列例句：

Yesterday Karen and Jim played tennis. They started at 10 o'clock and finished at 11.30.
So, at 10.30 they **were playing** tennis.

they **were playing** 表示他们当时正在打网球，还没有结束。
was/were + -ing 是过去进行时的构成形式：

I/he/she/it	**was**	**playing**
we/you/they	**were**	**doing**
		working 等

B

过去进行时表示过去某个时间某人正在进行的动作。这个动作或情形在这个时间点之前已经开始了，而且还没有完成或结束。

I started doing → **I was doing** → **I finished doing**

过去 ... 过去 ... 现在

- This time last year I **was living** in Brazil.
- What **were** you **doing** at 10 o'clock last night?
- I waved to Helen, but she **wasn't looking**.

C

请比较过去进行时（I **was doing**）与一般过去时（I **did**）：

过去进行时（动作在进行中）	一般过去时（完成的动作）
I **was walking** home when I met Dan.（在步行回家途中）	I **walked** home after the party last night.（全程步行，已完成）
Kate **was watching** TV when we arrived.	Kate **watched** TV a lot when she was ill last year.

D

一般过去时经常与过去进行时配合使用，表示一个动作发生时，另一动作正在进行：

- Matt **phoned** while we **were having** dinner.
- It **was raining** when I **got** up.
- I **saw** you in the park yesterday. You **were sitting** on the grass and **reading** a book.
- I **hurt** my back while I **was working** in the garden.

但是一般过去时也用来说明动作发生的先后顺序：

- I **was walking** along the road when I **saw** Dan. So I **stopped**, and we **had** a chat.

请比较：

When Karen arrived, we **were having** dinner.（在卡伦来之前，我们已经开始吃晚餐）	When Karen arrived, we **had** dinner.（卡伦来之后，我们开始吃晚餐）

E

有些动词（如 **know** 和 **want**）通常不用于进行时（参见Unit 4A）：

- We were good friends. We **knew** each other well.（而不用 We were knowing）
- I was enjoying the party, but Chris **wanted** to go home.（而不用 was wanting）

Exercises

6.1 下列时间你在做什么？仿照示例造句，有时可以不用过去进行时（参见示例2）。

1 (at 8 o'clock yesterday evening) I was having dinner.
2 (at 5 o'clock last Monday) I was on a bus on my way home.
3 (at 10.15 yesterday morning) ....
4 (at 4.30 this morning) ....
5 (at 7.45 yesterday evening) ....
6 (half an hour ago) ....

6.2 根据你自己的想法，用过去进行时完成下列句子。

1 Matt phoned while we were having dinner.
2 The doorbell rang while I ....
3 The car began to make a strange noise when we ....
4 Jessica fell asleep while she ....
5 The television was on, but nobody ....

6.3 用括号内动词的过去进行时或一般过去时形式填空。

1

I saw (see) Sue in town yesterday, but she .... (not / see) me. She .... (look) the other way.

2

I .... (meet) Tom and Jane at the airport a few weeks ago. They .... (go) to Paris and I .... (go) to Rome. We .... (have) a chat while we .... (wait) for our flights.

I .... (cycle) home yesterday when a man .... (step) out into the road in front of me. I .... (go) quite fast, but luckily I .... (manage) to stop in time and .... (not / hit) him.

6.4 用动词的过去进行时或一般过去时形式填空。

1 Jenny was waiting (wait) for me when I arrived (arrive).
2 'What .... (you / do) at this time yesterday?' 'I was asleep.'
3 '.......... (you / go) out last night?' 'No, I was too tired.'
4 How fast .... (you / drive) when the accident .... (happen)?
5 Sam .... (take) a picture of me while I .... (not / look).
6 We were in a very difficult position. We .... (not / know) what to do.
7 I haven't seen Alan for ages. When I last .... (see) him, he .... (try) to find a job.
8 I .... (walk) along the street when suddenly I .... (hear) footsteps behind me. Somebody .... (follow) me. I was scared and I .... (start) to run.
9 When I was young, I .... (want) to be a pilot.
10 Last night I .... (drop) a plate when I .... (do) the washing-up. Fortunately it .... (not / break).

➜ 补充练习（第302页）

Unit 7 现在完成时 (1) (I have done)

A

请看下列例句：

Tom is looking for his key. He can't find it.
He **has lost** his key.

He **has lost** his key 表示他把钥匙弄丢了且仍未找到。

have/has lost 是现在完成时的构成形式：

I/we/they/you **have** (= **I've** 等)	**finished** **lost**
he/she/it **has** (= **he's** 等)	**done** **been** 等

现在完成时由 **have/has** + 过去分词构成。规则动词的过去分词是在动词原形后加 **-ed**（finish**ed**/decid**ed** 等），但许多重要动词的过去分词是不规则的（**lost/done/written** 等）。

不规则动词表参见附录1。

B

现在完成时常用于提供新的信息或告知最近发生的事情：

- Ow! **I've cut** my finger.
- The road is closed. There**'s been** (there **has been**) an accident.
- (*from the news*) Police **have arrested** two men in connection with the robbery.

现在完成时总是与现在有着密切的联系，表示过去的动作对现在有影响：

- 'Where's your key?' 'I don't know. **I've lost** it.' (= I don't have it *now*)
- He told me his name, but **I've forgotten** it. (= I can't remember it *now*)
- 'Is Sally here?' 'No, she**'s gone** out.' (= She is out *now*)
- I can't find my bag. **Have** you **seen** it? (= Do you know where it is *now*)

C

注意 **gone (to)** 和 **been (to)** 的区别：

- James is on holiday. He **has gone to** Italy. (= he is there now or on his way there)
- Jane is back home now. She **has been to** Italy. (= she has now come back)

D

现在完成时可以与 **just**，**already** 和 **yet** 连用：

just 表示"方才，刚刚"：

- 'Are you hungry?' 'No, **I've just had** lunch.'
- Hello. **Have** you **just arrived**?

already 用于说明动作在预计的时间之前发生了：

- 'Don't forget to pay your electricity bill.' '**I've already paid** it.'
- 'What time is Mark leaving?' 'He**'s already left**.'

yet 表示"到目前为止"。**yet** 表明说话者期待某事发生，只用于疑问句和否定句：

- **Has** it **stopped** raining **yet**?
- I've written the email, but I **haven't sent** it **yet**.

E

本页中给出的例句也可以用一般过去时 (**did**，**went**，**had** 等)，如可以说：

- 'Is Sally here?' 'No, she **went** out.' 或 'No, she**'s gone** out.'
- 'Are you hungry?' 'No, I **just had** lunch.' 或 'No, I**'ve just had** lunch.'

现在完成时 ➔ Units 8，11　been to ➔ Units 8A，126A　现在完成进行时 ➔ Units 9–10
现在完成时与一般过去时比较 ➔ Units 12–14　yet 与 already 比较 ➔ Unit 111　美国英语 ➔ 附录 7

Exercises

7.1 根据所给情况，用下列动词的现在完成时形式造句。

arrive **break** **fall** **go up** **grow** **improve** ~~**lose**~~

1 Tom is looking for his key. He can't find it. Tom has lost his key.
2 Lisa can't walk and her leg is in plaster. Lisa ......
3 Last week the bus fare was £1.80. Now it is £2. The bus fare ......
4 Maria's English wasn't very good. Now it is better. Her English ......
5 Dan didn't have a beard before. Now he has a beard. Dan ......
6 This morning I was expecting a letter. Now I have it. The letter ......
7 The temperature was 20 degrees. Now it is only 12. The ......

7.2 用**been** 或 **gone** 填空。

1 James is on holiday. He's gone to Italy.
2 Hello! I've just ...... to the shops. I've bought lots of things.
3 Alice isn't here at the moment. She's ...... to the shop to get a newspaper.
4 Tom has ...... out. He'll be back in about an hour.
5 'Are you going to the bank?' 'No, I've already ...... to the bank.'

7.3 用括号内的词完成B所说的话。

	A	B
1	Would you like something to eat?	No, thanks. I've just had lunch. (I / just / have / lunch)
2	Do you know where Julia is?	Yes, ... (I / just / see / her)
3	What time is David leaving?	...... (he / already / leave)
4	What's in the newspaper today?	I don't know. ...... (I / not / read / it yet)
5	Is Sue coming to the cinema with us?	No, ... (she / already / see / the film)
6	Are your friends here yet?	Yes, ... (they / just / arrive)
7	What does Tim think about your plan?	...... (we / not / tell / him yet)

7.4 根据所给情况，用 **just**，**already** 或 **yet** 造句。

1 After lunch you go to see a friend at her house. She says, 'Would you like something to eat?'
You say: No thank you. I've just had lunch. (have lunch)
2 Joe goes out. Five minutes later, the phone rings and the caller says, 'Can I speak to Joe?'
You say: I'm afraid .... (go out)
3 You are eating in a restaurant. The waiter thinks you have finished and starts to take your plate away. You say: Wait a minute! .... (not / finish)
4 You plan to eat at a restaurant tonight. You phoned to reserve a table. Later your friend says, 'Shall I phone to reserve a table?' You say: No, ... (do it)
5 You know that a friend of yours is looking for a place to live. Perhaps she has been successful. Ask her. You say: ...... ? (find)
6 You are still thinking about where to go for your holiday. A friend asks, 'Where are you going for your holiday?' You say: .... (not / decide)
7 Linda went shopping, but a few minutes ago she returned. Somebody asks, 'Is Linda still out shopping?' You say: No, ... (come back)

Unit 8

现在完成时 (2) (I have done)

A

请看下列对话：

DAVE: **Have** you **travelled** a lot, Jane?
JANE: Yes, **I've been** to lots of places.
DAVE: Really? **Have** you ever **been** to China?
JANE: Yes, **I've been** to China twice.
DAVE: What about India?
JANE: No, I **haven't been** to India.

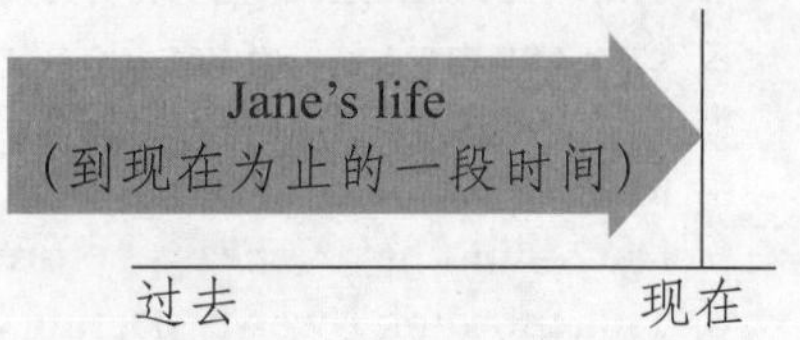

现在完成时（**have been** / **have travelled** 等）表示从过去某一个时间点开始一直持续到现在的动作。在这里，戴夫和简正在谈论简曾去过的地方，指开始于过去持续到现在的一段时间。

再看一些例句：

- **Have** you ever **eaten** caviar?
- We**'ve** never **had** a car.
- '**Have** you **read** *Hamlet*?' 'No, I **haven't read** any of Shakespeare's plays.'
- Susan really loves that film. She**'s seen** it eight times!
- What a boring film! It's the most boring film **I've ever seen**.

been (to) 意为"去过，到过，参观过"：

- **I've** never **been to** China. Have you **been** there?

B

在下列例句中，说话者也正在谈论从过去持续到现在的一段时间内 (**recently** / **in the last few days** / **so far** / **since breakfast** 等)发生的动作：

- **Have** you **heard** anything from Brian **recently**?
- **I've met** a lot of people **in the last few days**.
- Everything is going well. We **haven't had** any problems **so far**.
- I'm hungry. I **haven't eaten** anything **since breakfast**. (= from breakfast until now)
- It's good to see you again. We **haven't seen** each other **for a long time**.

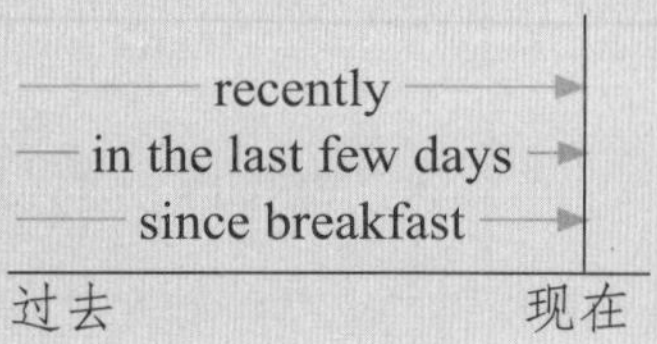

C

如果说话的当时仍处于"今天/今晚/今年等"时间段，现在完成时也可以与 **today** / **this evening** / **this year** 等连用：

- **I've drunk** four cups of coffee today.
- **Have** you **had** a holiday **this year**?
- I **haven't seen** Tom **this morning**. **Have** you?
- Rob **hasn't worked** very hard **this term**.

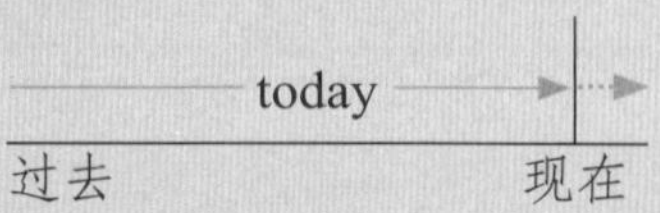

D

可以说 It's the (first) time something **has happened**。例如：

- Don is having a driving lesson. It's his first one.
  It's the first time he **has driven** a car. （而不用 drives）
  或 He **has never driven** a car **before**.
- Sarah has lost her passport again. This is the second time this **has happened**. （而不用 happens）
- Bill is phoning his girlfriend again. That's the third time he**'s phoned** her **this evening**.

现在完成时 (1) ➜ Unit 7　　现在完成时与 for/since 连用 ➜ Units 11–12
现在完成时与一般过去时比较 ➜ Units 12–14

Exercises

8.1 用 **ever** 造句，询问人们都做了什么。

1 (ride / horse?) Have you ever ridden a horse?
2 (be / California?) Have ……
3 (run / marathon?) ……
4 (speak / famous person?) ……
5 (most beautiful place / visit?) What's ……

8.2 用下列动词完成对话。有些用肯定形式，有些用否定形式。

be be eat happen ~~have~~ have ~~meet~~ play read see try

	A	B
1	What's Mark's sister like?	I've no idea. I've never met her.
2	Is everything going well?	Yes, we haven't had any problems so far.
3	Are you hungry?	Yes. I …… much today.
4	Can you play chess?	Yes, but …… for ages.
5	Are you enjoying your holiday?	Yes, it's the best holiday …… for a long time.
6	What's that book like?	I don't know. …… it.
7	Is Brussels an interesting place?	I've no idea. …… there.
8	I hear your car broke down again yesterday.	Yes, it's the second time …… this month.
9	Do you like caviar?	I don't know. …… it.
10	Mike was late for work again today.	Again? He …… late every day this week.
11	Who's that woman by the door?	I don't know. …… her before.

8.3 根据你自己的情况，用 **I haven't** 和方框中的词造句。

used a computer **travelled by bus** **eaten any fruit**
been to the cinema **read a book** **lost anything**

today
this week
recently
for ages
since ...
this year

1 I haven't used a computer today.
2 ……
3 ……
4 ……
5 ……

8.4 根据所给情况，仿照示例造句。

1 Jack is driving a car, but he's very nervous and not sure what to do.
You ask: Have you driven a car before?
He says: No, this is the first time I've driven a car.

2 Ben is playing tennis. He's not good at it and he doesn't know the rules.
You ask: Have ……
He says: No, this is the first ……

3 Sue is riding a horse. She doesn't look very confident or comfortable.
You ask: ……
She says: ……

4 Maria is in Japan. She has just arrived and it's very new for her.
You ask: ……
She says: ……

Unit 9 现在完成进行时 (I have been doing)

A

It has been raining.

请看下列例句：

Is it raining?

No, but the ground is wet.

It has been raining.

have/has been + -ing 是现在完成进行时的构成形式：

I/we/they/you **have** (= **I've** 等) he/she/it **has** (= **he's** 等)	**been**	**doing** **waiting** **playing** 等

现在完成进行时表示不久之前结束的或刚刚结束的动作，这个动作与现在有关联：

- You're out of breath. **Have** you **been running**? (= you're out of breath *now*)
- Paul is very tired. He**'s been working** very hard. (= he's tired *now*)
- Why are your clothes so dirty? What **have** you **been doing**?
- **I've been talking** to Amanda about the problem and she agrees with me.
- Where have you been? **I've been looking** for you everywhere.

B

It has been raining for two hours.

请看下列例句：

It began raining two hours ago and it is still raining.

How long **has** it **been raining**?

It **has been raining** for two hours.

用现在完成进行时表示某个动作仍在进行（如上述例句）或刚刚停止，尤其是与 **how long**，**for** 和 **since** 连用时。

- **How long have** you **been learning** English? (= you're still learning English)
- Tim is still watching TV. He**'s been watching** TV **all day**.
- Where have you been? **I've been looking** for you **for the last half hour**.
- Chris **hasn't been feeling** well **recently**.

现在完成进行时也可以用来表示在一段时间内重复发生的动作：

- Silvia is a very good tennis player. She**'s been playing since she was eight**.
- Every morning they meet in the same café. They**'ve been going** there **for years**.

C

请比较 **I am doing** (参见Unit 1) 与 **I have been doing**：

I am doing 现在进行时 (现在)	**I have been doing** 现在完成进行时 (现在)
Don't disturb me now. **I'm working**.	**I've been working** hard. Now I'm going to have a break.
We need an umbrella. It**'s raining**.	The ground is wet. It**'s been raining**.
Hurry up! We**'re waiting**.	We**'ve been waiting** for an hour.

现在完成进行时与现在完成时比较 ➜ **Units 10–11**　　现在完成时与 **for/since** 连用 ➜ **Units 11–12**

Exercises

9.1 根据下列图片，说说他们刚刚在做什么事。

1
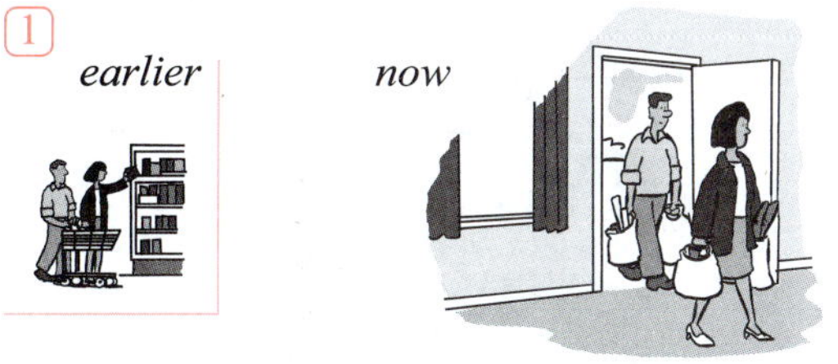

They 've been shopping.

2

She ....

3

They ....

4

He ....

9.2 根据所给情况提问。

1 You meet Paul as he is leaving the swimming pool.
You ask: (you / swim?) Have you been swimming?
2 You have just arrived to meet a friend who is waiting for you.
You ask: (you / wait / long?) ....
3 You meet a friend in the street. His face and hands are very dirty.
You ask: (what / you / do?) ....
4 A friend of yours is now working in a shop. You want to know how long.
You ask: (how long / you / work / there?) ....
5 A friend tells you about his job – he sells mobile phones. You want to know how long.
You ask: (how long / you / sell / mobile phones?) ....

9.3 根据所给情况，完成下列句子。

1 It's raining. The rain started two hours ago.
It 's been raining for two hours.
2 We are waiting for the bus. We started waiting 20 minutes ago.
We .... for 20 minutes.
3 I'm learning Spanish. I started classes in December.
I .... since December.
4 Jessica is working in a supermarket. She started working there on 18 January.
.... since 18 January.
5 Our friends always spend their holidays in Italy. They started going there years ago.
.... for years.

9.4 用括号内动词的现在进行时（**I am -ing** 等）或现在完成进行时（**I have been -ing** 等）形式填空。

1 Maria has been learning (Maria / learn) English for two years.
2 Hello, Tom. .... (I / look) for you. Where have you been?
3 Why .... (you / look) at me like that? Stop it!
4 Linda is a teacher. .... (she / teach) for ten years.
5 .... (I / think) about what you said and I've decided to take your advice.
6 'Is Paul on holiday this week?' 'No, ... (he / work).'
7 Sarah is very tired. .... (she / work) very hard recently.

Unit 10 现在完成进行时 (I have been doing) 与现在完成时 (I have done) 比较

A

请看下列例句：

There is paint on Kate's clothes.
She **has been painting** her bedroom.

has been painting 是现在完成进行时的形式。

现在完成进行时用于说明动作本身，不管这个动作是否已完成。在上述例句中，动作 (painting the bedroom) 尚未完成。

Her bedroom was green. Now it is yellow.
She **has painted** her bedroom.

has painted 是现在完成时的形式。

这里强调的是动作已经完成 (**has painted**)。现在完成时用于说明动作的结果，而不是动作本身。

B

请比较下列例句：

- My hands are very dirty. **I've been repairing** my bike.
- Joe **has been eating** too much recently. He should eat less.
- It's nice to see you again. What **have** you **been doing** since we last met?
- Where have you been? **Have** you **been playing** tennis?

- My bike is OK again now. **I've repaired** it.
- Somebody **has eaten** all the chocolates. The box is empty.
- Where's the book I gave you? What **have** you **done** with it?
- **Have** you ever **played** tennis?

C

现在完成进行时用于询问或说明动作的延续性（该动作仍然在进行）：

- How long **have** you **been reading** that book?
- Lisa is writing emails. She**'s been writing** emails all morning.
- They**'ve been playing** tennis since 2 o'clock.
- I'm learning Arabic, but **I haven't been learning** it very long.

现在完成时用于询问或说明已经完成动作的多少或次数：

- How much of that book **have** you **read**?
- Lisa is writing emails. She**'s sent** lots of emails this morning.
- They**'ve played** tennis three times this week.
- I'm learning Arabic, but I **haven't learnt** very much yet.

D

有些动词 (如 **know/like/believe**) 通常不用于进行时：

- I**'ve known** about the problem for a long time. (而不用 I've been knowing)
- How long **have** you **had** that camera? (而不用 have you been having)

更多类似的动词参见Unit 4A。有关 **have** 的用法，参见 Unit 17。
但注意，**want** 和 **mean** 可以用于现在完成进行时：

- **I've been meaning** to phone Jane, but I keep forgetting.

现在完成时 ➜ Units 7–8　现在完成进行时 ➜ Unit 9　现在完成时与 for/since 连用 ➜ Units 11–12

Exercises

10.1 根据所给情况，用括号内的动词造句。

1 Tom started reading a book two hours ago. He is still reading it and now he is on page 53.
He has been reading .... for two hours. (read)
He has read .... 53 pages so far. (read)

2 Rachel is from Australia. She is travelling round Europe at the moment. She began her trip three months ago.
She .... for three months. (travel)
.... six countries so far. (visit)

3 Patrick is a tennis player. He began playing tennis when he was ten years old. This year he won the national championship again – for the fourth time.
.... the national championship four times. (win)
.... since he was ten. (play)

4 When they left college, Lisa and Sue started making films together. They still make films.
They .... films since they left college. (make)
.... five films since they left college. (make)

10.2 根据所给情况，用括号内的词语提问。

1 You have a friend who is learning Arabic. You ask:
(how long / learn / Arabic?) *How long have you been learning Arabic?*

2 You have just arrived to meet a friend. She is waiting for you. You ask:
(wait / long?) Have ....

3 You see somebody fishing by the river. You ask:
(catch / any fish?) ....

4 Some friends of yours are having a party next week. You ask:
(how many people / invite?) ....

5 A friend of yours is a teacher. You ask:
(how long / teach?) ....

6 You meet somebody who is a writer. You ask:
(how many books / write?) ....
(how long / write / books?) ....

7 A friend of yours is saving money to go on a world trip. You ask:
(how long / save?) ....
(how much money / save?) ....

10.3 用括号内动词的现在完成时 (**I have done**等) 或现在完成进行时 (**I have been doing**等) 形式填空。

1 Where have you been? *Have you been playing* .... (you / play) tennis?
2 Look! .... (somebody / break) that window.
3 You look tired. .... (you / work) hard?
4 ‘........ (you / ever / work) in a factory?’ ‘No, never.’
5 ‘Liz is away on holiday.’ ‘Is she? Where .... (she / go)?’
6 My brother is an actor. .... (he / appear) in several films.
7 ‘Sorry I’m late.’ ‘That’s all right. .... (I / not / wait) long.’
8 ‘Is it still raining?’ ‘No, ... (it / stop).’
9 .... (I / lose) my phone. .... (you / see) it anywhere?
10 .... (I / read) the book you lent me, but .... (I / not / finish) it yet. It’s very interesting.
11 .... (I / read) the book you lent me, so you can have it back now.
12 This is a very old book. .... (I / have) it since I was a child.

How long have you (been) ... ?

A

请看下列例句：

Dan and Jenny are married. They got married exactly 20 years ago, so today is their 20th wedding anniversary.

They **have been** married **for 20 years**.

可以说：They **are** married. （现在时）

可以说：**How long have** they **been** married? （现在完成时）
（而不用 How long are they married?）
They **have been** married **for 20 years**.
（而不用 They are married for 20 years）

现在完成时用来表示某个动作开始于过去，现在仍在继续。
请比较下列现在时与现在完成时的句子：

- Paul is in hospital.

可以说 He**'s been** in hospital **since Monday**. （= He **has** been ...）
（而不用 He's in hospital since Monday）

- **Do** you **know** each other well?

可以说 **Have** you **known** each other **for a long time**?
（而不用 Do you know）

- She**'s waiting** for somebody.

可以说 She**'s been waiting all morning**.

- **Do** they **have** a car?

可以说 **How long have** they **had** their car?

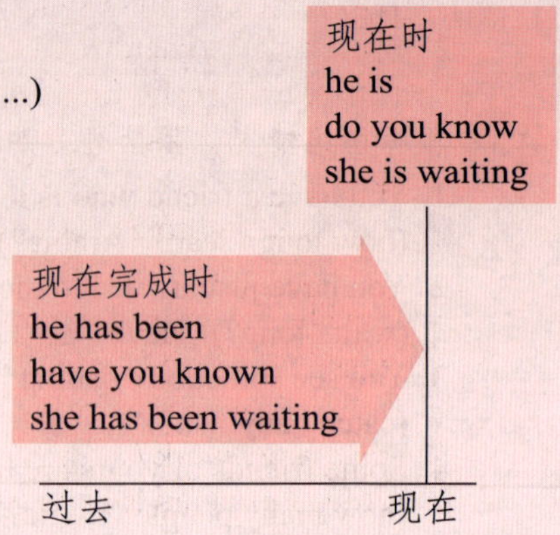

B

I have known/had/lived 等是一般现在完成时的形式。
I have been learning / been waiting / been doing 等是现在完成进行时的形式。

当询问或说明动作的延续性时，常用现在完成进行时 (参见Unit 10)：

- **I've been learning** English **for six months**.
- It**'s been raining since lunchtime**.
- Richard **has been doing** the same job **for 20 years**.
- '**How long have** you **been driving**?' 'Since I was 17.'

有些动词 (如 **know/like/believe**) 通常不用于进行时：

- How long **have** you **known** Jane? （而不用 have you been knowing)
- **I've had** a pain in my stomach all day. （而不用 I've been having)

另见Unit 4A，Unit 10C。有关 **have** 的用法，参见 Unit 17。

C

live 和 **work** 既可以用于现在完成进行时，也可以用于一般现在完成时：

- Julia **has been living** / **has lived** here for a long time.
- How long **have** you **been working** / **have** you **worked** here?

但用于一般现在完成时 (**I've lived / I've done** 等) 时，要与 **always** 连用：

- **I've always lived** in the country. （而不用 always been living)

D

可以说 **I haven't done** something **since/for** ... (一般现在完成时)：

- I **haven't seen** Tom since Monday. （= Monday was the last time I saw him)
- Sarah **hasn't phoned** for ages. （= the last time she phoned was ages ago)

I haven't ... since/for → Unit 8B　　现在完成进行时 → Units 9–10　　**for**与**since**比较 → Unit 12A

Exercises

11.1 画线部分的动词是否正确？如有错误，请改正。

1 Ben is a friend of mine. I know him very well. ......对......
2 Ben is a friend of mine. I know him for a long time. ......错，I've known him......
3 Sarah and Adam are married since July. ....
4 The weather is awful. It's raining again. ....
5 The weather is awful. It's raining all day. ....
6 I like your house. How long are you living there? ....
7 Gary is working in a shop for the last few months. ....
8 I don't know Tom well. We've only met a few times. ....
9 I gave up drinking coffee. I don't drink it for a year. ....
10 That's a very old bike. How long do you have it? ....

11.2 根据所给情况，用括号内的词语提问。

1 A friend tells you that Paul is in hospital. You ask him:
(how long / be / in hospital?) ......How long has Paul been in hospital?......
2 You meet a woman who tells you that she teaches English. You ask her:
(how long / teach / English?) ....
3 You know that Jane is a good friend of Katherine's. You ask Jane:
(how long / know / Katherine?) ....
4 Your friend's brother went to Australia some time ago and he's still there. You ask your friend:
(how long / be / in Australia?) ....
5 Tom always wears the same jacket. It's a very old jacket. You ask him:
(how long / have / that jacket?) ....
6 You are talking to a friend about Joe. Joe now works at the airport. You ask your friend:
(how long / work / at the airport?) ....
7 A friend of yours is having guitar lessons. You ask him:
(how long / have / guitar lessons?) ....
8 You meet somebody on a plane. She says that she lives in Chicago. You ask her:
(always / live / in Chicago?) ....

11.3 完成下列对话。

	A	B
1	Paul is in hospital, isn't he?	Yes, he ......has been...... in hospital since Monday.
2	Do you see Ann very often?	No, I ......haven't seen...... her for three months.
3	Is Amy married?	Yes, she .... married for ten years.
4	Are you waiting for me?	Yes, I .... for the last half hour.
5	You know Mel, don't you?	Yes, we .... each other for a long time.
6	Do you still play tennis?	No, I .... tennis for years.
7	Is Joe watching TV?	Yes, he .... TV all evening.
8	Do you watch TV a lot?	No, I .... TV for ages.
9	Do you have a headache?	Yes, I .... a headache all morning.
10	Adrian is never ill, is he?	No, he .... ill since I've known him.
11	Are you feeling ill?	Yes, I .... ill all day.
12	Sue lives in Berlin, doesn't she?	Yes, she .... in Berlin for the last few years.
13	Do you go to the cinema a lot?	No, I .... to the cinema for ages.
14	Would you like to go to New York one day?	Yes, I .... to go to New York. (*use* **always** / **want**)

for 与 since 比较　When … ?与 How long … ? 比较

A

for 与 **since** 用来表示事情发生了多久：

for 用于表示动作持续了一段时间 (**two hours**，**six weeks** 等)：

- I've been waiting **for two hours**.

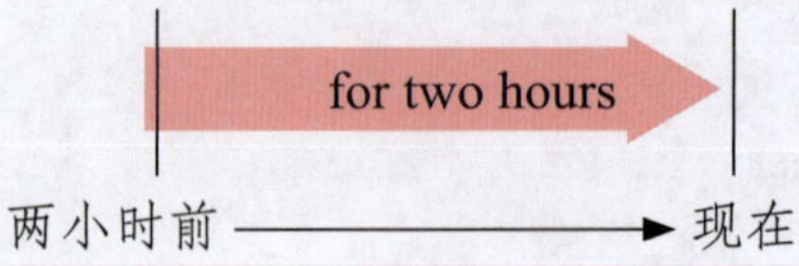

	for	
two hours	20 minutes	five days
a long time	six months	50 years
a week	ages	years

- Sally has been working here **for six months**.（而不用 since six months）
- I haven't seen Tom **for three days**.

since 用于表示动作开始于什么时候 (**8 o'clock**，**Monday**，**1999** 等)：

- I've been waiting **since 8 o'clock**.

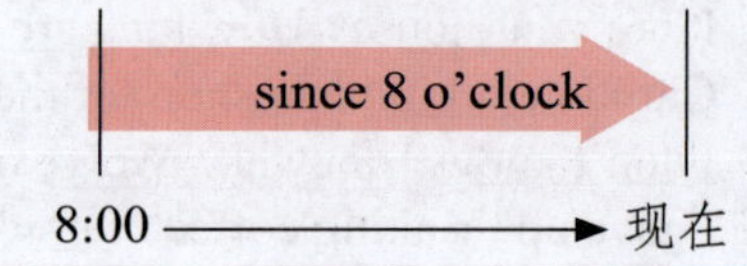

	since	
8 o'clock	Monday	12 May
April	2001	Christmas
lunchtime	we arrived	I got up

- Sally has been working here **since April**. (= from April until now)
- I haven't seen Tom **since Monday**.

for 在肯定句中有时可以省略，但在否定句中不能省略：

- They've been married (for) **ten years**.（用不用 **for** 均可）
- They **haven't had** a holiday **for** ten years.（必须用 **for**）

不用 **for** + **all** … (**all day** / **all my life** 等)：

- I've lived here **all my life**.（而不用 for all my life）

在否定句 (**I haven't** ... 等) 中，可以用 **in** 代替 **for**：

- They **haven't had** a holiday **in ten years**. (= for ten years)

B

请比较 **When** … ? (+ 一般过去时) 与 **How long** … ? (+ 现在完成时)：

A: **When** did it start raining?
B: It started raining **an hour ago** / **at 1 o'clock**.

A: **How long** has it been raining?
B: It's been raining **for an hour** / **since 1 o'clock**.

A: **When** did Joe and Carol first meet?
B: They first met { **a long time ago.** / **when they were at school.** }

A: **How long** have they known each other?
B: They've known each other { **for a long time.** / **since they were at school.** }

C

可以说：

It's (= It **is**) 或 **It's been** (= It **has been**)	a long time six months （等）	since something happened

- **It's two years since** I last saw Joe. 或 **It's been two years since** …
  (= I haven't seen Joe for two years)
- **It's ages since** we went to the cinema. 或 **It's been ages since** …
  (= We haven't been to the cinema for ages)
- **How long is it since** Mrs Hill died? 或 **How long has it been since** … ?
  (= When did Mrs Hill die?)

How long have you (been) … ? → Unit 11

Exercises

12.1 用 **for** 或 **since** 填空。

1 It's been raining ......since...... lunchtime.
2 Sarah has lived in Paris .... 1995.
3 Paul has lived in Brazil .... ten years.
4 I'm tired of waiting. We've been sitting here .... an hour.
5 Kevin has been looking for a job .... he left school.
6 I haven't been to a party .... ages.
7 I wonder where Joe is. I haven't seen him .... last week.
8 Jane is away. She's been away .... Friday.
9 The weather is dry. It hasn't rained .... a few weeks.

12.2 用 **how long** 和 **when** 提问。

1 It's raining.
(how long?) ......How long has it been raining?......
(when?) ......When did it start raining?......
2 Kate is learning Japanese.
(how long / learn?) ....
(when / start?) ....
3 I know Simon.
(how long / you / know?) ....
(when / you / first / meet?) ....
4 Rebecca and David are married.
(how long?) ....
(when?) ....

12.3 根据所给情况，仿照示例完成下列句子。

1 It's raining. It's been raining since lunchtime. It ......started raining...... at lunchtime.
2 Ann and Jess are friends. They first met years ago. They've ......known each other for...... years.
3 Mark is ill. He became ill on Sunday. He has .... Sunday.
4 Mark is ill. He became ill a few days ago. He has .... a few days.
5 Sarah is married. She's been married for a year. She got ....
6 You have a headache. It started when you woke up.
I've .... I woke up.
7 Sue has been in Italy for the last three weeks.
She went ....
8 You're working in a hotel. You started six months ago.
I've ....

12.4 完成下列对话。

1 A: Do you often go on holiday?
B: No, ...I haven't had a holiday for...... five years.
2 A: Do you often see Laura?
B: No, I .... about a month.
3 A: Do you often go to the cinema?
B: No, ... a long time.
4 A: Do you often eat in restaurants?
B: No, ... ages.

用 **It's ... since ...** 完成上面的对话。

5 (1) ......No, it's five years since I had a holiday......
6 (2) No, it's ....
7 (3) No, ...
8 (4) ....

Unit 13 现在完成时 (I have done) 与一般过去时 (I did) 比较 (1)

A

请看下列例句：

Tom is looking for his key. He can't find it.
He **has lost** his key. (现在完成时)
意为：他现在没有钥匙。

十分钟后：

Now Tom **has found** his key. He has it now.
Has he **lost** his key? No, he **has found** it.
Did he **lose** his key? Yes, he **did**.
He **lost** his key. (一般过去时)
但是现在，he **has found** it. (现在完成时)

现在完成时总是用来讲述现在的情况。Tom **has lost** his key 表示他现在没有钥匙 (参见 Unit 7)。

一般过去时只讲述过去发生的情况。如果某人说 Tom **lost** his key，这并没有告诉我们汤姆现在是否有钥匙，只说明他在过去某个时候把钥匙弄丢了。

如果现在的情况已与过去不同，不能用现在完成时。请比较：

- They**'ve gone** away. They'll be back on Friday. (他们现在不在)
  They **went** away, but I think they're back at home now. (而不用 They've gone)
- It **has stopped** raining now, so we don't need the umbrella. (现在没有在下雨)
  It **stopped** raining for a while, but now it's raining again. (而不用 It has stopped)

B

现在完成时可以用来表示新近发生的事情：

- '**I've repaired** the washing machine. It's working OK now.' 'Oh, that's good.'
- 'Sally **has had** a baby! It's a boy.' 'That's great news.'

通常，也可以用一般过去时：

- I **repaired** the washing machine. It's working OK now.

一般过去时（而不用现在完成时）可以用来谈论过去发生的事情：

- Mozart **was** a composer. He **wrote** more than 600 pieces of music.
  (而不用 has been … has written)
- My mother **grew** up in Italy. (而不用 has grown)

请比较：

- Did you know that somebody **has invented** a new type of washing machine?
- Who **invented** the telephone? (而不用 has invented)

C

现在完成时用于提供新的信息(参见Unit 7)。但如果谈话继续下去，通常会用到一般过去时：

- A: Ow! **I've burnt** myself.
  B: How **did** you **do** that? (而不用 have you done)
  A: I **picked** up a hot dish. (而不用 have picked)
- A: Look! Somebody **has spilt** something on the sofa.
  B: Well, it **wasn't** me. I **didn't do** it. (而不用 hasn't been … haven't done)

一般过去时 ➜ Unit 5　现在完成时 ➜ Units 7–8　现在完成时与一般过去时比较 (2) ➜ Unit 14
美国英语 ➜ 附录 7

Exercises

13.1 用括号内动词的现在完成时或一般过去时形式填空。

13.2 下列句子中画线的部分是否正确？如有错误，请改正。

1 Did you hear about Sue? <u>She's given</u> up her job. 对
2 My mother <u>has grown</u> up in Italy. 错：grew
3 How many poems <u>has William Shakespeare written</u>? ....
4 Ow! <u>I've cut</u> my finger. It's bleeding. ....
5 Drugs <u>have become</u> a big problem everywhere. ....
6 Who <u>has invented</u> paper? ....
7 Where <u>have you been born</u>? ....
8 Ellie isn't at home. <u>She's gone</u> shopping. ....
9 Albert Einstein <u>has been</u> the scientist who <u>has developed</u> the theory of relativity. ....

13.3 用括号内动词的现在完成时或一般过去时形式填空。

1 It stopped raining for a while, but now it's raining again. (it / stop)
2 The town where I live is very different now. It has changed a lot. (it / change)
3 I studied German at school, but .... most of it now. (I / forget)
4 The police .... three people, but later they let them go. (arrest)
5 What do you think of my English? Do you think ....? (it / improve)
6 A: Are you still reading the paper?
B: No, ... with it. You can have it. (I / finish)
7 .... for a job as a tourist guide, but I wasn't successful. (I / apply)
8 Where's my bike? .... outside the house, but it's not there now. (it / be)
9 Quick! We need to call an ambulance. .... an accident. (there / be)
10 A: Have you heard about Ben? .... his arm. (he / break)
B: Really? How ....? (that / happen)
A: .... off a ladder. (he / fall)

现在完成时 (I have done) 与一般过去时 (I did) 比较 (2)

A

谈论某个过去的时间 (如 **yesterday / ten minutes ago / in 2005 / when I was a child**) 时，不用现在完成时 (**I have done**)，而要用一般过去时：

- It **was** very cold **yesterday**. (而不用 has been)
- Paul and Lucy **arrived ten minutes ago**. (而不用 have arrived)
- **Did** you **eat** a lot of sweets **when you were a child**? (而不用 have you eaten)
- I **got** home late **last night**. I **was** very tired and **went** straight to bed.

在问句 **When** … ? 或 **What time** … ? 中使用过去时：

- **When did** your friends **arrive**? (而不用 have … arrived)
- **What time did** you **finish** work?

请比较：

现在完成时

- Tom **has lost** his key. He can't get into the house.
- Is Carla here or **has** she **left**?

一般过去时

- Tom **lost** his key **yesterday**. He couldn't get into the house.
- **When did** Carla **leave**?

B

请比较：

现在完成时 (**have done**)

- **I've done** a lot of work **today**.

现在完成时用于表示始于过去持续到现在的一段时间，如 **today / this week / since 2007**。

- It **hasn't rained this week**.
- **Have** you **seen** Anna **this morning**? (现在仍然是早晨)
- **Have** you **seen** Tim **recently**?
- I don't know where Lisa is. I **haven't seen** her. (= I haven't seen her recently)
- We**'ve been waiting** for an hour. (我们现在仍然在等)
- Jack lives in Los Angeles. He **has lived** there for seven years.
- I **have never played** golf. (我一生中)
- *It's the last day of your holiday. You say*: It**'s been** a really good holiday. **I've** really **enjoyed** it.

一般过去时 (**did**)

- **I did** a lot of work **yesterday**.

一般过去时用于表示发生在过去现在已经结束的一段时间，如 **yesterday / last week / from 2007 to 2010**。

- It **didn't rain last week**.
- **Did** you **see** Anna **this morning**? (现在是下午或晚上)
- **Did** you **see** Tim **on Sunday**?
- A: **Was** Lisa at the party **on Sunday**?
  B: I don't think so. I **didn't** see her.
- We **waited** (或 **were waiting**) for an hour. (我们现在已经没有在等了)
- Jack **lived** in New York for ten years. Now he lives in Los Angeles.
- I **didn't play** golf **last summer**.
- *After you come back from holiday you say*: It **was** a really good holiday. I really **enjoyed** it.

一般过去时 → Unit 5　现在完成时 → Units 7–8　现在完成时与一般过去时比较 (1) → Unit 13

Exercises

14.1 下列句子中画线的部分是否正确？如有错误，请改正。

1 I've lost my key. I can't find it anywhere. ..对..
2 Have you eaten a lot of sweets when you were a child? ..错：Did you eat..
3 I've bought a new car. You must come and see it. ....
4 I've bought a new car last week. ....
5 Where have you been yesterday evening? ....
6 Lucy has left school in 1999. ....
7 I'm looking for Mike. Have you seen him? ....
8 'Have you been to Paris?' 'Yes, many times.' ....
9 I'm very hungry. I haven't eaten much today. ....
10 When has this book been published? ....

14.2 根据括号内所给的词语，用现在完成时或一般过去时造句。

1 (it / not / rain / this week) ..It hasn't rained this week..
2 (the weather / be / cold / recently) The weather ....
3 (it / cold / last week) It ....
4 (I / not / read / a newspaper yesterday) I ....
5 (I / not / read / a newspaper today) ....
6 (Emily / earn / a lot of money / this year) ....
7 (she / not / earn / so much / last year) ....
8 (you / have / a holiday recently?) ....

14.3 用括号内动词的现在完成时或一般过去时形式填空。

1 'What's Madrid like?' 'I don't know. ..I haven't been.. (I / not / be) there.'
2 When ..I got.. (I / get) home last night, ..I was.. (I / be) very tired and ..I went.. (I / go) straight to bed.
3 A: .... (you / see) Lisa recently?
B: Yes, ... (I / see) her a few days ago.
4 I'm tired. .... (I / not / sleep) well last night.
5 The bus drivers were on strike last week. .... (there / be) no buses.
6 Mr Lee .... (work) in a bank for 15 years. Then .... (he / give) it up. Now he works as a gardener.
7 Mary lives in Dublin. .... (she / live) there all her life.
8 A: .... (you / go) to the cinema last night?
B: Yes, but .... (it / be) a mistake. The film .... (be) awful.
9 My grandfather .... (die) before I was born. .... (I / never / meet) him.
10 I don't know Karen's husband. .... (I / never / meet) him.
11 It's nearly lunchtime, and .... (I / not / see) Martin all morning. I wonder where he is.
12 'Where do you live?' 'In Boston.'
'How long .... (you / live) there?' 'Five years.'
'Where .... (you / live) before that?' 'In Chicago.'
'And how long .... (you / live) in Chicago?' 'Two years.'

14.4 根据括号内的提示，结合你自己的情况造句。

1 (something you haven't done today) ..I haven't eaten any fruit today..
2 (something you haven't done today) ....
3 (something you didn't do yesterday) ....
4 (something you did yesterday evening) ....
5 (something you haven't done recently) ....
6 (something you've done a lot recently) ....

→ 补充练习 2–4 (第303–304页)，14–15 (第310–311页)

过去完成时 (I had done)

A

请看下列例句：

10点30分　　11点

PAUL　　*SARAH*

Sarah went to a party last week. Paul went to the party too, but they didn't see each other. Paul left the party at 10.30 and Sarah arrived at 11 o'clock. 因此可以说：

When Sarah arrived at the party, Paul wasn't there.

He **had gone** home.

had gone 是过去完成时的构成形式：

I/we/they/you he/she/it	**had**	(= I'**d** 等) (= he'**d** 等)	**gone** **seen** **finished** 等

过去完成时由 **had** + 过去分词 (**gone/seen/finished** 等) 构成。

有时我们谈论过去发生的动作或行为：

- Sarah **arrived** at the party.

这是故事的开始。如果要谈论在这之前发生的动作或行为，就要使用过去完成时：

- When Sarah arrived at the party, Paul **had** already **gone** home.

其他一些例句：

- When we got home last night, we found that somebody **had broken** into the flat.
- Karen didn't want to go to the cinema with us because she'**d** already **seen** the movie.
- At first I thought **I'd done** the right thing, but I soon realised that **I'd made** a big mistake.
- The man sitting next to me on the plane was very nervous. He **hadn't flown** before.
  或 … He **had** never **flown** before.

B

请比较现在完成时 (**have seen** 等) 与过去完成时 (**had seen** 等)：

现在完成时

- Who is that woman? **I've seen** her before, but I can't remember where.
- We aren't hungry. We'**ve** just **had** lunch.
- The house is dirty. They **haven't cleaned** it for weeks.

过去完成时

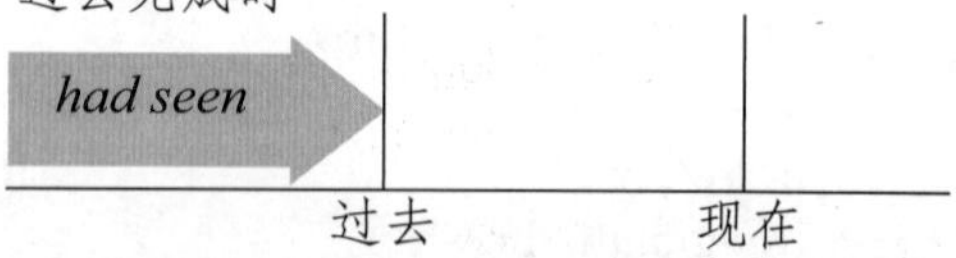

- I wasn't sure who she was. **I'd seen** her before, but I couldn't remember where.
- We weren't hungry. We'**d** just **had** lunch.
- The house was dirty. They **hadn't cleaned** it for weeks.

C

请比较一般过去时 (**left**，**was**等)与过去完成时 (**had left**，**had been**等)：

- A: Was Tom there when you arrived?
  B: Yes, but he **left** soon afterwards.
- Kate **wasn't** at home when I phoned. She **was** at her mother's house.

- A: Was Tom there when you arrived?
  B: No, he **had** already **left**.
- Kate **had** just **got** home when I phoned. She **had been** at her mother's house.

过去完成进行时 ➔ Unit 16　　不规则动词表 (gone/seen 等) ➔ 附录 1

Exercises

15.1 根据所给情况，用括号内的词语造句。

1 You went to Sue's house, but she wasn't there.
(she / go / out) She had gone out.
2 You went back to your home town after many years. It wasn't the same as before.
(it / change / a lot) ……
3 I invited Rachel to the party, but she couldn't come.
(she / arrange / to do something else) ……
4 You went to the cinema last night. You got to the cinema late.
(the film / already / start) ……
5 It was nice to see Daniel again after such a long time.
(I / not / see / him for five years) ……
6 I offered Sue something to eat, but she wasn't hungry.
(she / just / have / breakfast) ……

15.2 根据所给情况，用括号内的动词造句，使用 **never … before**。

1 The man sitting next to you on the plane was very nervous. It was his first flight.
(fly) He'd never flown before.
2 Somebody sang a song. I didn't know it.
(hear) I …… before.
3 Sam played tennis yesterday. He wasn't very good at it because it was his first game.
(play) He ……
4 Last year we went to Mexico. It was our first time there.
(be there) We ……

15.3 用左边的句子完成右边各段内容。这些句子按事情发生的先后顺序排列——（a）发生在（b）之前，（b）发生在（c）之前。你需要完成的段落是以带下划线的句子开头的，有时需用过去完成时。

1 (a) Somebody broke into the office during the night.
(b) <u>We arrived at work in the morning.</u>
(c) We called the police.

We arrived at work in the morning and found that somebody had broken into the office during the night. So …… the police.

2 (a) Laura went out this morning.
(b) <u>I rang her doorbell.</u>
(c) There was no answer.

I went to Laura's house this morning and rang her doorbell, but …… no answer. …… out.

3 (a) Jim came back from holiday a few days ago.
(b) <u>I met him the same day.</u>
(c) He looked very well.

I met Jim a few days ago. …… just …… holiday. …… very well.

4 (a) Kevin sent Sally lots of emails.
(b) She never replied to them.
(c) <u>Yesterday he got a phone call from her.</u>
(d) He was very surprised.

Yesterday Kevin …… from Sally. …… very surprised. …… lots of emails, but …… .

15.4 用括号内动词的过去完成时 (**I had done**等) 或一般过去时 (**I did**等) 形式填空。

1 'Was Paul at the party when you arrived?' 'No, he had gone (go) home.'
2 I felt very tired when I got home, so I …… (go) straight to bed.
3 The house was very quiet when I got home. Everybody …… (go) to bed.
4 Sorry I'm late. The car …… (break) down on my way here.
5 We were driving along the road when we …… (see) a car which …… (break) down, so we …… (stop) to help.

→ 补充练习 5–8 (第304–307页)

过去完成进行时 (I had been doing)

A 请看下列例句：

昨天早上

Yesterday morning I got up and looked out of the window.
The sun was shining, but the ground was very wet.

It **had been raining**.

It was *not* raining when I looked out of the window;
the sun was shining. But it **had been** raining before.

had been + -ing 是过去完成进行时的构成形式：

I/we/you/they he/she/it	**had**	(= I'**d** 等) (= he'**d** 等)	**been**	**doing** **working** **playing** 等

其他一些例句：

- When the boys came into the house, their clothes were dirty, their hair was untidy and one of them had a black eye. They**'d been fighting**.
- I was very tired when I got home. **I'd been working** hard all day.
- When I went to Madrid a few years ago, I stayed with a friend of mine. She **hadn't been living** there very long, but she knew the city very well.

B 如果某事在另外一件事发生之前的一段时间内发生，可以说 something **had been happening**：

- We**'d been playing** tennis for about half an hour when it started to rain heavily.
- Paul went to the doctor last Friday. He **hadn't been feeling** well for some time.

C 请比较现在完成进行时 (**have been -ing**) 与过去完成进行时 (**had been -ing**)：

现在完成进行时

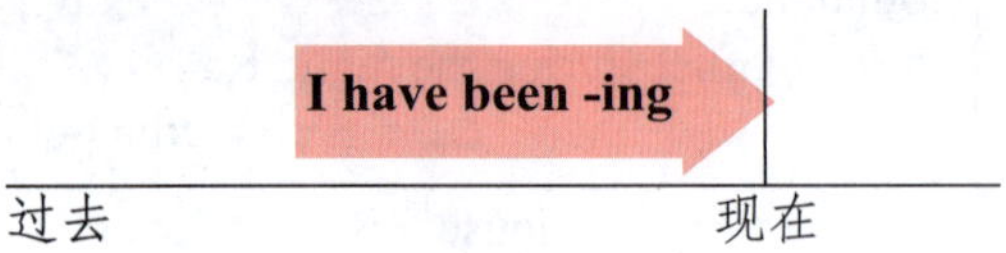

- I hope the bus comes soon. **I've been waiting** for 20 minutes. (现在之前)
- James is out of breath. He **has been running**.

过去完成进行时

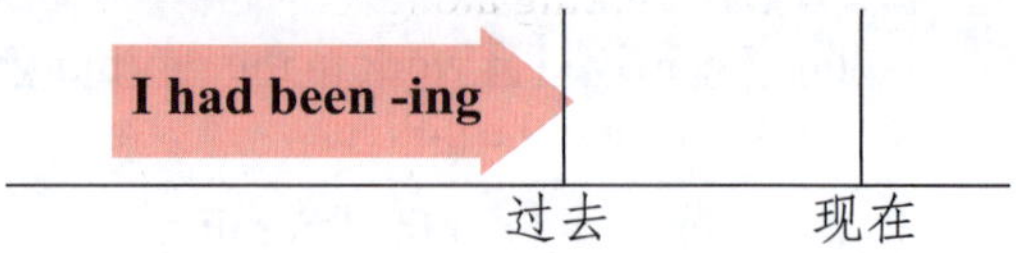

- At last the bus came. **I'd been waiting** for 20 minutes. (公共汽车来之前)
- James was out of breath. He **had been running**.

D 请比较**had been -ing** 与 **was -ing** (过去进行时)：

- It **wasn't raining** when we went out. The sun **was shining**. But it **had been raining**, so the ground was wet.
- Katherine **was sitting** in an armchair resting. She was tired because she**'d been working** very hard.

E 有些动词 (如 **know** 和 **like**) 通常不用于进行时：

- We were good friends. We **had known** each other for years. (而不用 had been knowing)
- I was surprised when Lisa cut her hair. She**'d had** long hair since I first met her. (而不用 she'd been having)

更多类似的动词参见Unit 4A。有关 **have** 的用法，参见 Unit 17。

现在完成进行时 ➜ Units 9–10　　过去完成时 ➜ Unit 15

Exercises

16.1 根据所给情况，用括号内的词语造句。

1 I was very tired when I arrived home.
(I / work / hard all day) I'd been working hard all day.
2 The two boys came into the house. They had a football and they were both very tired.
(they / play / football) ……
3 I was disappointed when I had to cancel my holiday.
(I / look / forward to it) ……
4 Ann woke up in the middle of the night. She was frightened and didn't know where she was.
(she / dream) ……
5 When I got home, Mark was sitting in front of the TV. He had just turned it off.
(he / watch / a film) ……

16.2 根据所给情况，完成下列句子。

1 We played tennis yesterday. Half an hour after we began playing, it started to rain.
We had been playing for half an hour when it started to rain .
2 I had arranged to meet Tom in a restaurant. I arrived and waited for him. After 20 minutes I realised that I was in the wrong restaurant.
I …… for 20 minutes when I …… the wrong restaurant.
3 Sarah got a job in a factory. Five years later the factory closed down.
At the time the factory ……, Sarah …… there for five years.
4 I went to a concert last week. The orchestra began playing. After about ten minutes a man in the audience suddenly started shouting.
The orchestra …… when ……

根据你自己的想法造句：

5 I began walking along the road. I ……
when ……

16.3 用括号内动词的过去进行时 (**I was doing**)、过去完成时 (**I had done**) 或过去完成进行时 (**I had been doing**) 形式填空。

1 It was very noisy next door. Our neighbours were having (have) a party.
2 We were good friends. We'd known (we / know) each other for years.
3 John and I went for a walk. I had difficulty keeping up with him because …… (he / walk) so fast.
4 Sue was sitting on the ground. She was out of breath. …… (she / run).
5 When I arrived, everybody was sitting round the table with their mouths full. …… (they / eat).
6 When I arrived, everybody was sitting round the table and talking. Their mouths were empty, but their stomachs were full. …… (they / eat).
7 James was on his hands and knees on the floor. …… (he / look) for his contact lens.
8 When I arrived, Kate …… (wait) for me. She was annoyed because I was late and …… (she / wait) for a long time.
9 I was sad when I sold my car. …… (I / have) it for a very long time.
10 We were extremely tired at the end of the journey. …… (we / travel) for more than 24 hours.

➜ 补充练习 5–8 (第304–307页)

have 与 have got

A

have 与 **have got** (表示所有、关系、疾病等)

have 单独使用，或与 **got** 一起使用，意思没有区别：

- They **have** a new car. 或 They**'ve got** a new car.
- Lisa **has** two brothers. 或 Lisa**'s got** two brothers.
- I **have** a headache. 或 **I've got** a headache.
- Our house **has** a small garden. 或 Our house **has got** a small garden.
- He **has** a few problems. 或 He**'s got** a few problems.

当 **have** 表示所有等含义时，不能用于进行时 (**am having** 等)：

- We're enjoying our holiday. We **have** / We**'ve got** a nice room in the hotel. (而不用 We're having a nice room)

have 的过去式为 **had** (通常不与 **got** 连用)：

- Lisa **had** long hair when she was a child. (而不用 Lisa had got)

B

下列三种形式可以用于疑问句和否定句中：

Do you have any questions?	I **don't have** any questions.
Have you got any questions?	I **haven't got** any questions.
Have you any questions? (不常用)	I **haven't** any questions. (不常用)
Does she have a car?	She **doesn't have** a car.
Has she got a car?	She **hasn't got** a car.
Has she a car? (不常用)	She **hasn't** a car. (不常用)

在过去时的疑问句和否定句中，使用 **did/didn't**：

- **Did** you **have** a car when you were living in Paris?
- I **didn't have** my phone, so I couldn't call you.
- Lisa **had** long hair, **didn't** she?

C

have breakfast / have a shower / have a good time 等

我们还可以用 **have** (而不用 have got) 来表示动作或经历。例如：

have	**breakfast / dinner / a cup of coffee / something to eat** 等 **a bath / a shower / a swim / a break / a rest / a party / a holiday** **an accident / an experience / a dream** **a look** (at something) **a chat / a conversation / a discussion** (with somebody) **trouble / difficulty / fun / a good time** 等 **a baby** (生小孩)

have got 不能用于上框内的表达中，请比较：

- Sometimes I **have** (= eat) a sandwich for my lunch. (而不用 I've got)

但是 **I've got / I have** some sandwiches. Would you like one?

在上框内的表达中，**have** 可以用于进行时 (**am having** 等)：

- We're enjoying our holiday. We**'re having** a great time. (而不用 We have)
- Mark **is having** a shower at the moment. He has a shower every day.

在疑问句和否定句中用 **do/does/did**：

- I **don't** usually **have** a big breakfast. (而不用 I usually haven't)
- What time **does** Chris **have** lunch? (而不用 has Chris lunch)
- **Did** you **have** trouble finding a place to live?

have (got) to ... ➔ Unit 31 **美国英语** ➔ 附录 7

Exercises

17.1 用 **have** 写出下列句子的否定形式。有些用现在时，有些用过去时。

1 I can't get into the house. (a key) I haven't got a key.
2 I couldn't read the letter. (my glasses) I didn't have my glasses.
3 I can't get onto the roof. (a ladder) I ......
4 We couldn't visit the museum. (enough time) We ......
5 He couldn't find his way to our house. (a map) ......
6 She can't pay her bills. (any money) ......
7 I can't go swimming today. (enough energy) ......
8 They couldn't take any pictures. (a camera) ......

17.2 选出正确的选项，有时答案不止一个。

1 Excuse me, ... a pen I could borrow?
A have you got **B** are you having **C** do you have (*both* A *and* C *are correct*)

2 ...... time to go to the bank yesterday?
A Had you got **B** Did you have **C** Had you

3 I need a stamp for this letter. ...... one?
A Do you have **B** Are you having **C** Have you got

4 What does Jack do? ...... a job?
A Does he have **B** Is he having **C** Has he got

5 ...... a lot of friends when you were a child?
A Did you have **B** Were you having **C** Had you

6 When you worked in your last job, ... your own office?
A had you **B** have you got **C** did you have

17.3 下列句子中画线的部分是否正确？如有错误，请改正。

1 Is there anything you want to ask? Do you have any questions? 对
2 Lisa had got long hair when she was a child. 错：Lisa had long hair.
3 Tom couldn't contact us because he hadn't our number. ......
4 'Are you feeling OK?' 'No, I'm having a toothache.' ......
5 Are you enjoying yourself? Are you having a good time? ......
6 It started to rain. I got wet because I hadn't an umbrella. ......
7 Will can't drive. He doesn't have a driving licence. ......
8 Did your trip go OK? Had you any problems? ......
9 My friend called me when I was having breakfast. ......

17.4 用下列所给表达的适当形式完成句子。

have a baby	**have a break**	**have a chat**	**have trouble**	**have a good flight**
have a look	**have lunch**	**have a party**	**have a nice time**	**have a shower**

1 I don't eat much during the day. I never have lunch .
2 David starts work at 8 o'clock and ...... at 10.30.
3 We ...... last week. It was great – we invited lots of people.
4 Excuse me, can I ...... at your newspaper, please?
5 Jim is away on holiday at the moment. I hope he ....
6 I met Ann in the supermarket yesterday. We stopped and ....
7 A: ...... finding the book you wanted?
B: No, I found it OK.
8 Suzanne ...... a few weeks ago. It's her second child.
9 A: Why didn't you answer the phone?
B: I ....
10 *You meet your friend Sally at the airport. She has just arrived. You say:*
Hi, Sally. How are you? ...... ?

used to (do)

A

请看下列例句：

几年前

现在

Nicola doesn't travel much these days.
She prefers to stay at home.

But she **used to travel** a lot.
She **used to go** away two or three times a year.

she **used to travel** a lot 意为她过去经常去旅行，但现在已经不了。

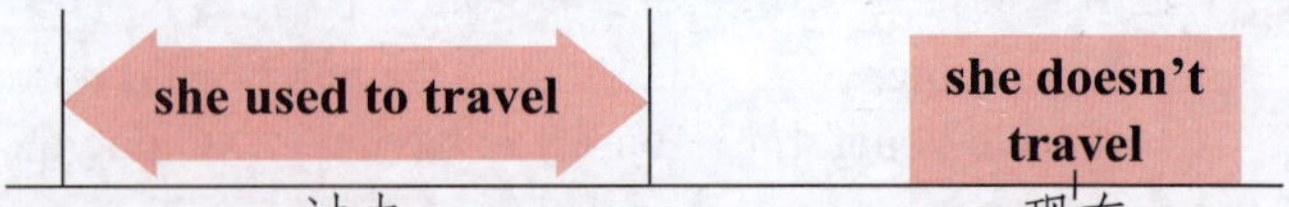

B

something **used to** happen 意为过去经常发生，但现在不再发生了：

- I **used to play** tennis a lot, but I don't play very much now.
- David **used to spend** a lot of money on clothes. These days he can't afford it.
- 'Do you go to the cinema much?' 'Not now, but I **used to**.' (= I used to go)

used to 还用来表示过去发生而现在已经不存在的事情或习惯：

- This building is now a furniture shop. It **used to be** a cinema.
- I **used to think** Mark was unfriendly, but now I realise he's a very nice person.
- I've started drinking tea recently. I never **used to like** it before.
- Lisa **used to have** very long hair when she was a child.

C

I **used to** do something 仅用于一般过去时，不能说 I use to do。表示现在的习惯，要用一般现在时(**I do**)。请比较：

过去	he **used to play**	we **used to live**	there **used to be**
现在	he **plays**	we **live**	there **is**

- We **used to live** in a small village, but now we **live** in London.
- There **used to be** four cinemas in the town. Now there **is** only one.

D

疑问句形式为 **did** (you) **use to** ... ?：

- **Did** you **use to eat** a lot of sweets when you were a child?

否定句形式为 **didn't use to** ... （也可以用 **used not to** ...）：

- I **didn't use to like** him. （或 I **used not to like** him.）

E

请比较 **I used to do** 与 **I was doing**：

- I **used to watch** TV a lot. (= I watched TV often in the past, but I no longer do this)
- I **was watching** TV when Rob called. (= I was in the middle of watching TV)

F

不要混淆 **I used to do** 与 **I am used to doing** 的用法 (参见Unit 61)，它们的形式与意义是不同的：

- I **used to live** alone. (= I lived alone in the past, but I no longer live alone)
- I **<u>am</u> used** to **livi<u>ng</u>** alone. (= I live alone, and I don't find it strange or difficult because I've been living alone for some time)

过去进行时 (I was doing) ➔ Unit 6　　would (= used to) ➔ Unit 36
be/get used to (doing) something ➔ Unit 61

Exercises

18.1 用 **use(d) to** + 适当的动词完成下列句子。

1 Nicola doesn't travel much now. She ....used to travel.... a lot, but she prefers to stay at home these days.
2 Sophie .... a motorbike, but last year she sold it and bought a car.
3 We moved to Spain a few years ago. We .... in Paris.
4 I rarely eat ice-cream now, but I .... it when I was a child.
5 Jackie .... my best friend, but we aren't good friends any more.
6 It only takes me about 40 minutes to get to work now that the new road is open. It .... more than an hour.
7 There .... a hotel near the airport, but it closed a long time ago.
8 When you lived in New York, ... to the theatre very often?

18.2 请比较卡伦五年前讲的话与现在讲的话：

FIVE YEARS AGO

~~I travel a lot.~~
I'm a hotel receptionist.
I play the piano.
I've got lots of friends.
I never read newspapers.
I'm very lazy.
I don't drink tea.
I don't like cheese.
I've got a dog.
I go to a lot of parties.

TODAY

My dog died two years ago.
I eat lots of cheese now.
I read a newspaper every day now.
I work very hard these days.
I haven't been to a party for ages.
I don't know many people these days.
I haven't played the piano for years.
I work in a bookshop now.
~~I don't go away much these days.~~
Tea's great! I like it now.

在句子的前半部分，使用 **used to / didn't use to / never used to**，写出有关卡伦变化的句子。

1 ....She used to travel a lot,.... but ....she doesn't go away much these days....
2 She used .... but ....
3 .... but ....
4 .... but ....
5 .... but ....
6 .... but ....
7 .... but ....
8 .... but ....
9 .... but ....
10 .... but ....

18.3 根据你自己的情况，仿照示例，以 **I used to ... (I used to be/work/like/play/read** 等**)** 开头造句。

1 ....I used to live in a small village, but now I live in London....
2 ....I used to play tennis a lot, but I don't play any more....
3 I used ...., but ....
4 I ....
5 ....

以 **I didn't use to ...** 开头造句。

6 ....I didn't use to read a lot, but I do now....
7 I didn't ....
8 ....

→ 补充练习 9（第 307 页）

Unit 19

现在时 (I am doing / I do) 表示将来

A

表示将来意义的现在进行时 (**I am doing**)

This is Ben's diary for next week.

He **is playing** tennis on Monday afternoon.
He **is going** to the dentist on Tuesday morning.
He **is having** dinner with Kate on Friday.

在这些例句中，本已经决定并安排要做这些事情。

现在进行时 (**I'm doing**) 可表示预先决定或预先安排要做的事：

- A: What **are** you **doing** on Saturday evening? (而不用 What do you do)
  B: **I'm going** to the theatre. (而不用 I go)
- A: What time **is** Katherine **arriving** tomorrow?
  B: Half past ten. **I'm meeting** her at the station.
- **I'm not working** tomorrow, so we can go out somewhere.
- Steve **isn't playing** football next Saturday. He's hurt his leg.

I'm **going to** (do) 也可以用于上述句子中：

- What **are** you **going to do** on Saturday evening?

但是表示预先安排的事情时，用现在进行时更自然。参见Unit 20B。

在表示安排要做的事情时，不要使用 **will**：

- What **are** you **doing** this evening? (而不用 What will you do)
- Alex **is getting** married next month. (而不用 will get)

现在进行时也可以用来表示即将进行的动作，尤其动词是表移动的动词 (**go/come/leave** 等) 时：

- I'm tired. **I'm going** to bed now. Goodnight. (而不用 I go to bed now)
- 'Jess, are you ready yet?' 'Yes, **I'm coming**.' (而不用 I come)

B

表示将来意义的一般现在时 (**I do**)

一般现在时可用来表示时间安排（如交通工具的时刻表、影片等节目的放映时间等）：

- My train **leaves** at 11.30, so I need to be at the station by 11.15.
- What time **does** the film **start** this evening?
- It**'s** Wednesday tomorrow. / Tomorrow **is** Wednesday.

一般现在时可用来表示像日程表那样已确定的计划：

- I **start** my new job on Monday.
- What time **do** you **finish** work tomorrow?

表示个人的安排时，现在进行时更常用：

- What time **are** you **meeting** Ann tomorrow? (而不用 do you meet)

请比较：

现在进行时	一般现在时
What time **are you arriving**?	What time **does the train arrive**?
I'm going to the cinema this evening.	**The film starts** at 8.15 (this evening).

I'm going to ➜ Units 20，23　**will** ➜ Units 21–22　**一般现在时用于 when/if 等之后** ➜ Unit 25

Exercises

19.1 你的一个朋友计划去度假。用括号内的词语询问她的计划。

1 (where / go?) Where are you going? — Scotland.
2 (how long / go for?) .... — Ten days.
3 (when / leave?) .... — Next Friday.
4 (go / alone?) .... — No, with a friend.
5 (travel / by car?) .... — No, by train.
6 (where / stay?) .... — In a hotel.

19.2 汤姆想让你去拜访他，但你很忙。根据你记事本中对接下来几天的安排，向他解释你为什么不能去。

TOM: Can you come on Monday evening?
YOU: Sorry, but I'm playing volleyball. (1)
TOM: What about Tuesday evening then?
YOU: No, not Tuesday. I .... (2)
TOM: And Wednesday evening?
YOU: .... (3)
TOM: Well, are you free on Thursday?
YOU: I'm afraid not. .... (4)

19.3 请写出你在下列时间的安排。

1 (this evening) I'm going out this evening. **or** I'm not doing anything this evening.
2 (tomorrow morning) I ....
3 (tomorrow evening) ....
4 (next Sunday) ....
5 (*choose another day or time*) ....

19.4 用括号内动词的现在进行时或一般现在时形式填空。

1 I'm going (I / go) to the cinema this evening.
2 Does the film start (the film / start) at 3.30 or 4.30?
3 .... (we / have) a party next Saturday. Would you like to come?
4 The art exhibition .... (finish) on 3 May.
5 .... (I / not / go) out this evening. .... (I / stay) at home.
6 '.................... (you / do) anything tomorrow morning?' 'No, I'm free. Why?'
7 .... (we / go) to a concert tonight. .... (it / start) at 7.30.
8 .... (I / leave) now. I've come to say goodbye.
9 A: Have you seen Liz recently?
B: No, but .... (we / meet) for lunch next week.
10 *You are on the train to London and you ask another passenger:*
Excuse me. What time .... (this train / get) to London?
11 *You are talking to Helen:*
Helen, ... (I / go) to the supermarket. .... (you / come) with me?
12 *You and a friend are watching television. You say:*
I'm bored with this programme. What time .... (it / end)?
13 .... (I / not / use) the car this evening, so you can have it.
14 Sue .... (come) to see us tomorrow. .... (she / travel) by train and her train .... (arrive) at 10.15.

→ 补充练习 10–13（第308–310页）

Unit 20

(I'm) going to (do)

A

I **am going to do** something 表示“我已决定去做某事，我试图或打算做某事”：

- '**Are** you **going to eat** anything?' 'No, I'm not hungry.'
- A: I hear Sarah has won some money. What **is** she **going to do** with it?
  B: She**'s going to buy** a new car.
- **I'm** just **going to make** a quick phone call. Can you wait for me?
- This cheese smells horrible. **I'm not going to eat** it.

B

I am doing 与 **I am going to do** 比较

I am doing (现在进行时) 一般用于表示已安排要做的事情，如去见某人、去某个地方 (参见 Unit 19A)：

- What time **are** you **meeting** Ann this evening?
- **I'm leaving** tomorrow. I've got my plane ticket.

I **am going to do** something 表示“我已决定做某事 (但可能还没有安排去做)”：

- 'Your shoes are dirty.' 'Yes, I know. **I'm going to clean** them.' (= I've decided to clean them, but I haven't *arranged* to clean them)
- I've decided not to stay here any longer. Tomorrow I**'m going to look** for somewhere else to stay.

两种形式常常区别很小，都可以使用。

C

表示将来时还可以说，something **is going to happen**。例如：

The man isn't looking where he is going.

He **is going to walk** into the wall.

something **is going to happen** 表示现在的情况预示着某事即将发生。例句中的那个人现在正往墙那边走，因此他将会撞墙。

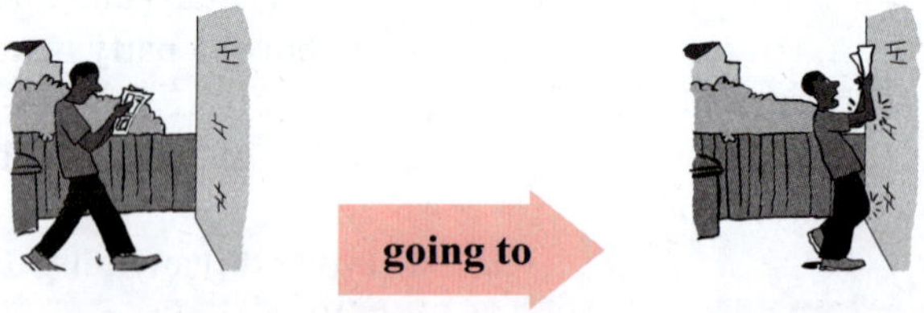

现在　　　　将来

再看一些例句：

- Look at those black clouds! It**'s going to rain**. (现在乌云密布)
- I feel terrible. I think **I'm going to be** sick. (我现在感觉不好)
- The economic situation is bad now and things **are going to get** worse.

D

I **was going to** do something 表示“我本来试图或打算做某事，但没做”：

- We **were going to travel** by train, but then we decided to go by car instead.
- Peter **was going to do** the exam, but he changed his mind.
- I **was** just **going to cross** the road when somebody shouted 'Stop!'

可以说 something **was going to happen** (但是没有发生)：

- I thought it **was going to rain**, but it didn't.

I am doing表示将来 → Unit 19A　　**I will**与**I'm going to**比较 → Unit 23

Exercises

20.1 根据所给情况，用 **going to** 提问。

1 Your friend has won some money. You ask:
(what / do with it?) What are you going to do with it?

2 Your friend is going to a party tonight. You ask:
(what / wear?) ……

3 Your friend has just bought a new table. You ask:
(where / put it?) ……

4 Your friend has decided to have a party. You ask:
(who / invite?) ……

20.2 根据所给情况，用 **going to**完成下列对话。

1 You have decided to clean your room this morning.
FRIEND: Are you going out this morning?
YOU: No, I'm going to clean my room.

2 You bought a sweater, but it doesn't fit you very well. You have decided to take it back to the shop.
FRIEND: That sweater is too big for you.
YOU: I know. ……

3 You have been offered a job, but you have decided not to accept it.
FRIEND: I hear you've been offered a job.
YOU: That's right, but ……

4 You have to phone Sarah. It's morning now, and you have decided to phone her tonight.
FRIEND: Have you phoned Sarah yet?
YOU: No, ……

5 You are in a restaurant. The food is awful and you've decided to complain.
FRIEND: This food is awful, isn't it?
YOU: Yes, it's disgusting. ……

20.3 根据所给情况，用括号内的词语完成下列句子。

1 There are a lot of black clouds in the sky.
(rain) It's going to rain.

2 It is 8.30. Tom is leaving his house. He has to be at work at 8.45, but the journey takes 30 minutes.
(late) He ……

3 There is a hole in the bottom of the boat. A lot of water is coming in through the hole.
(sink) The boat ……

4 Lucy and Chris are driving. There is very little petrol left in the tank. The nearest petrol station is a long way away.
(run out) They ……

20.4 用 **was/were going to** + 下列动词完成句子。

buy **give up** **phone** **play** **say** ~~**travel**~~

1 We were going to travel by train, but then we decided to go by car instead.
2 I …… some new clothes yesterday, but I was very busy and didn't have time to go to the shops.
3 Oliver and I …… tennis last week, but he had to cancel because he'd hurt his knee.
4 I …… Jane, but I decided to email her instead.
5 A: When I last saw Tim, he …… his job.
B: That's right, but in the end he decided to stay where he was.
6 I'm sorry I interrupted you. What …… you ……?

Unit 21

will/shall (1)

A

用 **I'll** (= **I will**) 表示在说话时决定做的事情：

- Oh, I've left the door open. **I'll go** and shut it.
- 'What would you like to drink?' **'I'll have** an orange juice, please.'
- 'Did you phone Lucy?' 'Oh no, I forgot. **I'll phone** her now.'

这些句子不能用一般现在时 (**I do** / **I go** 等)：

- **I'll go** and shut the door. (而不用 I go and shut)

常常用 **I think I'll** ... 及 **I don't think I'll** ... ：

- I feel a bit hungry. **I think I'll have** something to eat.
- **I don't think I'll go** out tonight. I'm too tired.

在口语中，**will** 的否定形式通常用 **won't** (= **will not**)：

- I can see you're busy, so **I won't stay** long.

B

不要用**will** 表示已决定并安排做的事情 (参见 Units 19–20)：

- **I'm going** on holiday next Saturday. (而不用 I'll go)
- **Are** you **working** tomorrow? (而不用 Will you work)

C

在下列情形中常用 **will**：

主动提出做某事

- That bag looks heavy. **I'll help** you with it. (而不用 I help)

赞同做某事

- A: Can you give Tim this book?
- B: Sure, **I'll give** it to him when I see him this afternoon.

承诺做某事

- Thanks for lending me the money. **I'll pay** you back on Friday.
- **I won't tell** anyone what happened. I promise.

请求某人做某事 (**Will you** ... ?)

- **Will you** please turn the music down? I'm trying to concentrate.

说某人拒绝做某事可以用 **won't**：

- I've tried to give her advice, but she **won't listen**.
- The car **won't start**. (= the car 'refuses' to start)

D

Shall I ... ? Shall we ... ?

shall 多用于疑问句 **Shall I** ... ? / **Shall we** ... ?中。
Shall I ... ? / **Shall we** ... ? 用于询问某人的观点 (特别是给予帮助或提建议)：

- **Shall I** open the window? (= Do you want me to open the window?)
- I've got no money. What **shall I** do? (= What do you suggest?)
- '**Shall we** go?' 'Just a minute. I'm not ready yet.'
- 'Where **shall we** have lunch?' 'Let's go to Marino's.'

请比较 **Shall I** ... ? 与 **Will you** ... ?：

- **Shall I** shut the door? (= Do you want me to shut it?)
- **Will you** shut the door? (= I want you to shut it)

will/shall (2) → Unit 22 **I will 与 I'm going to 比较** → Unit 23 **美国英语** → 附录 7

Exercises

21.1 用 **I'll** + 适当的动词完成下列句子。

1 I'm too tired to walk home. I think ......I'll take...... a taxi.
2 'It's cold in this room.' 'Is it? .... on the heating then.'
3 'Bye! Have a nice holiday!' 'Thanks. .... you a postcard.'
4 'Shall I do the washing-up?' 'No, it's all right. .... it later.'
5 'I don't know how to shut down this computer.' 'OK, ... you.'
6 'Would you like tea or coffee?' '.................................... coffee, please.'
7 'Are you coming with us?' 'No, I think .... here.'
8 Thanks for lending me the money. .... it back as soon as possible, OK?
9 A: I know you're busy, but can you finish this report this afternoon?
B: Well, ..., but I can't promise.

21.2 根据所给情况，用 **I think I'll ...** 或 **I don't think I'll ...** 造句。

1 It's a bit cold. The window is open and you decide to close it. You say:
......I think I'll close the window.......
2 You are feeling tired and it's getting late. You decide to go to bed. You say:
I think ....
3 A friend of yours offers you a lift in his car, but you decide to walk. You say:
Thank you, but ....
4 You were going to have lunch. Now you decide that you don't want to eat anything. You say:
I don't think ....
5 You planned to go swimming. Now you decide that you don't want to go. You say:
....

21.3 指出下列句子中哪个是正确的。(如需要，可参见Units 19–20。)

1 'Did you phone Lucy?' 'Oh no, I forgot. ~~I phone~~ / I'll phone her now.' (I'll phone *is correct*)
2 I can't meet you tomorrow. I'm playing / ~~I'll play~~ tennis. (I'm playing *is correct*)
3 'I meet / I'll meet you outside the hotel in half an hour, OK?' 'Yes, that's fine.'
4 'I need some money.' 'OK, I'm lending / I'll lend you some. How much do you need?'
5 I'm having / I'll have a party next Saturday. I hope you can come.
6 'Remember to get a newspaper when you go out.' 'OK, I don't forget / I won't forget.'
7 What time does your train leave / will your train leave tomorrow?
8 I asked Sue what happened, but she doesn't tell / won't tell me.
9 'Are you doing / Will you do anything tomorrow evening?' 'No, I'm free. Why?'
10 I don't want to go out alone. Do you come / Will you come with me?

21.4 在下列情景中你会说什么？用 **shall I ... ?** 或 **shall we ... ?**造句。

1 You and a friend want to do something this evening, but you don't know what.
You ask your friend: ......What shall we do this evening?......
2 You try on a jacket in a shop. You are not sure whether to buy it or not.
You ask a friend for advice: .... it?
3 It's Helen's birthday next week. You want to give her a present, but you don't know what.
You ask a friend for advice:
What ....
4 You and a friend are going on holiday together, but you have to decide where.
You ask him/her: ....
5 You and a friend are going out. You have to decide whether to go by car or to walk.
You ask him/her: .... or ....
6 Your friend wants you to come and see her. You don't know what time to come.
You ask her: ....

➜ 补充练习 10–13 (第308–310页)

will/shall (2)

A

不要用 **will** 来表示某人已安排好或决定要做的事：

- Diane **is working** next week. （而不用 Diane will work）
- **Are** you **going to watch** anything on TV this evening? （而不用 Will you watch）

有关 **is working** 与 **Are** you **going to** ... ? 的用法，参见Units 19–20。

当我们谈论将来时，我们往往并不是在谈论某人已决定要做某事，例如：

Kate is doing an exam next week. Chris and Joe are talking about it.

she'll pass 的意思并不是 she has decided to pass，而是乔在预测将来发生的事情。

will/won't 用来预测将来发生的事情或出现的情况。

再看一些例句：

- They've been away a long time. When they return, they'**ll find** a lot of changes here.
- 'Where **will** you **be** this time next year?' '**I'll be** in Japan.'
- That plate is hot. If you touch it, you'**ll burn** yourself.
- Tom **won't pass** the exam. He hasn't studied hard enough.
- Anna looks completely different now. You **won't recognise** her.
- When **will** you **get** your exam results?

B

will ('ll) 常与下列表达连用：

probably	I'**ll probably** be home late tonight.
(I'm) sure	Don't worry about the exam. I'm **sure** you'**ll** pass.
(I) think	Do you **think** Sarah **will** like the present we bought her?
(I) don't think	I **don't think** the exam **will** be very difficult.
I wonder	**I wonder** what **will** happen.

I hope 后面通常用现在时 (也可以用**will**)：

- I hope Kate **passes** the exam. （或 I hope Kate **will pass** ...）
- I hope it **doesn't rain** tomorrow.

C

will 通常用来表示将来，但有时也用来表示现在。例如：

- Don't phone Ann now. She'**ll be** busy. (= she'll be busy *now*)

D

I shall ... / **we shall** ...

通常 **shall** 只与第一人称 **I** 和 **we** 连用。
可以说 **I shall** 或 **I will (I'll)**，**we shall** 或 **we will (we'll)**：

- **I shall** be late this evening. （或 **I will** be）
- **We shall** probably go to France in June. （或 We **will** probably go）

口语中常用 **I'll** 和 **we'll**：

- **We'll** probably go to France.

shall 的否定形式为 **shall not** 或 **shan't**：

- I **shan't** be here tomorrow. （或 I **won't** be）

he/she/it/you/they 不能与**shall**连用：

- She **will** be very angry. （而不用 She shall be）

will/shall (1) → Unit 21 **I will 与 I'm going to 比较** → Unit 23 **will be doing 与 will have done 比较** → Unit 24
will have to → Unit 31A **将来时** → 附录 3 **美国英语** → 附录 7

Exercises

22.1 指出下列句子中画线部分的动词哪些是正确（或更自然些）的。

1 Diane isn't free on Saturday. ~~She'll work~~ / She's working. (She's working *is correct*)
2 I'll go / I'm going to a party tomorrow night. Would you like to come too?
3 I think Amy will get / is getting the job. She has a lot of experience.
4 I can't meet you this evening. A friend of mine will come / is coming to see me.
5 A: Have you decided where to go for your holidays?
B: Yes, we'll go / we're going to Italy.
6 Don't be afraid of the dog. It won't hurt / It isn't hurting you.

22.2 用 **will ('ll)** 或 **won't** 填空。

1 Can you wait for me? I ...won't... be long.
2 Don't ask Amanda for advice. She .... know what to do.
3 I'm glad you're coming to see us next week. It .... be good to see you again.
4 I'm sorry about what happened yesterday. It .... happen again.
5 You don't need to take an umbrella with you. I don't think it .... rain.
6 I've got some incredible news! You .... believe it.

22.3 用 **will ('ll)** 和下列词语完成句子。

it / be	**she / come**	**you / get**	**you / like**
people / live	**it / look**	**we / meet**	~~**you / pass**~~

1 Don't worry about your exam. I'm sure ...you'll pass... .
2 Why don't you try on this jacket? .... nice on you.
3 You must meet Daniel sometime. I think .... him.
4 It's raining. Don't go out. .... wet.
5 Do you think .... longer in the future?
6 Bye! I'm sure .... again before long.
7 I've invited Anna to the party, but I don't think ....
8 It takes me an hour to get to work at the moment, but when the new road is finished, ... much quicker.

22.4 用 **do you think ... will ... ?** 和下列词语提问。

be back	**cost**	**end**	**get married**	**happen**	~~**like**~~	**rain**

1 I've bought this picture for Karen. ...Do you think she'll like it...?
2 The weather doesn't look very good. Do you ....?
3 The meeting is still going on. When do you ....?
4 My car needs to be repaired. How much ....?
5 Sally and David are in love. Do ....?
6 'I'm going out now.' 'OK. What time ....?'
7 The future situation is uncertain. What ....?

22.5 根据你的真实情况，用下列句型造句。

I'll be ... ***or*** **I'll probably be ...** ***or*** **I don't know where I'll be**

1 (next Monday evening at 7.45) ...I'll be at home...
or ...I'll probably be at home...
or ...I don't know where I'll be...
2 (at 5 o'clock tomorrow morning) ....
3 (at 10.30 tomorrow morning) ....
4 (next Saturday afternoon at 4.15) ....
5 (this time next year) ....

I will 与 I'm going to 比较

A

将来的动作

请看 **will** 与 **(be) going to** 的区别：

Sarah is talking to Helen:

will ('ll) 表示在说话时决定要进行的动作或行为。说话人在此之前并未决定举办聚会。

Later that day, Helen meets Dan:

(be) going to 表示已决定进行的动作或行为。海伦在与丹说话之前就已经决定了要邀请很多人。

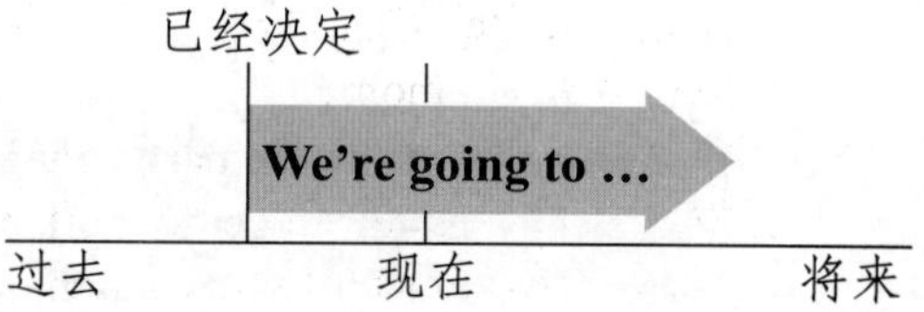

请比较：

- 'Gary phoned while you were out.' 'OK. **I'll call** him back.'
  'Gary **phoned** while you were out.' 'Yes, I know. **I'm going to call** him back.'
- 'Anna is in hospital.' 'Oh really? I didn't know. **I'll go** and visit her.'
  'Anna is in hospital.' 'Yes, I know. **I'm going to visit** her this evening.'

B

将来发生的事情或情景 (推测将来)

推测将来发生的事情或情景时，**will** 与 **going to** 有时并无区别：

- I think **the weather will be** nice later. 或
  I think **the weather is going to be** nice later.
- Those shoes are well-made. **They'll last** a long time. 或
  Those shoes are well-made. **They're going to last** a long time.

something **is going to** happen 用于表示在现在的情况下已经知道 (或想到) 将来会发生的动作或行为：

- Look at those black clouds. It'**s going to rain**. (而不用 It will rain)
  (现在乌云密布，预示要下雨)
- I feel terrible. I think I'**m going to be** sick. (而不用 I think I'll be sick)
  (我现在不舒服，感觉要生病)

在这种情况下，不使用 **will**。

I'm going to ➜ Unit 20 **will** ➜ Units 21–22 **将来时** ➜ 附录 3

Exercises

23.1 用 **will ('ll)** 或 **going to** 完成下列对话。

1 A: Why are you turning on the TV?
B: *I'm going to watch* the news. (I / watch)

2 A: Oh, I've just realised. I haven't got any money.
B: Haven't you? Well, don't worry. ………… you some. (I / lend)

3 A: I've got a headache.
B: Have you? Wait a second and ………… an aspirin for you. (I / get)

4 A: Why are you filling that bucket with water?
B: ………… the car. (I / wash)

5 A: I've decided to repaint this room.
B: Oh, have you? What colour ………… it? (you / paint)

6 A: Where are you going? Are you going shopping?
B: Yes, ………… some things for dinner. (I / buy)

7 A: I don't know how to use the washing machine.
B: It's easy. ………… you. (I / show)

8 A: What would you like to eat?
B: ………… a pizza, please. (I / have)

9 A: Did you call Lisa?
B: Oh, no. I completely forgot. ………… her now. (I / call)

10 A: Has Dan decided what to do when he leaves school?
B: Yes. Everything is planned. ………… a holiday for a few weeks. (he / have) Then ………… a management training course. (he / do)

23.2 根据所给情况，用 **will ('ll)** 或 **going to** 完成下列对话。

1 The phone rings and you answer. Somebody wants to speak to John.
CALLER: Hello. Can I speak to John, please?
YOU: Just a moment. *I'll get* him. (I / get)

2 It's a nice day, so you have decided to take a walk. Just before you go, you tell your friend.
YOU: The weather's too nice to stay in. ………… a walk. (I / take)
FRIEND: Good idea! I think ………… you. (I / join)

3 Your friend is worried because she has lost her driving licence.
YOU: Don't worry. I'm sure ………… it. (you / find)
FRIEND: I hope so.

4 There was a job advertised in the paper recently. At first you were interested, but then you decided not to apply.
FRIEND: Have you decided what to do about that job you were interested in?
YOU: Yes, ………… for it. (I / not / apply)

5 You and a friend are stuck in traffic. You have to be in a meeting in five minutes and you need at least another 20 minutes to get there.
YOU: The meeting begins in five minutes. ………… . (we / be late)

6 Ann and Sam are staying at a hotel. Their room is in very bad condition, especially the ceiling.
ANN: The ceiling doesn't look very safe, does it?
SAM: No, it looks as if ………… . (it / fall down)

7 Paul has to go to the airport to catch a plane tomorrow morning.
PAUL: Kate, I need somebody to take me to the airport tomorrow morning.
KATE: That's no problem. ………… you. (I / take) What time is your flight?
PAUL: 10.30.
KATE: OK, ………… you up at your house at about 8 o'clock then. (I / pick)
Later that day, Joe offers to take Paul to the airport.
JOE: Paul, do you want me to take you to the airport?
PAUL: No thanks, Joe. ………… me. (Kate / take)

→ 补充练习 10–13 (第308–310页)

Unit 24 will be doing 与 will have done 比较

A 请看下列例句：

These people are standing in a queue to get into the cinema.

现在

Half an hour from now, the cinema will be full.
Everyone **will be watching** the film.

半小时后

Three hours from now, the cinema will be empty.
The film **will have finished**.
Everyone **will have gone** home.

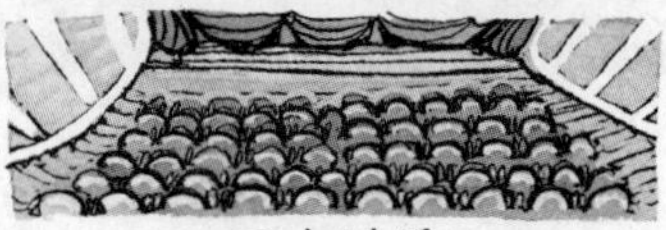

三小时后

B I **will be doing** something (将来进行时) 表示将来某时正在做某事：

- This time next week I'll be on holiday. **I'll be lying** on the beach or **swimming** in the sea.
- You have no chance of getting the job. You**'ll be wasting** your time if you apply for it.

请比较 **will be** (do)**ing** 与 **will** (do)：

- Don't phone between 7 and 8. We**'ll be having** dinner.
- Let's wait for Liz to arrive and then we**'ll have** dinner.

请比较 **will be -ing** 与其他进行时形式：

- At 10 o'clock yesterday, Sally **was** in her office. She **was working**. (过去进行时)
  It's 10 o'clock now. She **is** in her office. She **is working**. (现在进行时)
  At 10 o'clock tomorrow, she **will be** in her office. She **will be working**.

C **will be -ing** 还用于表示将来要做的事情：

- The government **will be making** a statement about the crisis later today.
- **Will** you **be going** away this summer?
- Later in the programme, I**'ll be talking** to the Minister of Education …
- Our best player is injured and **won't be playing** in the game on Saturday.

在这些例句中，**will be -ing** 与表示将来意义的现在进行时 **(be) going to …** 一样。

D **will have (done)** (将来完成时) 用于表示在将来某个时间点之前已完成的动作。例如：

- Sally always leaves for work at 8.30 in the morning. She won't be at home at 9 o'clock – she**'ll have gone** to work.
- We're late. The film **will** already **have started** by the time we get to the cinema.

请比较 **will have** (done) 与其他完成时形式：

- Ted and Amy **have been** married for 24 years. (现在完成时)
  Next year they **will have been** married for 25 years.
  When their son was born, they **had been** married for three years. (过去完成时)

will → Units 21–22 **by then / by the time** → Unit 120 **将来时** → 附录 3

Exercises

24.1 先读下面介绍安迪情况的一段话，然后在正确的句子后面打✓。每组至少有一句是正确的。

Andy goes to work every day. He leaves home at 8 o'clock and arrives at work at about 8.45. He starts work immediately and continues until 12.30 when he has lunch (which takes about half an hour). He starts work again at 1.15 and goes home at exactly 4.30. Every day he follows the same routine and tomorrow will be no exception.

1 

At 7.45
a he'll be leaving the house
b he'll have left the house
c he'll be at home ✓
d he'll be having breakfast ✓

2 

At 8.15
a he'll be leaving the house
b he'll have left the house
c he'll have arrived at work
d he'll be arriving at work

3 

At 9.15
a he'll be working
b he'll start work
c he'll have started work
d he'll be arriving at work

4 

At 12.45
a he'll have lunch
b he'll be having lunch
c he'll have finished his lunch
d he'll have started his lunch

5 

At 4 o'clock
a he'll have finished work
b he'll finish work
c he'll be working
d he won't have finished work

6 

At 4.45
a he'll leave work
b he'll be leaving work
c he'll have left work
d he'll have arrived home

24.2 用动词的 **will be (do)ing** 或 **will have (done)** 形式填空。

1 Don't phone between 7 and 8. We'll be having .... dinner then. (we / have)
2 Phone me after 8 o'clock. .... dinner by then. (we / finish)
3 Tomorrow afternoon we're going to play tennis from 3 o'clock until 4.30. So at 4 o'clock, ... tennis. (we / play)
4 A: Can we meet tomorrow?
B: Yes, but not in the afternoon. .... (I / work)
5 *B has to go to a meeting which begins at 10 o'clock. It will last about an hour.*
A: Will you be free at 11.30?
B: Yes, ... by then. (the meeting / end)
6 Ben is on holiday and he is spending his money very quickly. If he continues like this, ... all his money before the end of his holiday. (he / spend)
7 Do you think .... the same job in ten years' time? (you / still / do)
8 Lisa is from New Zealand. She is travelling around Europe at the moment. So far she has travelled about 1,000 miles. By the end of the trip, ... more than 3,000 miles. (she / travel)
9 If you need to contact me, ... at the Lion Hotel until Friday. (I / stay)
10 A: .... Laura tomorrow? (you / see)
B: Yes, probably. Why?
A: I borrowed this DVD from her. Can you give it back to her?

→ 补充练习 12–13 (第309–310页)

Unit 25

when I do / when I've done when 与 if 比较

A

请看下列例句：

I'll phone you when I get home 这句话包含两部分：

主句： **I'll** phone you

when 从句： **when** I **get** home

句子讲述的是将来 (明天) 要发生的事，但 **when** 后面的从句用的是一般现在时 (**get**)。

句中 **when** 引导的从句不用**will**。

再看一些例句：

- We'**ll go** out **when** it **stops** raining. (而不用 when it will stop)
- **When** you **are** in London again, come and see us. (而不用 When you will be)
- (*said to a child*) What do you want to be **when** you **grow** up? (而不用 will grow)

由 **while** / **before** / **after** / **as soon as** / **until** 或 **till** 引导的从句情况相同：

- What are you going to do **while** I'**m** away? (而不用 while I will be)
- I'll probably go back home on Sunday. **Before** I **go**, I'd like to visit the museum.
- Wait here **until** (或 **till**) I **come** back.

B

在 **when** / **after** / **until** / **as soon as** 后也可以用现在完成时：

- Can I borrow that book **when** you'**ve finished** with it?
- Don't say anything while Ian is here. Wait **until** he **has gone**.

现在完成时表示一个动作在另一个动作发生之前已完成。请比较：

- **When I've phoned** Kate, we can have dinner.
  (= First I'll phone Kate and *after* that we can have dinner.)

如果两个动作同时发生，不要用现在完成时：

- **When** I **phone** Kate, I'll ask her about the party. (而不用 When I've phoned)

经常既可以用一般现在时又可以用现在完成时：

- I'll come **as soon as I finish**. 或 I'll come **as soon as I've finished**.
- You'll feel better **after you have** something to eat. 或 You'll feel better **after you've had** something to eat.

C

if 后通常用一般现在时表示将来 (**if I do** / **if I see** 等)：

- It's raining hard. We'll get wet **if** we **go** out. (而不用 if we will go)
- I'll be angry **if** it **happens** again. (而不用 if it will happen)
- Hurry up! **If** we **don't hurry**, we'll be late.

D

when 与 **if** 比较

when 用于表示肯定发生的动作：

- I'm going out later. (肯定发生) **When** I go out, I'll get some bread.

if 用于表示可能发生的动作：

- I might go out later. (可能发生) **If** I go out, I'll get some bread.
- **If** it is raining this evening, I won't go out. (而不用 When it is raining)
- Don't worry **if** I'm late tonight. (而不用 when I'm late)
- **If** they don't come soon, I'm not going to wait. (而不用 When they don't come)

if ➜ Units 38–40 **even if / even when** ➜ Unit 112D **unless** ➜ Unit 115

Exercises

25.1 下列句子都用来讲述将来发生的事。用 **will/won't** 和括号内的动词或用一般现在时 **(I see / he plays / it is 等)** 完成句子。

1 When ......you are...... (you / be) in London again, come and see us.
2 I want to see Sophie before .... (she / go) out.
3 Call me when .... (you / know) what time you're going to get here.
4 I'm going out now. .... (you / be) here when .... (I / get) back?
5 I think everything will be fine, but if .... (there / be) any problems, ... (I / call) you, OK?
6 We must do something soon before .... (it / be) too late.
7 Anna looks very different now. When .... (you / see) her again, ... (you / not / recognise) her.
8 Steve has applied for the job, but he isn't really qualified for it. .... (I / be) surprised if .... (he / get) it.
9 I'm going to be away for a few days. If .... (you / need) to contact me while .... (I / be) away, here's my mobile number.
10 I don't want to go without you. .... (I / wait) for you until .... (you / be) ready.

25.2 将下列每组句子改写成一句。

1 It will stop raining soon. Then we'll go out.
......We'll go out...... when ......it stops raining......
2 I'll find somewhere to live. Then I'll give you my address.
I .... when ....
3 I'll do the shopping. Then I'll come straight back home.
.... after ....
4 It's going to get dark. Let's go home before that.
.... before ....
5 She must apologise to me first. I won't speak to her until then.
.... until ....

25.3 根据所给情况，完成下列句子。

1 A friend of yours is going on holiday. You want to know what she is going to do.
You ask: What are you going to do when ......you are on holiday......?
2 A friend is visiting you. She has to go soon, but you'd like to show her some pictures.
You ask: Do you have time to look at some pictures before ....?
3 You want to sell your car. Mark is interested in buying it, but he hasn't decided yet.
You ask: Can you let me know as soon as ....?
4 Your friends are going to Hong Kong soon. You want to know where they're going to stay.
You ask: Where are you going to stay when ....?
5 The traffic is very bad in your town, but they are going to build a new road.
You say: I think things will be better when they ....

25.4 用 **when** 或 **if** 填空。

1 Don't worry ......if...... I'm late tonight.
2 Be careful. You'll hurt yourself .... you fall.
3 I'm going to Rome next week. .... I'm there, I hope to visit a friend of mine.
4 I'm going shopping. .... you want anything, I can get it for you.
5 .... I don't see you tomorrow, when will I see you again?
6 I'm going away for a few days. I'll call you .... I get back.
7 I hope Sarah can come to the party. It will be a shame .... she can't come.
8 We can eat at home or, ... you prefer, we can go to a restaurant.

→ 补充练习 12–15 (第309–311页)，32 (第321页)

can，could 与 (be) able to 比较

A

can 用来表示某事可能发生或某人有能力做某事。我们用 **can** + 不带 **to** 的动词不定式 (**can do** / **can see** 等)：

- We **can see** the lake from our hotel.
- 'I don't have a pen.' 'You **can use** mine.'
- **Can** you **speak** any foreign languages?
- I **can come** and see you tomorrow if you like.
- The word 'dream' **can be** a noun or a verb.

否定形式为 **can't** (= **cannot**)：

- I'm afraid I **can't come** to the party on Friday.

B

可以用 **be able to** 代替 **can**，但 **can** 更常用：

- We **are able to see** the lake from our hotel.

但是 **can** 只有两种形式：**can** (现在时形式) 与 **could** (过去时形式)。因而有时需要用 **(be) able to …**。请比较：

I **can't** sleep.	**I haven't been able to** sleep recently.
Tom **can** come tomorrow.	Tom **might be able to** come tomorrow.
Maria **can** speak French, Spanish and English.	Applicants for the job **must be able to** speak two foreign languages.

C

could

could 有时用作 **can** 的过去式，尤与下列动词连用：

see **hear** **smell** **taste** **feel** **remember** **understand**

- We had a lovely room in the hotel. We **could see** the lake.
- As soon as I walked into the room, I **could smell** gas.
- I was sitting at the back of the theatre and **couldn't hear** very well.

could 也可以用来表示某人具有某种能力或被允许做某事：

- My grandfather **could speak** five languages.
- We were totally free. We **could do** what we wanted. (= we were allowed to do)

D

could 与 **was able to** 比较

could 表示具有某种能力。但若要表示某人在特定的情况下能够做某事，则需用 **was/were able to …** 或 **managed to …** (而不用 **could**)：

- The fire spread through the building very quickly, but fortunately everybody **was able to escape** / **managed to escape**. (而不用 could escape)
- We didn't know where David was, but we **managed to find** / **were able to find** him in the end. (而不用 could find)

请比较：

- Jack was an excellent tennis player when he was younger. He **could beat** anybody. (= he had the *general* ability to beat anybody)

但是 Jack and Andy played a match yesterday. Andy played well, but Jack **managed to beat** him. (= he managed to beat him this time)

否定式 **couldn't (could not)** 可以用于所有情况：

- My grandfather **couldn't swim**.
- We looked for David everywhere, but we **couldn't find** him.
- Andy played well, but he **couldn't beat** Jack.

could (do) 与 **could have (done)** 比较 ➔ Unit 27　　**must** 与 **can't** 比较 ➔ Unit 28
Can/Could you … ? ➔ Unit 37

Exercises

26.1 用 **can** 或 **(be) able to** 完成下列句子。

1 Gary has travelled a lot. He ...can... speak five languages.
2 I haven't ...been able to... sleep very well recently.
3 Nicole .... drive, but she doesn't have a car.
4 I used to .... stand on my head, but I can't do it any more.
5 I can't understand Mark. I've never .... understand him.
6 I can't see you on Friday, but I .... meet you on Saturday morning.
7 Ask Katherine about your problem. She might .... help you.

26.2 根据你自己的情况，用括号内的提示造句。

1 (something you used to be able to do)
...I used to be able to sing well....
2 (something you used to be able to do)
I used ....
3 (something you would like to be able to do)
I'd ....
4 (something you have never been able to do)
I've ....

26.3 用 **can/can't/could/couldn't** + 下列动词完成句子。

~~come~~	eat	hear	run	sleep	wait

1 I'm afraid I ...can't come... to your party next week.
2 When Dan was 16, he .... 100 metres in 11 seconds.
3 'Are you in a hurry?' 'No, I've got plenty of time. I ....'
4 I was feeling sick yesterday. I .... anything.
5 Can you speak a little louder? I .... you very well.
6 'You look tired.' 'Yes, I .... last night.'

26.4 用 **was/were able to ...** 完成下列对话。

1 A: Did everybody escape from the fire?
B: Yes, although the fire spread quickly, everybody ...was able to escape... .
2 A: Did you finish your work this afternoon?
B: Yes, there was nobody to disturb me, so I ....
3 A: Did you have problems finding our house?
B: Not really. Your directions were good and we ....
4 A: Did the thief get away?
B: Yes. No-one realised what was happening and the thief ....

26.5 用 **could**，**couldn't** 或 **managed to** 完成下列句子。

1 My grandfather travelled a lot. He ...could... speak five languages.
2 I looked everywhere for the book, but I ...couldn't... find it.
3 They didn't want to come with us at first, but we ...managed to... persuade them.
4 Laura had hurt her leg and .... walk very well.
5 I ran my first marathon recently. It was very hard, but I .... finish.
6 I looked very carefully and I .... see somebody in the distance.
7 I wanted to buy some tomatoes. The first shop I went to didn't have any, but I .... get some in the next shop.
8 My grandmother loved music. She .... play the piano very well.
9 A girl fell into the river, but fortunately we .... pull her out.
10 I had forgotten to bring my camera, so I .... take any pictures.

could (do) 与 could have (done) 比较

A

could 有下列几种用法。有时，**could** 用作 **can** 的过去式 (参见Unit 26C)：

- Listen. I **can hear** something. (现在)
- I listened. I **could hear** something. (过去)

could 还用于谈论现在或将来可能发生的动作 (尤用于提建议)，例如：

- A: What shall we do tonight?
  B: We **could go** to the cinema.
- A: When you go to Paris next month, you **could stay** with Sarah.
  B: Yes, I suppose I **could**.

can 也可以用于上述句子中 (We **can** go to the cinema 等)。**could** 的语气不像 **can** 那么确定。

B

could 还可以用来表示并不现实的行为 (不用**can**)。例如：

- I'm so tired, I **could sleep** for a week. (而不用 I can sleep for a week)

请比较 **can** 与 **could**：

- I **can stay** with Sarah when I go to Paris. (现实)
- Maybe I **could stay** with Sarah when I go to Paris. (有可能，但没那么确定)
- This is a wonderful place. I **could stay** here forever. (不现实)

C

could 用于谈论现在或将来有可能发生的事情或情形 (不用 **can**)，意思与 **might** 或 **may** 相近 (参见 Unit 29)：

- The story **could be** true, but I don't think it is. (而不用 can be true)
- I don't know what time Lisa is coming. She **could get** here at any time.

请比较 **can** 与 **could**：

- The weather **can** change very quickly in the mountains. (泛指)
- The weather is nice now, but it **could** change. (指当下的天气，而非泛指)

D

could have (done) 用于谈论过去：

- I'm so tired, I **could sleep** for a week. (现在)
  I was so tired, I **could have slept** for a week. (过去)
- The situation is bad, but it **could be** worse. (现在)
  The situation was bad, but it **could have been** worse. (过去)

could have 用于表示某事本来可能发生但实际却没有发生：

- Why did you stay at a hotel when you were in Paris? You **could have stayed** with Sarah.
  (你本来有机会同她在一起但实际你没有这样做)
- David was lucky. He **could have hurt** himself when he fell, but he's OK.

E

couldn't 用来表示某事不可能发生：

- I **couldn't live** in a big city. I'd hate it. (= it wouldn't be possible for me)
- Everything is fine right now. Things **couldn't be** better.

表示过去时用 **couldn't have** (done)：

- We had a really good holiday. It **couldn't have been** better.
- The trip was cancelled last week. Paul **couldn't have gone** anyway because he was ill.
  (= it would not have been possible for him to go)

couldn't have (done) ➜ Unit 28B **could 与 might 比较** ➜ Unit 29C **Could I/you … ?** ➜ Unit 37
could 与 if 连用 ➜ Units 38C，39E，40D **情态动词 (can/could/will/would 等)** ➜ 附录 4

Exercises

27.1 以提建议的方式，用 **could** 回答下列问题。

1	Where shall we go for our holidays?	(to Scotland) We could go to Scotland.
2	What shall we have for dinner tonight?	(fish) We ......
3	When shall I phone Vicky?	(now) You ......
4	What shall I give Ann for her birthday?	(a book) ......
5	Where shall we hang this picture?	(in the kitchen) ......

27.2 下列有些句子需要用 **could** 而非 **can**，必要时请改正。

1 The story can be true, but I don't think it is. could be true
2 It's a nice day. We can go for a walk. OK (could go *is also possible*)
3 I'm so angry with him. I can kill him! ......
4 If you're hungry, we can have dinner now. ......
5 It's so nice here. I can stay here all day, but unfortunately I have to go. ......
6 A: Where's my bag? Have you seen it?
B: No, but it can be in the car. ......
7 Peter is a keen musician. He plays the flute and he can also play the piano. ......
8 A: I need to borrow a camera.
B: You can borrow mine. ......
9 Be careful climbing that tree. You can fall. ......

27.3 用 **could** 或 **could have** + 适当的动词完成下列对话。

1 A: What shall we do this evening?
B: I don't mind. We could go to the cinema.
2 A: I spent a very boring evening at home yesterday.
B: Why did you stay at home? You ...... out with us.
3 A: Have you seen this job advertised in the paper? You ...... for it.
B: What sort of job? Show me the advertisement.
4 A: How was your exam? Was it difficult?
B: It wasn't so bad. It ...... worse.
5 A: I got very wet walking home in the rain last night.
B: Why did you walk? You ...... a taxi.
6 A: Where shall we meet tomorrow?
B: Well, I ...... to your house if you like.

27.4 用 **couldn't** 或 **couldn't have** + 下列动词的适当形式完成句子。

~~be~~ be come find get ~~live~~ wear

1 I couldn't live in a big city. I'd hate it.
2 We had a really good holiday. It couldn't have been better.
3 I ...... that hat. I'd look silly and people would laugh at me.
4 We managed to find the restaurant you recommended, but we ...... it without the map that you drew for us.
5 Paul has to get up at 4 o'clock every morning. I don't know how he does it. I ...... up at that time every day.
6 The staff at the hotel were really nice when we stayed there last summer. They ...... more helpful.
7 A: I tried to phone you last week. We had a party and I wanted to invite you.
B: That was nice of you, but I ...... anyway. I was away all last week.

→ 补充练习 16–18 (第311–313页)

Unit 28

must 与 can't 比较

A

请看下列例句：

must 用于表示肯定的推测：

- You've been travelling all day. You **must be** tired. (旅行很累人，而且你整日在旅途中，因此你一定很累)
- 'Joe is a hard worker.' 'Joe? You **must be joking**. He doesn't do anything.'
- Louise **must get** very bored in her job. She does the same thing every day.
- I'm sure Sally gave me her address. I **must have** it somewhere.

can't 用于表示否定的推测：

- You've just had lunch. You **can't be** hungry already. (人在饭后一般都不饿。你刚吃完饭，因此你肯定不饿)
- They haven't lived here for very long. They **can't know** many people.

请看下列构成方式：

I/you/he (等)	**must** **can't**	**be** (tired / hungry / at work 等) **be (doing / going / joking 等)** **do / get / know / have** 等

B

must have (done) 和 **can't have (done)** 用于谈论过去。
请看下列例句：

Martin and Lucy are standing at the door of their friends' house. They have rung the doorbell twice, but nobody has answered. Lucy says:

They **must have gone** out.

- 'We used to live very near the motorway.' 'Did you? It **must have been** noisy.'
- 'I've lost one of my gloves.' 'You **must have dropped** it somewhere.'
- Sarah hasn't contacted me. She **can't have got** my message.
- Tom walked into a wall. He **can't have been looking** where he was going.

请看下列构成方式：

I/you/he (等)	**must** **can't**	**have**	**been** (asleep / at work 等) **been (doing / looking 等)** **gone / got / known** 等

可以用 **couldn't have ...** 代替 **can't have ...**：

- Sarah **couldn't have got** my message.
- Tom **couldn't have been looking** where he was going.

can't → Unit 26　　**must** (I must go 等) → Units 31–32
情态动词 (can/could/will/would 等) → 附录 4　　**美国英语** → 附录 7

Exercises

28.1 用 **must** 或 **can't** 填空。

1 You've been travelling all day. You ...must... be tired.
2 That restaurant .... be very good. It's always full of people.
3 That restaurant .... be very good. It's always empty.
4 I'm sure I gave you the key. You .... have it. Have you looked in your bag?
5 I often see that woman walking along this street. She .... live near here.
6 It rained every day during their holiday, so they .... have had a very nice time.
7 Congratulations on passing your exam. You .... be very pleased.
8 You got here very quickly. You .... have walked very fast.
9 Bill and Sue always stay at luxury hotels, so they .... be short of money.

28.2 用动词的适当形式完成下列句子。

1 I've lost one of my gloves. I must ...have dropped... it somewhere.
2 Their house is very near the motorway. It must ...be... very noisy.
3 Sarah knows a lot about films. She must .... to the cinema a lot.
4 I left my bike outside the house last night and now it's gone. Somebody must .... it.
5 'How old is Ted?' 'He's older than me. He must .... at least 40.'
6 I didn't hear the phone ring. I must .... asleep.
7 A: You're going on holiday soon. You must .... forward to it.
B: Yes, it will be really good to get away.
8 The police have closed the road, so we have to go a different way. There must .... an accident.
9 I'm sure you know this song. You must .... it before.
10 There is a man walking behind us. He has been walking behind us for the last 20 minutes. He must .... us.

28.3 根据所给情况和下列括号中的词语，用 **must have** 或 **can't have** 造句。

1 We went to their house and rang the doorbell, but nobody answered. (they / go out)
They must have gone out.
2 Sarah hasn't contacted me. (she / get / my message)
She can't have got my message.
3 The jacket you bought is very good quality. (it / very expensive)
....
4 I haven't seen our neighbours for ages. (they / go away)
....
5 I can't find my umbrella. (I / leave / it in the restaurant last night)
....
6 Amy was in a very difficult situation when she lost her job. (it / easy for her)
....
7 There was a man standing outside the café. (he / wait / for somebody)
....
8 Rachel did the opposite of what I asked her to do. (she / understand / what I said)
....
9 When I got back to my car, the door was unlocked. (I / forget / to lock it)
....
10 I was woken up in the night by the noise next door. (my neighbours / have / a party)
....
11 The light was red, but the car didn't stop. (the driver / see / the red light)
....

➔ 补充练习 16–18（第311–313页）

may 与 might 比较（1）

A

请看下列例句：

You are looking for Ben. Nobody is sure where he is, but you get some suggestions.

(= perhaps he is in his office)
(= perhaps he is having lunch)
(= perhaps she knows)

may 或 **might** 用来表示“可能，也许”。通常 **may** 和 **might** 均可使用，可以说：

- It **may** be true. 或 It **might** be true. (= perhaps it is true)
- She **might** know. 或 She **may** know.

否定形式为 **may not** 和 **might not** (或 **mightn't**)：

- It **may not** be true. (= perhaps it isn't true)
- She **might not** work here any more. (= perhaps she doesn't work here)

请看下列构成方式：

I/you/he (等)	**may** **might**	**(not)**	**be** (true / in his office 等) **be (doing / working / having** 等) **know / work / want** 等

B

may have (done) 和 **might have (done)** 用来谈论过去：

- A: I wonder why Kate didn't answer her phone.
  B: She **may have been** asleep. (= perhaps she was asleep)
- A: I can't find my phone anywhere.
  B: You **might have left** it at work. (= perhaps you left it at work)
- A: Why wasn't Amy at the meeting yesterday?
  B: She **might not have known** about it. (= perhaps she didn't know)
- A: I wonder why David was in such a bad mood yesterday.
  B: He **may not have been feeling** well. (= perhaps he wasn't feeling well)

请看下列构成方式：

I/you/he (等)	**may** **might**	**(not) have**	**been** (asleep / at home 等) **been (doing / working / feeling** 等) **known / had / wanted / left** 等

C

有时 **could** 与 **may** 和 **might** 意思相同：

- It's a strange story, but it **could be** true. (= it is possible that it's true)
- You **could have left** your phone at work. (= it's possible that you left it there)

但是 **couldn't** 与 **may not** 和 **might not** 意思不同。请比较：

- Sarah **couldn't have** got my message. Otherwise she would have replied.
  (= it is not possible that she got my message)
- I wonder why Sarah hasn't replied to my message. I suppose she **might not have** got it.
  (= it's possible that she didn't get it – so perhaps she did, perhaps she didn't)

could ➜ Unit 27 **may 与 might 比较 (2)** ➜ Unit 30 **May I ... ?** ➜ Unit 37C
might 与 if 连用 ➜ Units 30B，38C，40D **情态动词 (can/could/will/would 等)** ➜ 附录 4

Exercises

29.1 用 **might** 造句。

1 Perhaps Helen is in her office. She might be in her office.
2 Perhaps Helen is busy. ....
3 Perhaps she is working. ....
4 Perhaps she wants to be alone. ....
5 Perhaps she was ill yesterday. ....
6 Perhaps she went home early. ....
7 Perhaps she had to go home early. ....
8 Perhaps she was working yesterday. ....

9–11 句用 **might not** 造句。

9 Perhaps she doesn't want to see me. ....
10 Perhaps she isn't working today. ....
11 Perhaps she wasn't feeling well yesterday. ....

29.2 用动词的适当形式完成下列对话。

1 'Where's Ben?' 'I'm not sure. He might be having lunch.'
2 'Who is that man with Anna?' 'I'm not sure. It might .... her brother.'
3 A: Who was the man we saw with Anna yesterday?
B: I'm not sure. It may .... her brother.
4 A: What are those people doing by the side of the road?
B: I don't know. I suppose they might .... for a bus.
5 'Is Sarah here?' 'I can't see her. She may not .... yet.'

29.3 根据所给情况和括号内的词语，用 **might** 造句。

1 I can't find Jeff anywhere. I wonder where he is.
a (he / go / shopping) He might have gone shopping.
b (he / play / tennis) He might be playing tennis.
2 I'm looking for Sophie. Do you know where she is?
a (she / watch / TV) ....
b (she / go / out) ....
3 I can't find my umbrella. Have you seen it?
a (it / be / in the car) ....
b (you / leave / in the restaurant) ....
4 Why didn't Dan answer the doorbell? I'm sure he was at home at the time.
a (he / go / to bed early) ....
b (he / not / hear / the doorbell) ....
c (he / be / in the shower) ....

29.4 用 **might not have** 或 **couldn't have** 完成下列对话。

1 A: Do you think Sarah got the message I sent her?
B: No, she would have replied. She couldn't have got it.
2 A: I was surprised Amy wasn't at the meeting. Perhaps she didn't know about it.
B: That's possible. She might not have known about it.
3 A: I wonder why they haven't replied to the email I sent. Do you think they received it?
B: Maybe not. They ....
4 A: I wonder how the fire started. Was it an accident?
B: No, the police say it ....
5 A: Mike says he needs to see you. He tried to find you yesterday.
B: Well, he .... very hard. I was in my office all day.
6 A: The man you spoke to – are you sure he was American?
B: No, I'm not sure. He ....

➜ 补充练习 16–18 (第311–313页)

Unit 30

may 与 might 比较 (2)

A

may 和 **might** 用来谈论将来可能发生的事情或动作：

- I haven't decided yet where to go on holiday. I **may go** to Ireland. (= perhaps I will go there)
- Take an umbrella with you. It **might rain** later. (= perhaps it will rain)
- The bus isn't always on time. We **might have** to wait a few minutes. (= perhaps we will have to wait)

否定形式为 **may not** 和 **might not (mightn't)**：

- Amy **may not go** out tonight. She isn't feeling well. (= perhaps she will not go out)
- There **might not be** enough time to discuss everything at the meeting. (= perhaps there will not be enough time)

请比较 **will** 和 **may/might**：

- **I'll** be late this evening. (肯定)
- I **may/might** be late this evening. (可能)

B

通常既可以用 **may**，也可以用 **might**。可以说：

- I **may go** to Ireland. 或 I **might go** to Ireland.
- Jane **might be** able to help you. 或 Jane **may be** able to help you.

但当情况是虚拟的时，只能用 **might** (不能用 **may**)：

- If they paid me better, I **might** work harder. (而不用 I may work)

这种情况不是真的，因为他们付给我的报酬并不丰厚，所以我不打算更努力地工作。

C

may/might 的进行时形式为**may/might be -ing**。请同 **will be -ing** 比较：

- Don't phone at 8.30. **I'll be watching** the football on television.
- Don't phone at 8.30. I **might be watching** (或 I **may be watching**) the football on TV. (= perhaps I'll be watching it)

may/might be -ing 表示可能的计划。请比较：

- **I'm going** to Ireland in July. (肯定)
- I **might be going** (或 I **may be going**) to Ireland soon. (可能)

也可以说 I **might go** / I **may go** ...，意义没有区别。

D

might as well

Helen and Clare have just missed the bus. The buses run every hour.

we **might as well** do something 意为"倒不如做某事"。

也可以说 **may as well**。

- A: What time are you going out?
  B: Well, I'm ready, so I **might as well go** now.
- Buses are so expensive these days, you **might as well get** a taxi. (= taxis are as good, no more expensive)

will be -ing → Unit 24 **may 与 might 比较 (1)** → Unit 29 **May I ... ?** → Unit 37C
might 与 if 连用 → Units 38C, 40D

Exercises

30.1 用 **might** 造句。

1 Where are you going for your holidays? (to Ireland???)
I haven't decided yet. I might go to Ireland.

2 What sort of car are you going to buy? (a Honda???)
I'm not sure yet. I ……

3 When is Tom coming to see us? (on Saturday???)
He hasn't said yet. ……

4 Where are you going to hang that picture? (in the dining room???)
I haven't made up my mind yet. ……

5 What is Tanya going to do when she leaves school? (go to university???)
She's still thinking about it. ……

30.2 用 **might** + 下列动词完成句子。

bite	**break**	**need**	~~**rain**~~	**slip**	**wake**

1 Take an umbrella with you when you go out. It might rain later.
2 Don't make too much noise. You …… the baby.
3 Be careful of that dog. It …… you.
4 Don't throw that letter away. We …… it later.
5 Be careful. The footpath is very icy. You …… .
6 Don't let the children play in this room. They …… something.

30.3 用 **might be able to** 或 **might have to** + 适当的动词完成下列句子。

fix	~~**help**~~	**leave**	**meet**	**sell**	**work**

1 Tell me about your problem. I might be able to help you.
2 I'm not free this evening, but I …… you tomorrow.
3 I don't know if I'll be free on Sunday. I …… .
4 I can come to the meeting, but I …… before the end.
5 I'm short of money. I want to keep my car, but I …… it.
6 A: There's something wrong with my bike.
B: Let me have a look. I …… it.

30.4 用 **might not** 造句。

1 I'm not sure that Liz will come to the party.
Liz might not come to the party.

2 I'm not sure that I'll go out this evening.
I ……

3 I'm not sure that we'll be able to get tickets for the game.
We ……

4 I'm not sure that Sam will be able to go out with us tonight.
……

30.5 根据所给情况，用 **might as well** 造句。

1 You and a friend have just missed the bus. The buses run every hour.
You say: We'll have to wait an hour for the next bus. We might as well walk.

2 You've been invited to a party. You're not very excited about it, but you decide to go.
You say: I'm not doing anything else, so I …… to the party.

3 You've just painted your kitchen. You still have a lot of paint, so why not paint the bathroom too?
You say: We …… . There's plenty of paint left.

4 You and a friend are at home. You're bored. There's a film on TV starting in a few minutes.
You say: …… . There's nothing else to do.

➜ 补充练习 16–18（第311–313页）

Unit 31 have to 与 must 比较

A

I **have to** do something 表示“必须或应当做某事”：

- You can't turn right here. You **have to turn** left.
- I **have to wear** glasses for reading.
- Robert can't come out with us this evening.
  He **has to work** late.
- Last week Tina broke her arm and **had to go** to hospital.
- I haven't **had to go** to the doctor for ages.

在一般现在时和一般过去时中，用 **do/does/did** 构成have to的疑问句和否定句：

- What **do** I **have to do** to get a new driving licence? （而不用 What have I to do?)
- Karen **doesn't have to work** Saturdays. （而不用 Karen hasn't to)
- Why **did** you **have to leave** early?

可以说 **I'll have to** ...， **I'm going to have to** ... 或 **I might / I may have to** ...：

- They can't fix my computer, so **I'll have to buy** a new one. 或
  I'm going to have to buy a new one.
- Tom **might have to work** late tomorrow. 或 Tom **may have to work** ...
  (= it's possible that he will have to)

B

must 的用法与 **have to** 相似：

- It's later than I thought. I **must go**. 或 I **have to go**.

must 和 **have to** 可用来表达观点（比如表达你认为需要做什么或建议某人做某事）：

- I haven't spoken to Sue for ages. I **must phone** her. / I **have to phone** her.
  (= I say this is necessary)
- Mark is a really nice person. You **must meet** him. / You **have to meet** him.
  （我建议如此）

have to（通常不用 **must**）用来表示某人不得不做某事，说话者并不是在表达自己的观点：

- I **have to work** from 8.30 to 5.30 every day. （事实而非观点）
- Jane **has to travel** a lot for her work.

但在书面规定、规则中用 **must**：

- Applications for the job **must be received** by 18 May.
- (*exam instruction*) Answer all the questions. You **must write** your answers in ink.

must 不用来谈论过去：

- We didn't have much time. We **had** to hurry. （而不用 we must hurry)

C

mustn't 与 **don't have to** 完全不同：

You **mustn't** do something 表示不许做（因此不做）：	You **don't have to** do something 表示不需要做（但如果想做也可以）：
You **must keep** this a secret. You **mustn't tell** anyone. (= don't tell anybody)	You **don't have to tell** Tom what happened. I can tell him myself.
I promised I would be on time. I **mustn't be** late. (= I must be on time)	I **don't have to be** at the meeting, but I think I'll go anyway.

D

可以用 **have got to** 代替 **have to**，可以说：

- **I've got to** work tomorrow. 或 I **have to** work tomorrow.
- When **has** Helen **got to** go? 或 When **does** Helen **have to** go?

must ('You must be tired') ➜ Unit 28 **must/mustn't/needn't** ➜ Unit 32

Exercises

31.1 用 **have to / has to / had to** 完成下列句子。

1 Bill starts work at 5 a.m. ....He has to get up.... at four. (he / get up)
2 'I broke my arm last week.' '....Did you have to go.... to hospital?' (you / go)
3 There was a lot of noise from the street. .... the window. (we / close)
4 Karen can't stay for the whole meeting. .... early. (she / leave)
5 How old .... to drive in your country? (you / be)
6 I don't have much time. .... soon. (I / go)
7 How is Paul enjoying his new job? .... a lot? (he / travel)
8 'I'm afraid I can't stay long.' 'What time ....?' (you / go)
9 'The bus was late again.' 'How long ....?' (you / wait)
10 There was nobody to help me. I .... everything by myself. (I / do)

31.2 用 **have to** + 所给的动词完成下列句子。有时需用否定形式。

ask do drive ~~get up~~ go make make pay ~~show~~

1 I'm not working tomorrow, so I ....don't have to get up.... early.
2 Steve didn't know how to turn off the computer, so I ....had to show.... him.
3 Excuse me a moment – I .... a phone call. I won't be long.
4 I'm not too busy. I have a few things to do, but I .... them now.
5 I couldn't find the street I wanted. I .... somebody for directions.
6 The car park is free. You .... to park your car there.
7 A man was injured in the accident, but he .... to hospital because it wasn't serious.
8 Jane has a senior position in the company. She .... important decisions.
9 When Patrick starts his new job next month, he .... 50 miles to work every day.

31.3 下列句子中有些使用 **must** 是不正确或不自然的，请改正。

1 It's later than I thought. I must go. ....OK (have to *is also correct*)....
2 I must work every day from 8.30 to 5.30. ....I have to work....
3 You must come and see us again soon. ....
4 Tom can't meet us tomorrow. He must work. ....
5 I must work late yesterday evening. ....
6 I must get up early tomorrow. I have a lot to do. ....
7 Julia wears glasses. She must wear glasses since she was very young. ....

31.4 用 **mustn't** 或 **don't/doesn't have to** 完成下列句子。

1 I don't want anyone to know about our plan. You ....mustn't.... tell anyone.
2 Richard ....doesn't have to.... wear a suit to work, but he usually does.
3 I can sleep late tomorrow morning because I .... go to work.
4 Whatever you do, you .... touch that switch. It's very dangerous.
5 There's a lift in the building, so we .... climb the stairs.
6 You .... forget what I told you. It's very important.
7 Silvia .... get up early, but she usually does.
8 Don't make so much noise. We .... wake the children.
9 I .... eat too much. I'm supposed to be on a diet.
10 You .... be a good player to enjoy a game of tennis.

→ 补充练习 16（第311页）

must mustn't needn't

A must 与 mustn't 比较

you **must** do something 表示必须做：

- Don't tell anybody what I said. You **must** keep it a secret.
- We haven't got much time. We **must** hurry.

you **mustn't** do something 表示不许做（因此不做）：

- You **must** keep it a secret. You **mustn't** tell anyone. (= don't tell anyone)
- We **must** be very quiet. We **mustn't** make any noise.

B needn't 与 don't need to 比较

you **needn't** do something 表示不需要做（但如果你想的话也可以做）：

- We've got plenty of time. We **needn't hurry**. (= it is not necessary to hurry)
- Joe can stay here. He **needn't come** with us. (= it is not necessary for him to come)

也可以用 **don't/doesn't need to**：

- We **don't need to** hurry.

注意，可以说 **don't need to do / doesn't need to do**，但要说 **needn't do**（不加 **to**）。

C needn't have (done)

请看下列例句：

Paul and Sue decided to go to a restaurant. They reserved a table.

But the restaurant was almost empty. So they **needn't have reserved** a table.

they **needn't have reserved** a table 表示他们预订了餐桌，但其实并没有必要。

请比较 **needn't** (do) 与 **needn't have** (done)：

- Everything will be OK. You **needn't worry**. （不必担心）
- Everything was OK. You **needn't have worried**. （担心了，但其实并没有必要）

D needn't have (done) 与 didn't need to (do) 比较

he **needn't have done** something 表示"他本不需要做某事（已经做了，但现在我们知道不必做）"：

- Why did he get up at 5 o'clock? He **needn't have got** up so early. He could have stayed in bed longer.

he **didn't need to** do something 表示"他不需要做某事（做了与不做无关紧要）"：

- He **didn't need to** get up early, so he didn't.
- He **didn't need to** get up early, but it was a beautiful morning, so he did.

上述句子中也可以用 **He didn't have to** ...。

must ('You must be tired') → Unit 28 **have to 与 must 比较** → Unit 31
情态动词 (can/could/will/would 等) → 附录 4 **美国英语** → 附录 7

Exercises

32.1 指出下列句子中画线的部分哪个是正确的。

1 We haven't got much time. We must / ~~mustn't~~ hurry. (must *is correct*)
2 We've got plenty of time. We mustn't / don't need to hurry.
3 I have to talk to Gary. I must / mustn't remember to call him.
4 I have to talk to Gary. I mustn't / needn't forget to call him.
5 There's plenty of time for you to make up your mind. You mustn't / don't need to decide now.
6 We needn't / mustn't wash these tomatoes. They've already been washed.
7 This is a valuable book. You must / needn't take good care of it and you mustn't / don't need to lose it.
8 A: What sort of house do you want to buy? Something big?
B: Well, it mustn't / needn't be big – that's not so important. But it must / mustn't have a nice garden – that's essential.

32.2 用 **needn't** + 下列动词完成句子。

ask **come** **explain** ~~**leave**~~ **walk**

1 We've got plenty of time. We needn't leave yet.
2 I can manage the shopping alone. You .... with me.
3 We .... all the way home. We can get a taxi.
4 Just help yourself if you'd like more to eat. You .... first.
5 I understand the situation perfectly. You .... further.

32.3 根据所给情况，仿照示例造句。第一句使用 **needn't have**，第二句使用 **could have**。**could have** 的用法参见Unit 27。

1 Why did you rush? Why didn't you take your time?
You needn't have rushed. You could have taken your time.
2 Why did you walk home? Why didn't you take a taxi?
....
3 Why did you stay at a hotel? Why didn't you stay with us?
....
4 Why did she phone me in the middle of the night? Why didn't she wait until the morning?
....
5 Why did you shout at me? Why weren't you more patient?
....
6 Why did you leave without saying anything? Why didn't you say goodbye to me?
....

32.4 下列句子如有错误请改正。

1 We have plenty of time. We don't need hurry. We don't need to hurry.
2 You must keep it a secret. You mustn't tell anybody else. OK
3 I'll be all right. You needn't to worry about me. ....
4 You mustn't wait for me. You go on and I'll join you later. ....
5 You don't need to keep these emails. You can delete them. ....
6 I needn't have gone out, so I stayed at home. ....
7 I needn't have bought eggs. We had some already. ....

→ 补充练习（第311–312页）

Unit 33 should (1)

A

you **should do** something 表示"应该做某事"。**should** 用来提出建议或表达观点：

- You look tired. You **should go** to bed.
- The government **should do** more to improve education.
- '**Should** we **invite** Stephanie to the party?' 'Yes, I think we **should**.'

I think / I don't think / Do you think … ? 后面的从句中常用 **should**：

- **I think** the government **should do** more to improve education.
- **I don't think** you **should work** so hard.
- '**Do you think** I **should apply** for this job?' 'Yes, **I think you should**.'

you **shouldn't** do something 表示"不应该做某事"：

- You **shouldn't believe** everything you read in the newspapers.

should 的语气不如 **must** 或 **have to** 那样肯定：

- You **should** apologise. (= it would be a good thing to do)
- You **must** apologise. / You **have to** apologise. (= you have no alternative)

B

should 还用来表示某事不太对头或不像我们想象的那样：

- Where's Tina? She **should be** here by now.
  (= she isn't here yet, and this is not normal)
- The price on this packet is wrong. It **should be** £2.50, not £3.50.
- That man on the motorbike **should be wearing** a helmet.

He **should be wearing** a helmet.

should 用于表示希望做某事或期待某事发生：

- Helen has been studying hard for the exam, so she **should pass**.
  (= I expect her to pass)
- There are plenty of hotels in the town. It **shouldn't be** hard to find a place to stay.
  (= I don't expect it to be hard)

C

you **should have done** something 表示"本应做某事(实际没有做)"：

- You missed a great party last night. You **should have come**. Why didn't you?
  (= you didn't come, but it would have been good to come)
- I wonder why they're so late. They **should have got** here long ago.

you **shouldn't have done** something 表示"本不该做某事(但实际上做了)"：

- I'm feeling sick. I **shouldn't have eaten** so much. (= I ate too much)
- She **shouldn't have been listening** to our conversation. It was private.
  (= she was listening)

请比较 **should** (do) 与 **should have** (done)：

- You look tired. You **should go** to bed now.
- You went to bed very late last night. You **should have gone** to bed earlier.

D

ought to …

本页给出的句子都可以用 **ought to** 代替 **should**。注意 ought to do … 中要加 **to**：

- Do you think I **ought to apply** for this job? (= Do you think I **should apply** … ?)
- Jack **ought not to go** to bed so late. (= Jack **shouldn't go** …)
- It was a great party last night. You **ought to have come**.
- Helen has been studying hard for the exam, so she **ought to pass**.

should (2) ➜ Unit 34 **should 与 had better 比较** ➜ Unit 35B
情态动词 (can/could/will/would 等) ➜ 附录 4

Exercises

33.1 根据所给情况，用 **should** 或 **shouldn't** + 下列短语造句。

~~go away for a few days~~	go to bed so late	look for another job
put some pictures on the walls	take a photo	use her car so much

1 Anna needs a change. She should go away for a few days.
2 Your salary is very low. You ……
3 Jack always finds it hard to get up. He ……
4 What a beautiful view! You ……
5 Sue drives everywhere. She never walks. She ……
6 Dan's room isn't very interesting. ……

33.2 根据所给情况，用 **I think / I don't think … should …** 造句。

1 Joe and Catherine are planning to get married. You think it's a bad idea.
I don't think they should get married.
2 Jane has a bad cold, but plans to go out tonight. You don't think this is a good idea. You say to her: ……
3 Peter needs a job. He's just seen an advert for a job which you think would be ideal for him, but he's not sure whether to apply or not. You say to him:
……
4 The government wants to increase taxes, but you don't think this is a good idea.
……

33.3 用 **should (have)** + 括号内的动词完成下列句子。

1 Helen should pass the exam. She's been studying very hard. (pass)
2 You missed a great party last night. You should have come. (come)
3 We don't see you enough. You …… and see us more often. (come)
4 I'm in a difficult position. What do you think I …… now? (do)
5 I'm sorry that I didn't take your advice. I …… what you said. (do)
6 We lost the game yesterday, but we …… . We were the better team. (win)
7 Tanya has a tennis match against Jane tomorrow. Jane …… – she's much better than Tanya. (win)
8 'Is Joe here yet?' 'Not yet, but he …… here soon.' (be)
9 We went the wrong way and got lost. We …… right, not left. (turn)

33.4 根据所给情况，用 **should/shouldn't** 造句。有些句子表示现在，有些表示过去。

1 I'm feeling sick. I ate too much. I shouldn't have eaten so much.
2 That man on the motorbike isn't wearing a helmet. That's dangerous.
He should be wearing a helmet.
3 When we got to the restaurant, there were no free tables. We hadn't reserved one.
We ……
4 The notice says that the shop is open every day from 8.30. It is 9 o'clock now, but the shop isn't open yet. ……
5 The speed limit is 30 miles an hour, but Kate is doing 50.
She ……
6 Laura told me her address, but I didn't write it down. Now I can't remember the house number.
I ……
7 I was driving behind another car. Suddenly, the driver in front stopped without warning and I drove into the back of his car. It wasn't my fault.
The driver in front ……
8 I walked into a wall. I was looking behind me. I wasn't looking where I was going.
……

→ 补充练习 16–18（第311–313页）

should (2)

A

should 可以用于下列动词之后：

insist **recommend** **suggest** **demand** **propose**

- I **insisted** that he **should apologise**.
- Doctors **recommend** that everyone **should eat** plenty of fruit.
- What do you **suggest** we **should do**?
- Many people are **demanding** that something **should be done** about the problem.

也可以说 **It's important/vital/necessary/essential** that … **should** …：

- **It's essential** that everyone **should be** here on time.

B

A节所给句子中的 **should** 可以省略：

- **It's essential** that everyone **be** here on time. (= … that everyone **should be** here)
- I **insisted** that he **apologise**. (= … that he **should apologise**)
- What do you **suggest** we **do**?
- Many people are **demanding** that something **be done** about the problem.

这种形式 (**be/do/apologise** 等) 被称为虚拟语气。
还可以使用现在时与过去时：

- **It's essential** that everyone **is** here on time.
- I **insisted** that he **apologised**.

C

注意 **suggest** 后不能带 **to …** (to do / to buy 等)。可以说：

- What do you **suggest we should do**?

或 What do you **suggest we do**? (而不用 What do you suggest us to do?)

- Jane won the lottery.
  I **suggested** that she **should buy** a car with the money she'd won.

或 I **suggested** that she **buy** a car.
或 I **suggested** that she **bought** a car. (而不用 I suggested her to buy)

suggest 后还可以用动词 **-ing** 形式 (What do you **suggest doing**?)。参见Unit 53。

D

should 可以用在一些形容词后，特别是：

strange **odd** **funny** **typical** **natural** **interesting** **surprised** **surprising**

- It's **strange** that he **should be** late. He's usually on time.
- I was **surprised** that he **should say** such a thing.

E

可以说 **if** something **should** happen …：

- We have no jobs at present, but **if** the situation **should change**, we will contact you.

should 还可以用于这些句子的句首 (**Should** something happen …)：

- **Should** the situation **change**, we will contact you.

意思与 **If** the situation **changes**, … 相同。使用 **should** 表明说话人感觉到可能性更小。

F

可以用**I should** … / **I shouldn't** … 提出劝告。例如：

- 'Shall I leave now?' 'No, **I should wait** a bit.'

在这里，**I should wait** 意为"如果我是你，我会等；我建议你等"。
再看两个例句：

- 'I'm going out now. Is it cold out?' 'Yes, **I should wear** a coat.'
- **I shouldn't stay** up too late. You have to be up early tomorrow.

should (1) ➜ Unit 33 **美国英语** ➜ 附录 7

Exercises

34.1 仿照示例改写下列句子，保持意思不变。

1 'I think it would be a good idea to see a specialist,' the doctor said to me.
The doctor recommended that I should see a specialist.
2 'You really must stay a little longer,' she said to me.
She insisted that I ....
3 'Why don't you visit the museum after lunch?' I said to them.
I suggested that ....
4 'You must pay the rent by Friday,' the landlord said to us.
The landlord demanded that ....
5 'Why don't we go away for a few days?' Jack said to me.
Jack suggested that ....

34.2 指出下列句子是否正确。

1 a Tom suggested that I should look for another job. 正确
b Tom suggested that I look for another job. ....
c Tom suggested that I looked for another job. ....
d Tom suggested me to look for another job. ....
2 a Where do you suggest I go for my holiday? ....
b Where do you suggest me to go for my holiday? ....
c Where do you suggest I should go for my holiday? ....

34.3 用 **should** + 下列动词完成句子。

ask ~~**be**~~ **leave** **listen** **say** **worry**

1 It's strange that he should be late. He's usually on time.
2 It's funny that you .... that. I was going to say the same thing.
3 It's only natural that parents .... about their children.
4 Isn't it typical of Joe that he .... without saying goodbye to anybody?
5 I was surprised that they .... me for advice. What advice could I give them?
6 I'm going to give you all some essential information, so it's important that everybody .... very carefully.

34.4 用 **If ... should ...** 完成下列句子。

1 We have no jobs at present. (the situation / change)
If the situation should change, we will contact you.
2 I've hung the washing out to dry on the balcony. (it / rain)
.........., can you bring the washing in, please?
3 I think everything will be OK. (there / be / any problems)
.........., I'm sure we'll be able to solve them.
4 I don't want anyone to know where I'm going. (anyone / ask)
.........., just say that you don't know.

以 **should** 开头，改写后两句。

5 (3) Should ...., I'm sure we'll be able to solve them.
6 (4) ...., just say that you don't know.

34.5 (F 节) 用 **I should** + 下列动词完成句子。

get **keep** **phone** ~~**wait**~~

1 'Shall I leave now?' 'No, I should wait a bit.'
2 'Shall I throw these things away?' 'No, ... them. You may need them.'
3 'Shall I go and see Paul?' 'Yes, but .... him first.'
4 'Is it worth getting this TV repaired?' 'No, ... a new one.'

Unit 35 had better It's time …

A had better (I'd better / you'd better 等)

I'd better do something 表示“最好做某事，否则会有问题或危险”：

- I have to meet Amy in ten minutes. **I'd better go** now or I'll be late.
- 'Shall I take an umbrella?' 'Yes, **you'd better**. It might rain.'
- **We'd better stop** for petrol soon. The tank is almost empty.

否定形式为 **I'd better not** (= I **had** better not)：

- 'The jacket looks good on you. Are you going to buy it?'
  '**I'd better not**. It's too expensive.'
- You don't look very well. **You'd better not go** out tonight.

请注意：

形式为 **had** better (通常在口语中用 **I'd** better / you'**d** better 等)：

- **I'd better** phone Chris, **hadn't** I?

had 是过去时形式，但 **had better** 表示的是现在或将来，而非过去：

- **I'd better go** to the bank **now** / **tomorrow**.

可以说 I'd better **do** (而不用 to do)：

- It might rain. We'd better **take** an umbrella. (而不用 We'd better to take)

B had better 与 should 比较

had better 与 **should** 意义相似，但并不完全一样。**had better** 只用来表示某一具体情况，不用来泛指；而 **should** 可用于表示提出看法或建议的所有情况中：

- It's late. You**'d better go**. / You **should go**. (具体情况)
- You're always at home. You **should go** out more often.
  (一般情况——不用had better go)

另外，**had better** 表示如不听从劝告总是会有危险或遇到困难的。而 **should** 仅表示 it is a good thing to do。请比较：

- It's a great film. You **should** go and see it. (但如果不去看也没问题)
- The film starts at 8.30. You**'d better** go now or you'll be late.

C It's time …

可以说 **It's time** (for somebody) **to** …：

- It's time **to go** home. / It's time for us **to go** home.

还可以说：

- It's late. It's time **we went** home.

it's time + 过去时 (we **went** / I **did** / they **were** 等) 表示的是现在，而非过去：

- **It's time** they **were** here. Why are they so late? (而不用 It's time they are here)

It's time somebody **did** something 表示本应做某事或开始做某事。这种结构常用来表示批评或抱怨：

- This situation can't continue. **It's time** you **did** something about it.
- He's very selfish. **It's time** he **realised** that he isn't the most important person in the world.

还可以用 **It's about time** … 表示更为强烈的批评：

- Jack is a great talker. But **it's about time** he **did** something instead of just talking.

should (1) ➜ Unit 33

Exercises

35.1 根据所给情况，用 **had better** 或 **had better not** 与括号内的词语造句。

1 You're going out for a walk with Tom. It looks as if it might rain. You say to Tom:
(an umbrella)
We'd better take an umbrella.

2 Oliver has just cut himself. It's a bad cut. You say to him:
(a plaster) ……

3 You and Kate plan to go to a restaurant this evening. It's a popular restaurant. You say to Kate:
(reserve) We ……

4 Rebecca doesn't look very well this morning – not well enough to go to work. You say to her:
(work) ……

5 You received your phone bill four weeks ago, but you haven't paid it yet. If you don't pay soon, you could be in trouble. You say to yourself:
(pay) ……

6 You want to ask your boss something, but he's very busy and you know he doesn't like to be disturbed. You say to a colleague:
(disturb) I ……

35.2 用 **had better** 或 **should** 填空。

1 I have an appointment in ten minutes. I 'd better go now or I'll be late.
2 It's a great film. You should go and see it. You'll really like it.
3 You …… set your alarm. You'll never wake up on time if you don't.
4 When people are driving, they …… keep their eyes on the road.
5 I'm glad you came to see us. You …… come more often.
6 She'll be upset if we don't invite her to the party, so we …… invite her.
7 These biscuits are delicious. You …… try one.
8 I think everybody …… learn a foreign language.

35.3 用一个或两个词完成下列句子。

1 a I have a toothache. I'd better go to the dentist.
  b John is expecting you to phone him. You …… better phone him now.
  c 'Shall I leave the window open?' 'No, you'd better …… it.'
  d We'd better leave as soon as possible, …… we?

2 a It's time the government …… something about the problem.
  b It's time something …… about the problem.
  c I think it's about time you …… about other people instead of only thinking about yourself.

35.4 根据所给情况，用 **It's time** (somebody **did** something) 造句。

1 You think the oil in the car needs to be changed. It hasn't been changed for a long time.
It's time we changed the oil in the car.

2 You haven't had a holiday for a very long time. You need one now.
It's time I ……

3 You're sitting on a train waiting for it to leave the station. It's already five minutes late.
……

4 You enjoy having parties. You haven't had one for a long time.
……

5 The company you work for has been badly managed for a long time. You think some changes should be made.
……

6 Andrew has been doing the same job for the last ten years. He should try something else.
……

→ 补充练习 16（第311页）

Unit 36 would

A

would ('d) / wouldn't 用于表示一种假设的情形或动作：

- It **would be** nice to buy a new car, but we can't afford it.
- **I'd love** to live by the sea.
- A: Shall I tell Chris what happened?
  B: No, I **wouldn't say** anything.
  (= I wouldn't say anything in your situation)

would have (done) 用于表示对过去的情形或动作的假设：

- They helped us a lot. I don't know what we**'d have done** (= we **would have done**) without their help.
- I didn't tell Sam what happened. He **wouldn't have been** pleased.

请比较 **would (do)** 与 **would have (done)**：

- I **would call** Lisa, but I don't have her number. (现在)
  I **would have called** Lisa, but I didn't have her number. (过去)
- I'm not going to invite them to the party. They **wouldn't come** anyway.
  I didn't invite them to the party. They **wouldn't have come** anyway.

would 常与 **if** 从句连用 (参见 Units 38–40)：

- I **would call** Lisa **if** I had her number.
- I **would have called** Lisa **if** I'd had her number.

B

请比较 **will ('ll)** 与 **would ('d)**：

- **I'll stay** a little longer. I've got plenty of time.
  I'd stay a little longer, but I really have to go now. (因此我不能再待下去了)
- **I'll call** Lisa. I have her number.
  I'd call Lisa, but I don't have her number. (因此我不能给她打电话)

would/wouldn't 有时用作 **will/won't** 的过去式。请比较：

现在		过去
TOM: **I'll call** you on Sunday.	→	Tom said he**'d call** me on Sunday.
AMY: I promise I **won't be** late.	→	Amy promised that she **wouldn't be** late.
LISA: Damn! The car **won't start**.	→	Lisa was annoyed because her car **wouldn't start**.

somebody **wouldn't do** something 意为"某人不肯做某事"：

- I tried to warn him, but he **wouldn't listen** to me. (= he refused to listen)
- The car **wouldn't start**. (= it 'refused' to start)

C

would 可用来谈论过去重复发生的动作：

- When we were children, we lived by the sea. In summer, if the weather was fine, we **would** all get up early and go for a swim. (= we did this regularly)
- Whenever Richard was angry, he **would** walk out of the room.

表示这个意义时，**would** 的用法与 **used to** 相似 (参见 Unit 18)：

- Whenever Richard was angry, he **used to walk** out of the room.

will → Units 21–22 **Would you ... ?** → Unit 37A **would ... if** → Units 38–40
wish ... would → Unit 41 **would like** → Units 37E，58 **would prefer / would rather** → Unit 59
情态动词 → 附录 4

Exercises

36.1 根据括号内的提示，结合你自己的情况造句。

1 (a place you'd love to live) I'd love to live by the sea.
2 (a job you wouldn't like to do) ....
3 (something you would love to do) ....
4 (something that would be nice to have) ....
5 (a place you'd like to go to) ....

36.2 用 **would** + 下列动词的适当形式完成句子。

be be ~~do~~ do enjoy enjoy have pass stop

1 They helped us a lot. I don't know what we would have done without their help.
2 You should go and see the film. You .... it.
3 It's a pity you couldn't come to the party last night. You .... it.
4 Shall I apply for the job or not? What .... you .... in my position?
5 I was in a hurry when I saw you. Otherwise I .... to talk.
6 We took a taxi home last night, but got stuck in the traffic. It .... quicker to walk.
7 Why don't you go and see Clare? She .... very pleased to see you.
8 Why didn't you do the exam? I'm sure you .... it.
9 In an ideal world, everybody .... enough to eat.

36.3 请搭配左右两栏的句子。

1 ~~I'd like to go to Australia one day.~~
2 I wouldn't like to live on a busy road.
3 I'm sorry the trip was cancelled.
4 I'm looking forward to going out tonight.
5 I'm glad we didn't go out in the rain.
6 I'm not looking forward to the trip.

a It wouldn't have been very nice.
b It would have been fun.
c ~~It would be nice.~~
d It won't be much fun.
e It wouldn't be very nice.
f It will be fun.

1 c
2 ....
3 ....
4 ....
5 ....
6 ....

36.4 用 **promised ... would/wouldn't** 造句。

1 I wonder why Laura is late. She promised she wouldn't be late.
2 I wonder why Steve hasn't called me. He promised ....
3 Why did you tell Jane what I said? You ....
4 I'm surprised they didn't wait for us. They ....

36.5 用 **wouldn't** + 恰当的动词完成下列句子。

1 I tried to warn him, but he wouldn't listen to me.
2 I asked Amanda what had happened, but she .... me.
3 Paul was very angry about what I'd said and .... to me for two weeks.
4 Martina insisted on carrying all her luggage. She .... me help her.

36.6 下列句子用于讲述过去经常发生的事情。用 **would** + 所给动词完成句子。

forget help shake share ~~walk~~

1 Whenever Richard was angry, he would walk out of the room.
2 We used to live next to a railway line. Every time a train went past, the house ....
3 Alan was a very kind man. He .... always .... you if you had a problem.
4 Katherine was always very generous. She didn't have much, but she .... what she had with everyone else.
5 You could never rely on Joe. It didn't matter how many times you reminded him to do something, he .... always ....

→ 补充练习 16–18（第311–313页）

Can/Could/Would you … ? 等 (请求，给予帮助，允许及邀请)

A 请求做事

can 或 **could** 用于表示请求某人做某事：
- **Can you** wait a moment, please?

或 **Could you** wait a moment, please?
- Helen, **can you** do me a favour?
- Excuse me, **could you** tell me how to get to the airport?

注意可以说 **Do you think** you **could** … ? (而不用 can)：
- **Do you think you could** take me to the station?

will 和 **would** 也用于表示请求 (但 **can/could** 更常用)：
- Helen, **will you** do me a favour?
- **Would you** please be quiet? I'm trying to concentrate.

B 请求给予

Can I have … ? / **Could I have** … ? 或 **Can I get** ... ? 用于表示请求给予：
- (*in a shop*) **Can I have** these postcards, please? 或
  Can I get these postcards, please?
- (*during a meal*) **Could I have** the salt, please?

May I have … ? 也可以用来表达同样的意思：
- **May I have** these postcards, please?

C 征求许可

can，**could** 或 **may** 用于表示征求许可：
- (*on the phone*) Hello, **can I** speak to Steve, please?
- '**Could I** use your phone?' 'Sure.'
- **Do you think I could** borrow your bike?
- '**May I** come in?' 'Yes, please do.'

may 比 **can** 或 **could** 更为正式。

征求许可还可以用 **Do you mind if I** … ?
或 **Is it all right / Is it OK if I** … ?：
- '**Do you mind if I** use your phone?' 'Sure. Go ahead.'
- '**Is it all right if I** come in?' 'Yes, of course.'

D 主动提出做某事

Can I … ? 用于表示主动提出做某事：
- '**Can I** get you a cup of coffee?' 'That would be nice.'
- '**Can I** help you?' 'No, it's all right. I can manage.'

E 给予和邀请

Would you like … ? (而不用 Do you like) 用于表示给予或邀请：
- '**Would you like** a cup of coffee?' 'Yes, please.'
- '**Would you like** to eat with us tonight?' 'I'd love to.'

I'd like … 是一种表达愿望的客气的说法：
- (*at a tourist information office*) **I'd like** some information about hotels, please.
- (*in a shop*) **I'd like** to try on this jacket, please.

can 与 **could** 比较 ➜ Units 26–27 **mind** + **-ing** 形式 ➜ Unit 53 **would like** ➜ Units 55A，58B
情态动词 (can/could/will/would 等) ➜ 附录 4

Exercises

37.1 根据所给情况，以 **Can …** 或 **Could …** 开头造句。

1 You're carrying a lot of things. You can't open the door yourself. There's a man standing near the door. You say to him: Could you open the door, please?

2 You phone Kate's office, but somebody else answers. Kate isn't there. You want to leave a message for her. You say: ……

3 You're a tourist. You want to go to the station, but you don't know how to get there. You ask at your hotel: ……

4 You are in a clothes shop. You see some trousers you like and you want to try them on. You say to the shop assistant: ……

5 You have a car. You have to go the same way as Steve, who is on foot. You offer him a lift. You say to him: ……

37.2 根据所给情况，用括号中的单词提问。

1 You want to borrow your friend's bike. What do you say to him?
(think) Do you think I could borrow your bike?

2 You are staying at a friend's house and you would like to make some coffee. What do you say?
(all right) Is it all right if I make some coffee?

3 You've filled in some forms in English. You want your friend to check them for you. What do you ask?
(think) ……

4 You want to leave work early. What do you ask your boss?
(mind) ……

5 The woman in the next room is playing music. It's very loud. You want her to turn it down. What do you say to her?
(think) ……

6 You're on a train. The window is open and you're feeling cold. You'd like to close it, but first you ask the woman next to you.
(OK) ……

7 You're still on the train. The woman next to you has finished reading her paper, and you'd like to have a look at it. You ask her.
(think) ……

37.3 根据所给情况，完成下列对话。

1 Paul has come to see you in your flat. You offer him something to eat.
YOU: Would you like something to eat?
PAUL: No, thank you. I've just eaten.

2 You need help to charge the battery in your camera. You ask Kate.
YOU: I don't know how to charge the battery. ……?
KATE: Sure. It's easy. All you have to do is this.

3 You're on a bus. You have a seat, but an elderly man is standing. You offer him your seat.
YOU: ……?
MAN: Oh, that's very kind of you. Thank you very much.

4 You're the passenger in a car. Your friend is driving very fast. You ask her to slow down.
YOU: You're making me very nervous. ……?
DRIVER: Oh, I'm sorry. I didn't realise I was going so fast.

5 You've finished your meal in a restaurant and now you want the bill. You ask the waiter:
YOU: ……?
WAITER: Sure. I'll get it for you now.

6 A friend of yours is interested in one of your books. You invite him to borrow it.
FRIEND: This looks very interesting.
YOU: Yes, it's a good book. ……?

If I do … 与 If I did … 比较

A

请看下列例句：

(1) LISA: Shall we go by bus or by train?
JESS: **If we go** by bus, it **will** be cheaper.

在这个例子中，杰丝觉得她们可能乘坐公共汽车去，因此她说：
If we **go** by bus, it **will** be …

(2) Lisa and Jess decide to go by train.
Later, Jess talks to Joe.

JOE: How are you going to travel?
JESS: We're going by train. **If we went** by bus, it **would** be cheaper, but the train is quicker.

说话时杰丝已经知道她们不会乘坐公共汽车去了，因此她说：
If we **went** by bus, it **would** be … (而不用 If we go …)

if + 过去时 (**if** we **went** / **if** there **was** / **if** you **found** 等)
表示虚拟的事情，而非过去发生的事情：

- What would you do **if** you **won** a lot of money? (我们并不认为会真实发生)
- **If** there **was** (或 **were**) an election tomorrow, who would you vote for?

有关 **if … was/were** 的用法，参见 Unit 39C。

请比较 **if I find** 与 **if I found**：

- I think I left my watch at your house. **If you find** it, can you call me?

但是 **If you found** a wallet in the street, what would you do with it?

B

if 从句中一般不用 **would**：

- I'd be very scared **if** somebody **pointed** a gun at me. (而不用 if somebody would point)
- **If** we **went** by bus, it would be cheaper. (而不用 If we would go)

if … would 可以用来表示请求某人做某事：

- (*from a formal letter*) I would be grateful **if** you **would let** me know your decision as soon as possible.

C

would ('**d**) / **wouldn't** 用于句子的主句 (而非 **if** 从句) 中：

- What **would** you **do** if you were bitten by a snake?
- I'm not going to bed yet. I'm not tired. If I went to bed now, I **wouldn't sleep**.
- **Would** you **mind** if I used your phone?

could 和 **might** 也可以使用：

- If I won a lot of money, I **might buy** a house. (= it is possible that I would buy a house)
- If it stopped raining, we **could go** out. (= we would be able to go out)

will → Units 21–22 **if** 与 **when** 比较 → Unit 25D **would** → Unit 36 **If I knew** → Unit 39
If I had known → Unit 40

Exercises

38.1 下列哪个表达是正确的？

1 Of course you don't expect to win the lottery. Which do you say?
 a If I win the lottery, I'll buy a big house. ☐
 b If I won the lottery, I'd buy a big house. ☑ (b *is correct*)

2 You're not going to sell your car because it's old and not worth much. Which do you say?
 a If I sell my car, I won't get much money for it. ☐
 b If I sold my car, I wouldn't get much money for it. ☐

3 You often see Sarah. A friend of yours wants to contact her. Which do you say?
 a If I see Sarah, I'll tell her to call you. ☐
 b If I saw Sarah, I'd tell her to call you. ☐

4 You don't expect that there will be a fire in the building. Which do you say?
 a What will you do if there is a fire in the building? ☐
 b What would you do if there was a fire in the building? ☐

5 You've never lost your passport. You can only imagine it.
 a I don't know what I'll do if I lose my passport. ☐
 b I don't know what I'd do if I lost my passport. ☐

6 Somebody stops you and asks the way to a bank. Which do you say?
 a If you go right at the end of this street, you'll see a bank on your left. ☐
 b If you went right at the end of this street, you'd see a bank on your left. ☐

7 You're in a lift. There is an emergency button. Nobody is going to press it. Which do you say?
 a What will happen if somebody presses that button? ☐
 b What would happen if somebody pressed that button? ☐

38.2 用括号内动词的适当形式填空。

1 I'd be very scared if somebody ...pointed... (point) a gun at me.
2 I can't afford to buy a car. If I .... (buy) a car, I'd have to borrow the money.
3 Don't lend Amy your car. If she .... (ask) me, I wouldn't lend her mine.
4 If the computer factory closed down, many people .... (lose) their jobs.
5 I don't think Gary and Emma will get married. I .... (be) amazed if they did.
6 What would you do if you .... (be) in a lift and it .... (stop) between floors?
7 If somebody .... (give) me £10,000, I .... (have) a very long holiday.

38.3 以 **If …** 开头造句。

1 We've decided not to catch the 10.30 train. (arrive too early)
 If we caught the 10.30 train, we'd arrive too early.
2 Kevin is not going to do his driving test now. (fail)
 If he ....
3 We've decided not to stay at a hotel. (cost too much)
 If ....
4 Sally isn't going to leave her job. (not / get another one)
 ....
5 We've decided not to invite Ben to the party. (have to invite his friends too)
 ....
6 I'm not going to tell him what happened. (not / believe me)
 ....

38.4 根据你自己的想法完成下列句子。

1 If I won a lot of money, ...I'd buy a house.
2 I'd be very angry if ....
3 If you bought a car, ...
4 I'd be surprised if ....
5 Would you mind if ....

If I knew … I wish I knew …

A 请看下列例句：

Sarah wants to phone Paul, but she can't do this because she doesn't know his number. She says:

If I knew his number, I **would phone** him.

萨拉说：**If I knew** his number … 表明她并不知道保罗的电话号码，她是在作假设。

if + 过去时 (**if** I **knew** / **if** you **were** / **if** we **didn't** 等) 用来表示对现在情况的虚拟，并非指过去：

- There are many things I'd like to do **if I had** more time. (但我没有很多时间)
- **If** I **didn't** want to go to the party, I wouldn't go. (但我想去)
- We wouldn't have any money **if** we **didn't** work. (但其实我们是工作的)
- **If** you **were** in my position, what would you do?
- It's a pity he can't drive. It would be useful **if** he **could**.

B **wish** 之后也可以用过去时 (I **wish** I **knew** / I **wish** you **were** 等)，表示因某事不能如自己所愿而感到遗憾：

- I **wish** I **knew** Paul's phone number. (= I don't know it and I regret this)
- Do you ever **wish** you **could** fly? (你不能飞行)
- It rains a lot here. I **wish** it **didn't** rain so much.
- It's very crowded here. I **wish** there **weren't** so many people. (有很多人)
- I **wish** I **didn't** have to work tomorrow, but unfortunately I do.

C if I **were** / if I **was**

if 和 **wish** 之后，可以用 **were** 代替 **was** (**if I were** / **I wish it were** 等)。
也可以用 **if I was** / **I wish it was**，例如：

- **If I were** you, I wouldn't buy that coat. 或 **If I was** you, …
- I'd go for a walk **if it weren't** so cold. 或 … **if it wasn't** so cold.
- I **wish she were** here. 或 I **wish she was** here.

D 在 **if** 从句或 **wish** 之后的句子中一般不使用 **would**：

- **If** I **were** rich, I **would** travel a lot. (而不用 If I would be rich)
- Who **would** you ask **if** you **needed** help? (而不用 if you would need)
- I **wish** I **had** something to read. (而不用 I wish I would have)

有时 **wish** … **would** 是可以使用的 (**I wish you would listen**)。参见Unit 41。

E 注意，**could** 有时意为 would be able to，而有时意为 was/were able to：

- She **could** get a better job if she **could** speak English. (she **could** get = shc would be able to get) (if she **could** speak = if she was/were able to speak)
- I wish I **could** help you. (I wish I could = I wish I was able)

could → Units 26–27 **If I do** 与 **If I did** 比较 → Unit 38
If I had known / **I wish I had known** → Unit 40 **wish** → Unit 41

Exercises

39.1 用动词的适当形式填空。

1 If I knew (I / know) his number, I would phone him.
2 I wouldn't buy (I / not / buy) that coat if I were you.
3 .... (I / help) you if I could, but I'm afraid I can't.
4 We don't need a car at present, but we would need a car if .... (we / live) in the country.
5 If we had the choice, ... (we / live) in the country.
6 This soup isn't very good. .... (it / taste) better if it wasn't so salty.
7 I wouldn't mind living in England if the weather .... (be) better.
8 If I were you, ... (I / not / wait). .... (I / go) now.
9 You're always tired. If .... (you / not / go) to bed so late every night, you wouldn't be tired all the time.
10 I think there are too many cars. If .... (there / not / be) so many cars, ... (there / not / be) so much pollution.

39.2 用 if ... 句式造句。

1 We don't see you very often because you live so far away.
If you didn't live so far away, we'd see you more often.
2 It's a nice book but it's too expensive, so I'm not going to buy it.
I .... it if .... so ....
3 We don't go out very often – we can't afford it.
We .... more often ....
4 I can't meet you tomorrow – I have to work late.
If ....
5 It would be nice to have lunch outside but it's raining, so we can't.
We ....
6 I don't want his advice, and that's why I'm not going to ask for it.
If ....

39.3 以 I wish ... 开头造句。

1 I don't know many people (and I'm lonely). I wish I knew more people.
2 I don't have a computer (and I need one). I wish ....
3 Helen isn't here (and I need to see her). ....
4 It's cold (and I hate cold weather). ....
5 I live in a big city (and I don't like it). ....
6 I can't go to the party (and I'd like to). ....
7 I have to get up early tomorrow (but I'd like to sleep late).
....
8 I don't know anything about cars (and my car has just broken down).
....
9 I'm not feeling well (and it's not nice).
....

39.4 以 I wish ... 开头造句。

1 (somewhere you'd like to be now – on the beach, in New York, in bed etc.)
I wish I ....
2 (something you'd like to have – a motorbike, more friends, lots of money etc.)
....
3 (something you'd like to be able to do – sing, travel more, cook etc.)
....
4 (something you'd like to be – beautiful, strong, younger etc.)
....

→ 补充练习 19–21 (第313–314页)

If I had known … I wish I had known …

A

请看下列例句：

Last month Gary was in hospital for a few days. Rachel didn't know this, so she didn't go to visit him. They met a few days ago.
Rachel said:

If I'd known you were in hospital, I **would have gone** to see you.

雷切尔说：**If I'd known** (= If I **had** known) you were in hospital … 真实的情况是她不知道加里住院了。

if + had ('d) … 用于谈论过去 (**if** I **had known/been/done** 等)：

- I didn't see you when you passed me in the street. **If I'd seen** you, of course I would have said hello. (但我没看见你)
- I didn't go out last night. I would have gone out **if** I **hadn't been** so tired. (但我累了)
- **If** he **had been looking** where he was going, he wouldn't have walked into the wall. (但他没看)
- The view was wonderful. **If** I'**d had** a camera with me, I would have taken some pictures. (但我没有照相机)

请比较：

- I'm not hungry. **If** I **was** hungry, I would eat something. (现在)
- I wasn't hungry. **If** I **had been** hungry, I would have eaten something. (过去)

B

if 从句不使用 **would**，**would** 用于主句中：

- **If** I **had seen** you, I **would have said** hello. (而不用 If I would have seen you)

注意，**'d** 既可以是 **would** 也可以是 **had** 的缩略形式：

- If I'**d seen** you, (I'**d** seen = I **had** seen)
- I'**d have said** hello. (I'**d** have said = I **would** have said)

C

wish 之后同样也可以用 **had (done)**。I **wish** something **had happened** 表示很遗憾某事没有发生：

- I **wish I'd known** that Gary was ill. I would have gone to see him. (但我不知道)
- I feel sick. I **wish** I **hadn't eaten** so much cake. (我吃了太多的蛋糕)
- Do you **wish** you'**d studied** science instead of languages? (你不是学理科的)

wish 之后不要用 **would have** …：

- The weather was cold when we were on holiday. I wish it **had been** warmer. (而不用 I wish it would have been)

D

请比较 **would (do)** 与 **would have (done)**：

- If I'd gone to the party last night, I **would be** tired now. (我现在不累——现在)
- If I'd gone to the party last night, I **would have met** lots of people. (我没见到许多人——过去)

请比较 **would have**，**could have** 与 **might have**：

- If the weather hadn't been so bad,
  - we **would have gone** out.
  - we **could have gone** out. (= we would have been able to go out)
  - we **might have gone** out. (= perhaps we would have gone out)

had done ➔ Unit 15 **If I do 与 If I did 比较** ➔ Unit 38 **If I knew / I wish I knew** ➔ Unit 39
wish ➔ Unit 41

Exercises

40.1 用动词的适当形式填空。

1 I didn't see you when you passed me in the street. If I'd seen (I / see) you, I would have said (I / say) hello.

2 Sam got to the station just in time to catch the train to the airport. If .... (he / miss) the train, ... (he / miss) his flight too.

3 I'm glad that you reminded me about Rachel's birthday. .... (I / forget) if .... (you / not / remind) me.

4 I wanted to send you an email, but I didn't have your email address. If .... (I / have) your address, ... (I / send) you an email.

5 A: How was your trip? Was it good?
B: It was OK, but .... (we / enjoy) it more if the weather .... (be) better.

6 I took a taxi to the hotel, but the traffic was bad. .... (it / be) quicker if .... (I / walk).

7 I'm not tired. If .... (I / be) tired, I'd go home now.

8 I wasn't tired last night. If .... (I / be) tired, I would have gone home earlier.

40.2 根据所给情况，以 **if** 开头造句。

1 I wasn't hungry, so I didn't eat anything.
If I'd been hungry, I would have eaten something.

2 The accident happened because the road was icy.
If the road ...., the accident ....

3 I didn't know that Joe had to get up early, so I didn't wake him up.
If I .... that he had to get up early, ...

4 Unfortunately I lost my phone, so I couldn't call you.
If ....

5 Karen wasn't injured in the crash because she was wearing a seat belt.
....

6 You didn't have breakfast – that's why you're hungry now.
....

7 I didn't get a taxi because I didn't have enough money.
....

40.3 假设你处在下列情况下，用 **I wish ...** 造句。

1 You've eaten too much and now you feel sick.
You say: I wish I hadn't eaten so much.

2 There was a job advertised in the paper. You decided not to apply for it. Now you think that your decision was wrong.
You say: I wish I ....

3 When you were younger, you never learned to play a musical instrument. Now you regret this.
You say: ....

4 You've painted the gate red. Now you think that red was the wrong colour.
You say: ....

5 You are walking in the country. You'd like to take some pictures, but you didn't bring your camera.
You say: ....

6 You have some unexpected guests. They didn't phone you first to say they were coming. You are very busy and you are not prepared for them.
You say (to yourself): ....

➜ 补充练习 19–21 (第313–314页)

wish

A

可以说 **I wish you luck / all the best / a happy birthday** 等：

- **I wish you all the best** in the future.
- I saw Mark before the exam and **he wished me luck**.

可以说 wish somebody *something* (**luck / a happy birthday** 等)。但不能说 I wish that something *happens*，这时应用 **hope**：

- I'm sorry you're not well. I **hope** you **feel** better soon. (而不用 I wish you feel)

请比较 **I wish** 与 **I hope**：

- **I wish** you **a pleasant stay** here.
- **I hope** you **have** a pleasant stay here. (而不用 I wish you have)

B

wish 用来表示很遗憾某事未能如愿。
wish 之后用过去时 (**knew/lived** 等)，但表示的意义却是现在：

- I **wish** I **knew** what to do about the problem. (我不知道，对此感到遗憾)
- I **wish** you **didn't** have to go so soon. (你必须得走)
- Do you **wish** you **lived** near the sea? (你不住在海边)
- Jack's going on a trip to Mexico soon. I **wish** I **was** going too. (我不会去)

表示对于发生在过去的某事未能如愿很遗憾，用 **wish** + **had** ... (**had known / had said**) 等：

- I **wish I'd known** about the party. I would have gone if I'd known. (我不知道)
- It was a stupid thing to say. I **wish** I **hadn't said** it. (我说了)

更多例句参见 Units 39–40。

C

I wish I could (**do** something) 表示很遗憾不能做某事：

- I'm sorry I have to go. I **wish** I **could stay** longer. (但我不能)
- I've met that man before. I **wish** I **could remember** his name. (但我不能)

I wish I could have (**done** something) 表示很遗憾过去不能做某事：

- I hear the party was great. I **wish** I **could have gone**. (但我没能去)

D

可以说 **I wish** (somebody) **would** (do something)，例如：

It's been raining all day. Tanya doesn't like it. She says:
I wish it **would stop** raining.

这句话意为塔尼娅在抱怨下雨，希望雨停下来。

I wish ... would ... 用于表示希望某事发生或改变。通常讲话人并不认为会真的发生。

I wish ... would ... 常用来表达抱怨：

- The phone has been ringing for five minutes. **I wish** somebody **would answer** it.
- **I wish** you**'d do** (= you **would** do) something instead of just sitting and doing nothing.

I wish ... wouldn't ... 可用来抱怨某人总是做某事：

- **I wish** you **wouldn't keep** interrupting me. (= please don't interrupt me)

I wish ... would ... 可用来表示希望某事发生，但不能用来表示希望某人或某事处于某种状态。请比较：

- I **wish** Sarah **would** come. (= I want her to come)

但是 I **wish** Sarah **was** (或 **were**) here now. (而不用 I wish Sarah would be)

- I **wish** somebody **would buy** me a car.

但是 I **wish** I **had** a car. (而不用 I wish I would have)

would ➔ Unit 36 **I wish I knew** ➔ Unit 39 **I wish I was / I wish I were** ➔ Unit 39C
I wish I had known ➔ Unit 40

Exercises

41.1 用 wish(ed) 或 hope(d) 填空。

1 I ......wish...... you a pleasant stay here.
2 Enjoy your holiday. I .... you have a great time.
3 Goodbye. I .... you all the best.
4 We said goodbye to each other and .... each other luck.
5 We're going to have a picnic tomorrow, so I .... the weather is nice.
6 I .... you luck in your new job. I .... it works out well for you.

41.2 根据所给情况，用 I wish … would … 造句。

1 It's raining. You want to go out, but not in the rain.
You say: ......I wish it would stop raining.......
2 You're waiting for Jane. She's late and you're getting impatient.
You say to yourself: I wish ....
3 You're looking for a job – so far without success. Nobody will give you a job.
You say: I wish somebody ....
4 You can hear a baby crying. It's been crying for a long time and you're trying to study.
You say: ....
5 Brian has been wearing the same clothes for years. You think he needs some new clothes.
You say to Brian: ....

在下列情况下用 **I wish … wouldn't …** 造句。

6 Your friend drives very fast. You don't like this.
You say to your friend: I wish you ....
7 Joe leaves the door open all the time. This annoys you.
You say to Joe: ....
8 A lot of people drop litter in the street. You don't like this.
You say: I wish people ....

41.3 下列句子是否正确？如有错误，请改正。

1 I wish Sarah would be here now. ......I wish Sarah were here now.......
2 I wish you would listen to me. ....
3 I wish I would have more free time. ....
4 I wish our flat would be a bit bigger. ....
5 I wish the weather would change. ....
6 I wish you wouldn't complain all the time. ....
7 I wish everything wouldn't be so expensive. ....

41.4 用动词的适当形式填空。

1 It was a stupid thing to say. I wish I ......hadn't said...... it. (I / not / say)
2 I'm fed up with this rain. I wish ......it would stop...... . (it / stop)
3 It's a difficult question. I wish .... the answer. (I / know)
4 I should have listened to you. I wish .... your advice. (I / take)
5 You're lucky to be going away. I wish .... with you. (I / can / come)
6 I have no energy at the moment. I wish .... so tired. (I / not / be)
7 Aren't they ready yet? I wish .... (they / hurry up)
8 It would be nice to stay here longer. I wish .... to go now. (we / not / have)
9 When we were in London last year, we didn't have time to see all the things we wanted to see. I wish .... longer. (we / can / stay)
10 It's freezing today. I wish .... so cold. I hate cold weather. (it / not / be)
11 Joe still doesn't know what he wants to do. I wish .... (he / decide)
12 I really didn't enjoy the party. I wish .... (we / not / go)

Unit 42 被动语态 (1) (is done / was done)

A

请看下列例句：

This house **was built** in 1961.

was built 是被动语态。

请比较主动语态与被动语态：

Somebody **built** this house in 1961. (主动)
主语 宾语

This house **was built** in 1961. (被动)
主语

主动语态用于说明动作的执行者：

- My grandfather was a builder. **He built** this house in 1961.
- It's a big company. **It employs** two hundred people.

被动语态用于说明动作的承受者：

- 'How old is this house?' '**It was built** in 1961.'
- **Two hundred people are employed** by the company.

B

使用被动语态时往往不知道或没有必要知道动作的执行者：

- A lot of money **was stolen** in the robbery. (有人偷了但不知道是谁)
- **Is** this room **cleaned** every day? (谁打扫的并不重要)

如果需要说明动作的执行者，可以用 **by…**：

- This house was built **by my grandfather**.
- Two hundred people are employed **by the company**.

C

被动语态由 **be (is/was** 等) + 过去分词 (**done/cleaned/seen** 等) 构成：

(be) done **(be) cleaned** **(be) damaged** **(be) built** **(be) seen** 等

不规则动词的过去分词 (**done/seen/known** 等)，参见附录1。

请看一般现在时和一般过去时的被动语态形式：

一般现在时

主动：**clean(s) / see(s)** 等 — Somebody **cleans** this room every day.

被动：**am/is/are + cleaned/seen** 等 — This room **is cleaned** every day.

- Many accidents **are caused** by careless driving.
- **I'm not invited** to parties very often.
- How **is** this word **pronounced**?

一般过去时

主动：**cleaned/saw** 等 — Somebody **cleaned** this room yesterday.

被动：**was/were + cleaned/seen** 等 — This room **was cleaned** yesterday.

- We **were woken** up by a loud noise during the night.
- 'Did you go to the party?' 'No, I **wasn't invited**.'
- How much money **was stolen** in the robbery?

被动语态 (2)，(3) ➜ Units 43–44 by ➜ Unit 128

Exercises

42.1 用下列动词的适当形式完成句子。

~~cause~~	damage	hold	invite	make
overtake	show	surround	translate	write

1 Many accidents ......are caused...... by dangerous driving.
2 Cheese .... from milk.
3 The roof of the building .... in a storm a few days ago.
4 You .... to the wedding. Why didn't you go?
5 A cinema is a place where films ....
6 In the United States, elections for president .... every four years.
7 Originally the book .... in Spanish, and a few years ago it .... into English.
8 Although we were driving fast, we .... by a lot of other cars.
9 You can't see the house from the road. It .... by trees.

42.2 用现在时或过去时的被动语态提问。

1 Ask about glass. (how / make?) ......How is glass made?......
2 Ask about television. (when / invent?) ....
3 Ask about mountains. (how / form?) ....
4 Ask about antibiotics. (when / discover?) ....
5 Ask about silver. (what / use for?) ....

42.3 用动词主动语态或被动语态的一般现在时或一般过去时形式填空。

1 It's a big factory. Five hundred people ......are employed...... (employ) there.
2 ......Did somebody clean...... (somebody / clean) this room yesterday?
3 Water .... (cover) most of the earth's surface.
4 How much of the earth's surface .... (cover) by water?
5 The park gates .... (lock) at 6.30 p.m. every evening.
6 The letter .... (send) a week ago and it (arrive) .... yesterday.
7 The boat hit a rock and .... (sink) quickly. Fortunately everybody .... (rescue).
8 Robert's parents .... (die) when he was very young. He and his sister .... (bring up) by their grandparents.
9 I was born in London, but I .... (grow up) in Canada.
10 While I was on holiday, my camera .... (steal) from my hotel room.
11 While I was on holiday, my camera .... (disappear) from my hotel room.
12 Why .... (Sue / resign) from her job? Didn't she enjoy it?
13 Why .... (Ben / fire) from his job? Did he do something wrong?
14 The company is not independent. It .... (own) by a much larger company.
15 I saw an accident last night. Somebody .... (call) an ambulance but nobody .... (injure), so the ambulance .... (not / need).
16 Where .... (these pictures / take)? In London? .... (you / take) them, or somebody else?
17 Sometimes it's quite noisy living here, but it's not a problem for me – I .... (not / bother) by it.

42.4 用被动语态改写下列句子。

1 Somebody cleans the room every day. ......The room is cleaned every day......
2 They cancelled all flights because of fog. All ....
3 People don't use this road much. ....
4 Somebody accused me of stealing money. I ....
5 How do people learn languages? How ....
6 People warned us not to go out alone. ....

Unit 43

被动语态 (2) (be done / been done / being done)

A

请看下列主动语态与被动语态形式：

动词不定式

主动：(to) **do/clean/see** 等 — Somebody **will clean** this room later.

被动：(to) **be + done/cleaned/seen** 等 — This room **will be cleaned** later.

- The situation is serious. Something must **be done** before it's too late.
- A mystery is something that can't **be explained**.
- The music was very loud and could **be heard** from a long way away.
- A new supermarket is going **to be built** next year.
- Please go away. I want **to be left** alone.

B

完成时

主动：(to) **have + done/cleaned/seen** 等 — Somebody **should have cleaned** the room.

被动：(to) **have been + done/cleaned/seen** 等 — The room **should have been cleaned**.

- I should have received the letter by now. It might **have been sent** to the wrong address.
- If you had locked the car, it wouldn't **have been stolen**.
- There were some problems at first, but they seem **to have been solved**.

C

现在完成时

主动：**have/has + done** 等 — The room looks nice. Somebody **has cleaned** it.

被动：**have/has been + done** 等 — The room looks nice. It **has been cleaned**.

- Have you heard? The trip **has been cancelled**.
- **Have** you ever **been bitten** by a dog?
- 'Are you going to the party?' 'No, I **haven't been invited**.'

过去完成时

主动：**had + done** 等 — The room looked nice. Somebody **had cleaned** it.

被动：**had been + done** 等 — The room looked nice. It **had been cleaned**.

- The vegetables didn't taste good. They **had been cooked** too long.
- The car was three years old, but **hadn't been used** very much.

D

现在进行时

主动：**am/is/are + (do)ing** — Somebody **is cleaning** the room at the moment.

被动：**am/is/are + being (done)** — The room **is being cleaned** at the moment.

- There's somebody walking behind us. I think we **are being followed**.
- (*in a shop*) 'Can I help you?' 'No, thanks. **I'm being served**.'

过去进行时

主动：**was/were + (do)ing** — Somebody **was cleaning** the room when I arrived.

被动：**was/were + being (done)** — The room **was being cleaned** when I arrived.

- There was somebody walking behind us. I think we **were being followed**.

被动语态 (1)，(3) ➜ Units 42，44

Exercises

43.1 用 **it can …** 或 **it can't …** 说明下列单词的含义。必要时可以查字典。

If something is

1 **washable**, it can be washed .
2 **unbreakable**, it ....
3 **edible**, ...
4 **unusable**, ...
5 **invisible**, ...
6 **portable**, ...

43.2 用下列动词的适当形式完成句子。

arrest carry cause ~~do~~ make repair ~~send~~ spend wake up

有时需要用 **have (might have, should have** 等)。

1 The situation is serious. Something must be done before it's too late.
2 I should have received the letter by now. It might have been sent to the wrong address.
3 A decision will not .... until the next meeting.
4 Do you think that more money should .... on education?
5 This road is in very bad condition. It should .... a long time ago.
6 The injured man couldn't walk and had to ....
7 I told the hotel receptionist I wanted to .... at 6.30 the next morning.
8 If you hadn't pushed the policeman, you wouldn't ....
9 It's not certain how the fire started, but it might .... by an electrical fault.

43.3 用被动语态改写下列句子。

1 Somebody has cleaned the room.
The room has been cleaned.
2 Somebody is using the computer right now.
The computer ....
3 I didn't realise that somebody was recording our conversation.
I didn't realise that ....
4 When we got to the stadium, we found that they had cancelled the game.
When we got to the stadium, we found that ....
5 They are building a new ring road round the city.
....
6 They have built a new hospital near the airport.
....

43.4 用括号内的词语造句。有些动词使用主动语态形式，有些使用被动语态形式。

1 There's somebody behind us. (I think / we / follow) I think we're being followed.
2 This room looks different. (you / paint / the walls?) Have you painted the walls?
3 My car has disappeared. (it / steal!) It ....
4 My umbrella has disappeared. (somebody / take) Somebody ....
5 Sam gets a higher salary now. (he / promote) He ....
6 Ann can't use her office this week. (it / redecorate) It ....
7 There was a problem with the photocopier yesterday, but now it's OK.
(it / work) It .... again. (it / repair) It ....
8 When I went into the room, I saw that the table and chairs were not in the same place.
(the furniture / move) The ....
9 A neighbour of mine disappeared six months ago. (he / not / see / since then)
He ....
10 I wonder how Jane is these days. (I / not / see / for ages)
I ....
11 A friend of mine was mugged on his way home a few nights ago. (you / ever / mug?)
....

→ 补充练习 22–24 (第314–315页)

被动语态 (3)

A I was offered … / we were given … 等

有些动词可以有两个宾语。例如 **give**：

- Somebody gave **the police** **the information**. (= somebody gave the information to the police)
  宾语1 宾语2

因此可以改写成两个被动语态的句子：

- **The police** were given the information. 或
  The information was given to the police.

其他可以有两个宾语的动词：

ask **offer** **pay** **show** **teach** **tell**

这些动词的被动句往往以"人"开头：

- **I've been offered** the job, but I don't think I'll accept it. (= they have offered me the job)
- **You will be given** plenty of time to decide. (= we will give you plenty of time)
- I didn't see the original document but **I was shown** a copy. (= somebody showed me)
- Tim has an easy job – **he's paid** a lot of money to do very little. (= they pay him a lot)

B I don't like being …

doing/seeing 等的被动式是 **being done** / **being seen** 等。请比较：

主动：I don't like **people telling me** what to do.
被动：I don't like **being told** what to do.

- I remember **being taken** to the zoo when I was a child.
  (= I remember somebody taking me to the zoo)
- Steve hates **being kept** waiting. (= he hates people keeping him waiting)
- We managed to climb over the wall without **being seen**. (= without anybody seeing us)

C I was born …

可以说 **I was** born … (而不用 I am born)：

- **I was born** in Chicago.
- Where **were** you **born**? (而不用 Where are you born?)

} 一般过去时

但是

- How many babies **are born** every day? 一般现在时

D get

有时，使用被动语态时可以用 **get** 代替 **be**：

- There was a fight at the party, but nobody **got hurt**. (= nobody **was** hurt)
- I don't **get invited** to many parties. (= **I'm** not invited)
- I'm surprised Liz **didn't get offered** the job. (= Liz **wasn't offered** the job)

get 只用来表示事情的发生及变化。例如 **get** 不能用于下列例句中：

- Jessica **is liked** by everybody. (而不用 gets liked ——这不是发生的事情)
- Peter was a mystery man. Very little **was known** about him. (而不用 got known)

get 主要用于口语中，**be** 可以用于所有场合。

get 还可以用于下列表达中 (非被动意义)：

get married，**get divorced**
get lost (= not know where you are)
get dressed (= put on your clothes)
get changed (= change your clothes)

被动语态 (1)，(2) ➜ Units 42–43

Exercises

44.1 按照给出的句子开头改写句子。

1 They didn't give me the information I needed.
I wasn't given the information I needed.
2 They asked me some difficult questions at the interview.
I ....
3 Amy's colleagues gave her a present when she retired.
Amy ....
4 Nobody told me about the meeting.
I wasn't ....
5 How much will they pay you for your work?
How much will you ....
6 I think they should have offered Tom the job.
I think Tom ....
7 Has anybody shown you what to do?
Have you ....

44.2 用 **being** + 下列动词的适当形式完成句子。

give **invite** ~~**keep**~~ **knock down** **stick** **treat**

1 Steve hates being kept waiting.
2 We went to the party without ....
3 I like giving presents and I also like .... them.
4 It's a busy road and I don't like crossing it. I'm afraid of ....
5 I'm an adult. I don't like .... like a child.
6 You can't do anything about .... in a traffic jam.

44.3 他们是哪年出生的？选出五个人物，仿照示例造句。(有两人同年出生。)

Ludwig van Beethoven	Mahatma Gandhi	Elvis Presley	1452	1869	1935
~~Walt Disney~~	Michael Jackson	William Shakespeare	1564	~~1901~~	1958
Galileo	Martin Luther King	Leonardo da Vinci	1770	1929	

1 Walt Disney was born in 1901.
2 ....
3 ....
4 ....
5 ....
6 ....
7 And you? I ....

44.4 用 **get/got** + 下列动词的适当形式完成句子。

ask **damage** ~~**hurt**~~ **pay** **steal** **sting** **stop** **use**

1 There was a fight at the party, but nobody got hurt.
2 Alex .... by a bee while he was sitting in the garden.
3 These tennis courts don't .... very often. Not many people want to play.
4 I used to have a bicycle, but it .... a few months ago.
5 Rachel works hard but doesn't .... very much.
6 Last night I .... by the police as I was driving home. One of the lights on my car wasn't working.
7 Please pack these things very carefully. I don't want them to ....
8 People often want to know what my job is. I .... that question a lot.

→ 补充练习 22–24 (第314–315页)

It is said that ... He is said to ... He is supposed to ...

A

请看下列例句：

George is very old. Nobody knows exactly how old he is, but:

It is said that he is 108 years old.

或 He **is said to be** 108 years old.

这两句话的意思都是：People say that he is 108 years old.

下列动词可以用于上述句型中：

alleged **believed** **considered** **expected** **known** **reported** **thought** **understood**

请比较下列两个构成方式：

- Cathy loves running.
  It is said that she runs ten miles a day. 或 She **is said to run** ten miles a day.
- The police are looking for a missing boy.
  It is believed that the boy is wearing a white sweater and blue jeans. 或 The boy **is believed to be wearing** a white sweater and blue jeans.
- The strike started three weeks ago.
  It is expected that the strike will end soon. 或 The strike **is expected to end** soon.
- A friend of mine has been arrested.
  It is alleged that he hit a policeman. 或 He **is alleged to have hit** a policeman.
- The two houses belong to the same family.
  It is said that there is a secret tunnel between them. 或 There **is said to be** a secret tunnel between them.

新闻报道中常用这些句型，如报道一场事故等：

- **It is reported that** two people were injured in the explosion. 或 Two people **are reported to have been injured** in the explosion.

B

(be) supposed to

有时用 **(it is) supposed to** ... 表示“据说……”“听说……”：

- I want to see that film. It**'s supposed to be** good. (= it is said to be good)
- Fireworks **are supposed to have been invented** in China. Is it true?

但有时 **supposed to** 表示不同的意思。something **is supposed to** happen 表示计划、安排或希望某事发生，但经常是事情并没有发生：

- The plan **is supposed to be** a secret, but everybody seems to know about it.
  (= the plan is intended to be a secret)
- What are you doing at work? You**'re supposed to be** on holiday.
  (= you arranged to be on holiday)
- Our guests **were supposed to come** at 7.30, but they were late.
- Jane **was supposed to phone** me last night, but she didn't.
- I'd better hurry. **I'm supposed to be meeting** Chris in ten minutes.

you're **not supposed to** do something 表示“不准”“不应当”：

- You**'re not supposed to park** your car here. It's private parking only.
- Jeff is much better after his illness, but he**'s still not supposed to do** any heavy work.

Exercises

45.1 按照给出的句子开头，用画线的单词改写句子。

1 It is expected that the strike will end soon. The strike is expected to end soon.
2 It is expected that the weather will be good tomorrow.
The weather is ……
3 It is believed that the thieves got in through a window in the roof.
The thieves ……
4 It is reported that many people are homeless after the floods.
Many people ……
5 It is thought that the prisoner escaped by climbing over a wall.
The prisoner ……
6 It is alleged that the man was driving at 110 miles an hour.
The man ……
7 It is reported that the building has been badly damaged by the fire.
The building ……
8 a It is said that the company is losing a lot of money.
The company ……
b It is believed that the company lost a lot of money last year.
The company ……
c It is expected that the company will make a loss this year.
The company ……

45.2 关于艾伦有很多传言，例如：

1 Alan speaks ten languages.
2 He knows a lot of famous people.
3 He is very rich.
4 He has twelve children.
5 He was an actor when he was younger.

Alan

没有人知道这些传言是否真实。用 **(be) supposed to** 就艾伦的情况造句。

1 Alan is supposed to speak ten languages.
2 He ……
3 ……
4 ……
5 ……

45.3 用 **supposed to be** + 下列词语完成句子。

on a diet	**a flower**	**my friend**	**a joke**	~~**a secret**~~	**working**

1 How is it that everybody seems to know about the plan? It is supposed to be a secret.
2 You shouldn't criticise me all the time. You ……
3 I shouldn't be eating this cake really. I ……
4 I'm sorry for what I said. I was trying to be funny. It ……
5 What's this drawing? Is it a tree? Or maybe it ……
6 You shouldn't be reading the paper now. You ……

45.4 用 **supposed to** + 下列动词完成句子。

block	**depart**	~~**park**~~	**phone**	**start**

必要时可用否定形式。

1 You 're not supposed to park here. It's private parking only.
2 We …… work at 8.15, but we rarely do anything before 8.30.
3 Oh, I …… Helen last night, but I completely forgot.
4 This door is a fire exit. You …… it.
5 My flight …… at 11.30, but it was an hour late.

→ 补充练习 22–24（第314–315页）

Unit 46 have something done

A

请看下列例句：

The roof of Lisa's house was damaged in a storm. So she called a builder, and yesterday a man came and repaired it.

Lisa **had** the roof **repaired** yesterday.

其意思是：莉萨安排人修了屋顶，不是她自己修。

have something done 用来表示"叫某人做某事"。

请比较：

- Lisa **repaired** the roof. (= she repaired it herself)
  Lisa **had** the roof **repaired**. (= she arranged for somebody else to repair it)
- 'Did you **make** those curtains yourself?' 'Yes, I enjoy making things.'
  'Did you **have** those curtains **made**?' 'No, I made them myself.'

B

注意词序，过去分词 (**repaired/cut** 等) 用于宾语之后：

have	宾语	过去分词
Lisa **had**	the roof	**repaired** yesterday.
Where did you **have**	your hair	**cut**?
Your hair looks nice. Have you **had**	it	**cut**?
Our neighbour has just **had**	a garage	**built**.
We are **having**	the house	**painted** this week.
How often do you **have**	your car	**serviced**?
I think you should **have**	that coat	**cleaned**.
I don't like **having**	my picture	**taken**.

C

get something done

还可以用 **get** something done 代替 **have** something done：

- When are you going to **get the roof repaired**? (= have the roof repaired)
- I think you should **get your hair cut** really short.

D

有时 **have something done** 有着完全不同的意思，例如：

- Paul and Karen **had their bags stolen** while they were travelling.

这句话的意思当然不是说他们安排人偷了他们的钱。They **had their bags stolen** 的含义是：Their bags were stolen.

在用作这个意义时，**have something done** 通常用来表示意外或不幸的遭遇：

- Gary **had** his nose **broken** in a fight. (= his nose was broken)
- Have you ever **had** your bike **stolen**?

Exercises

46.1 按每幅图所示，选择正确的句子。

1

SARAH
(a) Sarah is cutting her hair.
(b) Sarah is having her hair cut.

2

BILL
(a) Bill is cutting his hair.
(b) Bill is having his hair cut.

3

JOHN
(a) John is cleaning his shoes.
(b) John is having his shoes cleaned.

4

SUE
(a) Sue is taking a picture.
(b) Sue is having her picture taken.

46.2 用下列词语造句。

1 had / a few weeks ago / the house / we / painted
We had the house painted a few weeks ago.
2 serviced / her car / Sarah / once a year / has
Sarah ……
3 twelve pounds / have / cleaned / it / my suit / cost / to
……
4 my eyes / I / two years ago / had / tested / the last time / was
……
5 had / in the kitchen / fitted / some new cupboards / we've
……
6 as soon as possible / need / translated / we / to get / this document
……

46.3 仿照示例造句。

1 Lisa didn't repair the roof herself. She had it repaired.
2 I didn't cut my hair myself. I ……
3 We didn't clean the carpets ourselves. We ……
4 John didn't build that wall himself. ……
5 I didn't deliver the flowers myself. ……

46.4 用 **have something done** 结构及括号内的词语完成下列句子。

1 We're having the house painted (we / the house / paint) this week.
2 I lost my key. I'll have to …… (another key / make).
3 When was the last time …… (you / your hair / cut)?
4 …… (you / a newspaper / deliver) to your house every day, or do you go out and buy one?
5 A: What's happening in your garden?
B: Oh, …… (we / a garage / build).
6 A: …… (you / the washing machine / fix)?
B: Not yet. There's someone coming to look at it next week.
7 If you want to wear earrings, why don't you …… (you / your ears / pierce)?

用 **have something done** 结构的第二个含义回答下列问题 (参见 **D** 节)。

8 Gary was in a fight last night. He had his nose broken (he / his nose / break).
9 Did I tell you about Jane? …… (she / her credit cards / steal).
10 Security was very strict at the airport. …… (we all / our bags / search).

间接引语 (1) (He said that …)

A

请看下列例句：

You want to tell somebody what Paul said.
There are two ways of doing this:

你可以重复保罗的话 (直接引语)：
Paul said **'I'm feeling ill.'**

或者可以用间接引语：
Paul said **that he was feeling ill.**

请比较：

直接： Paul said '**I** **am** feeling ill.'

间接： Paul said that **he** **was** feeling ill.

在书面语中，用引号表示直接引语。

B

间接引语中句子的主要动词通常为过去式 (Paul said that … / I told her that … 等)，句子的其他部分通常也要用过去时态：

- Paul **said** that he **was feeling** ill.
- I **told** Lisa that I **didn't have** any money.

这时，**that** 可以省略：

- Paul **said that** he was feeling ill. 或 Paul **said** he was feeling ill.

一般情况下，直接引语变间接引语时，动词的现在时形式要变成过去时形式：

am/is → **was** do/does → **did** will → **would**
are → **were** have/has → **had** can → **could**
want/like/know/go 等 → **wanted/liked/knew/went** 等

请比较下列直接引语与间接引语：

你遇到了安娜，下面是她对你说的话：

My parents **are** fine.
I'm going to learn to drive.
I **want** to buy a car.
John **has** a new job.
I **can't** come to the party on Friday.
I **don't** have much free time.
I'm going away for a few days.
I'll phone you when I **get** back.

随后，你用间接引语向某人转述安娜的话：

- Anna said that her parents **were** fine.
- She said that she **was** going to learn to drive.
- She said that she **wanted** to buy a car.
- She said that John **had** a new job.
- She said that she **couldn't** come to the party on Friday.
- She said she **didn't** have much free time.
- She said that she **was** going away for a few days and **would** phone me when she **got** back.

C

直接引语中的一般过去时 **(did/saw/knew** 等) 在间接引语中通常可以保持不变，或者可以变成过去完成时 (**had done** / **had seen** / **had known** 等)：

- 直接 Paul said 'I **woke** up feeling ill, so I **didn't go** to work.'
  间接 Paul said (that) he **woke** up feeling ill, so he **didn't go** to work. 或
  Paul said (that) he **had woken** up feeling ill, so he **hadn't gone** to work.

间接引语 (2) ➔ Unit 48 间接疑问句 ➔ Unit 50B

Exercises

47.1 昨天，你遇到了你的朋友史蒂夫。你们已经很久没见面了，以下是史蒂夫对你讲的一些事情：

1 I'm living in London.
2 My father isn't very well.
3 Rachel and Mark are getting married next month.
4 My sister has had a baby.
5 I don't know what Joe is doing.
6 I saw Helen at a party in June and she seemed fine.
7 I haven't seen Amy recently.
8 I'm not enjoying my job very much.
9 You can come and stay at my place if you're ever in London.
10 My car was stolen a few days ago.
11 I want to go on holiday, but I can't afford it.
12 I'll tell Chris I saw you.

当天晚些时候，你使用间接引语，向另一个朋友转述了史蒂夫的话。

1 Steve said that he was living in London.
2 He said that ……
3 He ……
4 ……
5 ……
6 ……
7 ……
8 ……
9 ……
10 ……
11 ……
12 ……

47.2 有人说了一些出乎你意料的事，根据你自己的想法完成回答。

1 A: It's quite a long way from the hotel to the station.
B: Is it? The man on the reception desk said it was only five minutes' walk.
2 A: Sue is coming to the party tonight.
B: Is she? I saw her a few days ago and she said she …… .
3 A: Sarah gets on fine with Paul.
B: Does she? Last week you said …… each other.
4 A: Joe knows lots of people.
B: That's not what he told me. He said …… anyone.
5 A: Jane will be here next week.
B: Oh, really? When I spoke to her, she said …… away.
6 A: I'm going out tonight.
B: Are you? I thought you said …… home.
7 A: John speaks French quite well.
B: Does he? He told me …… any other languages.
8 A: I haven't seen Ben recently.
B: That's strange. He told me …… last weekend.

→ 补充练习 25（第316页）

间接引语 (2)

A

在间接引语中，动词的时态并不是都要改变。如果转述的情况仍然成立或有效，就不用改变动词的时态了：

- 直接　Paul said 'My new job **is** boring.'
  间接　Paul said that his new job **is** boring.
  (情况仍然相同，他的工作现在仍然枯燥乏味)
- 直接　Helen said '**I want** to go to Canada next year.'
  间接　Helen told me that **she wants** to go to Canada next year.
  (海伦仍然想明年去加拿大)

注意在以上情况下，将动词改成过去式也是正确的：

- Paul said that his new job **was** boring.
- Helen told me that she **wanted** to go to Canada next year.

但如果转述的情况已发生了变化，一定要用过去时：

- Paul left the room suddenly. He said **he had** to go. (而不用 has to go)

B

如果转述的情况与事实不相符合时，需要用过去时。例如：

You met Sonia a few days ago.
She said: **Joe is in hospital.**

几天之后，你在街上遇见了乔，你可以说：
Hi, Joe. I didn't expect to see you. Sonia said you **were** in hospital.
(而不用 Sonia said you are in hospital，因为显然他现在没病)

C

say 与 **tell** 比较

如果要讲明说话对象，用 **tell**：

- Sonia **told me** that you were in hospital. (而不用 Sonia said me)
- What did you **tell the police**? (而不用 say the police)

否则用 **say**：

- Sonia **said** that you were in hospital. (而不用 Sonia told that …)
- What did you **say**?

但是可以说 **say** something **to** somebody：

- Ann **said** goodbye **to** me and left. (而不用 Ann said me goodbye)
- What did you **say to** the police?

D

tell/ask somebody **to** do something

在间接引语中，特别是在 **tell** 和 **ask** (表示命令和请求) 之后，还可以使用动词的不定式：

- 直接　'**Drink** plenty of water,' the doctor said to me.
  间接　The doctor **told me to drink** plenty of water.
- 直接　'**Don't be** late,' I said to Joe.
  间接　**I told Joe not to be** late.
- 直接　'**Can you help** me, please,' Jackie said to me.
  间接　Jackie **asked me to help** her.

也可以用 somebody **said (not) to** do something：

- Paul **said not to worry** about him. (而不用 Paul said me)

间接引语 (1) ➜ Unit 47　　**间接疑问句 ➜ Unit 50B**

Exercises

48.1 下面是萨拉对你说过的一些话：

I've never been to the United States.
I don't have any brothers or sisters.
I can't drive.
I don't like fish.
Jane has a very well-paid job.
I'm working tomorrow evening.
Jane is a friend of mine.
~~Dave is lazy.~~

但后来萨拉的说法发生了变化。你会说些什么？

	Sarah	You
1	Dave works very hard.	But you said he was lazy.
2	Let's have fish for dinner.	But ....
3	I'm going to buy a car.	....
4	Jane is always short of money.	....
5	My sister lives in Paris.	....
6	I think New York is a great place.	....
7	Let's go out tomorrow evening.	....
8	I've never spoken to Jane.	....

48.2 用 **say** 或 **tell** 的适当形式完成句子，每空只填一个词。

1 Ann said goodbye to me and left.
2 .... us about your holiday. Did you have a nice time?
3 Don't just stand there! .... something!
4 I wonder where Sue is. She .... she would be here at 8 o'clock.
5 Dan .... me that he was bored with his job.
6 The doctor .... that I should rest for at least a week.
7 Don't .... anybody what I .... It's a secret just between us.
8 'Did she .... you what happened?' 'No, she didn't .... anything to me.'
9 Gary couldn't help me. He .... me to ask Chris.
10 Gary couldn't help me. He .... to ask Chris.

48.3 下面是一些直接引语：

Don't wait for me if I'm late.
Mind your own business.
Don't worry, Sue.
Please slow down!
Can you open your bag, please?
Could you get me a paper?
~~Hurry up!~~
Will you marry me?
Do you think you could give me a hand, Tom?

根据上面的话，用间接引语完成下列句子。

1 Will was taking a long time to get ready, so I told him to hurry up.
2 Sarah was driving too fast, so I asked ....
3 Sue was nervous about the situation. I told ....
4 I couldn't move the piano alone, so I ....
5 The security guard looked at me suspiciously and ....
6 Tom was going to the shop, so I ....
7 The man started asking me personal questions, so I ....
8 John was in love with Marianne, so he ....
9 I didn't want to delay Helen, so I ....

→ 补充练习 25 (第316页)

Unit 49

疑问句 (1)

A

陈述句变为疑问句时常改变词序，将助动词移到主语之前：

主语 + 助动词　　助动词 + 主语

Tom	will	→	will	Tom?
you	have	→	have	you?
the house	was	→	was	the house?

- **Will Tom** be here tomorrow?
- **Have you** been working hard?
- When **was the house** built?

注意，主语要跟在助动词之后：

- **Is Katherine** working today?（而不用 Is working Katherine）

B

在一般现在时的疑问句中，使用 **do/does**：

you	live	→	**do**	you **live**?
the film	starts	→	**does**	the film **start**?

- **Do** you **live** near here?
- What time **does** the film **start**?

在一般过去时的疑问句中，使用 **did**：

you	sold	→	**did**	you **sell**?
the train	stopped	→	**did**	the train **stop**?

- **Did** you **sell** your car?
- Why **did** the train **stop**?

如果 **who/what** 等作句子的主语，疑问句中不使用 **do/does/did**。请比较：

who 作宾语	**who** 作主语
Emma phoned somebody.	Somebody phoned Emma.
宾语	主语
Who **did** Emma **phone**?	Who **phoned** Emma?

在下列例句中，**who/what** 等作主语：

- **Who wants** something to eat?（而不用 Who does want）
- **What happened** to you last night?（而不用 What did happen）
- **How many people came** to the meeting?（而不用 did come）
- **Which bus goes** to the centre?（而不用 does go）

C

注意在以 **Who/What/Which/Where** ... ? 开头的疑问句中介词的位置：

- **Who** do you want to speak **to**?
- **Which** job has Tina applied **for**?
- **What** was the weather **like** yesterday?
- **Where** are you **from**?

在正式文体中，可以用介词 + **whom**：

- **To whom** do you wish to speak?

D

否定疑问句 (**Isn't it** ... ? / **Didn't you** ... ? 等)

否定疑问句尤用来表示惊讶：

- **Didn't you** hear the doorbell? I rang it three times.

或表示希望得到肯定的答复：

- '**Haven't we** met before?' 'Yes, I think we have.'

注意在回答否定疑问句时，**yes** 和 **no** 的含义：

- **Don't you** want to go? { **Yes.** (= Yes, I want to go) / **No.** (= No, I don't want to go) }

注意在以 **Why** ... ? 开头的否定疑问句中的词序：

- **Why don't we** eat out tonight?（而不用 Why we don't eat）
- **Why wasn't Emma** at work yesterday?（而不用 Why Emma wasn't）

疑问句 (2) ➜ Unit 50　　附加疑问 (do you? isn't it? 等) ➜ Unit 52

Exercises

49.1 根据乔的回答提问。

1	(where / live?) Where do you live?	In Manchester.
2	(born there?)	No, I was born in London.
3	(married?)	Yes.
4	(how long / married?)	17 years.
5	(children?)	Yes, two boys.
6	(how old / they?)	12 and 15.
7	(what / do?)	I'm a journalist.
8	(what / wife / do?)	She's a doctor.

Joe

49.2 用 **who** 或 **what** 提问。

1	Somebody hit me.	Who hit you?
2	I hit somebody.	Who did you hit?
3	Somebody paid the bill.	Who ....
4	Something happened.	What ....
5	Diane said something.	....
6	This book belongs to somebody.	....
7	Somebody lives in that house.	....
8	I fell over something.	....
9	Something fell off the shelf.	....
10	This word means something.	....
11	I borrowed the money from somebody.	....
12	I'm worried about something.	....

49.3 按照疑问句形式正确排列括号内词语的顺序。

1 (when / was / built / this house) When was this house built?
2 (how / cheese / is / made) ....
3 (when / invented / the computer / was) ....
4 (why / Sue / working / isn't / today) ....
5 (what time / coming / your friends / are) ....
6 (why / was / cancelled / the trip) ....
7 (where / your mother / was / born) ....
8 (why / you / to the party / didn't / come) ....
9 (how / the accident / did / happen) ....
10 (why / this machine / doesn't / work) ....

49.4 用括号内的词语写出否定疑问句以示惊讶。

1 A: We won't see Lisa this evening.
B: Why not? (she / not / come / out with us?) Isn't she coming out with us?

2 A: I hope we don't meet Luke tonight.
B: Why? (you / not / like / him?) ....

3 A: Don't go and see that film.
B: Why not? (it / not / good?) ....

4 A: I'll have to borrow some money.
B: Why? (you / not / have / any?) ....

Unit 50 疑问句 (2) (Do you know where ... ? / He asked me where ...)

A

Do you know where ... ? / **I don't know why** ... / **Could you tell me what** ... ? 等。

可以说： Where **has Tom** gone?

但是 Do you know where **Tom has** gone? （而不用 Do you know where has Tom gone?)

当疑问句 (**Where has Tom gone?**) 是长句 (**Do you know** ... ? / **I don't know** ... / **Can you tell me** ... ? 等) 的一部分时，句中词序要发生变化：

- What time **is it**? 但是 **Do you know** what time **it is**?
- Who **are those people**? **I don't know** who **those people are**.
- Where **can I** find Louise? **Can you tell me** where **I can** find Louise?
- How much **will it** cost? **Do you have any idea** how much **it will** cost?

注意 **do/does/did** 的问句：

- What time **does the film start**? 但是 **Do you know** what time **the film starts**? (而不用 does the film start)
- What **do you mean**? **Please explain** what **you mean**.
- Why **did she leave** early? **I wonder** why **she left** early.

在没有 **what** / **why** 等疑问词的情况下，可以使用 **if** 或 **whether**：

- Did anybody see you? 但是 Do you know **if** anybody saw you? 或 ... **whether** anybody saw you?

B

He asked me where ... (转述问题)

在转述问题时要改变词序，请比较：

- 直接 The police officer said to us 'Where **are you going**?'
  间接 The police officer asked us where **we were going**.
- 直接 Clare said 'What time **do the banks close**?'
  间接 Clare wanted to know what time **the banks closed**.

在间接疑问句中，动词通常改为过去式 (**were**，**closed** 等)。参见Unit 47。

下列例句是求职面试中的几个问题：

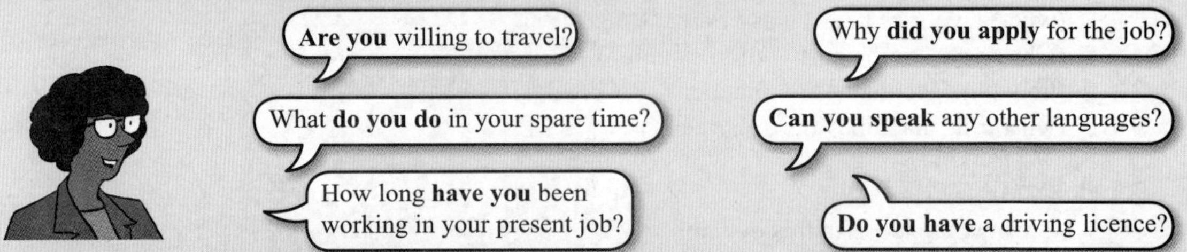

面试之后，你使用间接引语向一个朋友讲述面试人员对你提的问题：

- She asked if (或 whether) **I was** willing to travel.
- She wanted to know what **I did** in my spare time.
- She asked how long **I had** been working in my present job.
- She asked why **I had** applied for the job. （或 ... why I **applied**)
- She wanted to know if (或 whether) **I could** speak any other languages.
- She asked if (或 whether) **I had** a driving licence.

间接引语 ➜ Units 47–48

Exercises

50.1 在正确的表达后面画 ✓。

1 a Do you know what time the film starts? ✓
b Do you know what time does the film start?
c Do you know what time starts the film?

2 a Why Amy does get up so early every day?
b Why Amy gets up so early every day?
c Why does Amy get up so early every day?

3 a I want to know what this word means.
b I want to know what does this word mean.
c I want to know what means this word.

4 a I can't remember where did I park the car.
b I can't remember where I parked the car.
c I can't remember where I did park the car.

5 a Why you didn't phone me yesterday?
b Why didn't you phone me yesterday?
c Why you not phoned me yesterday?

6 a Do you know where does Helen work?
b Do you know where Helen does work?
c Do you know where Helen works?

7 a How much it costs to park here?
b How much does it cost to park here?
c How much it does cost to park here?

8 a Tell me what you want.
b Tell me what you do want.
c Tell me what do you want.

50.2 正确排列括号内词语的顺序。

1 (don't / Tom / where / know / gone / has) I don't know where Tom has gone .
2 (is / to the airport / far / it) How ...... ?
3 (wonder / is / how / old / Tom) I ....
4 (Lisa / on holiday / going / is) When ...... ?
5 (tell / the post office / you / me / is / where)
Could ...... ?
6 (in the accident / injured / anyone / don't / whether / know / was)
I ....
7 (what / tomorrow / know / time / will / arrive / you / you)
Do ...... ?

50.3 你外出了一段时间，刚回到家乡，遇到你的朋友托尼，他问了你一些问题。

1 How are you?
2 Where have you been?
3 How long have you been back?
4 What are you doing now?

Tony

5 Why did you come back?
6 Where are you living?
7 Are you glad to be back?
8 Do you have any plans to go away again?
9 Can you help me find a job?

用间接引语告诉另一位朋友托尼问你的问题。

1 He asked me how I was.
2 He asked me ......
3 He ......
4 ......
5 ......
6 ......
7 ......
8 ......
9 ......

→ 补充练习 25（第316页）

Unit 51

助动词 (have/do/can 等)
I think so / I hope so 等

A

下列句子都用了两个动词：

I	**have**	**lost**	my keys.
She	**can't**	**come**	to the party.
The hotel	**was**	**built**	ten years ago.
Where	**do** you	**live**?	

这些句子中的 **have/can't/was/do** 是助动词。

为了避免重复，在回答问题或写后半句话时可以只用助动词：

- 'Have you locked the door?' 'Yes, I **have**.' (= I have *locked the door*)
- Gary wasn't working, but Laura **was**. (= Laura was *working*)
- Jessica could lend me the money, but she **won't**. (= she won't *lend me the money*)

do/does/did 用于一般现在时和一般过去时：

- 'Do you like onions?' 'Yes, I **do**.' (= I *like onions*)
- 'Does Simon live in London?' 'He **did**, but he **doesn't** any more.'

助动词可以用来反驳某人说的话：

- 'You're sitting in my place.' 'No, **I'm not**.' (= I'm not *sitting in your place*)
- 'You didn't lock the door before you left.' 'Yes, I **did**.' (= I *locked the door*)

B

用 **have you**? / **isn't she**? / **do they**? 等表示对某人的话感兴趣或感到惊讶：

- 'I've just seen Stephen.' 'Oh, **have you**? How is he?'
- 'Lisa isn't very well today.' 'Oh, **isn't she**? What's wrong with her?'
- 'It rained every day during our holiday.' '**Did it**? What a shame!'
- 'James and Tanya are getting married.' '**Are they**? Really?'

C

so 和 **neither** 可与助动词连用：

- 'I'm tired.' '**So am I**.' (= I'm tired too)
- 'I never read newspapers.' '**Neither do I**.' (= I never read newspapers either)
- Sarah hasn't got a car and **neither has Mark**.

注意 **so** 和 **neither** 之后的词序 (动词置于主语前)：

- I passed the exam and **so did Paul**. (而不用 so Paul did)

可以用 **nor** 代替 **neither**，还可以用 **not … either**：

- 'I don't know.' '**Neither** do I.' 或 '**Nor** do I.' 或 'I do**n't either**.'

D

I think so / I hope so 等

为了避免重复，在有些动词之后可以用**so**：

- 'Are those people Korean?' '**I think so**.' (= I think *they are Korean*)
- 'Will you be at home this evening?' '**I expect so**.' (= I expect *I'll be at home* …)
- 'Do you think Kate has been invited to the party?' '**I suppose so**.'

还可以说 **I hope so**，**I guess so** 和 **I'm afraid so**。

否定形式通常是：

I think so / I expect so	→	I **don't think so** / I **don't expect so**
I hope so / I'm afraid so / I guess so	→	I **hope not** / **I'm afraid not** / I **guess not**
I suppose so	→	I **don't suppose so** 或 I **suppose not**

- 'Is that woman American?' '**I think so**. / **I don't think so**.'
- 'Do you think it will rain?' '**I hope so**. / **I hope not**.' (而不用 I don't hope so)

美国英语 ➜ 附录 7

Exercises

51.1 用助动词 (**do/was/could** 等) 完成下列句子。有时要用否定形式 (**don't/wasn't** 等)。

1 I wasn't tired, but my friends *were* .
2 I like hot weather, but Ann ....
3 'Is Andy here?' 'He .... five minutes ago, but I think he's gone home now.'
4 Liz said she might call me later this evening, but I don't think she ....
5 'Are you and Chris coming to the party?' 'I ...., but Chris ....'
6 I don't know whether to apply for the job or not. Do you think I .... ?
7 'Please don't tell anybody what I said.' 'Don't worry. I ....'
8 'You never listen to me.' 'Yes, I .... !'
9 I thought it was going to rain, but it ....
10 'Please help me.' 'I'm sorry. I .... if I ...., but I ....'

51.2 你不赞同休的话。仿照示例作出回答。

Sue

	Sue	You
1	I'm hungry.	*Are you? I'm not.*
2	I'm not tired.	*Aren't you? I am.*
3	I like football.	....
4	I didn't enjoy the film.	....
5	I've never been to Australia.	....
6	I thought the exam was easy.	....

You

51.3 根据你自己的情况，仿照示例1用 **So …** 或 **Neither …** 对蒂娜的话作出答复，或仿照示例2 提问。

Tina

	Tina	You
1	I'm tired.	*So am I.*
2	I work hard.	*Do you? What do you do?*
3	I watched television last night.	....
4	I won't be at home tomorrow.	....
5	I like reading. I read a lot.	....
6	I'd like to live somewhere else.	....
7	I can't go out tonight.	....

You

51.4 根据括号内的情况，用 **I think so / I hope not** 等作出回答。

1 (You don't like rain.)
A: Is it going to rain? B: (hope) *I hope not.*
2 (You need more money quickly.)
A: Do you think you'll get a pay rise soon? B: (hope) ....
3 (You think Katherine will probably get the job that she applied for.)
A: Do you think Katherine will get the job? B: (expect) ....
4 (You're not sure whether Amy is married – probably not.)
A: Is Amy married? B: (think) ....
5 (You are the receptionist at a hotel. The hotel is full.)
A: Have you got a room for tonight? B: (afraid) ....
6 (You're at a party. You have to leave early.)
A: Do you have to leave already? B: (afraid) ....
7 (Ann normally works every day, Monday to Friday. Tomorrow is Wednesday.)
A: Is Ann working tomorrow? B: (suppose) ....
8 (You are going to a party. You can't stand John.)
A: Do you think John will be at the party? B: (hope) ....
9 (You're not sure what time the concert is – probably 7.30.)
A: Is the concert at 7.30? B: (think) ....

Unit 52 附加疑问 (do you? isn't it? 等)

A

请看下列例句：

have you? 和 **wasn't it**? 是附加疑问，即口语中附加在句子后面的简略问话。在附加疑问中要用助动词 (**have/was/will** 等)，其中 **do/does/did** 用于一般现在时和一般过去时的附加疑问中(参见Unit 51)：

- 'Karen plays the piano, **does**n't she?' 'Well, yes, but not very well.'
- 'You didn't lock the door, **did** you?' 'No, I forgot.'

B

在肯定句后，我们一般用否定的附加疑问：

肯定句 +	否定疑问
Kate **will** be here soon,	**won't she**?
There **was** a lot of traffic,	**wasn't there**?
Joe **should** pass the exam,	**shouldn't he**?

在否定句后，一般用肯定的附加疑问：

否定句 +	肯定疑问
Kate **won't** be late,	**will she**?
They **don't** like us,	**do they**?
You **haven't** eaten yet,	**have you**?

注意对否定疑问句作出回答时**yes** 和 **no** 的含义：

- You're **not** going out today, **are you**? { **Yes.** (= Yes, I am going out) / **No.** (= No, I am not going out) }

C

附加疑问的意思取决于说话人的语调。如果用降调，说话人通常并不是在真的发问，而是希望得到对方的认可：

- 'It's a nice day, **isn't it**?' 'Yes, beautiful.'
- 'Paul doesn't look well today, **does he**?' 'No, he looks very tired.'
- 'Lisa's very funny. She's got a great sense of humour, **hasn't she**?' 'Yes, she has.'

如果说话人用升调，则是提出一个希望得到回答的真正的问句：

- 'You haven't seen Lisa today, **have you**?' 'No, I haven't.'
  (= Have you by chance seen Lisa today?)

否定句＋肯定附加疑问的形式可用来询问有关情况，或让某人做某事。这时附加疑问句用升调：

- 'You haven't got a pen, **have you**?' 'Yes, here you are.'
- 'You couldn't do me a favour, **could you**?' 'It depends what it is.'
- 'You don't know where Karen is, **do you**?' 'Sorry, I have no idea.'

D

let's 后的附加疑问用**shall we**：

- **Let's** go for a walk, **shall we**? (升调)

在祈使句 (**Don't** …等) 之后，附加疑问通常用 **will you**：

- **Don't** be late, **will you**? (降调)

I'm 之后的附加疑问用 **aren't I** (= am I not)：

- 'I'm right, **aren't I**?' 'Yes, you are.'

助动词 (have/do/can 等) ➜ Unit 51

Exercises

52.1 在下列句子中填入附加疑问。

1	Kate won't be late,	will she ?	No, she's never late.
2	You're tired,	aren't you ?	Yes, a little.
3	You travel a lot,	.... ?	Yes, I love travelling.
4	You weren't listening,	.... ?	Yes, I was!
5	Sarah doesn't know Ann,	.... ?	No, they've never met.
6	Jack's on holiday,	.... ?	Yes, he's in Australia.
7	Kate's been to China before,	.... ?	Yes, two or three times.
8	You can speak German,	.... ?	Yes, but not fluently.
9	They won't mind if I take a photo,	.... ?	No, of course they won't.
10	There are a lot of people here,	.... ?	Yes, more than I expected.
11	Let's go out tonight,	.... ?	Yes, that would be great.
12	This isn't very interesting,	.... ?	No, not really.
13	I'm too impatient,	.... ?	Yes, you are sometimes.
14	You wouldn't tell anyone,	.... ?	No, of course not.
15	Ann has lived here a long time,	.... ?	Yes, 20 years.
16	I shouldn't have lost my temper,	.... ?	No, but that's all right.
17	He'd never met her before,	.... ?	No, that was the first time.
18	Don't drop that vase,	.... ?	Don't worry. I won't.

52.2 根据所给的情况，写出附加疑问。

1 You look out of the window. The sky is blue and the sun is shining. What do you say to your friend? (beautiful day) It's a beautiful day, isn't it?

2 You're with a friend outside a restaurant. You're looking at the prices, which are very high. What do you say? (expensive) It ....

3 You and a colleague have just finished a training course. You really enjoyed it. What do you say to your colleague? (great) The course ....

4 Your friend's hair is much shorter than when you last met. What do you say to her/him? (have / your hair / cut) You ....

5 You and a friend are listening to a woman singing. You like her voice very much. What do you say to your friend? (a good voice) She ....

6 You are trying on a jacket in a shop. You look in the mirror and you don't like what you see. What do you say to your friend? (not / look / very good)
It ....

7 You and a friend are walking over a small wooden bridge. The bridge is very old and some parts are broken. What do you say? (not / very safe)
This bridge ....

52.3 根据下列情况，仿照示例造句。

1 You need a pen. Perhaps Jane has got one. Ask her.
Jane, you haven't got a pen, have you?

2 You have to move a heavy table. You want Joe to give you a hand with it. Ask him.
Joe, you ....

3 You're looking for Sarah. Perhaps Kate knows where she is. Ask her.
Kate, you ....

4 You need a bicycle pump. Perhaps Helen has got one. Ask her.
Helen, ...

5 Ann has a car and you need a lift to the station. Perhaps she'll take you. Ask her.
Ann, ...

6 You're looking for your keys. Perhaps Robert has seen them. Ask him.
Robert, ...

动词 + -ing 形式 (enjoy doing / stop doing 等)

A

请看下列例句：

- I **enjoy reading**. (而不用 I enjoy to read)
- Would you **mind closing** the door? (而不用 mind to close)
- Chris **suggested going** to the cinema. (而不用 suggested to go)

在 **enjoy**，**mind** 和 **suggest** 之后的动词要用-**ing** 形式 (而不用 **to** ...)。

下表中的动词之后均跟动词的 -**ing** 形式：

stop	**postpone**	**admit**	**avoid**	**imagine**
finish	**consider**	**deny**	**risk**	**fancy**

- Suddenly everybody **stopped talking**. There was silence.
- I'll do the shopping when I've **finished cleaning** the flat.
- He tried to **avoid answering** my question.
- I don't **fancy going** out this evening. (= I'm not enthusiastic about it)
- Have you ever **considered going** to live in another country?
- They said they were innocent. They **denied doing** anything wrong.

注意，否定形式是 **not -ing**：

- When I'm on holiday, I enjoy **not having** to get up early.

B

在一些短语后面也用动词的 -**ing** 形式：

give up (= stop)
put off (= postpone)
go on 或 **carry on** (= continue)
keep 或 **keep on** (= do something continuously or repeatedly)

- I've **given up reading** newspapers. I think it's a waste of time.
- Catherine doesn't want to retire. She wants to **go on working**. (或 ... to **carry on working**.)
- You **keep interrupting** when I'm talking! 或 You **keep on interrupting** ...

C

有些动词可以用动词 + 宾语 + -**ing** 形式的结构：

- I can't **imagine George riding** a motorbike.
- You can't **stop me doing** what I want.
- Did you really say that? I don't **remember you saying** that.
- 'Sorry to **keep you waiting** so long.' 'That's all right.'

注意-**ing** 形式的被动形式 (**being done/seen/kept** 等)：

- I don't **mind being kept** waiting. (= I don't mind **people keeping** me ...)

D

谈论已完成的动作时，可以用 **having done/stolen/said** 等：

- They admitted **having stolen** the money.

除了 **having** (done)，也可以用-**ing** 的一般式来表示已经完成的动作。如：

- They admitted **stealing** the money.
- I now regret **saying** (或 **having said**) what I said.

E

上述的一些动词 (尤其是 **admit/deny/suggest**) 之后，可以跟 **that** 从句：

- They **denied that** they had stolen the money. (或 They **denied stealing** ...)
- Chris **suggested that** we went to the cinema. (或 Sam **suggested going** ...)

suggest → Unit 34 **being done** (被动语态) → Unit 44B 动词 + to ... (动词不定式) → Unit 54
动词 + to ... 与 -ing 形式比较 → Units 55C，56–58 **remember / regret / go on** → Unit 56B
go on / carry on / keep on → Unit 141A

Exercises

53.1 根据下列情况，用动词的 **-ing** 形式完成句子。

1

She suggested going to the zoo.

2

He didn't fancy ....

3

She admitted ....

4

She suggested ....

5

He denied ....

6

They didn't mind ....

53.2 用下列动词的适当形式完成句子。

~~answer~~	apply	be	forget	listen	live
lose	make	pay	read	try	use

1 He tried to avoid answering my question.
2 Could you please stop .... so much noise?
3 I enjoy .... to music.
4 I considered .... for the job, but in the end I decided against it.
5 Have you finished .... the newspaper yet?
6 We need to change our routine. We can't go on .... like this.
7 I don't mind you .... my phone, but please ask me first.
8 My memory is getting worse. I keep .... things.
9 I've put off .... this bill so many times. I really must do it today.
10 What a stupid thing to do! Can you imagine anybody .... so stupid?
11 I've given up .... to lose weight – it's impossible.
12 If you gamble, you risk .... your money.

53.3 用动词的 **-ing** 形式改写下列句子，保持意思不变。

1 I can do what I want and you can't stop me.
You can't stop me doing what I want.
2 It's not a good idea to travel during the rush hour.
It's better to avoid .... during the rush hour.
3 Shall we paint the kitchen next weekend instead of this weekend?
Shall we postpone .... until next weekend?
4 Could you turn the music down, please?
Would you mind .... , please?
5 Please don't interrupt all the time.
Would you mind .... all the time?

53.4 根据你自己的想法，用动词的 **-ing** 形式完成下列句子。

1 She's a very interesting person. I always enjoy talking to her.
2 I'm not feeling very well. I don't fancy ....
3 I'm afraid there aren't any chairs. I hope you don't mind ....
4 It was a beautiful day, so I suggested ....
5 It was very funny. I couldn't stop ....
6 My car isn't very reliable. It keeps ....

动词 + to ... (动词不定式) (decide to ... / forget to ... 等)

A

offer	**decide**	**hope**	**deserve**	**promise**
agree	**plan**	**manage**	**afford**	**threaten**
refuse	**arrange**	**fail**	**forget**	**learn**

上述动词后面可以跟带 **to** 的动词不定式：

- It was late, so we **decided to take** a taxi home.
- Simon was in a difficult situation, so I **agreed to help** him.
- How old were you when you **learnt to drive**? (或 learnt **how** to drive)
- I waved to Karen, but **failed to attract** her attention.

注意，否定式为 **not to** ...：

- We **decided not to go** out because of the weather.
- I **promised not to be** late.

有些动词后面不能跟不定式，如 **enjoy/think/suggest**：

- I **enjoy reading**. (而不用 enjoy to read)
- Andy **suggested meeting** for coffee. (而不用 suggested to meet)
- Are you **thinking of buying** a car? (而不用 thinking to buy)

关于动词 + **-ing** 形式，参见Unit 53。关于动词 + 介词 + **-ing** 形式，参见Unit 62。

B

dare 之后的不定式可以带 **to**，也可以不带**to**：

- I wouldn't **dare to tell** him. 或 I wouldn't **dare tell** him.

dare not (或 **daren't**) 之后必须用不带 **to** 的不定式：

- I **daren't tell** him what happened. (而不用 I daren't to tell him)

C

下列动词之后跟带 **to** 的不定式：

seem **appear** **tend** **pretend** **claim**

例如：

- They **seem to have** plenty of money.
- I like Dan, but I think he **tends to talk** too much.
- Ann **pretended not to see** me when she passed me in the street.

不定式有进行式 (**to be** doing) 和完成式 (**to have** done)：

- I **pretended to be reading** the paper. (= I pretended that I **was reading**)
- You **seem to have lost** weight. (= it seems that you **have lost** weight)
- Joe **seems to be enjoying** his new job. (= it seems that he **is enjoying** it)

D

下列动词后可以用疑问词 (**what/whether/how** 等) + **to** ...：

ask **decide** **know** **remember** **forget** **explain** **learn** **understand** **wonder**

We **asked**	**how**	**to get**	to the station.
Have you **decided**	**where**	**to go**	for your holidays?
I don't **know**	**whether**	**to apply**	for the job or not.
Do you **understand**	**what**	**to do**?	

此外

show/tell/ask/advise/teach + 宾语 + **what/how/where** + **to** ...：

- Can somebody **show me how to use** this camera?
- Ask Jack. He'll **tell you what to do**.

动词 + -ing 形式 ➜ Unit 53　　动词 (want 等) + 宾语 + to ... ➜ Unit 55
动词 + to ... 与 -ing 形式比较 ➜ Units 55C，56–58

Exercises

54.1 依据下列情况完成句子。

1 

They decided to get married .

2 

She agreed ....

3 

He offered ....

4 

They arranged ....

5 

She refused ....

6 

She promised ....

54.2 用动词的适当形式完成下列句子。

1 Don't forget to lock the door when you go out.
2 There was a lot of traffic, but we managed .... to the airport in time.
3 We couldn't afford .... in London. It's too expensive.
4 We've got new computer software in our office. I haven't learnt .... it yet.
5 Mark doesn't know what happened. I decided not .... him.
6 We were all afraid to speak. Nobody dared .... anything.

54.3 用动词的 **-ing** 形式或不定式填空。(关于动词 **-ing** 形式的用法，参见 Unit 53。)

1 When I'm tired, I enjoy watching television. It's relaxing. (watch)
2 I've decided .... for another job. I need a change. (look)
3 Let's get a taxi. I don't fancy .... home. (walk)
4 I'm not in a hurry. I don't mind .... (wait)
5 Tina ran in a marathon last week, but she failed .... (finish)
6 I wish that dog would stop .... It's driving me crazy. (bark)
7 Our neighbour threatened .... the police if we didn't stop the noise. (call)
8 We were hungry, so I suggested .... dinner early. (have)
9 Hurry up! I don't want to risk .... the train. (miss)
10 They didn't know I was listening to them. I pretended .... asleep. (be)

54.4 用括号中的动词造句。

1 You've lost weight. (seem) You seem to have lost weight.
2 Tom is worried about something. (appear) Tom appears ....
3 You know a lot of people. (seem) You ....
4 My English is getting better. (seem) ....
5 That car has broken down. (appear) ....
6 David forgets things. (tend) ....
7 They have solved the problem. (claim) ....

54.5 用 **what/how/where/whether** + 不定式结构完成下列句子。

do ~~**get**~~ **go** **put** **ride** **use**

1 Do you know how to get to John's house?
2 Would you know .... if there was a fire in the building?
3 You'll never forget .... a bicycle once you've learnt.
4 I've been invited to the party, but I haven't decided .... or not.
5 My room is very untidy. I've got so many things and I don't know .... them.
6 I have some clothes to wash. Can you show me .... the washing machine?

→ 补充练习 26–28 (第317–319页)

动词 (+ 宾语) + to ... (I want you to ... 等)

A

want	**ask**	**help**	**would like**
expect	**beg**	**mean** (= intend)	**would prefer**

上述动词后面可以跟带 **to** 的不定式。结构为：

动词 + **to** ... 或 动词 + 宾语 + **to** ...

- We **expected to be** late. / We expected **Dan to be** late.
- **Would** you **like to go** now? / Would you like **me to go** now?
- He doesn't **want to know**. / He doesn't want **anybody to know**.

注意 **want** 的用法。不能说 want that ...：

- Do you **want me to come** with you? (而不用 Do you want that I come)

help 后面可以跟带 **to** 或不带 **to** 的不定式，可以说：

- Can you help me **to move** this table? 或 Can you help me **move** this table?

B

tell	**remind**	**force**	**encourage**	**teach**	**enable**
order	**warn**	**invite**	**persuade**	**get** (= persuade)	

上述动词之后可以跟宾语 + **to** ... 的结构：

- Can you **remind me to call** Sam tomorrow?
- Who **taught you to drive**?
- I didn't move the piano by myself. I **got somebody to help** me.
- Joe said the switch was dangerous and **warned me not to touch** it.

下面的例句是被动语态 (**I was warned** / **we were told** 等)：

- **I was warned not to touch** the switch.

注意 **suggest** 之后不能跟宾语 + **to** ...的结构：

- Jane **suggested that I ask** your advice. (而不用 Jane suggested me to ask)

C

advise 和 **allow** 后面可以跟两种结构。请比较：

动词 + **-ing** 形式 (不加宾语)

- I wouldn't **advise staying** in that hotel.
- They don't **allow parking** in front of the building.

动词 + 宾语 + **to** ...

- I wouldn't **advise anybody to stay** in that hotel.
- They don't **allow people to park** in front of the building.

将这些例句和 **(be) allowed** (被动语态) 作比较：

- Parking **isn't allowed** in front of the building.
- You **aren't allowed to park** in front of the building.

D

make 和 **let** 与宾语+不带 **to** 的不定式连用：

- I **made him promise** that he wouldn't tell anybody what happened. (而不用 to promise)
- Hot weather **makes me feel** tired. (= causes me to feel tired)
- Her parents wouldn't **let her go** out alone. (= wouldn't allow her to go out)
- **Let me carry** your bag for you.

说 **make** somebody **do** (而不用 to do)，但在被动语态中要说 **made to** do：

- **We were made to wait** for two hours. (= They **made us wait** ...)

suggest ➜ Units 34，53 **tell/ask somebody to ...** ➜ Unit 48D **动词 + -ing 形式** ➜ Unit 53
动词 + to ... ➜ Unit 54 **动词 + to ... 与 -ing 形式比较** ➜ Units 56–58 **help** ➜ Unit 57C

Exercises

55.1 用 **Do you want me to … ?** 或 **Would you like me to … ?** 的结构和下列动词完成句子。

~~come~~	lend	repeat	show	shut	wait

1 Do you want to go alone, or do you want me to come with you?
2 Do you have enough money, or do you want ……………… ?
3 Shall I leave the window open, or would you ……………… ?
4 Do you know how to use the machine, or would ……………… ?
5 Did you hear what I said, or do ……………… ?
6 Can I go now, or do ……………… ?

55.2 根据下列情况完成句子。

1

She told him to meet her at the station.

2

They invited him ……………… .

3

He reminded her ……………… .

4

She warned ……………… .

5

He asked ……………… .

55.3 完成下列句子，使其与前面的句子意思相近。

1 My father said I could use his car. — My father allowed me to use his car.
2 I was surprised that it rained. — I didn't expect ………………
3 Don't stop him doing what he wants. — Let ………………
4 Tim looks older when he wears glasses. — Tim's glasses make ………………
5 I think you should know the truth. — I want ………………
6 At first I didn't want to apply for the job, but Sarah persuaded me. — Sarah persuaded ………………
7 My lawyer said I shouldn't say anything to the police. — My lawyer advised ………………
8 I was told that I shouldn't believe everything he says. — I was warned ………………
9 If you've got a car, you are able to get around more easily. — Having a car enables ………………

55.4 用动词的正确形式 (**-ing** 形式或不定式) 填空。

1 They don't allow people to park in front of the building. (park)
2 I've never been to Hong Kong, but I'd like ……………… there. (go)
3 I'm in a difficult position. What do you advise me ……………… ? (do)
4 The film was very sad. It made me ……………… . (cry)
5 Lisa's parents always encouraged her ……………… hard at school. (study)
6 If you want to get a cheap flight, I'd advise ……………… early. (book)
7 Sarah wouldn't let me ……………… her car. She doesn't trust me. (borrow)
8 If you enter a country with a tourist visa, you are normally not allowed ……………… there. (work)
9 'I don't think Alex likes me.' 'What makes you ……………… that?' (think)

→ 补充练习 26–28 (第317–319页)

动词 (remember/regret 等) + -ing 形式或 to ... (1)

A

主要动词之后接另一个动词时，有些跟-ing 形式，有些跟带 to 的不定式。

动词 + -ing 形式

admit	**fancy**	**postpone**
avoid	**finish**	**risk**
consider	**imagine**	**stop**
deny	**keep (on)**	**suggest**
enjoy	**mind**	

例句参见 Unit 53。

动词 + to ...

afford	**fail**	**offer**
agree	**forget**	**plan**
arrange	**hope**	**promise**
decide	**learn**	**refuse**
deserve	**manage**	**threaten**

例句参见Unit 54。

B

有些动词既可与动词 -ing 形式也可与带 to 的不定式连用，但含义有所不同：

remember

I **remember doing** something 表示“我记得做过某事”。
remember doing 是先做某事再记起来。

- I know I locked the door. I clearly **remember locking** it. (= I locked it, and now I remember this)
- He could **remember driving** along the road just before the accident, but he couldn't remember the accident itself.

I **remembered to do** something 表示“我记住要做某事，所以去做了”。
remember to do 是记住去做某事。

- I **remembered to lock** the door, but I forgot to shut the windows. (= I remembered that I had to lock it, and so I locked it)
- I must **remember to pay** the electricity bill. (= I must not forget to pay it)

regret

I **regret doing** something 表示“我为做过某事而感到后悔”：

- I now **regret saying** what I said. I shouldn't have said it.
- Do you **regret not going** to college?

I **regret to say** / **to tell** you / **to inform** you 表示“我很遗憾地说/告诉你/通知你”：

- (*from a formal letter*) We **regret to inform** you that your application has been unsuccessful.

go on

go on doing something 表示继续同一件事情：

- The president paused for a moment and then **went on talking**.
- We need to change. We can't **go on living** like this.

go on to do something 表示做或说一件新的事情：

- After discussing the economy, the president then **went on to talk** about foreign policy.

C

下列动词后面可以跟动词 -ing 形式或带 to 的不定式而无含义上的差别：

begin **start** **continue** **intend** **bother**

因此可以说：

- It **started raining**. 或 It **started to rain**.
- Andy **intends buying** a house. 或 Andy **intends to buy** ...
- Don't **bother locking** the door. 或 Don't **bother to lock** ...

但通常动词的 -ing 形式后面不再接 -ing 形式：

- It's **starting to rain**. (而不用It's starting raining)

动词 + -ing 形式 ➜ Unit 53 动词 + to ... ➜ Units 54–55 其他动词 + -ing 形式或 to ... ➜ Units 57–58

Exercises

56.1 用动词的 **-ing** 形式或不定式填空。

1 They denied ....stealing.... the money. (steal)
2 I don't enjoy .... very much. (drive)
3 I can't afford .... out tonight. I don't have enough money. (go)
4 Has it stopped .... yet? (rain)
5 We were unlucky to lose the game. We deserved .... (win)
6 Why do you keep .... me questions? Can't you leave me alone? (ask)
7 Please stop .... me questions! (ask)
8 I refuse .... any more questions. (answer)
9 The driver of one of the cars admitted .... the accident. (cause)
10 Mark needed our help, and we promised .... what we could. (do)
11 I don't mind .... alone, but it's better to be with other people. (be)
12 The wall was quite high, but I managed .... over it. (climb)
13 'Does Sarah know about the meeting?' 'No, I forgot .... her.' (tell)
14 I've enjoyed .... to you. I hope .... you again soon. (talk, see)

56.2 汤姆能记起来童年的一些事情。根据所给情况完成下列句子。

1 He was in hospital when he was a small child. He can still remember this.
....He can remember being in hospital.... when he was a small child.
2 He went to Paris with his parents when he was eight. He remembers this.
He remembers .... with his parents when he was eight.
3 He cried on his first day at school. He doesn't remember this.
He doesn't .... on his first day at school.
4 Once he fell into the river. He can remember this.
He ....
5 He said he wanted to be a doctor. He can't remember this.
.... to be a doctor.
6 Once he was bitten by a dog. He doesn't remember this.
.... a dog.

56.3 用动词的适当形式 (**-ing** 形式或不定式) 完成下列句子。

1 a Please remember ....to lock.... the door when you go out.
b A: You lent me some money a few months ago.
B: Did I? Are you sure? I don't remember .... you any money.
c A: Did you remember .... your sister?
B: Oh no, I completely forgot. I'll phone her tomorrow.
d When you see Steve, remember .... hello to him from me.
e Someone must have taken my bag. I clearly remember .... it by the window and now it has gone.
2 a I believe that what I said was right. I don't regret .... it.
b I knew they were in trouble, but I regret .... I did nothing to help them.
c It started to get cold, and he regretted not .... his coat.
3 a Ben joined the company nine years ago. He became assistant manager after two years, and a few years later he went on .... manager of the company.
b I can't go on .... here any more. I want a different job.
c When I came into the room, Lisa was reading a newspaper. She looked up and said hello, and then went on .... her newspaper.
4 a If the company continues .... money, the factory may be closed.
b Julia has been ill, but now she's beginning .... better.
c The baby started .... in the middle of the night.

→ 补充练习 26–28 (第317–319页)

Unit 57 动词 (try/need/help) + -ing 形式或 to ... (2)

A try to ... 与 try -ing 比较

try to do 表示“试图或努力做某事”：

- I was very tired. I **tried to keep** my eyes open, but I couldn't.
- Please **try to be** quiet when you come home. Everyone will be asleep.

try 也有“尝试”的意思。例如：

- These cakes are delicious. You should **try** one.
  (= you should have one to see if you like it)
- We couldn't find anywhere to stay. We **tried** every hotel in the town, but they were all full. (= we went to every hotel to see if they had a room)

当 **try** 表示“尝试”时，后面跟动词的 **-ing** 形式：

- A: The photocopier doesn't seem to be working.
  B: **Try pressing** the green button.
  (= press the green button – perhaps this will help to solve the problem)

请比较：

- I **tried to move** the table, but it was too heavy. (所以我搬不动)
- I didn't like the way the furniture was arranged, so I **tried moving** the table to the other side of the room. But it didn't look right, so I moved it back again.

B need to ... 与 need -ing 比较

I need to do something 表示“我需要做某事”：

- I **need to get** more exercise.
- He **needs to work** harder if he wants to make progress.
- I don't **need to come** to the meeting, do I?

something **needs doing** 表示“某事需要被完成”：

- My phone **needs charging**.
  (= it needs to be charged)
- Do you think this jacket **needs cleaning**?
  (= ... needs to be cleaned)
- It's a difficult problem. It **needs thinking** about very carefully. (= it needs to be thought about)

C help 与 can't help

可以说 **help to do** 或 **help do** (带 **to** 或不带 **to** 的不定式)：

- Everybody **helped to clean** up after the party. 或
  Everybody **helped clean** up ...
- Can you **help** me **to move** this table? 或
  Can you **help** me **move** ...

I can't help doing something 表示“我忍不住做某事”：

- I don't like him, but he has a lot of problems. I **can't help feeling** sorry for him.
- She tried to be serious, but she **couldn't help laughing**.
  (= she couldn't stop herself laughing)
- I'm sorry I'm so nervous. I **can't help it**.
  (= I can't help **being** nervous)

She **couldn't help laughing**.

动词 + -ing 形式 → Unit 53　动词 + to ... → Units 54–55　其他动词 + -ing 形式或 to ... → Units 56，58

Exercises

57.1 仿照示例，用 **try** 和下列短语造句。

phone his office　　**restart it**　　**~~change the batteries~~**
turn it the other way　　**take an aspirin**

1 The radio isn't working. — Have you tried changing the batteries?
2 I can't open the door. The key won't turn. — Try ……
3 The computer isn't working properly. — Have you tried ……
4 Fred isn't answering his phone. What shall I do? — You could ……
5 I've got a terrible headache. I wish it would go. — Have you ……

57.2 根据图片内容，用 **need(s)** + 下列动词的适当形式造句。

~~clean~~　　**cut**　　**empty**　　**paint**　　**tighten**

1 This jacket is dirty. It needs cleaning.
2 The room isn't very nice. It ……
3 The grass is very long. ……
4 The screws are loose. ……
5 The bin is full. ……

57.3 用动词的适当形式 (**-ing** 形式或不定式) 填空。

1 a I was very tired. I tried to keep (keep) my eyes open, but I couldn't.
  b I rang the doorbell, but there was no answer. Then I tried …… (knock) on the door, but there was still no answer.
  c We tried …… (put) the fire out but without success. We had to call the fire brigade.
  d Sue needed to borrow some money. She tried …… (ask) Gary, but he was short of money too.
  e I tried …… (reach) the shelf, but I wasn't tall enough.
  f Please leave me alone. I'm trying …… (concentrate).

2 a I need a change. I need …… (go) away for a while.
  b My grandmother isn't able to look after herself any more. She needs …… (look) after.
  c The windows are dirty. They need …… (clean).
  d Your hair is getting very long. It needs …… (cut).
  e You don't need …… (iron) that shirt. It doesn't need …… (iron).

3 a They were talking very loudly. I couldn't help …… (overhear) what they said.
  b Can you help me …… (get) the dinner ready?
  c He looks so funny. Whenever I see him, I can't help …… (smile).
  d The fine weather helped …… (make) it a really nice holiday.

动词 (like / would like 等) + -ing 形式或 to ... (3)

A

like / love / hate

这些动词后面可用动词 **-ing** 形式或带 **to** 的不定式来谈论反复发生的动作。因此可以说：

- Do you **like getting** up early? 或 Do you **like to get** up early?
- Stephanie **hates flying**. 或 Stephanie **hates to fly**.
- I **love meeting** people. 或 I **love to meet** people.
- I don't **like being** kept waiting. 或 ... **like to be** kept waiting.
- I don't **like** friends **calling** me at work. 或 ... friends **to call** me at work.

但是

(1) 当谈论已经存在(或存在过)的情况时，我们用 **-ing** 形式(而不用带 **to** 的不定式)：

- Paul lives in Berlin now. He **likes living** there. (He **likes living** in Berlin = He lives there and he likes it)
- Do you **like being** a student? (你是个学生——你喜欢当学生吗？)
- The office I worked in was horrible. I **hated working** there. (我在那里工作过，我讨厌那里)

(2) 有时 **I like to do** 与 **I like doing** 之间存在区别：

I like doing something 表示"我喜欢做某事"：

- I **like cleaning** the kitchen. (= I enjoy it)

I **like to do** something 表示"我认为做某事很好，但我不一定喜欢"：

- It's not my favourite job, but I **like to clean** the kitchen as often as possible.

注意，**enjoy** 和 **mind** 后面跟动词的 **-ing** 形式(而不用带 **to** 的不定式)：

- I **enjoy cleaning** the kitchen. (而不用 I enjoy to clean)
- I **don't mind cleaning** the kitchen. (而不用 I don't mind to clean)

B

would like / would love / would hate / would prefer

would like / **would love** 等后面通常跟带 **to** 的动词不定式：

- **I'd like** (= I **would** like) to go away for a few days.
- **Would** you **like to come** to dinner on Friday?
- I **wouldn't like to go** on holiday alone.
- **I'd love to meet** your family.
- **Would** you **prefer to have** dinner now or later?

请比较 **I like** 与 **I would like (I'd** like)：

- I **like playing** tennis. / I **like to play** tennis. (= I like it in general)
- **I'd like to play** tennis today. (= I want to play today)

注意，**would mind** 后面跟动词的 **-ing** 形式(而不用带 **to** 的不定式)：

- **Would** you **mind closing** the door, please?

C

I would like **to have done** something 表示现在后悔之前没做某事或不能做某事：

- It's a shame we didn't see Anna when we were in London. I **would like to have seen** her again.
- We**'d like to have gone** away, but we were too busy at home.

would love / would hate / would prefer 之后也可以用同样的结构：

- Poor David! I **would hate to have been** in his position.
- **I'd love to have gone** to the party, but it was impossible.

enjoy/mind ➜ Unit 53　**would like** ➜ Units 37E，55A　**prefer** ➜ Unit 59

Exercises

58.1 根据你自己的情况，用下列动词和括号内表示活动的词语造句。

like / don't like　**love**　**hate**　**enjoy**　**don't mind**

1 (fly) I don't like flying. **or** I don't like to fly.
2 (play cards) ……
3 (be alone) ……
4 (go to museums) ……
5 (cook) ……

58.2 根据括号内的词语，用动词的 **-ing** 形式或带 **to** 的不定式造句。

1 Paul lives in Berlin now. It's nice. He likes it.
(he / like / live / there) He likes living there.
2 Jane is a biology teacher. She likes her job.
(she / like / teach / biology) She ……
3 Joe always has his camera with him and takes a lot of pictures.
(he / like / take / pictures) ……
4 I used to work in a supermarket. I didn't like it much.
(I / not / like / work / there) ……
5 Rachel is studying medicine. She likes it.
(she / like / study / medicine) ……
6 Dan is famous, but he doesn't like it.
(he / not / like / be / famous) ……
7 Jennifer is a very careful person. She doesn't take many risks.
(she / not / like / take / risks) ……
8 I don't like surprises.
(I / like / know / things / in advance) ……

58.3 用动词的适当形式 (**-ing** 形式或不定式) 填空，有时两种形式均可。

1 It's good to visit other places – I enjoy travelling .
2 'Would you like …… down?' 'No, thanks. I'll stand.'
3 I'm not quite ready yet. Would you mind …… a little longer?
4 When I was a child, I hated …… to bed early.
5 When I have to catch a train, I'm always worried that I'll miss it. So I like …… to the station in plenty of time.
6 I enjoy …… busy. I don't like it when there's nothing to do.
7 I would love …… to your wedding, but I'm afraid it isn't possible.
8 I don't like …… in this part of town. I want to move somewhere else.
9 Do you have a minute? I'd like …… to you about something.
10 If there's bad news and good news, I like …… the bad news first.

58.4 用 **would … to have (done)** 结构和括号内的动词改写句子。

1 It's a shame I couldn't go to the party. (like) I would like to have gone to the party.
2 It's a shame I didn't see the programme. (like) ……
3 I'm glad I didn't lose my watch. (hate) ……
4 It's too bad I didn't meet your parents. (love) ……
5 I'm glad I wasn't alone. (not / like) ……
6 It's a shame I couldn't travel by train. (prefer) ……

→ 补充练习 26–28 (第317–319页)

Unit 59

prefer与would rather 比较

A

prefer to do 与 **prefer doing** 比较

prefer to (do) 或 **prefer -ing** 形式可用来表示优先选择：

- I don't like cities. I **prefer to live** in the country. 或 I **prefer living** in the country.

请看下表中 **prefer** 后的不同结构：

	I prefer	something	**to** something else.
	I prefer	**doing** something	**to doing** something else.
但是	I prefer	**to do** something	**rather than** (**do**) something else.

- I **prefer** this coat to the coat you were wearing yesterday.
- I **prefer driving to travelling** by train.

但是
- I **prefer to drive rather than travel** by train.
- Sarah **prefers to live** in the country **rather than** (**live**) in a city.

B

would prefer (I'd prefer ...)

would prefer 可用来表示某人在特定情况（而非一般情况）下的愿望：

- '**Would** you **prefer** tea or coffee?' 'Coffee, please.'

可以说 would prefer **to do**（通常不用 doing）：

- 'Shall we go by train?' '**I'd prefer to drive**.' （而不用 I'd prefer driving）
- **I'd prefer to stay** at home tonight **rather than go** to the cinema.

C

would rather (I'd rather ...)

would rather (do) = **would prefer** (to do)。**would rather** 之后可以跟不带 **to** 的动词不定式。请比较：

- 'Shall we go by train?' { 'I'd **prefer to drive**.' / 'I'd **rather drive**.' （而不用to drive）}
- '**Would** you **rather have** tea or coffee?' 'Coffee, please.'

否定形式为 **I'd rather not** (do something)：

- I'm tired. **I'd rather not go** out this evening, if you don't mind.
- 'Do you want to go out this evening?' '**I'd rather not**.'

可以说 **would rather do** something **than do** something else：

- **I'd rather stay** at home tonight **than go** to the cinema.

D

I'd rather somebody **did** something

想要某人做某事，可以说 **I'd rather** you **did** something（而不用 I'd rather you do）。例如：

- 'Who's going to drive, you or me?' '**I'd rather** you **drove**.' (= I would prefer this)
- 'Jack says he'll repair your bike tomorrow, OK?' '**I'd rather** he **did** it today.'
- Are you going to tell Anna what happened, or **would** you **rather** I **told** her?

这时要用动词的过去式（**drove**，**did** 等），但表示的意思是现在而非过去。请比较：

- I'd rather **make** dinner now.
  I'd rather **you made** dinner now. （而不用 I'd rather you make）

I'd rather you **didn't** (do something) 表示"我希望你不要做某事"：

- **I'd rather you didn't tell** anyone what I said.
- 'Are you going to tell Anna what happened?' 'No. **I'd rather** she **didn't** know.'
- 'Shall I tell Anna what happened?' '**I'd rather you didn't**.'

would prefer ➜ Unit 58B   **prefer** (one thing) **to** (another) ➜ Unit 136D

Exercises

59.1 根据括号内的提示，用 **I prefer (something) to (something else)** 结构造句。

1 (drive / travel by train)
I prefer driving to travelling by train.
2 (basketball / football)
I prefer ……
3 (go to the cinema / watch DVDs at home)
I …… to …… at home.
4 (be very busy / have nothing to do)
I ……

用 **I prefer to (do something)** 结构改写后两句。

5 (1) I prefer to drive rather than travel by train.
6 (3) I prefer to ……
7 (4) ……

59.2 完成下列句子。

	A	B
1	Shall we walk home?	I'd rather get a taxi.
2	Do you want to eat now?	I'd prefer to wait till later.
3	Would you like to watch TV?	I'd …… to listen to some music.
4	Do you want to go to a restaurant?	I'd rather …… at home.
5	Let's leave now.	…… wait a few minutes.
6	What about a game of tennis?	I'd prefer …… for a swim.
7	I think we should decide now.	I'd …… think about it for a while.
8	Would you like to sit down?	…… to stand.
9	Do you want me to come with you?	I'd rather …… alone.

根据上述回答，用 **than** 或 **rather than** 造句。

10 I'd rather get a taxi than walk home.
11 I'd prefer …… for a swim ……
12 I'd rather …… at home ……
13 I'd prefer …… about it for a while ……
14 I'd rather …… some music ……

59.3 用 **would you rather I …** 的结构完成下列句子。

1 Are you going to make dinner or would you rather I made it?
2 Are you going to pay the bill or would you rather ……?
3 Are you going to do the shopping or ……?
4 Are you going to phone Tanya or ……?

59.4 根据你的判断完成下列句子。

1 'Shall I tell Anna what happened?' 'No, I'd rather she didn't know.'
2 Do you want me to go now or would you rather I …… here?
3 Do you want to go out this evening or would you rather …… at home?
4 This is a private matter. I'd rather you …… tell anybody else.
5 I don't want to make a decision without Jack and Sue. I'd rather they …… here.
6 A: Do you mind if I put some music on?
B: I'd rather you ……. I'm trying to study.

→ 补充练习27–28 (第318–319页)

Unit 60

介词 (in/for/about 等) + -ing 形式

A

介词 (**in/for/about** 等) 后面的动词要用 **-ing** 形式。例如：

	介词	动词 (-ing)	
Are you interested	**in**	**working**	for us?
I'm not good	**at**	**learning**	languages.
Sue must be fed up	**with**	**studying.**	
What are the advantages	**of**	**having**	a car?
Thanks very much	**for**	**inviting**	me to your party.
How	**about**	**meeting**	for lunch tomorrow?
Why don't you go out	**instead of**	**sitting**	at home all the time?
Amy went to work	**in spite of**	**feeling**	ill.

还可以说 instead of **somebody** doing something …， fed up with **people** doing something 等：

- I'm fed up with **people** telling me what to do.

B

请注意下列介词 + -ing 形式的用法：

before + -ing 形式和 **after + -ing** 形式：

- **Before going** out, I phoned Sarah. (而不用Before to go out)
- What did you do **after finishing** school?

也可以说 **Before I went** out … 和 … **after you finished** school。

by + -ing 形式 (表明某事发生的方式)：

- The burglars got into the house **by breaking** a window and **climbing** in.
- You can improve your English **by reading** more.
- She made herself ill **by** not **eating** properly.
- Many accidents are caused **by** people **driving** too fast.

without + -ing 形式：

- We ran ten kilometres **without stopping**.
- It was a stupid thing to say. I said it **without thinking**.
- She needs to work **without** people **disturbing** her. (或… **without being** disturbed.)
- I have enough problems of my own **without having** to worry about yours.

C

to + -ing 形式 (look forward **to doing** something 等)

to 常常是动词不定式的组成部分 (**to** do / **to** see 等)：

- We decided **to travel** by train.
- Would you like **to meet** for lunch tomorrow?

但是 **to** 也可以用作介词 (像 **in/for/about/with** 等)。例如：

- We went from Paris **to Geneva**.
- I prefer tea **to coffee**.
- Are you looking forward **to the weekend**?

介词后面的动词要用 **-ing** 形式：

- I'm fed up **with travelling** by train.
- How **about going** away this weekend?

因此当 **to** 用作介词时，后面的动词要用 **-ing** 形式：

- I prefer driving **to travelling** by train. (而不用 to travel)
- Are you looking forward **to going** on holiday? (而不用 looking forward to go)

be/get used to -ing → Unit 61　**动词 + 介词 + -ing 形式** → Unit 62
while/when -ing → Unit 68B　**in spite of** → Unit 113　**介词** → Units 121–136

Exercises

60.1 完成下列句子，使它们与上面的句子意思相同。

1 Why is it useful to have a car?
What are the advantages of *having a car* ?
2 I don't intend to apply for the job.
I have no intention of ....
3 Helen has a good memory for names.
Helen is good at ....
4 You probably won't win the lottery. You have little chance.
You have little chance of ....
5 Did you get into trouble because you were late?
Did you get into trouble for .... ?
6 We didn't eat at home. We went to a restaurant instead.
Instead of ....
7 We got into the exhibition. We didn't have to queue.
We got into the exhibition without ....
8 We played very well, but we lost the game.
We lost the game despite ....

60.2 根据下列短语，用 **by + -ing** 形式完成句子。

borrow too much money	~~**break a window**~~	**drive too fast**
put some pictures on the walls	**stand on a chair**	**turn a key**

1 The burglars got into the house *by breaking a window* .
2 I was able to reach the top shelf ....
3 You start the engine of a car ....
4 Kevin got himself into financial trouble ....
5 You can put people's lives in danger ....
6 We made the room look nicer ....

60.3 用动词的适当形式填空，每空只填一个单词。

1 We ran ten kilometres without *stopping* .
2 He left the hotel without .... his bill.
3 It's a nice morning. How about .... for a walk?
4 We were able to translate the letter into English without .... a dictionary.
5 Before .... to bed, I like to have a hot drink.
6 It was a long trip. I was very tired after .... on a train for 36 hours.
7 I was annoyed because the decision was made without anybody .... me.
8 After .... the same job for ten years, I felt I needed a change.
9 We got lost because we went straight on instead of .... left.
10 I like these pictures you took. You're good at .... pictures.

60.4 根据下列情况，用 **I'm (not) looking forward to** 造句。

1 You are going on holiday next week. How do you feel?
I'm looking forward to going on holiday.
2 Kate is a good friend of yours and she is coming to visit you soon. So you will see her again soon. How do you feel? I'm ....
3 You are going to the dentist tomorrow. You don't enjoy going to the dentist. How do you feel?
I'm not ....
4 Rachel hates school, but she's leaving next summer. How does she feel?
....
5 You've arranged to play tennis tomorrow. You haven't played for a while and you like tennis a lot. How do you feel?
....

➜ 补充练习 26–28（第317–319页）

Unit 61 be/get used to something (I'm used to ...)

A

请看下列例句：

Lisa is American, but she lives in Britain. When she first drove a car in Britain, she found it very difficult because she had to drive on the left, not on the right. Driving on the left was strange and difficult for her because:

She **wasn't used to it**.
She **wasn't used to driving** on the left.

But after a lot of practice, driving on the left became less strange. So:
She **got used to driving** on the left.

Now it's no problem for Lisa:
She **is used to driving** on the left.

B

I'm used to something 表示"我习惯某事"：

- Paul lives alone. He doesn't mind this because he has lived alone for 15 years. It is not strange for him. He **is used to it**. He **is used to living** alone.
- I bought some new shoes. They felt a bit strange at first because I **wasn't used to them**.
- Our new apartment is on a very busy street. I expect we'll **get used to the noise**, but at the moment it's very disturbing.
- Helen has a new job. She has to get up much earlier now than before – at 6.30. She finds this difficult because she **isn't used to getting** up so early.
- Katherine's husband is often away from home. She doesn't mind this. She **is used to him being** away.

C

be/get used 后面不能用动词不定式 (**to do** / **to drive** 等)，可以说：

- She is used **to driving** on the left. (而不用 She is used to drive)

I am used to something 中的 **to** 是介词而不是不定式符号。
因此可以说：

- We're not used **to the noise**. / We're not used **to it**.
- Paul is used **to living** alone. (而不用 Paul is used to live)
- Lisa had to get used **to driving** on the left. (而不用 get used to drive)

D

注意，不要混淆 **I am used to doing** 与 **I used to do**，它们在结构和含义上都不同。

I **am** used **to (doing)** something 表示"我习惯 (做) 某事"：

- I **am** used **to the weather** in this country.
- I **am** used **to driving** on the left because I've lived in Britain a long time.

I used **to do** something 表示"我过去经常做某事，但现在不再做了"。此结构仅用于表示过去的情况，不用于表示现在。(参见Unit 18)
注意此结构的形式为 I **used** to do (而不用 I **am** used to do)：

- I **used to drive** to work every day, but these days I usually go by bike.
- We **used to live** just outside the town, but now we live near the centre.

used to (do) ➜ **Unit 18**　　**to + 动词 -ing 形式** ➜ **Unit 60C**

Exercises

61.1 根据下列情况，用 **(be/get) used to** 的结构完成句子。

1 Jack has to drive two hours to his work every morning. Many years ago, when he first had to do this, it was difficult for him. But now it's OK.
When Jack started working in this job, he wasn't .... driving two hours to work every morning, but after some time he .... it. Now it's no problem for him. He .... two hours every morning.

2 Julia is a nurse. A year ago she started working nights. At first she found it hard and didn't like it.
She .... nights and it took her a few months to .... it. Now, after a year, it's OK for her.
She .... nights.

61.2 根据下列情况，用 **I'm (not) used to ...** 完成对话。

1 You live alone. You don't mind this. You have always lived alone.
FRIEND: Do you get lonely sometimes?
YOU: No, I'm used to living alone.

2 You sleep on the floor. You don't mind this. You have always slept on the floor.
FRIEND: Wouldn't you prefer to sleep in a bed?
YOU: No, I ....

3 You have to work long hours in your job. This is not a problem for you. You have always worked long hours.
FRIEND: You have to work very long hours in your job, don't you?
YOU: Yes, but I don't mind that. I ....

4 You usually go to bed early. Last night you went to bed very late (for you) and as a result you are very tired this morning.
FRIEND: You look tired this morning.
YOU: Yes, ...

61.3 根据下列情况，用 **get/got used to** 的结构完成句子。

1 Some friends of yours have just moved into an apartment on a busy street. It is very noisy.
They'll have to get used to the noise.

2 The children at school got a new teacher. She was different from the teacher before her, but this wasn't a problem for the children. They soon ....

3 Sue moved from a big house to a much smaller one. She found it strange at first. She had to .... in a much smaller house.

4 Some people you know from Britain are going to live in your country. What will they have to get used to?
They'll have to ....

61.4 用动词的适当形式填空，每空只填一个单词。

1 Lisa had to get used to driving on the left.
2 Dan used to .... a lot of coffee. Now he prefers tea.
3 I feel very full after that meal. I'm not used to .... so much.
4 I wouldn't like to share an office. I'm used to .... my own office.
5 I used to .... a car, but I sold it a few months ago.
6 When we were children, we used to .... swimming very often.
7 There used to .... a school here, but it was knocked down a few years ago.
8 I'm the boss here! I'm not used to .... told what to do.
9 We used to .... in a village. We moved to London a few years ago and had to get used to .... in a big city.

→ 补充练习 26–28（第317–319页）

Unit 62 动词 + 介词 + -ing 形式 (succeed in -ing / accuse somebody of -ing 等)

A

很多动词之后可以跟介词 (in/for/about 等) + 宾语的结构。
例如：

动词 +	介词	+ 宾语
We **talked**	**about**	the problem.
You must **apologise**	**for**	what you said.

如果宾语是动词，则要用 **-ing** 形式：

动词 +	介词	+ 宾语
We **talked**	**about**	**going** to South America.
You must **apologise**	**for**	not **telling** the truth.

可以用这种结构的动词还有：

approve (of)	He doesn't **approve**	**of**	**swearing**.
decide (against)	We have **decided**	**against**	**moving** to London.
dream (of)	I wouldn't **dream**	**of**	**asking** them for money.
feel (like)	Do you **feel**	**like**	**going** out tonight?
insist (on)	They **insisted**	**on**	**paying** for the meal.
look forward (to)	I'm **looking forward**	**to**	**meeting** her.
succeed (in)	Have you **succeeded**	**in**	**finding** a job yet?
think (of/about)	I'm **thinking**	**of/about**	**buying** a house.

可以说 approve of **somebody** doing something，look forward to **somebody** doing something 等：
- I don't approve **of people killing** animals for fun.
- We are all looking forward **to Andy coming** home.

B

下列动词可以跟宾语 + 介词 + **-ing** 形式的结构：

	动词	+ 宾语	+ 介词	+ **-ing** 形式 (宾语)
accuse (of)	They **accused**	us	**of**	**telling** lies.
congratulate (on)	We all **congratulated**	Lisa	**on**	**winning** the first prize.
excuse (for)	**Excuse**	me	**for**	**phoning** you so late.
prevent (from)	What **prevented**	you	**from**	**coming** to see us?
stop (from)	The rain didn't **stop**	us	**from**	**enjoying** our holiday.
suspect (of)	Nobody **suspected**	the general	**of**	**being** a spy.
thank (for)	I forgot to **thank**	them	**for**	**helping** me.

可以说 **stop** somebody **doing** 或 **stop** somebody **from doing**：
- You can't **stop** me **doing** what I want. 或 You can't **stop** me **from doing** what I want.

下列例句用的是 **not -ing** 形式：
- They accused us of **not telling** the truth.
- Excuse me for **not replying** to your email until now.

上述动词有的常用被动语态。例如：
- We **were accused of telling** lies.
- The general **was suspected of being** a spy.

注意，要说 apologise **to somebody** for …：
- I apologised **to them** for keeping them waiting. (而不用 I apologised them)

decide to … ➜ Unit 54A 介词 + **-ing** 形式 ➜ Unit 60 动词 + 介词 ➜ Units 132–136

Exercises

62.1 完成下列句子，每空只填一个单词。

1 Our neighbours apologised for ...making... so much noise.
2 I feel lazy. I don't feel like .... any work.
3 I wanted to go out alone, but Joe insisted on .... with me.
4 Where are you thinking of .... your holiday this year?
5 We have decided against .... a car because we can't really afford it.
6 It's good Dan and Amy are coming to stay with us. I'm looking forward to .... them again.
7 Some parents don't approve of their children .... a lot of TV.
8 It took us a long time, but we finally succeeded in .... the problem.
9 I've always dreamed of .... a small house by the sea.

62.2 用介词 + 下列动词的适当形式完成句子。

be	**cause**	**do**	**eat**	**escape**	~~**go**~~
interrupt	**invite**	**tell**	**use**	**walk**	**wear**

1 Do you feel ...like going... out this evening?
2 The driver of the other car accused me .... the accident.
3 There's a fence around the lawn to stop people .... on the grass.
4 Excuse me .... you, but may I ask you something?
5 The man who has been arrested is suspected .... a false passport.
6 I'm fed up with my job. I'm thinking .... something else.
7 The guards weren't able to prevent the prisoner ....
8 I didn't want to hear the story, but Dan insisted .... me.
9 I'm getting hungry. I'm really looking forward .... something.
10 I think you should apologise to Sue .... so rude to her.
11 I'm sorry I can't come to your party, but thank you very much .... me.
12 The police stopped the car because they suspected the driver .... not .... a seat belt.

62.3 根据下列情况完成句子。

1

Kevin thanked ...me for helping him... .

2

Tom insisted .... Ann ....

3

Dan congratulated me ....

4
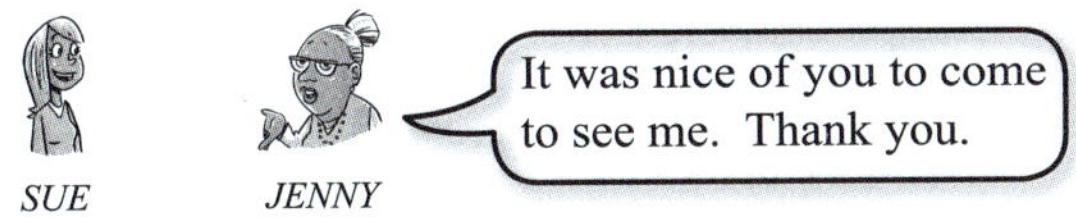

Jenny thanked ....

5

Kate apologised ....

6

Jane accused ....

➔ 补充练习 27–28 (第318–319页)

Unit 63

含有 -ing 形式的表达

A 下列表达后面跟动词时要用 **-ing** 形式：

It's no use / It's no good ...

- There's nothing you can do about the situation, so **it's no use worrying** about it.
- **It's no good trying** to persuade me. You won't succeed.

There's no point in ...

- **There's no point in having** a car if you never use it.
- **There was no point in waiting** any longer, so we left.

也可以说 **the** point **of doing** something：

- **What's the point of having** a car if you never use it?

B

It's (not) **worth ...**

- I live only a short walk from here, so **it's not worth taking** a taxi.
- Our flight was very early in the morning, so **it wasn't worth going** to bed.

可以说 a film is **worth seeing**，a book is **worth reading** 等：

- What was the film like? Was it **worth seeing**?
- Thieves broke into the house, but didn't take anything. There was nothing **worth stealing**.

C **have trouble -ing**，**have difficulty -ing** 等：

have **trouble / difficulty / a problem doing** something：

- I had no **trouble finding** a place to stay. （而不用 trouble to find）
- Did you have any **difficulty getting** a visa?
- People sometimes have **problems reading** my writing.

D **spend time / waste time / be busy**

spend/waste (time) **doing** something：

- He **spent** hours **trying** to repair the clock.
- I **waste** a lot of time **doing** nothing.

(be) **busy doing** something：

- She said she couldn't see me. She was too **busy doing** other things.

E **go swimming / go fishing** 等

常用**go + -ing** 形式来表示一些活动（尤其是体育运动）：

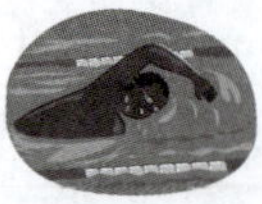

go sailing	**go swimming**	**go fishing**	**go skiing**
go camping	**go surfing**	**go scuba diving**	**go jogging**
go riding	**go hiking**	**go sightseeing**	**go shopping**

- How often do you **go swimming**?
- I'd like to **go skiing**.
- When was the last time you **went shopping**?
- I've never **been sailing**. （有关 **gone** 和 **been** 的用法，参见Unit 7C。）

Exercises

63.1 以 **There's no point ...** 开头改写下列句子。

1 Why have a car if you never use it?
There's no point in having a car if you never use it.
2 Why work if you don't need money?
....
3 Don't try to study if you feel tired.
....
4 Why hurry if you've got plenty of time?
....

63.2 根据下列情况完成句子。

1	Shall we get a taxi home?	No, it isn't far. It's not worth getting a taxi .
2	If you need help, why don't you ask David?	It's no use .... He won't be able to do anything.
3	I don't really want to go out tonight.	Well, stay at home! There's no point .... if you don't want to.
4	Shall I phone Lisa now?	No, it's no good .... now. She won't be at home.
5	Are you going to complain about what happened?	No, it's not worth .... Nobody will do anything about it.
6	Do you want to keep these old clothes?	No, let's throw them away. They're not worth ....

63.3 改写下列句子。

1 I managed to get a visa, but it was difficult.
I had difficulty getting a visa .
2 I find it hard to remember people's names.
I have a problem ....
3 Lucy managed to get a job. It wasn't a problem.
She had no trouble ....
4 It won't be difficult to get a ticket for the game.
You won't have any problem ....
5 Do you find it difficult to understand him?
Do you have difficulty .... ?

63.4 完成下列句子，每空只填一个单词。

1 I waste a lot of time doing nothing.
2 Every morning I spend about an hour .... the newspaper.
3 'What's Karen doing?' 'She's going away tomorrow, so she's busy ....'
4 I think you waste too much time .... TV.
5 There's a beautiful view from that hill. It's worth .... to the top.
6 Just stay calm. There's no point in .... angry.

63.5 用下列短语的适当形式完成句子。

go riding ~~**go sailing**~~ **go shopping** **go skiing** **go swimming**

1 Ben lives by the sea and he's got a boat, so he often goes sailing .
2 It was a very hot day, so we .... in the lake.
3 There's plenty of snow in the mountains, so we'll be able to ....
4 Helen has got two horses. She .... regularly.
5 'Where's Dan?' 'He's .... There were a few things he needed to buy.'

→ 补充练习 27–28 (第318–319页)

Unit 64

to …, for … 与 so that … 比较（表目的）

A

请看下列例句：

- I phoned the restaurant **to reserve** a table.
- What do you need **to make** bread?
- We shouted **to warn** everybody of the danger.
- This letter is **to confirm** the decisions we made at our meeting last week.
- The president has a team of bodyguards **to protect** him.

这些例句中的 **to ... (to reserve ... / to make ...** 等**)** 表明某事物的目的：某人为什么做某事、拥有某物或需要某物等，或某事物为什么存在。

B

我们说 a place **to park**，something **to eat**，work **to do** 等：

- It's difficult to find **a place to park** in the centre. (= a place where you can park)
- Would you like **something to eat**? (= something that you can eat)
- Do you have **much work to do**? (= work that you must do)
- I get lonely if there's **nobody to talk to**.
- I need **something to open** this bottle **with**.

此外，**money/time/chance/opportunity/energy/courage** 等名词后面也跟 **to** (do something)：

- They gave us **money to buy** food.
- Do you have **much opportunity to practise** your English?
- I need **a few days to think** about your proposal.

C

请比较 **for** … 与 **to** …：

for + 名词	**to** + 动词
We stopped **for petrol**.	We stopped **to get** petrol.
I had to run **for the bus**.	I had to run **to catch** the bus.

可以说 **for** somebody **to do** something：

- There weren't any chairs **for us to sit on**, so we sat on the floor.

for -ing 或 **to** … 可用来谈论某事物的一般性目的或用途：

- I use this brush **for washing** the dishes. 或 … **to wash** the dishes.

但是 **for -ing** 不用于表示某人为什么做某事：

- I went into the kitchen **to wash** the dishes. (而不用 for washing)

What … **for**? 可用于询问目的或用途：

- **What** is this switch **for**?
- **What** did you do that **for**?

D

so that

有时必须用 **so that** 来表示目的 (而不用 **to** …)。

当表示目的的部分为否定含义时 (**so that** … **won't/wouldn't**)：

- I hurried **so that** I **wouldn't** be late. (= because I didn't want to be late)
- Eat something now **so that** you **won't** (或 **don't**) **get** hungry later.

与 **can** 或 **could** 连用时 (**so that** … **can/could**)：

- She's learning English **so that** she **can** study in Canada.
- We moved to London **so that** we **could** see our friends more often.

此结构中的 **that** 可省略，因此可以说：

- I hurried **so that** I wouldn't be late. 或 I hurried **so** I wouldn't be late.

Exercises

64.1 从左右两框中各选一个句子，用 to … 结构把它们组成新句。

A

1 ~~I shouted~~
2 I opened the box
3 I'm saving money
4 I need a knife
5 I'm wearing two sweaters
6 I phoned the police

B

I want to keep warm
I want to go to Canada
I wanted to report the accident
~~I wanted to warn people of the danger~~
I want to chop these onions
I wanted to see what was in it

1 I shouted to warn people of the danger.
2 I opened the box ……
3 I ……
4 ……
5 ……
6 ……

64.2 用 to + 适当的动词填空。

1 The president has a team of bodyguards to protect him.
2 I didn't have enough time …… the newspaper today.
3 I came home by taxi. I didn't have the energy …… .
4 'Would you like something …… ?' 'Yes, please. A cup of coffee.'
5 We need a bag …… these things in.
6 There will be a meeting next week …… the problem.
7 Do you need a visa …… to the United States?
8 I saw Helen at the party, but we didn't have a chance …… to each other.
9 I need some new clothes. I don't have anything nice …… .
10 They've just passed their exams. They're having a party …… .
11 I can't do all this work alone. I need somebody …… me.

64.3 用 to 或 for 填空。

1 We stopped for petrol.
2 You need a lot of experience …… this job.
3 You need a lot of experience …… do this job.
4 We'll need more time …… make a decision.
5 I went to the dentist …… a check-up.
6 I had to put on my glasses …… read the paper.
7 Do you have to wear glasses …… reading?
8 I wish we had a garden …… the children …… play in.

64.4 用 so that 改写下列句子。

1 I hurried. I didn't want to be late. I hurried so that I wouldn't be late.
2 I wore warm clothes. I didn't want to be cold.
I wore warm clothes ……
3 I gave Dan my phone number. I wanted him to be able to contact me.
I gave Dan my phone number ……
4 We whispered. We didn't want anybody else to hear our conversation.
We whispered …… nobody ……
5 Please arrive early. We want to be able to start the meeting on time.
Please arrive early ……
6 We made a list of things to do. We didn't want to forget anything.
We made a list of things to do ……
7 I slowed down. I wanted the car behind me to be able to overtake.
I slowed down ……

形容词 + to ...

A difficult to understand 等

请比较 (a) 和 (b) 两句：

- James doesn't speak very clearly. (a) **It** is difficult to understand him.
  (b) He is **difficult to understand**.

两句意思相同，但要注意后一句的说法：

- He is difficult **to understand**. (而不用 He is difficult to understand him.)

可以用于这种结构的形容词有：

easy **nice** **safe** **cheap** **exciting** **impossible**
hard **good** **dangerous** **expensive** **interesting**

- Do you think it is **safe** (for us) **to drink this water**?
  Do you think this water is **safe** (for us) **to drink**? (而不用 to drink it)
- The questions in the exam were very difficult. It was **impossible to answer them**.
  The questions in the exam were very difficult. They were **impossible to answer**.
  (而不用 to answer them)
- Nicola has lots of interesting ideas. It's **interesting to talk** to her.
  Nicola is **interesting to talk to**. (而不用 to talk to her.)

这种结构中的形容词后还可以跟名词：

- This is a **difficult question** (for me) **to answer**. (而不用 to answer it)

B nice of (you) to ...

可以用 It's **nice of** somebody **to** do something 来表明你对某人的看法：

- It was **nice of you to take** me to the airport. Thank you very much.

可以这样用的形容词有很多，例如：

kind **(in)considerate** **generous** **mean** **careless** **silly** **stupid** **unfair**

- It's **silly of Ruth to give up** her job when she needs the money.
- I think it was **unfair of him to criticise** me.

C sorry to ... / surprised to ... 等

形容词 + **to** ... 可用来表明某人对于某事的反应：

- I'm **sorry to hear** that your mother isn't well.

可以这样用的形容词还有：

glad **pleased** **relieved** **surprised** **amazed** **sad** **disappointed**

- Was Julia **surprised to see** you?
- It was a long and tiring journey. We were **glad to get** home.

D the first / the next (等) + to ...

to ... 可用于 **the first/second/third** 等以及 **the last / the next / the only** 的后面：

- If I have any more news, you will be **the first** (person) **to know**.
- **The next** train **to arrive** at platform 4 will be the 10.50 to Liverpool.
- Everybody was late except me. I was **the only** one **to arrive** on time.

E

可以说 something is **sure/certain/likely/bound to** happen：

- Carla is a very good student. She's **bound to pass** the exam. (= she is sure to pass)
- I'm **likely to get** home late tonight. (= I will probably get home late)

afraid/interested/sorry ➜ Unit 66 **it ...** ➜ Unit 84C **enough 与 too 和形容词连用比较** ➜ Unit 103

Exercises

65.1 参照 A 节的例句改写下列句子。

1 It's difficult to understand him. He *is difficult to understand.*
2 It's easy to use this machine. This machine is ....
3 It was very difficult to open the window. The window ....
4 It's impossible to translate some words. Some words ....
5 It's expensive to maintain a car. A ....
6 It's not safe to stand on that chair. That ....

65.2 仿照示例，用括号内的形容词和 **to …** 的结构完成下列句子。

1 I couldn't answer the question. (difficult) It was a *difficult question to answer.*
2 Everybody makes that mistake. (easy) It's an ....
3 I like living in this place. (nice) It's a ....
4 We enjoyed watching the game. (good) It was a ....

65.3 参照 B 节，用下列形容词造句，以 **It …** 开头。

careless **inconsiderate** ~~**kind**~~ **nice**

1 Sue has offered to help me. *It's kind of Sue to offer to help me.*
2 You make the same mistake again and again.
It ....
3 Dan and Jenny invited me to stay with them.
....
4 The neighbours make so much noise.
....

65.4 参照 C 节，用下列词语完成句子。

~~**I / sorry / hear**~~ **I / glad / hear** **pleased / meet** **we / surprised / see**

1 *I'm sorry to hear* that your mother isn't well. I hope she gets better soon.
2 I got your message. .... that you're keeping well.
3 .... Paula at the party last night. We didn't expect her to come.
4 'Tom, this is Chris.' 'Hi Chris. .... you.'

65.5 参照 D 节，用括号内的词 + **to …** 完成下列句子。

1 Nobody spoke before me. (the first) I was *the first person to speak.*
2 Everybody else arrived before Paul.
(the last) Paul was the ....
3 Emily passed the exam. All the other students failed.
(the only) Emily was ....
4 I complained to the restaurant manager about the service. Another customer had already complained.
(the second) I was ....
5 Neil Armstrong walked on the moon in 1969. Nobody had done this before him.
(the first) Neil Armstrong was ....

65.6 参照 E 节，用括号内的词及适当的动词完成下列句子。

1 Carla is a very good student. She *is bound to pass* the exam. (bound)
2 I'm not surprised you're tired. After such a long journey you .... tired. (bound)
3 Andy has a very bad memory. He .... what you tell him. (sure)
4 I don't think you need to take an umbrella. It .... (not likely)
5 The holidays begin this weekend. There .... a lot of traffic on the roads. (likely)

to ... (如 afraid **to do**) 与介词 + **-ing** 形式 (如 afraid **of -ing**) 比较

A afraid to (do) 与 afraid of (do)ing 比较

I am **afraid to do** something 表示由于某事危险或后果不好而不想做。
afraid to do 可用来谈论计划要做，但可以选择不做的事：

- This part of town is dangerous. People are **afraid to walk** here at night. (= they don't want to walk here because it is dangerous – so they don't)
- James was **afraid to tell** his parents what had happened. (= he didn't want to tell them because he knew they would be angry or worried)

I am **afraid of** something **happening** 表示不好的事情可能会发生 (如事故等)。
afraid of -ing 不用于谈论计划要做的事：

- The path was icy, so we walked very carefully. We were **afraid of falling**. (= it was possible that we would fall，而不用 we were afraid to fall)
- I don't like dogs. I'm always **afraid of being** bitten. (而不用 afraid to be bitten)

因此可以说，you are **afraid to do** something because you are **afraid of something happening** as a result：

- I was **afraid to go** near the dog because I **was afraid of being** bitten.

B interested in (do)ing 与 interested to (do) 比较

I'm **interested in doing** something 表示"我正考虑做某事或想要做某事"：

- Let me know if you're **interested in joining** the club. (而不用 to join)
- I tried to sell my car, but nobody was **interested in buying** it. (而不用 to buy)

interested to 常与 **hear/see/read/learn/know/find** 连用，表明某人的反应。
例如，I was **interested to hear** it = I heard it and it was interesting for me：

- I was **interested to hear** that Tanya left her job.
- Ask Mike for his opinion. I would be **interested to know** what he thinks. (= it would be interesting for me to know it)

类似的结构还有 **surprised to** ... / **glad to** ... 等 (参见Unit 65C)：

- I was **surprised to hear** that Tanya left her job.

C sorry to (do) 与 sorry for/about (do)ing 比较

sorry to ... 表示对某事感到遗憾 (参见Unit 65C)：

- I was **sorry to hear** that Nicky lost her job. (= I was sorry when I heard that ...)
- I've enjoyed my stay here. I'll be **sorry to leave**.

sorry to ... 还可以用于为正在做的事表达歉意：

- I'm **sorry to phone** you so late, but I need to ask you something.

sorry for 或 **sorry about** (doing something) 可用于为已经做过的事而道歉：

- I'm **sorry for** (或 **about**) **shouting** at you yesterday. (而不用 sorry to shout)

也可以说：

- I'm **sorry I shouted** at you yesterday.

D

注意下列用法：

I want to (do) / **I'd like to** (do)	但是	I'm **thinking of** (do)**ing** / I **dream of** (do)**ing**
I failed to (do)	但是	I **succeeded in** (do)**ing**
I allowed them to (do)	但是	I **prevented** them **from** (do)**ing**
		I **stopped** them **from** (do)**ing**

更多例句参见 Units 54、55 和 62。

动词 + 介词 + -ing 形式 ➔ Unit 62　形容词 + 介词 ➔ Units 130–131
sorry about/for ➔ Unit 130

Exercises

66.1 根据下列情况和括号内的词，用 **afraid to …** 或 **afraid of -ing** 结构造句。

1 The streets are unsafe at night.
(a lot of people / afraid / go / out) A lot of people are afraid to go out.
2 We walked very carefully along the icy path.
(we / afraid / fall) We were afraid of falling.
3 I don't usually carry my passport with me.
(I / afraid / lose / it) ……
4 I thought she would be angry if I told her what had happened.
(I / afraid / tell / her) ……
5 We rushed to the station.
(we / afraid / miss / our train) ……
6 In the middle of the film there was an especially horrifying scene.
(we / afraid / look) ……
7 The vase was very valuable, so I held it carefully.
(I / afraid / drop / it) ……
8 I thought the food on my plate didn't look fresh.
a (I / afraid / eat / it) ……
b (I / afraid / get / sick) ……

66.2 用下列动词的适当形式 (**in …** 或 **to …**) 填空。

~~buy~~ **get** **know** **look** **read** **start**

1 I'm trying to sell my car, but nobody is interested in buying it.
2 Julia is interested …… her own business.
3 I was interested …… your article in the newspaper last week. It was very well written.
4 Ben wants to stay single. He's not interested …… married.
5 I heard from Mark recently. You'll be interested …… that he's now working in Paris.
6 I don't enjoy sightseeing. I'm not interested …… at old buildings.

66.3 用括号内的动词和 **sorry for / about …** 或 **sorry to …** 结构完成下列句子。

1 I'm sorry to phone you so late, but I need to ask you something. (phone)
2 I was …… that you didn't get the job you applied for. (hear)
3 I'm …… all those bad things about you. I didn't mean them. (say)
4 I'm …… you, but do you have a pen I could borrow? (disturb)
5 I'm …… the book you lent me. I'll buy you another one. (lose)

66.4 用括号内的动词完成下列句子。

1 a We wanted to leave the building. (leave)
b We weren't allowed …… the building. (leave)
c We were prevented …… the building. (leave)
2 a Peter failed …… the problem. (solve)
b Chris succeeded …… the problem. (solve)
3 a I'm thinking …… away next week. (go)
b I'm hoping …… away next week. (go)
c I'd like …… away next week. (go)
d I'm looking forward …… away next week. (go)
4 a Helen wanted …… me lunch. (buy)
b Helen insisted …… me lunch. (buy)
c Helen promised …… me lunch. (buy)
d Helen wouldn't dream …… me lunch. (buy)

→ 补充练习 27 (第318页)

see somebody do 与 see somebody doing 比较

A 请看下列例句：

Tom got into his car and drove away. You saw this.
可以说：

- I saw Tom **get** into his car and **drive** away.

在这种结构中用 **get/drive/do** 等不带 **to** 的不定式(而不用 to get / to drive / to do)：

somebody **did** something + I saw this

→ I **saw** somebody **do** something

但在被动语态后面 (he **was seen** 等)，要加 **to**：

- He was seen **to** get in the car.

B 请看下列例句：

Yesterday you saw Kate. She was waiting for a bus.
可以说：

- I saw Kate **waiting** for a bus.

在这种结构中要用 **-ing** 形式 (**waiting/doing** 等)：

somebody **was doing** something + I saw this

→ I **saw** somebody **doing** something

C 请区分这两种结构在意思上的差别：

I saw him **do** something = he **did** something (一般过去时) and I saw this (我见到了动作的全过程)：

- He **fell** off the wall. I saw this. → I saw him **fall** off the wall.
- The accident **happened**. Did you see it? → Did you see the accident **happen**?

I saw him **doing** something = he **was doing** something (过去进行时) and I saw this (我只见到他正在做某事，并没有看见动作的全过程)：

- He **was walking** along the street. I saw this when I drove past in my car. } I saw him **walking** along the street.

有时这种区别并不重要，两者可以互换：

- I've never seen her **dance**. 或 I've never seen her **dancing**.

D 除了 **see** 和 **hear** 以外，还有一些动词也可以这样用：

- I didn't **hear** you **come** in. (你进来了，我没有听见)
- Lisa suddenly **felt** somebody **touch** her on the shoulder.
- Did you **notice** anyone **go** out?

- I could **hear** it **raining**. (当时正在下雨，我听得见)
- A man was **seen running** away a short time after the break-in.
- **Listen to** the birds **singing**!
- Can you **smell** something **burning**?
- We looked everywhere for Paul, and finally we **found** him **sitting** under a tree in the garden and **eating** an apple.

Exercises

67.1 根据下列情况回答问题。

1. Did anybody go out? — I don't think so. I didn't see anybody go out .
2. Has Sarah arrived yet? — Yes, I think I heard her ....
3. How do you know I took the money? — I know because I saw you ....
4. Did the doorbell ring? — I don't think so. I didn't hear ....
5. Can Tom play the piano? — I've never heard ....
6. Did I lock the door when I went out? — Yes, I saw ....
7. How did the woman fall? — I don't know. I didn't see ....

67.2 根据下列图片以及你和朋友的谈话完成句子。

1. We saw Kate waiting for a bus .
2. We saw David and Helen ....
3. We saw .... in a restaurant.
4. We heard ....
5. We could ....
6. ....

67.3 用下列动词的适当形式完成句子。

climb	~~**come**~~	**crawl**	**cry**	**explode**	**ride**
run	**say**	~~**sing**~~	**slam**	**sleep**	**tell**

1. Listen to the birds singing !
2. I didn't hear you come in.
3. We listened to the old man .... his story from beginning to end.
4. Listen! Can you hear a baby .... ?
5. I looked out of the window and saw Dan .... his bike along the road.
6. I thought I heard somebody .... 'Hi', so I looked round.
7. We watched two men .... across the garden and .... through an open window into the house.
8. Everybody heard the bomb .... It was a tremendous noise.
9. Oh! I can feel something .... up my leg! It must be an insect.
10. I heard somebody .... the door in the middle of the night. It woke me up.
11. When we got home, we found a cat .... on the kitchen table.

-ing 分句 (例如：**Feeling tired**, I went to bed early.)

A

请看下列例子：

Joe was playing football. He hurt his knee.
可以说：
- Joe hurt his knee **playing football**.

You were feeling tired. So you went to bed early.
可以说：
- **Feeling tired**, I went to bed early.

playing football 和 **feeling tired** 为 **-ing** 分句。
如果**-ing** 分句位于句首 (如第二个例句)，要用逗号与主句隔开。

B

同一主语的两个动作同时发生时，其中一个动作常可用 **-ing** 分句来表示：
- Kate is in the kitchen **making coffee**.
  (= she is in the kitchen *and* she is making coffee)
- A man ran out of the house **shouting**.
  (= he ran out of the house *and* he was shouting)
- Do something! Don't just stand there **doing nothing**!

如果一个动作发生时，另一个动作正在进行，则正在进行的动作可以用 **-ing** 分句来表示：
- Joe hurt his knee **playing football**. (= while he was playing)
- Did you cut yourself **shaving**? (= while you were shaving)

上述情况也可用 **while** 或 **when** + **-ing** 的结构表示：
- Joe hurt his knee **while playing** football.
- Be careful **when crossing** the road. (= when you are crossing)

C

如果一个动作发生在另一个动作之前，发生在先的动作用 **having (done)** 表示：
- **Having found** a hotel, we looked for somewhere to have dinner.
- **Having finished** her work, she went home.

这时也可用 **after** + **-ing** 的结构：
- **After finishing** her work, she went home.

如果一个短暂动作紧接着另一个短暂动作，发生在先的动作用 **-ing** 的一般形式 (**doing**)，而不用完成形式 (**having done**)：
- **Taking** a key out of his pocket, he opened the door.

这些结构在书面语中更常见。

D

-ing 分句还可以用来解释某事或说明原因，这时它常位于句首：
- **Feeling** tired, I went to bed early. (= because I felt tired)
- **Being** unemployed, he doesn't have much money. (= because he is unemployed)
- **Not having** a car, she finds it difficult to get around.
  (= because she doesn't have a car)

having (done) 用于解释或说明发生在先的事情：
- **Having** already **seen** the film twice, I didn't want to see it again.
  (= because I had already seen it twice)

这些结构在书面语中更常见。

-ing 与 -ed 分句比较 ➜Unit 97

Exercises

68.1 从左右两框中各选一个句子，用 **-ing** 分句将它们改写成新句。

A	B
1 ~~Kate was in the kitchen.~~	She was trying not to make a noise.
2 Amy was sitting in an armchair.	She looked at the sights and took pictures.
3 Sue opened the door carefully.	She said she would be back in an hour.
4 Sarah went out.	She was reading a book.
5 Lisa was in London for two years.	~~She was making coffee.~~
6 Anna walked around the town.	She worked in a bookshop.

1 Kate was in the kitchen making coffee.
2 Amy was sitting ....
3 Sue ....
4 ....
5 ....
6 ....

68.2 用 **-ing** 分句将下列每两个句子改写成一句。

1 Joe was playing football. He hurt his knee. Joe hurt his knee playing football.
2 I was watching TV. I fell asleep. I ....
3 A friend of mine slipped and fell. He was getting off a bus.
A friend of mine ....
4 I was walking home in the rain. I got very wet.
I ....
5 Laura was driving to work yesterday. She had an accident.
....
6 Two people were overcome by smoke. They were trying to put out the fire.
....

68.3 以 **Having ...** 开头，用括号内的词语造句。

1 (went / she / work / her / home / finished)
Having finished her work, she went home.
2 (tickets / the theatre / bought / into / our / went / we)
Having ...., ...
3 (journey / their / had / they / lunch / continued)
Having ...., ...
4 (the / coffee / shopping / I / a cup / went / done / for / of)
Having ...., ...

68.4 以 **-ing** 或 **Not -ing** 开头改写下列句子，有的需以完成时 **Having** (done something) 开头。

1 I felt tired. So I went to bed early.
Feeling tired, I went to bed early.
2 I thought they might be hungry. So I offered them something to eat.
........, I offered them something to eat.
3 Robert is a vegetarian. So he doesn't eat any kind of meat.
........, Robert doesn't eat any kind of meat.
4 I didn't know his email address. So I wasn't able to contact him.
........, I wasn't able to contact him.
5 Sarah has travelled a lot. So she knows a lot about other countries.
........, Sarah knows a lot about other countries.
6 I wasn't able to speak the local language. So I had trouble communicating.
........, I had trouble communicating.
7 We had spent nearly all our money. So we couldn't afford to stay at a hotel.
........, we couldn't afford to stay at a hotel.

Unit 68 数名词与不可数名词 (1)

名词分为可数名词与不可数名词。请比较：

可数

- I eat **a banana** every day.
- I like **bananas**.

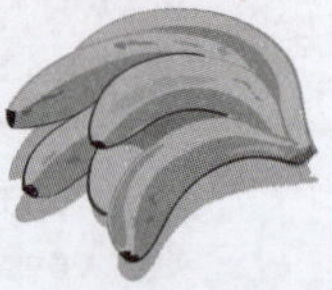

banana 是可数名词。

可数名词分单数 (**banana**) 和复数 (**bananas**) 形式。

可数名词的数量可用数词来表示，因此可以说 one banana，two bananas 等。

常见的可数名词有：

- Kate was singing **a song**.
- There's **a** nice **beach** near here.
- Do you have **a** ten-pound **note**?
- It wasn't your fault. It was **an accident**.
- There are no **batteries** in the radio.
- We don't have enough **cups**.

不可数

- I eat **rice** every day.
- I like **rice**.

rice 是不可数名词。

不可数名词只有一种表示形式 (**rice**)。

不可数名词不能用数词来修饰，不能说 one rice，two rices 等。

常见的不可数名词有：

- Kate was listening to (some) **music**.
- There's **sand** in my shoes.
- Do you have any **money**?
- It wasn't your fault. It was bad **luck**.
- There is no **electricity** in this house.
- We don't have enough **water**.

B

可数名词单数前面可以加 **a/an**：

a beach **a student** **an umbrella**

可数名词单数不能单独使用，前面必须有 **a/the/my** 等：

- I want **a banana**. (而不用 I want banana)
- There's been **an accident**. (而不用 There's been accident)

可数名词复数可以单独使用：

- I like **bananas**. (= bananas in general)
- **Accidents** can be prevented.

不可数名词前面一般不加 **a/an**。例如不能说 a sand，a music，a rice，但常说 **a … of**：

a bowl / a packet / a grain of rice

不可数名词可以单独使用 (不加 **the/my/some** 等)：

- I eat **rice** every day.
- There's **blood** on your shirt.
- Can you hear **music**?

C

可数名词的复数前面可以用 **some** 和 **any**：

- We sang **some songs**.
- Did you buy **any apples**?

可数名词的复数前面可以用 **many** 和 **few** 表示多少：

- We didn't take **many pictures**.
- I have a **few things** to do.

不可数名词前面可以用 **some** 和 **any**：

- We listened to **some music**.
- Did you buy **any** apple **juice**?

不可数名词前面则用 **much** 和 **little** 表示多少：

- We didn't do **much shopping**.
- I have a **little work** to do.

可数名词与不可数名词 (2) ➔ Unit 70 **some 与 any 比较 ➔ Unit 85**
many/much/few/little ➔ Unit 87 **children / the children ➔ Unit 75**

Exercises

69.1 在下列句子中合适的地方加上 **a/an**。如果句子是正确的，写上：对。

1 Joe goes everywhere by bike. He hasn't got car. ......He hasn't got a car......
2 Helen was listening to music when I arrived. ......对......
3 We went to very nice restaurant last weekend. ....
4 I brush my teeth with toothpaste. ....
5 I use toothbrush to brush my teeth. ....
6 Can you tell me if there's bank near here? ....
7 My brother works for insurance company in Frankfurt. ....
8 I don't like violence. ....
9 Can you smell paint? ....
10 When we were in Rome, we stayed in big hotel. ....
11 We need petrol. I hope we come to petrol station soon. ....
12 I wonder if you can help me. I have problem. ....
13 I like your suggestion. It's very interesting idea. ....
14 John has interview for job tomorrow. ....
15 I like volleyball. It's good game. ....
16 Lisa doesn't usually wear jewellery. ....
17 Jane was wearing beautiful necklace. ....

69.2 用所给单词完成下列句子，在必要的地方加上 **a/an**。

~~**accident**~~	**biscuit**	**blood**	**coat**	**decision**	**electricity**
interview	**key**	**moment**	~~**music**~~	**question**	**sugar**

1 It wasn't your fault. It was ......an accident...... .
2 Listen! Can you hear ......music...... ?
3 I couldn't get into the house because I didn't have ....
4 It's very warm today. Why are you wearing .... ?
5 Do you take .... in your coffee?
6 Are you hungry? Would you like .... with your coffee?
7 Our lives would be very difficult without ....
8 'I had .... for a job yesterday.' 'Did you? How did it go?'
9 The heart pumps .... through the body.
10 Excuse me, but can I ask you .... ?
11 I'm not ready yet. Can you wait .... , please?
12 We can't delay much longer. We have to make .... soon.

69.3 用所给单词完成下列句子。有时需用名词的复数形式，有时需加上 **a/an**。

air	**day**	**friend**	**joke**	**language**	**meat**
patience	**people**	~~**picture**~~	**queue**	**space**	**umbrella**

1 I had my camera, but I didn't take any ......pictures...... .
2 There are seven .... in a week.
3 A vegetarian is a person who doesn't eat ....
4 Outside the cinema there was .... of people waiting to see the film.
5 I'm not very good at telling ....
6 Last night I went out with some .... of mine.
7 There were very few .... in town today. The streets were almost empty.
8 I'm going out for a walk. I need some fresh ....
9 Gary always wants things quickly. He doesn't have much ....
10 I think it's going to rain. Do you have .... I could borrow?
11 Do you speak any foreign .... ?
12 Our flat is very small. We don't have much ....

可数名词与不可数名词 (2)

A

很多名词既可以是可数名词也可以是不可数名词，但其意义不同：

可数	不可数
Did you hear **a noise** just now? (= a specific noise)	I can't work here. There's too much **noise**. (= noise in general)
I bought **a paper** to read. (= a newspaper)	I need **some paper** to write on. (= material for writing on)
There's **a hair** in my soup! (= one single hair)	You've got very long **hair**. (而不用 hairs) (= all the hair on your head)
You can stay with us. There's **a** spare **room**. (= a room in a house)	You can't sit here. There isn't **room**. (= space)
I had some interesting **experiences** while I was travelling. (= things that happened to me)	They offered me the job because I had a lot of **experience**. (而不用 experiences)
Enjoy your trip. Have **a** good **time**!	I can't wait. I don't have **time**.

coffee/tea/juice/beer 等 (饮料) 通常为不可数名词：

- I don't like **coffee** very much.

但可以说 **a coffee** (= a cup of coffee)，**two coffees** (= two cups) 等：

- **Two coffees** and **an orange juice**, please.

B

下列名词通常为不可数名词：

accommodation	**behaviour**	**damage**	**luck**	**permission**	**traffic**
advice	**bread**	**furniture**	**luggage**	**progress**	**weather**
baggage	**chaos**	**information**	**news**	**scenery**	**work**

这些名词前不加 **a/an**：

- I'm going to buy **some bread**. 或 … **a loaf of bread**. (而不用 a bread)
- Enjoy your holiday! I hope you have good **weather**. (而不用 a good weather)

这些名词通常没有复数形式 (不说 breads，furnitures 等)：

- Where are you going to put all your **furniture**? (而不用 furnitures)
- Let me know if you need more **information.** (而不用 informations)

news 是不可数名词，而非名词的复数形式：

- The **news was** very depressing. (而不用 The news were)

travel (名词) 指笼统意义上的"旅行"，不能说 a travel，可以用 **a trip** 或 **a journey** 来表示"一次旅行"：

- They spend a lot of money on **travel**.
- We had a very good **trip/journey**. (而不用 a good travel)

请比较下列可数与不可数名词：

可数	不可数
I'm looking for **a job**.	I'm looking for **work**. (而不用 a work)
What **a** beautiful **view**!	What beautiful **scenery**!
It's **a** nice **day** today.	It's nice **weather** today.
We had a lot of **bags** and **cases**.	We had a lot of **baggage/luggage**.
These chairs are mine.	**This furniture** is mine.
That's **a** good **suggestion**.	That's good **advice**.

可数名词与不可数名词 (1) ➜ Unit 69　美国英语 ➜ 附录 7

Exercises

70.1 判断下列句子中画线部分的词哪一个是正确的。

1 'Did you hear ~~noise~~ / a noise just now?' 'No, I didn't hear anything.' (a noise *is correct*)
2 a If you want to know the news, you can read paper / a paper.
  b I want to print some documents, but the printer is out of paper / papers.
3 a Light / A light comes from the sun.
  b I thought there was somebody in the house because there was light / a light on inside.
4 a I was in a hurry this morning. I didn't have time / a time for breakfast.
  b 'Did you have a good holiday?' 'Yes, we had wonderful time / a wonderful time.'
5 This is nice room / a nice room. Did you decorate it yourself?
6 Sue was very helpful. She gave us some very useful advice / advices.
7 Did you have nice weather / a nice weather when you were away?
8 We were very unfortunate. We had bad luck / a bad luck.
9 Is it difficult to find a work / job at the moment?
10 Our travel / journey from Paris to Moscow by train was very tiring.
11 When the fire alarm rang, there was total chaos / a total chaos.
12 I had to buy a bread / some bread because I wanted to make some sandwiches.
13 Bad news don't / doesn't make people happy.
14 Your hair is / Your hairs are too long. You should have it / them cut.
15 The damage / The damages caused by the storm will cost a lot to repair.

70.2 用所给名词填空，有时需用复数形式。

advice	**chair**	**experience**	**experience**	**furniture**	**hair**
information	**job**	~~**luggage**~~	**permission**	**progress**	**work**

1 I didn't have much luggage – just two small bags.
2 They'll tell you all you want to know. They'll give you plenty of ....
3 There is room for everybody to sit down. There are plenty of ....
4 We have no ...., not even a bed or a table.
5 'What does Alan look like?' 'He's got a long beard and very short ....'
6 Carla's English is better than it was. She's made ....
7 Mike is unemployed. He can't get a ....
8 Mike is unemployed. He can't get ....
9 If you want to leave early, you have to ask for ....
10 I didn't know what to do. So I asked Chris for ....
11 I don't think Dan should get the job. He doesn't have enough ....
12 Nicola has done many interesting things. She could write a book about her ....

70.3 根据所给情况，用B节中的词 (**luggage**，**weather** 等) 完成下列句子。

1 Your friends have just arrived at the station. You can't see any cases or bags.
  You ask them: Do you have any luggage?
2 You go into the tourist office. You want to know about places to see in the town.
  You say: I'd like ....
3 You are a student. You want your teacher to advise you about which courses to do.
  You say: Can you give me ....?
4 You want to watch the news on TV, but you don't know when it is on.
  You ask your friend: What time ....?
5 You are at the top of a mountain. You can see a very long way. It's beautiful.
  You say: It ...., isn't it?
6 You look out of the window. The weather is horrible – cold, wet and windy.
  You say: What ....!

Unit 71

可数名词的单复数

A

可数名词有单复数之分：

a **dog**	a **child**	the **evening**	this **party**	an **umbrella**
dogs	some **children**	the **evenings**	these **parties**	two **umbrellas**

单数可数名词前面要加 **a/an**：

- Bye! Have **a** nice **evening**.
- Do you need **an umbrella**?

单数可数名词不能单独使用，必须与 **a/the/my** 等连用：

- She never wears **a** hat. (而不用 She never wears hat)
- Be careful of **the** dog. (而不用 Be careful of dog)
- What **a** beautiful day!
- I've got **a** headache.

B

a/an 可用来表示某物或某人属于哪一类别：

- That's **a nice table**.

复数名词可以单独使用，而不必与 some 连用：

- Those are **nice chairs**. (而不用 some nice chairs)

请比较下列可数名词的单复数：

- A dog is **an animal**.
- I'm **an optimist**.
- Tom's father is **a doctor**.
- Are you **a good driver**?
- Jane is **a really nice person**.
- What **a lovely dress**!

- Dogs are **animals**.
- We're **optimists**.
- Most of my friends are **students**.
- Are they **good students**?
- Jane's parents are **really nice people**.
- What **awful shoes**!

也可以说 somebody has **a long nose** / **a nice face** / **blue eyes** / **small hands** 等：

- Jack has **a** long **nose**.
  (而不用 the long nose)

- Jack has **blue eyes**.
  (而不用 the blue eyes)

注意，在表示职业的名词前面要加 **a/an**：

- Sandra is **a nurse**. (而不用 Sandra is nurse)
- Would you like to be **an English teacher**?

C

some 可以和复数可数名词连用，有两种用法：

(1) **some** = a number of / a few of / a pair of：

- I've seen **some** good **movies** recently. (而不用 I've seen good movies)
- **Some friends** of mine are coming to stay at the weekend.
- I need **some** new **sunglasses**. (= a new pair of sunglasses)

表示全体的含义时不能用 **some** (参见 Unit 75)：

- I love **bananas**. (而不用 some bananas)
- My aunt is a writer. She writes **books**. (而不用 some books)

(2) **some** = some but not all：

- **Some children** learn very quickly. (但不是所有的孩子)
- Tomorrow there will be rain in **some places**, but most of the country will be dry.

可数名词与不可数名词 ➜ Units 69–70　　a/an 与 the 比较 ➜ Unit 72　　some 与 any 比较 ➜ Unit 85

Exercises

71.1 指出下列事物属于哪一类。

1 an ant? It's an insect.
2 ants and bees? They're insects.
3 a cauliflower? ....
4 chess? ....
5 a pigeon, an eagle and a crow? ....
6 a skyscraper? ....
7 Earth, Mars, Venus and Jupiter? ....
8 a tulip? ....
9 the Nile, the Rhine and the Mekong? ....
10 a violin, a trumpet and a flute? ....

指出下列人物属于哪一类。

11 Beethoven? He was a composer.
12 Shakespeare? ....
13 Albert Einstein? ....
14 Washington, Lincoln and Kennedy? ....
15 Marilyn Monroe? ....
16 Michael Jackson and John Lennon? ....
17 Van Gogh, Renoir and Picasso? ....

71.2 根据所给提示，用下列表示职业的名词造句。

chef	**interpreter**	**journalist**	~~**nurse**~~
plumber	**surgeon**	**tour guide**	**waiter**

1 Sarah looks after patients in hospital. She's a nurse.
2 Gary works in a restaurant. He brings the food to the tables. He ....
3 Jane writes articles for a newspaper. ....
4 Kevin works in a hospital. He operates on people. ....
5 Jonathan cooks in a restaurant. ....
6 Dave installs and repairs water pipes. ....
7 Martina takes visitors round her city and tells them about it. She ....
8 Lisa translates what people are saying from one language into another so that they can understand each other. ....

71.3 在必要的地方填上 **a/an** 或 **some**，在不需要的地方画"–"。

1 I've seen some good films recently.
2 What's wrong with you? Have you got a headache?
3 I know a lot of people. Most of them are – students.
4 When I was .... child, I used to be very shy.
5 Would you like to be .... actor?
6 Questions, questions, questions! You're always asking .... questions!
7 What .... beautiful garden!
8 .... birds, for example the penguin, cannot fly.
9 Do you like staying in .... hotels?
10 I've been walking for three hours. I've got .... sore feet.
11 I don't feel very well this morning. I've got .... sore throat.
12 Maria speaks .... English, but not very much.
13 It's a shame we don't have .... camera. I'd like to take .... picture of that house.
14 Those are .... nice shoes. Where did you get them?
15 I'm going shopping. I want to buy .... new shoes.
16 You need .... visa to visit .... countries, but not all of them.
17 Jane is .... teacher. Her parents were .... teachers too.
18 I don't believe him. He's .... liar. He's always telling .... lies.

a/an 与 the 比较

A

请看下列例句：

乔在这里说 **a** sandwich 和 **an** apple，是因为这是他第一次谈论这些东西。

乔现在说 **the** sandwich 和 **the** apple，是因为卡伦已经知道他所指的具体对象——他午饭时吃的那个三明治和苹果。

请比较下列例句中的 **a** 和 **the**：

- **A man** and **a woman** were sitting opposite me. **The man** was American, but I think **the woman** was British.
- When we were on holiday, we stayed at **a hotel**. Sometimes we ate at **the hotel** and sometimes we went to **a restaurant**.

B

the 用来表示某个特定的东西。试比较 **a/an** 和 **the**：

- Tim sat down on **a chair**. (可能是房间里许多椅子中的一把)
  Tim sat down on **the chair nearest the door**. (特指的一把椅子)
- Paula is looking for **a job**. (非特指)
  Did Paula get **the job she applied for**? (特指)
- Do you have **a car**? (非特指)
  I cleaned **the car** yesterday. (= my car)

C

the 也可用来表示彼此都知其所指的东西。例如，我们在房间里谈论 **the light** / **the floor** / **the ceiling** / **the door** / **the carpet** 等：

- Can you turn off **the light**, please? (= the light in this room)
- I took a taxi to **the station**. (= the station in that town)
- (*in a shop*) I'd like to speak to **the manager**, please. (= the manager of this shop)

同样地，可以说 (go to) **the bank** / **the post office**：

- I have to go to **the bank** and then I'm going to **the post office**.
  (指说话人通常会去的银行和邮局)

还可以说 (go to) **the doctor** / **the dentist**：

- Clare isn't very well. She's gone to **the doctor.** (= her usual doctor)
- I don't like going to **the dentist**.

请比较 **the** 和 **a**：

- I have to go to **the bank** today.
  Is there **a bank** near here?
- I don't like going to **the dentist**.
  My sister is **a dentist**.

D

可以说 once **a week** / three times **a day** / £1.50 **a kilo** 等：

- 'How often do you go to the cinema?' 'About once **a month**.'
- 'How much are those potatoes?' '£1.50 **a kilo**.'
- Helen works eight hours **a day**, six days **a week**.

a/an ➜ Unit 71   **the** ➜ Units 73–78

Exercises

72.1 用 **a/an** 或 **the** 填空。

1 This morning I bought ..a.... newspaper and .... magazine. .... newspaper is in my bag, but I can't remember where I put .... magazine.
2 I saw .... accident this morning. .... car crashed into .... tree. .... driver of .... car wasn't hurt, but .... car was badly damaged.
3 There are two cars parked outside: .... blue one and .... grey one. .... blue one belongs to my neighbours; I don't know who .... owner of .... grey one is.
4 My friends live in .... old house in .... small village. There is .... beautiful garden behind .... house. I would like to have .... garden like that.

72.2 用 **a/an** 或 **the** 填空。

1 a This house is very nice. Has it got .... garden?
  b It's a beautiful day. Let's sit in .... garden.
  c I like living in this house, but it's a shame that .... garden is so small.
2 a Can you recommend .... good restaurant?
  b We had dinner in .... very nice restaurant.
  c We had dinner in .... best restaurant in town.
3 a She has .... French name, but in fact she's English, not French.
  b What's .... name of that man we met yesterday?
  c We stayed at a very nice hotel – I can't remember .... name now.
4 a There isn't .... airport near where I live. .... nearest airport is 70 miles away.
  b Our flight was delayed. We had to wait at .... airport for three hours.
  c Excuse me, please. Can you tell me how to get to .... airport?
5 a 'Are you going away next week?' 'No, ... week after next.'
  b I'm going away for .... week in September.
  c Gary has a part-time job. He works three mornings .... week.

72.3 在必要的地方加上 **a/an** 或 **the**。

1 Would you like apple? ......Would you like an apple?......
2 How often do you go to dentist? ....
3 Could you close door, please? ....
4 I'm sorry. I didn't mean to do that. It was mistake. ....
5 Excuse me, where is bus station, please? ....
6 I have problem. Can you help me? ....
7 I'm just going to post office. I won't be long. ....
8 There were no chairs, so we sat on floor. ....
9 Have you finished with book I lent you? ....
10 My sister has just got job in bank in Zurich. ....
11 We live in small apartment in city centre. ....
12 There's supermarket at end of street I live in. ....

72.4 参照 **D** 节的结构 (**once a week / three times a day** 等)，根据你自己的情况回答下列问题。

1 How often do you go to the cinema? ......Three or four times a year.......
2 How often do you go to the dentist? ....
3 How often do you go away on holiday? ....
4 What's the usual speed limit in towns in your country? ....
5 How much sleep do you need? ....
6 How often do you go out in the evening? ....
7 How much television do you watch (on average)? ....
8 How much does it cost to rent a small car in your country? ....

→ 补充练习 29 (第319页)

the (1)

A

在表示世界上独一无二的东西的名词前面要加 **the**：

- Have you ever crossed **the equator**?
  (世界上只有一条赤道)
- What's **the longest river in Europe**?
- Our apartment is on **the tenth floor**.
- Buenos Aires is **the capital of Argentina**.
- I'm going away at **the end of this month**.

same 前面要加 **the** (**the same**)：

- Your sweater is **the same** colour as mine. (而不用 is same colour)
- 'Are these keys **the same**?' 'No, they're different.'

B

可以说：

the sun	**the moon**	**the earth**	**the world**	**the universe**
the sky	**the sea**	**the ground**	**the environment**	**the internet**

- I love to look at the stars in **the sky**. (而不用 in sky)
- **The internet** has changed the way we live.
- We need to do more to protect **the environment**. (= the natural world around us)
- **The earth** goes round **the sun**, and **the moon** goes round **the earth**.

earth 用于表示"地球"时也可不加 **the**，写成 **Earth** (像 **Mars**，**Jupiter** 等)：

- Which planet is nearest **Earth**?

注意，**space** 作"宇宙"讲时，前面不加 **the**：

- There are millions of stars **in space**. (而不用 in the space)
- I tried to park my car, but **the space** was too small.

a/an 可用于表明事物的类别 (参见 Unit 71B)。请比较下列例句中的 **the** 和 **a**：

- **The** sun is **a** star. (= one of many stars)
- **The** hotel we stayed at was **a** very nice hotel.

C

可以说 (go to) **the cinema**，**the theatre**：

- I go to **the cinema** a lot, but I haven't been to **the theatre** for ages.

但是 **the cinema / the theatre** 并不都是指某个特定的电影院或剧院。

通常说 **the radio**，但是说 **television/TV** (不带 **the**)。请比较：

- I listen to **the radio** a lot. 但是 I watch **television** a lot.
- We heard it on **the radio**. 但是 We watched it on **TV**.

the television / **the** TV 指的是"电视机"：

- Can you turn off **the television**, please?

D

breakfast/lunch/dinner 前面通常不加 **the**：

- What did you have for **breakfast**?
- We had **lunch** in a very nice restaurant.

但可以说 a **big** lunch，a **wonderful** dinner，an **early** breakfast 等：

- We had **a** very **nice lunch**. (而不用 We had very nice lunch)

E

在名词 + 基数词的结构前面不用 **the**：

- Our train leaves from **Platform 5**. (而不用 the Platform 5)
- (*In a shop*) Do you have these shoes in **size 43**? (而不用 the size 43)

同样可以说：**Room 126** (in a hotel)，**page 29** (of a book)，**question 3** (in an exam)，**Gate 10** (at an airport) 等。

a/an 与 the 比较 ➜ Unit 72 **the (2)–(4)** ➜ Units 74–76 **the 与名词连用** ➜ Units 77–78

Exercises

73.1 在必要的地方填上 **a** 或 **the**，在不需要的地方画“–”。

1 A: Our apartment is on ...the... tenth floor.
B: Is it? I hope there's ...a... lift.
2 A: Did you have .... nice holiday?
B: Yes, it was .... best holiday I've ever had.
3 A: Where's .... nearest shop?
B: There's one at .... end of this street.
4 A: It's .... lovely day, isn't it?
B: Yes, there isn't .... cloud in .... sky.
5 A: I've got a problem with my computer. It isn't connecting to .... internet.
B: That's interesting. I've got .... same problem with mine.
6 A: We spent all our money because we stayed at .... most expensive hotel in town.
B: Why didn't you stay at .... cheaper hotel?
7 A: Would you like to travel in .... space?
B: Yes, I'd love to go to .... moon.
8 A: What's Jupiter? Is it .... star?
B: No, it's .... planet. It's .... largest planet in .... solar system.

73.2 在必要的地方填上 **the**，在不需要的地方画“–”。

1 I haven't been to ...the... cinema for ages.
2 Sarah spends most of her free time watching .... TV.
3 Do you ever listen to .... radio?
4 .... television was on, but nobody was watching it.
5 Have you had .... dinner yet?
6 Lisa and I arrived at .... same time.
7 What's .... capital city of Canada?
8 What do you want for .... breakfast?
9 I lay down on .... ground and looked up at .... sky.

73.3 在必要的地方填上 **the** 或 **a** (参见 Unit 72)。

1 Sun is star. ...The sun is a star....
2 I'm fed up with doing same thing every day. ....
3 Room 25 is on second floor. ....
4 Moon goes round earth every 27 days. ....
5 It was very hot day. It was hottest day of year. ....
6 We had lunch in nice restaurant by sea. ....
7 What's on at cinema this week? ....
8 I like to eat good breakfast before I go to work. ....
9 We missed our train because we were waiting on wrong platform. ....
10 Next train to London leaves from Platform 3. ....
11 You'll find information you need at top of page 15. ....

73.4 用下列词语填空，在必要的地方加上 **the**。

breakfast **cinema** ~~**dinner**~~ **gate** **Gate 21** **question 8** **sea**

1 'Are you going out this evening?' 'Yes, after ...dinner... .'
2 There was no wind, so .... was very calm.
3 The test wasn't too difficult, but I couldn't answer ....
4 'I'm going to .... tonight.' 'Are you? What film are you going to see?'
5 I didn't have time for .... this morning because I was in a hurry.
6 Oh, ... is open. I must have forgotten to shut it.
7 (*airport announcement*) Flight AB123 to Rome is now boarding at ....

➜ 补充练习 29 (第319页)

the (2) (school / the school 等)

A 请比较 **school** 与 **the school**：

Ellie is ten years old. Every day she goes **to school**. She's **at school** now. **School** starts at 9 and finishes at 3.

可以说 a child goes **to school** 或 is **at school** (as a student)。这里 **school** 并不是指某个特定的学校，而是泛指学生在教室里学习。

Today Ellie's mother wants to speak to her daughter's teacher. So she has gone to **the school** to see her. She's at **the school** now.

埃莉的妈妈不是学生，因此不能说 at school, go to school。可以说：If she wants to see Ellie's teacher, she goes to **the school**. 这里 **school** 指埃莉的学校，某座特定的建筑。

B **prison** (或 **jail**)，**hospital**，**university**，**college** 和 **church** 的用法与 school 类似。当这些地点名词只表示抽象的意义或用途时，前面不用加 **the**。请比较：

- Ken's brother is **in prison** for robbery. (不是指某个特定的监狱，而是指"坐牢")
- Joe had an accident last week. He was taken **to hospital**. He's still **in hospital** now. (作为病人)
- When I leave school, I plan to go **to university** / go **to college**. (作为学生)
- Sally's father goes **to church** every Sunday. (做礼拜)

- Ken went to **the prison** to visit his brother. (指作为访客去探监)
- Jane has gone to **the hospital** to visit Joe. She's at **the hospital** now. (作为访客)
- I went to **the university** to meet Professor Thomas. (作为访客)
- Some workmen went to **the church** to repair the roof. (不是做礼拜)

但大多数表示地点的名词前面需要加 **the**。例如：**the station**，**the cinema** (参见 Units 72C和73)。

C 可以说 **go to bed** / **be in bed** 等 (而不用 the bed)：

- I'm going **to bed** now. Goodnight.
- Do you ever have breakfast **in bed**?

但是
- I sat down on **the bed**. (特定的一件家具)

go to work / **be at work** / **start work** / **finish work** 等 (而不用 the work)：

- Chris didn't go to **work** yesterday.
- What time do you usually finish **work**?

go home / **come home** / **arrive home** / **get home** / **be at home** 等：

- It's late. Let's go **home**.
- Will you be at **home** tomorrow afternoon?

D **go to sea** / **be at sea** (不带 **the**) 意为"航海"：

- Keith works on ships. He's **at sea** most of the time.

但是
- I'd like to live near **the sea.**
- It can be dangerous to swim in **the sea**.

the ➜ Units 72–73，75–78　　介词 (**at school** / **in hospital** 等) ➜ Units 123–125
home ➜ Unit 126C　　美国英语 ➜ 附录 7

Exercises

74.1 用介词 (**to/at/in** 等) + 下列名词完成句子。

bed	**home**	~~**hospital**~~	**hospital**	**prison**	**school**	**university**	**work**

1 Two people were injured in the accident and were taken to hospital .
2 In Britain, children from the age of five have to go ....
3 Mark didn't go out last night. He stayed ....
4 There is a lot of traffic in the morning when everybody is going ....
5 Kate's mother has just had an operation. She is still ....
6 When Sophie leaves school, she wants to study economics ....
7 Ben never gets up before 9 o'clock. It's 8.30 now, so he is still ....
8 If people commit crimes, they may be sent ....

74.2 用 **school** 或 **the school** 完成下列句子。

1 Why aren't your children at school today? Are they ill?
2 When he was younger, Tim hated ....
3 There were some parents waiting outside .... to meet their children.
4 .... usually starts at 8.30 in the morning.
5 A: How do your children get to and from .... ? By bus?
B: No, they walk. .... isn't very far.
6 What sort of job does Emily want to do when she leaves .... ?

74.3 在下列句子中必要的地方加上 **the**。

1 a 'How old is university?' 'About 200 years.' — the university
b In your country do many people go to university? — 对
c If you want to get a degree, you normally have to study at university. ....
d This is a small town, but university is the biggest in the country. ....

2 a My brother has always been healthy. He's never been in hospital. ....
b When Ann was ill, I went to hospital to visit her. When I was there, I met Lisa, who is a nurse at hospital. ....
c A woman was injured in the accident and was taken to hospital. ....

3 a John's mother is a regular churchgoer. She goes to church every Sunday. ....
b John himself doesn't go to church. ....
c John went to church to take some pictures of the building. ....

4 a Why is she in prison? What did she do? ....
b A few days ago firefighters were called to prison to put out a fire. ....
c Do you think too many people are sent to prison? ....

74.4 指出下列句子画线的部分中哪个是正确的。

1 How did you get home / ~~get to home~~ after the party? (get home *is correct*)
2 I like to read in bed / in the bed before I go to sleep.
3 Shall we meet after work / after the work tomorrow evening?
4 I love swimming in sea / in the sea.
5 It's nice to travel around, but there's no place like home / like the home!
6 Sam likes to go to bed / go to the bed early, and get up early.
7 I didn't sleep well in the hotel. Bed / The bed was uncomfortable.
8 How long did it take to cross the ocean? How long were you at sea / at the sea?
9 What time do you usually start work / the work in the morning?

→ 补充练习 29 (第319页)

the (3) (children / the children 等)

A

泛指某些事物或人时，不加 **the**：

- I'm afraid of **dogs**. (而不用 the dogs)
  (**dogs** 泛指狗这种动物，而非特指某些狗)
- **Doctors** are usually paid more than **teachers**.
- Do you know anybody who collects **stamps**?
- **Crime** is a problem in most big cities. (而不用 The crime)
- **Life** has changed a lot in the last thirty years. (而不用 The life)
- Do you like **classical music** / **Chinese food** / **fast cars**?
- My favourite sport is **football/skiing/athletics**.
- My favourite subject at school was **history/physics/English**.

可以说 **most** people / **most** books / **most** cars 等 (而不用 the most …)：

- **Most shops** accept credit cards. (而不用 The most shops)

B

特指某些事物或人时，要加 **the**。请比较：

泛指 (不带 **the**)	特指 (带 **the**)
Children learn from playing. (= children in general)	We took **the children** to the zoo. (= a specific group, perhaps the speaker's children)
I couldn't live without **music**.	The film wasn't very good, but I liked **the music**. (= the music in the film)
All **cars** have wheels.	All **the cars in this car park** belong to people who work here.
Sugar isn't very good for you.	Can you pass **the sugar**, please? (= the sugar on the table)
English people drink a lot of tea. (= English people in general)	**The English people I know** drink a lot of tea. (= only the English people I know, not English people in general)

C

泛指和特指之间的区别有时并不明显。请比较：

泛指 (不带 **the**)	特指 (带 **the**)
I like working with **people**. (= people in general)	
I like working with **people who say what they think**. (不是指所有人，但仍然是泛指的含义)	I like **the people I work with**. (= a specific group of people)
Do you like **coffee**? (= coffee in general)	
Do you like **strong black coffee**? (不是指所有咖啡，但仍然是泛指的含义)	I didn't like **the coffee we had after dinner**. (= specific coffee)

the (1)，(2) ➔ **Units 73–74**　　**the +** 形容词 (**the young / the English** 等) ➔ **Unit 76**

Exercises

75.1 根据你自己的情况，从方框中选出四个词，并用下列句型造句。

bananas	**boxing**	**cats**	**crowds**	**fast food**	**horror movies**
~~**hot weather**~~	**maths**	**opera**	**snow**	**supermarkets**	**zoos**

I like … / I don't like … **I don't mind …**
I love … / I hate … **I'm interested in … / I'm not interested in …**

1 I don't like hot weather very much.
2 ……
3 ……
4 ……
5 ……

75.2 用下列单词完成句子，在必要的地方加上 **the**。

~~**(the) basketball**~~	**(the) grass**	**(the) patience**	**(the) people**
(the) questions	**(the) meat**	~~**(the) information**~~	**(the) hotels**
(the) history	**(the) water**	**(the) spiders**	**(the) lies**

1 My favourite sport is basketball .
2 The information we were given wasn't correct.
3 Some people are afraid of …… .
4 A vegetarian is somebody who doesn't eat …… .
5 The test wasn't very difficult. I answered …… without difficulty.
6 Do you know …… who live next door?
7 …… is the study of the past.
8 It's better to tell the truth. Telling …… usually causes problems.
9 We couldn't find anywhere to stay in the town. …… were full.
10 …… in the pool didn't look very clean, so we didn't go for a swim.
11 Don't sit on …… . It's wet after the rain.
12 You need …… to teach young children.

75.3 从下列句子画线的部分中选择正确的答案。

1 I'm afraid of dogs / ~~the dogs~~. (dogs *is correct*)
2 Apples / The apples are good for you.
3 Look at apples / the apples on that tree! They're very big.
4 Women / The women live longer than men / the men.
5 I don't drink tea / the tea. I don't like it.
6 We had a very good meal. Vegetables / The vegetables were especially good.
7 Life / The life is strange sometimes. Some very strange things happen.
8 I enjoy holidays / the holidays by the sea.
9 How much money does the government spend on education / the education?
10 Who are people / the people in this picture?
11 What makes people / the people violent? What causes aggression / the aggression?
12 All books / All the books on the top shelf belong to me.
13 Don't stay in that hotel. It's very noisy and rooms / the rooms are very small.
14 A pacifist is somebody who is against war / the war.
15 First World War / The First World War lasted from 1914 until 1918.
16 I don't like films / the films that don't have happy endings.
17 Someone gave me a book about history / the history of modern art / the modern art.
18 Rob and Louise got married, but marriage / the marriage didn't last very long.
19 Most people / The most people believe that marriage / the marriage and family life / the family life are the basis of society / the society.

→ 补充练习 29 (第319页)

Unit 76

the (4) (the giraffe / the telephone / the piano 等；the + 形容词)

A

请看下列例句：

- **The giraffe** is the tallest of all animals.
- **The bicycle** is an excellent means of transport.
- When was **the telephone** invented?
- **The dollar** is the currency of the United States.

这些例句中的 **the ...** 不是指某个具体的东西。**the giraffe** 不是指某一只长颈鹿，而是特指一类动物。**the** + 单数可数名词用来指整个类属。

同样地，乐器前面也用 **the**：

- Can you play **the** guitar?
- **The** piano is my favourite instrument.

请比较 **a** 和 **the**：

- I'd like to have **a piano**. 但是 I can't play **the piano**.
- We saw **a giraffe** at the zoo. 但是 **The giraffe** is my favourite animal.

注意，**man** (泛指人类) 前面不用 **the**：

- What do you know about the origins of **man**? (而不用 the man)

B

the + 形容词

the 可以和形容词连用，代表一类人。例如：

the young	**the rich**	**the sick**	**the injured**
the old	**the poor**	**the disabled**	**the dead**
the elderly	**the homeless**	**the unemployed**	

the young 表示"年轻人"，**the rich** 表示"富人"等：

- Do you think **the rich** should pay higher taxes?
- We need to do more to help **the homeless**.

the young / the rich / the injured 等表示复数含义。例如，不能用 **a young** 或 **the injured** 来指代某一个人，而要说 **a** young **person**，**the** injured **woman** 等。

注意：要说 the **poor** (而不用 the poors)，the **young** (而不用 the youngs) 等。

C

the + 国籍

the + 以 **-ch** 或 **-sh** 结尾的表示国籍的形容词可用来表示某个国家的人 (**the French / the English / the Spanish** 等)：

- **The French** are famous for their food. (= the people of France)

the French / the English 等表示复数含义，因此不能说 **a French / an English**，而要说 **a Frenchman / an Englishwoman** 等。

也可以用 **the** + 以 **-ese** 结尾的表示国籍的词 (**the Chinese / the Sudanese / the Japanese** 等)：

- **The Chinese** invented printing.

这些词也可以用作单数 (**a** Chinese，**a** Japanese 等)。
此外：**a Swiss** (单数) / **the Swiss** (= the people of Switzerland)

下列表示国籍的词的复数是在词尾加**-s**：

an Italian → Italians　　**a Mexican → Mexicans**　　**a Turk → Turks**

这些词 (**Italians** 等) 用于泛指某些人时通常不加 **the** (参见 Unit 75)。

a/an 与 the 比较 → Unit 72　　**the (1)，(2)，(3) → Units 73–75**　　**the + 名词 → Units 77–78**

Exercises

76.1 从对应题号的方框中选择正确答案，回答下列问题。

1	2	3	4
animals tiger elephant rabbit cheetah giraffe kangaroo	*birds* eagle penguin swan owl parrot pigeon	*inventions* telephone wheel telescope laser helicopter typewriter	*currencies* dollar peso euro rupee rouble yen

1 a Which of the animals is tallest? ......the giraffe......
  b Which animal can run fastest? ....
  c Which of these animals is found in Australia? ....
2 a Which of these birds has a long neck? ....
  b Which of these birds cannot fly? ....
  c Which bird flies at night? ....
3 a Which of thcsc invcntions is oldcst? ....
  b Which one is most recent? ....
  c Which one was especially important for astronomy? ....
4 a What is the currency of India? ....
  b What is the currency of Canada? ....
  c And the currency of your country? ....

76.2 用 **the** 或 **a** 填空。

1 When was ...the... telephone invented?
2 Can you play .... musical instrument?
3 Jessica plays .... violin in an orchestra.
4 There was .... piano in the corner of the room.
5 Can you play .... piano?
6 Our society is based on .... family.
7 Martin comes from .... large family.
8 .... computer has changed the way we live.

76.3 用 **the** + 下列形容词完成句子。

injured poor rich sick unemployed ~~young~~

1 ...The young... have the future in their hands.
2 Ambulances arrived at the scene of the accident and took .... to hospital.
3 Life is all right if you have a job, but things are not so easy for ....
4 Helen has been a nurse all her life. She has spent her life caring for ....
5 In England there is an old story about a man called Robin Hood. It is said that he robbed .... and gave the money to ....

76.4 将下列国家的人的称呼填在空白处。

	one person (**a/an ...**)	*the people in general*
1 Canada	a Canadian	Canadians
2 Germany	....	....
3 France	....	....
4 Russia	....	....
5 China	....	....
6 Brazil	....	....
7 England	....	....
8 and your country	....	....

带 the 与不带 the 的名称 (1)

A

人名前不加 **the** (如 Helen，Helen Taylor 等)。同样地，地名前一般也不加 **the**。例如：

大洲	Africa (而不用 the Africa)，Europe，South America
国家等	France (而不用 the France)，Japan，Brazil，Texas
岛屿	Sicily，Bermuda，Tasmania
城镇等	Cairo，New York，Bangkok
山峰	Qomolangma，Etna，Kilimanjaro

但在某些带有 **Republic**，**Kingdom**，**States** 等词的国名前，要加 **the**：

the Czech **Republic**　　**the** United **Kingdom** (**the** UK)

the Dominican **Republic**　　**the** United **States** of America (**the** USA)

请比较：

- Have you been to **Canada** or **the United States**?

B

在 **Mr/Mrs/Captain/Doctor** 等 + 人名前，不加 **the**。因此可以说：

Mr Johnson / **Doctor** Johnson / **Captain** Johnson / **President** Johnson 等　(而不用 the ...)

Uncle Robert / **Saint** Catherine / **Princess** Maria 等　(而不用 the ...)

请比较：

- We called **the doctor**.
  We called **Doctor** Johnson.　(而不用 the Doctor Johnson)

Mount (= mountain) 和 **Lake** 前也不加 **the**：

Mount Qomolangma (而不用 the ...)　**Mount** Etna　**Lake** Superior　**Lake** Victoria

- They live near **the lake**.
  They live near **Lake Superior**.　(而不用 the Lake Superior)

C

江河海洋等地理名称前面要加 **the**：

the Atlantic (Ocean)　**the** Red Sea　**the** Amazon

the Indian Ocean　**the** Channel (between France and Britain)　**the** Nile

the Mediterranean (Sea)　**the** Suez Canal

沙漠的名称前要加 **the**：

the Sahara (Desert)　**the** Gobi Desert

D

复数的人名、地名前要加 **the**：

人	**the** Taylors (= the Taylor family)，**the** Johnsons
国家	**the** Netherlands，**the** Philippines，**the** United States
群岛	**the** Canaries / **the** Canary Islands，**the** Bahamas
山脉	**the** Rocky Mountains / **the** Rockies，**the** Andes，**the** Alps

- The highest mountain in **the Andes** is (**Mount**) **Aconcagua**.

E

可以说：

the north (of Brazil)　或　**northern** Brazil (不用 the)

the south-east (of Spain)　或　**south-eastern** Spain

请比较：

- Sweden is in **northern Europe**; Spain is in **the south**.

此外：**the** Middle East，**the** Far East

north/south 等也可以和地名连用，不加 **the**：

North America　**South Africa**

注意：地图上的地名前通常省略了 **the**。

带 the 与不带 the 的名称 (2) ➔ Unit 78

Exercises

77.1 在必要的地方填上 **the**，在不需要的地方画“–”。

1 Who is ...–... Doctor Johnson? (*the sentence is complete without* the)
2 I was ill, so I went to see .... doctor.
3 The most powerful person in .... United States is .... president.
4 .... President Kennedy was assassinated in 1963.
5 Do you know .... Wilsons? They're a very nice couple.
6 I'm looking for .... Professor Brown. Do you know where she is?

77.2 在下列句子中必要的地方加上 **the**，在正确的句子后写上：对。

1 Qomolangma was first climbed in 1953. ...对...
2 Milan is in north of Italy. ...in the north of Italy...
3 Africa is much larger than Europe. ....
4 Last year I visited Mexico and United States. ....
5 South of England is warmer than north. ....
6 Portugal is in western Europe. ....
7 France and Britain are separated by Channel. ....
8 James has travelled a lot in Middle East. ....
9 Chicago is on Lake Michigan. ....
10 Next year we're going skiing in Swiss Alps. ....
11 UK consists of Great Britain and Northern Ireland. ....
12 Seychelles are a group of islands in Indian Ocean. ....
13 The highest mountain in Africa is Kilimanjaro. ....
14 River Volga flows into Caspian Sea. ....

77.3 从方框中选出正确答案回答下列问题，在必要的地方加上 **the**，框内的地理名词不必全用。

continents	*countries*	*oceans and seas*	*mountains*	*rivers and canals*	
Africa	Canada	~~Atlantic~~	Alps	Amazon	Rhine
Asia	Denmark	Indian Ocean	Andes	Danube	Thames
Australia	Indonesia	Pacific	Himalayas	Nile	Volga
Europe	Sweden	Black Sea	Rockies	Suez Canal	
North America	Thailand	Mediterranean	Urals	Panama Canal	
South America	United States	Red Sea			

1 What do you have to cross to travel from Europe to America? ...the Atlantic...
2 Where is Argentina? ....
3 Which is the longest river in Africa? ....
4 Of which country is Stockholm the capital? ....
5 Of which country is Washington the capital? ....
6 What is the name of the mountain range in the west of North America? ....
7 What is the name of the sea between Africa and Europe? ....
8 Which is the smallest continent in the world? ....
9 What is the name of the ocean between North America and Asia? ....
10 What is the name of the ocean between Africa and Australia? ....
11 Which river flows through London? ....
12 Which river flows through Vienna, Budapest and Belgrade? ....
13 Of which country is Bangkok the capital? ....
14 What joins the Atlantic and Pacific oceans? ....
15 Which is the longest river in South America? ....

带 the 与不带 the 的名称 (2)

A

不带 the 的名称

大多数街道、道路、广场、公园等的名称前面不用 **the**：

Union **Street** (而不用 the ...) Fifth **Avenue** Hyde **Park**
Queens **Road** **Broadway** Times **Square**

重要的建筑物和机构的名称常由两个词构成 (如机场、车站、大学)：

Manchester Airport **Harvard University**

第一个词往往是人名 (Manchester) 或地名 (Harvard)，所以这些名称前面通常不加 **the**：

Victoria Station (而不用 the ...) **Canterbury Cathedral** **Edinburgh Castle**
Buckingham Palace **Cambridge University** **Sydney Harbour**

请比较：

Buckingham Palace (而不用 the ...) 但是 **the Royal Palace**
(Royal 是形容词，而 Buckingham 是地名。)

B

许多其他建筑的名称前要加 **the**，例如：

酒店	**the** Sheraton Hotel，**the** Holiday Inn
剧院/影院	**the** Palace Theatre，**the** Odeon (cinema)
博物馆/美术馆	**the** Guggenheim Museum，**the** National Gallery
其他建筑	**the** Empire State (Building)，**the** White House，**the** Eiffel Tower

这些名称中的名词经常省略：

the Sheraton (Hotel) **the Palace** (Theatre) **the Guggenheim** (Museum)

有的名称仅用 **the** + 名词来表示。例如：

the Acropolis **the Kremlin** **the Pentagon**

C

带 **of** 的名称前面通常加 **the**。例如：

the Bank **of** England **the** Museum **of** Modern Art
the Great Wall **of** China **the** Tower **of** London

注意可以说：

the University **of** Cambridge 但是 **Cambridge University** (不用 the)

D

许多商店、餐馆、旅馆、银行等是以创办人的名字而命名的，这些名称后面加 **-'s** 或 **-s**，前面不加 **the**：

McDonald's (而不用 the ...) **Barclays** (bank)
Joe's Diner (restaurant) **Macy's** (department store)

教堂常常以圣贤的名字命名 (St = Saint)：

St John's Church (而不用 the St Johns Church) **St Patrick's Cathedral**

E

大多数报纸以及许多组织机构的名称前要加 **the**：

报纸	***The*** *Washington Post*，***The*** *Financial Times*，***The*** *Sun*
组织机构	**the** European Union，**the** BBC，**the** Red Cross

公司等名称前面通常不加 **the**：

Fiat (而不用 the Fiat) **Sony** **Singapore Airlines**
Kodak **IBM** **Yale University Press**

带 the 与不带 the 的名称 (1) ➜ Unit 77

Exercises

78.1 看图回答下列问题，写出建筑的名称和它所处的街道，在必要的地方加上 **the**。

1 Is there a cinema near here? — Yes, the Odeon in Market Street .
2 Is there a supermarket near here? — Yes, ... in ....
3 Is there a hotel near here? — Yes, ... in ....
4 Is there a church near here? — Yes, ... in ....
5 Is there a museum near here? — Yes, ... in ....
6 Is there a bookshop near here? — Yes, ... in ....
7 Is there a restaurant near here? — Yes, ... in ....
8 Is there a park near here? — Yes, ... at the end of ....

78.2 从方框中选出正确的名称填入下列句子，在必要的地方加上 **the**。

Acropolis	**Broadway**	**Buckingham Palace**	**Eiffel Tower**
Kremlin	**White House**	**Gatwick Airport**	~~**Times Square**~~

1 Times Square is in New York.
2 .... is in Paris.
3 .... is in London.
4 .... is in Washington.
5 .... is in Moscow.
6 .... is in New York.
7 .... is in Athens.
8 .... is near London.

78.3 从下列句子画线的部分中选择正确的名称。

1 Have you ever been to ~~British Museum~~ / the British Museum? (the British Museum *is correct*)
2 The biggest park in New York is Central Park / the Central Park.
3 My favourite park in London is St James's Park / the St James's Park.
4 Imperial Hotel / The Imperial Hotel is in Baker Street / the Baker Street.
5 Dublin Airport / The Dublin Airport is situated about 12 kilometres from the city centre.
6 Jack is a student at Liverpool University / the Liverpool University.
7 If you're looking for a department store, I would recommend Harrison's / the Harrison's.
8 If you're looking for a hotel, I would recommend Park Plaza / the Park Plaza.
9 Statue of Liberty / The Statue of Liberty is at the entrance to New York Harbour / the New York Harbour.
10 You should go to Science Museum / the Science Museum. It's very interesting.
11 Andy works for IBM / the IBM now. He used to work for British Telecom / the British Telecom.
12 'Which cinema are you going to this evening?' 'Classic / The Classic.'
13 I'd like to go to China and see Great Wall / the Great Wall.
14 'Which newspaper do you want?' 'Times / The Times.'
15 This book is published by Cambridge University Press / the Cambridge University Press.
16 'What's that building?' 'It's College of Art / the College of Art.'

→ 补充练习 29 (第319页)

Unit 79 单数与复数

A

有时，名词以复数形式出现，表示一件物品由两部分构成：

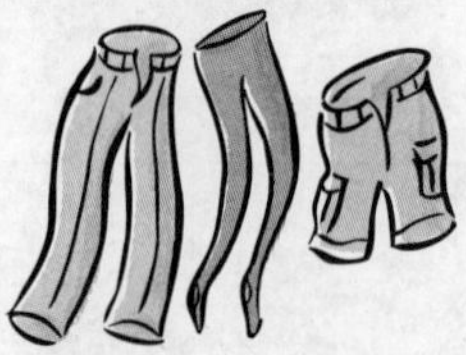	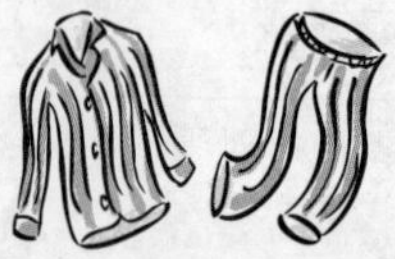			
trousers (*two legs*) 以及 jeans/tights/shorts/pants	pyjamas (*top and bottom*)	glasses	binoculars	scissors

这些名词是复数形式，后面跟复数动词：

- My trousers **are** too long. (而不用 my trousers is)

也可以用 **a pair of** + 复数名词：

- **Those are** nice **jeans**. 或 That'**s a** nice **pair of** jeans. (而不用 a nice jeans)
- I need **some** new **glasses**. 或 I need **a** new **pair of** glasses.

B

一些以-**ics** 结尾的名词并不都是复数，例如：

athletics **economics** **electronics** **gymnastics**
maths (= mathematics) **physics** **politics**

- **Gymnastics is** my favourite sport. (而不用 Gymnastics are)

news 不是复数名词 (参见 Unit 70B)：

- What time **is the news** on TV? (而不用 are the news)

以 **-s** 结尾的一些词可以是单数，也可以是复数。例如：

means	**a means** of transport	**many means** of transport
series	**a** television **series**	**two** television **series**
species	**a species** of bird	**200 species** of bird

C

一些单数名词常常和复数动词连用。例如：

audience **committee** **company** **family** **firm** **government** **staff** **team**

这些名词常用来指组成整体的若干人 (they)，而不是指这个整体 (it)，所以后面常跟复数动词：

- **The government** (= they) **have decided** to increase taxes.
- **The staff** at the company (= they) **are** not happy with **their** working conditions.

同样，运动队或公司的名称后面常常用复数动词：

- **Italy are** playing Brazil next Sunday (in a football match).
- **Shell have** increased the price of petrol.

这些名词也可以与单数动词连用 (The government **wants** … / Shell **has** … 等)。

police 后总是用复数动词：

- **The police are** investigating the crime, but **haven't** arrested anyone yet.
(而不用 The police is … hasn't)

注意：指某一个警察要用 **a police officer** / **a policeman** / **a policewoman** (而不用 a police)。

D

person 一词的复数形式不常用 persons，一般用 **people** (复数名词)：

- He's **a** nice **person**. 但是 They are nice **people**. (而不用 nice persons)
- **Many people don't** have enough to eat. (而不用 Many people doesn't)

E

一笔钱、一段时间、一段距离等所指的是一个整体数量时，后面跟单数动词：

- **Fifty thousand pounds** (= it) **was** stolen in the robbery. (而不用 were stolen)
- **Three years** (= it) **is** a long time to be without a job. (而不用 Three years are)
- **Two miles isn't** very far to walk.

美国英语 ➜ 附录 7

Exercises

79.1 用 **A** 节或 **B** 节中的词填空，有时需要加 **a** 或 **some**。

1 My eyesight isn't very good. I need glasses .
2 A species is a group of animals or plants that have the same characteristics.
3 Footballers don't wear trousers when they play. They wear ....
4 The bicycle is .... of transport.
5 The bicycle and the car are .... of transport.
6 I want to cut this piece of material. I need ....
7 A friend of mine is writing .... of articles for the local newspaper.
8 There are a lot of American TV .... shown on TV in Britain.
9 While we were out walking, we saw many different .... of bird.

79.2 左侧的词均与某种事项有关（例如体育或科研），根据给出的字母提示，写出事项的名称。

1 calculate algebra equation — mathematics
2 government election minister — p........
3 finance trade employment — e........
4 running jumping throwing — a........
5 light heat gravity — ph........
6 exercises somersault parallel bars — gy........
7 processor silicon chip gigabyte — el........

79.3 从下列句子画线的部分中选择正确的动词，其中有两句用单、复数动词均可。

1 Gymnastics <u>is / ~~are~~</u> my favourite sport. (<u>is</u> *is correct*)
2 The trousers you bought for me <u>doesn't / don't</u> fit me.
3 The police <u>want / wants</u> to interview two men about the robbery last week.
4 Physics <u>was / were</u> my best subject at school.
5 Can I borrow your scissors? Mine <u>isn't / aren't</u> sharp enough.
6 It's a nice place to visit. The people <u>is / are</u> very friendly.
7 Fortunately the news <u>wasn't / weren't</u> as bad as we expected.
8 Where <u>does / do</u> your family live?
9 I can't find my binoculars. Do you know where <u>it is / they are</u>?
10 <u>Does / Do</u> the police know how the accident happened?
11 Germany <u>is / are</u> playing Spain tomorrow night, but it's not on TV.
12 Most people <u>enjoy / enjoys</u> music.

79.4 找出下列句子中的错误并改正，在正确的句子后写上：对。

1 Three years are a long time to be without a job. — Three years is a long time
2 The government have decided to increase taxes. — 对 (has decided *is also correct*)
3 Susan was wearing a black jeans. ....
4 I don't like hot weather. Thirty degrees is too hot for me. ....
5 I like Martin and Jane. They're very nice persons. ....
6 Ten pounds aren't enough. I need more money than that. ....
7 I'm going to buy a new pyjama. ....
8 The committee haven't made a decision yet. ....
9 There was a police directing traffic in the street. ....
10 What is the police going to do? ....
11 This scissors isn't very sharp. ....
12 Four days isn't enough for a good holiday. ....

Unit 80

名词 + 名词 (a tennis ball / a headache)

A

两个名词可连在一起组成复合名词，表示一件东西/一个人/一个观点等。例如：

a **tennis ball**　　**income tax**　　the **city centre**

第一个名词起形容词的作用，表示东西/人/观点等的类别：

a **tennis ball** = a **ball** used to play **tennis**
a **bus driver** = the **driver** of a **bus**
a **road accident** = an **accident** that happens on the **road**
income tax = **tax** that you pay on your **income**
the **city centre** = the **centre** of the **city**
a **Paris hotel** = a **hotel** in **Paris**
my **life story** = the **story** of my **life**

因此可以说：

a **television** camera　　a **television** programme　　a **television** studio　　a **television** producer
(这些词都表示与电视有关的事物或人)

language **problems**　　marriage **problems**　　health **problems**　　work **problems**
(这些词都表示不同种类的问题)

请比较：

garden vegetables (= **vegetables** that are grown in a garden)
a **vegetable garden** (= a **garden** where vegetables are grown)

有时第一个词以 **-ing** 结尾，表示某种用途：

a **frying** pan (= a pan for frying)　　a **washing** machine　　a **swimming** pool

有时复合名词由两个以上的名词组成：

- I waited at the **hotel reception desk**.
- We watched the **World Swimming Championships** on television.
- If you want to play **table tennis** (= a game), you need a **table tennis table** (= a table).

B

由两个名词组成的复合名词可以写成一个词，也可以写成两个词：

a **headache**　　**toothpaste**　　a **weekend**　　a **car park**　　a **road sign**

对此没有明确规定。在不确定的情况下，最好将它写成两个词。

C

注意两者的区别：

a **sugar bowl** (可能是空的) 与 a **bowl of sugar** (= a bowl with sugar in it)
a **shopping bag** (可能是空的) 与 a **bag of shopping** (= a bag full of shopping)

D

复合名词的第一个名词起形容词的作用，通常是单数，但表示复数的含义。例如：a **book**shop 意为 a shop where you can buy **books**，an **apple** tree 意为 a tree that has **apples**。

同样地，可以说：

a **three-hour** journey　(= a journey that takes three **hours**)
a **ten-pound** note　(而不用 pounds)
a **four-week** course　(而不用 weeks)
a **six-mile** walk　(而不用 miles)
two **14-year-**old girls　(而不用 years)

请比较：

- It was **a** four-**week** course.

但是　The course lasted four **weeks**.

-'s 与 of ... 比较 ➔ Unit 81　　**a week's holiday / three weeks' holiday 等** ➔ Unit 81E

Exercises

80.1 用名词+名词的结构写出下列事物或人的名称。

1 A ticket for a concert is a concert ticket.
2 Problems concerning health are health problems.
3 An interview for a job is ....
4 Pictures taken on your holiday are your ....
5 Chocolate made with milk is ....
6 Somebody whose job is to inspect factories is ....
7 A horse that runs in races is ....
8 A race for horses is ....
9 Shoes for running are ....
10 A student studying at university is ....
11 The results of your exams are your ....
12 The carpet in the living room is ....
13 A scandal involving an oil company is ....
14 Workers at a car factory are ....
15 A scheme for the improvement of a road is ....
16 A department store in New York is ....
17 A course that lasts five days is ....
18 A question that has two parts is ....
19 A man who is thirty years old is ....

80.2 从下列单词中选出两个组成复合名词并填空。

~~accident~~	**belt**	**birthday**	**card**	**credit**	**driver**
editor	**forecast**	**newspaper**	**number**	**party**	**~~road~~**
room	**seat**	**shop**	**truck**	**weather**	**window**

1 This can be caused by bad driving. a road accident
2 You should wear this when you're in a car. a ....
3 You can use this to pay for things instead of cash. a ....
4 If you want to know if it's going to rain, this is what you need. the ....
5 This person is a top journalist. a ....
6 You might stop to look in this when you're walking along a street. a ....
7 If you're staying at a hotel, you need to remember this. your ....
8 This is a way to celebrate getting older. a ....
9 This person transports things by road. a ....

80.3 指出下列句子画线的部分中哪一个是正确的。

1 It's quite a long book. There are ~~450 page~~ / 450 pages. (450 pages *is correct*)
2 I didn't have any change. I only had a twenty-pound / twenty pounds note.
3 I looked down and there were two ten-pound / ten pounds notes on the ground.
4 At work in the morning I usually have a 15-minute / 15 minutes break for coffee.
5 There are 60-minute / 60 minutes in an hour.
6 It's only a two-hour / two hours flight from London to Madrid.
7 My office is on the tenth floor of a twelve-storey / twelve storeys building.
8 I work five-day / five days a week. Saturday and Sunday are free.
9 Five-star / Five stars hotels are the most expensive.
10 Sam's daughter is six-year-old / six years old.
11 The oldest building in the city is the 500-year-old / 500 years old castle.
12 Do you use the twelve-hour / twelve hours clock or the 24-hour / 24 hours clock?

Unit 81 -'s (your sister's name) 与 of ... (the name of the book) 比较

A

-'s 通常用来表示人或动物的所有关系：

- **Tom's** computer isn't working. （而不用 the computer of Tom）
- How old are **Chris's** children? （而不用 the children of Chris）
- What's (= What is) **your sister's** name?
- What's **Tom's sister's** name?
- Be careful. Don't step on **the cat's** tail.

注意-**'s** 后面可以不跟名词：

- This isn't my book. It's **my sister's**. (= my sister's book)

-'s 可用于单个名词的后面 (**Tom/friend/teacher** 等)，而不用于一长串词语之后。因此可以说：

your friend's name

但是 the name **of the woman sitting by the door**

可以说 **a woman's hat** (= a hat for a woman)，**a boy's name** (= a name for a boy)，**a bird's egg** (= an egg laid by a bird) 等。

B

单数名词后面用 **-'s**：

my **sister's** room (= **her** room – one sister)　　**Mr Carter's** house (= **his** house)

复数名词 (sisters，friends 等) 后面只加省字号 "'"：

my sisters' room (= **their** room – *two or more* sisters)
the Carters' house (= **their** house – Mr and Mrs Carter)

如果复数名词不以 **-s** 结尾 (如 **men/women/children/people**)，则仍加 **-'s**：

the men's changing room　　a **children's** book (= a book for children)

注意：两个及两个以上的名词后也能用 **-'s**。例如：

Jack and Karen's wedding　　**Mr and Mrs Carter's** house

C

of + 名词结构 (... **of the water** / ... **of the book** 等) 通常用来表示事物、观点等无生命物的所有关系：

the temperature **of the water** （而不用 the water's temperature）
the name **of the book**　　the owner **of the restaurant**

有时，可以用名词+名词的结构来代替 (参见Unit 80)：

the **water temperature**　　the **restaurant owner**

可以说 **the beginning/end/middle of** ... / **the top/bottom of** ... / **the front/back/side of** ...：

the beginning of the month （而不用 the month's beginning）
the top of the hill　　**the back of** the car

D

与机构有关的可以用 **-'s** 或 **of** ... 结构：

the government's decision　或　the decision **of the government**
the company's success　或　the success **of the company**

与地点相关的也可以用 **-'s**：

the city's streets　　**the world's** population　　**Italy's** prime minister

E

-'s 可以用于时间表达法 (**yesterday** / **next week** 等)：

- Do you still have **yesterday's** newspaper?
- **Next week's** meeting has been cancelled.

同样地，可以说 **today's** / **tomorrow's** / **this evening's** / **Monday's** 等。

-'s (或与复数名词连用的 **-s'**) 也可用于表示持续的时间：

- I've got **a week's** holiday starting on Monday.
- Julia has got **three weeks'** holiday.
- I live near the station – it's only about **ten minutes'** walk.

名词 + 名词 (a tennis ball) ➔ Unit 80　　a **three-hour** journey，a **ten-pound** note ➔ Unit 80D

Exercises

81.1

下列句子画线的部分中，有些表达用 -'s 或 -' 更自然，请找出并加以改正。在正确的句子后写上：对。

1 Who is the owner of this restaurant? 对
2 How old are the children of Chris? Chris's children
3 Is this the umbrella of your friend? ……
4 Write your name at the top of the page. ……
5 I've never met the daughter of Charles. ……
6 Have you met the son of Helen and Dan? ……
7 We don't know the cause of the problem. ……
8 Do we still have the newspaper of last Monday? ……
9 I don't know the words of this song. ……
10 What is the cost of a new computer? ……
11 The friends of your children are here. ……
12 The garden of our neighbours is very nice. ……
13 I work on the ground floor of the building. ……
14 The hair of David is very long. ……
15 I couldn't go to the party of Katherine. ……
16 Do you know the number of the man I need to speak to? ……
17 Have you seen the car of the parents of Mike? ……
18 What's the meaning of this expression? ……
19 Do you agree with the economic policy of the government? ……

81.2

用 -'s 或 -s' 的形式替换下列表达。

1 a hat for a woman a woman's hat
2 a name for a boy ……
3 clothes for children ……
4 a school for girls ……
5 a nest for a bird ……
6 a magazine for women ……

81.3

以所给句子中画线的词开头造句。

1 The meeting tomorrow has been cancelled.
Tomorrow's meeting has been cancelled.
2 The storm last week caused a lot of damage.
Last ……
3 The only cinema in the town has closed down.
The ……
4 The weather in Britain is very changeable.
……
5 Tourism is the main industry in the region.
……

81.4

用所给信息和括号中的单词完成下列句子。

1 If I leave my house at 9 o'clock and drive to the airport, I arrive at about 11.
So it's about two hours' drive from my house to the airport. (drive)
2 If I leave my house at 8.40 and walk to the centre, I get there at 9 o'clock.
So it's …… from my house to the centre. (walk)
3 I'm going on holiday on the 12th. I have to be back at work on the 26th.
So I've got …… . (holiday)
4 I went to sleep at 3 o'clock this morning and woke up an hour later. After that I couldn't sleep. So last night I only had …… . (sleep)

→ 补充练习 1（第302页）

myself/yourself/themselves 等

A

请看下列例句：

Steve **introduced himself** to the other guests.

句中主语和宾语是同一个人时，可以用 **myself/yourself/himself** 等反身代词。

Steve introduced himself

主语　　宾语

反身代词有：

单数：	myself	yourself (一个人)	him**self**/her**self**/it**self**
复数：	ourselves	yourselves (不止一个人)	them**selves**

- I don't want you to pay for me. **I'**ll pay for **myself**. (而不用 I'll pay for me)
- Amy had a great holiday. **She** really enjoyed **herself**.
- Do **you** talk to **yourself** sometimes? (只对一个人讲)
- If **you** want more to eat, help **yourselves**. (对不止一个人讲)

请比较：

- It's not our fault. **You** can't blame **us**.
- It's our own fault. **We** should blame **ourselves**.

B

feel/relax/concentrate/meet 后面不用反身代词：

- I **feel** nervous. I can't **relax**.
- You must try and **concentrate**. (而不用 concentrate yourself)
- What time shall we **meet**? (而不用 meet ourselves，meet us)

wash/shave/dress 后通常不用反身代词：

- He got up, **washed**, **shaved** and **dressed**. (而不用 washed himself 等)

也可以说 **get dressed** (He **got dressed**)。

C

请比较 **-selves** 与 **each other**：

- Kate and Joe stood in front of the mirror and looked at **themselves**. (= *Kate and Joe* looked at *Kate and Joe*)
- Kate looked at Joe; Joe looked at Kate. They looked at **each other**.

themselves

each other

one another 与 **each other** 可以互换：

- How long have you and Ben known **each other**? 或 … known **one another**?
- Sue and Alice don't like **each other**. 或 … don't like **one another**.
- Do you and Sarah live near **each other**? 或 … near **one another**?

D

反身代词还有另一种用法：

- 'Who repaired your bike for you?' '**I** repaired it **myself**.'

I repaired it myself 表示是我自己修的，而不是其他人。这时，**myself** 用来强调 I。再看几个例句：

- I'm not going to do your work for you. **You** can do it **yourself**. (= you, not me)
- **Let's** paint the house **ourselves**. It will be much cheaper.
- **The film itself** wasn't very good, but I loved the music.
- I don't think Lisa will get the job. **Lisa herself** doesn't think so. (或 **Lisa** doesn't think so **herself**.)

get dressed / get married 等 ➜ Unit 44D　　**by myself / by yourself 等 ➜ Unit 83D**

Exercises

82.1 用 **myself/yourself** 等和下列动词的适当形式完成句子。

blame burn enjoy express hurt ~~introduce~~ put

1 Steve introduced himself to the other guests at the party.
2 Ben fell down some steps, but fortunately he didn't ....
3 It isn't Sue's fault. She really shouldn't ....
4 Please try and understand how I feel. .... in my position.
5 The children had a great time at the beach. They really ....
6 Be careful! That pan is very hot. Don't ....
7 Sometimes I can't say exactly what I mean. I wish I could .... better.

82.2 用 **myself/yourself/ourselves** 等或 **me/you/us** 等填空。

1 Amy had a great holiday. She enjoyed herself .
2 It's not my fault. You can't blame ....
3 What I did was really bad. I'm ashamed of ....
4 We've got a problem. I hope you can help ....
5 'Can I take another biscuit?' 'Of course. Help .... !'
6 You must meet Sarah. I'll introduce .... to her.
7 Don't worry about us. We can take care of ....
8 Don't worry about the children. I'll take care of ....
9 I gave them a key to our house so that they could let .... in.

82.3 用所给动词的适当形式填空，有些地方需用反身代词。

concentrate defend dry feel meet relax ~~shave~~

1 Martin decided to grow a beard because he was fed up with shaving .
2 I wasn't very well yesterday, but I .... much better today.
3 I climbed out of the swimming pool and .... with a towel.
4 I tried to study, but I couldn't ....
5 If somebody attacks you, you need to be able to ....
6 I'm going out with Chris this evening. We're .... at 7.30.
7 You're always rushing around. Why don't you sit down and .... ?

82.4 用 **ourselves/themselves** 或 **each other** 填空。

1 How long have you and Ben known each other ?
2 If people work too hard, they can make .... ill.
3 I need you and you need me. We need ....
4 In Britain friends often give .... presents at Christmas.
5 Some people are very selfish. They only think of ....
6 Tracy and I don't see .... very often these days.
7 We couldn't get back into the house. We had locked .... out.
8 They've had an argument. They're not speaking to .... at the moment.
9 We'd never met before, so we introduced .... to ....

82.5 用反身代词回答下列问题。

1	Who repaired the bike for you?	Nobody. I repaired it myself.
2	Who cuts Brian's hair for him?	Nobody. He cuts ....
3	Do you want me to tell Amy about your idea?	No, I'll ....
4	Who told you that Linda was going away?	Linda ....
5	Can you phone John for me?	Why can't you .... ?

→ 补充练习 30（第320页）

Unit 83 a friend of mine   my own house   on my own / by myself

A a friend of mine / a friend of yours 等

通常说 a friend **of mine/yours/his/hers/ours/theirs**：
a friend of mine = one of my friends：

- I'm going to a wedding on Saturday. **A friend of mine** is getting married. (而不用 a friend of me)
- We went on holiday with **some friends of ours**. (而不用 some friends of us)
- Mike had an argument with **a neighbour of his**.
- It was **a good idea of yours** to go to the cinema.

同样地，可以说 a friend **of my sister's**，a friend **of Tom's** 等：

- That woman over there is **a friend of my sister's**. (= one of my sister's friends)
- It was **a good idea of Tom's** to go to the cinema.

B my own ... / your own ... 等

own 的前面要用 **my/your/his/her/its/our/their**：

my own house   **your own** car   **her own** room
(而不用 an own house，an own car 等)

my own ... / **your own** ... 等表示只属于某人自己的东西，不是共享或借来的：

- I don't want to share a room with anybody. I want **my own room**.
- Vicky and Gary would like to have **their own house**.
- It's a shame that the apartment hasn't got **its own parking space**.
- It's **my own fault** that I've got no money. I buy too many things I don't need.
- Why do you want to borrow my car? Why don't you use **your own**? (= your own car)

也可以说 a room **of my own**，a house **of your own**，problems **of his own** 等：

- I'd like to have a room **of my own**.
- He won't be able to help you with your problems. He has too many problems **of his own**.

C

... **own** ... 也可以用来表示某人自己做某事，而不是他人代替：

- Brian usually cuts **his own hair**. (= he cuts it himself; he doesn't go to a barber)
- I'd like to have a garden so that I could grow **my own vegetables**. (= grow them myself instead of buying them from shops)

D on my own / by myself

on my own 和 **by myself** 都是"独自"的意思。可以说：

on { my / your ; his / her / its ; our / their } **own** = **by** { myself / yourself (单数) ; himself / herself / itself ; ourselves / yourselves (复数) / themselves }

- I like living **on my own / by myself**.
- 'Did you go on holiday **on your own / by yourself**?' 'No, with a friend.'
- Jack was sitting **on his own / by himself** in a corner of the café.
- Learner drivers are not allowed to drive **on their own / by themselves**.

myself/yourself/themselves 等 → Unit 82

Exercises

83.1 用 **A** 节中的结构 **(a friend of mine** 等) 改写下列句子中的画线部分。

1 I am meeting <u>one of my friends</u> tonight. — I'm meeting a friend of mine tonight.
2 We met <u>one of your relatives</u>. — We met a ……
3 Jason borrowed <u>one of my books</u>. — Jason ……
4 Lisa invited <u>some of her friends</u> to her flat. — Lisa …… to her flat.
5 We had dinner with <u>one of our neighbours</u>. — ……
6 I went on holiday with <u>two of my friends</u>. — ……
7 Is that man <u>one of your friends</u>? — ……
8 I met <u>one of Jane's friends</u> at the party. — …… at the party.
9 It's always been <u>one of my ambitions</u> to travel round the world. — …… to travel round the world.

83.2 用 **my own / our own** 等 + 下列名词的结构完成句子。

~~bedroom~~ business opinions private beach words

1 I share a kitchen and bathroom, but I have my own bedroom.
2 Gary doesn't think the same as me. He's got …… .
3 Julia is fed up with working for other people. She wants to start …… .
4 In the test we had to read a story, and then write it in …… .
5 We stayed at a luxury hotel by the sea. The hotel had …… .

83.3 用 **my own / your own** 等完成下列句子。

1 Why do you want to borrow my car? Why don't you use your own car?
2 How can you blame me? It's not my fault. It's …… .
3 She's always using my ideas. Why can't she use ……?
4 Please don't worry about my problems. You've got …… .
5 I can't make his decisions for him. He must make …… .

83.4 用所给动词及 **my own / your own** 等完成下列句子。

bake clean ~~cut~~ make write

1 Brian never goes to a barber.
He cuts his own hair.
2 Helen doesn't often buy clothes.
She usually …… .
3 We don't often buy bread.
We usually …… .
4 I'm not going to clean your shoes.
You can …… .
5 Paul and Joe are singers.
They sing songs written by other people, but they also …… .

83.5 用 **my own / myself** 等填空。

1 Did you go on holiday on your own?
2 I'm glad I live with other people. I wouldn't like to live on …… .
3 The box was too heavy for me to lift by …… .
4 'Who was Tom with when you saw him?' 'Nobody. He was by …….'
5 Very young children should not go swimming by …… .
6 I don't think she knows many people. When I see her, she is always by …… .
7 I don't like strawberries with cream. I like them on …… .
8 Do you like working with other people or do you prefer working by ……?
9 We had no help decorating the flat. We did it completely on …… .
10 I went out with Sally because she didn't want to go out on …… .

there ... 与 it ... 比较

A

请看下列例句：

第一次谈论到某事物时，用 **there** ... 表明它的存在：

- **There's** a new restaurant in Hill Street. （而不用 A new restaurant is in Hill Street)
- I'm sorry I'm late. **There was** a lot of traffic. （而不用 It was a lot of traffic)
- Things are more expensive now. **There has been** a big rise in the cost of living.

it 则用来指某个特定的东西、地点、事实、情形等 (参见 C 节)：

- We went to the new restaurant. **It**'s very good. (**It** = the restaurant)
- I wasn't expecting them to come. **It** was a complete surprise. (**It** = that they came)

请比较 **there** 和 **it**：

- I don't like this town. **There**'s nothing to do here. **It**'s a boring place.

注意 **there** 也可以指"在那儿"：

- When we got to the party, there were already a lot of people **there**. (= at the party)

B

可以说 **there will be / there must be / there might be / there used to be** 等：

- Will you be busy tomorrow? **Will there be** much to do?
- '**Is there** a flight to Rome tonight?' '**There might be**. I'll check the website.'
- If people drove more carefully, **there wouldn't be** so many accidents.

此外，可以说 **there must have been**，**there should have been** 等：

- I could hear music coming from the house. **There must have been** somebody at home.

请比较**there** 和 **it**：

- They live on a busy road. **There must be** a lot of noise from the traffic.
- They live on a busy road. **It must be** very noisy.
- **There used to be** a cinema here, but it closed a few years ago.
- That building is now a supermarket. **It used to be** a cinema.

也可以说 **there is sure / bound** (= sure) / **likely** to be ... 。请比较**there** 和 **it**：

- **There's sure to be** a flight to Rome tonight. （或 **There's bound to be** ...)
- There's a flight to Rome tonight, but **it's sure to be** full. (**it** = the flight)

C

下面的例句要用 **it**：

- **It**'s dangerous **to walk in the road**.

通常以 **It** ...开头，而不说 To walk in the road is dangerous。再看一些例句：

- **It** didn't take us long **to get here**.
- **It**'s a shame **(that) you can't come to the party**.
- Let's go. **It**'s not worth **waiting any longer**.

it 也可以用来表示距离、时间和天气：

- How far is **it** from here to the airport?
- What day is **it** today?
- **It**'s a long time since we saw you last.
- **It** was windy yesterday. （或 **There** was **a cold wind**.)

it's worth / it's no use / there's no point ➜ **Unit 63**　　**sure to / bound to** ... 等 ➜ **Unit 65E**
there is + -ing/-ed ➜ **Unit 97**

Exercises

84.1 用 **there is/was** 或 **it is/was** 填空，有些句子要用疑问形式 (**is there … ? / is it … ?** 等) 或否定形式 (**isn't/wasn't**)。

1 The journey took a long time. ......There was...... a lot of traffic.
2 What's this restaurant like? ......Is it...... good?
3 .... something wrong with the computer. Can you check it for me?
4 I wanted to visit the museum, but .... enough time.
5 'What's that building? .... a hotel?' 'No, ... a theatre.'
6 How do we get across the river? .... a bridge?
7 A few days ago .... a big storm, which caused a lot of damage.
8 I can't find my phone. .... in my bag – I just looked.
9 It's often cold here, but .... much snow.
10 'How was your trip?' '.................... a disaster. Everything went wrong.'
11 .... anything on television, so I turned it off.
12 '.................... a bookshop near here?' 'Yes, ... one in Hudson Street.'
13 When we got to the cinema, ... a queue outside. .... a very long queue, so we decided not to wait.
14 I couldn't see anything. .... completely dark.
15 .... difficult to get a job right now. .... a lot of unemployment.

84.2 以 **There …** 开头改写下列句子。

1 The roads were busy yesterday. ......There was a lot of traffic......
2 This soup is very salty. There .... in the soup.
3 The box was empty. .... in the box.
4 The film is very violent. ....
5 The shopping mall was crowded. ....
6 I like this town – it's lively. ....

84.3 从方框中选择恰当的词，用 **there will be / there would be** 等结构完成下列句子。

will **may** ~~**would**~~ **wouldn't** **should** **used to** **(be) going to**

1 If people drove more carefully, ...there would be...... fewer accidents.
2 'Do we have any eggs?' 'I'm not sure. .... some in the fridge.'
3 I think everything will be OK. I don't think .... any problems.
4 Look at the sky. .... a storm.
5 'Is there a school in the village?' 'Not now. .... one, but it closed.'
6 People drive too fast on this road. I think .... a speed limit.
7 If people weren't aggressive, ... any wars.

84.4 指出下列句子是否正确，如有错误，请改正。在正确的句子后写上：对。

1 They live on a busy road. It must be a lot of noise. ......There must be a lot of noise......
2 It's a long way from my house to the nearest shop. ....
3 After the lecture it will be an opportunity to ask questions. ....
4 I like where I live, but it would be nicer to live by the sea. ....
5 Why was she so unfriendly? It must have been a reason. ....
6 It's three years since I last went to the theatre. ....
7 A: Where can we park the car?
B: Don't worry. It's sure to be a car park somewhere. ....
8 It was Ken's birthday yesterday. We had a party. ....
9 The situation is still the same. It has been no change. ....
10 It used to be a church here, but it was knocked down. ....
11 I was told that it would be somebody to meet me at the station, but it wasn't anybody. ....
12 I don't know who'll win, but it's sure to be a good game. ....

Unit 85

some 与 any 比较

A

一般来说，肯定句中用 **some** (还有 **somebody/someone/something**)，否定句中用**any** (还有 **anybody** 等)。

some	**any**
We bought **some** flowers.	We did**n't** buy **any** flowers.
He's busy. He's got **some** work to do.	He's lazy. He **never** does **any** work.
There's **somebody** at the door.	There is**n't anybody** at the door.
I want **something** to eat.	I do**n't** want **anything** to eat.

在下列含有否定意思的句中要用 **any**：

- She went out **without any** money. (she **didn't** take **any** money with her)
- He **refused** to eat **anything**. (he **didn't** eat **anything**)
- It's a very easy exam. **Hardly anybody** fails. (= almost **nobody** fails)

B

some 和 **any** 都可用于疑问句中。**some/somebody/something** 可用来表示我们知道或认为其存在的人或事物：

- Are you waiting for **somebody**? (我认为你是在等某人)

some 用于表示提供或要求某物的疑问句中：

- Would you like **something** to eat? (有东西可以吃)
- Can I have **some** sugar, please? (认为有糖可以拿)

但在大多数疑问句中要用 **any**，表示不知道某事物或某人是否存在：

- 'Do you have **any** luggage?' 'No, I don't.'
- I can't find my bag. Has **anybody** seen it?

C

if 从句中常用 **any**：

- **If anyone** has **any** questions, I'll be pleased to answer them.
- Let me know **if** you need **anything**.

下列句中有 **if** 的含义，因此要用 **any**：

- I'm sorry for **any** trouble I've caused. (= if I have caused any trouble)
- **Anyone** who wants to do the exam should tell me by Friday. (= if there is anyone)

D

any 可以表示"无论哪个""任何"：

- You can take **any** bus. They all go to the centre. (= it doesn't matter which bus you take)
- 'Sing a song.' 'Which song shall I sing?' '**Any** song. I don't mind.'
  (= it doesn't matter which song)
- Come and see me **any** time you want.

anybody/anyone/anything/anywhere 也可以这样用：

- We forgot to lock the door. **Anybody** could have come in.
- 'Let's go out somewhere.' 'Where shall we go?' '**Anywhere**. I just want to go out.'

请比较 **something** 与 **anything**：

- A: I'm hungry. I want **something** to eat.
  B: What would you like?
  A: I don't mind. **Anything**. (= it doesn't matter what)

E

somebody/someone/anybody/anyone 表示单数：

- **Someone** is here to see you.

但在这些词后常用 **they/them/their**：

- **Someone** has forgotten **their** umbrella. (= his or her umbrella)
- If **anybody** wants to leave early, **they** can. (= he or she can)

not … any ➜ Unit 86 **some of / any of …** ➜ Unit 88 **hardly any** ➜ Unit 101D

Exercises

85.1 用 **some** 或 **any** 填空。

1 We didn't buy ......any...... flowers.
2 Tonight I'm going out with .... friends of mine.
3 A: Have you seen .... good movies recently?
B: No, I haven't been to the cinema for ages.
4 I didn't have .... money, so I had to borrow ....
5 Can I have .... milk in my coffee, please?
6 We wanted to buy .... grapes, but they didn't have .... in the shop.
7 He did everything himself – without .... help.
8 You can use this card to withdraw money at .... cash machine.
9 I'd like .... information about places of interest in the town.
10 With the special tourist train ticket, you can travel on .... train you like.
11 Those apples look nice. Shall we buy .... ?

85.2 用 **some-** 或 **any-** + **-body/-thing/-where** 的结构完成下列句子。

1 I was too surprised to say ......anything...... .
2 There's .... at the door. Can you go and see who it is?
3 Does .... mind if I open the window?
4 I wasn't feeling hungry, so I didn't eat ....
5 You must be hungry. Why don't I get you .... to eat?
6 Quick, let's go! There's .... coming and I don't want .... to see us.
7 Sarah was upset about .... and refused to talk to ....
8 This machine is very easy to use. .... can learn to use it very quickly.
9 There was hardly .... on the beach. It was almost deserted.
10 'Do you live .... near Joe?' 'No, he lives in another part of town.'
11 'Where shall we go on holiday?' 'Let's go .... warm and sunny.'
12 They stay at home all the time. They never seem to go ....
13 I'm going to a meeting now. If .... needs me, tell them I'll be back at 11.30.
14 Why are you looking under the bed? Have you lost .... ?
15 This is a no-parking area. .... who parks here will have to pay a fine.
16 Jonathan stood up and left the room without saying ....
17 'Can I ask you .... ?' 'Sure. What do you want to ask?'
18 Sue is very secretive. She never tells .... (*2 words*)

85.3 用 **any** (+ 名词) 或 **anybody/anything/anywhere** 完成下列句子。

1	Which bus do I have to catch?	......Any bus...... . They all go to the centre.
2	Which day shall I come?	I don't mind. ....
3	What do you want to eat?	.... I don't mind. Whatever you have.
4	Where shall I sit?	It's up to you. You can sit .... you like.
5	What sort of job are you looking for?	.... It doesn't matter.
6	What time shall I call you tomorrow?	.... Leave a message if I don't answer and I'll get back to you.
7	Who shall I invite to the party?	I don't mind. .... you like.
8	Which newspaper shall I buy?	.... See what they have in the shop.

no/none/any nothing/nobody 等

A

no 与 none

no 可与名词连用。**no** = **not a** 或 **not any**：

- We had to walk home because there was **no bus**. (= there **wasn't a** bus)
- Sue will have **no trouble** finding a job. (= Sue **won't** have **any** trouble …)
- There were **no shops** open. (= There **weren't any** shops open.)

no + 名词的结构可用于句首：

- **No reason** was given for the change of plan.

none 不能与名词连用：

- 'How much money do you have?' '**None**.' (= no money)
- All the tickets have been sold. There are **none** left. (= no tickets left)

或者可以用 **none of** …：

- This money is all yours. **None of it** is mine.

请比较 **none** 与 **any**：

- 'How much luggage do you have?' '**None**.' / 'I **don't** have **any**.'

none of + 复数名词 (none of **the students**, none of **them** 等) 后面的动词用单复数形式均可，但复数形式更为常见：

- None of the shops **were** (或 **was**) open.

B

nothing **nobody/no-one** **nowhere**

回答问句时，这些词可用于句首或单独使用：

- 'What's going to happen?' '**Nobody** (或 **No-one**) knows.'
- 'What happened?' '**Nothing**.'
- 'Where are you going?' '**Nowhere**. I'm staying here.'

这些词也可用于动词之后，尤其是 **be** 和 **have**：

- The house is empty. There**'s nobody** living there.
- We **had nothing** to eat.

nothing/nobody etc. = **not** + **anything/anybody** etc.：

- I said **nothing**. = I **didn't** say **anything**.
- Jane told **nobody** about her plans. = Jane **didn't** tell **anybody** about her plans.
- They have **nowhere** to live. = They **don't** have **anywhere** to live.

nothing/nobody 等不能与否定动词 (**isn't**, **didn't** 等) 同时使用：

- I **said** nothing. (而不用 I didn't say nothing)

C

nobody/no-one 后面可用 **they/them/their** (参见 Unit 85E)：

- **Nobody** is perfect, are **they**? (= is he or she perfect)
- **No-one** did what I asked **them** to do. (= him or her)
- **Nobody** in the class did **their** homework. (= his or her homework)

D

any/anything/anybody 有时意为"无论哪个/无论什么/无论是谁"(参见 Unit 85D)。请比较 **no-** 与 **any-**：

- There was **no** bus, so we walked home.
  You can take **any** bus. They all go to the centre. (= it doesn't matter which)
- 'What do you want to eat?' '**Nothing**. I'm not hungry.'
  I'm so hungry. I could eat **anything**. (= it doesn't matter what)
- The exam was extremely difficult. **Nobody** passed. (= everybody failed)
  The exam was very easy. **Anybody** could have passed. (= it doesn't matter who)

some 与 any 比较 ➜ Unit 85 **none of … ➜ Unit 88** **any bigger / no better 等 ➜ Unit 106B**

Exercises

86.1 用 **no**, **none** 或 **any** 填空。

1 It was a public holiday, so there were ...no... shops open.
2 I haven't got ...any... money. Can you lend me some?
3 We had to walk home because there were .... taxis.
4 We had to walk home because there weren't .... taxis.
5 'How many eggs have we got?' '.................... . Do you want me to get some?'
6 We took a few pictures, but .... of them were very good.
7 'Did you take lots of pictures?' 'No, I didn't take ....'
8 What a stupid thing to do! .... intelligent person would do such a thing.
9 There's nowhere to cross the river. There's .... bridge.
10 I haven't read .... of the books you lent me.
11 We cancelled the party because .... of the people we invited were able to come.
12 'Do you know when Chris will be back?' 'I'm sorry. I have .... idea.'

86.2 用 **none/nobody/nothing/nowhere** 回答下列问题。

1 What did you do?	Nothing.
2 Who were you talking to?	....
3 How much sugar do you want?	....
4 Where are you going?	....
5 How many emails did you get?	....
6 How much did you pay?	....

用 **any/anybody/anything/ anywhere** 将上述回答改写成完整的句子。

7 (1) I didn't do anything.
8 (2) I ....
9 (3) ....
10 (4) ....
11 (5) ....
12 (6) ....

86.3 用 **no-** 或 **any-** + **-body/-thing/-where** 完成下列句子。

1 I don't want ...anything... to drink. I'm not thirsty.
2 The bus was completely empty. There was .... on it.
3 'Where did you go for your holidays?' '.................... . I stayed at home.'
4 I went to the shops, but I didn't buy ....
5 'What did you buy?' '.................... . I couldn't find .... I wanted.'
6 The town is still the same as it was years ago. .... has changed.
7 Have you seen my watch? I can't find it ....
8 There was complete silence in the room. .... said ....

86.4 从下列句子画线的部分中选择正确答案。

1 She didn't tell ~~nobody~~ / anybody about her plans. (anybody *is correct*)
2 The accident looked bad, but fortunately nobody / anybody was badly injured.
3 I looked out of the window, but I couldn't see no-one / anyone.
4 My job is very easy. Nobody / Anybody could do it.
5 'What's in that box?' 'Nothing / Anything. It's empty.'
6 The situation is uncertain. Nothing / Anything could happen.
7 I don't know nothing / anything about economics.
8 I'll try and answer no / any questions you ask me.
9 'Who were you talking to just now?' 'No-one / Anyone. I wasn't talking to no-one / anyone.'

→ 补充练习 30 (第320页)

Unit 87

much, many, little, few, a lot, plenty

A

much 和 **little** 与不可数名词连用：

much time **much luck** **little energy** **little money**

many 和 **few** 与复数名词连用：

many friends **many people** **few cars** **few countries**

a lot of / lots of / plenty of 与不可数名词或复数名词连用均可：

a lot of luck **lots of time** **plenty of money**
a lot of friends **lots of people** **plenty of ideas**

plenty = more than enough：

- There's no need to hurry. We've got **plenty of time**.

B

much 通常用于否定句和疑问句中（尤用于口语中）。请比较：

- We **didn't** spend **much** money.

但是 We **spent a lot of** money. （而不用 We spent much money）

- **Do** you **see** David **much**?

但是 I **see** David **a lot**. （而不用 I see David much）

many 和 **a lot of** 可用于各种类型的句子中：

- **Many** people drive too fast. 或 **A lot of** people drive too fast.
- Do you know **many** people? 或 Do you know **a lot of** people?
- There aren't **many** tourists here. 或 There aren't **a lot of** tourists here.

注意，可以说 **many years / many weeks / many days** （而不用 a lot of ...）：

- We've lived here for **many years**. （而不用 a lot of years）

C

little 和 **few** （不带 **a**）具有否定的含义（= not much / not many）：

- Gary is very busy with his job. He has **little time** for other things. (= not much time, less time than he would like)
- Vicky doesn't like living in London. She has **few** friends there. (= not many, not as many as she would like)

可以说 **very little** 和 **very few**：

- Gary has **very little** time for other things.
- Vicky has **very few** friends in London.

D

a little = some, a small amount：

- Let's go and have a coffee. We have **a little** time before the train leaves.
 (a little time = some time, enough time to have a coffee)
- 'Do you speak English?' '**A little**.' （因此我们可以简单交流）

a few = some, a small number：

- I enjoy my life here. I have **a few** friends and we meet quite often.
 (a few friends = not many but enough to have a good time)
- 'When was the last time you saw Clare?' '**A few** days ago.' (= some days ago)

请比较 **little** 与 **a little**，**few** 与 **a few**：

- He spoke **little** English, so it was difficult to communicate with him.
 He spoke **a little** English, so we were able to communicate with him.
- She's lucky. She has **few** problems. (= not many problems)
 Things are not going so well for her. She has **a few** problems. (= some problems)

可以说 **only a little** 和 **only a few**：

- Hurry! We **only** have **a little** time. （而不用 only little time）
- The village was very small. There were **only a few** houses. （而不用 only few houses）

可数名词与不可数名词 ➜ Units 69–70

Exercises

87.1 下列句子有的使用 **much** 是不正确或不自然的，请改为 **many** 或 **a lot (of)**。在正确的句子后写上：对。

1 We didn't spend much money. ......对......
2 Sue drinks much tea. ......a lot of tea......
3 Joe always puts much salt on his food. ....
4 We'll have to hurry. We don't have much time. ....
5 It cost much to repair the car. ....
6 Did it cost much to repair the car? ....
7 I don't know much people in this town. ....
8 Mike travels much. ....
9 There wasn't much traffic this morning. ....
10 You need much money to travel round the world. ....

87.2 用 **plenty** 或 **plenty of** + 所给的词语完成下列句子。

hotels	money	room	~~time~~	to learn	to see

1 There's no need to hurry. There's ......plenty of time.......
2 He doesn't have any financial problems. He has ....
3 Come and sit with us. There's ....
4 She knows a lot, but she still has ....
5 It's an interesting town to visit. There ....
6 I'm sure we'll find somewhere to stay. ....

87.3 用 **much/many/little/few** 填空，每空只填一个单词。

1 She isn't very popular. She has ......few...... friends.
2 Ann is very busy these days. She has .... free time.
3 Did you take .... pictures when you were on holiday?
4 I'm not very busy today. I don't have .... to do.
5 This is a very modern city. There are .... old buildings.
6 The weather has been very dry recently. We've had .... rain.
7 'Do you know Rome?' 'No, I haven't been there for .... years.'

87.4 在下列句中必要的地方加上 **a**，在正确的句子后写上：对。

1 She's lucky. She has few problems. ......对......
2 Things are not going so well for her. She has few problems. ......a few problems......
3 Can you lend me few dollars? ....
4 There was little traffic, so the journey didn't take very long. ....
5 I can't give you a decision yet. I need little time to think. ....
6 It was a surprise that he won the match. Few people expected him to win. ....
7 I don't know much Spanish – only few words. ....
8 I wonder how Sam is. I haven't seen him for few months. ....

87.5 用 **little / a little / few / a few** 填空。

1 Gary is very busy with his job. He has ......little...... time for other things.
2 Listen carefully. I'm going to give you .... advice.
3 Do you mind if I ask you .... questions?
4 It's not a very interesting place to visit, so .... tourists come here.
5 I don't think Amy would be a good teacher. She has .... patience.
6 'Would you like milk in your coffee?' 'Yes, ...'
7 This is a very boring place to live. There's .... to do.
8 'Have you ever been to Paris?' 'Yes, I've been there .... times.'

Unit 88

all / all of   most / most of   no / none of 等

A

all	some	any	most	much/many	little/few	no

上表中的词可以和名词连用 (**some food / few books** 等)：

- **All cars** have wheels.
- **Some cars** can go faster than others.
- (*on a notice*) **NO CARS**. (= no cars allowed)
- **Many people** drive too fast.
- I don't go out very often. I'm at home **most days**.

不能说 all of cars，some of people 等 (参见 B 节)：

- **Some people** learn languages more easily than others. (而不用 Some of people)

注意：要说 **most** (而不用 the most)。例如：

- **Most tourists** don't visit this part of the town. (而不用 The most tourists)

B

all	some	any	most	much/many	little/few	half	none

上表中的词可以和 **of** 连用，可以说 **some of / most of** 等。

可以用		+		
	some of **most of** **none of** 等	+	**the …** **this …** **those …**	**my …** **these …** **those …** 等

可以说：

some **of the people**，some **of those people** (而不用 some of people)
most **of my time**，most **of the time** (而不用 most of time)

- **Some of the people I work with** are not very friendly.
- **None of this money** is mine.
- Have you read **any of these books**?
- I was sick yesterday. I spent **most of the day** in bed.

有时 **all** 或 **half** 之后加不加 **of** 均可：

- **All my friends** live in Los Angeles. 或 All **of** my friends …
- **Half this money** is mine. 或 Half **of** this money …

请比较：

- **All flowers** are beautiful. (= all flowers in general)
  All (of) **the flowers in this garden** are beautiful. (= a specific group of flowers)
- **Most problems** have a solution. (= most problems in general)
  We were able to solve **most of the problems we had**. (= a specific group of problems)

C

可以用 **all of / some of / none of** 等 + **it/us/you/them**：

- 'How many of these people do you know?' '**None of them**. / **A few of them**.'
- Do **any of you** want to come to a party tonight?
- 'Do you like this music?' '**Some of it**. Not **all of it**.'

可以说 **all of us / all of you / half of it / half of them** 等。**it/us/you/them** 前需加 **of**：

- **All of us** were late. (而不用 All us)
- I haven't finished the book yet. I've only read **half of it**. (而不用 half it)

D

上表中的词可以单独使用，后面不跟名词：

- Some cars have four doors and **some** have two.
- A few of the shops were open, but **most** (of them) were closed.
- Half this money is mine, and **half** (of it) is yours. (而不用 the half)

all ➜ Units 75B，90，110D   **some / any ➜ Unit 85**   **no / none ➜ Unit 86**
much/many/little/few ➜ Unit 87   **all of whom / most of which 等 ➜ Unit 96B**

Exercises

88.1 在必要的地方填入 **of**，在不需要的地方画“–”。

1 All ....–....... cars have wheels. (*the sentence is already complete*)
2 None ....of....... this money is mine.
3 Some .... films are very violent.
4 Some .... the films I've seen recently have been very violent.
5 Joe never goes to museums. He says that all .... museums are boring.
6 I think some .... people watch too much TV.
7 'Do you want any .... these magazines?' 'No, I've finished with them.'
8 Kate has lived in London most .... her life.
9 Joe has lived in Chicago all .... his life.
10 Most .... days I get up before 7 o'clock.

88.2 根据所给的词语完成下列句子，在必要的地方加上 **of** (如 **some of / most of** 等)。

accidents	**European countries**	**my dinner**	**the players**
birds	**her friends**	**my spare time**	**the population**
~~**cars**~~	**her opinions**	**the buildings**	~~**these books**~~

1 I haven't read many ....of these books....... .
2 All ....cars....... have wheels.
3 I spend much .... gardening.
4 Many .... are caused by bad driving.
5 It's a historic town. Many .... are over 400 years old.
6 When she got married, she kept it a secret. She didn't tell any ....
7 Not many people live in the north of the country. Most .... live in the south.
8 Not all .... can fly. For example, the penguin can't fly.
9 Our team played badly and lost the game. None .... played well.
10 Emma and I have very different ideas. I don't agree with many ....
11 Sarah travels a lot in Europe. She has been to most ....
12 I had no appetite. I could only eat half ....

88.3 根据你自己的想法完成下列句子。

1 The building was damaged in the explosion. All ....the windows....... were broken.
2 We argue sometimes, but get on well most of ....
3 I went to the cinema by myself. None of .... wanted to come.
4 The test was difficult. I could only answer half ....
5 Some of .... you took at the wedding were very good.
6 'Did you spend all .... I gave you?' 'No, there's still some left.'

88.4 用 **all of / some of / none of + it/them/us (all of it / some of them** 等) 的结构完成下列句子。

1 These books are all Jane's. ....None of them....... belong to me.
2 'How many of these books have you read?' '.................. . Every one.'
3 We all got wet in the rain because .... had an umbrella.
4 Some of this money is yours and .... is mine.
5 I asked some people for directions, but .... was able to help me.
6 She invented the whole story from beginning to end. .... was true.
7 Not all the tourists in the group were Spanish. .... were French.
8 I watched most of the film, but not ....

Unit 89 both / both of neither / neither of either / either of

A

both/neither/either 可以和名词连用 (**both books**，**neither book** 等)，用来谈论两个人或事物。
例如，你们打算出去吃饭，有两家餐馆可以选择。可以说：

- **Both restaurants** are very good. (而不用 The both restaurants)
- **Neither restaurant** is expensive.
- We can go to **either restaurant**. I don't mind.
  (**either** = one or the other, it doesn't matter which one)

both/neither/either 也可以单独使用：

- I couldn't decide which of the two shirts to buy. I liked **both**. (或 I liked **both** of them.)
- 'Is your friend British or American?' '**Neither**. She's Australian.'
- 'Do you want tea or coffee?' '**Either**. I don't mind.'

B

both of … / neither of … / either of …

both of / neither of / either of 的结构后面总是要加 **the/these/my/Tom's** 等。不能说 both of restaurants，必须说 both of **the** restaurants，both of **those** restaurants 等：

- **Both of these** restaurants are very good.
- **Neither of the** restaurants we went to was (*or* were) expensive.
- I haven't been to **either of those** restaurants. (= I haven't been to one or the other)

有时 **both** 后面加不加 **of** 均可：

- **Both my parents** are from Egypt. 或 Both **of** my parents …

可以用 **both of / neither of / either of + us/you/them**：

- (*talking to two people*) Can **either of you** speak Russian?
- I asked two people the way to the station, but **neither of them** could help me.

both 和 **us/you/them** 之间一定要加 **of**：

- **Both of us** were very tired. (而不用 Both us were …)

neither of … 之后的动词用单复数形式均可：

- Neither of the children **wants** (*or* **want**) to go to bed.

C

可以说：

both … **and** …	**Both** Chris **and** Paul were late. I was **both** tired **and** hungry when I arrived home.
neither … **nor** …	**Neither** Chris **nor** Paul came to the party. There was an accident in the street where we live, but we **neither** saw **nor** heard anything.
either … **or** …	I'm not sure where Maria's from. She's **either** Spanish **or** Italian. **Either** you apologise, **or** I'll never speak to you again.

D

请比较 **either/neither/both** (两个) 与 **any/none/all** (两个以上)：

There are **two** good hotels here. You could stay at **either** of them.	There are **many** good hotels here. You could stay at **any** of them.
We tried **two** hotels. { **Neither** of them had any rooms. / **Both** of them were full.	We tried **a lot of** hotels. { **None** of them had any rooms. / **All** of them were full.

neither do I / I don't either ➜ Unit 51C both of whom / neither of which ➜ Unit 96B
both ➜ Unit 110D

Exercises

89.1 用 **both/neither/either** 填空。

1 'Do you want tea or coffee?' '......Either...... . I really don't mind.'
2 'What day is it today – the 18th or the 19th?' '.................................. . It's the 20th.'
3 A: Where did you go on your trip – South Korea or Japan?
B: We went to .... A week in South Korea and a week in Japan.
4 'Shall we sit in the corner or by the window?' '.................................. . I don't mind.'
5 'Where's Lisa? Is she at work or at home?' '.................................. . She's away on holiday.'

89.2 用 **both/neither/either** 完成下列句子，在必要的地方加上 **of**。

1 ......Both...... my parents are from London.
2 To get to the town centre, you can go along the footpath by the river or you can go along the road. You can go .... way.
3 I tried twice to phone Carl, but .... times he was out.
4 .... Tom's parents is English. His father is Polish and his mother is Italian.
5 I saw an accident this morning. One car drove into the back of another. Fortunately .... driver was injured, but .... cars were badly damaged.
6 I've got two sisters and a brother. My brother is working, but .... my sisters are still at school.

89.3 用 **both/neither/either + of us / of them** 填空。

1 I asked two people the way to the station, but ......neither of them...... could help me.
2 I was invited to two parties last week, but I couldn't go to ....
3 There were two windows in the room. It was very warm, so I opened ....
4 Sarah and I play tennis together regularly, but we're not very good. .... can play very well.
5 I tried two bookshops for the book I wanted, but .... had it.

89.4 用 **both ... and ... / neither ... nor ... / either ... or ...** 造句。

1 Chris was late. So was Pat. ......Both Chris and Pat were late......
2 He didn't say hello, and he didn't smile. ......He neither said hello nor smiled......
3 Joe is on holiday and so is Sam.
....
4 Joe doesn't have a car. Sam doesn't have one either.
....
5 Brian doesn't watch TV and he doesn't read newspapers.
....
6 It was a boring movie. It was long too.
The movie ....
7 Is that man's name Richard? Or is it Robert? It's one of the two.
That man's name ....
8 I haven't got time to go on holiday. And I don't have the money.
I have ....
9 We can leave today or we can leave tomorrow – whichever you prefer.
We ....

89.5 用 **neither/either/none/any** 完成下列句子。

1 We tried a lot of hotels, but ......none...... of them had any rooms.
2 I took two books with me on holiday, but I didn't read .... of them.
3 I took five books with me on holiday, but I didn't read .... of them.
4 There are a few shops at the end of the street, but .... of them sells newspapers.
5 You can phone me at .... time during the evening. I'm always at home.
6 I can meet you next Monday or Friday. Would .... of those days suit you?
7 John and I couldn't get into the house because .... of us had a key.

Unit 90 all，every 与 whole 比较

A

all 与 everybody/everyone 比较

all 通常不用来表示“每个人”：

- **Everybody** had a great time at the party. （而不用 All had a great time）

可以说 **all of us / all of you / all of them**：

- **All of us** had a great time at the party. （而不用 Everybody of us）

B

all 与 everything 比较

有时 **all** 和 **everything** 可以互换：

- I'll do **all I can** to help. 或 I'll do **everything I can** to help.

通常不单独使用**all**，但可以说 all **I can** / all **you need** 等。例如：

- He thinks he knows **everything**. （而不用 he knows all）
- Our holiday was a disaster. **Everything** went wrong. （而不用 All went wrong）

可以说 **all about**：

- He knows **all about** computers.

all 还可以用来表示“唯一”：

- **All** I've eaten today is a sandwich. （= the only thing I've eaten today）

C

every / everybody / everyone / everything 是单数，后面跟单数动词：

- **Every seat** in the theatre **was** taken.
- **Everybody has** arrived. （而不用 have arrived）

但在 **everybody/everyone** 之后，常用 **they/them/their**：

- **Everybody** said **they** enjoyed **themselves**. （= everybody enjoyed himself or herself）

D

all 与 whole 比较

whole 可表示“全部的，整个的”，通常和单数名词连用：

- Did you read **the whole book**? （= all the book, not just a part of it）
- Emily has lived **her whole life** in the same town.
- I was so hungry, I ate **a whole packet** of biscuits. （= a complete packet）

whole 的前面通常有 **the/my/her** 等。请比较 **whole** 与 **all**：

her whole life 或 **all her life**

whole 通常不与不可数名词连用。可以说：

- I've spent **all the money** you gave me. （而不用 the whole money）

E

every/all/whole 与表示时间的词连用

every 可用来表明某事发生的频率。因此可以说 **every day / every Monday / every ten minutes / every three weeks** 等：

- When we were on holiday, we went to the beach **every day**. （而不用 all days）
- The bus service is excellent. There's a bus **every ten minutes**.
- We don't see each other very often – about **every six months**.

all day / the whole day 表示“一整天”：

- We spent **all day / the whole day** on the beach.
- Dan was very quiet. He didn't say a word **all evening / the whole evening**.

注意：可以说 **all day** (而不用 all the day)，**all week** (而不用 all the week) 等。

请比较 **all the time** 与 **every time**：

- They never go out. They are at home **all the time**. （= always, continuously）
- **Every time** I see you, you look different. （= each time, on every occasion）

可数名词与不可数名词 ➜ Units 69–70 **all / all of** ➜ Unit 88 **each 与 every 比较** ➜ Unit 91
every one ➜ Unit 91D **all (词序)** ➜ Unit 110D

Exercises

90.1 用 **all**，**everything** 或 **everybody/everyone** 填空。

1 It was a good party. ....Everybody.... had a great time.
2 ....All.... I've eaten today is a sandwich.
3 .... has their faults. Nobody is perfect.
4 Nothing has changed. .... is the same as it was.
5 Kate told me .... about her new job. It sounds quite interesting.
6 Can .... write their names on a piece of paper, please?
7 Why are you always thinking about money? Money isn't ....
8 I didn't have much money with me. .... I had was ten pounds.
9 When the fire alarm rang, ... left the building immediately.
10 Sarah didn't say where she was going. .... she said was that she was going away.
11 We have completely different opinions. I disagree with .... she says.
12 We all did well in the exam. .... in our class passed.
13 We all did well in the exam. .... of us passed.
14 Why are you so lazy? Why do you expect me to do .... for you?

90.2 根据下列情况，用 **whole** 造句。

1 I read the book from beginning to end. ....I read the whole book....
2 Everyone in the team played well.
The ....
3 Paul opened a box of chocolates. When he finished eating, there were no chocolates left in the box. He ate ....
4 The police came to the house. They were looking for something. They searched everywhere, every room. They ....
5 Everyone in Ed and Jane's family plays tennis. Ed and Jane play, and so do all their children. The ....
6 Ann worked from early in the morning until late in the evening.
....
7 Jack and Lisa had a week's holiday by the sea. It rained from the beginning of the week to the end. It ....

再用 **all** 重写第6句和第7句。

8 (6) Ann ....
9 (7) ....

90.3 用 **every** + 下列表示时间的短语完成句子。

five minutes	~~**ten minutes**~~	**four hours**	**six months**	**four years**

1 The bus service is very good. There's a bus ....every ten minutes.... .
2 Tom is ill. He has some medicine. He has to take it ....
3 The Olympic Games take place ....
4 We live near a busy airport. A plane flies over our house ....
5 Martin goes to the dentist for a check-up ....

90.4 从下列句子画线的部分中选择正确答案。

1 I've spent ~~the whole money~~ / all the money you gave me. (all the money *is correct*)
2 Sue works every day / all days except Sunday.
3 I'm tired. I've been working hard all the day / all day.
4 It was a terrible fire. Whole building / The whole building was destroyed.
5 I've been trying to contact her, but every time / all the time I phone there's no answer.
6 I don't like the weather here. It rains every time / all the time.
7 When I was on holiday, all my luggage / my whole luggage was stolen.

→ 补充练习 30（第320页）

each 与 every 比较

A

each 和 **every** 意思相近，常常可以互换：

- **Each** time (*or* **Every** time) I see you, you look different.
- There are computers in **each** classroom (*or* **every** classroom) in the school.

但是 **each** 和 **every** 并不完全一样。区别如下：

each 强调事物的分离性、个体性。

- Study **each sentence** carefully.
  (= study the sentences one by one)

each = X + X + X + X

each 通常用来表示小数目：

- There were four books on the table. **Each book** was a different colour.
- (*in a card game*) At the beginning of the game, **each player** has three cards.

every 强调总体概念，意思同 **all** 相近。

- **Every sentence** must have a verb.
  (= all sentences in general)

every = 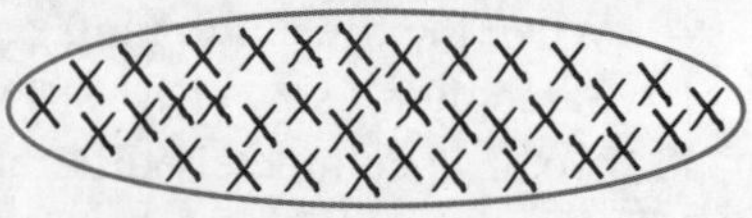

every 常常用来表示大数目：

- Kate loves reading. She has read **every book** in the library. (= all the books)
- I'd like to visit **every country** in the world. (= all the countries)

each 可以用来指两个人或物：

- In football, **each team** has eleven players. (而不用 every team)

every 可用来表明某事发生的频率：

- 'How often do you use your car?' '**Every day**.' (而不用 Each day)
- There's a bus **every ten minutes**. (而不用 each ten minutes)

B

请比较 **each** 与 **every** 的构成方式：

each 可与名词连用：

each book **each student**

each 可以单独使用，后面不接名词：

- None of the rooms was the same.
  Each (= each room) was different.

或者可以用 **each one**：

- **Each one** was different.

可以说 **each of (the … / these … / them** 等)：

- Read **each of these** sentences carefully.
- **Each of the** books is a different colour.
- **Each of them** is a different colour.

every 可与名词连用：

every book **every student**

every 不能单独使用，但可以说 **every one**：

- A: Have you read all these books?
  B: Yes, **every one**.

可以说 **every one of** … (而不用 every of)：

- I've read **every one of those** books.
  (而不用 every of those books)
- I've read **every one of them**.

C

each 可以放在句末，也可以放在句子中间：

- The students were **each** given a book. (= Each student was given a book.)
- These oranges cost 40 pence **each**.

D

everyone 与 **every one** 比较

everyone (写成一个词) 仅用来指人 (= everybody)。

every one (写成两个词) 可用来指人或物，用法与 **each one** 相似 (参见 B 节)：

- **Everyone** enjoyed the party. (= **Everybody** …)
- Sarah is invited to lots of parties and she goes to **every one**. (= to **every party**)

each other ➜ Unit 82C **all 与 every 比较** ➜ Unit 90

Exercises

91.1 看下列图片，用 **each** 或 **every** 完成句子。

1 ....Each.... player has three cards.
2 Kate has read ....every.... book in the library.
3 .... side of a square is the same length.
4 .... seat in the theatre was taken.
5 There are six apartments in the building. .... one has a balcony.
6 There's a train to London .... hour.
7 She was wearing four rings – one on .... finger.
8 Our football team is playing well. We've won .... game this season.

91.2 用 **each** 或 **every** 填空。

1 There were four books on the table. ....Each.... book was a different colour.
2 The Olympic Games are held ....every.... four years.
3 .... parent worries about their children.
4 In a game of tennis there are two or four players. .... player has a racket.
5 Nicola plays volleyball .... Thursday evening.
6 I understood most of what they said but not .... word.
7 The book is divided into five parts and .... of these has three sections.
8 I get paid .... four weeks.
9 I called the office two or three times, but .... time it was closed.
10 Car seat belts save lives. .... driver should wear one.
11 A friend of mine has three children. I always give .... of them a present at Christmas.
12 (*from an exam*) Answer all five questions. Write your answer to .... question on a separate sheet of paper.

91.3 用 **each** 改写下列句子。

1 The price of one of those oranges is 30 pence. ....Those oranges are 30 pence each.... .
2 I had ten pounds and so did Sonia. Sonia and I ....
3 One of those postcards costs 80 pence. Those ....
4 The hotel was expensive. I paid £150 and so did you. We ....

91.4 用 **everyone** 或 **every one** 填空。

1 Sarah is invited to a lot of parties and she goes to ....every one.... .
2 As soon as .... had arrived, we began the meeting.
3 I asked her lots of questions and she answered .... correctly.
4 Amy is very popular. .... likes her.
5 I dropped a tray of glasses. Unfortunately .... broke.

Unit 92

定语从句 (1) —— 由关系代词 who/that/which 引导的从句

A

请看下列例句：

The woman | who lives next door | is a doctor.
（定语从句）

从句是句子的一部分，定语从句表明说话人所指的人或物：

- The woman **who lives next door** … (who lives next door 起限定作用，表明是哪个女人)
- People **who live in the country** … (who live in the country 起限定作用，表明是什么人)

who 引导的定语从句修饰人，而不是物，**who** 取代了 **he/she/they**：

the woman – she lives next door – is a doctor

→ The woman **who lives next door** is a doctor.

we know a lot of people – they live in the country

→ We know a lot of people **who live in the country**.

- An architect is someone **who designs buildings**.
- What was the name of the person **who phoned**?
- Anyone **who wants to apply for the job** must do so by Friday.

who 也可以用 **that** 替换，但不可用 **which**：

- The woman **that lives next door** is a doctor. (而不用 the woman which)

但有时只能用 **who** 修饰人，参见 Unit 95。

B

谈论事物时，使用 **that** 或 **which** 引导的定语从句：

where is the cheese? – it was in the fridge

→ Where is the cheese { **that** / **which** } **was in the fridge?**

- I don't like stories **that have unhappy endings**. (或 stories **which** have …)
- Grace works for a company **that makes furniture**. (或 a company **which** makes furniture)
- The machine **that broke down** is working again now. (或 The machine **which** broke down)

that 比 **which** 更常见，但有时只能用 **which** 来修饰，参见 Unit 95。

C

定语从句必须由关系代词 **who/that/which** 引导，而不能用 **he/she/they/it**。

请比较：

- 'Who's that woman?' '**She** lives next door to me.'
  I've never spoken to the woman **who** lives next door. (而不用 the woman she lives)
- Where is the cheese? **It** was in the fridge.
  Where is the cheese **that** was in the fridge? (而不用 the cheese it was)

D

what = the thing(s) that。请比较 **what** 与 **that**：

- **What happened** was my fault. (= the thing that happened)

但是

- Everything **that happened** was my fault. (而不用 Everything what happened)
- The machine **that broke down** is now working again. (而不用 The machine what broke down)

定语从句 (2)–(5) → Units 93–96

Exercises

92.1 根据下列提示，用 **who** 引导的定语从句给括号内的词下定义。

he/she	steals from a shop ~~designs buildings~~ doesn't believe in God is not brave	he/she	buys something from a shop pays rent to live in a house or apartment breaks into a house to steal things expects the worst to happen

1 (an architect) An architect is someone who designs buildings.
2 (a burglar) A burglar is someone ……
3 (a customer) ……
4 (a shoplifter) ……
5 (a coward) ……
6 (an atheist) ……
7 (a pessimist) ……
8 (a tenant) ……

92.2 用 **who/that/which** 引导的定语从句改写下列句子。

1 A girl was injured in the accident. She is now in hospital.
The girl who was injured in the accident is now in hospital.
2 A waitress served us. She was impolite and impatient.
The ……
3 A building was destroyed in the fire. It has now been rebuilt.
The ……
4 Some people were arrested. They have now been released.
The ……
5 A bus goes to the airport. It runs every half hour.
The ……

92.3 用方框中的表达和定语从句的结构将下列句子补充完整。

invented the telephone	~~**makes furniture**~~
runs away from home	**gives you the meaning of words**
stole my wallet	**can support life**
were hanging on the wall	**cannot be explained**

1 Helen works for a company that makes furniture.
2 The book is about a girl …… .
3 What happened to the pictures …… ?
4 A mystery is something …… .
5 The police have arrested the man …… .
6 A dictionary is a book …… .
7 Alexander Bell was the man …… .
8 It seems that Earth is the only planet …… .

92.4 指出下列句子是否正确。如有错误，请改正。

1 I don't like stories who have unhappy endings. stories that have
2 What was the name of the person who phoned? 对
3 Where's the nearest shop who sells bread? ……
4 The driver which caused the accident was fined £500. ……
5 Do you know the person that took these pictures? ……
6 We live in a world what is changing all the time. ……
7 Dan said some things about me that were not true. ……
8 What was the name of the horse it won the race? ……

定语从句 (2) —— who/that/which 的省略

A

请看Unit 92 中的例句：

- The woman **who** lives next door is a doctor. (或 The woman **that** lives …)

  The woman lives next door. **who** (= the woman) 是主语。

- Where is the cheese **that** was in the fridge? (或 the cheese **which** was …)

  The cheese was in the fridge. **that** (= the cheese) 是主语。

who/that/which 在充当定语从句的主语时不能省略。因此不能说 The woman lives next door is a doctor，也不能说Where is the cheese was in the fridge?

B

有时 **who/that/which** 充当定语从句中动词的宾语。例如：

- The woman **who** **I wanted to see** was away on holiday.

  I wanted to see the woman. **who** (= the woman) 是宾语，**I** 是主语。

- Have you found the keys **that** **you lost**?

  You lost the keys. **that** (= the keys) 是宾语，**you** 是主语。

这时的 **who/that/which** 可以省略：

- **The woman I wanted to see** was away. 或 The woman **who** I wanted to see …
- Have you found **the keys you lost**? 或 … the keys **that** you lost?
- **The dress Lisa bought** doesn't fit her very well. 或 The dress **that** Lisa bought …
- Is there **anything I can do**? 或 … anything **that** I can do?

注意下列用法：

the keys you lost (而不用 the keys you lost them)
the dress Lisa bought (而不用 the dress Lisa bought it)

C

注意介词 (**in/to/for** 等) 在定语从句中的位置：

Tom is talking to a woman – do you know her?

→ Do you know the woman (who/that) Tom is **talking to** ?

I slept in a bed last night – it wasn't very comfortable

→ The bed (that/which) I **slept in** last night wasn't very comfortable.

- Are these the books **you were looking for**? 或 … the books **that/which** you were …
- The woman **he fell in love with** left him after a month. 或 The woman **who/that** he …
- The man **I was sitting next to on the plane** talked all the time. 或
  The man **who/that** I was sitting next to …

注意下列用法：

the books you were looking for (而不用 the books you were looking for them)

D

what 不能用于下列句子中 (参见Unit 92D)：

- Everything **(that) they said** was true. (而不用 Everything what they said)
- I gave her all the money **(that) I had**. (而不用 all the money what I had)

what = the thing(s) that：

- Did you hear **what they said**? (= the things that they said)

定语从句 (1) → Unit 92 定语从句 (3)–(5) → Units 94–96 **whom** → Unit 94B

Exercises

93.1 下列句子中有的需要使用 **who** 或 **that**，如有必要请改正。

1 The woman lives next door is a doctor. ......The woman who lives next door......
2 Have you found the keys you lost? ......对......
3 The people we met last night were very nice. ......
4 The people work in the office are very nice. ......
5 The people I work with are very nice. ......
6 What have you done with the money I gave you? ......
7 What happened to the money was on the table? ......
8 What's the worst film you've ever seen? ......
9 What's the best thing it has ever happened to you? ......

93.2 根据下列情况，用定语从句完成句子。

1 Your friend lost some keys. You want to know if he has found them. You say:
Have you found ......the keys you lost......?
2 A friend is wearing a dress. You like it. You tell her:
I like the dress ....
3 A friend is going to see a film. You want to know the name of the film. You say:
What's the name of the film ......?
4 You wanted to visit a museum. It was shut when you got there. You tell a friend:
The museum ...... was shut when we got there.
5 You invited some people to your party. Some of them couldn't come. You tell someone:
Some of the people ...... couldn't come.
6 Your friend had to do some work. You want to know if she has finished. You say:
Have you finished the work ......?
7 You rented a car. It broke down after a few miles. You tell a friend:
The car ...... broke down after a few miles.

93.3 用定语从句完成下列句子，注意介词的位置。

1 Did you find (looking / for / you / the books / were)?
Did you find ......the books you were looking for......?
2 We couldn't go to (we / invited / to / were / the wedding).
We couldn't go to ....
3 What's the name of (the hotel / about / me / told / you)?
What's the name of ......?
4 Unfortunately I didn't get (applied / I / the job / for).
Unfortunately I didn't get ....
5 Did you enjoy (you / the concert / to / went)?
Did you enjoy ......?
6 Gary is a good person to know. He's (on / rely / can / somebody / you).
Gary is a good person to know. He's ....
7 Who was (the man / were / with / you) in the restaurant last night?
Who was ...... in the restaurant last night?

93.4 用 **that** 或 **what** 填空，在不需要的地方画"–"。

1 I gave her all the money ......–...... I had. (all the money **that** I had *is also correct*)
2 Did you hear ......what...... they said?
3 They give their children everything ...... they want.
4 Tell me ...... you want and I'll try to get it for you.
5 Why do you blame me for everything ...... goes wrong?
6 I won't be able to do much, but I'll do ...... I can.
7 I won't be able to do much, but I'll do the best ...... I can.
8 I don't agree with ...... you've just said.
9 I don't trust him. I don't believe anything ...... he says.

定语从句 (3) —— whose/whom/where

A whose

可以用 **whose** 代替定语从句中的 **his/her/their**：

we helped some people – their car had broken down

→ We helped some people **whose car had broken down.**

whose 大多用来修饰人：

- A widow is a woman **whose husband is dead.** (**her** husband is dead)
- What's the name of the man **whose car you borrowed**? (you borrowed **his** car)
- I met someone **whose brother I went to school with.** (I went to school with **his/her** brother)

请比较 **who** 与 **whose**：

- I met a man **who** knows you. (**he** knows you)
- I met a man **whose sister** knows you. (**his sister** knows you)

B whom

whom 可以代替 **who**，充当定语从句中动词的宾语 (例如 Unit 93B中的句子)：

- George is a person **whom I admire** very much. (I admire **him**)

whom 也可与介词连用 (**to whom** / **from whom** / **with whom** 等)：

- I like the people **with whom I work.** (I work **with them**)

但 **whom** 这个词较为正式，在上述用法中 **who** 或 **that** 更常见，或者不用关系代词 (参见 Unit 93)：

- … a person **who/that** I admire a lot 或 … a person **I admire** a lot
- … the people **who/that** I work with 或 … the people **I work with**

C where

where 可用于定语从句中表示地点：

the restaurant – we had lunch there – it was near the airport

→ The restaurant **where we had lunch** was near the airport.

- I recently went back to **the town where I grew up.**
  (或 … the town I grew up in 或 … the town **that** I grew up in)
- I would like to live in **a place where there is plenty of sunshine.**

D

可以说：

the day / the year / the time 等 { something happens 或 / **that** something happens }

- I can't meet you on Friday. That's **the day (that) I'm going away.**
- **The last time (that) I saw Anna,** she looked great.
- I haven't seen Jack and Helen since **the year (that) they got married.**

E

可以说：

the reason { something happens 或 / **that/why** something happens }

- **The reason I'm phoning** is to ask your advice.
  (或 The reason **that** I'm phoning / The reason **why** I'm phoning)

定语从句 (1)，(2) ➔ Units 92–93 定语从句 (4)，(5) ➔ Units 95–96 whom ➔ Unit 96

Exercises

94.1 下图是你在聚会上遇见的人：

第二天你向朋友谈起这些人，用 **who …** 或 **whose …**完成下列句子。

1 I met somebody ......whose mother writes detective stories...... .
2 I met a man ....
3 I met a woman ....
4 I met somebody ....
5 I met a couple ....
6 I met somebody ....

94.2 根据下列情况，用 **where** 引导的定语从句完成句子。

1 You grew up in a small town. You went back there recently. You tell someone this.
I recently went back to ......the small town where I grew up...... .
2 You're thirsty and you want a drink. You ask a friend where you can get some water.
Is there a shop near here ...... ?
3 You work in a factory. The factory is going to close down next month. You tell a friend.
The ...... is going to close down next month.
4 Sue is staying at a hotel. You want to know the name of the hotel. You ask a friend.
Do you know the name of ...... ?
5 You play football in a park on Sundays. You show a friend the park. You say:
This is the ...... on Sundays.

94.3 用 **who/whom/whose/where** 填空。

1 What's the name of the man ......whose...... car you borrowed?
2 A cemetery is a place ...... people are buried.
3 A pacifist is a person ...... believes that all wars are wrong.
4 An orphan is a child ...... parents are dead.
5 What was the name of the person to ...... you spoke on the phone?
6 The place ...... we spent our holidays was really beautiful.
7 This school is only for children ...... first language is not English.
8 The woman with ...... he fell in love left him after a month.

94.4 根据你自己的情况完成下列句子。

1 I can't meet you on Friday. That's the day ......I'm going away...... .
2 The reason ...... was that the salary was too low.
3 I'll never forget the time ....
4 Do you remember the day ...... ?
5 The reason ...... is that they don't need one.
6 ...... was the year ....

定语从句 (4) —— 非限定性从句 (1)

A 定语从句分为两类。比较下列例句，画线部分为定语从句：

类型1	类型2
▢ The woman who lives next door is a doctor. ▢ Grace works for a company that makes furniture. ▢ We stayed at the hotel (that) you recommended.	▢ My brother Ben, who lives in Hong Kong, is an architect. ▢ Anna told me about her new job, which she's enjoying a lot. ▢ We stayed at the Park Hotel, which a friend of ours recommended.
以上例句中，定语从句表明说话人所指为何人或何物： the woman **who lives next door** 表明是哪个女人。 a company **that makes furniture** 表明是什么样的公司。 the hotel **(that) you recommended** 表明是哪家旅馆。	以上例句中，定语从句不起限定作用，我们已经知道说话人所指为何人或何物，如 My brother Ben，Anna's new job和 the Park Hotel。 这时的定语从句只对被修饰的人或物作补充说明。
从句与被修饰的词之间没有逗号： ▢ We know a lot of people who live in London.	从句与被修饰的词之间用逗号隔开： ▢ My brother Ben, who lives in Hong Kong, is an architect.

B 两种类型的定语从句中都可用 **who** 指代人，用 **which** 指代物。请比较：

类型1	类型2
从句中可用 **that**： ▢ Do you know anyone **who/that** speaks French and Italian? ▢ Grace works for a company **which/that** makes furniture.	从句中不可用 **that**： ▢ John, **who** (而不用 that) speaks French and Italian, works as a tour guide. ▢ Anna told me about her new job, **which** (而不用 that) she's enjoying a lot.
who/which/that 作宾语时可以省略 (参见 Unit 93)： ▢ We stayed at the hotel (that/which) you recommended. ▢ This morning I met somebody (who/that) I hadn't seen for ages.	不能省略 **who** 或 **which**： ▢ We stayed at the Park Hotel, **which** a friend of ours recommended. ▢ This morning I met Chris, **who** I hadn't seen for ages.
这种类型的从句中不常用 **whom** (参见Unit 94B)。	从句中关系代词作宾语指代人时，可以用 **whom** 来表示： ▢ This morning I met Chris, **whom** I hadn't seen for ages.

C **whose** 和 **where** 可以用于两种类型的从句中：

▢ We met some people **whose** car had broken down. ▢ What's the name of the place **where** you went on holiday?	▢ Lisa, **whose** car had broken down, was in a very bad mood. ▢ Kate has just been to Sweden, **where** her daughter lives.

定语从句 (类型 1) ➜ Units 92–94　　定语从句 (类型 2) ➜ Unit 96

Exercises

95.1 用 **who(m)/whose/which/where** 将下列括号内的句子改写为非限定性定语从句，并与前一句合并成一句话。

1 Catherine is very friendly. (She lives next door.)
Catherine, who lives next door, is very friendly.

2 We stayed at the Park Hotel. (A friend of ours recommended it.)
We stayed at the Park Hotel, which a friend of ours recommended.

3 We often go to visit our friends in Cambridge. (It is not far from London.)
We often go to visit our friends in Cambridge ……

4 I went to see the doctor. (She told me I needed to change my diet.)
I went to see ……

5 Steven is one of my closest friends. (I have known him for a very long time.)
Steven ……

6 Lisa is away from home a lot. (Her job involves a lot of travelling.)
Lisa ……

7 The new stadium will be finished next month. (It can hold 90,000 people.)
……

8 Alaska is the largest state in the USA. (My brother lives there.)
……

9 Our teacher was very kind. (I have forgotten her name.)
……

95.2 根据所给情况，用限定性或非限定性定语从句完成下列句子。

1 There's a woman living next door to me. She's a doctor.
The woman who lives next door to me is a doctor.

2 I've got a brother called Ben. He lives in Hong Kong. He's an architect.
My brother Ben, who lives in Hong Kong, is an architect.

3 There was a strike at the factory. It began ten days ago. It is now over.
The strike at the factory ……

4 I was looking for a book this morning. I've found it now.
I've found ……

5 I've had my car for 15 years. It has never broken down.
My car ……

6 A job was advertised. A lot of people applied for it. Few of them had the necessary qualifications.
Few of ……

7 Amy has a son. She showed me a picture of him. He's a police officer.
Amy showed me ……

95.3 指出下列句子是否正确，如有错误请改正。在正确的句子下方写上：对。

1 Anna told me about her new job that she's enjoying very much.
Anna told me about her new job, **which** she's enjoying very much.

2 My office that is on the second floor is very small.
……

3 The office I'm using at the moment is very small.
……

4 Mark's father that used to be in the army now works for a TV company.
……

5 The doctor that examined me couldn't find anything wrong.
……

6 The sun that is one of millions of stars in the universe provides us with heat and light.
……

Unit 96 定语从句 (5) —— 非限定性从句 (2)

A

介词+ **whom/which**

在非限定性定语从句中，介词可以用于 **whom** (指代人) 和 **which** (指代物) 之前，因此可以说 **to whom / with whom / about which / without which** 等：

- Mr Lee, **to whom** I spoke at the meeting, is very interested in our proposal.
- Fortunately we had a good map, **without which** we would have got lost.

在非正式用法中，定语从句中的介词常常位于动词之后。这时，通常用 **who** (而不用 whom) 来指代人：

- This is my friend from Canada, **who** I was telling you **about**.
- Yesterday we visited the City Museum, **which** I'd never been **to** before.

B

all of / most of 等 + **whom/which**

请看下列例句：

Helen has three brothers. All of them are married. (两个句子)

→ Helen has three brothers, **all of** whom are married. (一个句子)

They asked me a lot of questions. I couldn't answer most of them. (两个句子)

→ They asked me a lot of questions, **most of** which I couldn't answer. (一个句子)

同样地，可以说：

none of / neither of / any of / either of
some of / many of / much of / (a) few of
both of / half of / each of / one of / two of 等
} + **whom** (指代人) / + **which** (指代物)

- Martin tried on three jackets, **none of which** fitted him.
- Two men, **neither of whom** I had seen before, came into the office.
- They have three cars, **two of which** they rarely use.
- Sue has a lot of friends, **many of whom** she was at school with.

也可以说 **the cause of which / the name of which** 等：

- The building was destroyed in a fire, **the cause of which** was never established.
- We stayed at a beautiful hotel, **the name of which** I can't remember now.

C

which (而不用 what)

请看下列例句：

Joe got the job. This surprised everybody. (两个句子)

Joe got the job, which surprised everybody. (一个句子)
定语从句

本例中，**which** = the fact that he got the job。在下列句子中，必须用 **which** (而不用 what)：

- Sarah couldn't meet us, **which** was a shame. (而不用 what was a shame)
- The weather was good, **which** we hadn't expected. (而不用 what we hadn't expected)

关于 **what** 的用法，参见 Unit 92D 和 Unit 93D。

all of / most of 等 → Unit 88 **both of 等** → Unit 89 **定语从句 (1)– (4)** → Units 92–95

Exercises

96.1 用介词 + **whom/which** 引导的定语从句完成下列句子。

1 Yesterday we visited the City Museum, which I'd never been to before.
Yesterday we visited the City Museum, *to which I'd never been before* .
2 My brother showed us his new car, which he's very proud of.
My brother showed us his new car, ...
3 This is a picture of our friends Chris and Sam, who we went on holiday with.
This is a picture of our friends Chris and Sam, ...
4 The wedding, which only members of the family were invited to, took place on Friday.
The wedding, ... ,
took place on Friday.

96.2 根据下列所给的信息，用 **all of / most of** 等或 **the … of + whom/which** 的结构造句。

1 All of Helen's brothers are married.
Helen has three brothers, *all of whom are married* .
2 Most of the information we were given was useless.
We were given a lot of information, ...
3 None of the ten people who applied for the job was suitable.
Ten people applied for the job, ...
4 Kate hardly ever uses one of her computers.
Kate has got two computers, ...
5 Mike won £100,000. He gave half of it to his parents.
Mike won £100,000, ...
6 Both of Julia's sisters are lawyers.
Julia has two sisters, ...
7 Jane replied to neither of the emails I sent her.
I sent Jane two emails, ...
8 I went to a party – I knew only a few of the people there.
There were a lot of people at the party, ...
9 The sides of the road we drove along were lined with trees.
We drove along the road, the ....
10 The aim of the company's new business plan is to save money.
The company has a new business plan, ...

96.3 从左右两框中各选一个句子，用 **which** 将它们改写成一句。

1 ~~Laura couldn't come to the party.~~ 2 Jane doesn't have a phone. 3 Alex has passed his exams. 4 Our flight was delayed. 5 Kate offered to let me stay at her house. 6 The street I live in is very noisy at night. 7 Our car has broken down.	This was very kind of her. This means we can't go away tomorrow. This makes it difficult to contact her. This makes it difficult to sleep sometimes. ~~This was a shame.~~ This is good news. This meant we had to wait three hours at the airport.

1 Laura couldn't come to the party, *which was a shame.*
2 Jane ....
3 ....
4 ....
5 ....
6 ....
7 ....

Unit 97 -ing 与 -ed 分句比较 (the woman **talking to Tom**, the boy **injured in the accident**)

A 分句是句子的一部分，一些分句以 **-ing** 或 **-ed** 开头。例如：

Do you know the woman **talking to Tom**?
（**talking to Tom**：-ing 分句）

The boy **injured in the accident** was taken to hospital.
（**injured in the accident**：-ed 分句）

B **-ing** 分句表明某人或某物在特定的时间正在进行的行为：

- Do you know the woman **talking to Tom**? (the woman **is talking** to Tom)
- Police **investigating the crime** are looking for three men. (police **are investigating** the crime)
- Who were those people **waiting outside**? (they **were waiting**)
- I was woken up by a bell **ringing**. (a bell **was ringing**)

-ing 分句也可用来表示一般性的事实。例如：

- The road **connecting the two villages** is very narrow. (the road **connects** the two villages)
- I have a large room **overlooking the garden**. (the room **overlooks** the garden)
- Can you think of the name of a flower **beginning with T**? (the name **begins** with T)

C **-ed** 分句有被动含义：

- The boy **injured in the accident** was taken to hospital. (he **was injured** in the accident)
- George showed me some pictures **painted by his father**. (they **had been painted** by his father)

injured 和 **invited** 为过去分词形式，但也有很多动词的过去分词不以 **-ed** 结尾 (如 **stolen/made/written** 等)：

- The police never found the money **stolen in the robbery**.
- Most of the goods **made in this factory** are exported.

left 也可这样用，意为"剩下的，未被使用的"：

- We've eaten nearly all the chocolates. There are only a few **left**.

D **there is / there was** 等后面常常用-**ing** 或 **-ed** 短语：

- **There were** some children **swimming** in the river.
- **Is there** anybody **waiting**?
- **There was** a big red car **parked** outside the house.

see/hear somebody **doing** something ➜ Unit 67   **-ing 分句** ➜ Unit 68   **there (is)** ➜ Unit 84
不规则过去分词 (**made/stolen** 等) ➜ 附录 1

Exercises

97.1 用 **-ing** 分句将所给的两个句子合并为一句。

1 A bell was ringing. I was woken up by it.
I was woken up by ...a bell ringing... .
2 A man was sitting next to me on the plane. I didn't talk much to him.
I didn't talk much to the ....
3 A taxi was taking us to the airport. It broke down.
The .... broke down.
4 There's a path at the end of this street. The path leads to the river.
At the end of the street there's a ....
5 A factory has just opened in the town. It employs 500 people.
A .... has just opened in the town.
6 The company sent me a brochure. It contained the information I needed.
The company sent me ....

97.2 仿照示例，用 **-ed** 分句将两个句子合并为一句。

1 A boy was injured in the accident. He was taken to hospital.
The boy ...injured in the accident... was taken to hospital.
2 A gate was damaged in the storm. It has now been repaired.
The gate .... has now been repaired.
3 A number of suggestions were made at the meeting. Most of them were not very practical.
Most of the .... were not very practical.
4 Some paintings were stolen from the museum. They haven't been found yet.
The .... haven't been found yet.
5 A man was arrested by the police. What's his name?
What's the name of .... ?

97.3 用下列动词的适当形式填空。

blow call ~~invite~~ live offer read ~~ring~~ sit study work

1 I was woken up by a bell ...ringing... .
2 Some of the people ...invited... to the party can't come.
3 Life must be very unpleasant for people .... near busy airports.
4 A few days after the interview, I received an email .... me the job.
5 Somebody .... Jack phoned while you were out.
6 There was a tree .... down in the storm last night.
7 The waiting room was empty except for a young man .... by the window .... a magazine.
8 Ian has a brother .... in a bank in London and a sister .... economics at university in Manchester.

97.4 根据下列情况和括号内的词语，以 **There is / There was** 等开头造句。

1 That house is empty. (nobody / live / in it) ...There's nobody living in it....
2 The accident wasn't serious. (nobody / injure) ...There was nobody injured....
3 I can hear footsteps. (somebody / come)
There ....
4 The train was full. (a lot of people / travel)
....
5 We were the only guests at the hotel. (nobody else / stay there)
....
6 The piece of paper was blank. (nothing / write / on it)
....
7 The college offers English courses in the evening. (a course / begin / next Monday)
....

以 -ing 和 -ed 结尾的形容词 (boring/bored 等) 比较

A

许多形容词以-ing 或 -ed 结尾，如 **boring** 和 **bored**。请看下列例句：

Jane has been doing the same job for a very long time. Every day she does exactly the same thing again and again. She doesn't enjoy her job any more and would like to do something different.

Jane's job is **boring**.

Jane is **bored** (with her job).

Somebody is **bored** if something (or somebody else) is **boring**. 或 If something is **boring**, it makes you **bored**. 这就表明了两者的区别。因此可以说：

- Jane is **bored** because her job is **boring**.
- Jane's job is **boring**, so Jane is **bored**. (而不用 Jane is boring)

boring 用于形容人时意为 they make other people **bored**。例如：

- George always talks about the same things. He's really **boring**.

B

请比较以-ing 和 -ed 结尾的形容词：

My job is { **boring**. / **interesting**. / **tiring**. / **satisfying**. / **depressing**. (等) }	I'm **bored** with my job. I'm not **interested** in my job any more. I get very **tired** doing my job. I'm not **satisfied** with my job. My job makes me **depressed**. (等)
以 -ing 结尾的形容词表达事物给人的感觉。	以 -ed 结尾的形容词表达人对事物的感觉。

请比较下列例句：

interesting Julia thinks politics is **interesting**. Did you meet anyone **interesting** at the party?	**interested** Julia is **interested** in politics. (而不用 interesting in politics) Are you **interested** in buying a car? I'm trying to sell mine.
surprising It was **surprising** that he passed the exam.	**surprised** Everybody was **surprised** that he passed the exam.
disappointing The movie was **disappointing**. We expected it to be much better.	**disappointed** We were **disappointed** with the movie. We expected it to be much better.
shocking The news was **shocking**.	**shocked** I was **shocked** when I heard the news.

Exercises

98.1 根据所给情况，将括号内的词加上 **-ing** 或 **-ed** 填入句中。

1 The movie wasn't as good as we had expected. (**disappoint**...)
a The movie was disappointing .
b We were disappointed with the movie.

2 Donna teaches young children. It's a very hard job, but she enjoys it. (**exhaust**...)
a She enjoys her job, but it's often ....
b At the end of a day's work, she is often ....

3 It's been raining all day. I hate this weather. (**depress**...)
a This weather is ....
b This weather makes me ....
c It's silly to get .... because of the weather.

4 Clare is going to Mexico next month. She has never been there before. (**excit**...)
a It will be an .... experience for her.
b Going to new places is always ....
c She is really .... about going to Mexico.

98.2 从下列句子画线的部分中选择正确答案。

1 I was ~~disappointing~~ / disappointed with the film. I had expected it to be better. (disappointed *is correct*)
2 Are you interesting / interested in football?
3 The new project sounds exciting / excited. I'm looking forward to working on it.
4 It's embarrassing / embarrassed when you have to ask people for money.
5 Do you easily get embarrassing / embarrassed?
6 I had never expected to get the job. I was really amazing / amazed when I was offered it.
7 She has really learnt very fast. She has made amazing / amazed progress.
8 I didn't find the situation funny. I was not amusing / amused.
9 It was a really terrifying / terrified experience. Everybody was very shocking / shocked.
10 Why do you always look so boring / bored? Is your life really so boring / bored?
11 He's one of the most boring / bored people I've ever met. He never stops talking and he never says anything interesting / interested.

98.3 从方框中选择恰当的词填空。

amusing/amused	**annoying/annoyed**	**boring/bored**
confusing/confused	**disgusting/disgusted**	**exciting/excited**
exhausting/exhausted	**interesting/interested**	**~~surprising~~ /surprised**

1 He works very hard. It's not surprising that he's always tired.
2 I've got nothing to do. I'm ....
3 The teacher's explanation was .... Most of the students didn't understand it.
4 The kitchen hadn't been cleaned for ages. It was really ....
5 I don't visit art galleries very often. I'm not particularly .... in art.
6 There's no need to get .... just because I'm a few minutes late.
7 The lecture was .... I fell asleep.
8 I've been working very hard all day and now I'm ....
9 I'm starting a new job next week. I'm very .... about it.
10 Steve is good at telling funny stories. He can be very ....
11 Helen is a very .... person. She knows a lot, she's travelled a lot and she's done lots of different things.

Unit 99 形容词词序 (a **nice new** house) 动词后面的形容词 (you look **tired**)

A

有时两个或两个以上的形容词可以连用：

- My brother lives in a **nice new** house.
- In the kitchen there was a **beautiful large round wooden** table.

new/large/round/wooden 是事实类形容词，表明物体的大小、颜色、新旧等客观信息。而 **nice/beautiful** 等形容词表明说话人的观点。

表示观点的形容词一般位于事实类形容词之前：

	观点	事实	
a	**nice**	**long**	summer holiday
an	**interesting**	**young**	man
	delicious	**hot**	vegetable soup
a	**beautiful**	**large round wooden**	table

B

有时两个或两个以上的事实类形容词连用，词序排列一般如下所示：

1 大小 → 2 年龄 → 3 颜色 → 4 国籍 → 5 材质 | 名词

a **tall young** man (1 → 2)
big blue eyes (1 → 3)
a **small black plastic** bag (1 → 3 → 5)
a **large wooden** table (1 → 5)
an **old Russian** song (2 → 4)
an **old white cotton** shirt (2 → 3 → 5)

表示大小、长度的形容词 (**big/small/tall/short/long** 等) 一般位于表示形状、宽度的形容词 (**round/fat/thin/slim/wide** 等) 之前：

a **large round** table　　a **tall thin** girl　　a **long narrow** street

两个或两个以上表明颜色的形容词连用时，最后两词之间用 **and** 连接：

a **black and white** dress　　a **red, white and green** flag

其他形容词通常不这样用：

a **long black** dress　(而不用 a long and black dress)

C

be/get/become/seem 后面跟形容词：

- **Be careful**!
- **I'm tired** and **I'm getting hungry**.
- As the film went on, it **became** more and more **boring**.
- Your friend **seems** very **nice**.

形容词也可用于 **look** / **feel** / **sound** / **taste** / **smell** 等动词后，描述某人或某物的外观、触觉、味道等：

- You **look tired**. / I **feel tired**. / She **sounds tired**.
- The dinner **smells good**.
- This tea **tastes** a bit **strange**.

但是谈论某人做某事的方式时，则要用副词 (参见 Units 100–101)：

- Drive **carefully**!　(而不用 Drive careful)
- Susan plays the piano very **well**.　(而不用 plays … very good)

D

可以说 the **first two** days / the **next few** weeks / the **last ten** minutes 等：

- I didn't enjoy the **first two** days of the course.　(而不用 the two first days)
- They'll be away for the **next few** weeks.　(而不用 the few next weeks)

副词 ➔ Units 100–101　　比较级 (cheaper 等) ➔ Units 105–107
最高级 (cheapest 等) ➔ Unit 108

Exercises

99.1 将括号内的形容词放入正确的位置。

1 a beautiful table (wooden / round) .... a beautiful round wooden table
2 an unusual ring (gold) ....
3 an old house (beautiful) ....
4 black gloves (leather) ....
5 an American film (old) ....
6 a long face (thin) ....
7 big clouds (black) ....
8 a sunny day (lovely) ....
9 an ugly dress (yellow) ....
10 a wide avenue (long) ....
11 a lovely restaurant (little) ....
12 a red car (old / little) ....
13 a new sweater (green / nice) ....
14 a metal box (black / small) ....
15 a big cat (fat / black) ....
16 long hair (black / beautiful) ....
17 an old painting (interesting / French) ....
18 an enormous umbrella (red / yellow) ....

99.2 用方框中动词的适当形式和形容词完成下列句子。

feel	**look**	~~**seem**~~
smell	**sound**	**taste**

awful	**fine**	**interesting**
nice	~~**upset**~~	**wet**

1 Helen .... seemed upset .... this morning. Do you know what was wrong?
2 I can't eat this. I've just tried it and it ....
3 I wasn't very well yesterday, but I .... today.
4 What beautiful flowers! They .... too.
5 You .... Have you been out in the rain?
6 James was telling me about his new job. It .... – much better than his old job.

99.3 选择恰当的词填空。

1 This tea tastes a bit .... strange .... (strange / strangely)
2 I always feel .... when the sun is shining. (happy / happily)
3 The children were playing .... in the garden. (happy / happily)
4 The man became .... when the manager of the restaurant asked him to leave. (violent / violently)
5 You look .... ! Are you all right? (terrible / terribly)
6 There's no point in doing a job if you don't do it .... (proper / properly)
7 The soup tastes .... (good / well)
8 Hurry up! You're always so .... (slow / slowly)

99.4 用 **the first … / the next … / the last …** 改写下列短语。

1 the first day and the second day of the course .... the first two days of the course
2 next week and the week after .... the next two weeks
3 yesterday and the day before yesterday ....
4 the first week and the second week of May ....
5 tomorrow and a few days after that ....
6 questions 1, 2 and 3 in the exam ....
7 next year and the year after ....
8 the last day of our holiday and the two days before that ....

→ 补充练习 31 (第320页)

Unit 100 形容词与副词比较 (1) (quick/quickly)

A

请看下列例句：

- Our holiday was too short – the time passed very **quickly**.
- Two people were **seriously** injured in the accident.

quickly 和 **seriously** 为副词。很多副词由形容词 + **-ly** 构成：

形容词：	quick	serious	careful	quiet	heavy	bad
副词：	**quickly**	**seriously**	**carefully**	**quietly**	**heavily**	**badly**

拼写法参见附录 6。

并不是所有以 **-ly** 结尾的词都是副词，一些形容词词尾也是 **-ly**。例如：

friendly **lively** **elderly** **lonely** **silly** **lovely**

B

是形容词还是副词？

形容词 (**quick/careful** 等) 修饰名词 (人或物)，位于名词之前：

- Sam is a **careful driver**. (而不用 a carefully driver)
- We didn't go out because of the **heavy rain**.

副词 (**quickly/carefully** 等) 修饰动词，表示行为或动作的方式：

- Sam **drove carefully** along the narrow road. (而不用 drove careful)
- We didn't go out because it was **raining heavily**. (而不用 raining heavy)

请比较：

- She speaks **perfect English**.
  形容词 + 名词
- She **speaks English perfectly**.
  动词 + 宾语 + 副词

动词 **be** 和 **look/feel/sound** 等后面也可用形容词。
请比较：

- Please **be quiet**.
- I was disappointed that my exam results **were** so **bad**.
- Why do you always **look** so **serious**?
- I **feel happy**.

- Please **speak quietly**.
- I was unhappy that I **did** so **badly** in the exam. (而不用 did so bad)
- Why do you never **take** me **seriously**?
- The children were **playing happily**.

C

副词也可以用于形容词或其他副词之前。例如：

reasonably cheap	(副词 + 形容词)
terribly sorry	(副词 + 形容词)
incredibly quickly	(副词 + 副词)

- It's a **reasonably cheap** restaurant and the food is **extremely good**.
- I'm **terribly sorry**. I didn't mean to push you. (而不用 terrible sorry)
- Maria learns languages **incredibly quickly**.
- The exam was **surprisingly easy**.

副词也可以用于过去分词 (**injured/organised/written** 等) 之前：

- Two people were **seriously injured** in the accident. (而不用 serious injured)
- The meeting was **badly organised**.

be/look/feel 等动词后的形容词 ➜ Unit 99C 形容词与副词比较 (2) ➜ Unit 101

Exercises

100.1 根据字母提示，在下列句中填入副词。

1 We didn't go out because it was raining he*avily*........ .
2 Our team lost the game because we played very ba.................................... .
3 I didn't have any problems finding a place to live. I found a flat quite ea.................................... .
4 We had to wait for a long time, but we didn't complain. We waited pat.................................... .
5 Nobody knew Steve was coming to see us. He arrived unex.................................... .
6 Mike keeps fit by playing tennis reg.................................... .
7 I don't speak French very well, but I can understand per.................................... if people speak sl.................................... and cl.................................... .

100.2 选择恰当的词填空。

1 Two people were ......*seriously*...... injured in the accident. (serious / seriously)
2 The driver of the car had ......*serious*...... injuries. (serious / seriously)
3 I think you behaved very .... (selfish / selfishly)
4 Tanya is .... upset about losing her job. (terrible / terribly)
5 There was a .... change in the weather. (sudden / suddenly)
6 Everybody at the carnival was .... dressed. (colourful / colourfully)
7 Linda usually wears .... clothes. (colourful / colourfully)
8 Liz fell and hurt herself really .... (bad / badly)
9 Joe says he didn't do well at school because he was .... taught. (bad / badly)
10 Don't go up that ladder. It doesn't look .... (safe / safely)

100.3 从方框中选择恰当的词填空。

careful(ly)	**complete(ly)**	**continuous(ly)**	**financial(ly)**	**fluent(ly)**
happy/happily	**nervous(ly)**	**perfect(ly)**	~~**quick(ly)**~~	**special(ly)**

1 Our holiday was too short. The time passed very ......*quickly*...... .
2 Steve doesn't take risks when he's driving. He's always ....
3 Sue works .... She never seems to stop.
4 Rachel and Patrick are very .... married.
5 Maria's English is very .... although she makes quite a lot of mistakes.
6 I cooked this meal .... for you, so I hope you like it.
7 Everything was very quiet. There was .... silence.
8 I tried on the shoes and they fitted me ....
9 Do you usually feel .... before exams?
10 I'd like to buy a car, but it's .... impossible for me at the moment.

100.4 从下列两个方框中各选一个词完成句子。

absolutely	**badly**	**completely**
~~**reasonably**~~	**seriously**	**slightly**
unnecessarily	**unusually**	

changed	~~**cheap**~~	**damaged**
enormous	**ill**	**long**
planned	**quiet**	

1 I thought the restaurant would be expensive, but it was ......*reasonably cheap*...... .
2 Will's mother is .... in hospital.
3 What a big house! It's ....
4 It wasn't a serious accident. The car was only ....
5 The children are normally very lively, but they're .... today.
6 When I returned home after 20 years, everything had ....
7 The movie was .... It could have been much shorter.
8 A lot went wrong during our holiday because it was ....

→ 补充练习 31（第320页）

Unit 101 形容词与副词比较 (2) (well/fast/late，hard/hardly)

A

good/well

good 是形容词，**well** 是副词：

- Your English is **good**. 或 You **speak** English **well**.
- Susan is a **good** pianist. 或 Susan **plays** the piano **well**.

well (而不用 good) 可与过去分词连用 (**dressed/known** 等)：

well-dressed **well-known** **well-educated** **well-paid**

- Gary's father is a **well-known** writer.

well 也可以用作形容词，意思是"健康的"：

- 'How are you today?' 'I'm very **well**, thanks.'

B

fast/hard/late

这些词既可以作形容词也可以作副词：

形容词	副词
Darren is a very **fast runner**.	Darren can **run** very **fast**.
Kate is a **hard worker**.	Kate **works hard**. (而不用 works hardly)
I was **late**.	I **got up late** this morning.

lately 意为"最近"：

- Have you seen Tom **lately**?

C

hardly

hardly 意为"几乎没有，几乎不"。请看下列例句：

- Sarah wasn't very friendly at the party. She **hardly** spoke to me. (= she spoke to me very little, almost not at all)
- We've only met once or twice. We **hardly** know each other.

hard 和 **hardly** 不同。请比较：

- He tried **hard** to find a job, but he had no luck. (= he tried a lot, with a lot of effort)
- I'm not surprised he didn't find a job. He **hardly** tried. (= he tried very little)

I **can hardly** do something 表示某事非常困难，几乎不可能做到：

- Your writing is terrible. I **can hardly** read it. (= it is almost impossible to read it)
- My leg was hurting. I **could hardly** walk.

D

可以用 **hardly** + **any/anybody/anyone/anything/anywhere**：

- A: How much money have we got?
  B: **Hardly any**. (= very little, almost none)
- These two cameras are very similar. There's **hardly any** difference between them.
- The exam results were very bad. **Hardly anybody** in our class passed. (= very few students passed)

注意 **hardly** 的位置：

- She said **hardly anything**. 或 She **hardly** said **anything**.
- We've got **hardly any** money. 或 We've **hardly** got **any** money.

hardly ever 表示"几乎从不"：

- I'm nearly always at home in the evenings. I **hardly ever** go out.

hardly 也可表示"当然不"。例如：

- It's **hardly surprising** that you're tired. You haven't slept for three days. (= it's certainly not surprising)
- The situation is serious, but it's **hardly a crisis**. (= it's certainly not a crisis)

动词后跟形容词 (you look tired 等) ➜ Unit 99C　　形容词与副词比较 (1) ➜ Unit 100

Exercises

101.1 用 **good** 或 **well** 填空。

1 I play tennis but I'm not very ......good...... .
2 Your exam results were very ....
3 You did .... in your exams.
4 The weather was .... while we were away.
5 I didn't sleep .... last night.
6 Lucy speaks German .... She's .... at languages.
7 Our new business isn't doing very .... at the moment.
8 I like your hat. It looks .... on you.
9 I've met her a few times, but I don't know her ....

101.2 用 **well** + 下列过去分词的结构完成句子。

~~behaved~~	dressed	informed	kept	known	paid	written

1 The children were very good. They were ......well-behaved...... .
2 I'm surprised you haven't heard of her. She is quite ....
3 Our neighbours' garden is neat and tidy. It is very ....
4 I enjoyed the book you lent me. It's a great story and it's very ....
5 Tanya knows a lot about many things. She is very ....
6 Mark's clothes are always smart. He is always ....
7 Jane has a lot of responsibility in her job, but she isn't very ....

101.3 句中画线部分是否正确？如有错误，请改正。

1 I'm tired because I've been working <u>hard</u>. ......对......
2 I tried <u>hard</u> to remember her name, but I couldn't. ....
3 This coat is practically unused. I've <u>hardly</u> worn it. ....
4 Laura is a good tennis player. She hits the ball <u>hardly</u>. ....
5 Don't walk so <u>fast</u>! I can't keep up with you. ....
6 I had plenty of time, so I was walking <u>slow</u>. ....

101.4 用 **hardly** 和下列动词的适当形式完成句子。

change	hear	~~know~~	recognise	say	sleep	speak

1 Scott and Tracy have only met once before. They ......hardly know...... each other.
2 You're speaking very quietly. I can .... you.
3 I'm very tired this morning. I .... last night.
4 We were so shocked when we heard the news, we could ....
5 Kate was very quiet this evening. She .... a word.
6 You look the same now as you looked 15 years ago. You've ....
7 I met David a few days ago. I hadn't seen him for a long time and he looks very different now. I .... him.

101.5 用 **hardly + any/anybody/anything/anywhere/ever** 的结构完成下列句子。

1 I'll have to go shopping. There's ......hardly anything...... to eat.
2 It was a very warm day and there was .... wind.
3 'Do you know much about computers?' 'No, ...'
4 The hotel was almost empty. There was .... staying there.
5 I listen to the radio a lot, but I .... watch television.
6 Our new boss is not very popular. .... likes her.
7 It was very crowded in the room. There was .... to sit.
8 We used to be good friends, but we .... see each other now.
9 It was nice driving this morning. There was .... traffic.
10 I hate this town. There's .... to do and .... to go.

→ 补充练习 31（第320页）

Unit 102

so 与 such 比较

A

请比较 so 与 such：

可以用 so + 形容词/副词： **so stupid** **so quick** **so nice** **so quickly** I didn't like the book. The story was **so stupid**. I like Liz and Joe. They are **so nice**.	可以用 such + 名词： **such a story** **such people** 可以用 such + 形容词 + 名词： **such** a stupid **story** **such** nice **people** I didn't like the book. It was **such** a stupid **story**. (而不用 a so stupid story) I like Liz and Joe. They are **such nice people**. (而不用 so nice people) 注意要说 **such a** ... (而不用 a such)： **such a** big **dog** (而不用 a such big dog)

B

so 和 **such** 用于加强形容词（或副词）的词义：

It's a beautiful day, isn't it? It's **so warm**. (= really warm) It's difficult to understand him because he talks **so quietly**. 可以用 **so ... that**： The book was **so good that** I couldn't put it down. I was **so tired that** I fell asleep in the armchair. 在这些例句中通常可以省略 **that**： I was **so tired** I fell asleep.	It was a great holiday. We had **such a good time**. (= a really good time) You always think good things are going to happen. You're **such an optimist**. 可以用 **such ... that**： It was **such a good book that** I couldn't put it down. It was **such nice weather that** we spent the whole day on the beach. 在这些例句中通常可以省略 **that**： It was **such nice weather** we spent ...

C

so 和 **such** 还可以用于表示"这么"：

Somebody told me the house was built 100 years ago. I didn't realise it was **so old**. (= as old as it is) I'm tired because I got up at six. I don't usually get up **so early**. I expected the weather to be cooler. I'm surprised it is **so warm**.	I didn't realise it was **such an old house**. You know it's not true. How can you say **such a thing**? 注意 **no such** ... 这种表达： You won't find the word 'blid' in the dictionary. There's **no such word**. (= this word does not exist)

D

请比较：

so long I haven't seen her for **so long** I've forgotten what she looks like.	**such a long time** I haven't seen her for **such a long time**. (而不用 so long time)
so far I didn't know it was **so far**.	**such a long way** I didn't know it was **such a long way**.
so much, **so many** I'm sorry I'm late – there was **so much** traffic.	**such a lot (of)** I'm sorry I'm late – there was **such a lot of** traffic.

not so ... as ➜ Unit 107A **such as** ➜ Unit 117A

Exercises

102.1 用 **so**，**such** 或 **such a** 填空。

1 It's difficult to understand him because he speaks ~~so~~ quietly.
2 I like Liz and Joe. They're ~~such~~ nice people.
3 It was a great holiday. We had ~~such a~~ good time.
4 I was surprised that he looked .... well after his recent illness.
5 Everything is .... expensive these days, isn't it?
6 The weather is beautiful, isn't it? I didn't expect it to be .... nice day.
7 I think she works too hard. She looks .... tired all the time.
8 He always looks good. He wears .... nice clothes.
9 It was .... boring movie that I fell asleep while I was watching it.
10 I couldn't believe the news. It was .... shock.
11 I have to go. I didn't realise it was .... late.
12 The food at the hotel was .... awful. I've never eaten .... awful food.
13 They've got .... much money they don't know what to do with it.
14 I didn't realise you lived .... long way from the city centre.
15 The party was really great. It was .... shame you couldn't come.

102.2 将下列句子配对，然后用 **so** 或 **such** 把它们改写成一句。

1 ~~She worked hard.~~	You could hear it from miles away.
2 ~~It was a beautiful day.~~	You would think it was her native language.
3 I was tired.	We spent the whole day indoors.
4 We had a good time on holiday.	~~She made herself ill.~~
5 She speaks English well.	I couldn't keep my eyes open.
6 I've got a lot to do.	I didn't eat anything else for the rest of the day.
7 The music was loud.	~~We decided to go to the beach.~~
8 I had a big breakfast.	I didn't know what to say.
9 It was horrible weather.	I don't know where to begin.
10 I was surprised.	We didn't want to come home.

1 She worked so hard she made herself ill.
2 It was such a beautiful day we decided to go to the beach.
3 I was ....
4 ....
5 ....
6 ....
7 ....
8 ....
9 ....
10 ....

102.3 根据你自己的想法，完成下列句子。

1 a We enjoyed our holiday. It was so relaxing.
b We enjoyed our holiday. We had such a good time.
2 a I like Catherine. She's so ....
b I like Catherine. She's such ....
3 a I like New York. It's so ....
b I like New York. It's such ....
4 a I wouldn't like to be a teacher. It's so ....
b I wouldn't like to be a teacher. It's such ....
5 a It's great to see you again! I haven't seen you for so ....
b It's great to see you again! I haven't seen you for such ....

Unit 103

enough 与 too 比较

A

enough 用于形容词和副词之后：

- I can't run very far. I'm not **fit enough**. (而不用 enough fit)
- Let's go. We've waited **long enough**.
- I can let you know tomorrow. Is that **soon enough**?

请比较 **too** … 和 **not** … **enough**：

- You never stop working. You work **too hard**. (= more than is necessary)
- You're lazy. You **don't** work **hard enough**. (= less than is necessary)

B

enough 一般用于名词之前：

- I can't run very far. I don't have **enough energy**. (而不用 energy enough)
- Do we have **enough petrol**, or should we stop and get some?
- We've got **enough money**. We don't need any more.
- Some of us had to sit on the floor because there weren't **enough chairs**.

enough 还可以单独使用 (不加名词)：

- We don't need to stop for petrol. We've got **enough**.

请比较 **too much/many** 和 **enough**：

- There's **too much furniture** in this room. There's not **enough space**.
- There were **too many people** and not **enough chairs**.

C

可以说 **enough/too** … **for** somebody/something：

- Does Joe have enough experience **for the job**?
- This bag isn't big enough **for all my clothes**.
- That shirt is too small **for you**. You need a larger size.

可以说 **enough/too** … **to** do something。例如：

- Does Joe have enough experience **to do the job**? (而不用 for doing)
- We don't have enough money **to go on holiday right now**.
- She's not old enough **to have a driving licence**.
  She's too young **to have a driving licence**.
- Let's get a taxi. It's too far **to walk home from here**.

下面的例句同时含有 **for** … 和 **to** … 的结构：

- The bridge is just wide enough **for two cars to pass each other**.

D

可以说：

	The food was very hot. We couldn't eat **it**.
或	The food was so hot that we couldn't eat **it**.
或	The food was **too** hot **to eat**. (不加 it)

再看一些例句：

- These boxes are **too heavy to carry**. (而不用 to carry them)
- The wallet was **too big to put** in my pocket. (而不用 to put it)
- This chair isn't **strong enough to stand on**. (而不用 to stand on it)

to … 与 **for** … (表目的) 比较 ➜ Unit 64　　形容词 + **to** … (**difficult to understand** 等) ➜ Unit 65

Exercises

103.1 用 **enough** 和下列形容词或名词完成句子。

big ~~**chairs**~~ **cups** ~~**fit**~~ **milk** **money** **room** **time** **warm** **well**

1 I can't run very far. I'm not fit enough .
2 Some of us had to sit on the floor because there weren't enough chairs .
3 I'd like to buy a car, but I don't have .... at the moment.
4 Do you have .... in your coffee or would you like some more?
5 Are you .... ? Or shall I switch on the heating?
6 It's only a small car. There isn't .... for all of us.
7 Steve didn't feel .... to go to work this morning.
8 I enjoyed my trip to Paris, but there wasn't .... to do everything I wanted.
9 Try this jacket on and see if it's .... for you.
10 There weren't .... for everybody to have coffee at the same time.

103.2 用 **too** 或 **enough** 及括号内的词语回答下列问题。

1	Does she have a driving licence?	(old)	No, she's not old enough to have a driving licence.
2	I need to talk to you about something.	(busy)	Well, I'm afraid I'm .... to you now.
3	Let's go to the cinema.	(late)	No, it's .... to the cinema.
4	Why don't we sit outside?	(warm)	It's not .... outside.
5	Would you like to be a politician?	(shy)	No, I'm .... a politician.
6	Would you like to be a teacher?	(patience)	No, I don't have .... a teacher.
7	Did you hear what he was saying?	(far away)	No, we were .... what he was saying.
8	Can he read a newspaper in English?	(English)	No, he doesn't know .... a newspaper.

103.3 用 **too** 或 **enough** 将两个句子改写成一句。

1 We couldn't carry the boxes. They were too heavy.
The boxes were too heavy to carry.
2 I can't drink this coffee. It's too hot.
This coffee is ....
3 Nobody could move the piano. It was too heavy.
The piano ....
4 Don't eat these apples. They're not ripe enough.
These apples ....
5 I can't explain the situation. It is too complicated.
The situation ....
6 We couldn't climb over the wall. It was too high.
The wall ....
7 Three people can't sit on this sofa. It isn't big enough.
This sofa ....
8 You can't see some things without a microscope. They are too small.
Some ....

quite，pretty，rather 与 fairly 比较

A

可以用 **quite/pretty/rather/fairly** + 形容词或副词。因此可以说：

- It's **quite cold**. It's **pretty cold**. It's **rather cold**. It's **fairly cold**.

quite/pretty/rather/fairly 表示的程度比"很……"弱，但比"有点……"强。

B

quite 和 **pretty** 意思相近：

- I'm surprised you haven't heard of her. She's **quite famous / pretty famous**. (= less than 'very famous', but more than 'a little famous')
- Anna lives **quite near** me, so we see each other **pretty often**.

pretty 作为非正式用语主要用于口语中。

quite 置于 **a/an** 之前：

- We live in **quite an old house**. (而不用 a quite old house)

请比较：

- Sarah has **quite a** good job.
  Sarah has **a pretty** good job.

quite (而不用 **pretty**) 还可以用于以下用法中：

quite a/an + 名词 (不加形容词)：

- I didn't expect to see them. It was **quite a surprise**. (= quite a big surprise)

quite a lot (of …)：

- There were **quite a lot of** people at the meeting.

quite + 动词 (特别是 **like** 和 **enjoy**)：

- I **quite like** tennis, but it's not my favourite sport.

C

rather 的意思与 **quite** 和 **pretty** 相近，常用来表示否定观点 (认为这样不好)：

- The weather isn't so good. It's **rather cloudy**.
- Paul is **rather shy**. He doesn't talk very much.

这些例句中的 **rather** 也可用 **quite** 和 **pretty** 代替。

rather 用于表示肯定观点时 (后接 **good/nice** 等)，意为"异常地"或"出奇地"：

- These oranges are **rather good**. Where did you get them?

D

fairly 表示的程度比 **quite/rather/pretty** 弱。例如，**fairly good** 意为"还好，尚可"：

- My room is **fairly big**, but I'd prefer a bigger one.
- We see each other **fairly often**, but not as often as we used to.

E

quite 还意为"完全地"：

- 'Are you sure?' 'Yes, **quite sure**.' (= completely sure)

quite 特别是与下列形容词连用时表示"完全地"：

sure	**right**	**true**	**clear**	**different**	**incredible**	**amazing**
certain	**wrong**	**safe**	**obvious**	**unnecessary**	**extraordinary**	**impossible**

- She was **quite different** from what I expected. (= completely different)
- Everything they said was **quite true**. (= completely true)

quite (完全地) 还可以与一些动词连用。例如：

- I **quite agree** with you. (= I completely agree)

not quite 表示"不完全"：

- They **haven't quite finished** eating yet.
- I **don't quite understand** what you mean.
- 'Are you ready yet?' '**Not quite**.' (= not completely)

Exercises

104.1 用 **quite** + 下列词语完成句子。

~~famous~~	good	hungry	late	noisy	often	old	surprised

1 I'm surprised you haven't heard of her. She's quite famous .
2 I'm .... Is there anything to eat?
3 'How were the pictures you took?' '........ . Better than usual.'
4 I go to the cinema .... – maybe once a month.
5 We live near a very busy road, so it's often ....
6 I didn't expect Laura to contact me. I was .... when she phoned.
7 I went to bed .... last night, so I'm a bit tired this morning.
8 I don't know exactly when these houses were built, but they're ....

104.2 用括号内的词语完成下列句子。

1 The weather was better than we had expected.
It was quite a nice day (a / nice / quite / day).
2 Tom likes to sing.
He has .... (voice / quite / good /a).
3 The bus stop wasn't very near the hotel.
We had to walk .... (quite / way / a / long).
4 It's not so warm today.
There's .... (a / wind / cold / pretty).
5 The journey took longer than I expected.
There was .... (lot / traffic / a / of / quite).
6 I'm tired.
I've had .... (pretty / day / a / busy).

104.3 根据你自己的想法，用 **rather** + 形容词完成下列句子。

1 The weather isn't so good. It's rather cloudy .
2 I enjoyed the film, but it was ....
3 The hotel we stayed at wasn't very good. I was ....
4 I think it's .... that Chris went away without telling anybody.
5 Lucy doesn't like having to wait. Sometimes she's ....

104.4 在下列句子中，**quite** 有什么含义？在正确处画✓。

	比"很……"弱，比"有点……"强	完全地
1 It's quite cold. You'd better wear your coat.	✓	
2 'Are you sure?' 'Yes, quite sure.'		✓
3 Anna's English is quite good.		
4 I couldn't believe it. It was quite incredible.		
5 My bedroom is quite big.		
6 I'm quite tired. I think I'll go to bed.		
7 I quite agree with you.		

104.5 用 **quite** 及下列形容词完成句子。

different	impossible	right	safe	sure	~~true~~	unnecessary

1 I didn't believe her at first, but in fact what she said was quite true .
2 You won't fall. The ladder is ....
3 I'm afraid I can't do what you ask. It's ....
4 I couldn't agree with you more. You are ....
5 You can't compare the two things. They are ....
6 You needn't have done that. It was ....
7 I think I saw them go out, but I'm not ....

比较级 (1) (cheaper，more expensive 等)

A

请看下列例句：

How shall we travel? Shall we drive or go by train?

Let's drive. It's **cheaper**.
Don't go by train. It's **more expensive**.

cheaper 和 **more expensive** 都是比较级的形式。

比较级后面可用 **than** (参见 Unit 107)：

- It's **cheaper** to drive **than** go by train.
- Going by train is **more expensive than** driving.

B

比较级的构成方式是将原级变成以 **-er** 结尾或在原级前面加 **more**：

单音节的词变成以**-er** 结尾：

cheap → cheaper　　**fast** → faster
large → larger　　**thin** → thinner

以**-y** 结尾的双音节词也变成以**-er** 结尾 (**-y** → **ier**)：

lucky → luck**ier**　　early → earl**ier**
easy → eas**ier**　　pretty → prett**ier**

拼写法参见附录6。

双音节或多音节的词在原级前面加 **more**：

more serious　　**more often**
more expensive　　**more comfortable**

以 **-ly** 结尾的副词在原级前面加 **more**：

more slowly　　**more seriously**
more easily　　**more quietly**

请比较下列例句：

- You're **older** than me.
- The exam was quite easy – **easier** than I expected.
- Can you walk a bit **faster**?
- I'd like to have a **bigger** car.
- Last night I went to bed **earlier** than usual.

- You're **more patient** than me.
- The exam was quite difficult – **more difficult** than I expected.
- Can you walk a bit **more slowly**?
- I'd like to have a **more reliable** car.
- I don't play tennis much these days. I used to play **more often**.

有些双音节形容词的比较级既可以以 **-er** 结尾，也可以在原级前面加 **more**：

clever　　**narrow**　　**quiet**　　**shallow**　　**simple**

- It's too noisy here. Can we go somewhere **quieter** / **more quiet**?

C

有些形容词或副词的比较级形式是不规则的：

good/well → **better**

- The garden looks **better** since you tidied it up.
- I know him **well** – probably **better** than anybody else knows him.

bad/badly → **worse**

- 'How's your headache? Better?'　'No, it's **worse**.'
- He did very badly in the exam – **worse** than expected.

far → **further** (或 **farther**)

- It's a long walk from here to the park – **further** than I thought.　(或 **farther** than)

further (而不用 farther) 也可以用来表示"更多的"或"附加的"：

- Let me know if you hear any **further** news.　(= any more news)

比较级 (2)，(3) → **Units 106–107**　　**最高级 (cheapest / most expensive 等)** → **Unit 108**

Exercises

105.1 用比较级形式 (**older / more important** 等) 完成下列句子。

1 It's too noisy here. Can we go somewhere *quieter* ?
2 This coffee is very weak. I like it ....
3 The hotel was surprisingly big. I expected it to be ....
4 The hotel was surprisingly cheap. I expected it to be ....
5 The weather is too cold here. I'd like to live somewhere ....
6 My job is a bit boring sometimes. I'd like to do something ....
7 It's a shame you live so far away. I wish you lived ....
8 I was surprised how easy it was to get a job. I thought it would be ....
9 Your work isn't very good. I'm sure you can do ....
10 Don't worry. The situation isn't so bad. It could be ....
11 I was surprised we got here so quickly. I expected the trip to take ....
12 You're talking very loudly. Can you speak .... ?
13 You hardly ever call me. Why don't you call me .... ?
14 You're standing too near the camera. Can you move a bit .... away?
15 You were a little depressed yesterday, but you look .... today.

105.2 用方框中词语的比较级形式完成下列句子，必要时加上 **than**。

big	**crowded**	~~**early**~~	**easily**	**high**	**important**
interested	**peaceful**	~~**reliable**~~	**serious**	**simple**	**thin**

1 I was feeling tired last night, so I went to bed *earlier than* usual.
2 I'd like to have a *more reliable* car. The one I have keeps breaking down.
3 Unfortunately her illness was .... we thought at first.
4 You look .... Have you lost weight?
5 I want a .... apartment. We don't have enough space here.
6 He doesn't study very hard. He's .... in having a good time.
7 Health and happiness are .... money.
8 The instructions were very complicated. They could have been ....
9 There were a lot of people on the bus. It was .... usual.
10 I like living in the country. It's .... living in a town.
11 You'll find your way around the town .... if you have a good map.
12 In some parts of the country, prices are .... in others.

105.3 根据所给情况，用比较级形式 (**-er** 或 **more ...**) 完成下列句子。

1 Yesterday the temperature was six degrees. Today it's only three degrees.
It's *colder today than* it was yesterday.

2 The journey takes four hours by car and five hours by train.
It takes .... by car.

3 Dan and I went for a run. I ran ten kilometres. Dan stopped after eight kilometres.
I ran .... Dan.

4 Chris and Joe both did badly in the test. Chris got 30%, but Joe only got 25%.
Joe did .... Chris in the test.

5 I expected my friends to arrive at about 4 o'clock. In fact they arrived at 2.30.
My friends .... I expected.

6 You can go by bus or by train. The buses run every 30 minutes. The trains run every hour.
The buses .... the trains.

7 We were very busy in the office today. We're not usually so busy.
We .... usual in the office today.

Unit 106

比较级 (2) (much better / any better / better and better / the sooner the better)

A

在比较级之前可以使用：

much **a lot** **far** (= a lot) **a bit** **a little** **slightly** (= a little)

- Let's go by car. It's **much cheaper**. (或 **a lot cheaper**)
- 'How do you feel now?' '**Much better**, thanks.'
- Don't go by train. It's **a lot more expensive**. (或 **much more expensive**)
- Could you speak **a bit more slowly**? (或 **a little more slowly**)
- This bag is **slightly heavier** than the other one.
- Her illness was **far more serious** than we thought at first. (或 **much more serious** / **a lot more serious**)

B

可以用 **any** 和 **no** + 比较级 (**any longer** / **no bigger** 等)：

- I've waited long enough. I'm not waiting **any longer**. (= not even a little longer)
- We expected their apartment to be very big, but it's **no bigger** than ours. 或 … it is**n't any bigger** than ours. (= not even a little bigger)
- How do you feel now? Do you feel **any better**?
- This hotel is better than the other one, and it's **no more expensive**.

C

better and better / **more and more** 等

比较级的叠加使用 (**better and better** 等) 可用来表示持续的变化：

- Your English is improving. It's getting **better and better**.
- The city has grown fast in recent years. It's got **bigger and bigger**.
- As I listened to his story, I became **more and more convinced** that he was lying.
- These days **more and more people** are learning English.

D

the … the …

可以说 **the** (sooner/bigger/more etc.) **the better**：

- 'What time shall we leave?' '**The sooner the better**.' (= as soon as possible)
- A: What sort of box do you want? A big one?
  B: Yes, **the bigger the better**. (= as big as possible)
- When you're travelling, **the less luggage** you have **the better**.

还可以用 **the** + 比较级 + **the** + 比较级这个结构表示"越……就越……"：

- **The warmer** the weather, **the better** I feel. (= if the weather is warmer, I feel better)
- **The sooner** we leave, **the earlier** we will arrive.
- **The younger** you are, **the easier** it is to learn.
- **The more expensive** the hotel, **the better** the service.
- **The more** electricity you use, **the higher** your bill will be.
- **The more** I thought about the plan, **the less** I liked it.

E

older 与 **elder** 比较

old 的比较级形式是 **older**：

- David looks **older** than he really is.

谈论家人时可以用 **elder** (或 **older**)，如 (**my/your** etc.) **elder sister/brother/daughter/son**：

- **My elder sister** is a TV producer. (或 My **older** sister …)

可以说 my **elder sister**，但不能说 somebody is elder：

- My sister is **older** than me. (而不用 elder than me)

any/no ➜ **Unit 86** **比较级 (1)，(3)** ➜ **Units 105，107** **eldest** ➜ **Unit 108C**
even + **比较级** ➜ **Unit 112C**

Exercises

106.1 根据括号内的词，用 **much / a bit** 等 + 比较级形式完成下列句子，必要时加上 **than**。

1 Her illness was *much more serious than* we thought at first. (much / serious)
2 This bag is too small. I need something ....(much / big)
3 I liked the museum. It was .... I expected.(much / interesting)
4 It was very hot yesterday. Today it's .... (a bit / cool)
5 I'm afraid the problem is .... it seems.(far / complicated)
6 You're driving too fast. Can you drive .... ? (a bit / slowly)
7 It's .... to learn a language in a country where it is spoken.(a lot / easy)
8 I thought she was younger than me, but in fact she's .... (slightly / old)

106.2 用 **any/no** + 比较级形式完成下列句子，必要时加上 **than**。

1 I've waited long enough. I'm not waiting *any longer* .
2 I'm sorry I'm a bit late, but I couldn't get here ....
3 This shop isn't expensive. The prices are .... anywhere else.
4 I need to stop for a rest. I can't walk ....
5 The traffic isn't particularly bad today. It's .... usual.

106.3 用 **C** 节中的结构 (**… and …**) 完成下列句子。

1 It's getting *more and more difficult* to find a job. (difficult)
2 That hole in your sweater is getting .... (big)
3 My bags seemed to get .... as I carried them. (heavy)
4 As I waited for my interview, I became .... (nervous)
5 As the day went on, the weather got .... (bad)
6 Health care is becoming .... (expensive)
7 Since Anna went to Canada, her English has got .... (good)
8 As the conversation went on, Paul became .... (talkative)

106.4 用 **D** 节中的结构 (**the … the …**)完成下列句子。

1 I like warm weather.
The warmer the weather, *the better I feel* . (feel)
2 I didn't really like him when we first met.
But the more I got to know him, ...(like)
3 If you're in business, you want to make a profit.
The more goods you sell, ...(profit)
4 It's hard to concentrate when you're tired.
The more tired you are, ... (hard)
5 Kate had to wait a very long time.
The longer she had to wait, ... (impatient / become)

106.5 从下列右框中选择恰当的单词填空。

1 I like to travel light. The *less* luggage, the better.
2 The problem is getting .... and more serious.
3 The more time I have, the .... it takes me to do things.
4 I'm walking as fast as I can. I can't walk .... faster.
5 The higher your income, ... more tax you have to pay.
6 I'm surprised Anna is only 25. I thought she was ....
7 Jane's .... sister is a nurse.
8 I was a little late. The journey took .... longer than I expected.
9 We have a lot to discuss. We need to start the meeting .... later than 9.30.
10 Don't tell him anything. The .... he knows, the ....

any
better
elder
~~**less**~~
less
longer
more
no
older
slightly
the

比较级 (3) (as … as / than)

A

请看下列例句：

Sarah, Joe and David are all very rich. Sarah has \$20 million, Joe has \$15 million and David has \$10 million. So:

Joe is rich.

He is **richer than** David.

But he **isn't as rich as** Sarah.
(= Sarah is **richer than** he is)

再看一些含 **not as … (as)** 结构的例句：

- Jack **isn't as old as** he looks. (= he looks **older than** he is)
- The town centre **wasn't as crowded as** usual. (= it is usually **more crowded**)
- Lisa **didn't** do **as well** in the exam **as** she had hoped. (= she had hoped to do **better**)
- The weather is better today. It's **not as cold**. (= yesterday was **colder than** today)
- I **don't** know **as many** people **as** you do. (= you know **more** people **than** me)
- 'How much did it cost? Fifty pounds?' 'No, **not as much as** that.' (= **less than** fifty pounds)

还可以说 **not so … (as)**：

- It's not warm, but it is**n't so** cold **as** yesterday. (= it isn't **as** cold **as** …)

less … than 与 **not as … as** 表示的意义相似：

- I spent **less** money **than** you. (= I **didn't** spend **as** much money **as** you)
- The city centre was **less** crowded **than** usual. (= it **wasn't as** crowded **as** usual)
- I play tennis **less than** I used to. (= I **don't** play **as** much **as** I used to)

B

as … as (而不用 so … as) 可以用于肯定句和疑问句中：

- I'm sorry I'm late. I got here **as fast as** I could.
- There's plenty of food. You can have **as much as** you want.
- Let's walk. It's **just as quick as** taking the bus.
- Can you send me the information **as soon as possible**, please?

还可以说 **twice as … as**，**three times as … as** 等：

- Petrol is **twice as expensive as** it was a few years ago.
- Their house is about **three times as big as** ours.

C

可以说 **the same as** (而不用 the same like)：

- Laura's salary is **the same as** mine. 或 Laura gets **the same** salary **as** me.
- David is **the same** age **as** James.
- Sarah hasn't changed. She still looks **the same as** she did ten years ago.

D

than me / than I am 等

可以说：

- You're taller **than me**. 或 You're taller **than I am**.
  (而不常用 You're taller than I)
- He's not as clever **as her**. 或 He's not as clever **as she is**.
- They have more money **than us**. 或 They have more money **than we have**.
- I can't run as fast **as him**. 或 I can't run as fast **as he can**.

比较级 (1)，(2) ➜ Units 105–106 **as long as** ➜ Unit 115B **as 与 like 比较** ➜ Unit 117

Exercises

107.1 用 **as … as** 完成下列句子。

1 I'm tall, but you are taller. I'm not ...as tall as you... .
2 My salary is high, but yours is higher. My salary isn't ....
3 You know a bit about cars, but I know more.
You don't ....
4 We are busy today, but we were busier yesterday.
We aren't ....
5 I still feel bad, but I felt a lot worse earlier.
I don't ....
6 Our neighbours have lived here for quite a long time, but we've lived here longer.
Our neighbours haven't ....
7 I was a little nervous before the interview, but usually I'm a lot more nervous.
I wasn't ....

107.2 改写下列句子，保持意思不变。

1 Jack is younger than he looks. Jack isn't ...as old as he looks... .
2 I didn't spend as much money as you. You ...spent more money than me... .
3 The station was nearer than I thought. The station wasn't ....
4 The meal didn't cost as much as I expected. The meal cost ....
5 I go out less than I used to. I don't ....
6 Karen's hair isn't as long as it used to be. Karen used to ....
7 I know them better than you do. You don't ....
8 There are fewer people at this meeting than at the last one.
There aren't ....

107.3 用 **as … as** 与下列词语完成句子。

bad	comfortable	~~fast~~	hard	long	often	quietly	soon	well

1 I'm sorry I'm late. I got here ...as fast as... I could.
2 It was a difficult question. I answered it .... I could.
3 'How long can I stay with you?' 'You can stay .... you like.'
4 I need the information quickly, so let me know .... possible.
5 I like to keep fit, so I go swimming .... I can.
6 I didn't want to wake anybody, so I came in .... I could.

用 **just as … as** 和方框中词语完成下列句子。

7 I'm going to sleep on the floor. It's .... the bed.
8 You always say how tiring your job is, but I work .... you.
9 At first I thought he was nice, but really he's .... everybody else.

107.4 用 **the same as** 完成下列句子。

1 David and James are both 22 years old. David ...is the same age as... James.
2 You and I both have dark brown hair. Your hair .... mine.
3 I arrived at 10.25 and so did you. I arrived .... you.
4 My birthday is 5 April. It's Tom's birthday too. My birthday .... Tom's.

107.5 用 **than …** 或 **as …** 完成下列句子。

1 I can't reach as high as you. You are taller ...than me... .
2 He doesn't know much. I know more ....
3 I don't work particularly hard. Most people work as hard ....
4 We were very surprised. Nobody was more surprised ....
5 She's not a very good player. I'm a better player ....
6 They've been very lucky. I wish we were as lucky ....

Unit 108 最高级 (the longest / the most enjoyable 等)

A

请看下列例句：

What is **the longest** river in the world?
What was **the most enjoyable** holiday you've ever had?

longest 和 **most enjoyable** 是最高级的形式。

最高级是将原级变成以 **-est** 结尾或在原级前加 **most**。通常，单音节或少数双音节的形容词或副词的最高级形式是将原级变成以 **-est** 结尾。多数双音节或多音节的形容词或副词的最高级形式是在原级前加 **most**。（与比较级的规则相同，参见 Unit 105。）

	long → long**est**	**hot** → hott**est**	**easy** → easi**est**	**hard** → hard**est**
但是	**most** famous	**most** boring	**most** difficult	**most** expensive

不规则形容词的最高级：

good → **best**　　bad → **worst**　　far → **furthest/farthest**

拼写法参见附录 6。

B

在最高级形式之前通常要用定冠词 **the** (**the** longest / **the** most famous 等)：

- Yesterday was **the hottest** day of the year.
- The movie was really boring. It's **the most boring** movie I've ever seen.
- She is a really nice person – one of **the nicest** people I know.
- Why does he always come to see me at **the worst** possible time?

请比较下列最高级与比较级形式：

- This hotel is **the cheapest** in town. （最高级）
  It's **cheaper** than all the others in town. （比较级）
- He's **the most patient** person I've ever met.
  He's much **more patient** than I am.

C

oldest 与 **eldest** 比较

old 的最高级形式是 **oldest**：

- That church is **the oldest** building in the town. （而不用 the eldest）

eldest (或 **oldest**) 可用来谈论家人：

- **My eldest son** is 13 years old. （或 My **oldest** son）
- Are you **the eldest** in your family? （或 the **oldest**）

D

最高级形式之后接地点名词（城市 / 建筑等）时要用介词 **in**：

- What's the longest river **in the world**? （而不用 of the world）
- We had a nice room. It was one of the best **in the hotel**. （而不用 of the hotel）

后接表示组织和人群的集体名词（班级/队伍/公司等）时也要用介词 **in**：

- Who is the youngest student **in the class**? （而不用 of the class）

后接表示一段时间的词时通常用介词 **of**：

- Yesterday was the hottest day **of the year**.
- What was the happiest day **of your life**?

E

最高级形式之后常使用动词的现在完成式 (另参见 Unit 8A)：

- What's **the most important** decision **you've ever had** to make?
- That was **the best** holiday **I've had** for a long time.

比较级 (cheaper / more expensive 等) ➜ Units 105–107　　elder ➜ Unit 106E

Exercises

108.1 用最高级形式 (**-est** 或 **most ...**) + 介词完成下列句子。

1 It's a very good room. It's *the best room in* the hotel.
2 It's a very cheap restaurant. It's .... the town.
3 It was a very happy day. It was .... my life.
4 She's a very intelligent student. She's .... the class.
5 It's a very valuable painting. It's .... the gallery.
6 Spring is a very busy time for me. It's .... the year.

用 **one of** + 最高级 + 介词完成下列句子。

7 It's a very good room. It's *one of the best rooms in* the hotel.
8 He's a very rich man. He's one .... the country.
9 It's a very big castle. It's .... Europe.
10 She's a very good player. She's .... the team.
11 It was a very bad experience. It was .... my life.
12 It's a very famous university. It's .... the world.

108.2 用最高级 (**-est** 或 **most ...**) 或比较级 (**-er** 或 **more ...**) 形式完成下列句子。

1 We stayed at *the cheapest* hotel in the town. (cheap)
2 Our hotel was *cheaper* than all the others in the town. (cheap)
3 The United States is very large, but Canada is .... (large)
4 What's .... country in the world? (small)
5 I wasn't feeling well yesterday, but I feel a bit .... today. (good)
6 It was an awful day. It was .... day of my life. (bad)
7 What is .... sport in your country? (popular)
8 Qomolangma is .... mountain in the world. It is .... than any other mountain. (high)
9 This building is over 250 metres high, but it's not .... in the city. (tall)
10 I prefer this chair to the other one. It's .... (comfortable)
11 What's .... way to get to the station? (quick)
12 Which is .... – the bus or the train? (quick)
13 What's .... thing you've ever bought? (expensive)
14 Sue and Kevin have got three daughters. .... is 14 years old. (old)

108.3 根据下列情况和括号内的词，用最高级 + **ever ...** 完成下列句子。

1 You've just been to the cinema. The movie was extremely boring. You tell your friend:
(boring / movie / see) That's *the most boring movie I've ever seen* .

2 Your friend has just told you a joke, which you think is very funny. You say:
(funny / joke / hear) That's ....

3 You're drinking coffee with a friend. It's really good coffee. You say:
(good / coffee / taste) This ....

4 You are talking to a friend about Sarah. Sarah is very generous. You tell your friend about her:
(generous / person / meet) She ....

5 You have just run ten kilometres. You've never run further than this. You say to your friend:
(far / run) That ....

6 You decided to give up your job. Now you think this was a bad mistake. You say to your friend:
(bad / mistake / make) It ....

7 Your friend meets a lot of people, some of them famous. You ask your friend:
(famous / person / meet) Who .... ?

Unit 109

词序 (1) —— 动词 + 宾语；地点和时间

A

动词 + 宾语

动词一般和宾语连用，中间不加入其他词语：

	动词	+ 宾语	
I	**like**	**my job**	very much. (而不用 I like very much my job)
Did you	**see**	**your friends**	yesterday?
Helen never	**drinks**	**coffee**.	

请看下列例句。注意动词和动词宾语的连用：

- Do you **eat** **meat** every day? (而不用 Do you eat every day meat?)
- Everybody **enjoyed** **the party** very much. (而不用 enjoyed very much the party)
- Our guide **spoke** **English** fluently. (而不用 spoke fluently English)
- I lost all my money and I also **lost** **my passport**.
  (而不用 I lost also my passport)
- At the end of the street you'll **see** **a supermarket** on your left.
  (而不用 see on your left a supermarket)

B

地点和时间

动词通常与表示地点的词连用：

go home **live in a city** **walk to work** 等

如果动词本身带宾语，表示地点的词用于动词 + 宾语之后：

take somebody home **meet a friend in the street**

表示时间的词一般用于表示地点的词之后：

	地点 +	时间
Ben walks	**to work**	**every morning**. (而不用 every morning to work)
Sam has been	**in Canada**	**since April**.
We arrived	**at the airport**	**early**.

请看下列例句。注意表示地点和时间的词的先后顺序：

- I'm going **to Paris** **on Monday**. (而不用 I'm going on Monday to Paris)
- They have lived **in the same house** **for a long time**.
- Don't be late. Make sure you're **here** **by 8 o'clock**.
- Sarah gave me a lift **home** **after the party**.
- You really shouldn't go **to bed** **so late**.

表示时间的词常可以用于句首：

- **On Monday** I'm going to Paris.
- **Every morning** Ben walks to work.

某些表示时间的词 (例如 **always/never/usually**) 通常与动词连用，位于句子中间。参见 Unit 110。

疑问句语序 → Units 49–50 **形容词词序 → Unit 99** **词序 (2) → Unit 110**

Exercises

109.1 下列句中词语的排列顺序是否正确？如有错误，请改正。

1 Everybody enjoyed the party very much. 对
2 Ben walks every morning to work. Ben walks to work every morning.
3 Joe doesn't like very much football. ....
4 I drink three or four cups of coffee every morning. ....
5 I ate quickly my breakfast and went out. ....
6 Are you going to invite to the party a lot of people? ....
7 I phoned Tom immediately after hearing the news. ....
8 Did you go late to bed last night? ....
9 Did you learn a lot of things at school today? ....
10 I met on my way home a friend of mine. ....

109.2 正确排列下列括号内词语的顺序，写成一句话。

1 (the party / very much / everybody enjoyed) Everybody enjoyed the party very much.
2 (we won / easily / the game) ....
3 (quietly / the door / I closed) ....
4 (Tanya / quite well / speaks / German)
....
5 (Sam / all the time / TV / watches)
....
6 (again / please don't ask / that question)
....
7 (football / every weekend / does Kevin play?)
....
8 (some money / I borrowed / from a friend of mine)
....

109.3 正确排列下列括号内词语的顺序，完成句子。

1 (for a long time / have lived / in the same house)
They have lived in the same house for a long time.
2 (to the supermarket / every Friday / go)
I ....
3 (home / did you come / so late)
Why .... ?
4 (her children / takes / every day / to school)
Sarah ....
5 (been / recently / to the cinema)
I haven't ....
6 (at the top of the page / your name / write)
Please ....
7 (her name / after a few minutes / remembered)
I ....
8 (around the town / all morning / walked)
We ....
9 (on Saturday night / didn't see you / at the party)
I ....
10 (some interesting books / found / in the library)
We ....
11 (her umbrella / last night / in a restaurant / left)
Laura ....
12 (opposite the park / a new hotel / are building)
They ....

词序 (2) —— 副词与动词

A

有些副词 (如 **always**，**also**，**probably**) 与动词连用，位于句子中间：

- Helen **always drives** to work.
- We were feeling very tired and we **were also** hungry.
- The concert **will probably be cancelled**.

B

如果谓语动词是单个词 (**drives/fell/cooked** 等)，那么副词用于动词之前：

	副词	动词	
Helen	always	**drives**	to work.
I	almost	**fell**	as I was going down the stairs.

- I cleaned the house and **also cooked** the dinner. (而不用 cooked also)
- Lucy **hardly ever watches** television and **rarely reads** newspapers.
- 'Shall I give you my address?' 'No, I **already have** it.'

注意，这些副词 (**always/often/also** 等) 用于 **have to** … 之前：

- Joe never phones me. I **always have to** phone him. (而不用 I have always to phone)

但是副词要用于 **am/is/are/was/were** 之后：

- We were feeling very tired and we **were also** hungry.
- Why are you always late? You**'re never** on time.
- The traffic **isn't usually** as bad as it was this morning.

C

如果谓语动词由两个或两个以上的词组成 (如 **can remember / doesn't eat / will be cancelled**)，副词通常用于第一个动词之后 (**can/doesn't/will** 等)：

	动词 1	副词	动词 2	
I	**can**	**never**	**remember**	her name.
Clare	**doesn't**	**often**	**eat**	meat.
	Are you	**definitely**	**going**	away next week?
The concert	**will**	**probably**	**be**	cancelled.

- You**'ve always been** very kind to me.
- Jack can't cook. He **can't even boil** an egg.
- **Do** you **still work** for the same company?
- The house **was only built** a year ago and it**'s already falling** down.

注意，**probably** 用于否定词之前 (**isn't/won't** 等)。因此可以说：

- I **probably won't see** you. 或 I will **probably not** see you. (而不用 I won't probably)

D

all 和 **both** 也可以用于下列位置：

- We **all felt** ill after the meal. (而不用 we felt all ill)
- My parents **are both** teachers. (而不用 my parents both are teachers)
- Sarah and Jane **have both applied** for the job.
- We **are all going** out tonight.

E

有时使用 **is/will/did** 等避免句子的重复 (参见 Unit 51A)：

- Tom says he isn't clever, but I think he **is**. (= he **is clever**)

在这种用法中，**always/never** 等副词用于动词之前：

- He always says he won't be late, but he **always is**. (= he **is always** late)
- I've never done it and I **never will**. (= I **will never** do it)

词序 (1) → Unit 109

Exercises

110.1 下列画线的词语在句中的位置是否正确？如有错误，请改正。

1 Helen drives always to work. ......Helen always drives to work.......
2 I cleaned the house and also cooked the dinner. ......对......
3 I have usually a shower in the morning. ....
4 We soon found the solution to the problem. ....
5 Steve gets hardly ever angry. ....
6 I did some shopping and I went also to the bank. ....
7 Jane has always to hurry in the morning. ....
8 I never have worked in a factory. ....
9 I never have enough time. I always am busy. ....

110.2 用括号内的单词改写下列句子。

1 Clare doesn't eat meat. (often) ......Clare doesn't often eat meat.......
2 Katherine is very generous. (always) ....
3 I don't have to work on Saturdays. (usually) ....
4 Do you watch TV in the evenings? (always) ....
5 Martin is learning Spanish and he is learning Japanese. (also)
Martin is learning Spanish and he ....
6 a We were on holiday in Spain. (all) ....
b We were staying at the same hotel. (all) ....
c We enjoyed ourselves. (all) ....
7 a The new hotel is very expensive. (probably) ....
b It costs a lot to stay there. (probably) ....
8 a I can help you. (probably) ....
b I can't help you. (probably) ....

110.3 正确排列下列括号内词语的顺序，完成句子。

1 ......I can never remember...... (remember / I / never / can) her name.
2 .... (take / I / usually) sugar in coffee.
3 .... (am / usually / I) hungry when I get home from work.
4 Mark and Amy .... (both / were / born) in Manchester.
5 Lisa is a good pianist. .... (sing / she / also / can) very well.
6 Our cat .... (usually / sleeps) under the bed.
7 They live in the same building as me, but ....
(never / I / have / spoken) to them.
8 This shop is always very busy. ....
(have / you / always / to wait) a long time to be served.
9 My eyesight isn't very good. ....
(I / read / can / only) with glasses.
10 .... (all / were / we) tired, so ....
(all / we / fell) asleep.
11 A: Are you tired?
B: Yes, ... (am / I / always) at this time of day.
12 .... (I / probably / leaving / will / be) early tomorrow.
13 I'm afraid .... (probably / I / be / won't) able to come to the party.
14 Helen is away a lot. .... (is / hardly ever / she) at home.
15 .... (we / still / are / living) in the same place. We haven't moved.
16 If we hadn't taken the same train, ...
(never / met / we / would / have) each other.
17 Tanya .... (says / always) that she'll phone me, but .... (does / she / never).

Unit 111 still，yet 与 already 比较 any more / any longer / no longer

A still

still 用于表示情况或动作持续进行着，没有变化或停止：

- It's 10 o'clock and Joe is **still** in bed.
- When I went to bed, Chris was **still** working.
- Do you **still** want to go away or have you changed your mind?

still 通常与动词连用，位于句子中间。参见 Unit 110。

B any more / any longer / no longer

not … **any more** 或 **not** … **any longer** 用于表示情况已发生了变化。**any more** 和 **any longer** 用于句子的结尾部分：

- Lucy **doesn't** work here **any more** (或 **any longer**). She left last month.
  (而不用 Lucy doesn't still work here.)
- We used to be good friends, but we **aren't any more** (或 **any longer**).

也可以用 **no longer**，位于句子中间：

- Lucy **no longer** works here.

注意 **no more** 一般不这样使用：

- We are **no longer** friends. (而不用 We are no more friends.)

请比较 **still** 和 **not** … **any more**：

- Sally **still** works here, but Lucy **doesn't** work here **any more**.

C yet

yet 表示"到目前为止"，主要用于否定句 (**He isn't** here **yet**) 和疑问句 (**Is he** here **yet**?) 中。**yet** 表示说话人期待某事发生，通常用于句子的结尾部分：

- It's 10 o'clock and Joe **isn't** here **yet**.
- **Have** you **met** your new neighbours **yet**?
- 'Where are you going on holiday?' 'We **don't** know **yet**.'

yet 常用于现在完成时 (**Have** you **met** … **yet**?) 中。参见 Unit 7D。

请比较 **yet** 与 **still**：

- Mike lost his job six months ago and **is still** unemployed.
  Mike lost his job six months ago and **hasn't found** another job **yet**.
- **Is** it **still** raining?
  Has it **stopped** raining **yet**?

still 也可以用于否定句中（在否定词前）：

- She said she would be here an hour ago and she **still hasn't** come.

后半句话与 she hasn't come **yet** 表示的意义相似，但 **still** … **not** 强调说话人惊讶或不耐烦的语气。

请比较：

- I sent him an invitation last week. He **hasn't** replied **yet**. (但是我希望他会很快回信)
- I sent him an invitation weeks ago and he **still hasn't** replied. (在这之前他本应该回信了)

D already

already 表示某事比预期提前发生，通常用于句子中间 (参见 Unit 110)：

- 'What time is Sue leaving?' 'She has **already** left.' (= sooner than you expected)
- Shall I tell Joe what happened or does he **already** know?
- I've just had lunch and I'm **already** hungry.

现在完成时与 already/yet 连用 ➜ Unit 7D　词序 ➜ Unit 110

Exercises

111.1 比较保罗几年前和现在所说的话，用 **still** 或 **not … any more** 造句。

Paul a few years ago

Paul now

1 (travel) He still travels a lot.
2 (shop) He doesn't work in a shop any more.
3 (poems) He ……
4 (teacher) ……
5 (politics) ……
6 (single) ……
7 (fishing) ……
8 (beard) ……

根据保罗讲述的情况，用 **no longer** 造句。

9 He no longer works in a shop.
10 ……
11 ……
12 ……

111.2 用 **not … yet** 和方框中动词的适当形式，写出与下列含 **still** 的句子意思相近的句子。

decide	**find**	**finish**	**go**	~~**stop**~~	**take off**	**wake up**

1 It's still raining. It hasn't stopped raining yet.
2 Gary is still here. He ……
3 They're still repairing the road. They ……
4 The children are still asleep. ……
5 Is Ann still looking for a place to live? …… ?
6 I'm still wondering what to do. ……
7 The plane is still waiting on the runway. ……

111.3 仿照示例，将 **still**，**yet**，**already** 或 **any more** 填入画线部分。

1 Mike lost his job a year ago and he is unemployed. he is still unemployed
2 Shall I tell Joe what happened or does he know? does he already know?
3 I'm hungry. Is dinner ready? Is dinner ready yet?
4 I was hungry earlier, but I'm not hungry. I'm not hungry any more
5 Can we wait a few minutes? I don't want to go out. ……
6 Amy used to work at the airport, but she doesn't work there. ……
7 I used to live in Amsterdam. I have a lot of friends there. ……
8 'Shall I introduce you to Joe?' 'There's no need. We've met.' ……
9 Do you live in the same place or have you moved? ……
10 Would you like to eat with us or have you eaten? ……
11 'Where's John?' 'He's not here. He'll be here soon.' ……
12 Tim said he'd be here at 8.30. It's 9 o'clock now and he isn't here. ……
13 Do you want to join the club or are you a member? ……
14 It happened a long time ago, but I can remember it very clearly. ……
15 I've put on weight. These trousers don't fit me. ……
16 'Have you finished with the paper?' 'No, I'm reading it.'
……

even

A

请看下列例句：

Tina loves watching television.

She has a TV in every room of the house, **even** the bathroom.

even 用于表示某事不同寻常或令人惊奇。例如把电视放在浴室里就很不寻常。

再看一些例句：

- These pictures are really awful. **Even I** take better pictures than these. (我当然也不是个好的摄影师)
- He always wears a coat, **even in hot weather**.
- The print was very small. I couldn't read it, **even with glasses**.
- Nobody would help her, **not even her best friend**.

或 **Not even** her best friend would help her.

B

even 可与动词连用，位于句子中间 (参见 Unit 110)：

- Sue has travelled all over the world. She has **even** been to the Antarctic. (去南极洲是件不同寻常的事，所以她一定去过很多地方旅行)
- They are very rich. They **even** have their own private jet.

请看下列例句，注意 **even** 接在否定式 (**not/can't/don't** 等) 后面的用法：

- I can't cook. I **can't even** boil an egg. (煮鸡蛋非常容易，而我却不会)
- They weren't very friendly to us. They **didn't even** say hello.
- Jessica is very fit. She's just run five miles and she's **not even** out of breath.

C

可以用 **even** + 比较级 (**cheaper** / **more expensive** 等)：

- I got up very early, but Jack got up **even earlier**.
- I knew I didn't have much money, but I've got **even less** than I thought.
- We were surprised to get an email from her. We were **even more surprised** when she came to see us a few days later.

D

even though / **even when** / **even if**

even + **though** / **when** / **if** 可以作连词连接句子：

- **Even though she can't** drive, she bought a car.
  (she can't：主语 + 动词)
- He never shouts, **even when he's** angry.
- This river is dangerous. It's dangerous to swim in it, **even if you're** a strong swimmer.

注意不能单独使用 **even** 连接句子。可以说：

- **Even though she can't** drive, she bought a car. (而不用 Even she can't drive)
- I can't reach the shelf **even if I stand** on a chair. (而不用 even I stand)

请比较 **even if** 与 **if**：

- We're going to the beach tomorrow. It doesn't matter what the weather is like. We're going **even if** it's raining.
- We want to go to the beach tomorrow, but we won't go **if** it's raining.

if 与 when 比较 ➜ Unit 25D **though / even though** ➜ Unit 113E

Exercises

112.1 埃米、凯特和莉萨三个朋友一起外出度假。根据所给信息，用 **even** 或 **not even** 完成句子。

Amy	*Kate*	*Lisa*
is usually happy	isn't very keen on art	is almost always late
is usually on time	is usually miserable	is a keen photographer
likes getting up early	usually hates hotels	loves staying in hotels
is very interested in art	hasn't got a camera	isn't very good at getting up

1 They stayed at a hotel. Everybody liked it, even Kate.
2 They arranged to meet. They all arrived on time, ...
3 They went to an art gallery. Nobody enjoyed it, ...
4 Yesterday they had to get up early. They all managed to do this, ...
5 They were together yesterday. They were all in a good mood, ...
6 None of them took any pictures, ...

112.2 用 **even** 及括号内的词语改写下列句子。

1 Sue has been all over the world. (the Antarctic) She has even been to the Antarctic.
2 We painted the whole room. (the floor) We ....
3 Rachel has met lots of famous people. (the prime minister)
She ....
4 You could hear the noise from a long way away. (from the next street)
You ....

用 **not … even** 改写下列句子。

5 They didn't say anything to us. (hello) They didn't even say hello.
6 I can't remember anything about her. (her name)
I ....
7 There isn't anything to do in this town. (a cinema)
....
8 He didn't tell anybody where he was going. (his wife)
....
9 I don't know anyone in our street. (the people next door)
....

112.3 用 **even** + 形容词或副词的比较级完成句子。

1 It was very hot yesterday, but today it's even hotter.
2 The church is 500 years old, but the house next to it is ....
3 That's a very good idea, but I've got an .... one.
4 The first question was very difficult to answer. The second one was ....
5 I did very badly in the exam, but most of my friends did ....
6 Neither of us was hungry. I ate very little and my friend ate ....

112.4 用 **if**, **even**, **even if** 或 **even though** 填空。

1 Even though she can't drive, she has bought a car.
2 The bus leaves in five minutes, but we can still catch it .... we run.
3 The bus leaves in two minutes. We won't catch it now .... we run.
4 His Spanish isn't very good, ... after three years in Spain.
5 His Spanish isn't very good, ... he lived in Spain for three years.
6 .... with the heating on, it was cold in the house.
7 I couldn't sleep .... I was very tired.
8 I won't forgive them for what they did, ... they apologise.
9 .... I hadn't eaten anything for 24 hours, I wasn't hungry.

→ 补充练习 32 (第321页)

Unit 113

although / though / even though in spite of / despite

A

请看下列例句：

Last year Paul and Sarah had a holiday by the sea. It rained a lot, but they enjoyed it.

可以说：

Although it rained a lot, they enjoyed it.
(= It rained a lot, *but* they …)

或

In spite of / **Despite** **the rain**, they enjoyed it.

B

在 **although** 之后使用主语 + 动词：

- **Although it rained** a lot, we enjoyed our holiday.
- I didn't get the job **although I had** the necessary qualifications.

请比较 **although** 与 **because** 所表示的不同含义：

- We went out **although** it was raining heavily.
- We didn't go out **because** it was raining heavily.

C

在 **in spite of** 与 **despite** 之后使用名词、代词 (**this/that/what** 等) 或动词的 **-ing** 形式：

- **In spite of the rain**, we enjoyed our holiday.
- I didn't get the job **in spite of having** the necessary qualifications.
- She wasn't well, but **in spite of this** she continued working.
- **In spite of what** I said yesterday, I still love you.

despite 与 **in spite of** 表示相同含义，但是 **despite** 后面不加 **of**：

- She wasn't well, but **despite this** she continued working. (而不用 despite of this)

可以说 **in spite of the fact (that)** … 和 **despite the fact (that)** …：

- I didn't get the job { **in spite of the fact (that)** / **despite the fact (that)** } I had the necessary qualifications.

请比较 **in spite of** 与 **because of**：

- We went out **in spite of the rain**. (或 … **despite the rain**.)
- We didn't go out **because of the rain**.

D

请比较 **although** 与 **in spite of / despite**：

- **Although the traffic was** bad, / **In spite of the traffic**, } we arrived on time. (而不用 In spite of the traffic was bad)
- I couldn't sleep { **although I was** very tired. (而不用 despite I was tired) / **despite being** very tired.

E

有时用 **though** 代替 **although**：

- I didn't get the job **though** I had the necessary qualifications.

在口语中，**though** 常用于句子的结尾：

- The house isn't so nice. I like the garden **though**. (= but I like the garden)
- I see them every day. I've never spoken to them **though**. (= but I've never spoken to them)

even though (而不用 even) 比 **although** 的语气更强烈：

- **Even though** I was really tired, I couldn't sleep. (而不用 Even I was really tired …)

even ➔ **Unit 112**

Exercises

113.1 用 **although** + 下框中的表达完成句子。

I didn't speak the language well	~~he has a very important job~~
I had never seen her before	we don't like them very much
it was quite cold	the heating was on
I'd met her twice before	we've known each other a long time

1 Although he has a very important job, he isn't particularly well-paid.
2 ……………… , I recognised her from a photograph.
3 She wasn't wearing a coat ……………… .
4 We thought we'd better invite them to the party ……………… .
5 ……………… , I managed to make myself understood.
6 ……………… , the room wasn't warm.
7 I didn't recognise her ……………… .
8 We're not very good friends ……………… .

113.2 用 **although / in spite of / because / because of** 完成下列句子。

1 Although it rained a lot, we enjoyed our holiday.
2 a ……………… all our careful plans, a lot of things went wrong.
b ……………… we'd planned everything carefully, a lot of things went wrong.
3 a I went home early ……………… I was feeling unwell.
b I went to work the next day ……………… I was still feeling unwell.
4 a She only accepted the job ……………… the salary, which was very high.
b She accepted the job ……………… the salary, which was rather low.
5 a I managed to get to sleep ……………… there was a lot of noise.
b I couldn't get to sleep ……………… the noise.

根据你自己的想法完成下列句子。

6 a He passed the exam although ……………… .
b He passed the exam because ……………… .
7 a I didn't eat anything although ……………… .
b I didn't eat anything in spite of ……………… .

113.3 用括号内的词语，将两句话改写成一句。

1 I couldn't sleep. I was very tired. (despite)
I couldn't sleep despite being very tired.
2 They have very little money. They are happy. (in spite of)
In spite ………………
3 My foot was injured. I managed to walk home. (although)
………………
4 I enjoyed the film. The story was silly. (in spite of)
………………
5 We live in the same street. We hardly ever see each other. (despite)
………………
6 I got very wet in the rain. I was only out for five minutes. (even though)
………………

113.4 用括号内的词语，以 **though** 结尾造句。

1 The house isn't very nice. (like / garden) I like the garden though.
2 It's warm today. (very windy) ………………
3 We didn't like the food. (ate) ………………
4 Liz is very nice. (don't like / husband) I ………………

→ 补充练习 32（第321页）

Unit 114

in case

A

请看下列例句：

Your car should have a spare wheel because it is possible you will have a puncture.

Your car should have a spare wheel **in case** you have a puncture.

in case you have a puncture = because it is possible you will have a puncture

再看几个使用 **in case** 的例句：

- I'll leave my mobile phone switched on **in case Jane calls**. (= because it is possible she will call)
- I'll draw a map for you **in case you have problems finding our house**. (= because it is possible you will have problems)
- I'll remind them about the meeting **in case they've forgotten**. (= because it is possible they have forgotten)

just in case 用于表示较小的可能性：

- I don't think it will rain, but I'll take an umbrella **just in case**. (= **just in case** it rains)

在 **in case** 之后用一般现在时表示将来，而不用将来时 (参见 Unit 25)：

- I'll leave my phone switched on **in case** Jane **calls**. (而不用 in case Jane will call)

B

in case 与 **if** 不同。**in case** 表示某种行为的原因，现在做是为了防止以后某事的发生。

请比较：

in case	if
We'll buy some more food **in case** Tom comes. (= Maybe Tom will come. We'll buy some more food now, whether he comes or not; then we'll *already* have the food *if* he comes.)	We'll buy some more food **if** Tom comes. (= Maybe Tome will come. If he comes, we'll buy some more food; if he doesn't come, we won't buy any more food.)
I'll give you my phone number **in case** you need to contact me.	You can call me on this number **if** you need to contact me.
You should insure your bike **in case** it is stolen.	You should inform the police **if** your bike is stolen.

C

in case (+ 过去时) 可用来表示过去的原因：

- I left my phone switched on **in case Jane called**. (= because it was possible that Jane would call)
- I drew a map for Sarah **in case she had problems finding the house**.
- We rang the doorbell again **in case they hadn't heard it the first time**.

D

in case of 与 **in case** 不同。**in case of** ... 表示“要是……，在……的时候”(尤用于告示等)：

- **In case of fire**, please leave the building as quickly as possible. (= if there is a fire)
- **In case of emergency**, call this number. (= if there is an emergency)

if → Units 25，38–40

Exercises

114.1 索菲准备在乡间作一次长途步行。你认为她应该带上下列物品：

~~some chocolate~~ | a map | an anorak | a camera | some water

因为：

it's possible she'll get lost
perhaps she'll be thirsty
she might want to take some pictures
~~she might get hungry~~
maybe it will rain

用 **in case** 造句，说服索菲带上这些物品。

1 Take some chocolate in case you get hungry.
2 Take ……
3 ……
4 ……
5 ……

114.2 根据下列情况，用 **in case** 完成句子。

1 It's possible that Jane will need to contact you, so you agree to give her your phone number.
You say: I'll give you my phone number in case you need to contact me.
2 A friend of yours is going away for a long time. Maybe you won't see her again before she goes, so you decide to say goodbye now.
You say: I'll say goodbye now …… .
3 You are shopping in a supermarket with a friend. You think you have everything you need, but maybe you forgot something. Your friend has the list. You ask her to check it.
You say: Can you …… ?
4 You advise a friend about using a computer. You think he should back up (= *copy*) his files because maybe there will be a problem with his computer (and he could lose all his data).
You say: You should back up …… .

114.3 用 **in case** 完成下列句子。

1 There was a possibility that Jane would call. So I left my phone switched on.
I left my phone switched on in case Jane called.
2 I thought that I might forget the name of the book. So I wrote it down.
I wrote down the name of the book …… .
3 I thought my parents might be worried about me. So I phoned them.
I phoned my parents …… .
4 I sent an email to Lisa, but she didn't reply. So I sent another email because maybe she didn't get the first one.
I sent her another email …… .
5 I met some people when I was on holiday in France. They said they might come to London one day. I live in London, so I gave them my phone number.
I gave them my phone number …… .

114.4 用 **in case** 或 **if** 填空。

1 I'll draw a map for you in case you have problems finding our house.
2 You should tell the police if you have any information about the crime.
3 I hope you'll come to Australia sometime. …… you come, you must visit us.
4 This book belongs to Susan. Can you give it to her …… you see her?
5 Write your name and phone number on your bag …… you lose it.
6 Go to the lost property office …… you lose your bag.
7 The burglar alarm will ring …… somebody tries to break into the house.
8 You should lock your bike to something …… somebody tries to steal it.
9 I was advised to get insurance …… I needed medical treatment while I was abroad.

→ 补充练习 32（第321页）

unless as long as provided/providing

A unless

请看下列例句：

The club is for members only.

You can't go in **unless you are a member**.

意为：

You can't go in *except if* you are a member.
You can go in *only if* you are a member.

unless 表示"如果不……，除非……"。

再看一些含 **unless** 的例句：

- I'll see you tomorrow **unless I have to work late**. (= except if I have to work late)
- There are no buses to the beach. **Unless you have a car**, it's difficult to get there. (= except if you have a car)
- 'Shall I tell Liz what happened?' '**Not unless** she asks you.' (= only if she asks you)
- Sally hates to complain. She wouldn't complain about something **unless it was really bad**. (= except if it was really bad)
- We can take a taxi to the restaurant – **unless you'd prefer to walk**. (= except if you'd prefer to walk)

if … not 常可以代替 **unless**：

- **Unless we leave now**, we'll be late. 或 **If we don't leave now**, we'll ...

B as long as / provided / providing

as long as 或 **so long as** / **provided (that)** 或 **providing (that)** } 其共同意义是"如果"或"在……条件下"。

例如：

- You can borrow my car { **as long as** / **so long as** } you promise not to drive too fast. (= you can borrow my car, but you must promise not to drive too fast—this is a condition)
- Travelling by car is convenient { **provided (that)** / **providing (that)** } you have somewhere to park. (= but only if you have somewhere to park)
- { **Providing (that)** / **Provided (that)** } the room is clean, I don't mind which hotel we stay at. (= the room must be clean – otherwise I would mind)

C unless / as long as 等表示将来

unless / **as long as** / **so long as** /**provided** / **providing** 之后用一般现在时表示将来，而不用将来时 (参见 Unit 25)：

- I'm not going out **unless** it **stops** raining. (而不用 unless it will stop)
- **Providing** the weather **is** good, we're going to have a picnic tomorrow. (而不用 providing the weather will be good)

if ➜ **Units 25，38–40**

Exercises

115.1 用 **unless** 改写句子，保持意思不变。

1 You must try a bit harder or you won't pass the exam.
You won't pass the exam unless you try a bit harder.

2 Listen carefully or you won't know what to do.
You won't know what to do ……

3 She must apologise to me or I'll never speak to her again.
……

4 You have to speak very slowly or he won't be able to understand you.
……

5 Business must improve soon or the company will have to close.
……

115.2 用 **unless** 将下列句子合并成一句。

1 The club isn't open to everyone. You're allowed in only if you're a member.
You aren't allowed in the club unless you're a member.

2 I don't want to go to the party alone. I'm going only if you go too.
I'm not going ……

3 Don't worry about the dog. It will attack you only if you move suddenly.
The dog ……

4 Ben isn't very talkative. He'll speak to you only if you ask him something.
Ben ……

5 Today is a public holiday. The doctor will see you only if it's an emergency.
The doctor ……

115.3 从下列句子画线的部分中选择正确答案。

1 You can borrow my car <u>unless / as long as</u> you promise not to drive too fast.
(<u>as long as</u> *is correct*)
2 I'm playing tennis tomorrow <u>unless / providing</u> it rains.
3 I'm playing tennis tomorrow <u>unless / providing</u> it doesn't rain.
4 I don't mind if you come home late <u>unless / as long as</u> you come in quietly.
5 I'm going now <u>unless / provided</u> you want me to stay.
6 I don't watch TV <u>unless / as long as</u> I've got nothing else to do.
7 Children are allowed to use the swimming pool <u>unless / provided</u> they are with an adult.
8 <u>Unless / Provided</u> they are with an adult, children are not allowed to use the swimming pool.
9 We can sit here in the corner <u>unless / as long as</u> you'd rather sit over there by the window.
10 A: Our holiday cost a lot of money.
B: Did it? Well, that doesn't matter <u>unless / as long as</u> you enjoyed yourselves.

115.4 根据你自己的想法完成下列句子。

1 We'll be late unless we get a taxi.
2 I like hot weather as long as …… .
3 It takes about 20 minutes to drive to the airport provided …… .
4 I don't mind walking home long as …… .
5 I like to walk to work in the morning unless …… .
6 We can meet tomorrow unless …… .
7 I can lend you the money providing …… .
8 You won't achieve anything unless …… .

→ 补充练习 32（第321页）

as (As I walked along the street … / As I was hungry …)

A

as 作连词时可指“在……的同时”：

这时 **as** 可用来表示两件事同时发生：

- We all waved goodbye to Liz **as** she drove away.
  (“我们挥手”和“她开车离开”同时发生)
- **As** I walked along the street, I looked in the shop windows.
- Can you turn off the light **as** you go out, please?

或者用 **as** + 过去进行时表示在做某事的过程中发生了另外一件事：

- Kate slipped **as she was getting off** the bus.
- We met Paul **as we were leaving** the hotel.

有关过去进行时的用法 (**was getting** / **were going** 等)，参见 Unit 6。

也可以用 **just as**，意为“正当……时”：

- **Just as** I sat down, the doorbell rang.
- I had to leave **just as** the conversation was getting interesting.

as 也可用来表示两件事在一段时间内同时发生：

- **As** the day went on, the weather got worse.
- I began to enjoy the job more **as** I got used to it.

the day went on
the weather got worse

请比较 **as** 与 **when**：

as 仅用于两件事同时发生的情况：	**when** (而不用 as) 可用来表示两件事先后发生：
As I drove home, I listened to music. (= at the same time)	**When I got home**, I had something to eat. (而不用 As I got home)

B

as 还可指“因为”：

- **As I was hungry**, I decided to find somewhere to eat. (= because I was hungry)
- **As we have plenty of time** before our flight, let's go and have a coffee.
- We watched TV all evening **as we didn't have anything better to do**.
- **As I don't watch television any more**, I gave my TV to a friend of mine.

这时也可用 **since** 代替 **as**：

- **Since** we have plenty of time, let's go and have a coffee.

请比较 **as** (因为) 与 **when**：

I couldn't contact David **as he was on holiday**. (= because he was on holiday)	David's passport was stolen **when he was on holiday**. (= during the time he was away)
As they lived near us, we used to see them quite often. (= because they lived near us)	**When they lived near us**, we used to see them quite often. (= at the time they lived near us)

as … as → Unit 107 **like** 与 **as** 比较 → Unit 117 **as if** → Unit 118

Exercises

116.1 仿照示例，将下列两框中的句子配对，并用 **as** 把它们连接成一句话。

1 ~~We all waved goodbye to Liz~~	we were driving along the road
2 I listened	I was taking a hot dish out of the oven
3 I burnt myself	~~she drove away~~
4 The crowd cheered	she told me her story
5 A dog ran out in front of the car	the two teams came onto the field

1 We all waved goodbye to Liz as she drove away.
2 ……
3 ……
4 ……
5 ……

116.2 仿照示例，将下列两框中的句子配对，并用 **as** 把它们连接成一句话。

1 ~~I was hungry~~	I need some advice
2 today is a public holiday	I was very quiet
3 I didn't want to disturb anybody	~~I decided to find somewhere to eat~~
4 I don't know what to do	we didn't know what time it was
5 none of us had a watch	many of the shops are shut

1 As I was hungry, I decided to find somewhere to eat.
2 ……
3 ……
4 ……
5 ……

116.3 指出 **as** 在下列句子中的含义。

	因为	同时
1 **As** they live near us, we see them quite often.	✓	
2 Kate slipped **as** she was getting off the bus.		✓
3 **As** I was tired, I went to bed early.		
4 Unfortunately, **as** I was parking the car, I hit the car behind me.		
5 **As** we climbed the hill, we got more and more tired.		
6 We decided to go out to eat **as** we had no food at home.		
7 **As** we don't use the car very often, we've decided to sell it.		

116.4 下列有些句子中的 **as** 需用 **when** 代替。如有必要，请改正。

1 Julia got married as she was 22. …… when she was 22
2 As the day went on, the weather got worse. …… 对
3 He dropped the glass as he was taking it out of the cupboard. ……
4 I lost my phone as I was in London. ……
5 As I left school, I didn't know what to do. ……
6 The train slowed down as it approached the station. ……
7 I used to live near the sea as I was a child. ……

116.5 根据你自己的想法完成下列句子。

1 I saw you as ……
2 It started to rain just as ……
3 As I didn't have enough money for a taxi, ……
4 Just as I took the picture, ……

→ 补充练习 32（第321页）

Unit 117 like 与 as 比较

A

like 可表示“与……相似，和……一样”。注意 **as** 不可以这样用：

- What a beautiful house! It's **like a palace**. (而不用 as a palace)
- 'What does Sandra do?' 'She's a teacher, **like me**.' (而不用 as me)
- Be careful! The floor has been polished. It's **like walking on ice**. (而不用 as walking)
- It's raining again. I hate weather **like this**. (而不用 as this)

在这些句子中，**like** 用作介词，后面加名词 (like **a palace**)、代词 (like **me** / like **this**) 或动词的 **-ing** 形式 (like **walking**)。

还可以说 **like** (somebody/something) **doing** something：

- 'What's that noise?' 'It sounds **like a baby crying**.'

有时 **like** 表示举例，意为“例如，像”：

- I enjoy water sports, **like surfing, scuba diving and water-skiing**.

这时还可以用 **such as** 代替 **like**：

- I enjoy water sports, **such as surfing, scuba diving and water-skiing**.

B

as 可指“按……的方式，如同”，用于主语 + 动词之前：

- I didn't move anything. I left everything **as it was**.
- You should have done it **as I showed you**.

这时也可用 **like** 代替 **as**：

- I left everything **like it was**.

请比较下列句中的 **as** 与 **like**：

- You should have done it **as I showed you**. 或 ... **like I showed you**.
- You should have done it **like this**. (而不用 as this)

注意要说 **as usual** / **as always**：

- You're late **as usual**.
- **As always**, Nick was the first to complain.

C

as 后接主语 + 动词时还可表示其他含义，例如跟在动词 **do** 之后：

- You can do **as you like**. (= do what you like)
- They did **as they promised**. (= They did what they promised.)

还可以说 **as you know** / **as I said** / **as she expected** / **as I thought** 等：

- **As you know**, it's Emma's birthday next week. (= you know this already)
- Andy failed his driving test, **as he expected**. (= he expected this before)

like 通常不这样用，除了 **like I said**：

- **As I said** yesterday, I'm sure we can solve the problem. 或 **Like I said** yesterday ...

D

as 也可以用作介词，但与 **like** 的含义不同。
请比较：

As a taxi driver, I spend most of my working life in a car. (我是出租车司机)	Everyone wants me to drive them to places. I'm **like a taxi driver**. (我像出租车司机)

as (介词) 表示“作为，以……身份”等：

- Many years ago I worked **as a photographer**. (而不用 like a photographer)
- Many words, for example 'work' and 'rain', can be used **as verbs or nouns**.
- London is fine **as a place to visit**, but I wouldn't like to live there.
- The news of the tragedy came **as a great shock**.

as ... as ➜ Unit 107　**as** (时间与原因) ➜ Unit 116　**as if** ➜ Unit 118

Exercises

117.1 下列有些句子中的 **as** 需用 **like** 代替。如有必要，请改正。

1 It's raining again. I hate weather as this. .... weather like this
2 Andy failed his driving test, as he expected. .... 对
3 Do you think Lisa looks as her mother? ....
4 Tim gets on my nerves. I can't stand people as him. ....
5 Why didn't you do it as I told you to do it? ....
6 Brian is a student, as most of his friends. ....
7 You never listen. Talking to you is as talking to the wall. ....
8 As I said before, I'm thinking of changing my job. ....
9 Tom's idea seems a good one. Let's do as he suggests. ....
10 I'll phone you tomorrow as usual, OK? ....
11 Suddenly there was a terrible noise. It was as a bomb exploding. ....
12 She's a very good swimmer. She swims as a fish. ....

117.2 用 **like** 或 **as** + 下列词语完成句子。

a beginner	**blocks of ice**	~~**a palace**~~	**a birthday present**
a child	**a theatre**	**winter**	**a tour guide**

1 This house is beautiful. It's .... like a palace ....
2 My feet are really cold. They're ....
3 I've been playing tennis for years, but I still play ....
4 Marion once had a part-time job ....
5 I wonder what that building is. It looks ....
6 My brother gave me this watch .... a long time ago.
7 It's very cold for the middle of summer. It's ....
8 He's 22 years old, but he sometimes behaves ....

117.3 用 **like** 或 **as** 填空，有时两者均可。

1 We heard a noise .... like .... a baby crying.
2 Your English is very fluent. I wish I could speak .... you.
3 Don't take my advice if you don't want to. You can do .... you like.
4 You waste too much time doing things .... sitting in cafés all day.
5 I wish I had a car .... yours.
6 You don't need to change clothes. You can go out .... you are.
7 My neighbour's house is full of interesting things. It's .... a museum.
8 We saw Kevin last night. He was very cheerful, ... always.
9 Sally has been working .... a waitress for the last two months.
10 In several countries in Asia, ... Japan, Indonesia and Thailand, traffic drives on the left.
11 You're different from the other people I know. I don't know anyone else .... you.
12 We don't need all the bedrooms in the house, so we use one of them .... a study.
13 The news that Sarah and Gary were getting married came .... a complete surprise to me.
14 .... her father, Catherine has a very good voice.
15 At the moment I've got a temporary job in a bookshop. It's not great, but it's OK .... a temporary job.
16 .... you can imagine, we were very tired after such a long journey.
17 This tea is awful. It tastes .... water.
18 I think I prefer this room .... it was, before we decorated it.

Unit 118

like / as if / as though

A

like 可以与 **look/sound/feel** 等动词连用：

- That house **looks like** it's going to fall down.
- Helen **sounded like** she had a cold, didn't she?
- I've just got back from holiday, but I feel very tired. I don't **feel like** I've had a holiday.

这些例句中的 **like** 也可用 **as if** 或 **as though** 代替：

- That house **looks as if** it's going to fall down.
- Helen **sounded as if** she had a cold, didn't she?
- I don't **feel as though** I've had a holiday.

请比较：

- You **look tired**. (**look** + 形容词)
  You **look like you haven't slept**. (**look like** + 主语 + 动词)

as if 和 **as though** 比 **like** 更为正式。

B

还可以说 **It looks like** ... / **It sounds like** ...：

- Sarah is very late, isn't she? **It looks like** she isn't coming.
- We took an umbrella because **it looked like** it was going to rain.
- The noise is very loud next door. **It sounds like** they're having a party.

这时也可用 **as if** 或 **as though** 代替 **like**：

- It **looks as if** she isn't coming. 或
  It **looks as though** she isn't coming.
- It **looked as if** it was going to rain.
- It **sounds as though** they're having a party.

C

like / as if / as though 可以与一些动词连用来描述行为方式：

- He ran **like he was running for his life**.
- After the interruption, the speaker went on talking **as if nothing had happened**.
- When I told them my plan, they looked at me **as though I was mad**.

D

as if (或 **as though**) 之后有时用过去时表示现在：

- I don't like Tim. He talks as if he **knew** everything.

这个句子的含义并不是指过去，而是用过去时 (as if he **knew**) 表示虚拟：Tim does *not* know everything。这种用法与 **if** 和 **wish** 的用法相同 (参见 Unit 39)。
like 通常不这样用。

再看一些例句：

- She's always asking me to do things for her – **as if I didn't** have enough to do already. (我还有很多事要做)
- Gary's only 40. Why do you talk about him **as if he was** an old man? (他不是很老)

在这类句子中，可以用 **were** 代替 **was**：

- Why do you talk about him **as if he were** (或 **was**) an old man?
- They treat me **as if I were** (或 **was**) their own son. (我不是他们的儿子)

if I was/were → Unit 39C　**look/sound 等 + 形容词** → Unit 99C　**like 与 as 比较** → Unit 117

Exercises

118.1 根据所给情况，用括号内的词语造句。

1 You meet Bill. He has a black eye and some plasters on his face. (look / like / be / a fight)
You say to him: You look like you've been in a fight.
2 Claire comes into the room. She looks absolutely terrified. (look / like / see / a ghost)
You say to her: What's the matter? You ……
3 Joe is on holiday. He's talking to you on the phone and sounds happy. (sound / as if / have / a good time)
You say to him: You ……
4 You have just run one kilometre. You are absolutely exhausted. (feel / like / run / a marathon)
You say to a friend: I ……

118.2 根据所给情况和下框中的句子，以 **It looks like … / It sounds like …** 开头造句。

you should see a doctor	there's been an accident	they're having an argument
it's going to rain	~~she isn't coming~~	we'll have to walk

1 Sarah said she would be here an hour ago.
You say: It looks like she isn't coming.
2 The sky is full of black clouds.
You say: It ……
3 You hear two people shouting at each other next door.
You say: ……
4 You see an ambulance, some policemen and two damaged cars at the side of the road.
You say: ……
5 You and a friend have just missed the last bus home.
You say: ……
6 Dave isn't feeling well. He tells you all about it.
You say: ……

118.3 用下框中的信息与 **as if** 完成句子。

she / enjoy / it	I / go / be sick	he / not / eat / for a week
~~he / need / a good rest~~	she / hurt / her leg	he / mean / what he / say
I / not / exist	she / not / want / come	

1 Mark looks very tired. He looks as if he needs a good rest.
2 I don't think Paul was joking. He looked …… .
3 What's the matter with Amanda? She's walking …… .
4 Peter was extremely hungry and ate his dinner very quickly.
He ate …… .
5 Tanya had a bored expression on her face during the movie.
She didn't look …… .
6 I've just eaten too many chocolates. Now I don't feel well.
I feel …… .
7 I phoned Liz and invited her to the party, but she wasn't very enthusiastic about it.
She sounded …… .
8 I went into the office, but nobody spoke to me or looked at me.
Everybody ignored me …… .

118.4 根据 **D** 节，用 **as if** 完成下列句子。

1 Andy is a terrible driver. He drives as if he were the only driver on the road.
2 I'm 20 years old, so please don't talk to me …… I …… a child.
3 Steve has never met Nicola, but he talks about her …… his best friend.
4 It was a long time ago that we first met, but I remember it …… yesterday.

Unit 119

for，during 与 while 比较

A for 与 during 比较

用 **for** + 一段时间表示时间的持续：

for **two hours**　　for **a week**　　for **ages**

- We watched TV **for two hours** last night.
- Jess is going away **for a week** in September.
- Where have you been? I've been waiting **for ages.**
- Are you going away **for the weekend**?

I fell asleep **during the movie.**

用 **during** + 名词表示事情发生的时间：

during **the movie**　　during **our holiday**　　during **the night**

- I fell asleep **during the movie.**
- We met some really nice people **during our holiday.**
- The ground is wet. It must have rained **during the night.**

表示时间的词 (例如 **the morning / the afternoon / the summer**) 常可与 **in** 或 **during** 连用：

- It must have rained **in the night.**　或　... **during the night.**
- I'll phone you sometime **during the afternoon.**　或　... **in the afternoon.**

不能用 **during** 来表示时间的持续：

- It rained **for** three days without stopping.（而不用 during three days)

请比较 **during** 与 **for**：

- I fell asleep **during the movie.** I was asleep **for half an hour.**

B during 与 while 比较

请比较：

during + 名词	**while** + 主语 + 动词
I fell asleep **during the movie.** └ 名词 ┘	I fell asleep **while I was watching TV.** └ 主语 + 动词 ┘
We met a lot of interesting people **during our holiday.**	We met a lot of interesting people **while we were on holiday.**
Robert suddenly began to feel ill **during the exam.**	Robert suddenly began to feel ill **while he was doing the exam.**

再看几个含 **while** 的例句：

- We saw Clare **while we were waiting** for the bus.
- **While you were** out, there was a phone call for you.
- Alex read a book **while I watched** TV.

Alex read a book **while I watched** TV.

在 **while** 之后用一般现在时（而不用将来时）表示将来：

- I'm going to Singapore next week. I hope to see some friends of mine **while I'm** there. (而不用 while I will be there)
- What are you going to do **while** you**'re** waiting? (而不用 while you'll be waiting)

更多信息参见 Unit 25。

for 与 since 比较 ➔ Unit 12A　　while + -ing ➔ Unit 68B

Exercises

119.1 用 **for** 或 **during** 填空。

1 It rained ....for.... three days without stopping.
2 I fell asleep ....during.... the movie.
3 I went to the theatre last night. I met Sue .... the interval.
4 Martin hasn't lived in Britain all his life. He lived in Brazil .... four years.
5 Production at the factory was seriously affected .... the strike.
6 I felt really ill last week. I could hardly eat anything .... three days.
7 I waited for you .... half an hour and decided that you weren't coming.
8 Sarah was very angry with me. She didn't speak to me .... a week.
9 We usually go out at weekends, but we don't go out .... the week very often.
10 Jack started a new job a few weeks ago. Before that he was out of work .... six months.
11 I need a break. I think I'll go away .... a few days.
12 The president gave a long speech. She spoke .... two hours.
13 We were hungry when we arrived. We hadn't had anything to eat .... the journey.
14 We were hungry when we arrived. We hadn't had anything to eat .... eight hours.

119.2 用 **during** 或 **while** 填空。

1 We met a lot of interesting people ....while.... we were on holiday.
2 We met a lot of interesting people ....during.... our holiday.
3 I met Mike .... I was shopping.
4 .... I was on holiday, I didn't read any newspapers or watch TV.
5 .... our stay in Paris, we went to a lot of museums and galleries.
6 My phone rang .... we were having dinner.
7 There was a lot of noise .... the night. What was it?
8 I'd been away for many years. .... that time, many things had changed.
9 What did they say about me .... I was out of the room?
10 I went out for dinner last night. Unfortunately I began to feel ill .... the meal and had to go home.
11 Please don't interrupt me .... I'm speaking.
12 There were many interruptions .... the president's speech.
13 Can you hold my bag .... I try on this jacket?
14 We were hungry when we arrived. We hadn't had anything to eat .... we were travelling.

119.3 根据你自己的想法完成下列句子。

1 I fell asleep while ....I was watching TV.
2 I fell asleep during ....the movie.
3 Nobody came to see me while ....
4 Can you wait for me while ....
5 Most of the students looked bored during ....
6 I was asked a lot of questions during ....
7 Don't open the car door while ....
8 The lights suddenly went out while ....
9 It started to rain during ....
10 It started to rain while ....
11 What are you going to do while ....

→ 补充练习 33（第321页）

Unit 120 by 与 until 比较　by the time ...

A

by ... 表示“不晚于……”：

- I sent the documents to them today, so they should receive them **by Monday**. (= on or before Monday, not later than Monday)
- We'd better hurry. We have to be home **by 5 o'clock**. (= at or before 5 o'clock, not later than 5 o'clock)
- Where's Sarah? She should be here **by now**. (= now or before now – so she should have already arrived)

This milk has to be used **by 14 August**.

B

until (或 **till**) 可用来表示情况的持续：

- 'Shall we go now?' 'No, let's **wait until** it stops raining.' 或 '... **till** it stops raining.'
- I couldn't get up this morning. { I **stayed in bed until** half past ten. / I **didn't** get up **until** half past ten.

请比较 **until** 与 **by**：

until 表示事情持续到将来：	**by** 表示事情在将来某时之前发生：
Joe **will be away until** Monday. (因此他会在星期一回来)	Joe **will be back by** Monday. (= he'll be back not later than Monday)
I'll be working until 11.30. (因此我会在11点30分时停止工作)	**I'll have finished my work by** 11.30. (= I'll finish my work not later than 11.30)

C

可以说 **by the time** something happens，请看下列例句：

- It's too late to go to the bank now. **By the time we get there**, it will be closed. (= the bank will close between now and the time we get there)
- (*from a postcard*) Our holiday ends tomorrow. So **by the time you receive this postcard**, I'll be back home. (= I will arrive home between tomorrow and the time you receive this postcard)
- Hurry up! **By the time we get to the cinema**, the film will already have started.

可以说 **by the time** something happened (指过去)：

- Karen's car broke down on the way to the party last night. **By the time she arrived**, most of the other guests had left. (= it took her a long time to get to the party and most of the guests left during this time)
- I had a lot of work to do yesterday evening. I was very tired **by the time I finished**. (= it took me a long time to do the work, and I became more and more tired during this time)
- We went to the cinema last night. It took us a long time to find somewhere to park the car. **By the time we got to the cinema**, the film had already started.

还可以用 **by then** 或 **by that time**：

- Karen finally got to the party at midnight, but **by then**, most of the other guests had left. 或 ... but **by that time**, most of the other guests had left.

will be doing 与 will have done 比较 → Unit 24　　**by (其他用法) → Units 42B，60B，128**

Exercises

120.1 根据所给情况，用 **by** 完成下列句子。

1 We have to be home not later than 5 o'clock.
We have to be home by 5 o'clock.

2 I have to be at the airport not later than 8.30.
I have to be at the airport ....

3 Let me know not later than Saturday whether you can come to the party.
.... whether you can come to the party.

4 Please make sure that you're here not later than 2 o'clock.
Please make sure that ....

5 If we leave now, we should arrive not later than lunchtime.
If we leave now, ...

120.2 用 **by** 或 **until** 填空。

1 Steve has gone away. He'll be away until Monday.
2 Sorry, but I must go. I have to be home .... 5 o'clock.
3 I've been offered a job. I haven't decided yet whether to accept it or not. I have to decide .... Friday.
4 I think I'll wait .... Thursday before making a decision.
5 It's too late to go shopping. The shops are open only .... 5.30 today. They'll be closed .... now.
6 I need to pay the phone bill. It has to be paid .... tomorrow.
7 Don't pay the bill today. Wait .... tomorrow.
8 A: Have you finished redecorating your house?
B: Not yet. We hope to finish .... the end of the week.
9 A: I'm going out now. I'll be back at about 10.30. Will you still be here?
B: I don't think so. I'll probably have gone out .... then.
10 I'm moving into my new flat next week. I'm staying with a friend .... then.
11 I've got a lot of work to do. .... the time I finish, it will be time to go to bed.
12 If you want to take part in the competition, you have to apply .... 3 April.

120.3 根据你自己的想法，用 **by** 或 **until** 完成下列句子。

1 David is away at the moment. He'll be away until Monday.
2 David is away at the moment. He'll be back by Monday.
3 I'm just going out. I won't be very long. Wait here ....
4 I'm going out to buy a few things. It's 4.30 now. I won't be long. I'll be back ....
5 If you want to apply for the job, your application must be received ....
6 Last night I watched TV ....

120.4 根据所给情况，以 **By the time ...** 开头完成下列句子。

1 I was invited to a party, but I got there much later than I intended.
By the time I got to the party, most of the other guests had left.

2 I intended to catch a train, but it took me longer than expected to get to the station.
.........., my train had already left.

3 I wanted to go shopping after finishing my work. But I finished much later than expected.
.........., it was too late to go shopping.

4 I saw two men who looked as if they were trying to steal a car. I called the police, but it was some time before they arrived.
.........., the two men had disappeared.

5 We climbed a mountain and it took us a very long time to get to the top. There wasn't much time to enjoy the view.
.........., we had to come down again.

→ 补充练习 33（第321页）

Unit 121

at/on/in (时间)

A

请比较 **at**，**on** 与 **in**：

- They arrived **at 5 o'clock**.
- They arrived **on Friday**.
- They arrived **in October**. / They arrived **in 1998**.

请看下列用法：

at 用来表示一天之内的某个时间：
at five o'clock **at 11.45** **at midnight** **at lunchtime** **at sunset** 等

on 用来表示星期几和日期等：
on Friday / on Fridays **on 16 May 2009** **on Christmas Day** **on my birthday**

in 用来表示较长一段时间 (例如，月/季/年)：
in October **in 1998** **in the 18th century** **in the past**
in (the) winter **in the 1990s** **in the Middle Ages** **in (the) future**

B

at 可用于下列短语：

at night	I don't like working **at night**.
at the weekend / at weekends	Will you be here **at the weekend**?
at Christmas	Do you give each other presents **at Christmas**?
at the moment / at present	The manager isn't here **at the moment / at present**.
at the same time	Kate and I arrived **at the same time**.

C

可以说：

in the morning(s) 或 **on Friday morning(s)**
in the afternoon(s) **on Sunday afternoon(s)**
in the evening(s) **on Monday evening(s)** 等

- I'll see you **in the morning**.
- Do you work **in the evenings**?
- I'll see you **on Friday morning**.
- Do you work **on Saturday evenings**?

D

last/next/this/every 前不用 **at/on/in**：

- I'll see you **next Friday**. (而不用 on next Friday)
- They got married **last March**.

口语中，在表示星期几的词 (**Sunday/Monday** 等) 前面通常不加 **on**。因此可以说：

- I'll see you **on Friday**. 或 I'll see you **Friday**.
- I don't work **on Monday mornings**. 或 I don't work **Monday mornings**.

E

in a few minutes / in six months 等表示将来某时：

- The train will be leaving **in a few minutes**. (= a few minutes from now)
- Andy has gone away. He'll be back **in a week**. (= a week from now)
- They'll be here **in a moment**. (= a moment from now)

还可以说 in six months' **time**，in a week's **time** 等：

- They're getting married **in six months' time**. 或 … **in six months**.

还可以用 **in** 表示用时多久：

- I learnt to drive **in four weeks**. (= it took me four weeks to learn)

on/in time，**at/in the end** ➜ Unit 122 **in/at/on (地点)** ➜ Units 123–125
in/at/on (其他用法) ➜ Unit 127 **美国英语** ➜ 附录 7

Exercises

121.1 用 **at**，**on** 或 **in** 填空。

1 Mozart was born in Salzburg ...in... 1756.
2 I've been invited to a wedding .... 14 February.
3 Electricity prices are going up .... October.
4 .... weekends, we often go for long walks in the country.
5 I haven't seen Kate for a few days. I last saw her .... Tuesday.
6 Jonathan is 63. He'll be retiring from his job .... two years' time.
7 I'm busy right now, but I'll be with you .... a moment.
8 My brother is an engineer, but he doesn't have a job .... the moment.
9 There are usually a lot of parties .... New Year's Eve.
10 I don't like driving .... night.
11 My car is being repaired at the garage. It will be ready .... two hours.
12 My phone and the doorbell rang .... the same time.
13 Mary and David always go out for dinner .... their wedding anniversary.
14 It was a short book and easy to read. I read it .... a day.
15 .... Saturday night I went to bed .... midnight.
16 We travelled overnight and arrived .... 5 o'clock .... the morning.
17 The course begins .... 7 January and ends sometime .... April.
18 I might not be at home .... Tuesday morning, but I'll be there .... the afternoon.

121.2 用 **at**，**on** 或 **in** + 下列词语完成句子。

the evening	**about 20 minutes**	~~**1492**~~	**the same time**
the moment	**21 July 1969**	**the 1920s**	**night**
Saturdays	**the Middle Ages**	**11 seconds**	

1 Columbus made his first voyage from Europe to America ...in 1492... .
2 If the sky is clear, you can see the stars ....
3 After working hard during the day, I like to relax ....
4 Neil Armstrong was the first man to walk on the moon ....
5 It's difficult to listen if everyone is speaking ....
6 Jazz became popular in the United States ....
7 I'm just going out to the shop. I'll be back ....
8 'Can I speak to Dan?' 'I'm afraid he's busy ....'
9 Many of Europe's great cathedrals were built ....
10 Ben is a very fast runner. He can run 100 metres ....
11 Liz works from Monday to Friday. Sometimes she also works ....

121.3 指出下列 **a**、**b** 两句中正确的句子。

1 a I'll see you on Friday. b I'll see you Friday. ...both...
2 a I'll see you on next Friday. b I'll see you next Friday. ...b...
3 a Paul got married in April. b Paul got married April. ....
4 a They never go out on Sunday evenings. b They never go out Sunday evenings. ....
5 a We often have a short holiday on Christmas. b We often have a short holiday at Christmas. ....
6 a What are you doing the weekend? b What are you doing at the weekend? ....
7 a Will you be here on Tuesday? b Will you be here Tuesday? ....
8 a We were ill at the same time. b We were ill in the same time. ....
9 a Sue got married at 18 May 2008. b Sue got married on 18 May 2008. ....
10 a He left school last June. b He left school in last June. ....

→ 补充练习 33（第321页）

on time 与 in time 比较　at the end 与 in the end 比较

A on time 与 in time 比较

on time 表示“准时，按时”，指某事按计划时间发生：

- The 11.45 train left **on time**. (= it left at 11.45)
- 'I'll meet you at 7.30.' 'OK, but please be **on time**.' (= don't be late, be there at 7.30)
- The conference was well-organised. Everything began and finished **on time**.

on time 的反义词是 **late**：

- Be **on time**. Don't be **late**.

in time (for something / to do something) 表示“及时（地）（做某事）”：

- Will you be home **in time for dinner**? (= soon enough for dinner)
- I've sent Tracey a birthday present. I hope it arrives **in time** (for her birthday). (= on or before her birthday)
- I'm in a hurry. I want to get home **in time to see** the game on TV. (= soon enough to see the game)

in time 的反义词是 **too late**：

- I got home **too late** to see the game on TV.

可以说 **just in time** (差点晚了)：

- We got to the station **just in time** for our train.
- A child ran into the road in front of the car – I managed to stop **just in time**.

B at the end 与 in the end 比较

at the end (of something) 表示“在……结束时”：

at the end of the month	**at the end of January**	**at the end of the game**
at the end of the film	**at the end of the course**	**at the end of the concert**

- I'm going away **at the end of January / at the end of the month**.
- **At the end of the concert**, everyone applauded.
- The players shook hands **at the end of the game**.

不能用 **in** the end of …，例如不能说 in the end of January 或 in the end of the concert。

at the end (**of** …) 的反义词是 **at the beginning** (**of** …)：

- I'm going away **at the beginning of January**. (而不用 in the beginning)

in the end 表示最终的结果或情况：

- We had a lot of problems with our car. We sold it **in the end**. (= finally we sold it)
- He got more and more angry. **In the end** he just walked out of the room.
- Alan couldn't decide where to go for his holidays. He didn't go anywhere **in the end**. (而不用 at the end)

in the end 的反义词通常用 **at first**：

- **At first** we didn't get on very well, but **in the end** we became good friends.

at/on/in (时间) ➜ Unit 121

Exercises

122.1 用 **on time** 或 **in time** 填空。

1 The bus was late this morning, but it's usually ...on time... .
2 The film was supposed to start at 8.30, but it didn't begin ....
3 I like to get up .... to have a big breakfast before going to work.
4 We want to start the meeting ...., so please don't be late.
5 I've just washed this shirt. I want to wear it this evening, so I hope it will be dry.......... .
6 The train service isn't very good. The trains are rarely ....
7 I nearly missed my flight this morning. I got to the airport just ....
8 I almost forgot that it was Joe's birthday. Fortunately I remembered ....
9 Why are you never ....? You always keep everybody waiting.

122.2 根据所给情况，用 **just in time** 造句。

1 A child ran into the road in front of your car. You saw the child at the last moment.
(manage / stop) ...I managed to stop just in time...
2 You were walking home. Just after you got home, it started to rain very heavily.
(get / home) I ....
3 Tim was going to sit on the chair you had just painted. You said, 'Don't sit on that chair!', so he didn't. (stop / him) I ....
4 You and a friend went to the cinema. You were late, and you thought you would miss the beginning of the film. But the film began just as you sat down in the cinema.
(get / cinema / beginning / film)
We ....

122.3 用 **at the end of** + 下列词语完成句子。

the course	~~the game~~	the interview	the month	the race

1 The players shook hands ...at the end of the game... .
2 I usually get paid ....
3 The students had a party ....
4 Two of the runners collapsed ....
5 To my surprise, I was offered the job ....

122.4 以 **In the end ...**开头，用括号内动词的适当形式造句。

1 We had a lot of problems with our car. (sell) ...In the end we sold it...
2 Anna got more and more fed up with her job.
(resign) ....
3 I tried to learn German, but I found it too difficult.
(give up) ....
4 We couldn't decide whether to go to the party or not.
(not / go) ....

122.5 用 **at** 或 **in** 填空。

1 I'm going away ...at... the end of the month.
2 It took me a long time to find a job. .... the end I got a job in a hotel.
3 Are you going away .... the beginning of August or .... the end?
4 I couldn't decide what to buy Laura for her birthday. I didn't buy her anything .... the end.
5 We waited ages for a taxi. We gave up .... the end and walked home.
6 I'll be moving to a new address .... the end of September.
7 We had a few problems at first, but .... the end everything was OK.
8 I'm going away .... the end of this week.
9 A: I didn't know what to do.
B: Yes, you were in a difficult position. What did you do .... the end?

in/at/on (地点) (1)

A in

in a room
in a building
in a box

in a garden
in a town/country
in the city centre

in a pool
in the sea
in a river

- There's no-one **in the room / in the building / in the garden**.
- What have you got **in your hand / in your mouth**?
- When we were **in Italy**, we spent a few days **in Venice**.
- I have a friend who lives **in a small village in the mountains**.
- There were some people swimming **in the pool / in the sea / in the river**.

B at

at the bus stop

at the door

at the roundabout

at reception

- Who is that man standing **at the bus stop / at the door / at the window**?
- Turn left **at the traffic lights / at the church / at the roundabout / at the junction**.
- We have to get off the bus **at the next stop**.
- When you leave the hotel, please leave your key **at reception**. (= at the reception desk)

C on

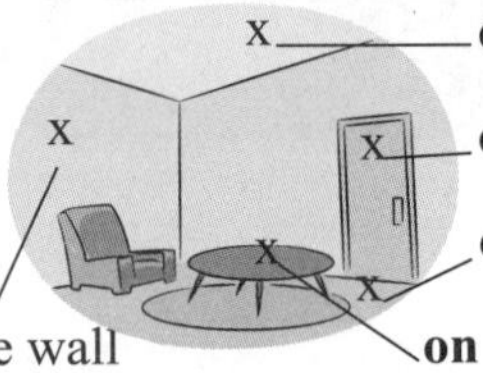

on the ceiling
on the door
on the floor
on the wall
on the table

on her nose

on a page

on an island

- I sat **on the floor / on the ground / on the grass / on the beach / on a chair**.
- There's a dirty mark **on the wall / on the ceiling / on your nose / on your shirt**.
- Have you seen the notice **on the notice board / on the door**?
- You'll find details of TV programmes **on page seven** (of the newspaper).
- The hotel is **on a small island** in the middle of a lake.

D

请比较 **in** 与 **at**：

- There were a lot of people **in the shop**. It was very crowded.
  Go along this road, then turn left **at the shop**.
- I'll meet you **in the hotel lobby**.
  I'll meet you **at the entrance to the hotel**.

请比较 **in** 与 **on**：

- There is some water **in the bottle**.
  There is a label **on the bottle**.

in the bottle
on the bottle

请比较 **at** 与 **on**：

- There is somebody **at the door**. Shall I go and see who it is?
  There is a notice **on the door**. It says 'Do not disturb'.

in/at/on (地点) (2)，(3) ➜ Units 124–125

Exercises

123.1 用 **in**，**at** 或 **on** 与图中所给的词语回答下列问题。

1 
(bottle)

2 
(arm)

3 
(traffic lights)

4 

(door)

5 
(wall)

6 
(Paris)

7 
(gate)

8 
(beach)

1 Where's the label? On the bottle.
2 Where's the fly? ....
3 Where is the car waiting? ....
4 a Where's the notice? ....
b Where's the key? ....
5 Where are the shelves? ....
6 Where's the Eiffel Tower? ....
7 a Where's the man standing? ....
b Where's the bird? ....
8 Where are the children playing? ....

123.2 用 **in**，**at** 或 **on** + 下列词语完成句子。

the window	**your coffee**	**the mountains**	**that tree**
my guitar	~~**the river**~~	**the island**	**the next petrol station**

1 Look at those people swimming in the river .
2 One of the strings .... is broken.
3 There's something wrong with the car. We'd better stop ....
4 Would you like sugar .... ?
5 The leaves .... are a beautiful colour.
6 Last year we had a wonderful skiing holiday ....
7 There's nobody living .... It's uninhabited.
8 He spends most of the day sitting .... and looking outside.

123.3 用 **in**，**at** 或 **on** 填空。

1 There was a long queue of people at the bus stop.
2 Nicola was wearing a silver ring .... her little finger.
3 There was an accident .... the crossroads this morning.
4 I wasn't sure whether I had come to the right office. There was no name .... the door.
5 There are some beautiful trees .... the park.
6 You'll find the sports results .... the back page of the newspaper.
7 I wouldn't like an office job. I couldn't spend the whole day sitting .... a computer.
8 My brother lives .... a small village .... the south-west of England.
9 The man the police are looking for has a scar .... his right cheek.
10 The headquarters of the company are .... Milan.
11 I like that picture hanging .... the wall .... the kitchen.
12 If you come here by bus, get off .... the stop after the traffic lights.

➜ 补充练习 34 (第322页)

Unit 124 in/at/on (地点) (2)

A

下列短语可用来谈论某人/某物：

in a line / **in a row** / **in a queue**	**in bed**
in the sky / **in the world**	**in the country** / **in the countryside**
in an office / **in a department**	**in a picture** / **in a photo** / **in a photograph**
in a book / **in a paper** (= newspaper) / **in a magazine** / **in a letter**	

- When I go to the cinema, I like to sit **in the front row**.
- James isn't up yet. He's still **in bed**.
- It was a lovely day. There wasn't a cloud **in the sky**.
- I've just started working **in the sales department**.
- Who is the woman **in that photo**?
- Have you seen this picture **in today's paper**?

in a row

B

on the left / **on the right**　**on the left-hand side** / **on the right-hand side**
on the ground floor / **on the first floor** / **on the second floor** 等
on a map / **on a menu** / **on a list**
on a farm

- In Britain we drive **on the left**. 或 … **on the left-hand side**.
- Our apartment is **on the second floor** of the building.
- Here's a shopping list. Don't buy anything that's not **on the list**.
- Have you ever worked **on a farm**?

可以用 **on a river** / **on a road** / **on the coast** 来表示地理位置：

- Budapest is **on the** (River) **Danube**.
- The town where you live – is it **on the coast** or inland?

可以用 **on the way** 来表示"在(去某地的)路上"：

- We stopped to buy some things in a shop **on the way** home.

C

at the top (of) / **at the bottom** (of) / **at the end** (of)

- Write your name **at the top of the page**.
- Jane's house is **at the other end of the street**.

D

可以说 **in the front** / **in the back** of a car：

- I was sitting **in the back** (of the car) when we crashed.

可以说 **at the front** / **at the back** of a building / theatre / group of people 等：

- The garden is **at the back of the house**.
- Let's sit **at the front** (of the cinema).
- We were **at the back**, so we couldn't see very well.

另外还可以说 **on the front** / **on the back** of a letter / piece of paper 等：

- I wrote the date **on the back of the photo**.

at the back

at the front

E

可以说 **in the corner** of a room：

- The TV is **in the corner** of the room.

可以说 **at the corner** 或 **on the corner** of a street：

- There is a small shop **at/on the corner** of the street.

in the corner

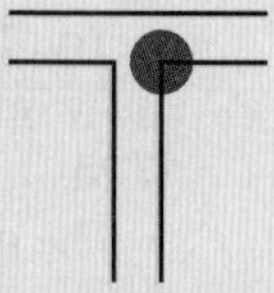

at/on the corner

in the world ➜ Unit 108D　**in/at/on (地点)** ➜ Units 123，125　**美国英语** ➜ 附录 7

Exercises

124.1 用 **in**，**at** 或 **on** 及图中所给词语回答下列问题。

1 Where does Sue work? In the sales department.
2 Sue lives in this building. Where's her flat exactly? ....
3 Where is the woman standing? ....
4 Where is the man standing? ....
5 Where's the cat? ....
6 Where's the dog? ....
7 Liz is in this group of people. Where is she? ....
8 Where's the post office? ....
9 Gary is at the cinema. Where is he sitting? ....
10 Where does Kate work? ....

124.2 用 **in**，**at** 或 **on** + 下列词语完成句子。

the west coast	**the world**	**the back of the class**	~~**the sky**~~
the front row	**the right**	**the back of this card**	**the way to work**

1 It was a lovely day. There wasn't a cloud in the sky.
2 In most countries people drive ....
3 What is the tallest building .... ?
4 I usually buy a newspaper .... in the morning.
5 San Francisco is .... of the United States.
6 We went to the theatre last night. We had seats ....
7 I couldn't hear the teacher. She spoke quietly and I was sitting ....
8 I don't have your address. Could you write it .... ?

124.3 用 **in**，**at** 或 **on** 填空。

1 Write your name at the top of the page.
2 Is your sister .... this photograph? I don't recognise her.
3 I didn't feel very well when I woke up, so I stayed .... bed.
4 We normally use the front entrance to the building, but there's another one .... the back.
5 Is there anything interesting .... the paper today?
6 There was a list of names, but my name wasn't .... the list.
7 .... the end of the street, there is a path leading to the river.
8 I love to look up at the stars .... the sky at night.
9 When I'm a passenger in a car, I prefer to sit .... the front.
10 I live in a very small village. You probably won't find it .... your map.
11 Joe works .... the furniture department of a large store.
12 Paris is .... the River Seine.
13 I don't like cities. I'd much prefer to live .... the country.
14 My office is .... the top floor. It's .... the left as you come out of the lift.

➔ 补充练习 34 (第322页)

in/at/on (地点) (3)

A

in hospital / at work 等

谈论某人时可以说 **in hospital / in prison / in jail**：

- Anna's mother is **in hospital**.

可以说 **at work / at school / at university / at college**：

- I'll be **at work** until 5.30.
- Julia is studying chemistry **at university**.

可以说 **be at home** 或 **be home** (带不带 **at** 均可)，但要说 **do something at home** (带 **at**)：

- I'll **be at home** all evening. 或 I'll **be home** all evening.
- Shall we go to a restaurant or **eat at home**?

B

at a party / at a concert 等

at 可用来表示某人在某个场合 (**at a party / at a conference** 等)：

- Were there many people **at the party / at the meeting / at the wedding**?
- I saw Steve **at a conference / at a concert** on Saturday.

C

in 与 at 用于谈论建筑物

in 或 **at** 常可用来谈论建筑物。例如，可以说 **in a restaurant** 或 **at a restaurant**，**in a supermarket** 或 **at a supermarket**。**at** 通常用来表示某活动发生的地点 (例如：a concert，a film，a party，a meeting)：

- We went to a concert **at the National Concert Hall**.
- The meeting took place **at the company's head office** in Frankfurt.
- There was a robbery **at the supermarket**.

可以说 **at the station / at the airport**：

- There's no need to meet me **at the station**. I can get a taxi.

可以说 **at** somebody's house：

- I was **at Helen's house** last night. 或 I was **at Helen's** last night.

还可以说 **at the doctor's / at the hairdresser's** 等。

in 用于表示建筑物本身：

- We had dinner **at the hotel**.
  All the rooms **in the hotel** have air conditioning. (而不用 at the hotel)
- I was **at Helen's (house)** last night.
  It's always cold **in Helen's house**. The heating doesn't work well. (而不用 at Helen's house)

D

in 与 at 用于谈论城镇等

in 通常可用来表示在城镇或村庄里：

- The Louvre is a famous art museum **in Paris**. (而不用 at Paris)
- Sam's parents live **in a village** in the south of France. (而不用 at a village)

at 可后接地点表示在旅途中的某地或某站：

- Does this train stop **at Oxford**? (= at Oxford station)

E

on a bus / in a car 等

通常说 **on a bus / on a train / on a plane / on a ship** 或 **in a car / in a taxi**：

- **The bus** was very full. There were too many people **on it**.
- Laura arrived **in a taxi**.

可以说 **on a bike** (= bicycle) / **on a motorbike / on a horse**：

- Jane passed me **on her bike**.

at school / in hospital 等 ➔ Unit 74 **in/at/on (地点) (1)，(2)** ➔ Units 123–124
to/at/in/into ➔ Unit 126 **by car / by bike 等** ➔ Unit 128B

Exercises

125.1 用 **in**，**at** 或 **on** 及图中所给词语完成下列句子。

1

(the airport)

2

(a train)

3

(a conference)

4

(hospital)

5

(the hairdresser's)

6

(his bike)

7

(New York)

8

(the Savoy Theatre)

1 You can hire a car ....at the airport.... .
2 Dave is ....
3 Karen is ....
4 Martin is ....
5 Judy is ....
6 I saw Gary ....
7 We spent a few days ....
8 We went to a show ....

125.2 用 **in**，**at** 或 **on** + 下列词语完成句子。

the plane	**hospital**	**a taxi**	~~**the station**~~	**the cinema**
Tokyo	**school**	**prison**	**the airport**	**the sports centre**

1 My train arrives at 11.30. Can you meet me ....at the station.... ?
2 We walked to the restaurant, but we went home ....
3 I'd like to see a film. What's on .... this week?
4 Some people are .... for crimes that they did not commit.
5 'What does your sister do? Does she have a job?' 'No, she's still ....'
6 I play basketball .... on Friday evenings.
7 A friend of mine was injured in an accident a few days ago. She's still ....
8 Our flight was delayed. We had to wait .... for four hours.
9 I enjoyed the flight, but the food .... wasn't very nice.
10 Vicky has gone to Japan. She's living ....

125.3 用 **in**，**at** 或 **on** 填空。

1 We went to a concert ....at.... the National Concert Hall.
2 It was a very slow train. It stopped .... every station.
3 My parents live .... a small village about 50 miles from London.
4 I haven't seen Kate for some time. I last saw her .... David's wedding.
5 We stayed .... a very comfortable hotel when we were .... Amsterdam.
6 There were about fifty rooms .... the hotel.
7 I don't know where my umbrella is. Perhaps I left it .... the bus.
8 'Where were you on Monday evening?' 'I was .... a friend's house.'
9 There must be somebody .... the house. The lights are on.
10 The exhibition .... the Museum of Modern Art finishes on Saturday.
11 Shall we travel .... your car or mine?
12 I didn't expect you to be .... home. I thought you'd be .... work.
13 'Did you like the movie?' 'Yes, but it was too hot .... the cinema.'
14 Paul lives .... Birmingham. He's a student .... Birmingham University.

→ 补充练习 34（第322页）

Unit 126 to/at/in/into

A

可以说 **go/come/travel** (etc.) **to** a place or an event。例如：

go to China	**go to** bed	**come to** my house
go back to Italy	**go to** the bank	**be taken to** hospital
return to London	**go to** a concert	**be sent to** prison
welcome somebody **to** a place		**drive to** the airport

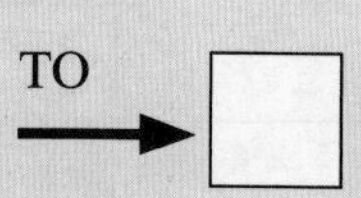

- When are your friends **going back to** Italy?（而不用 going back in Italy）
- Three people were injured in the accident and **taken to** hospital.
- **Welcome to** our country!（而不用 Welcome in）

同样可以说 a **journey to** / a **trip to** / a **visit to** / on **my way to** … 等：

- Did you enjoy **your trip to** Paris / **your visit to** the zoo?

请比较 **to** (表示移动) 与 **in/at** (表示位置)：

- They are **going to** France.　或　They **live in** France.
- Can you **come to** the party?　或　I'll **see you at** the party.

可以说 **been to** a place or an event：

- I've **been to Italy** four times, but I've never **been to Rome**.
- Amanda has never **been to a football match** in her life.

B

get 与 **arrive** 比较

可以说 **get to** a place：

- What time did they **get to London** / **to work** / **to the hotel**?

但是要说 **arrive in** … 或 **arrive at** …（而不用 arrive to）。
可以说 **arrive in** a town，city or country：

- They **arrived in London** / **in Spain** a week ago.

其他地点（建筑物等）或活动用 **arrive at** 表示：

- When did they **arrive at the hotel** / **at the airport** / **at the party**?

C

home

可以说 **go home** / **come home** / **get home** / **arrive home** / **on the way home** 等（不带介词）。
不能说 to home：

- I'm tired. Let's **go home** now.（而不用 go to home）
- I met Lisa **on my way home**.（而不用 my way to home）

D

into

go into，**get into** … etc. 表示"进入（房间 / 建筑物 / 汽车等）"：

- I opened the door, **went into** the room and sat down.
- A bird **flew into** the kitchen through the window.
- Every month, my salary **is paid** directly **into** my bank account.

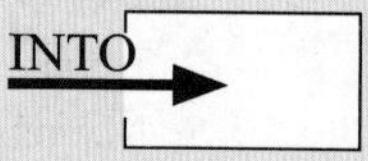

某些动词（尤其是 **go/get/put**）后面常用 **in** 代替 **into**：

- She **got in** the car and drove away.（或 She **got into** the car …）
- I read the letter and **put it** back **in** the envelope.

into 的反义词是 **out of**：

- She **got out of** the car and **went into** a shop.

注意通常说 **get on/off** a bus / a train / a plane（而不常用 into / out of）：

- She **got on the bus** and I never saw her again.

been to → Units 7–8　**in/at/on (地点)** → Units 123–125　**at home** → Unit 125A
into 与 in 比较 → Unit 138A

Exercises

126.1 用 **to/at/in/into** 填空，在不需要介词的地方画“–”。

1 Three people were taken ..*to*.. hospital after the accident.
2 I met Kate on my way ..*–*.. home. (*no preposition*)
3 We left our luggage .... the station and went to find something to eat.
4 Shall we take a taxi .... the station or shall we walk?
5 I have to go .... the bank today. What time does it open?
6 The Amazon flows .... the Atlantic Ocean.
7 'Do you have your camera with you?' 'No, I left it .... the car.'
8 Have you ever been .... China?
9 I had lost my key, but I managed to climb .... the house through a window.
10 We got stuck in a traffic jam on our way .... the airport.
11 We had lunch .... the airport while we were waiting for our plane.
12 Welcome .... the hotel. We hope you enjoy your stay here.
13 We drove along the main road for about a kilometre and then turned .... a narrow side street.
14 Did you enjoy your visit .... the museum?
15 I'm tired. As soon as I get .... home, I'm going .... bed.
16 Marcel is French. He has just returned .... France after two years .... Brazil.
17 Carl was born .... Chicago, but his family moved .... New York when he was three. He still lives .... New York.

126.2 根据你自己的情况，选择下框中的三个地名，仿照示例用 **been to** 造句。

Athens	**Australia**	**Hong Kong**	**Mexico**	**Paris**
Rome	**Singapore**	**Sweden**	**Tokyo**	**the United States**

1 (*example answers*) ..*I've never been to Australia. / I've been to Mexico once.*..
2 ....
3 ....
4 ....

126.3 用 **to/at/in** 填空，在不需要介词的地方画“–”。

1 What time does this train get ..*to*.. London?
2 We arrived .... Barcelona a few days ago.
3 What time did you get .... home last night?
4 What time do you usually arrive .... work in the morning?
5 When we got .... the cinema, there was a long queue outside.
6 I arrived .... home feeling very tired.

126.4 根据所给情况，用 **got + into / out of / on / off** 造句。

1 You were walking home. A friend passed you in her car. She saw you, stopped and offered you a lift. She opened the door. What did you do? ..*I got into the car.*..
2 You were waiting for the bus. At last your bus came. The doors opened. What did you do then?
I .... the bus.
3 You drove home in your car. You stopped outside your house and parked the car. What did you do then? ....
4 You were travelling by train to Manchester. When the train got to Manchester, what did you do?
....
5 You needed a taxi. After a few minutes a taxi stopped for you. You opened the door. What did you do then? ....
6 You were travelling by air. At the end of your flight, your plane landed at the airport and stopped. The doors were opened, you took your bag and stood up. What did you do then?
....

→ 补充练习 34（第322页）

Unit 127

in/on/at (其他用法)

A

in

in the rain / in the sun / in the shade / in the dark / in bad weather 等

- We sat **in the shade**. It was too hot to sit **in the sun**.
- Don't go out **in the rain**. Wait until it stops.

the shade

(write) **in ink / in pen / in pencil**

- When you do the exam, you're not allowed to write **in pencil**.

还可以用 (write) **in words / in figures / in capital letters** 等：

- Please write your name **in capital letters**.
- Write the story **in your own words**. (= don't copy somebody else)

(be/fall) **in love (with** somebody)

- They're very happy together. They're **in love**.

in (my) **opinion**

- **In my opinion**, the movie wasn't very good.

B

on

on TV / **on television** / **on the radio**

- I didn't watch the news **on television**, but I heard it **on the radio**.

on the phone

- I've never met her, but I've spoken to her **on the phone** a few times.

(be/go) **on strike**

- There are no trains today. The drivers are **on strike**.

(be/go) **on a diet**

- I've put on a lot of weight. I'll have to go **on a diet**.

(be) **on fire**

- Look! That car is **on fire**.

on the whole (总之，大体上)

- Sometimes I have problems at work, but **on the whole** I enjoy my job.

on purpose (有目的地，有意地)

- I'm sorry. I didn't mean to annoy you. I didn't do it **on purpose**.

C

on holiday / on a trip 等

可以说 (be/go) **on holiday** / **on business** / **on a trip** / **on a tour** / **on a cruise** 等：

- I'm going **on holiday** next week.
- Emma's away **on business** at the moment.
- One day I'd like to go **on a world tour**.

也可以说 go to a place **for a** holiday / **for my** holiday(s)：

- Steve has gone to France **for a holiday**.

D

at the age of … 等

可以说 **at the age of 16** / **at 120 miles an hour** / **at 100 degrees** 等：

- Tracy left school **at 16**. 或 … **at the age** of 16.
- The train was travelling **at 120 miles an hour**.
- Water boils **at 100 degrees Celsius**.

in/at/on (时间) ➜ Unit 121 in/at/on (地点) ➜ Units 123–125

Exercises

127.1 用 **in** + 下列词语完成句子。

capital letters	**cold weather**	**love**	**my opinion**
pencil	~~**the rain**~~	**the shade**	

1 Don't go out ......*in the rain*...... . Wait until it stops.
2 Matt likes to keep warm, so he doesn't go out much ....
3 If you write .... and make a mistake, you can rub it out and correct it.
4 They fell .... almost immediately and were married in a few weeks.
5 Please write your address clearly, preferably ....
6 It's too hot in the sun. I'm going to sit ....
7 Amanda thought the restaurant was OK, but .... it wasn't very good.

127.2 用 **on** + 下列词语完成句子。

business	**a diet**	~~**fire**~~	**holiday**	**the phone**
purpose	**strike**	**TV**	**a tour**	**the whole**

1 Look! That car is ......*on fire*...... ! Somebody call the fire brigade.
2 Workers at the factory have gone .... for better pay and conditions.
3 Soon after we arrived, we were taken .... of the city.
4 I feel lazy this evening. Is there anything worth watching .... ?
5 I'm sorry. It was an accident. I didn't do it ....
6 Richard has put on a lot of weight recently. I think he should go ....
7 Jane's job involves a lot of travelling. She often has to go away ....
8 A: I'm going .... next week.
B: Where are you going? Somewhere nice?
9 A: Is Sarah here?
B: Yes, but she's .... at the moment. She won't be long.
10 A: How was your exam?
B: Well, there were some difficult questions, but .... it was OK.

127.3 用 **in**，**on** 或 **at** 填空。

1 Water boils ......*at*...... 100 degrees Celsius.
2 When I was 14, I went .... a trip to France organised by my school.
3 There was panic when people realised that the building was .... fire.
4 Julia's grandmother died recently .... the age of 79.
5 Can you turn the light on, please? I don't want to sit .... the dark.
6 We didn't go .... holiday last year. We stayed at home.
7 I hate driving .... fog. You can't see anything.
8 I won't be here next week. I'll be .... holiday.
9 Technology has developed .... great speed.
10 Alan got married .... 17, which is rather young to get married.
11 I heard an interesting programme .... the radio this morning.
12 .... my opinion, violent films should not be shown .... television.
13 I wouldn't like to go .... a cruise. I think I'd get bored.
14 I shouldn't eat too much. I'm supposed to be .... a diet.
15 I wouldn't like his job. He spends most of his time talking .... the phone.
16 The earth travels round the sun .... 107,000 kilometres an hour.
17 'Did you enjoy your holiday?' 'Not every minute, but .... the whole, yes.'
18 A lot of houses were damaged .... the storm last week.

→ 补充练习 34（第322页）

by

A

by 可用于很多表达中表示做某事的方式。例如可以说：

send something **by post** | contact somebody **by phone** / **by email**
do something **by hand** | pay **by credit card** / **by cheque**

- Can I pay **by credit card**?
- You can contact me **by phone** or **by email**.

但要说 **pay cash** 或 **pay in cash** (而不常用 by cash)。

也可以说 **by mistake** / **by accident** / **by chance**：

- We hadn't arranged to meet. We met **by chance**.

但要说 do something **on purpose**，表示“有意做某事”：

- I didn't do it **on purpose**. It was an accident.

注意要说 **by chance**，**by credit card** 等 (而不用 by the chance / by a credit card)。这些表达是由 **by** + 名词构成，不加冠词 **the** 或 **a**。

B

by 同样可以表示出行方式：

by car / **by train** / **by plane** / **by boat** / **by ship** / **by bus** / **by bike** 等
by road / **by rail** / **by air** / **by sea**

- Jess usually goes to work **by bus**.

但要说 **on foot**：

- Did you come here **by car** or **on foot**?

by 后面要使用不带冠词或物主代词的名词，因此在 **my car** / **the train** / **a taxi** 等之前不能使用 **by**。可以说：

by car 或 **in my** car (而不用 by my car)
by train 或 **on the** train (而不用 by the train)

in 用于汽车、出租车等名词前：

- They didn't come **in their car**. They came **in a taxi**.

on 用于自行车和公共交通 (如公交、火车) 等名词前：

- We travelled **on the 6.45 train**.

C

可以说 something is done **by** somebody/something (被动语态)：

- Have you ever been bitten **by a dog**?
- The programme was watched **by millions of people**.

请比较 **by** 与 **with**：

- The door must have been opened **with a key**. (而不用 by a key)
  (= somebody used a key to open it)
- The door must have been opened **by somebody** with a key.

可以说 a play **by Shakespeare**，a painting **by Rembrandt**，a novel **by Tolstoy** 等：

- Have you read anything **by** Ernest Hemingway?

D

by 还有“在……近旁，在……旁边”的意思：

- Come and sit **by me**. (= next to me)
- 'Where's the light switch?' **'By the door.'**

SWITCH →

E

注意下列 **by ...** 的用法：

- Clare's salary has just gone up **from** £2,500 a month **to** £2,750. So it has increased **by £250** / **by ten per cent**.
- Carl and Mike had a race over 200 metres. Carl won **by** about **three metres**.

new salary £2,750
increased **by** £250
old salary £2,500

被动语态 + **by** ➜ Unit 42B **by** + **-ing** ➜ Unit 60B **by myself** ➜ Unit 83D **by** (时间) ➜ Unit 120

Exercises

128.1 用 **by** + 下列词语完成句子。

canal	~~**chance**~~	**credit card**	**hand**	**mistake**

1 We hadn't arranged to meet. We met ...by chance... .
2 I didn't intend to take your umbrella. I took it ....
3 Don't put the sweater in the washing machine. It has to be washed ....
4 I don't need cash. I can pay the bill ....
5 The town is not on the coast, but is connected to the sea ....

128.2 用 **by**，**in** 或 **on** 填空。

1 Jess usually goes to work ...by... bus.
2 I saw Jane this morning. She was .... the bus.
3 How did you get here? Did you come .... train?
4 I decided not to go .... car. I went .... my bike instead.
5 I didn't feel like walking home, so I came home .... a taxi.
6 Sorry we're late. We missed the bus, so we had to come .... foot.
7 How long does it take to cross the Atlantic .... ship?

128.3 下列每句中都有一处错误，请指出并改正。

1 Did you come here by Kate's car or yours? ...in Kate's car...
2 I don't like travelling on bus. ....
3 These photographs were taken by a very good camera. ....
4 I know this music is from Beethoven, but I can't remember what it's called. ....
5 I couldn't pay by cash – I didn't have any money on me. ....
6 We lost the game because of a mistake of one of our players. ....

128.4 仿照示例造句，分别描述一本书、一首歌、一幅画或一部电影等。

1 ...War and Peace is a book by Tolstoy....
2 ...Romeo and Juliet is a play by Shakespeare....
3 ....
4 ....
5 ....

128.5 用 **by**，**in**，**on** 或 **with** 填空。

1 Have you ever been bitten ...by... a dog?
2 The plane was badly damaged .... lightning.
3 We managed to put the fire out .... a fire extinguisher.
4 Who is that man standing .... the window?
5 These photographs were taken .... a friend of mine.
6 I don't mind going .... car, but I don't want to go .... your car.
7 There was a small table .... the bed .... a lamp and a clock .... it.

128.6 仿照示例，用 **by** ...完成下列句子。

1 Clare's salary was £2,500 a month. Now it is £2,750.
Her salary ...has increased by £250....
2 My daily newspaper used to cost 80 pence. From today it costs 90.
The price has gone up ....
3 There was an election. Helen won. She got 25 votes and James got 23.
Helen won ....
4 I went to Kate's house to see her, but she had gone out five minutes before I arrived.
I missed ....

➜ 补充练习 34（第322页）

Unit 129 名词 + 介词 (reason for， cause of 等)

A

名词 + **for** …

a **demand** / a **need FOR** …

- The company closed down because there wasn't enough **demand for** its product.
- There's no excuse for behaviour like that. There's no **need for** it.

a **reason FOR** …

- The train was late, but nobody knew the **reason for** the delay. (而不用 reason of)

B

名词 + **of** …

an **advantage** / a **disadvantage OF** …

- The **advantage of living alone** is that you can do what you like.

但是说

there is an advantage **in** (*or* **to**) doing something

- **There are** many advantages **in** living alone. 或 … many advantages **to** living alone.

a **cause OF** …

- The **cause of** the explosion is unknown.

a **picture** / a **photo** / a **photograph** / a **map** / a **plan** / a **drawing** (etc.) **OF** …

- Rachel showed me some **pictures of** her family.
- I had a **map of** the town, so I was able to find my way around.

C

名词 + **in** …

an **increase** / a **decrease** / a **rise** / a **fall IN** (prices etc.)

- There has been an **increase in** the number of road accidents recently.
- Last year was a bad one for the company. There was a big **fall in** sales.

D

名词 + **to** …

damage TO …

- The accident was my fault, so I had to pay for the **damage to** the other car.

an **invitation TO** … (a party / a wedding etc.)

- Did you get an **invitation to** the party?

a **solution TO** (a problem) / a **key TO** (a door) / an **answer TO** (a question) / a **reply TO** (a letter) / a **reaction TO** …

- I hope we find a **solution to** the problem. (而不用 a solution of the problem)
- I was surprised at her **reaction to** my suggestion.

an **attitude TO** … 或 an **attitude TOWARDS** …

- His **attitude to** his job is very negative. 或 His **attitude towards** his job …

E

名词 + **with** … / **between** …

a **relationship** / a **connection** / **contact WITH** …

- Do you have a good **relationship with** your parents?
- The police want to question a man in **connection with** the robbery.

但是说

a **relationship** / a **connection** / **contact** / a **difference BETWEEN** two things or people

- The police believe that there is no **connection between** the two crimes.
- There are some **differences between** British and American English.

Exercises

129.1 完成下列句子，使它与前一个句子表达的意思相同。

1 What caused the explosion? What was the cause *of the explosion* ?
2 We're trying to solve the problem.
We're trying to find a solution ....
3 Sue gets on well with her brother.
Sue has a good relationship ....
4 The cost of living has gone up a lot.
There has been a big increase ....
5 I don't know how to answer your question.
I can't think of an answer ....
6 I don't think that a new road is necessary.
I don't think there is any need ....
7 I think that working at home has many advantages.
I think that there are many advantages ....
8 The number of people without jobs fell last month.
Last month there was a fall ....
9 Nobody wants to buy shoes like these any more.
There is no demand ....
10 In what way is your job different from mine?
What is the difference .... ?

129.2 用下列名词＋适当的介词完成句子。

cause	**connection**	**contact**	**damage**	**invitation**
key	~~**map**~~	**photographs**	**reason**	**reply**

1 On the wall there were some pictures and a *map of* the world.
2 Thank you for the .... your party next week.
3 Since she left home two years ago, Sophie has had little .... her family.
4 I can't open this door. Do you have a .... the other door?
5 The .... the fire at the hotel last week is still unknown.
6 Did you get a .... the email you sent to the company?
7 The two companies are completely independent. There is no .... them.
8 Jane showed me some old .... the city as it looked 100 years ago.
9 Carol has decided to give up her job. I don't know her .... doing this.
10 It wasn't a bad accident. The .... the car wasn't serious.

129.3 用适当的介词填空。

1 There are some differences *between* British and American English.
2 Money isn't the solution .... every problem.
3 There has been an increase .... the amount of traffic using this road.
4 The advantage .... having a car is that you don't have to rely on public transport.
5 There are many advantages .... being able to speak a foreign language.
6 Everything can be explained. There's a reason .... everything.
7 When Paul left home, his attitude .... his parents seemed to change.
8 Ben and I used to be good friends, but I don't have much contact .... him now.
9 There has been a sharp rise .... property prices in the past few years.
10 What was Sarah's reaction .... the news?
11 If I give you the camera, can you take a picture .... me?
12 The company has rejected the workers' demands .... a rise .... pay.
13 What was the answer .... question 3 in the test?
14 The fact that Jane was offered a job has no connection .... the fact that she is a friend of the managing director.

→ 补充练习 35（第322页）

Unit 130

形容词 + 介词 (1)

A

It was **nice of** you to …

nice / kind / good / generous / polite / stupid / silly etc. **OF** somebody (to do something)

- Thank you. It was very **kind of you** to help me.
- It is **stupid of me** to go out without a coat in such cold weather.

但是说

(be) **nice / kind / good / generous / polite / rude / friendly / cruel** etc. **TO** somebody

- They have always been very **nice to** me. (而不用 with me)
- Why were you so **unfriendly to** Lucy?

B

形容词 + **about / with**

angry / annoyed / furious / upset { **ABOUT** something / **WITH** somebody **FOR** doing something }

- There's no point in getting **angry about** things that don't matter.
- Are you **annoyed with** me **for** being late?
- Lisa is **upset about** not being invited to the party.

表示对某种情况有某种情绪时用 **excited / worried / nervous / happy** etc. **ABOUT**：

- Are you **nervous about** the exam?

表示对收到的东西或某事的结果具有某种感情或态度时用 **pleased / satisfied / happy / delighted / disappointed WITH**：

- They were **delighted with** the present I gave them.
- Were you **happy with** your exam results?

C

形容词 + **at / by / with / of**

surprised / shocked / amazed / astonished / upset AT *or* **BY** something

- Everybody was **surprised at** (*or* **by**) the news.
- I hope you weren't **shocked by** (*or* **at**) what I said.

impressed WITH *or* **BY** somebody/something

- I'm very **impressed with** (*or* **by**) her English. It's very good.

fed up / bored WITH something

- I don't enjoy my job any more. I'm **fed up with** it. / I'm **bored with** it.

tired / sick OF something

- Come on, let's go! I'm **tired of** waiting. / I'm **sick of** waiting.

D

sorry about / for

表示对某种情况或发生的事感到报歉时用 **sorry ABOUT**：

- I'm **sorry about** the mess. I'll clear it up later.
- **Sorry about** last night. (= Sorry about something that happened last night)

表示因做过的事而感到歉疚时用 **sorry FOR** *or* **ABOUT**：

- Alex is very **sorry for** what he said. (或 **sorry about** what he said)
- I'm **sorry for** shouting at you yesterday. (或 **sorry about** shouting)

还可以说 I'm sorry I (did something)：

- I'm **sorry I shouted** at you yesterday.

表示为处境糟糕的人感到难过时用 **feel / be sorry FOR**：

- I **feel sorry for** Matt. He's had a lot of bad luck. (而不用 I feel sorry about Matt)

介词 + -ing ➜ Unit 60　形容词 + to … ➜ Unit 65　sorry to … / sorry for … ➜ Unit 66C
形容词 + 介词 (2) ➜ Unit 131

Exercises

130.1 根据下列情况，用 **nice of ...**，**kind of ...** 等造句。

1	I went out in the cold without a coat.	(silly) That was silly of you.
2	Tom offered to drive me to the airport.	(nice) That was .... him.
3	I needed money and Sue gave me some.	(generous) That ....
4	They didn't invite us to their party.	(not very nice) That wasn't ....
5	Can I help you with your luggage?	(very kind) ....
6	Kevin never says 'thank you'.	(not very polite) ....
7	They've had an argument and now they refuse to speak to each other.	(a bit childish) ....

130.2 用下列形容词 + 适当的介词完成句子。

amazed angry bored careless excited impressed kind ~~nervous~~

1 Are you nervous about the exam?
2 Thank you for all you've done. You've been very .... me.
3 What have I done wrong? Why are you .... me?
4 You must be very .... your trip next week. It sounds really great.
5 I wasn't .... the service in the restaurant. We had to wait ages before our food arrived.
6 Ben isn't very happy at college. He says he's .... the course he's doing.
7 I'd never seen so many people before. I was .... the crowds.
8 It was .... you to leave the door unlocked when you went out.

130.3 用适当的介词填空。

1 They were delighted with the present I gave them.
2 It was nice .... you to come and see me when I was ill.
3 Why are you so rude .... people? Why can't you be more polite?
4 We always have the same food every day. I'm fed up .... it.
5 We enjoyed our holiday, but we were a bit disappointed .... the hotel.
6 I can't understand people who are cruel .... animals.
7 I was surprised .... the way he behaved. It was completely out of character.
8 I've been trying to learn Spanish, but I'm not very satisfied .... my progress.
9 Tanya doesn't look very well. I'm worried .... her.
10 They told me they were sorry .... the situation, but there was nothing they could do.
11 I wouldn't like to be in her position. I feel sorry .... her.
12 Are you still upset .... what I said to you yesterday?
13 Some people say Kate is unfriendly, but she's always been very nice .... me.
14 I'm tired .... doing the same thing every day. I need a change.
15 The man we interviewed for the job was intelligent and we were impressed .... the way he answered our questions.
16 I'm sorry .... the smell of paint in this room. I've just finished redecorating it.
17 I was shocked .... what I saw. I'd never seen anything like it before.
18 Our neighbours were very angry .... the noise we made.
19 Our neighbours were furious .... us .... making so much noise.
20 I'm sorry .... what I did. I hope you're not angry .... me.

→ 补充练习 35（第322页）

Unit 131

形容词 + 介词 (2)

A 形容词 + of (1)

afraid / frightened / terrified / scared OF …
- ▢ 'Are you **afraid of** spiders?' 'Yes, I'm **terrified of** them.'

fond / proud / ashamed / jealous / envious OF …
- ▢ Why are you always so **jealous of** other people?

suspicious / critical / tolerant OF …
- ▢ He didn't trust me. He was **suspicious of** my motives.

B 形容词 + of (2)

aware / conscious OF …
- ▢ 'Did you know he was married?' 'No, I wasn't **aware of** that.'

capable / incapable OF …
- ▢ I'm sure you are **capable of** passing the examination.

full / short OF …
- ▢ Amy is a very active person. She's always **full of** energy.
- ▢ I'm **short of** money. Can you lend me some?

typical OF …
- ▢ He's late again. It's **typical of** him to keep everybody waiting.

certain / sure OF *or* ABOUT …
- ▢ I think she's arriving this evening, but I'm not **sure of** that. 或 … not **sure about** that.

C 形容词 + at / to / from / in / on / with / for

good / bad / brilliant / better / hopeless etc. AT …
- ▢ I'm not very **good at** repairing things. (而不用 good in repairing things)

married / engaged TO …
- ▢ Louise is **married to** an American. (而不用 married with)

但是 Louise is married **with three children**. (= she is married and has three children)

similar TO …
- ▢ Your writing is **similar to** mine.

different FROM 或 different TO …
- ▢ The film was **different from** what I'd expected. 或 ... **different to** what I'd expected.

interested IN …
- ▢ Are you **interested in** art?

keen ON …
- ▢ We stayed at home because Chris wasn't very **keen on** going out.

dependent ON … (但是说 **independent OF …**)
- ▢ I don't want to be **dependent on** anybody.

crowded WITH (people etc.)
- ▢ The streets were **crowded with** tourists. (但是说 ... **full of** tourists)

famous FOR …
- ▢ The Italian city of Florence is **famous for** its art treasures.

responsible FOR …
- ▢ Who was **responsible for** all that noise last night?

介词 + -ing ➜ Unit 60　afraid of/to … ➜ Unit 66A　形容词 + 介词 (1) ➜ Unit 130
美国英语 ➜ 附录 7

Exercises

131.1 用下列形容词+适当的介词完成句子。

afraid capable different interested proud responsible similar ~~sure~~

1 I think she's arriving this evening, but I'm not ....sure of.... that.
2 Your camera is .... mine, but it isn't exactly the same.
3 Don't worry. I'll look after you. There's nothing to be ....
4 I never watch the news on TV. I'm not .... the news.
5 The editor is the person who is .... what appears in a newspaper.
6 Sarah is a keen gardener. She's very .... her garden and loves showing it to visitors.
7 I was surprised when I met Lisa for the first time. She was .... what I expected.
8 He could become world champion one day. He's .... it.

131.2 完成下列句子，使它与前一个句子表达的意思相同。

1 There were lots of tourists in the streets. The streets were crowded ....with tourists.... .
2 There was a lot of furniture in the room. The room was full ....
3 I don't like sport very much. I'm not very keen ....
4 We don't have enough time. We're short ....
5 I'm not a very good tennis player. I'm not very good ....
6 Catherine's husband is Russian. Catherine is married ....
7 I don't trust Robert. I'm suspicious ....
8 My problem is not the same as yours. My problem is different ....

131.3 用适当的介词填空。

1 Amy is always full ....of.... energy.
2 My home town is not a very interesting place. It's not famous .... anything.
3 Kate is very fond .... her younger brother.
4 I don't like going up ladders. I'm scared .... heights.
5 You look bored. You don't seem interested .... what I'm saying.
6 'Our flight departs at 10.35.' 'Are you sure .... that?'
7 I'm not ashamed .... what I did. In fact I'm quite proud .... it.
8 I wanted to go out for a meal, but nobody else was keen .... the idea.
9 These days everybody is aware .... the dangers of smoking.
10 The station platform was crowded .... people waiting for the train.
11 Sue is much more successful than I am. Sometimes I feel a bit jealous .... her.
12 Do you know anyone who might be interested .... buying an old car?
13 We've got plenty to eat. The fridge is full .... food.
14 She's very honest. I don't think she is capable .... telling a lie.
15 Helen works hard and she's extremely good .... her job.
16 It's typical .... him to change his mind at the last minute.
17 Mark has no money of his own. He's totally dependent .... his parents.
18 We're short .... staff in our office at the moment. We need more people to do the work.

131.4 根据你自己的情况和括号内的提示，用下列词语造句。

good pretty good not very good hopeless

1 (repairing things) ....I'm not very good at repairing things....
2 (telling jokes) ....
3 (maths) ....
4 (remembering names) ....
5 (sport) ....

→ 补充练习 35（第322页）

动词 + 介词 (1) —— to 与 at 比较

A

动词 + **to**

talk / **speak TO** somebody (有时也可用 **with**)
- Who was that man you were **talking to**?

listen TO …
- We spent the evening **listening to** music. (而不用 listening music)

apologise TO somebody (for …)
- They **apologised to me** for what happened. (而不用 They apologised me)

explain something **TO** somebody
- Can you **explain** this word **to me**? (而不用 explain me this word)

explain / **describe** (**to** somebody) what/how/why …
- I **explained to them** why I was worried. (而不用 I explained them)
- Let me **describe to you** what I saw. (而不用 Let me describe you)

B

下列动词后面不加 **to**:

phone / **call** / **email** / **text** somebody
- I **called the airline** to cancel my flight. (而不用 called to the airline)

但是说 **write** (a letter) **to** somebody

answer somebody/something
- He refused to **answer my question**. (而不用 answer to my question)

但是说 **reply to** an email / a letter etc.

ask somebody
- Can I **ask you** a question? (而不用 ask to you)

thank somebody (for something)
- He **thanked me** for helping him. (而不用 He thanked to me)

C

动词 + **at**

look / **stare** / **glance AT** …, **have a look** / **take a look AT** …
- Why are you **looking at** me like that?

laugh AT …
- I look stupid with this haircut. Everybody will **laugh at** me.

aim / **point** (something) **AT** …, **shoot** / **fire** (a gun) **AT** …
- Don't **point** that knife **at** me. It's dangerous.
- We saw someone with a gun **shooting at** birds, but he didn't hit any.

D

有些动词后可以使用 **at** 或 **to**,表示不同的含义:

shout AT somebody 表示生气时叫骂:
- He got very angry and started **shouting at** me.

shout TO somebody 表示大声喊叫:
- He **shouted to** me from the other side of the street.

throw something **AT** somebody/something 意为"朝……扔东西":
- Somebody **threw** an egg **at** the minister.

throw something **TO** somebody 意为"扔东西给某人":
- Lisa shouted 'Catch!' and **threw** the keys **to** me from the window.

动词 + 介词 (2)–(5) ➜ Units 133–136　**ask for ➜ Unit 133B**
apologise for / thank somebody for ➜ Unit 135B　**其他动词 + to ➜ Unit 136D**

Exercises

132.1 请在正确的句子后面画✓。

1 a Can you explain this word to me? ✓
  b Can you explain me this word? ☐
2 a I got angry with Mark. Afterwards, I apologised to him. ☐
  b I got angry with Mark. Afterwards I apologised him. ☐
3 a Amy won't be able to help you. There's no point in asking to her. ☐
  b Amy won't be able to help you. There's no point in asking her. ☐
4 a I need somebody to explain me what I have to do. ☐
  b I need somebody to explain to me what I have to do. ☐
5 a They didn't understand the system, so I explained it to them. ☐
  b They didn't understand the system, so I explained it them. ☐
6 a I like to sit on the beach and listen to the sound of the sea. ☐
  b I like to sit on the beach and listen the sound of the sea. ☐
7 a I asked them to describe me exactly what happened. ☐
  b I asked them to describe to me exactly what happened. ☐
8 a We'd better phone the restaurant to reserve a table. ☐
  b We'd better phone to the restaurant to reserve a table. ☐
9 a It was a difficult question. I couldn't answer to it. ☐
  b It was a difficult question. I couldn't answer it. ☐
10 a I explained everybody the reasons for my decision. ☐
  b I explained to everybody the reasons for my decision. ☐
11 a I thanked everybody for all the help they had given me. ☐
  b I thanked to everybody for all the help they had given me. ☐
12 a My friend texted to me to let me know she was going to be late. ☐
  b My friend texted me to let me know she was going to be late. ☐

132.2 用下列动词＋适当的介词完成句子。

~~explain~~ ~~laugh~~ **listen** **look** **point** **reply** **speak** **throw** **throw**

1 I look stupid with this haircut. Everybody will laugh at me.
2 I don't understand this. Can you explain it to me?
3 Sue and Kevin had an argument and now they're refusing to .... each other.
4 Be careful with those scissors! Don't .... them .... me!
5 I'm not sure where we are. I'll have to .... the map.
6 Please .... me! I've got something important to tell you.
7 Don't .... stones .... the birds! It's cruel.
8 If you don't want that sandwich, ... it .... the birds. They'll eat it.
9 I tried to contact Tina, but she didn't .... my emails.

132.3 用 **to** 或 **at** 填空。

1 They apologised to me for what happened.
2 I glanced .... my watch to see what time it was.
3 Please don't shout .... me! Try to calm down.
4 I saw Sue as I was cycling along the road. I shouted .... her, but she didn't hear me.
5 Don't listen .... what he says. He doesn't know what he's talking about.
6 What's so funny? What are you laughing .... ?
7 Could I have a look .... your magazine, please?
8 I'm lonely. I need somebody to talk ....
9 She was so angry she threw a book .... the wall.
10 The woman sitting opposite me on the train kept staring .... me.
11 Can I speak .... you a moment? There's something I want to ask you.

→ 补充练习 36 (第323页)

Unit 133 动词 + 介词 (2) —— about/for/of/after

A 动词 + about

talk / read / know ABOUT …， **tell** somebody **ABOUT** …

- We **talked about** a lot of things at the meeting.

have a discussion ABOUT something 或 **discuss** something (不用介词)

- We had **a discussion about** what we should do.
- We **discussed** a lot of things at the meeting. (而不用 discussed about)

do something **ABOUT** something 表示"想办法改善某种不好的情况"：

- If you're worried about the problem, you should **do** something **about** it.

B 动词 + for

ask (somebody) **FOR** …

- I sent an email to the company **asking** them **for** more information about the job.

但是 I **asked** him **the way** to …， She **asked** me **my name** (不用介词)

apply (**TO** a person, a company etc.) **FOR** a job etc.

- I think you'd be good at this job. Why don't you **apply for** it?

wait FOR …

- Don't **wait for** me. I'll join you later.
- I'm not going out yet. I'm **waiting for** the rain to stop.

search (a person / a place / a bag etc.) **FOR** …

- I've **searched** the house **for** my keys, but I still can't find them.

leave (a place) **FOR** another place

- I haven't seen her since she **left** (home) **for** the office this morning.
  (而不用 left to the office)

C care about，care for 与 take care of 比较

care ABOUT somebody/something 表示"在乎"：

- He's very selfish. He doesn't **care about** other people.

可以说 **care what/where/how**…等 (不带 about)：

- You can do what you like. I don't **care what** you do.

care FOR somebody/something

(1) 表示"喜欢(某物)"(通常用于否定句中)：

- I don't **care for** very hot weather. (= I don't like …)

(2) 表示"照顾，看护 (某人)"：

- Alan is 85 and lives alone. He needs somebody to **care for** him.

take care OF … 表示"照顾，看护，负责"：

- Don't worry about me. I can **take care of** myself.
- I'll **take care of** the travel arrangements. You don't need to do anything.

D look for 与 look after 比较

look FOR … 表示"寻找"：

- I've lost my keys. Can you help me to **look for** them?

look AFTER … 表示"照顾，看护"：

- Alan is 85 and lives alone. He needs somebody to **look after** him. (而不用 look for)
- You can borrow this book, but you must promise to **look after** it.

动词 (think/hear 等) + about/of ➜ Unit 134 其他动词 + for ➜ Unit 135B

Exercises

133.1 用适当的介词填空，在不需要介词的地方画“–”。

1 I'm not going out yet. I'm waiting ......for...... the rain to stop.
2 Don't ask me .... money. I don't have any.
3 I've applied .... a job at the factory. I don't know if I'll get it.
4 I've applied .... three colleges. I hope one of them accepts me.
5 I've searched everywhere .... Joe, but I haven't been able to find him.
6 I don't want to talk .... what happened last night. Let's forget it.
7 I don't want to discuss .... what happened last night. Let's forget it.
8 We had an interesting discussion .... the problem, but we didn't reach a decision.
9 We discussed .... the problem, but we didn't reach a decision.
10 I sent her an email. Now I'm waiting .... her to reply.
11 Ken and Sonia are travelling in Italy. They're in Rome right now, and tomorrow they leave .... Venice.
12 The roof of the house is in very bad condition. I think we ought to do something .... it.
13 We waited .... Steve for half an hour, but he never came.
14 Tomorrow morning I have to catch a plane. I'm leaving my house .... the airport at 7.30.

133.2 在 **care** 后填写适当的介词，在不需要介词的地方画“–”。

1 He's very selfish. He doesn't care ......about...... other people.
2 Who's going to take care .... you when you are old?
3 She doesn't care .... the exam. She doesn't care whether she passes or fails.
4 'Do you like this coat?' 'Not really. I don't care .... the colour.'
5 Don't worry about the shopping. I'll take care .... that.
6 He gave up his job to care .... his elderly father.
7 I want to have a good holiday. I don't care .... the cost.
8 I want to have a good holiday. I don't care .... how much it costs.

133.3 用 **look for** 或 **look after** 的适当形式完成下列句子。

1 I ......looked for...... my keys, but I couldn't find them anywhere.
2 Kate is .... a job. I hope she finds one soon.
3 Who .... you when you were ill?
4 I'm .... Liz. I need to ask her something. Have you seen her?
5 The car park was full, so we had to .... somewhere else to park.
6 A babysitter is somebody who .... other people's children.

133.4 用下列动词的适当形式＋介词完成句子。

apply	ask	do	leave	look	~~search~~	talk	wait

1 Police are ......searching for...... the man who escaped from prison.
2 Sarah wasn't ready. We had to .... her.
3 I think Ben likes his job, but he doesn't .... it much.
4 When I'd finished my meal, I .... the waiter .... the bill.
5 Cathy is unemployed. She has .... several jobs, but she hasn't had any luck.
6 If something is wrong, why don't you .... something .... it?
7 Helen's car is very old, but it's in excellent condition. She .... it very well.
8 Diane is from Boston, but now she lives in Paris. She .... Boston .... Paris when she was 19.

➜ 补充练习 36 (第323页)

动词 + 介词 (3) —— about 与 of 比较

A

hear ABOUT … 表示“被告知 (某事)”：
- ▢ Did you **hear about** the fire at the hotel yesterday?

hear OF … 表示“听说 (某人或某事)”：
- ▢ 'Who is Tom Hart?' 'I have no idea. I've never **heard of** him.' (而不用 heard from him)

hear FROM … 表示“得到 (某人的消息)”：
- ▢ 'Have you **heard from** Jane recently?' 'Yes, she called me a few days ago.'

B

think ABOUT … 与 **think OF** … 比较

think ABOUT something 表示“考虑，思考”：
- ▢ I've **thought about** what you said and I've decided to take your advice.
- ▢ 'Will you lend me the money?' 'I'll **think about** it.'

think OF something 表示“想到，想起”：
- ▢ It was my idea. I **thought of** it first. (而不用 thought about it)
- ▢ I felt embarrassed. I couldn't **think of** anything to say. (而不用 think about anything)

think of 也可用来表示询问或表达看法：
- ▢ 'What did you **think of** the movie?' 'I didn't **think** much **of** it.' (= I didn't like it much)

of 或 **about** 有时差别不大，可以互换：
- ▢ When I'm alone, I often **think of** (*or* **about**) you.

think of 或 **think about** doing something 可用来表示“考虑 (将来做某事)”：
- ▢ My sister is **thinking of** (*or* **about**) going to Canada. (= she is considering it)

C

dream ABOUT … 表示“(睡觉时) 梦见”：
- ▢ I **dreamt about** you last night.

dream OF *or* **ABOUT** being something / doing something 表示“梦想”：
- ▢ Do you **dream of** (或 **about**) being rich and famous?

I **wouldn't dream OF** doing something 表示“无论如何也不会做某事”：
- ▢ 'Don't tell anyone what I said.' 'No, I **wouldn't dream of** it.' (= I would never do it)

D

complain (**TO** somebody) **ABOUT** … 表示“申诉，控诉”：
- ▢ We **complained to** the manager of the restaurant **about** the food.

complain OF a pain, an illness etc. 表示“诉说有疼痛等”：
- ▢ We called the doctor because George was **complaining of** a pain in his stomach.

E

remind somebody **ABOUT** … 表示“提醒”：
- ▢ I'm glad you **reminded** me **about** the meeting. I'd completely forgotten about it.

remind somebody **OF** … 表示“使记起，使想起”：
- ▢ This house **reminds** me **of** the one I lived in when I was a child.
- ▢ Look at this photograph of Richard. Who does he **remind** you **of**?

F

警告某人要注意危险的或不同寻常的人/事时用 **warn** somebody **ABOUT**：
- ▢ I knew he was a strange person. I had been **warned about** him. (而不用 warned of him)
- ▢ Vicky **warned me** about the traffic. She said it would be bad.

警告某人有某种危险或可能要发生不好的事时用 **warn** somebody **ABOUT** *or* **OF**：
- ▢ Scientists have **warned** us **about** (*or* **of**) the effects of climate change.

remind/warn somebody **to** … ➜ **Unit 55B**

Exercises

134.1 用 **hear** 或 **heard** + 适当的介词 (**about/of/from**) 完成下列句子。

1 I've never ......heard of...... Tom Hart. Who is he?
2 'Did you .... the accident last night?' 'Yes, Vicky told me.'
3 Jane used to call me quite often, but I haven't .... her for a long time now.
4 A: Have you .... a writer called William Hudson?
B: No, I don't think so. What sort of writer is he?
5 Thanks for your email. It was good to .... you.
6 'Do you want to .... our holiday?' 'Not now. Tell me later.'
7 I live in a small town in the north of England. You've probably never .... it.

134.2 用 **think about** 或 **think of** 的适当形式完成下列句子。

1 You look serious. What are you ......thinking about...... ?
2 I need time to make decisions. I like to .... things carefully.
3 That's a good idea. Why didn't I .... that?
4 A: I've finished reading the book you lent me.
B: What did you .... it? Did you think it was good?
5 We're .... going out to eat this evening. Would you like to come?
6 I don't really want to go out with Tom tonight. I'll have to .... an excuse.
7 When I was offered the job, I didn't accept immediately. I went away and .... it for a while. In the end I decided to take the job.
8 I don't .... much .... this coffee. It's like water.
9 Katherine is homesick. She's always .... her family back home.
10 A: Do you think I should apply to do the course?
B: I can't .... any reason why not.

134.3 用适当的介词填空。

1 Did you hear ......about...... the fire at the hotel yesterday?
2 'I had a strange dream last night.' 'Did you? What did you dream ....?'
3 Our neighbours complained .... us .... the noise we made last night.
4 Kevin was complaining .... pains in his chest, so he went to the doctor.
5 I love this music. It reminds me .... a warm day in spring.
6 He loves his job. He thinks .... his work all the time, he dreams .... it, he talks .... it and I'm fed up with hearing .... it.
7 'We've got no money. What can we do?' 'Don't worry. I'll think .... something.'
8 Jackie warned me .... the water. She said it wasn't safe to drink.
9 We warned our children .... the dangers of playing in the street.

134.4 用下列动词的适当形式 + 介词完成句子。

complain	dream	hear	remind	remind	~~think~~	think	warn

1 It was my idea. I ......thought of...... it first.
2 Ben is never satisfied. He's always .... something.
3 I can't make a decision yet. I need time to .... your proposal.
4 Before you go into the house, I must .... you .... the dog. He's bitten people before, so be careful.
5 She's not a well-known singer. Not many people have .... her.
6 A: You wouldn't go away without telling me, would you?
B: Of course not. I wouldn't .... it.
7 I would have forgotten my appointment if Jane hadn't .... me .... it.
8 Do you see that man over there? Does he .... you .... anybody you know?

→ 补充练习 36 (第323页)

Unit 135 动词 + 介词 (4) —— of/for/from/on

A 动词 + of

accuse / **suspect** somebody **OF** …
- ▢ Sue **accused** me **of** being selfish.
- ▢ Some students were **suspected of** cheating in the exam.

approve / **disapprove OF** …
- ▢ His parents don't **approve of** what he does, but they can't stop him.

die OF *or* **FROM** an illness etc.
- ▢ 'What did he **die of**?' 'A heart attack.'

consist OF …
- ▢ We had an enormous meal. It **consisted of** seven courses.

B 动词 + for

pay (somebody) **FOR** …
- ▢ I didn't have enough money to **pay for** the meal. (而不用 pay the meal)

但是说 **pay** a bill / a fine / a fee / tax / rent / a sum of money 等 (不用介词)：
- ▢ I didn't have enough money to **pay the rent**.

thank / **forgive** somebody **FOR** …
- ▢ I'll never **forgive** them **for** what they did.

apologise (**TO** somebody) **FOR** …
- ▢ When I realised I was wrong, I **apologised** (**to** them) **for** my mistake.

blame somebody/something **FOR** …, somebody is **to blame FOR** …
- ▢ Everybody **blamed** me **for** the accident.
- ▢ Everybody said that I was **to blame for** the accident.

blame (a problem etc.) **ON** …
- ▢ The accident wasn't my fault. Don't **blame** it **on** me.

C 动词 + from

suffer FROM an illness etc.
- ▢ There's been an increase in the number of people **suffering from** heart disease.

protect somebody/something **FROM** …
- ▢ Sun block **protects** the skin **from** the sun.

D 动词 + on

depend / **rely ON** …
- ▢ 'What time will you be home?' 'I don't know. It **depends on** the traffic.'
- ▢ You can **rely on** Anna. She always keeps her promises.

depend 后面接 **when/where/how** 等 (疑问词) 时用不用 **on** 均可：
- ▢ 'Are you going to buy it?' 'It **depends how much** it is.' (或 It depends **on** how much)

live ON money / food
- ▢ Michael's salary is very low. It isn't enough to **live on**.

congratulate / **compliment** somebody **ON** …
- ▢ **I congratulated** her **on** doing so well in her exams.
- ▢ The meal was really good. I **complimented** Mark **on** his cooking skills.

动词 + 介词 + 动词 -ing 形式 ➔ Unit 62 其他动词 + for ➔ Unit 133 其他动词 + on ➔ Unit 136E

Exercises

135.1 用适当的介词填空，在不需要介词的地方画“–”。

1 Some students were suspected ...of... cheating in the exam.
2 Are you going to apologise .... what you did?
3 The apartment consists .... three rooms, a kitchen and bathroom.
4 I was accused .... lying, but I was telling the truth.
5 We finished our meal, paid .... the bill, and left the restaurant.
6 The accident was my fault, so I had to pay .... the repairs.
7 Some people are dying .... hunger, while others eat too much.
8 I called Helen to thank her .... the present she sent me.
9 The government is popular. Most people approve .... what they're doing.
10 Do you blame the government .... the economic situation?
11 When something goes wrong, you always blame it .... other people.

135.2 完成下列句子，使它与前一个句子表达的意思相同。

1 Sue said that I was selfish.
Sue accused me ...of being selfish... .
2 The misunderstanding was my fault, so I apologised.
I apologised ....
3 Jane won the tournament, so I congratulated her.
I congratulated ....
4 He has enemies, and he has a bodyguard to protect him.
He has a bodyguard to protect ....
5 There are eleven players in a football team.
A football team consists ....
6 Sandra eats only bread and eggs.
Sandra lives ....
7 You can't say that your problems are my fault.
You can't blame ....

135.3 用下列动词的适当形式＋介词完成句子。

accuse apologise ~~approve~~ congratulate depend live pay suffer

1 His parents don't ...approve of... what he does, but they can't stop him.
2 When you went to the theatre with Paul, who .... the tickets?
3 It's not pleasant when you are .... something you didn't do.
4 We hope to go to the beach tomorrow, but it .... the weather.
5 Things are cheap there. You can .... very little money.
6 You were rude to Lisa. I think you should .... her.
7 Alex .... back pain. He spends too much time working at his desk.
8 When I saw David, I .... him .... passing his driving test.

135.4 用适当的介词填空，在不需要介词的地方画“–”。

1 I'll never forgive them ...for... what they did.
2 They wore warm clothes to protect themselves .... the cold.
3 You know you can always rely .... me if you need any help.
4 Sophie doesn't have enough money to pay .... her college fees.
5 She's often unwell. She suffers .... very bad headaches.
6 I don't know whether I'll go out tonight. It depends .... how I feel.
7 She hasn't got a job. She depends .... her parents for money.
8 My usual breakfast consists .... fruit, cereal and coffee.
9 I complimented her .... her English. She spoke really well.

→ 补充练习 36（第323页）

Unit 136

动词 + 介词 (5) —— in/into/with/to/on

A

动词 + in

believe IN …

- Do you **believe in** God? (= Do you believe that God exists?)
- I **believe in** saying what I think. (= I believe it is right to say what I think)

但是用 **believe** something 表示"相信某事"，**believe** somebody 表示"相信某人说的话"：

- The story can't be true. I don't **believe it**. (而不用 believe in it)

specialise IN …

- Helen is a lawyer. She **specialises in** company law.

succeed IN …

- I hope you **succeed in** finding the job you want.

B

动词 + into

break INTO …

- Our house was **broken into** a few days ago, but nothing was stolen.

crash / **drive** / **bump** / **run INTO** …

- He lost control of the car and **crashed into** a wall.

divide / **cut** / **split** something **INTO** two or more parts

- The book is **divided into** three parts.

translate a book etc. **FROM** one language **INTO** another

- She's a famous writer. Her books have been **translated into** many languages.

C

动词 + with

collide WITH …

- There was an accident this morning. A bus **collided with** a car.

fill something **WITH** … (但是 **full** 要与 **of** 搭配，参见 Unit 131B)

- Take this saucepan and **fill** it **with** water.

provide / **supply** somebody **WITH** …

- The school **provides** all its students **with** books.

D

动词 + to

happen TO …

- What **happened to** that gold watch you used to have? (= where is it now?)

invite somebody **TO** a party / a wedding etc.

- They only **invited** a few people **to** their wedding.

prefer one thing / person **TO** another

- I **prefer** tea **to** coffee.

E

动词 + on

concentrate ON …

- I tried to **concentrate on** my work, but I kept thinking about other things.

insist ON …

- I wanted to go alone, but some friends of mine **insisted on** coming with me.

spend (money) **ON** …

- How much do you **spend on** food each week?

动词 + 介词 + 动词 -ing 形式 ➜ Unit 62　其他动词 + to ➜ Unit 132　其他动词 + on ➜ Unit 135D

Exercises

136.1 用下列动词的适当形式＋介词完成句子。

believe	concentrate	divide	drive	fill	happen	~~insist~~	invite	succeed

1 I wanted to go alone, but my friends insisted on coming with me.
2 I haven't seen Mike for ages. I wonder what has .... him.
3 We've been .... the party, but unfortunately we can't go.
4 It's a very large house. It's .... four apartments.
5 I don't .... ghosts. I think people imagine that they see them.
6 Steve gave me an empty bucket and told me to .... it .... water.
7 I was driving along when the car in front stopped suddenly. I couldn't stop in time and .... the back of it.
8 Don't try and do two things together. .... one thing at a time.
9 It wasn't easy, but in the end we .... finding a solution to the problem.

136.2 完成下列句子，使它与前一个句子表达的意思相同。

1 There was a collision between a bus and a car.
A bus collided with a car ....
2 I don't mind big cities, but I prefer small towns.
I prefer ....
3 I got all the information I needed from Jane.
Jane provided me ....
4 This morning I bought a pair of shoes which cost £70.
This morning I spent ....
5 There are ten districts in the city.
The city is divided ....

136.3 用适当的介词填空，在不需要介词的地方画"–"。

1 The school provides all its students with books.
2 A strange thing happened .... me a few days ago.
3 Mark decided to give up sport to concentrate .... his studies.
4 Money should be used well. I don't believe .... wasting it.
5 My present job isn't wonderful, but I prefer it .... what I did before.
6 I hope you succeed .... getting what you want.
7 As I was coming out of the room, I collided .... somebody who was coming in.
8 There was an awful noise as the car crashed .... a tree.
9 Patrick is a photographer. He specialises .... sports photography.
10 Do you spend a lot of money .... clothes?
11 I was amazed when Joe walked into the room. I couldn't believe .... it.
12 Somebody broke .... my car and stole the radio.
13 I was quite cold, but Tom insisted .... having the window open.
14 The teacher decided to split the class .... four groups.
15 I filled the tank, but unfortunately I filled it .... the wrong kind of petrol.
16 Some words are difficult to translate .... one language .... another.

136.4 根据你自己的想法，用适当的介词短语完成下列句子。

1 I wanted to go out alone, but my friend insisted on coming with me ....
2 I spend a lot of money ....
3 I saw the accident. The car crashed ....
4 Chris prefers basketball ....
5 The restaurant we went to specialises ....
6 Shakespeare's plays have been translated ....

➜ 补充练习 36（第323页）

Unit 137

短语动词 (1) —— 概述

A

下列单词通常跟在动词后使用：

in	**on**	**up**	**away**	**by**	**about**	**over**	**round** 或 **around**
out	**off**	**down**	**back**	**through**	**along**	**forward**	

因此可以说 **look out / get on / take off / run away** 等，这些就是短语动词。

on/off/out 等常与表示移动的动词连用。例如：

- **get on** — The bus was full. We couldn't **get on**.
- **drive off** — A woman got into the car and **drove off**.
- **come back** — Sarah is leaving tomorrow and **coming back** on Saturday.
- **turn round** — When I touched him on the shoulder, he **turned round**.

但通常是 **on/off/out** 等词赋予了动词特殊的含义：

- **break down** — Sorry I'm late. The car **broke down**. (= the engine stopped working)
- **look out** — **Look out**! There's a car coming. (= be careful)
- **take off** — It was my first flight. I was nervous as the plane **took off**. (= went into the air)
- **get on** — How was the exam? How did you **get on**? (= How did you do?)
- **get by** — My French isn't very good, but it's enough to **get by**. (= manage)

有关短语动词的更多用法，参见 Units 138–145。

B

有时短语动词后面使用介词：

短语动词	介词	
run away	**from**	Why did you **run away from** me?
keep up	**with**	You're walking too fast. I can't **keep up with** you.
look up	**at**	We **looked up at** the plane as it flew above us.
look forward	**to**	Are you **looking forward to** your trip?

C

有时短语动词有宾语，这时宾语在句中的位置通常有两种。
可以说：

I **turned on** the light. (宾语: the light) 或 I **turned** the light **on**. (宾语: the light)

如果宾语是代词 (**it/them/me/him** 等)，那么它在句中的位置只有下面一种：

I **turned** it **on**. (而不用 I turned on it)

再看一些例句：

- Can you { **fill in** this form? / **fill** this form **in**? }

但是 They gave me a form and told me to **fill it in**. (而不用 fill in it)

- Don't { **throw away** this box. / **throw** this box **away**. }

但是 I want to keep this box, so don't **throw it away**. (而不用 throw away it)

- I'm going to { **take off** my shoes. / **take** my shoes **off**. }

但是 These shoes are uncomfortable. I'm going to **take them off**. (而不用 take off them)

- Don't { **wake up** the baby. / **wake** the baby **up**. }

但是 The baby is asleep. Don't **wake her up**. (而不用 wake up her)

短语动词 (2)–(9) ➜Units 138–145　美国英语 ➜ 附录 7

Exercises

137.1 从A、B两框中各选一个词完成下列句子。有些词可以重复使用。

A: **fly** **get** **go** **look** **sit** **speak**

B: **away** **by** **down** **on** **out** **round** **up**

1 The bus was full. We couldn't get on .
2 I've been standing for the last two hours. I'm going to ………… for a bit.
3 A cat tried to catch the bird, but it ………… just in time.
4 We were trapped in the building. We couldn't ………… .
5 I can't hear you very well. Can you ………… a little?
6 'Do you speak German?' 'Not very well, but I can ………… .'
7 Everything has got so expensive. Prices have ………… a lot.
8 I thought there was somebody behind me, but when I ………… , there was nobody there.

137.2 从A、B两框中各选一个词完成下列句子。有些词可以重复使用。

A: **away** **back** **forward** **in** **up**

B: **at** **through** **to** **with**

1 You're walking too fast. I can't keep up with you.
2 My holidays are nearly over. Next week I'll be ………… work.
3 We went ………… the top floor of the building to admire the view.
4 The meeting tomorrow is going to be difficult. I'm not looking ………… it.
5 There was a bank robbery last week. The robbers got ………… £50,000.
6 I love to look ………… the stars in the sky at night.
7 I was sitting in the kitchen when a bird flew ………… the open window.

137.3 用下列短语动词和 **it/them/me** 完成句子。

~~fill in~~ **get out** **give back** **switch on** **take off** **wake up**

1 They gave me a form and told me to fill it in .
2 I'm going to bed now. Can you ………… at 6.30?
3 I've got something in my eye and I can't ………… .
4 I don't like it when people borrow things and don't ………… .
5 I want to use the hair dryer. How do I ………… ?
6 My shoes are dirty. I'd better ………… before going into the house.

137.4 根据你自己的想法，用名词 (**this box** 等) 或代词 (**it/them** 等) 及括号内的词完成句子。

1 Don't throw away this box . I want to keep it. (away)
2 I don't want this newspaper. You can throw it away . (away)
3 I borrowed these books from the library. I have to take ………… tomorrow. (back)
4 We can turn ………… . Nobody is watching it. (off)
5 A: How did the vase get broken?
B: I'm afraid I knocked ………… while I was cleaning. (over)
6 Shh! My mother is asleep. I don't want to wake ………… . (up)
7 It's cold today. You should put ………… if you're going out. (on)
8 It was only a small fire. I was able to put ………… easily. (out)
9 A: Is this hotel more expensive than when we stayed here last year?
B: Yes, they've put ………… . (up)
10 It's a bit dark in this room. Shall I turn ………… ? (on)

→ 补充练习 37–41 (第323–325页)

短语动词 (2) —— in/out

A

请比较 **in** 与 **out**：

in 表示“进入 (房间、建筑物、汽车等)”：

- How did the thieves **get in**?
- Here's a key, so you can **let yourself in**.
- Lisa walked up to the edge of the pool and **dived in**. (= into the water)
- I've got a new apartment. I'm **moving in** on Friday.
- As soon as I got to the airport, I **checked in**.

同样地，还可以说 **go in**，**come in**，**walk in**，**break in** 等。

请比较 **in** 与 **into**：

- I'm moving **in** next week.
- I'm moving **into my new flat** on Friday.

out 表示“(从房间、建筑物、汽车等中) 出来”：

- He just stood up and **walked out**.
- I had no key, so I was **locked out**.
- She swam up and down the pool, and then **climbed out**.
- Andy opened the window and **looked out**.
- (*at a hotel*) What time do we have to **check out**?

同样地，还可以说 **go out**，**get out**，**move out**，**let** somebody **out** 等。

请比较 **out** 与 **out of**：

- He walked **out**.
- He walked **out of the room**.

B

其他动词 + **in**

drop in 表示“临时拜访”：

- I **dropped in** to see Chris on my way home.

join in 表示“参加 (活动)，加入进来”：

- They were playing cards, so I **joined in**.

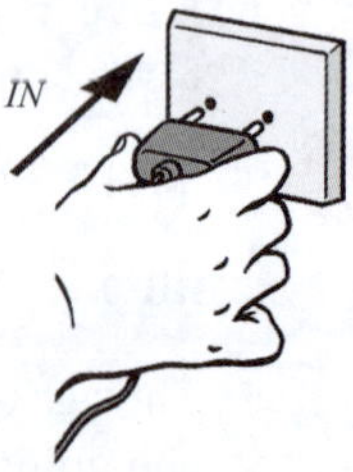

plug in 表示“接通 (电器) 电源”：

- The fridge isn't working because you haven't **plugged** it **in**.

fill in 表示“填写（表格、问卷等）”：

- Please **fill in** the application form and send it to us by 28 February.

这时也可以用 **fill out**。

take somebody **in** 表示“欺骗 (某人)”：

- The man said he was a policeman and I believed him. I was completely **taken in**.

C

其他动词 + **out**

eat out 表示“下馆子吃饭”：

- There wasn't anything to eat at home, so we decided to **eat out**.

drop out 表示“中途退出 (大学、课程、比赛等)”：

- Gary went to university but **dropped out** after a year.

get out 表示“逃避 (计划要做的事)”：

- I promised I'd go to the wedding. I don't want to go, but I can't **get out** of it now.

cut something **out** (of a newspaper etc.)

- There was a beautiful picture in the magazine, so I **cut** it **out** and kept it.

leave something **out** 表示“遗漏，不包括”：

- In the sentence 'She said that she was ill', you can **leave out** the word 'that'.

cross something **out** / **rub** something **out**

- Some of the names on the list had been **crossed out**. ~~Sarah~~ *cross out*

短语动词 (1) —— 概述 → Unit 137　　更多动词 + out → Unit 139

Exercises

138.1 用动词的适当形式完成下列句子。

1 Here's a key so that you can ...let... yourself in.
2 Liz doesn't like cooking, so she .... out a lot.
3 Amy isn't living in this apartment any more. She .... out a few weeks ago.
4 If you're in our part of town, you should .... in and say hello.
5 When I .... in at the airport, I was told my flight would be delayed.
6 There was an article in the paper that I wanted to keep, so I .... it out.
7 I wanted to iron some clothes, but there was nowhere to .... the iron in.
8 I hate .... in questionnaires.
9 Steve was upset because he'd been .... out of the team.
10 Be careful! The water's not very deep here, so don't .... in.
11 If you write in pencil and you make a mistake, you can .... it out.
12 Paul started doing a Spanish course, but he .... out after a few weeks.

138.2 用 **in**，**into**，**out** 或 **out of** 填空。

1 I've got a new flat. I'm moving ...in... on Friday.
2 We checked .... the hotel as soon as we arrived.
3 As soon as we arrived at the hotel, we checked ....
4 The car stopped and the driver got ....
5 Thieves broke .... the house while we were away.
6 Why did Sarah drop .... college? Did she fail her exams?

138.3 用动词的适当形式 + **in** 或 **out (of)** 完成下列句子。

1 Lisa walked to the edge of the pool, ...dived in... and swam to the other end.
2 Not all the runners finished the race. Three of them ....
3 I went to see Joe and Sophie in their new house. They .... last week.
4 I've told you everything you need to know. I don't think I've .... anything.
5 Some people in the crowd started singing. Then a few more people .... and soon everybody was singing.
6 We go to restaurants a lot. We like ....
7 Don't be .... by him. If I were you, I wouldn't believe anything he says.
8 I .... to see Laura a few days ago. She was fine.
9 A: Can we meet tomorrow morning at 10?
B: Probably. I'm supposed to go to another meeting, but I think I can .... it.

138.4 用下列括号内动词的适当形式完成句子。

1 A: The fridge isn't working.
B: That's because you haven't ...plugged it in... . (plug)

2 A: What do I have to do with these forms?
B: .... and send them to this address. (fill)

3 A: I've made a mistake on this form.
B: That's all right. Just .... and correct it. (cross)

4 A: Did you believe the story they told you?
B: Yes, I'm afraid they completely .... (take)

5 A: Have you been to that new club in Bridge Street?
B: We wanted to go there a few nights ago, but they wouldn't .... because we weren't members. (let)

→ 补充练习 37–41（第323–325页）

Unit 139

短语动词 (3) —— out

A

out 可用来表示“熄灭的，关掉的”：

go out — Suddenly all the lights in the building **went out**.
put out a fire / a cigarette / a light — We managed to **put** the fire **out**.
turn out a light — I **turned** the lights **out** before leaving.
blow out a candle — We don't need the candle. You can **blow** it **out**.

B

work out

work out 可指“锻炼”：
- Rachel **works out** at the gym three times a week.

work out 也可表示“好转，进展”：
- Good luck for the future. I hope everything **works out** well for you.
- A: Why did James leave the company?
  B: Things didn't **work out**. (= things didn't work out well)

work out (用于数学计算)
- The total bill for three people is £84.60. That **works out** at £28.20 each.

work something **out** 可表示“计算出，设法弄懂”：
- 345 × 76? I need to do this on paper. I can't **work** it **out** in my head.

C

其他动词 + **out**

carry out 可表示“执行(命令、实验、调查、计划等)”：
- Soldiers are expected to **carry out** orders.
- An investigation into the accident will be **carried out** as soon as possible.

fall out (**with** somebody) 意为“争吵”：
- They used to be very good friends. I'm surprised to hear that they have **fallen out**.
- David **fell out with** his father and left home.

find out that/what/when … etc.，**find out about** something 意为“了解”：
- The police never **found out** who committed the murder.
- I just **found out** that it's Helen's birthday today.
- I checked a few websites to **find out about** hotels in the town.

give/hand things **out** 意为“分发”：
- At the end of the lecture, the speaker **gave out** information sheets to the audience.

point something **out** (**to** somebody) 意为“指出”：
- As we drove through the city, our guide **pointed out** all the sights.
- I didn't realise I'd made a mistake until somebody **pointed** it **out to** me.

run out (**of** something)
- We **ran out of** petrol on the motorway. (= we used all our petrol)

sort something **out** 意为“解决，整理”：
- There are a few problems we need to **sort out**.
- All these papers are mixed up. I'll have to **sort** them **out**.

turn out to be …，**turn out** good/nice etc.，**turn out** that …
- Nobody believed Paul at first, but he **turned out** to be right. (= it became clear in the end that he was right)
- The weather wasn't so good in the morning, but it **turned out** nice later.
- I thought they knew each other, but it **turned out** that they'd never met.

try out 表示“试验(机器、系统、新想法等)”：
- The company is **trying out** a new computer system at the moment.

短语动词 (1) —— 概述 → Unit 137　　更多动词 + out → Unit 138

Exercises

139.1 从下框中选择可搭配的词填空。

a candle	a cigarette	~~a light~~	a mess	a mistake	a new product	an order

1 turn out ...a light...
2 point out ......
3 blow out ......
4 carry out ......
5 put out ......
6 try out ......
7 sort out ......

139.2 用动词的适当形式 + **out** 填空。

1 The company is ...trying out... a new computer system at the moment.
2 Steve is very fit. He does a lot of sport and ...... regularly.
3 The road will be closed for two days next week while building work is ....
4 We didn't manage to discuss everything at the meeting. We ...... of time.
5 You have to ...... the problem yourself. I can't do it for you.
6 I don't know what happened exactly. I need to ....
7 The new drug will be ...... on a small group of patients.
8 I thought the two books were the same until a friend of mine ...... the difference.
9 They got married a few years ago, but it didn't ...... and they separated.
10 There was a power cut and all the lights ....
11 We thought she was American at first, but she ...... to be Swedish.
12 Sometimes it ...... cheaper to eat in a restaurant than to cook at home.
13 I haven't applied for the job yet. I want to ...... more about the company first.
14 It took the fire brigade two hours to ...... the fire.

139.3 根据下列图片，用动词的适当形式 + **out** 完成句子。

1

They've ...run out of petrol... .

2

The man with the beard is ...... leaflets.

3

The weather has ....

4

Sally and Kim are ...... at the gym.

5

They've ....

6

Lisa is trying to ...... how ....

139.4 用动词的适当形式 + **out** 完成下列句子。

1 A: Was the fire serious?
B: No, we were able to ...put it out... .
2 A: This recipe looks interesting.
B: Yes, let's ....
3 A: How much money do I owe you exactly?
B: Just a moment. I'll have to ....
4 A: What happened about your problem with your bank?
B: It's OK now. I went to see them and we ....

→ 补充练习 37–41 (第323–325页)

Unit 140 短语动词 (4) —— on/off (1)

A

on 和 **off** 可表示灯、机器等的开和关

可以说：the light **is on** / **put** the light **on** / **leave** the light **on** 等
turn the light **on/off** 或 **switch** the light **on/off**

- ▢ Shall I **leave** the lights **on** or **turn** them **off**?
- ▢ '**Is** the heating **on**?' 'No, I **switched** it **off**.'
- ▢ We need some boiling water, so I'll **put** the kettle **on**.

也可以说 **put on** some music / a CD 等：

- ▢ I haven't listened to this CD yet. Shall I **put** it **on**? (= shall I play it)

B

on 和 **off** 可表示事件等的发生和取消

go on 意为"发生"：

- ▢ What's all that noise? What's **going on**? (= what's happening)

call something **off** 意为"取消"：

- ▢ The open air concert had to be **called off** because of the weather.

put something **off**，**put off** doing something 意为"推迟"：

- ▢ The wedding has been **put off** until January.
- ▢ We can't **put off** making a decision. We have to decide now.

C

on 和 **off** 还可表示穿、脱衣物等

put on 可表示"穿上 (衣服)，戴上 (眼镜)，涂 (化妆品)，系上 (安全带)"等：

- ▢ My hands were cold, so I **put** my gloves **on**.

put on weight 表示"增重"：

- ▢ I've **put on** two kilograms in the last month.

try on 意为"试穿 (衣服)"：

- ▢ I **tried on** a jacket in the shop, but it didn't fit me very well.

take off 可表示"脱下 (衣服)，摘下(眼镜)"：

- ▢ It was warm, so I **took off** my jacket.

D

off 可表示"离开"

be off (to + 地点)

- ▢ Tomorrow I'**m off** to Paris / I'**m off** on holiday.
  (= I'm going to Paris / I'm going on holiday)

walk off / **run off** / **drive off** / **ride off** / **go off** (与 **walk away** / **run away** 等意义相近)

- ▢ Diane got on her bike and **rode off**.
- ▢ Mark left home at the age of 18 and **went off** to Canada.

set off 意为"启程"：

- ▢ We **set off** very early to avoid the traffic. (= We left early)

take off 意为"(飞机) 起飞"：

- ▢ After a long delay the plane finally **took off**.

see somebody **off** 意为"(到机场、车站等) 给某人送行"：

- ▢ Helen was going away. We went to the station with her to **see her off**.

短语动词 (1) —— 概述 ➜ Unit 137 更多动词 + on/off ➜ Unit 141

Exercises

140.1 用 **put on** 和下列词语完成句子。

a CD **the heating** **the kettle** ~~**the light**~~ **the oven**

1 It was getting dark, so I put the light on .
2 It was getting cold, so I ....
3 I wanted to bake a cake, so I ....
4 I wanted to make some tea, so I ....
5 I wanted to listen to some music, so I ....

140.2 用动词的适当形式 + **on** 或 **off** 填空。

1 It was warm, so I took off my jacket.
2 What are all these people doing? What's .... ?
3 The weather was too bad for the plane to ...., so the flight was delayed.
4 I didn't want to be disturbed, so I .... my phone.
5 Rachel got into her car and .... at high speed.
6 Tim has .... weight since I last saw him. He used to be quite thin.
7 A: What time are you leaving tomorrow?
B: I'm not sure yet, but I'd like to .... as early as possible.
8 Don't .... until tomorrow what you can do today.
9 There was going to be a strike by bus drivers, but now they have been offered more money and the strike has been ....
10 Are you cold? Shall I get you a sweater to .... ?
11 When I go away, I prefer to be alone at the station or airport. I don't like it when people come to .... me ....

140.3 根据下列图片完成句子。

1

Her hands were cold, so she put her gloves on .

2

The plane .... at 10.55.

3

Maria ...., but it was too big for her.

4

The match .... because of the weather.

5

Mark's parents went to the airport to ....

6

He took his sunglasses out of his pocket and ....

→ 补充练习 37–41 (第323–325页)

Unit 141

短语动词 (5) —— on/off (2)

A

动词 + **on** 可表示继续某种行为

drive on / **walk on** / **play on** 意为"继续开车/步行/比赛等"：

- Shall we stop at this petrol station or shall we **drive on** to the next one?

go on 意为"持续"：

- The party **went on** until 4 o'clock in the morning.

go on / **carry on** doing something 意为"继续做某事"：

- We can't **go on** spending money like this. We'll have nothing left soon.
- I don't want to **carry on** working here. I'm going to look for another job.

也可以说 **go on with** / **carry on with** something：

- Don't let me disturb you. Please **carry on with** what you're doing.

keep on doing something 意为"一直做某事"：

- He **keeps on** criticising me. I'm fed up with it!

B

get on

get on 可意为"进展"：

- How are you **getting on** in your new job? (= How is it going?)

get on (**with** somebody) 意为"友好相处"：

- Joanne and Karen don't **get on**. They're always arguing.
- Richard **gets on** well **with** his neighbours. They're all very friendly.

get on with something 意为"(被打断后) 继续做要做的事"：

- I must **get on with** my work. I have a lot to do.

C

动词 + **off**

doze off / **drop off** / **nod off** 意为"睡着"：

- The lecture wasn't very interesting. In fact I **dozed off** in the middle of it.

finish something **off** 意为"对某事物作最后加工"：

- A: Have you finished painting the kitchen?
  B: Nearly. I'll **finish** it **off** tomorrow.

go off 意为"爆炸"：

- A bomb **went off** in the city centre, but fortunately nobody was hurt.

也可用 **go off** 来表示"(闹钟、警报器等) 发出响声"：

- Did you hear the alarm **go off**?

put somebody **off** (doing something) 意为"使某人不想 (做) 某事"：

- We wanted to go to the exhibition, but we were **put off** by the long queue.
- What **put** you **off** applying for the job? Was the salary too low?

rip somebody **off** 意为"敲某人竹杠" (非正式)：

- Did you really pay £2,000 for that painting? I think you were **ripped off**.
  (= you paid too much)

show off 意为"炫耀，卖弄"：

- Look at that boy on the bike riding with no hands. He's just **showing off**.

tell somebody **off** 意为"斥责，训斥"：

- Clare's mother **told** her **off** for wearing dirty shoes in the house.

go on / carry on / keep on ➜ Unit 53B　短语动词 (1) ——概述 ➜ Unit 137
更多动词 + on/off ➜ Unit 140　美国英语 ➜ 附录 7

Exercises

141.1 用动词的适当形式 + **on** 或 **off** 填空，使其与画线部分意思相同。

1 Did you hear the bomb explode?
Did you hear the bomb ....go off.... ?
2 The meeting continued longer than I expected.
The meeting .... longer than I expected.
3 We didn't stop to rest. We continued walking.
We didn't stop to rest. We ....
4 I fell asleep while I was watching TV.
I .... while I was watching TV.
5 Gary doesn't want to retire. He wants to continue working.
Gary doesn't want to retire. He wants to .... working.
6 The fire alarm rang in the middle of the night.
The fire alarm .... in the middle of the night.
7 Martin phones me continuously. It's very annoying.
Martin .... It's very annoying.

141.2 用动词的适当形式 + **on** 或 **off** 完成下列句子。

1 We can't ....go on.... spending money like this. We'll have nothing left soon.
2 I was standing by the car when suddenly the alarm ....
3 I'm not ready to go home yet. I have a few things to ....
4 'Shall I stop the car here?' 'No, ...'
5 Bill paid too much for the car he bought. I think he was ....
6 'Is Emma enjoying her course at university?' 'Yes, she's .... very well.'
7 I was very tired at work today. I nearly .... at my desk a couple of times.
8 Ben was .... by his boss for being late for work repeatedly.
9 I really like working with my colleagues. We all .... really well together.
10 There was a very loud noise. It sounded like a bomb ....
11 I .... making the same mistake. It's very frustrating.
12 I've just had a coffee break, and now I must .... with my work.
13 Peter is always trying to impress people. He's always ....
14 We decided not to go to the concert. We were .... by the cost of tickets.

141.3 用下列动词的适当形式 + **on** 或 **off** 完成句子。

carry	**finish**	~~**get**~~	**get**	**get**	**go**	**rip**	**tell**

1 A: How ....are you getting on.... in your new job?
B: Fine, thanks. It's going very well.
2 A: Have you written the letter you had to write?
B: I've started it. I'll .... in the morning.
3 A: We took a taxi to the airport. It cost £40.
B: £40! Normally it costs about £20. You ....
4 A: Why were you late for work this morning?
B: I overslept. My alarm clock didn't ....
5 A: How .... in your interview? Do you think you'll get the job?
B: I hope so. The interview was OK.
6 A: Did you stop playing tennis when it started to rain?
B: No, we .... The rain wasn't very heavy.
7 A: Some children at the next table in the restaurant were behaving very badly.
B: Why didn't their parents .... ?
8 A: Why does Paul want to leave his job?
B: He .... his boss.

→ 补充练习 37–41 (第323–325页)

短语动词 (6) —— up/down

A

请比较 **up** 与 **down**：

put something **up** (on a wall 等)
- I **put** a picture **up** on the wall.

pick something **up**
- There was a letter on the floor. I **picked** it **up** and looked at it.

stand up
- Alan **stood up** and walked out.

turn something **up**
- I can't hear the TV. Can you **turn** it **up** a bit?

take something **down** (from a wall 等)
- I didn't like the picture, so I **took** it **down**.

put something **down**
- I stopped writing and **put down** my pen.

sit down / bend down / lie down
- I **bent down** to tie my shoelace.

turn something **down**
- The oven is too hot. **Turn** it **down** to 150 degrees.

B

knock down，**cut down** 等

knock down a building，**blow** something **down**，**cut** something **down** 等
- Some old houses were **knocked down** to make way for the new shopping centre.
- Why did you **cut down** the tree in your garden?

be **knocked down** (by a car 等)
- A man was **knocked down** by a car and taken to hospital.

burn down 意为“被烧毁”：
- They were able to put out the fire before the house **burnt down**.

C

down 可表示“减少”之意

slow down 意为“减速”：
- You're driving too fast. **Slow down**.

calm (somebody) **down** 意为“(使) 平静，(使) 镇定”：
- **Calm down**. There's no point in getting angry.

cut down (**on** something) 意为“少吃，少喝，减少”：
- I'm trying to **cut down on** coffee. I drink too much of it.

D

其他动词 + **down**

break down 可表示“(机器、汽车等) 停止运转，(关系等) 破裂”：
- The car **broke down** and I had to phone for help.
- Their marriage **broke down** after only a few months.

close down / **shut down** 意为“停业”：
- There used to be a shop at the end of the street; it **closed down** a few years ago.

let somebody **down** 意为“使某人失望”：
- You can always rely on Paul. He'll never **let** you **down**.

turn somebody/something **down** 意为“拒绝 (申请，建议等)”：
- I applied for several jobs, but I was **turned down** for all of them.
- Rachel was offered the job, but she decided to **turn** it **down**.

write something **down** 意为“(在纸上) 记下”：
- I can't remember Tim's address. I **wrote** it **down**, but I can't find it.

短语动词 (1) ——概述 ➜ Unit 137　　更多动词 + up ➜ Units 143–144

Exercises

142.1 根据下列图片，用动词的适当形式 + **up** 或 **down** 完成句子。

1 There used to be a tree next to the house, but we ..cut it down.. .
2 There used to be some shelves on the wall, but I ....
3 The ceiling was so low, he couldn't .... straight.
4 She couldn't hear the radio very well, so she ....
5 While they were waiting for the bus, they .... on the ground.
6 A few trees .... in the storm last week.
7 We've got some new curtains, but we haven't .... yet.
8 Lisa dropped her keys, so she .... and ....

142.2 用下列动词的适当形式 + **down** 完成句子。

calm **let** ~~**take**~~ **turn** **turn** **write**

1 I don't like this picture on the wall. I'm going to ..take it down.. .
2 The music is too loud. Can you .... ?
3 David was very angry. I tried to ....
4 Sarah gave me her phone number. I .... on a piece of paper.
5 I promised I would help Anna. I don't want to ....
6 I was offered the job, but I decided I didn't want it. So I ....

142.3 用动词的适当形式 + **down** 完成下列句子。

1 I stopped writing and ..put down.. my pen.
2 I was really angry. It took me a long time to ....
3 The train .... as it approached the station.
4 Sarah applied to study medicine at university, but she ....
5 Our car is very reliable. It has never ....
6 I need to spend less money. I'm going to .... on things I don't really need.
7 I didn't play very well. I felt that I had .... the other players in the team.
8 The shop .... because it was losing money.
9 This is a very ugly building. Many people would like it to ....
10 I can't understand why you .... the chance of working abroad for a year. It would have been a great experience for you.
11 A: Did you see the accident? What happened exactly?
B: A man .... by a car as he was crossing the road.
12 Peter got married when he was 20, but unfortunately the marriage .... a few years later.

→ 补充练习 37–41 (第323–325页)

短语动词 (7) —— up (1)

A

go up / **come up** / **walk up** (**to** …) 意为“走近……”：

- A man **came up to** me in the street and asked me for money.

catch up (**with** somebody)，**catch** somebody **up** 意为“赶上，追上”：

- I'm not ready to go yet. You go on and I'll **catch up with** you / I'll **catch** you **up**.

keep up (**with** somebody) 意为“跟上，保持同步”：

- You're walking too fast. I can't **keep up** (**with** you).
- You're doing well. **Keep** it **up**!

B

set up 表示“成立(机构、公司、体制、网站等)”：

- The government has **set up** a committee to investigate the problem.

take up 表示“开始(某项爱好、运动、活动等)”：

- Laura **took up** photography a few years ago. She takes really good pictures.

fix up 表示“安排(会议等)”：

- We've **fixed up** a meeting for next Monday.

C

grow up 意为“长大成人”：

- Ann was born in Hong Kong but **grew up** in Australia.

bring up 表示“抚养(孩子)”：

- Her parents died when she was a child and she was **brought up** by her grandparents.

D

clean up / **clear up** / **tidy up** something 意为“整理，使整洁”：

- Look at this mess! Who's going to **tidy up**? (或 **tidy** it **up**)

wash up 指“洗餐具”：

- I hate **washing up**. (或 I hate **doing the washing-up**.)

E

end up somewhere，**end up** doing something 等

- There was a fight in the street and three men **ended up** in hospital. (= that's what happened to these men in the end)
- I couldn't find a hotel and **ended up** sleeping on a bench at the station. (= that's what happened to me in the end)

give up 意为“放弃(努力)”，**give** something **up** 意为“放弃某事”：

- Don't **give up**. Keep trying!
- Sue got bored with her job and decided to **give** it **up**. (= stop doing it)

make up something，be **made up of** something

- Children under 16 **make up** half the population of the city. (= half the population are children under 16)
- Air is **made up** mainly **of** nitrogen and oxygen. (= Air consists of …)

take up 可表示“占据(空间或时间)”：

- Most of the space in the room was **taken up** by a large table.

turn up / **show up** 意为“到达，出现”：

- We arranged to meet David last night, but he didn't **turn up**.

use something **up** 意为“用完，用光”：

- I'm going to make some soup. We have a lot of vegetables and I want to **use them up**.

短语动词 (1) ——概述 → Unit 137　更多动词 + up → Units 142，144

Exercises

143.1 根据下列图片，从 **A** 节中选择动词完成句子，每空只填三个单词。

1

A man ..came up to.. me in the street and asked me the way to the station.

2

Sue .... the front door of the house and rang the doorbell.

3

Tom was a long way behind the other runners, but he managed to .... them.

4

Tanya was running too fast for Paul. He couldn't .... her.

143.2 用下列动词的适当形式 + **up** 完成句子。

~~end~~ end give give grow make take take turn use wash

1 I couldn't find a hotel and ..ended up.. sleeping on a bench at the station.
2 I'm feeling very tired now. I've .... all my energy.
3 After dinner I .... and put the dishes away.
4 People often ask children what they want to be when they ....
5 We invited Tom to the party, but he didn't ....
6 Two years ago James .... his studies to be a professional footballer.
7 A: Do you do any sports?
B: Not at the moment, but I'm thinking of .... tennis.
8 You don't have enough determination. You .... too easily.
9 Karen travelled a lot for a few years and .... in Canada, where she still lives.
10 I do a lot of gardening. It .... most of my free time.
11 There are two universities in the city, and students .... 20 per cent of the population.

143.3 用下列动词的适当形式 + **up** 完成句子。

bring ~~catch~~ fix ~~give~~ go keep keep make set tidy

1 Sue got bored with her job and decided to ..give it up.. .
2 I'm not ready yet. You go on and I'll ..catch up with.. you.
3 The room is in a mess. I'd better ....
4 We expect to go away on holiday sometime in July, but we haven't .... yet.
5 Stephen is having problems at school. He can't .... the rest of the class.
6 Although I .... in the country, I have always preferred cities.
7 Our team started the game well, but we couldn't .... and in the end we lost.
8 I saw Mike at the party, so I .... him and said hello.
9 When I was on holiday, I joined a tour group. The group .... two Americans, three Germans, five Italians and myself.
10 Helen has her own internet website. A friend of hers helped her to ....

→ 补充练习 37–41（第323–325页）

Unit 144

短语动词 (8) —— up (2)

A

bring up 可表示"提起 (某个话题等)"：

- I don't want to hear any more about this matter. Please don't **bring** it **up** again.

come up 意为"被提到"：

- Some interesting points **came up** in our discussion yesterday.

come up with 意为"想出 (主意、建议等)"：

- Sarah is very creative. She's always **coming up with** new ideas.

make something **up** 意为"编造"：

- What Kevin told you about himself wasn't true. He **made** it all **up**.

B

cheer up 意为"高兴/振作起来"，**cheer** somebody **up** 意为"使某人高兴/振作起来"：

- You look so sad! **Cheer up**!
- Helen is depressed at the moment. What can we do to **cheer her up**?

save up for something / to do something 意为"存钱……"：

- Dan is **saving up** for a trip round the world.

clear up 指"(天气) 放晴"：

- It was raining when I got up, but it **cleared up** later.

C

blow up 指"爆炸"，**blow** something **up** 指"炸毁"：

- The engine caught fire and **blew up**.
- The bridge was **blown up** during the war.

tear something **up** 意为"撕碎"：

- I didn't read the letter. I just **tore** it **up** and threw it away.

beat somebody **up** 意为"痛打某人"：

- A friend of mine was attacked and **beaten up** a few days ago. He was badly hurt and had to go to hospital.

D

break up / **split up** (with somebody) 表示"(与某人) 分手"：

- I'm surprised to hear that Sue and Paul have **split up**. They seemed very happy together.

do up 意为"系上或扣上 (外套、鞋带、纽扣等)"：

- It's quite cold. **Do up** your coat before you go out.

do up 也可指"修缮 (建筑物、房间等)"：

- The kitchen looks great now that it has been **done up**.

look something **up** in ... 表示"查阅 (词典、百科全书等)"：

- If you don't know the meaning of a word, you can **look** it **up** in a dictionary.

put up with something 意为"忍受"：

- We live on a busy road, so we have to **put up with** a lot of noise from the traffic.

hold up 意为"耽搁（某人），阻延（计划）"：

- Don't wait for me. I don't want to **hold** you **up**.
- Plans to build a new factory have been **held up** because of the company's financial problems.

mix up people/things，**get** people/things **mixed up** 意为"混淆 (人/物)"：

- The two brothers look very similar. Many people **mix** them **up**. (或 ... **get** them **mixed up**)

短语动词 (1) ——概述 ➜ Unit 137　　更多动词 + up ➜ Units 142–143
美国英语 ➜ 附录 7

Exercises

144.1 请将下列两框中的信息正确搭配。

1 I'm going to tear up
2 Jane came up with
3 Paul is always making up
4 I think you should do up
5 I don't think you should bring up
6 I'm saving up for
7 We had to put up with

a a new camera
b a lot of bad weather
c your jacket
d an interesting suggestion
e excuses
f ~~the letter~~
g that subject

1 ...f...
2 ....
3 ....
4 ....
5 ....
6 ....
7 ....

144.2 根据下列图片，用两个或三个单词完成句子。

1

The weather was horrible this morning, but it's ...cleared up... now.

2

Amy was late because she was .... in the traffic.

3

They bought an old house and .... It's really nice now.

4

Joe was really depressed. We took him out for a meal to ....

144.3 用动词的适当形式 + **up** 完成下列句子。

1 Some interesting matters ...came up... in our discussion yesterday.
2 The ship .... and sank. The cause of the explosion was never discovered.
3 Two men have been arrested after a man was .... outside a restaurant last night. The injured man was taken to hospital.
4 'Is Robert still going out with Tina?' 'No, they've ....'
5 My hands were so cold, I found it hard to .... my shoelaces.
6 I wish it would stop raining! I hope it .... soon.
7 I wanted to phone Chris, but I dialled Laura's number by mistake. I got their phone numbers ....

144.4 用动词的适当形式 + **up** 完成下列句子。

1 Don't wait for me. I don't want to ...hold you up... .
2 I don't know what this word means. I'll have to ....
3 There's nothing we can do about the problem. We'll just have to .... it.
4 'Was that story true?' 'No, I ....'
5 I think we should follow Tom's suggestion. Nobody has .... a better plan.
6 I hate this photo. I'm going to ....
7 I'm trying to spend less money at the moment. I'm .... a trip to Australia.

➔ 补充练习 37–41 (第323–325页)

Unit 145

短语动词 (9) —— away/back

A

请比较 away 与 back：

away 可表示"不在家"：

- We're **going away** on holiday today.

away 可表示"离开 (某地、某人等)"：

- The woman got into her car, started the engine and **drove away**.
- I tried to take a picture of the bird, but it **flew away**.
- I dropped the ticket and it **blew away** in the wind.
- The police searched the house and **took away** a computer.

同样地，可以说：

walk away，**run away**，**look away** 等

back 可表示"回家"：

- We'll **be back** in three weeks.

back 可表示"回到 (某地)，还给 (某人)"：

- A: I'm going out now.
  B: What time will you **be back**?
- After eating at a restaurant, we **walked back** to our hotel.
- I've still got Jane's keys. I forgot to **give** them **back** to her.
- When you've finished with that book, can you **put** it **back** on the shelf?

同样地，可以说：

go back，**come back**，**get back**，**take** something **back** 等

B

其他动词 + **away**

get away 表示"逃离，逃脱"：

- We tried to catch the thief, but she managed to **get away**.

get away with something 表示"(做错事而) 不被发现"：

- I parked in a no-parking zone, but I **got away with** it. I didn't have to pay a fine.

keep away (from …) 表示"远离"：

- **Keep away from** the edge of the pool. You might fall in.

give something **away** 表示"分送 (不需要的东西)"：

- 'Did you sell your old computer?' 'No, I **gave** it **away**.'

put something **away** 表示"放回 (原处)"：

- When the children had finished playing with their toys, they **put** them **away**.

throw something **away** 表示"扔掉，丢弃"：

- I kept the letter, but I **threw away** the envelope.

C

其他动词 + **back**

wave back / **smile back** / **shout back** / **write back** / **hit** somebody **back**

- I waved to her and she **waved back**.

call/phone/ring (somebody) **back** 表示"回 (某人) 电话"：

- I can't talk to you now. I'll **call** you **back** in ten minutes.

get back to somebody 表示"给某人答复"：

- I sent him an email, but he never **got back to** me.

look back (on something) 表示"回想，回顾"：

- My first job was in a travel agency. I didn't like it very much at the time but, **looking back on** it, I learnt a lot and it was a very useful experience.

pay back money，**pay** somebody **back**

- If you borrow money, you have to **pay** it **back**.
- Thanks for lending me the money. I'll **pay** you **back** next week.

短语动词 (1) ——概述 ➔ Unit 137

Exercises

145.1 根据下列图片完成句子。

1

She waved to him and he waved back.

2

It was windy. I dropped a twenty-pound note and it ....

3

Sue opened the letter, read it and .... in the envelope.

4

He tried to talk to her, but she just ....

5

Ellie threw the ball to Ben and he ....

6

His shoes were worn out, so he ....

145.2 用动词的适当形式 + **away** 或 **back** 完成下列句子。

1 I was away all day yesterday. I got back very late.
2 I haven't seen our neighbours for a while. I think they must ....
3 'I'm going out now.' 'OK. What time will you ....?'
4 A man was trying to break into a car. When he saw me, he ....
5 I smiled at him, but he didn't ....
6 If you cheat in the exam, you might .... with it. But you might get caught.
7 Be careful! That's an electric fence. .... from it.

145.3 用动词的适当形式填空。

1 The woman got into her car, started the engine and drove away.
2 Here's the money you need. .... me back when you can.
3 Don't .... that box away. It could be useful.
4 Jane doesn't do anything at work. I don't know how she .... away with it.
5 I'm going out now. I'll .... back in about an hour.
6 You should think more about the future; don't .... back all the time.
7 Gary is very generous. He won some money in the lottery and .... it all away.
8 I'll .... back to you as soon as I have the information you need.

145.4 用括号内动词的适当形式 + **away** 或 **back** 完成下列句子。

1 A: Do you still have my keys?
B: No. Don't you remember? I gave them back to you yesterday. (give)
2 A: Do you want this magazine?
B: No, I've finished with it. You can .... (throw)
3 A: How are your new jeans? Do they fit you OK?
B: No, I'm going to .... to the shop. (take)
4 A: Here's the money you asked me to lend you.
B: Thanks. I'll .... as soon as I can. (pay)
5 A: What happened to all the books you used to have?
B: I didn't want them any more, so I .... (give)
6 A: Did you phone Sarah?
B: She wasn't there. I left a message asking her to .... (call)

→ 补充练习 37–41 (第323–325页)

附录 1
规则动词与不规则动词

1.1 规则动词

规则动词的过去式与过去分词在拼写上都以 **-ed** 结尾。例如：

动词原形	**clean**	**finish**	**use**	**paint**	**stop**	**carry**
过去式 过去分词	**cleaned**	**finished**	**used**	**painted**	**stopped**	**carried**

拼写法参见附录6。

有关一般过去时 (I **cleaned** / they **finished** / she **carried** 等)，参见 Unit 5。

过去分词用于构成各种完成时和被动语态。

各种完成时 (**have**/**has**/**had** cleaned)：

- I **have cleaned** the windows. (现在完成时——参见 Units 7–8)
- They were still working. They **hadn't finished**. (过去完成时——参见 Unit 15)

被动语态 (**is** cleaned / **was** cleaned 等)：

- He **was carried** out of the room. (一般过去时被动语态)
- This gate **has** just **been painted**. (现在完成时被动语态)

} 参见 Units 42–44

1.2 不规则动词

不规则动词的过去式和过去分词在拼写上不以 **-ed** 结尾 (例如 **I saw** / **I have seen**)。

有些不规则动词的原形、过去式和过去分词的拼写都相同。例如 **hit**：

- Don't **hit** me. (动词原形)
- Somebody **hit** me as I came into the room. (过去式)
- I've never **hit** anybody in my life. (过去分词——现在完成时)
- George was **hit** on the head by a stone. (过去分词——被动语态)

有些不规则动词的过去式和过去分词的拼写相同。例如：**tell → told**：

- Can you **tell** me what to do? (动词原形)
- She **told** me to come back the next day. (过去式)
- Have you **told** anybody about your new job? (过去分词——现在完成时)
- I was **told** to come back the next day. (过去分词——被动语态)

有些不规则动词的原形、过去式和过去分词的拼写都不相同。例如 **wake → woke/woken**：

- I'll **wake** you up. (动词原形)
- I **woke** up in the middle of the night. (过去式)
- The baby has **woken** up. (过去分词——现在完成时)
- I was **woken** up by a loud noise. (过去分词——被动语态)

1.3 下列动词既可以用作规则动词，也可以用作不规则动词：

burn	→	burned	或	burnt	**smell**	→	smelled	或	smelt
dream	→	dreamed	或	dreamt [dremt]*	**spell**	→	spelled	或	spelt
lean	→	leaned	或	leant [lent]*	**spill**	→	spilled	或	spilt
learn	→	learned	或	learnt	**spoil**	→	spoiled	或	spoilt

* 发音

可以说：

- I **leant** out of the window. 或 I **leaned** out of the window.
- The dinner has been **spoiled**. 或 The dinner has been **spoilt**.

英国英语中常把它们作不规则动词使用。

美国英语参见附录7。

1.4 不规则动词表

动词原形	过去式	过去分词
be	was/were	been
beat	beat	beaten
become	became	become
begin	began	begun
bend	bent	bent
bet	bet	bet
bite	bit	bitten
blow	blew	blown
break	broke	broken
bring	brought	brought
broadcast	broadcast	broadcast
build	built	built
burst	burst	burst
buy	bought	bought
catch	caught	caught
choose	chose	chosen
come	came	come
cost	cost	cost
creep	crept	crept
cut	cut	cut
deal	dealt	dealt
dig	dug	dug
do	did	done
draw	drew	drawn
drink	drank	drunk
drive	drove	driven
eat	ate	eaten
fall	fell	fallen
feed	fed	fed
feel	felt	felt
fight	fought	fought
find	found	found
flee	fled	fled
fly	flew	flown
forbid	forbade	forbidden
forget	forgot	forgotten
forgive	forgave	forgiven
freeze	froze	frozen
get	got	got/gotten
give	gave	given
go	went	gone
grow	grew	grown
hang	hung	hung
have	had	had
hear	heard	heard
hide	hid	hidden
hit	hit	hit
hold	held	held
hurt	hurt	hurt
keep	kept	kept
kneel	knelt	knelt
know	knew	known
lay	laid	laid
lead	led	led
leave	left	left
lend	lent	lent
let	let	let
lie	lay	lain

动词原形	过去式	过去分词
light	lit	lit
lose	lost	lost
make	made	made
mean	meant	meant
meet	met	met
pay	paid	paid
put	put	put
read	read [red]*	read [red]*
ride	rode	ridden
ring	rang	rung
rise	rose	risen
run	ran	run
say	said	said
see	saw	seen
seek	sought	sought
sell	sold	sold
send	sent	sent
set	set	set
sew	sewed	sewn/sewed
shake	shook	shaken
shine	shone	shone
shoot	shot	shot
show	showed	shown/showed
shrink	shrank	shrunk
shut	shut	shut
sing	sang	sung
sink	sank	sunk
sit	sat	sat
sleep	slept	slept
slide	slid	slid
speak	spoke	spoken
spend	spent	spent
spit	spat	spat
split	split	split
spread	spread	spread
spring	sprang	sprung
stand	stood	stood
steal	stole	stolen
stick	stuck	stuck
sting	stung	stung
stink	stank	stunk
strike	struck	struck
swear	swore	sworn
sweep	swept	swept
swim	swam	swum
swing	swung	swung
take	took	taken
teach	taught	taught
tear	tore	torn
tell	told	told
think	thought	thought
throw	threw	thrown
understand	understood	understood
wake	woke	woken
wear	wore	worn
weep	wept	wept
win	won	won
write	wrote	written

* 发音

附录 2
现在时与过去时比较

	一般时态	进行时态
现在时	**I do** 一般现在时 (参见 Units 2–4) ☐ Ann often **plays** tennis. ☐ I **work** in a bank, but I **don't enjoy** it much. ☐ **Do** you **like** parties? ☐ It **doesn't rain** so much in summer.	**I am doing** 现在进行时 (参见Units 1，3–4) ☐ 'Where's Ann?' 'She**'s playing** tennis.' ☐ Please don't disturb me now. **I'm working**. ☐ Hello. **Are** you **enjoying** the party? ☐ It **isn't raining** at the moment.
现在完成时	**I have done** 现在完成时 (参见Units 7–8，10–14) ☐ Ann **has played** tennis many times. ☐ **I've lost** my key. **Have** you **seen** it anywhere? ☐ How long **have** you and Sam **known** each other? ☐ A: Is it still raining? B: No, it **has stopped**. ☐ The house is dirty. I **haven't cleaned** it for weeks.	**I have been doing** 现在完成进行时 (参见Units 9–11) ☐ Ann is tired. She **has been playing** tennis. ☐ You're out of breath. **Have** you **been running**? ☐ How long **have** you **been learning** English? ☐ It's still raining. It **has been raining** all day. ☐ I **haven't been feeling** well recently. Perhaps I should go to the doctor.
过去时	**I did** 一般过去时 (参见Units 5–6，13–14) ☐ Ann **played** tennis yesterday afternoon. ☐ I **lost** my key a few days ago. ☐ There was a film on TV last night, but we **didn't watch** it. ☐ What **did** you **do** when you finished work yesterday?	**I was doing** 过去进行时 (参见Unit 6) ☐ I saw Ann at the sports centre yesterday. She **was playing** tennis. ☐ I dropped my key when I **was trying** to open the door. ☐ The television was on, but we **weren't watching** it. ☐ What **were** you **doing** at this time yesterday?
过去完成时	**I had done** 过去完成时 (参见Unit 15) ☐ It wasn't her first game of tennis. She **had played** many times before. ☐ They couldn't get into the house because they **had lost** the key. ☐ The house was dirty because I **hadn't cleaned** it for weeks.	**I had been doing** 过去完成进行时 (参见 Unit 16) ☐ Ann was tired yesterday evening because she **had been playing** tennis in the afternoon. ☐ James decided to go to the doctor because he **hadn't been feeling** well.

被动语态参见Units 42–44。

附录 3
将来时

3.1 将来时的形式列表如下：

I'm leaving tomorrow.	现在进行时	(参见 Unit 19A)
My train **leaves** at 9.30.	一般现在时	(参见 Unit 19B)
I'm going to leave tomorrow.	(be) **going to**	(参见 Units 20，23)
I'll leave tomorrow.	**will**	(参见 Units 21–23)
I'll be leaving tomorrow.	将来进行时	(参见 Unit 24)
I'll have left by this time tomorrow.	将来完成时	(参见 Unit 24)
I hope to see you before I **leave** tomorrow.	一般现在时	(参见 Unit 25)

3.2 将来的动作或行为

表示安排时，使用现在进行时 (**I'm doing**)：
- **I'm leaving** tomorrow. I've got my plane ticket. (已经计划或安排好)
- 'When **are** they **getting** married?' 'On 24 July.'

表示时间表、节目等时，使用一般现在时 (I **leave** / it **leaves** 等)：
- My train **leaves** at 11.30. (根据列车时刻表)
- What time **does** the film **begin**?

(be) **going to** 用于表示已经决定做的事情：
- I've decided not to stay here any longer. **I'm going to leave** tomorrow. (或 **I'm leaving** tomorrow.)
- 'Your shoes are dirty.' 'Yes, I know. **I'm going to clean** them.'

will ('ll) 用于表示在说话时决定或同意做的事情：
- A: I don't want you to stay here any longer.
  B: OK. **I'll leave** tomorrow. (B在说话时决定的)
- That bag looks heavy. **I'll help** you with it.
- I **won't tell** anybody what happened. I promise. (**won't** = **will not**)

3.3 将来发生的事情与情况

will 常用来表示将来发生的事情 (something **will happen**) 或情况 (something **will be**)：
- I don't think John is happy at work. I think **he'll leave** soon.
- This time next year **I'll be** in Japan. Where **will** you **be**?

(be) **going to** 用来表示现在的情况预示将来要发生的事情：
- Look at those black clouds. **It's going to rain**. (你现在能看见乌云)

3.4 将来进行时与将来完成时比较

will be (do)**ing** 表示“将在做……”：
- This time next week I'll be on holiday. **I'll be lying** on a beach or **swimming** in the sea.

还可以用 **will be -ing** 表示将来的动作 (参见 Unit 24C)：
- What time **will** you **be leaving** tomorrow?

will have (done) 表示将来某时已经完成的事情：
- I won't be here this time tomorrow. **I'll have** already **left**.

3.5 **when/if/while/before** 等之后用现在时 (不能用将来时，参见 Unit 25)：
- I hope to see you **before I leave** tomorrow. (而不用 before I will leave)
- **When** you **are** in London again, come and see us. (而不用 When you will be)
- **If** we **don't hurry**, we'll be late.

附录 4
情态动词 (can/could/will/would 等)

下面简单总结了情态动词的用法，详细介绍参见 Units 21–41。

4.1 请比较表示动作的 can/could 等：

can	I **can go** out tonight. (= there is nothing to stop me) I **can't go** out tonight.
could	I **could go** out tonight, but I'm not very keen. I **couldn't go** out last night. (= I wasn't able)
can 或 **may**	**Can** / **May** I **go** out tonight? (= do you allow me?)
will/won't	I think **I'll go** out tonight. I promise I **won't go** out.
would	I **would go** out tonight, but I have too much to do. I promised I **wouldn't go** out.
shall	**Shall** I **go** out tonight? (你认为这是个好主意吗？)
should 或 **ought to**	I **should** / **ought to** **go** out tonight. (= it would be a good thing to do)
must	I **must go** out tonight. (= it is necessary) I **mustn't go** out tonight. (= it is necessary that I do *not* go out)
needn't	I **needn't go** out tonight. (= it is not necessary)

请比较 **could have** … / **would have** … 等：

could	I **could have gone** out last night, but I decided to stay at home.
would	I **would have gone** out last night, but I had too much to do.
should 或 **ought to**	I **should** / **ought to** **have gone** out last night. I'm sorry I didn't.
needn't	I **needn't have gone** out last night. (= I went out, but it was not necessary)

4.2 will/would/may 等可用来表示事情的可能性。请比较：

will	'What time **will** she **be** here?' 'She**'ll be** here soon.'
would	She **would be** here now, but she's been delayed.
should 或 **ought to**	She **should** / **ought to** **be** here soon. (= I expect she will be here soon)
may 或 **might** 或 **could**	She **may** / **might** / **could** **be** here now. I'm not sure. (= it's possible that she is here)
must	She **must be** here. I saw her come in.
can't	She **can't** possibly **be** here. I know for certain that she's away on holiday.

请比较 **would have** … / **should have** … 等：

will	She **will have arrived** by now. (= before now)
would	She **would have arrived** earlier, but she was delayed.
should 或 **ought to**	I wonder where she is. She **should** / **ought to** **have arrived** by now.
may 或 **might** 或 **could**	She **may** / **might** / **could** **have arrived**. I'm not sure. (= it's possible that she has arrived)
must	She **must have arrived** by now. (= I'm sure – there is no other possibility)
can't	She **can't** possibly **have arrived** yet. It's much too early. (= it's impossible)

附录 5
缩略形式 (I'm / you've / didn't 等)

5.1 在口语中通常使用 **I'm / you've / didn't** 等缩略形式，而不用 **I am / you have / did not** 等。缩略形式还可以用于非正式的书面语中（如给朋友的信中）。

缩略形式使用 (') 表示省略的字母：

I'm = I am　　you've = you have　　didn't = did not

5.2 助动词的缩略形式表：

'm = am	I'**m**						
's = is 或 has		he'**s**	she'**s**	it'**s**			
're = are					you'**re**	we'**re**	they'**re**
've = have	I'**ve**				you'**ve**	we'**ve**	they'**ve**
'll = will	I'**ll**	he'**ll**	she'**ll**		you'**ll**	we'**ll**	they'**ll**
'd = would 或 had	I'**d**	he'**d**	she'**d**		you'**d**	we'**d**	they'**d**

's 既是 **is** 也是 **has** 的缩略形式：

- She**'s** ill.　(= She **is** ill.)
- She**'s** gone away.　(= She **has** gone)

但是 **let's** = let **us**：

- Let**'s** go now.　(= Let **us** go)

'd 既是 **would** 也是 **had** 的缩略形式：

- I**'d** see a doctor if I were you.　(= I **would** see)
- I**'d** never seen her before.　(= I **had** never seen)

在疑问词 (**who/what** 等) 及 **that/there/here** 后常使用缩略形式 (特别是 **'s**)：

who**'s**　what**'s**　where**'s**　how**'s**　that**'s**　there**'s**　here**'s**　who**'ll**　there**'ll**　who**'d**

- **Who's** that woman over there?　(= who **is**)
- **What's** happened?　(= what **has**)
- Do you think **there'll** be many people at the party?　(= there **will**)

名词后也可以使用缩略形式 (特别是 **'s**)：

- **Katherine's** going out tonight.　(= Katherine **is**)
- **My best friend's** just got married.　(= My best friend **has**)

句子结尾部分不能使用 **'m / 's / 're / 've / 'll / 'd** (因为句末使用的动词要重读)：

- 'Are you tired?'　'Yes, I **am**.'　(而不用 Yes, I'm.)
- Do you know where she **is**?　(而不用 Do you know where she's?)

5.3 缩略形式的否定式

isn't	(= is not)	**don't**	(= do not)	**haven't**	(= have not)
aren't	(= are not)	**doesn't**	(= does not)	**hasn't**	(= has not)
wasn't	(= was not)	**didn't**	(= did not)	**hadn't**	(= had not)
weren't	(= were not)				
can't	(= cannot)	**couldn't**	(= could not)	**mustn't**	(= must not)
won't	(= will not)	**wouldn't**	(= would not)	**needn't**	(= need not)
shan't	(= shall not)	**shouldn't**	(= should not)	**daren't**	(= dare not)

is 和 **are** 的缩略形式的否定式可以是：

he **isn't** / she **isn't** / it **isn't**　或　he**'s not** / she**'s not** / it**'s not**

you **aren't** / we **aren't** / they **aren't**　或　you**'re not** / we**'re not** / they**'re not**

附录 6
拼写法

6.1 名词、动词和形容词有下列词尾：

名词 + **-s/-es** (复数)	books	ideas	matches
动词 + **-s/-es** (在 **he/she/it**后使用)	works	enjoys	washes
动词 + **-ing**	work**ing**	enjoy**ing**	wash**ing**
动词 + **-ed**	work**ed**	enjoy**ed**	wash**ed**
形容词 + **-er** (比较级)	cheap**er**	quick**er**	bright**er**
形容词 + **-est** (最高级)	cheap**est**	quick**est**	bright**est**
形容词 + **-ly** (副词)	cheap**ly**	quick**ly**	bright**ly**

当词尾发生上述变化时，词的拼写有时也相应发生了变化。

6.2 名词与动词 + **-s/-es**

以 **-s/-ss/-sh/-ch/-x** 结尾的词后加 **-es**：

bus/bus**es** miss/miss**es** wash/wash**es**
match/match**es** search/search**es** box/box**es**

另外注意：

potato/potato**es** tomato/tomato**es**
do/do**es** go/go**es**

6.3 以 **-y** 结尾的词 (baby，carry，easy 等)

以辅音字母* + **y** (**-by/-ry/-sy/-vy** 等) 结尾的词：

在加 **-s** 前把**y** 改为 **ie**：

baby/bab**ies** story/stor**ies** country/countr**ies** secretary/secretar**ies**
hurry/hurr**ies** study/stud**ies** apply/appl**ies** try/tr**ies**

在加 **-ed** 前把**y** 改为 **i**：

hurry/hurr**ied** study/stud**ied** apply/appl**ied** try/tr**ied**

在加 **-er** 及**-est** 前把 **y** 改为 **i**：

easy/eas**ier**/eas**iest** heavy/heav**ier**/heav**iest** lucky/luck**ier**/luck**iest**

在加 **-ly** 前把**y** 改为 **i**：

easy/eas**ily** heavy/heav**ily** temporary/temporar**ily**

在加 **-ing** 时 **y** 不变：

hurry**ing** study**ing** apply**ing** try**ing**

以元音字母* + **y** (**-ay/-ey/-oy/-uy**) 结尾的词词尾变化时，**y** 不发生变化：

play/play**s**/play**ed** monkey/monkey**s** enjoy/enjoy**s**/enjoy**ed** buy/buy**s**

day/daily 例外。

还要注意：**pay/paid** **lay/laid** **say/said**

6.4 以 **-ie** 结尾的动词 (die，lie，tie)

以 **-ie** 结尾的动词变成 **-ing** 形式时，**ie** 变成 **y**：

d**y**ing/d**ying** l**ie**/l**ying** t**ie**/t**ying**

---

*a e i o u 是元音字母，其他都是辅音字母 (b c d f g 等)。

6.5 以 -e 结尾的词 (hope，dance，wide 等)

动词

以-e 结尾的动词变成 -ing 形式时，去掉 e：

hope/hoping　smile/smiling　dance/dancing　confuse/confusing

例外：be/being

及以 -ee 结尾的动词：　see/seeing　agree/agreeing

以 -e 结尾的规则动词的过去式在词尾加 -d：

hope/hoped　smile/smiled　dance/danced　confuse/confused

形容词与副词

以-e 结尾的形容词，加 -r 及 -st 变为比较级与最高级：

wide/wider/widest　late/later/latest　large/larger/largest

以 -e 结尾的形容词，e 不变，加 -ly 变为副词：

polite/politely　extreme/extremely　absolute/absolutely

以 -le 结尾的形容词 (simple，terrible 等)，变为副词后的词尾是 -ply，-bly 等：

simple/simply　terrible/terribly　reasonable/reasonably

6.6 双写辅音字母 (stop/stopping/stopped，wet/wetter/wettest 等)

有的词以元音字母 + 辅音字母结尾。例如：

stop　plan　rub　big　wet　thin　prefer　regret

这些词在加 -ing/-ed/-er/-est 前，要将词尾的辅音字母双写，如 p → pp，n → nn 等。例如：

stop	p → pp	stopping	stopped
plan	n → nn	planning	planned
rub	b → bb	rubbing	rubbed
big	g → gg	bigger	biggest
wet	t → tt	wetter	wettest
thin	n → nn	thinner	thinnest

如果单词由两个或两个以上的音节构成 (prefer，begin 等)，且最后一个音节是重读音节时，结尾的辅音字母要双写：

preFER / preferring / preferred　perMIT / permitting / permitted

reGRET / regretting / regretted　beGIN / beginning

最后一个音节是非重读音节时，结尾的辅音字母不双写：

VISit / visiting / visited　deVELop / developing / developed

HAPpen / happening / happened　reMEMber / remembering / remembered

在英国英语中，以 -l 作词尾的动词在变成 -ing 及 -ed 形式时，不管最后一个音节是否重读，都要变成双写的形式 (-ll-)：

travel / travelling / travelled　cancel / cancelling / cancelled

美国英语的拼写法参见附录7。

注意：

以两个辅音字母结尾的词 (-rt，-lp，-ng 等)，后面一个辅音字母不双写：

start / starting / started　help / helping / helped　long / longer / longest

词尾的辅音字母前有两个元音字母时 (-oil，-eed 等)，辅音字母不双写：

boil / boiling / boiled　need / needing / needed　explain / explaining / explained

cheap / cheaper / cheapest　loud / louder / loudest　quiet / quieter / quietest

以y 或 w 结尾的词，y 和 w 不双写 (词尾的 y 和 w 不是辅音字母)：

stay / staying / stayed　grow / growing　new / newer / newest

附录 7
美国英语

英国英语与美国英语在语法上有一些区别：

Unit	英国英语	美国英语
7A–B和 13A	现在完成时或一般过去时可用来表示刚刚或最近发生的事情。更常用现在完成时： □ **I've lost** my key. **Have** you **seen** it? (或 I **lost** my key. **Did** you **see** it?) □ Sally isn't here. She**'s gone** out. 现在完成时或一般过去时可与 **just**，**already** 和 **yet** 连用。更常用现在完成时： □ I'm not hungry. **I've just had** lunch. (或 I **just had** lunch.) □ A: What time is Mark leaving? B: He**'s already left**. □ **Have** you **finished** your work **yet**?	现在完成时或一般过去时可用来表示刚刚或最近发生的事情。更常用一般过去时： □ I **lost** my key. **Did** you **see** it? (或 **I've** lost my key. **Have** you **seen** it?) □ Sally isn't here. She **went** out. 现在完成时或一般过去时可与 **just**，**already** 和 **yet** 连用。更常用一般过去时： □ I'm not hungry. I **just had** lunch. (或 **I've just had** lunch.) □ A: What time is Mark leaving? B: He **already left**. □ **Did** you **finish** your work **yet**?
17C	通常说： **have** a bath　**have** a shower **have** a break　**have** a holiday	通常说： **take** a bath　**take** a shower **take** a break　**take** a vacation
21D和 22D	**will** 或 **shall** 都可以与 **I/we** 连用： □ I **will/shall** be late this evening. **Shall I** ...？及 **Shall we** ...？用于征求意见等： □ Which way **shall we** go?	**shall** 不太常用： □ I **will** be late this evening. **Should I** ...？及 **Should we** ...？用于征求意见等： □ Which way **should we** go?
28	**can't** 可用来表示认为某事不大可能发生： □ Sarah hasn't contacted me. She **can't** have got my message.	同样情况下常用 **must not**： □ Sarah hasn't contacted me. She **must not** have gotten my message.
32	既可以用 **needn't** 也可以用 **don't need to**： □ We **needn't** hurry. 或　We **don't need to** hurry.	通常不用 **needn't**，常用的形式是 **don't need to**： □ We **don't need to** hurry.
34 A–B	在 **insist**，**demand** 等词后可以使用 **should**： □ I insisted that he **should apologise**. □ Many people are demanding that something **should be** done about the problem.	虚拟语气正常使用，但是 **insist**，**demand** 等词后通常不用 **should**： □ I insisted that he **apologize**.* □ Many people are demanding that something **be done** about the problem.
51B	通常用 **Have you?** / **Isn't she?** 等： □ A: Lisa isn't very well today. B: **Isn't she?** What's wrong with her?	通常用 **You have?** / **She isn't?** 等： □ A: Lisa isn't very well today. B: **She isn't?** What's wrong with her?
70B	**accommodation** 通常作不可数名词： □ There isn't enough **accommodation**.	**accommodation** 可作可数名词： □ There aren't enough **accommodations**.

* 英国英语中许多以 **-ise** 结尾的动词 (apolog**ise**/organ**ise**/special**ise** 等)，在美国英语中拼作 **-ize** (apolog**ize**/organ**ize**/special**ize** 等)。

Unit	英国英语	美国英语
74B	使用 to/in **hospital** (不加 **the**)： ▢ Three people were injured and taken to **hospital**.	使用 to/in **the hospital**： ▢ Three people were injured and taken to **the hospital**.
79C	集体名词 **government/team/family** 等作主语时，谓语动词既可用单数形式，也可用复数形式： ▢ The team **is/are** playing well.	集体名词作主语时，谓语动词一般使用单数形式： ▢ The team **is** playing well.
121B	**at the weekend** / **at weekends**： ▢ Will you be here **at the weekend**?	**on the weekend** / **on weekends**： ▢ Will you be here **on the weekend**?
124D	**at** the front / **at** the back (of a group 等)： ▢ Let's sit **at** the front (of the cinema).	**in** the front / **in** the back (of a group 等)： ▢ Let's sit **in** the front (of the movie theater).
131C	**different from** 或 **different to**： ▢ It was **different from/to** what I'd expected.	**different from** 或 **different than**： ▢ It was **different from/than** what I'd expected.
137A	可用 **round** 或 **around**： ▢ He turned **round**. 或 He turned **around**.	常用 **around** (不太常用 round)： ▢ He turned **around**.
137C	可用 **fill in** 或 **fill out**： ▢ Can you **fill in** this form? 或 Can you **fill out** this form?	常用 **fill out**： ▢ Can you **fill out** this form?
141B	**get on** 可用来表示"进展"： ▢ How are you **getting on** in your new job? **get on** (with somebody)： ▢ Richard **gets on** well with his new neighbours.	**get on** 没有这种用法。 表达相同意思时要用 **get along** (with somebody)： ▢ Richard **gets along** well with his new neighbors.
144D	**do up** a house 等： ▢ That old house looks great now that it has been **done up**.	**fix up** a house 等： ▢ That old house looks great now that it has been **fixed up**.

附录	英国英语	美国英语
1.3	这一部分的动词 (**burn**，**spell** 等) 既可以用作规则动词，也可以用作不规则动词 (**burned** 或 **burnt**，**spelled** 或 **spelt** 等)。 **get** 的过去分词为 **got**： ▢ Your English has **got** much better. (= has become much better) **have got** 也可以代替 **have** 使用： ▢ **I've got** two brothers. (= I have two brothers.)	这部分的动词一般用作规则动词 (如 **burned**，**spelled** 等)。 **get** 的过去分词为 **gotten**： ▢ Your English has **gotten** much better. **have got** = have (与英国英语相同)： ▢ **I've got** two brothers.
6.6	英式拼写： travel → travelling / travelled cancel → cancelling / cancelled	美式拼写： travel → traveling / traveled cancel → canceling / canceled

补充练习

这部分的练习包括下列内容：

现在时与过去时 (Units 1–6)	Exercise 1
现在时与过去时 (Units 1–14)	Exercises 2–4
现在时与过去时 (Units 1–17)	Exercises 5–8
过去进行时与 **used to** 比较 (Units 6，18)	Exercise 9
将来时 (Units 19–25)	Exercises 10–13
过去时、现在时与将来时 (Units 1–25)	Exercises 14–15
情态动词 (**can/must/would** 等) (Units 26–36)	Exercises 16–18
条件句 (Units 25，38–40)	Exercises 19–21
被动语态 (Units 42–45)	Exercises 22–24
间接引语 (Units 47–48，50)	Exercise 25
动词的**-ing** 形式与不定式比较 (Units 53–66)	Exercises 26–28
冠词 (Units 69–78)	Exercise 29
代词与限定词 (Units 82–91)	Exercise 30
形容词与副词 (Units 98–108)	Exercise 31
连词 (Units 25，38，112–118)	Exercise 32
介词 (时间) (Units 12，119–122)	Exercise 33
介词 (地点与其他用法) (Units 123–128)	Exercise 34
名词/形容词 + 介词 (Units 129–131)	Exercise 35
动词 + 介词 (Units 132–136)	Exercise 36
短语动词 (Units 137–145)	Exercises 37–41

现在时与过去时

Units 1–6，附录 2

1 用动词的一般现在时 **(I do)**，现在进行时 **(I am doing)**，一般过去时 **(I did)** 或过去进行时 **(I was doing)** 的形式填空。

1 We can go out now. It isn't raining (it / not / rain) any more.
2 Katherine was waiting (wait) for me when I arrived (I / arrive).
3 .... (I / get) hungry. Let's go and have something to eat.
4 What .... (you / do) in your spare time? Do you have any hobbies?
5 The weather was horrible when .... (we / arrive). It was cold and .... (it / rain) hard.
6 Louise usually .... (phone) me on Fridays, but .... (she / not / phone) last Friday.
7 A: When I last saw you, ... (you / think) of moving to a new flat.
B: That's right, but in the end .... (I / decide) to stay where I was.
8 Why .... (you / look) at me like that? What's the matter?
9 It's usually dry here at this time of the year. .... (it / not / rain) much.
10 Sorry I'm late. My phone .... (ring) three times while .... (I / get) ready to go out.
11 Lisa was busy when .... (we / go) to see her yesterday. She had an exam today and .... (she / prepare) for it. .... (we / not / want) to disturb her, so .... (we / not / stay) very long.
12 When I first .... (tell) Tom what happened, ... (he / not / believe) me. .... (he / think) that .... (I / joke).

现在时与过去时

Units 1–14，附录 2

2 从下列句子画线的部分中选择正确答案。

1 Everything is going well. We ~~didn't have~~ / haven't had any problems so far. (haven't had *is correct*)
2 Lisa didn't go / hasn't gone to work yesterday. She wasn't feeling well.
3 Look! That man over there wears / is wearing the same sweater as you.
4 I went / have been to New Zealand last year.
5 I didn't hear / haven't heard from Jess recently. I hope she's OK.
6 I wonder why James is / is being so nice to me today. He isn't usually like that.
7 Jane had a book open in front of her, but she didn't read / wasn't reading it.
8 I wasn't very busy. I didn't have / wasn't having much to do.
9 It begins / It's beginning to get dark. Shall I turn on the light?
10 After finishing school, Tim got / has got a job in a factory.
11 When Sue heard the news, she wasn't / hasn't been very pleased.
12 This is a nice restaurant, isn't it? Is this the first time you are / you've been here?
13 I need a new job. I'm doing / I've been doing the same job for too long.
14 'Anna has gone out.' 'Oh, has she? What time did she go / has she gone?'
15 'You look tired.' 'Yes, I've played / I've been playing basketball.'
16 Where are you coming / do you come from? Are you American?
17 I'd like to see Tina again. It's a long time since I saw her / that I didn't see her.
18 Robert and Maria have been married since 20 years / for 20 years.

3 用适当的动词完成下列问句。

1 A: I'm looking for Paul. Have you seen him?
B: Yes, he was here a moment ago.

2 A: Why did you go to bed so early last night?
B: I was feeling very tired.

3 A: Where .... ?
B: Just to the shop at the end of the street. I'll be back in a few minutes.

4 A: .... TV every evening?
B: No, only if there's something special on.

5 A: Your house is very beautiful. How long .... here?
B: Nearly ten years.

6 A: How was your holiday? .... a nice time?
B: Yes, thanks. It was great.

7 A: .... Sarah recently?
B: Yes, we had lunch together a few days ago.

8 A: Can you describe the woman you saw? What .... ?
B: A red sweater and black jeans.

9 A: I'm sorry to keep you waiting. .... long?
B: No, only about ten minutes.

10 A: How long .... you to get to work in the morning?
B: Usually about 45 minutes. It depends on the traffic.

11 A: .... a horse before?
B: No, this is the first time. I'm a little nervous.

12 A: .... to the United States?
B: No, never, but I went to Canada a few years ago.

4 根据你自己的想法完成 **B** 所说的话。

1 A: What's the new restaurant like? Is it good?
B: I've no idea. I've never been .... there.

2 A: How well do you know Ben?
B: Very well. We .... since we were children.

3 A: Did you enjoy your holiday?
B: Yes, it was really good. It's the best holiday ....

4 A: Is David still here?
B: No, I'm afraid he isn't. .... about ten minutes ago.

5 A: I like your suit. I haven't seen it before.
B: It's new. It's the first time ....

6 A: How did you cut your knee?
B: I slipped and fell when .... tennis.

7 A: Do you ever go swimming?
B: Not these days. I haven't .... a long time.

8 A: How often do you go to the cinema?
B: Very rarely. It's nearly a year .... to the cinema.

9 A: I've bought some new shoes. Do you like them?
B: Yes, they're very nice. Where .... them?

现在时与过去时

Units 1–17，110，附录 2

5 用动词的一般过去时 **(I did)**，过去进行时 **(I was doing)**，过去完成时 **(I had done)** 或过去完成进行时 **(I had been doing)** 的形式填空。

1

Yesterday afternoon Sarah went (go) to the station to meet Paul. When she .... (get) there, Paul .... (already / wait) for her. His train .... (arrive) early.

2

When I got home, Ben .... (lie) on the sofa. The TV was on, but he .... (not / watch) it. He .... (fall) asleep and .... (snore) loudly. I .... (turn) the TV off and just then he .... (wake) up.

3

Last night I .... (just / go) to bed and .... (read) a book when suddenly I .... (hear) a noise. I .... (get) up to see what it was, but I .... (not / see) anything, so I .... (go) back to bed.

4

Lisa had to go to New York last week, but she almost .... (miss) the plane. She .... (stand) in the queue at the check-in desk when she suddenly .... (realise) that she .... (leave) her passport at home. Fortunately she lives near the airport, so she .... (have) time to take a taxi home to get it. She .... (get) back to the airport just in time for her flight.

5

I .... (meet) Peter and Lucy yesterday as I .... (walk) through the park. They .... (be) to the sports centre where they .... (play) tennis. They .... (go) to a café and .... (invite) me to join them, but I .... (arrange) to meet another friend and .... (not / have) time.

6 用括号内动词的现在完成时 **(I have done)**，现在完成进行时 **(I have been doing)**，过去完成时 **(I had done)** 或过去完成进行时 **(I had been doing)** 的形式造句。

1 Amanda is sitting on the ground. She's out of breath.
(she / run) She has been running.

2 Where's my bag? I left it under this chair.
(somebody / take / it) ....

3 We were all surprised when Jess and Nick got married last year.
(they / only / know / each other / a few weeks)
....

4 It's still raining. I wish it would stop.
(it / rain / all day) ....

5 Suddenly I woke up. I was confused and didn't know where I was.
(I / dream) ....

6 I wasn't hungry at lunchtime, so I didn't have anything to eat.
(I / have / a big breakfast) ....
7 Every year Robert and Tina spend a few days at the same hotel by the sea.
(they / go / there for years) ....
8 I've got a headache.
(I / have / it / since I got up) ....
9 Next month Gary is going to run in a marathon.
(he / train / very hard for it) ....

7 用动词的适当形式填空。

Sarah and Joe are old friends. They meet by chance at a train station.

SARAH: Hello, Joe. (1) .... (I / not / see) you for ages. How are you?

JOE: I'm fine. How about you? (2) .... (you / look) good.

SARAH: Thanks. You too. So, (3) .... (you / go) somewhere or (4) .... (you / meet) somebody?

JOE: (5) .... (I / go) to London for a business meeting.

SARAH: Oh. (6) .... (you / often / go) away on business?

JOE: Quite often, yes. And you? Where (7) .... (you / go)?

SARAH: Nowhere. (8) .... (I / meet) a friend. Unfortunately her train (9) .... (be) delayed – (10) .... (I / wait) here for nearly an hour.

JOE: How are your children?

SARAH: They're all fine, thanks. The youngest (11) .... (just / start) school.

JOE: How (12) .... (she / get) on? (13) .... (she / like) it?

SARAH: Yes, (14) .... (she / think) it's great.

JOE: (15) .... (you / work) at the moment? The last time I (16) .... (speak) to you, (17) .... (you / work) in a travel agency.

SARAH: That's right. Unfortunately the company (18) .... (go) out of business a couple of months after (19) .... (I / start) work there, so (20) .... (I / lose) my job.

JOE: And (21) .... (you / not / have) a job since then?

SARAH: Not a permanent job. (22) .... (I / have) a few temporary jobs. By the way, (23) .... (you / see) Matt recently?

JOE: Matt? He's in Canada.

SARAH: Really? How long (24) .... (he / be) in Canada?

JOE: About a year now. (25) .... (I / see) him a few days before (26) .... (he / go). (27) .... (he / be) unemployed for months, so (28) .... (he / decide) to try his luck somewhere else. (29) .... (he / really / look forward) to going.

SARAH: So, what (30) .... (he / do) there?

JOE: I have no idea. (31) .... (I / not / hear) from him since (32) .... (he / leave). Anyway, I have to go and catch my train. It was really nice to see you again.

SARAH: You too. Bye. Have a good trip.

JOE: Thanks. Bye.

8 用动词的适当形式填空。

1 Who .... (invent) the bicycle?
2 'Do you still have a headache?' 'No, ... (it / go). I'm OK now.'
3 I was the last to leave the office last night. Everybody else .... (go) home when I .... (leave).
4 What .... (you / do) last weekend? .... (you / go) away?
5 I like your car. How long .... (you / have) it?
6 It's a shame the trip was cancelled. I .... (look) forward to it.
7 Jane is an experienced teacher and loves her job. .... (she / teach) for 15 years.
8 .... (I / buy) a new jacket last week, but .... (I / not / wear) it yet.
9 A few days ago .... (I / see) a man at a party whose face .... (be) very familiar. At first I couldn't think where .... (I / see) him before. Then suddenly .... (I / remember) who .... (it / be).
10 .... (you / hear) of Agatha Christie? .... (she / be) a writer who .... (die) in 1976. .... (she / write) more than 70 detective novels. .... (you / read) any of them?
11 A: What .... (this word / mean)?
B: I've no idea. .... (I / never / see) it before. Look it up in the dictionary.
12 A: .... (you / get) to the theatre in time for the play last night?
B: No, we were late. By the time we got there, ... (it / already / start).
13 I went to Sarah's room and .... (knock) on the door, but there .... (be) no answer. Either .... (she / go) out or .... (she / not / want) to see anyone.
14 Patrick asked me how to use the photocopier. .... (he / never / use) it before, so .... (he / not / know) what to do.
15 Lisa .... (go) for a swim after work yesterday. .... (she / need) some exercise because .... (she / sit) in an office all day in front of a computer.

过去进行时与 used to 比较

Units 6, 18

9 用括号内动词的适当形式完成下列句子：过去进行时的形式 **(was/were -ing)** 或 **used to ...**。

1 I haven't been to the cinema for ages now. We *used to go* a lot. (go)
2 Ann didn't see me wave to her. She *was looking* in the other direction. (look)
3 I .... a lot, but I don't use my car very much these days. (drive)
4 I asked the taxi driver to slow down. She .... too fast. (drive)
5 Rosemary and Jonathan met for the first time when they .... in the same bank. (work)
6 When I was a child, I .... a lot of bad dreams. (have)
7 I wonder what Joe is doing these days. He .... in Spain when I last heard from him. (live)
8 'Where were you yesterday afternoon?' 'I .... volleyball.' (play)
9 'Do you do any sports?' 'Not these days, but I .... volleyball.' (play)
10 George looked very nice at the party. He .... a very smart suit. (wear)

将来时

Units 19–25，附录 3

10 根据下列情况，用括号内词语的适当形式填空：现在进行时 **(I am doing)**、**going to** 或 **will (I'll)**。

1 You have made all your holiday arrangements. Your destination is Jamaica.
FRIEND: Have you decided where to go for your holiday yet?
YOU: I'm going to Jamaica. (I / go)

2 You have made an appointment with the dentist for Friday morning.
FRIEND: Shall we meet on Friday morning?
YOU: I can't on Friday. .... (I / go)

3 You and some friends are planning a holiday in Spain. You have decided to hire a car, but you haven't arranged this yet.
FRIEND: How do you plan to travel round Spain? By train?
YOU: No, ... (we / hire)

4 Your friend has two young children. She wants to go out tomorrow evening. You offer to look after the children.
FRIEND: I want to go out tomorrow evening, but I don't have a babysitter.
YOU: That's no problem. .... (I / look after)

5 You have already arranged to have lunch with Sue tomorrow.
FRIEND: Are you free at lunchtime tomorrow?
YOU: No, ... (have lunch)

6 You are in a restaurant. You and your friend are looking at the menu. Maybe your friend has decided what to have. You ask her/him.
YOU: What ....? (you / have)
FRIEND: I don't know. I can't make up my mind.

7 You and a friend are reading. It's getting a bit dark and your friend is having trouble reading. You decide to turn on the light.
FRIEND: It's getting a bit dark, isn't it? It's difficult to read.
YOU: Yes. .... (I / turn on)

8 You and a friend are reading. It's getting a bit dark and you decide to turn on the light. You stand up and walk towards the light switch.
FRIEND: What are you doing?
YOU: .... (I / turn on)

11 用动词的适当形式填空：一般现在时、现在进行时、**will (I'll)** 或 **shall** 的形式。

对话 1 (*in the morning*)

JENNY: (1) Are you doing (you / do) anything tomorrow evening, Helen?
HELEN: No, why?
JENNY: Well, would you like to go to the cinema? *Strangers on a Plane* is on. I want to see it, but I don't want to go alone.
HELEN: OK, (2) .... (I / come) with you. What time (3) .... (we / meet)?
JENNY: Well, the film (4) .... (start) at 8.45, so (5) .... (I / meet) you at about 8.30 outside the cinema, OK?
HELEN: Fine. (6) .... (I / see) Tina later this evening. (7) .... (I / ask) her if she wants to come too?
JENNY: Yes, do that. (8) .... (I / see) you tomorrow then. Bye.

对话 2 (*later the same day*)

HELEN: Jenny and I (9) .... (go) to the cinema tomorrow night to see *Strangers on a Plane*. Why don't you come too?
TINA: I'd love to come. What time (10) .... (the film / start)?
HELEN: 8.45.
TINA: (11) .... (you / meet) outside the cinema?
HELEN: Yes, at 8.30. Is that OK for you?
TINA: Yes, (12) .... (I / be) there at 8.30.

12 用动词的适当形式填空，有时答案不止一个。

1 *A has decided to learn a language.*

A: I've decided to try and learn a foreign language.
B: Have you? Which language (1) are you going to learn (you / learn)?
A: Spanish.
B: (2) .... (you / do) a course?
A: Yes, (3) .... (it / start) next week.
B: That's great. I'm sure (4) .... (you / enjoy) it.
A: I hope so. But I think (5) .... (it / be) difficult.

2 *A wants to know about B's holiday plans.*

A: I hear (1) .... (you / go) on holiday soon.
B: That's right. (2) .... (we / go) to Finland.
A: I hope (3) .... (you / have) a nice time.
B: Thanks. (4) .... (I / send) you a postcard and (5) .... (I / get) in touch with you when (6) .... (I / get) back.

3 *A invites B to a party.*

A: (1) .... (I / have) a party next Saturday. Can you come?
B: On Saturday? I'm not sure. Some friends of mine (2) .... (come) to stay with me next week, but I think (3) .... (they / leave) by Saturday. But if (4) .... (they / be) still here, (5) .... (I / not / be) able to come to the party.
A: OK. Well, tell me as soon as (6) .... (you / know).
B: Right. (7) .... (I / call) you during the week.

4 *A and B are two secret agents arranging a meeting. They are talking on the phone.*

A: Well, what time (1) .... (we / meet)?
B: Come to the café by the station at 4 o'clock. (2) .... (I / wait) for you when (3) .... (you / arrive). (4) .... (I / sit) by the window and (5) .... (I / wear) a bright green sweater.
A: OK. (6) .... (Agent 307 / come) too?
B: No, she can't be there.
A: Oh. (7) .... (I / bring) the documents?
B: Yes. (8) .... (I / explain) everything when (9) .... (I / see) you. And don't be late.
A: OK. (10) .... (I / try) to be on time.

13 用动词的下列形式填空：

现在进行时 **(I am doing)**	**will ('ll) / won't**
一般现在时 **(I do)**	**will be doing**
going to (I'm going to do)	**shall**

1 I feel a bit hungry. I think .... (I / have) something to eat.
2 Why are you putting on your coat? .... (you / go) somewhere?
3 What time .... (I / phone) you tonight? About 7.30?
4 Look! That plane is flying towards the airport. .... (it / land).
5 We must do something soon, before .... (it / be) too late.
6 I'm sorry you've decided to leave the company. .... (I / miss) you when .... (you / go).
7 .... (I / give) you my phone number? If .... (I / give) you my number, ... (you / call) me?
8 Are you still watching that programme? What time .... (it / end)?
9 .... (I / go) to a wedding next weekend. A friend of mine .... (get) married.
10 I'm not ready yet. .... (I / tell) you when .... (I / be) ready. I promise .... (I / not / be) very long.
11 A: Where are you going?
B: To the hairdresser's. .... (I / have) my hair cut.
12 She was very rude to me. I refuse to speak to her again until .... (she / apologise).
13 I wonder where .... (we / live) ten years from now?
14 What do you plan to do when .... (you / finish) your course at college?

过去时、现在时与将来时

Units 1–25

14 根据你自己的想法完成 **B** 所说的话。

1 A: How did the accident happen?
B: I was going too fast and couldn't stop in time.
2 A: Is that a new camera?
B: No, I .... it a long time.
3 A: Is that a new computer?
B: Yes, I .... it a few weeks ago.
4 A: I can't talk to you right now. You can see I'm very busy.
B: OK. I .... back in about half an hour.
5 A: This is a nice restaurant. Do you come here often?
B: No, it's the first time I .... here.
6 A: Do you do any sport?
B: No, I .... football, but I gave it up.
7 A: I'm sorry I'm late.
B: That's OK. I .... long.
8 A: When you went to the US last year, was it your first visit?
B: No, I .... there twice before.
9 A: Do you have any plans for the weekend?
B: Yes, I .... to a party on Saturday night.
10 A: Do you know what Steve's doing these days?
B: No, I .... him for ages.
11 A: Will you still be here by the time I get back?
B: No, I .... by then.

15 罗伯特正在北美洲旅行。下面是他给在加拿大温尼伯的朋友写的邮件，请用括号内动词的适当形式填空。

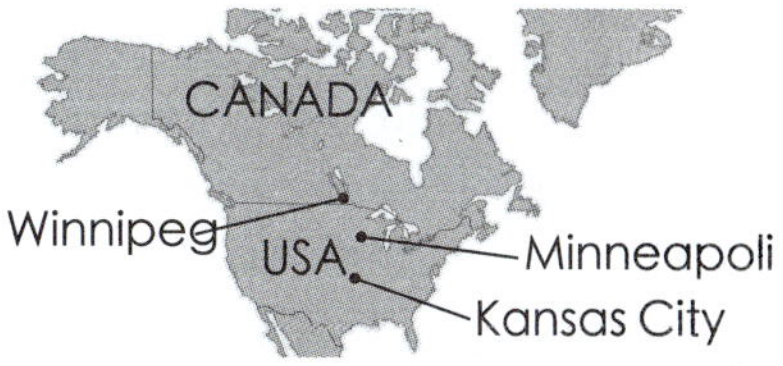

Delete Junk Reply Reply All Forward Print To Do

Subject:
To:

Hi

(1) ....I've just arrived.... (I / just / arrive) in Minneapolis. (2) .... (I / travel) for more than a month now, and (3) .... (I / begin) to think about coming home. Everything (4) .... (I / see) so far (5) .... (be) really interesting, and (6) .... (I / meet) some really kind people.

(7) .... (I / leave) Kansas City a week ago. (8) .... (I / stay) there with Emily, the aunt of a friend from college. She was really helpful and hospitable and although (9) .... (I / plan) to stay only a couple of days, (10) .... (I / end up) staying more than a week.

(11) .... (I / enjoy) the journey from Kansas City to here. (12) .... (I / take) the Greyhound bus and (13) .... (meet) some really interesting people – everybody was really friendly.

So now I'm here, and (14) .... (I / stay) here for a few days before (15) .... (I / continue) up to Canada. I'm not sure exactly when (16) .... (I / get) to Winnipeg – it depends what happens while (17) .... (I / be) here. But (18) .... (I / let) you know as soon as (19) .... (I / know) myself.

(20) .... (I / stay) with a family here – they're friends of some people I know at home. Tomorrow (21) .... (we / visit) some people they know who (22) .... (build) a house in the mountains. It isn't finished yet, but (23) .... (it / be) interesting to see what it's like.

Anyway, that's all for now. (24) .... (I / be) in touch again soon.

Robert

情态动词（can/must/would 等）

Units 26–36，附录 4

16 从下列选项中选择正确答案，有时答案不止一个。

1 'What time will you be home tonight?' 'I'm not sure. I .... late.'
A may be **B** might be **C** can be (*both* A *and* B *are correct*)

2 I can't find the theatre tickets. They .... out of my pocket.
A must have fallen **B** should have fallen **C** had to fall

3 Somebody ran in front of the car as I was driving. Fortunately I .... just in time.
A could stop **B** could have stopped **C** managed to stop

4 We've got plenty of time. We .... yet.
A mustn't leave **B** needn't leave **C** don't need to leave

5 I .... out but I didn't feel like it, so I stayed at home.
A could go **B** could have gone **C** must have gone

6 I'm sorry I .... come to your party last week.
A couldn't come **B** couldn't have come **C** wasn't able to come

7 'What do you think of my theory?' 'I'm not sure. You .... right.'
A could be **B** must be **C** might be

8 I couldn't wait for you any longer. I ...., and so I went.
A must go **B** must have gone **C** had to go

9 'Do you know where Sarah is?' 'No. I suppose she .... shopping.'
A should have gone **B** may have gone **C** could have gone

10 At first they didn't believe me when I told them what had happened, but in the end I .... them that I was telling the truth.
A was able to convince **B** managed to convince **C** could convince

11 I promised I'd call Gary this evening. I ....
A mustn't forget **B** needn't forget **C** don't have to forget

12 Why did you leave without me? You .... for me.
A must have waited **B** had to wait **C** should have waited

13 Lisa called me and suggested .... lunch together.
A we have **B** we should have **C** to have

14 You look nice in that jacket, but you hardly ever wear it. .... it more often.
A You'd better wear **B** You should wear **C** You ought to wear

15 Shall I buy a car? What's your advice? What .... ?
A will you do **B** would you do **C** shall you do

17 用括号内的词语造句。

1 Don't phone them now.
They *might be having* lunch. (might / have)

2 I've eaten too much. Now I feel sick.
I .... so much. (shouldn't / eat)

3 I wonder why Tom didn't phone me.
He .... (must / forget)

4 Why did you go home so early?
You .... home so early. (needn't / go)

5 You've signed the contract.
It .... now. (can't / change)

6 'What's Linda doing?' 'I'm not sure.'
She .... TV. (may / watch)

7 Laura was standing outside the cinema.
She .... for somebody. (must / wait)

8 He was in prison at the time that the crime was committed.
He .... it. (couldn't / do)

9 Why weren't you here earlier?
You .... here earlier. (ought / be)

10 Why didn't you ask me to help you?
I .... you. (would / help)

11 I'm surprised you weren't told that the road was dangerous.
You .... about it. (should / warn)

12 Gary was in a strange mood yesterday.
He .... very well. (might not / feel)

18 用 **can/could/might/must/should/would** + 括号内的动词完成 B 所说的话。有些句子需要用 **have (must have ... / should have ...** 等)，有些句子需要用否定形式 **(can't/couldn't** 等)。

1 A: I'm hungry.
B: But you've just had lunch. You *can't be* hungry already. (be)
2 A: I haven't seen our neighbours for ages.
B: No. They *must have gone* away. (go)
3 A: What's the weather like? Is it raining?
B: Not at the moment, but it .... later. (rain)
4 A: Where's Julia?
B: I'm not sure. She .... out. (go)
5 A: I didn't see you at Michael's party last week.
B: No, I had to work that night, so I .... (go)
6 A: I think I saw you at Michael's party last week.
B: No, you .... me. I didn't go to Michael's party. (see)
7 A: What time will we get to Sue's house?
B: Well, it takes about one and a half hours, so if we leave at 3 o'clock, we .... there by 4.30. (get)
8 A: When was the last time you saw Bill?
B: Years ago. I .... him if I saw him now. (recognise)
9 A: Did you hear the explosion?
B: What explosion?
A: There was a loud explosion about an hour ago. You .... it. (hear)
10 A: We weren't sure which way to go. In the end we turned right.
B: You went the wrong way. You .... left. (turn)

条件句

Units 25，38–40

19 用动词的适当形式填空。

1 If *you found* a wallet in the street, what would you do with it? (you / find)
2 I must hurry. My friend will be annoyed if *I'm not* on time. (I / not / be)
3 I didn't realise that Gary was in hospital. If *I'd known* he was in hospital, I would have gone to visit him. (I / know)
4 If the phone .... , can you answer it? (ring)
5 I can't decide what to do. What would you do if .... in my position? (you / be)
6 A: What shall we do tomorrow?
B: Well, if .... a nice day, we can go to the beach. (it / be)
7 A: Let's go to the beach.
B: No, it's too cold. If .... warmer, I wouldn't mind going. (it / be)
8 A: Did you go to the beach yesterday?
B: No, it was too cold. If .... warmer, we might have gone. (it / be)
9 If .... enough money to go anywhere in the world, where would you go? (you / have)
10 I'm glad we had a map. I'm sure we would have got lost if .... one. (we / not / have)
11 The accident was your fault. If .... more carefully, it wouldn't have happened. (you / drive)
12 A: Why do you read newspapers?
B: Well, if .... newspapers, I wouldn't know what was happening in the world. (I / not / read)

20 根据所给情况完成下列句子。

1 Lisa is tired all the time. She shouldn't go to bed so late.
If Lisa *didn't go* to bed so late, she *wouldn't be* tired all the time.
2 It's getting late. I don't think Sarah will come to see us now.
I'd be surprised if Sarah .... to see us now.
3 I'm sorry I disturbed you. I didn't know you were busy.
If .... you were busy, I .... you.
4 I don't want them to be upset, so I've decided not to tell them what happened.
.... upset if I .... them what happened.
5 The dog attacked you, but only because you frightened it.
If you .... the dog, it .... you.
6 Unfortunately I didn't have an umbrella and so I got very wet in the rain.
I .... so wet if .... an umbrella.
7 Martin failed his driving test. He was very nervous and that's why he failed.
If he .... so nervous, he .... the test.

21 根据你自己的想法完成下列句子。

1 I'd go out tonight if ....
2 I'd have gone out last night if ....
3 If you hadn't reminded me, ...
4 If I had my camera, ...
5 If you give me the camera, ...
6 Who would you phone if .... ?
7 We wouldn't have been late if ....
8 If I'd been able to get a ticket, ...
9 If I'd done better at the interview, ...
10 You wouldn't be hungry now if ....
11 Cities would be nicer places if ....
12 If there was no TV, ...

被动语态

Units 42–45

22 用动词被动语态的适当形式填空。

1 There's somebody behind us. I think *we're being followed* (we / follow).
2 A mystery is something that *can't be explained* (can't / explain).
3 We didn't play football yesterday. The game .... (cancel).
4 The TV .... (repair). It's working again now.
5 In the middle of the village there is a church which .... (restore) at the moment. The work is almost finished.
6 The tower is the oldest part of the church. .... (it / believe) to be over 600 years old.
7 If I didn't do my job properly, ... (I / would / sack).
8 A: I left a newspaper on the desk last night and it isn't there now.
B: .... (it / might / throw) away.
9 I learnt to swim when I was very young. .... (I / teach) by my mother.
10 After .... (arrest), I was taken to the police station.
11 '.................... (you / ever / arrest)?' 'No, never.'
12 Two people .... (report) to .... (injure) in an explosion at a factory in Birmingham early this morning.

23 用动词的主动语态或被动语态形式填空。

1 This house is quite old. It ..was built.. (build) over 100 years ago.
2 My grandfather was a builder. He ..built.. (build) this house many years ago.
3 'Is your car still for sale?' 'No, I .... (sell) it.'
4 A: Is the house at the end of the street still for sale?
B: No, it .... (sell).
5 Sometimes mistakes .... (make). It's inevitable.
6 I wouldn't leave your car unlocked. It .... (might / steal).
7 My bag has disappeared. It .... (must / steal).
8 I can't find my hat. Somebody .... (must / take) it by mistake.
9 It's a serious problem. I don't know how it .... (can / solve).
10 We didn't leave early enough. We .... (should / leave) earlier.
11 Nearly every time I travel by plane, my flight .... (delay).
12 A new bridge .... (build) across the river. Work started last year and the bridge .... (expect) to open next year.

24 阅读下列报道，用动词的适当形式填空。

1

Castle Fire

Winton Castle (1) ..was damaged.. (damage) in a fire last night. The fire, which (2) .... (discover) at about 9 o'clock, spread very quickly. Nobody (3) .... (injure), but two people had to (4) .... (rescue) from an upstairs room. A number of paintings (5) .... (believe / destroy). It (6) .... (not / know) how the fire started.

2

SHOP ROBBERY

In Paxham yesterday a shop assistant (1) .... (force) to hand over £500 after (2) .... (threaten) by a man with a knife. The man escaped in a car which (3) .... (steal) earlier in the day. The car (4) .... (later / find) in a car park where it (5) .... (abandon) by the thief. A man (6) .... (arrest) in connection with the robbery and (7) .... (still / question) by the police.

3

ROAD DELAYS

Repair work started yesterday on the Paxham–Longworth road. The road (1) .... (resurface) and there will be long delays. Drivers (2) .... (ask) to use an alternative route if possible. The work (3) .... (expect) to last two weeks. Next Sunday the road (4) .... (close), and traffic (5) .... (divert).

4

Accident

A woman (1) .... (take) to hospital after her car collided with a lorry near Norstock yesterday. She (2) .... (allow) home later after treatment. The road (3) .... (block) for an hour after the accident, and traffic had to (4) .... (divert). A police inspector said afterwards: 'The woman was lucky. She could (5) .... (kill).'

间接引语

Units 47–48，50

25 用间接引语完成下列句子。

1

A woman phoned at lunchtime yesterday and asked *if she could speak to Paul* ………… . I told ………… and ………… . I asked ………… , but she said ………… later. But she never did.

2

I went to London recently, but my visit didn't begin well. I had reserved a hotel room, but when I got to the hotel they told ………… . When I asked ………… , they said ………… , but ………… . There was nothing I could do. I just had to look for somewhere else to stay.

3

After getting off the plane, we had to queue for an hour to get through immigration. Finally it was our turn. The immigration official asked us ………… , and we told ………… . Then he wanted to know ………… and ………… . He seemed satisfied with our answers, checked our passports and wished us a pleasant stay.

4

A: What time is Sue arriving this afternoon?
B: About three. She said ………… us ………… .
A: Aren't you going to meet her?
B: No, she said ………… . She said ………… .

5

A few days ago a man phoned from a marketing company and started asking me questions. He wanted to know .... and asked .... I don't like people phoning and asking questions like that, so I told .... and I put the phone down.

6

Louise and Sarah are in a restaurant waiting for Paul.

LOUISE: I wonder where Paul is. He said ....
SARAH: Maybe he's got lost.
LOUISE: I don't think so. He said ....
And I told ....

7

Five minutes later

JOE: Is there anything to eat?
JANE: You just said ....
JOE: Well, I am now. I'd love a banana.
JANE: A banana? But you said ....
You told ....

动词的-ing 形式与不定式比较

Units 53–66

26 用动词的适当形式填空。

1 How old were you when you learnt *to drive* ? (drive)
2 I don't mind *walking* home, but I'd rather *get* a taxi. (walk, get)
3 I can't make a decision. I keep .... my mind. (change)
4 He had made his decision and refused .... his mind. (change)
5 Why did you change your decision? What made you .... your mind? (change)
6 It was a really good holiday. I really enjoyed .... by the sea again. (be)
7 Did I really tell you I was unhappy? I don't remember .... that. (say)
8 'Remember .... Tom tomorrow.' 'OK. I won't forget.' (call)

9 The water here is not very good. I'd avoid .... it if I were you. (drink)
10 I pretended .... interested in the conversation, but really it was very boring. (be)
11 I got up and looked out of the window .... what the weather was like. (see)
12 I have a friend who claims .... able to speak five languages. (be)
13 I like .... carefully about things before .... a decision. (think, make)
14 I had a flat in the centre of town but I didn't like .... there, so I decided .... (live, move)
15 Steve used .... a footballer. He had to stop .... because of an injury. (be, play)
16 After .... by the police, the man admitted .... the car, but denied .... at 100 miles an hour. (stop, steal, drive)
17 A: How do you make this machine .... ? (work)
B: I'm not sure. Try .... that button and see what happens. (press)

27 用括号内的词语造句。

1 I can't find the tickets. (I / seem / lose / them)
I seem to have lost them.

2 I don't have far to go. (it / not / worth / take / a taxi)
It's not worth taking a taxi.

3 I'm feeling a bit tired. (I / not / fancy / go / out)
....

4 Tim isn't very reliable. (he / tend / forget / things)
....

5 I've got a lot of luggage. (you / mind / help / me?)
....

6 There's nobody at home. (everybody / seem / go out)
....

7 We don't like our apartment. (we / think / move)
....

8 The vase was very valuable. (I / afraid / touch / it)
....

9 Ben never carries a lot of money with him. (he / afraid / robbed)
....

10 I wouldn't go to see the film. (it / not / worth / see)
....

11 I'm very tired after that long walk. (I / not / used / walk / so far)
....

12 Sue is on holiday. I received a postcard from her yesterday. (she / seem / enjoy / herself)
....

13 Dan had lots of photographs he'd taken while on holiday. (he / insist / show / them to me)
....

14 I don't want to do the shopping. (I'd rather / somebody else / do / it)
....

28 完成下列句子，使它与前一个句子表达的意思相近。

1 I was surprised I passed the exam.
I didn't expect ...to pass the exam... .

2 Did you manage to solve the problem?
Did you succeed ...in solving the problem... ?

3 I don't read newspapers any more.
I've given up ....

4 I'd prefer not to go out tonight.
I'd rather ....

5 He finds it difficult to sleep at night.
He has trouble ....

6 Shall I phone you this evening?
Do you want .... ?

7 Nobody saw me come in.
I came in without ....

8 They said I was a cheat.
I was accused ....

9 It will be good to see them again.
I'm looking forward ....

10 What do you think I should do?
What do you advise me .... ?

11 It's a pity I couldn't go out with you last night.
I'd like ....

12 I wish I'd taken your advice.
I regret ....

冠词

Units 69–76

29 用 **a/an** 或 **the** 填空，在不需要冠词的地方画"–"。

1 I don't usually like staying at ...–... hotels, but last summer we spent two weeks at ...a... very nice hotel by ...the... sea.

2 If you go to live in .... foreign country, you should try and learn .... language.

3 Helen is .... economist. She lives in .... United States and works for .... investment company.

4 I love .... sport, especially .... tennis . I play two or three times .... week if I can, but I'm not .... very good player.

5 I won't be home for .... dinner this evening. I'm meeting some friends after .... work and we're going to .... cinema.

6 When .... unemployment is high, it's difficult for .... people to find .... work. It's .... big problem.

7 There was .... accident as I was going .... home last night. Two people were taken to .... hospital. I think .... most accidents are caused by .... people driving too fast.

8 A: What's .... name of .... hotel where you're staying?
B: .... Ambassador. It's in .... Queen Street in .... city centre. It's near .... station.

9 I have two brothers. .... older one is training to be .... pilot with .... British Airways. .... younger one is still at .... school. When he leaves .... school, he wants to go to .... university to study .... law.

代词与限定词

Unit 82–91

30 从下列选项中选择正确答案，有时答案不止一个。

1 I don't remember .... about the accident.
(A) anything **B** something **C** nothing (*A is correct*)

2 Chris and I have known .... for quite a long time.
A us **B** each other **C** ourselves

3 'How often do the buses run?' '........................ twenty minutes.'
A All **B** Each **C** Every

4 I shouted for help, but .... came.
A nobody **B** no-one **C** anybody

5 Last night we went out with some friends of ....
A us **B** our **C** ours

6 It didn't take us a long time to get here. .... traffic.
A It wasn't much **B** There wasn't much **C** It wasn't a lot

7 Can I have .... milk in my coffee, please?
A a little **B** any **C** some

8 Sometimes I find it difficult to ....
A concentrate **B** concentrate me **C** concentrate myself

9 There's .... on at the cinema that I want to see, so there's no point in going.
A something **B** anything **C** nothing

10 I drink .... water every day.
A much **B** a lot of **C** lots of

11 .... in the centre are open on Sunday.
A Most of shops **B** Most of the shops **C** The most of the shops

12 There were about twenty people in the photo. I didn't recognise .... of them.
A any **B** none **C** either

13 I've been waiting .... for Sarah to phone.
A all morning **B** the whole morning **C** all the morning

14 I can't afford to buy anything in this shop. .... so expensive.
A All is **B** Everything is **C** All are

形容词与副词

Units 98–108

31 指出下列句子是否正确。如有错误，请改正。在正确的句子后面写上：**OK**。

1 The building was total destroyed in the fire. .... totally destroyed
2 I didn't like the book. It was such a stupid story. .... OK
3 The city is very polluted. It's the more polluted place I've ever been to. ....
4 I was disappointing that I didn't get the job. I was well-qualified and the interview went well. ....
5 It's warm today, but there's quite a strong wind. ....
6 Joe works hardly, but he doesn't get paid very much. ....
7 The company's offices are in a modern large building. ....
8 Dan is a very fast runner. I wish I could run as fast as him. ....
9 I missed the three last days of the course because I was ill. ....
10 You don't look happy. What's the matter? ....

11 The weather has been unusual cold for the time of the year. ....
12 The water in the pool was too dirty to swim in it. ....
13 I got impatient because we had to wait so long time. ....
14 Is this box big enough or do you need a bigger one? ....
15 This morning I got up more early than usual. ....

连词

Units 25, 38, 112–118

32 从下列句子画线的部分中选择正确答案。

1 I'll try to be on time, but don't worry <u>if / ~~when~~</u> I'm late. (<u>if</u> *is correct*)
2 Don't throw that bag away. <u>If / When</u> you don't want it, I'll have it.
3 Please report to reception <u>if / when</u> you arrive at the hotel.
4 We've arranged to go to the beach tomorrow, but we won't go <u>if / when</u> it's raining.
5 Tanya is in her final year at school. She still doesn't know what she's going to do <u>if / when</u> she leaves.
6 What would you do <u>if / when</u> you lost your keys?
7 I hope I'll be able to come to the party, but I'll let you know <u>if / unless</u> I can't.
8 I don't want to be disturbed, so don't phone me <u>if / unless</u> it's something important.
9 Please sign the contract <u>if / unless</u> you're happy with the conditions.
10 I like travelling by ship <u>as long as / unless</u> the sea is not rough.
11 You might not remember the name of the hotel, so write it down <u>if / in case</u> you forget it.
12 It's not cold now, but take your coat with you <u>if / in case</u> it gets cold later.
13 Take your coat with you and then you can put it on <u>if / in case</u> it gets cold later.
14 They always have the TV on, <u>even if / if</u> nobody is watching it.
15 <u>Even / Although</u> I left home early, I got to work late.
16 <u>Despite / Although</u> we've known each other a long time, we're not particularly close friends.
17 'When did you leave school?' '<u>As / When</u> I was 17.'
18 I think Ann will be very pleased <u>as / when</u> she hears the news.

介词（时间）

Units 12, 119–122

33 用下列介词填空： **at on in during for since by until**

1 Jack has gone away. He'll be back ...in... a week.
2 We're having a party .... Saturday. Can you come?
3 I've got an interview next week. It's .... 9.30 .... Tuesday morning.
4 Sue isn't usually here .... weekends. She goes away.
5 The train service is very good. The trains are nearly always .... time.
6 It was a confusing situation. Many things were happening .... the same time.
7 I couldn't decide whether or not to buy the sweater. .... the end I decided not to.
8 The road is busy all the time, even .... night.
9 I met a lot of nice people .... my stay in New York.
10 I saw Helen .... Friday, but I haven't seen her .... then.
11 Robert has been doing the same job .... five years.
12 Lisa's birthday is .... the end of March. I'm not sure exactly which day it is.
13 We have some friends staying with us .... the moment. They're staying .... Friday.
14 If you're interested in applying for the job, your application must be received .... Friday.
15 I'm just going out. I won't be long – I'll be back .... ten minutes.

介词 (地点与其他用法)

Units 123–128

34 用适当的介词填空。

1 I'd love to be able to visit every country .... the world.
2 Jessica White is my favourite author. Have you read anything .... her?
3 'Is there a bank near here?' 'Yes, there's one .... the end of this road.'
4 Tim is away at the moment. He's .... holiday.
5 We live .... the country, a long way from the nearest town.
6 I've got a stain .... my jacket. I'll have to have it cleaned.
7 We went .... a party .... Lisa's house on Saturday.
8 Boston is .... the east coast of the United States.
9 Look at the leaves .... that tree. They're a beautiful colour.
10 'Have you ever been .... Tokyo?' 'No, I've never been .... Japan.'
11 Mozart died .... Vienna in 1791 .... the age of 35.
12 'Are you .... this photo?' 'Yes, that's me, ... the left.'
13 We went .... the theatre last night. We had seats .... the front row.
14 'Where's the light switch?' 'It's .... the wall .... the door.'
15 It was late when we arrived .... the hotel.
16 I couldn't decide what to eat. There was nothing .... the menu that I liked.
17 We live .... a tower block. Our apartment is .... the fifteenth floor.
18 A: What did you think of the film?
B: Some parts were a bit stupid, but .... the whole I enjoyed it.
19 'When you paid the restaurant bill, did you pay cash?' 'No, I paid .... credit card.'
20 'How did you get here? Did you come .... the bus?' 'No, ... car.'
21 A: I wonder what's .... TV this evening. Do you have a newspaper?
B: Yes, the TV programmes are .... the back page.
22 Helen works for a telecommunications company. She works .... the customer services department.
23 Anna spent two years working .... Chicago before returning .... Italy.
24 'Did you enjoy your trip .... the beach?' 'Yes, it was great.'
25 Next summer we're going .... a trip to Canada.

名词/形容词 + 介词

Units 129–131

35 用适当的介词填空。

1 The plan has been changed, but nobody seems to know the reason .... this.
2 Don't ask me to decide. I'm not very good .... making decisions.
3 Some people say that Sue is unfriendly, but she's always very nice .... me.
4 What do you think is the best solution .... the problem?
5 There has been a big increase .... the price of oil recently.
6 He lives a rather lonely life. He doesn't have much contact .... other people.
7 Paul is a keen photographer. He likes taking pictures .... people.
8 Michael got married .... a woman he met when he was studying at college.
9 He's very brave. He's not afraid .... anything.
10 I'm surprised .... the amount of traffic today. I didn't think it would be so busy.
11 Thank you for lending me the guidebook. It was full .... useful information.
12 I'm afraid I've had to change my plans, so I can't meet you tomorrow. I'm sorry .... that.

动词 + 介词

Units 132–136

36 用适当的介词填空，在不需要介词的地方画“–”。

1 She works quite hard. You can't accuse her .... being lazy.
2 Who's going to look .... your children while you're at work?
3 The problem is becoming serious. We have to discuss .... it.
4 The problem is becoming serious. We have to do something .... it.
5 I prefer this chair .... the other one. It's more comfortable.
6 I need to phone .... the office to tell them I won't be at work today.
7 The river divides the city .... two parts.
8 'What do you think .... your new boss?' 'She's all right, I suppose.'
9 Can somebody please explain .... me what I have to do?
10 I said hello to her, but she didn't answer .... me.
11 'Do you like staying at hotels?' 'It depends .... the hotel.'
12 'Have you ever been to Borla?' 'No, I've never heard .... it. Where is it?'
13 You remind me .... somebody I knew a long time ago. You look just like her.
14 This is wonderful news! I can't believe .... it.
15 George is not an idealist – he believes .... being practical.
16 What's funny? What are you laughing .... ?
17 What did you do with all the money you had? What did you spend it .... ?
18 If Alex asks .... you .... money, don't give him any.
19 I apologised .... Sarah .... keeping her waiting so long.
20 Lisa was very helpful. I thanked .... her .... everything she'd done.

短语动词

Units 137–145

37 请将下列 **A**、**B** 两人所说的话正确配对。

A

1 ~~I've made a mistake on this form.~~
2 I'm too warm with my coat on.
3 This jacket looks nice.
4 My phone number is 576920.
5 This room is in a mess.
6 What's 45 euros in dollars?
7 How did you find the mistake?
8 I'm not sure whether to accept their offer or not.
9 I need a place to stay when I'm in London.
10 It's a subject he doesn't like to talk about.
11 I don't know what this word means.

B

a Don't worry. I'll clear it up.
b No problem. I can fix it up.
c Kate pointed it out.
d ~~That's OK. Cross it out and correct it.~~
e Yes, why don't you try it on?
f OK, I won't bring it up.
g Just a minute. I'll write it down.
h Why don't you take it off then?
i You can look it up.
j I think you should turn it down.
k Give me a moment. I'll work it out.

1 d
2 ....
3 ....
4 ....
5 ....
6 ....
7 ....
8 ....
9 ....
10 ....
11 ....

38 请从下列选项中选择正确答案。

1 Nobody believed Paul at first but he ....B.... to be right. (B *is correct*)
A came out **B** turned out **C** worked out **D** carried out

2 Here's some good news. It will ....
A turn you up **B** put you up **C** blow you up **D** cheer you up

3 I was annoyed with the way the children were behaving, so I ....
A told them up **B** told them off **C** told them out **D** told them over

4 The club committee is .... of the president, the secretary and seven other members.
A set up **B** made up **C** set out **D** made out

5 You were going to apply for the job, and then you decided not to. So what .... ?
A put you off **B** put you out **C** turned you off **D** turned you away

6 I had no idea that he was lying to me. I was completely ....
A taken in **B** taken down **C** taken off **D** taken over

7 Helen started a course at college, but she .... after six months.
A went out **B** fell out **C** turned out **D** dropped out

8 You can't predict everything. Often things don't .... as you expect.
A make out **B** break out **C** work out **D** get out

9 Why are all these people here? What's .... ?
A going off **B** getting off **C** going on **D** getting on

10 It's a very busy airport. There are planes .... or landing every few minutes.
A going up **B** taking off **C** getting up **D** driving off

11 The traffic was moving slowly because a bus had .... and was blocking the road.
A broken down **B** fallen down **C** fallen over **D** broken up

12 How are you .... in your new job? Are you enjoying it?
A keeping on **B** going on **C** carrying on **D** getting on

39 完成下列句子，每空需填两个单词。

1 Keep ....away from.... the edge of the pool. You might fall in.
2 I didn't notice that the two pictures were different until Tanya pointed it .... me.
3 I asked Dan if he had any suggestions about what we should do, but he didn't come .... anything.
4 I'm glad Sarah is coming to the party. I'm really looking .... seeing her again.
5 Things are changing all the time. It's difficult to keep .... all these changes.
6 I don't want to run .... food for the party. Are you sure we have enough?
7 Don't let me interrupt you. Carry .... your work.
8 Steve was very happy in his job until he fell .... his boss. After that, it was impossible for them to work together, and Steve decided to leave.
9 I've had enough of being treated like this. I'm not going to put .... it any more.
10 I didn't enjoy the trip very much at the time, but when I look .... it now, I realise it was a good experience and I'm glad I went on it.
11 The wedding was supposed to be a secret, so how did you find .... it? Did Jess tell you?
12 There is a very nice atmosphere in the office where I work. Everybody gets .... everybody else.

40 用短语动词填空，使其与括号内的词语意思相同。

1 The football match had to be ......called off...... because of the weather. (cancelled)
2 The story Kate told wasn't true. She ......made it up...... . (invented it)
3 A bomb .... near the station, but no-one was injured. (exploded)
4 Paul finally .... nearly an hour late. (arrived)
5 Here's an application form. Can you .... and sign it, please? (complete it)
6 A number of buildings are going to be .... to make way for the new road. (demolished)
7 I'm having a few problems with my computer which need to be .... as soon as possible. (put right)
8 Be positive! You must never .... ! (stop trying)
9 I was very tired and .... in front of the television. (fell asleep)
10 After eight years together, they've decided to .... (separate)
11 The noise is terrible. I can't .... any longer. (tolerate it)
12 We don't have a lot of money, but we have enough to .... (manage)
13 I'm sorry I'm late. The meeting .... longer than I expected. (continued)
14 We need to make a decision today at the latest. We can't .... any longer. (delay it)

41 完成下列句子，每空只填一个单词。

1 You're driving too fast. Please ......slow...... down.
2 It was only a small fire and I managed to .... it out with a bucket of water.
3 The house is empty at the moment, but I think the new tenants are .... in next week.
4 I've .... on weight. My clothes don't fit any more.
5 Their house is really nice now. They've .... it up really well.
6 I was talking to the woman sitting next to me on the plane, and it .... out that she works for the same company as my brother.
7 'Do you know what happened?' 'Not yet, but I'm going to .... out.'
8 There's no need to get angry. .... down!
9 If you're going on a long walk, plan your route carefully before you .... off.
10 Sarah has just phoned to say that she'll be late. She's been .... up.
11 You've written my name wrong. It's Martin, not Marin – you .... out the T.
12 Three days at £45 a day – that .... out at £135.
13 We had a really interesting discussion, but Jane didn't .... in. She just listened.
14 Jonathan is pretty fit. He .... out in the gym every day.
15 Come and see us more often. You can .... in any time you like.
16 We are still discussing the contract. There are still a couple of things to .... out.
17 My alarm clock .... off in the middle of the night and .... me up.

学习指导将帮助你找出需要认真学习的单元。这里的句子是参照目录中的单元顺序分组排列的(现在时与过去时比较、冠词与名词等)。

学习指导以选择填空形式出现，每个句子下方列有2—5个选项，有时答案不止一个。

如果你不知道或不确定正确选项是哪个，说明你需要认真学习右边数字所指示的单元。在这些单元中你会找到正确答案。(如果句子右边列有2—3个单元，正确答案则在第一个数字所指的单元中。)

书后第372页附有答案。

IF YOU ARE NOT SURE WHICH IS RIGHT — STUDY UNIT

现在时与过去时

1.1 At first I didn't like my job, but .... to enjoy it now. — 1, 3
A I'm beginning **B** I begin

1.2 I don't understand this sentence. What .... ? — 2, 49
A does mean this word **B** does this word mean **C** means this word

1.3 Robert .... away two or three times a year. — 2, 3, 110
A is going usually **B** is usually going **C** usually goes **D** goes usually

1.4 How .... now? Better than before? — 4
A you are feeling **B** do you feel **C** are you feeling

1.5 It was a boring weekend. .... anything. — 5
A I didn't **B** I don't do **C** I didn't do

1.6 Matt .... while we were having dinner. — 6, 14
A phoned **B** was phoning **C** has phoned

现在完成时与一般过去时

2.1 James is on holiday. He .... to Italy. — 7
A is gone **B** has gone **C** has been

2.2 Everything is going well. We .... any problems so far. — 8
A didn't have **B** don't have **C** haven't had

2.3 Sarah has lost her passport again. It's the second time this .... — 8
A has happened **B** happens **C** happened **D** is happening

2.4 You're out of breath. .... ? — 9
A Are you running **B** Have you run **C** Have you been running

2.5 Where's the book I gave you? What .... with it? — 10
A have you done **B** have you been doing **C** are you doing

2.6 '.................... each other for a long time?' 'Yes, since we were at school.' — 11, 10
A Do you know **B** Have you known **C** Have you been knowing

2.7 Sally has been working here .... — 12
A for six months **B** since six months **C** six months ago

IF YOU ARE NOT SURE WHICH IS RIGHT

		STUDY UNIT
2.8	It's two years .... Joe. **A** that I don't see **B** that I haven't seen **C** since I didn't see **D** since I last saw	12
2.9	It .... raining for a while, but now it's raining again. **A** stopped **B** has stopped **C** was stopped	13
2.10	My mother .... in Italy. **A** grew up **B** has grown up **C** had grown up	13
2.11	.... a lot of sweets when you were a child? **A** Have you eaten **B** Had you eaten **C** Did you eat	14
2.12	Jack .... in New York for ten years. Now he lives in Los Angeles. **A** lived **B** has lived **C** has been living	14, 11
2.13	The man sitting next to me on the plane was very nervous. He .... before. **A** hasn't flown **B** didn't fly **C** hadn't flown **D** wasn't flying	15
2.14	Katherine was sitting in an armchair resting. She was tired because .... very hard. **A** she was working **B** she's been working **C** she'd been working	16
2.15	.... a car when you were living in Paris? **A** Had you **B** Were you having **C** Have you had **D** Did you have	17, 14
2.16	I .... tennis a lot, but I don't play very much now. **A** was playing **B** was used to play **C** used to play	18

将来时

3.1	I'm tired. .... to bed now. Goodnight. **A** I go **B** I'm going	19
3.2	.... tomorrow, so we can go out somewhere. **A** I'm not working **B** I don't work **C** I won't work	19, 21
3.3	That bag looks heavy. .... you with it. **A** I'm helping **B** I help **C** I'll help	21
3.4	I think the weather .... be nice later. **A** will **B** shall **C** is going to	23, 22
3.5	'Anna is in hospital.' 'Yes, I know. .... her this evening.' **A** I visit **B** I'm going to visit **C** I'll visit	23, 20
3.6	We're late. The film .... by the time we get to the cinema. **A** will already start **B** will be already started **C** will already have started	24
3.7	Don't worry .... late tonight. **A** if I'm **B** when I'm **C** when I'll be **D** if I'll be	25

IF YOU ARE NOT SURE WHICH IS RIGHT

STUDY UNIT

情态动词

4.1 The fire spread through the building very quickly, but fortunately everybody 26
A was able to escape **B** managed to escape **C** could escape

4.2 I'm so tired I .... for a week. 27
A can sleep **B** could sleep **B** could have slept

4.3 The story .... be true, but I don't think it is. 27, 29
A might **B** can **C** could **D** may

4.4 Why did you stay at a hotel when you were in Paris? You .... with Sarah. 27
A can stay **B** could stay **C** could have stayed

4.5 'I've lost one of my gloves.' 'You .... it somewhere.' 28
A must drop **B** must have dropped **C** must be dropping
D must have been dropping

4.6 'Why wasn't Amy at the meeting yesterday?' 'She .... about it.' 29
A might not know **B** may not know **C** might not have known
D may not have known

4.7 What was the problem? Why .... leave early? 31
A had you to **B** did you have to **C** must you **D** you had to

4.8 We've got plenty of time. We .... hurry. 32
A don't need to **B** mustn't **C** needn't

4.9 You missed a great party last night. You .... Why didn't you? 33
A must have come **B** should have come **C** ought to have come
D had to come

4.10 Jane won the lottery. I .... a car with the money she'd won. 34
A suggested that she buy **B** suggested that she should buy
C suggested her to buy **D** suggested that she bought

4.11 You're always at home. You .... out more often. 35
A should go **B** had better go **C** had better to go

4.12 It's late. It's time .... home. 35
A we go **B** we must go **C** we should go **D** we went **E** to go

4.13 .... a little longer, but I really have to go now. 36
A I'd stay **B** I'll stay **C** I can stay **D** I'd have stayed

条件句与wish

5.1 I'm not going to bed yet. I'm not tired. If I .... to bed now, I wouldn't sleep. 38
A go **B** went **C** had gone **D** would go

5.2 If I were rich, ... a lot. 39
A I'll travel **B** I can travel **C** I would travel **D** I travelled

5.3 I wish I .... have to work tomorrow, but unfortunately I do. 39, 41
A don't **B** didn't **C** wouldn't **D** won't

IF YOU ARE NOT SURE WHICH IS RIGHT

STUDY UNIT

5.4 The view was wonderful. If .... a camera with me, I would have taken some pictures. 40
A I had **B** I would have **C** I would have had **D** I'd had

5.5 The weather is horrible. I wish it .... raining. 41
A would stop **B** stopped **C** stops **D** will stop

被动语态

6.1 We .... by a loud noise during the night. 42
A woke up **B** are woken up **C** were woken up **D** were waking up

6.2 A new supermarket is going to .... next year. 43
A build **B** be built **C** be building **D** building

6.3 There's somebody walking behind us. I think 43
A we are following **B** we are being following **C** we are followed
D we are being followed

6.4 'Where .... ?' 'In Chicago.' 44
A were you born **B** are you born **C** have you been born
D did you born

6.5 There was a fight at the party, but nobody 44
A was hurt **B** got hurt **C** hurt

6.6 Jane .... to phone me last night, but she didn't. 45
A supposed **B** is supposed **C** was supposed

6.7 Where .... ? Which hairdresser did you go to? 46
A did you cut your hair **B** have you cut your hair
C did you have cut your hair **D** did you have your hair cut

间接引语

7.1 Paul left the room suddenly. He said he .... to go. 48, 47
A had **B** has **C** have

7.2 Hi, Joe. I didn't expect to see you. Sonia said you .... in hospital. 48, 47
A are **B** were **C** was **D** should be

7.3 Ann .... and left. 48
A said goodbye to me **B** said me goodbye **C** told me goodbye

疑问句与助动词

8.1 'What time .... ?' 'At 8.30.' 49
A starts the film **B** does start the film **C** does the film start

8.2 'Do you know where .... ?' 'No, he didn't say.' 50
A Tom has gone **B** has Tom gone **C** has gone Tom

8.3 The police officer stopped us and asked us where 50
A were we going **B** are we going **C** we are going **D** we were going

IF YOU ARE NOT SURE WHICH IS RIGHT

STUDY UNIT

8.4 'Do you think it will rain?' '.......................... .' **51**
A I hope not. **B** I don't hope. **C** I don't hope so.

8.5 'You don't know where Karen is, ... ?' 'Sorry, I have no idea.' **52**
A don't you **B** do you **C** is she **D** are you

动词的 -ing 形式与不定式比较

9.1 You can't stop me .... what I want. **53**
A doing **B** do **C** to do **D** that I do

9.2 I must go now. I promised .... late. **54, 36**
A not being **B** not to be **C** to not be **D** I wouldn't be

9.3 Do you want .... with you or do you want to go alone? **55**
A me coming **B** me to come **C** that I come **D** that I will come

9.4 I know I locked the door. I clearly remember .... it. **56**
A locking **B** to lock **C** to have locked

9.5 She tried to be serious, but she couldn't help **57**
A laughing **B** to laugh **C** that she laughed **D** laugh

9.6 Paul lives in Berlin now. He likes .... there. **58**
A living **B** to live

9.7 It's not my favourite job, but I like .... the kitchen as often as possible. **58**
A cleaning **B** clean **C** to clean **D** that I clean

9.8 I'm tired. I'd rather .... out this evening, if you don't mind. **59**
A not going **B** not to go **C** don't go **D** not go

9.9 I'd rather .... anyone what I said. **59**
A you don't tell **B** not you tell **C** you didn't tell **D** you wouldn't tell

9.10 Are you looking forward .... on holiday? **60, 62**
A going **B** to go **C** to going **D** that you go

9.11 When Lisa came to Britain, she had to get used .... on the left. **61**
A driving **B** to driving **C** to drive

9.12 I'm thinking .... a house. Do you think that's a good idea? **62, 66**
A to buy **B** of to buy **C** of buying **D** about buying

9.13 I had no .... a place to stay. In fact it was surprisingly easy. **63**
A difficulty to find **B** difficulty finding **C** trouble to find
D trouble finding

9.14 I phoned the restaurant .... a table. **64**
A for reserve **B** to reserve **C** for reserving **D** for to reserve

9.15 James doesn't speak very clearly. **65**
A It is difficult to understand him. **B** He is difficult to understand.
C He is difficult to understand him.

IF YOU ARE NOT SURE WHICH IS RIGHT | STUDY UNIT

9.16 The path was icy, so we walked very carefully. We were afraid 66
A of falling **B** from falling **C** to fall **D** to falling

9.17 I didn't hear you .... in. You must have been very quiet. 67
A come **B** to come **C** came

9.18 .... a hotel, we looked for somewhere to have dinner. 68
A Finding **B** After finding **C** Having found **D** We found

冠词与名词

10.1 It wasn't your fault. It was 69
A accident **B** an accident **C** some accident

10.2 Where are you going to put all your .... ? 70
A furniture **B** furnitures

10.3 'Where are you going?' 'I'm going to buy ....' 70
A a bread **B** some bread **C** a loaf of bread

10.4 Sandra is .... She works at a large hospital. 71, 72
A nurse **B** a nurse **C** the nurse

10.5 Helen works six days .... week. 72
A in **B** for **C** a **D** the

10.6 There are millions of stars in 73
A space **B** a space **C** the space

10.7 Every day .... begins at 9 and finishes at 3. 74
A school **B** a school **C** the school

10.8 .... a problem in most big cities. 75
A Crime is **B** The crime is **C** The crimes are

10.9 When .... invented? 76
A was telephone **B** were telephones **C** were the telephones
D was the telephone

10.10 Have you been to .... ? 77
A Canada or United States **B** the Canada or the United States
C Canada or the United States **D** the Canada or United States

10.11 On our first day in Moscow, we visited 78
A Kremlin **B** a Kremlin **C** the Kremlin

10.12 What time .... on TV? 79, 70
A is the news **B** are the news **C** is news **D** is the new

10.13 It took us quite a long time to get here. It was .... journey. 80
A three hour **B** a three-hours **C** a three-hour

10.14 This isn't my book. It's 81
A my sister **B** my sister's **C** from my sister **D** of my sister
E of my sister's

IF YOU ARE NOT SURE WHICH IS RIGHT

STUDY UNIT

代词与限定词

11.1 What time shall we .... tomorrow? 82
A meet **B** meet us **C** meet ourselves

11.2 I'm going to a wedding on Saturday. .... is getting married. 83
A A friend of me **B** A friend of mine **C** One my friends

11.3 They live on a busy road. .... a lot of noise from the traffic. 84
A It must be **B** It must have **C** There must have **D** There must be

11.4 He's lazy. He never does .... work. 85
A some **B** any **C** no

11.5 'What would you like to eat?' 'I don't mind. .... – whatever you have.' 85
A Something **B** Anything **C** Nothing

11.6 We couldn't buy anything because .... of the shops were open. 86
A all **B** no-one **C** none **D** nothing

11.7 We went shopping and spent .... money. 87
A a lot of **B** much **C** lots of **D** many

11.8 .... don't visit this part of the town. 88
A The most tourists **B** Most of tourists **C** Most tourists

11.9 I asked two people the way to the station, but .... of them could help me. 89
A none **B** either **C** both **D** neither

11.10 .... had a great time at the party. 90
A Everybody **B** All **C** All of us **D** Everybody of us

11.11 The bus service is excellent. There's a bus .... ten minutes. 90, 91
A each **B** every **C** all

定语从句

12.1 I don't like stories .... have unhappy endings. 92
A that **B** they **C** which **D** who

12.2 I didn't believe them at first, but in fact everything .... was true. 93
A they said **B** that they said **C** what they said

12.3 What's the name of the man .... ? 94
A you borrowed his car **B** which car you borrowed
C whose car you borrowed **D** his car you borrowed

12.4 Anna told me about her new job, ... a lot. 95
A that she's enjoying **B** which she's enjoying **C** she's enjoying
D she's enjoying it

12.5 Sarah couldn't meet us, ... was a shame. 96
A that **B** it **C** what **D** which

12.6 George showed me some pictures .... by his father. 97, 92
A painting **B** painted **C** that were painted **D** they were painted

IF YOU ARE NOT SURE WHICH IS RIGHT — STUDY UNIT

形容词与副词

13.1 Jane doesn't enjoy her job any more. She's .... because every day she does exactly the same thing. 98
A boring **B** bored

13.2 Lisa was carrying a .... bag. 99
A black small plastic **B** small and black plastic **C** small black plastic
D plastic small black

13.3 Maria's English is excellent. She speaks 100
A perfectly English **B** English perfectly **C** perfect English
D English perfect

13.4 He .... to find a job, but he had no luck. 101
A tried hard **B** tried hardly **C** hardly tried

13.5 I haven't seen her for .... , I've forgotten what she looks like. 102
A so long **B** so long time **C** a such long time **D** such a long time

13.6 We don't have .... on holiday right now. 103
A money enough to go **B** enough money to go
C money enough for going **D** enough money for go

13.7 Sarah is doing OK at the moment. She has 104
A a quite good job **B** quite a good job **C** a pretty good job

13.8 The exam was quite easy – .... I expected. 105
A more easy that **B** more easy than **C** easier than **D** easier as

13.9 The more electricity you use, ... 106
A your bill will be higher **B** will be higher your bill
C the higher your bill will be **D** higher your bill will be

13.10 Patrick is a fast runner. I can't run as fast as 107
A he **B** him **C** he can

13.11 The movie was really boring. It's .... I've ever seen. 108
A most boring movie **B** the more boring movie **C** the movie more boring
D the most boring movie

13.12 Ben likes walking. 109
A Every morning he walks to work. **B** He walks to work every morning.
C He walks every morning to work. **D** He every morning walks to work.

13.13 Joe never phones me. 110
A Always I have to phone him. **B** I always have to phone him.
C I have always to phone him. **D** I have to phone always him.

13.14 Lucy .... She left last month. 111
A still doesn't work here **B** doesn't still work here
C no more works here **D** doesn't work here any more

13.15 .... she can't drive, she bought a car. 112, 113
A Even **B** Even when **C** Even if **D** Even though

IF YOU ARE NOT SURE WHICH IS RIGHT

STUDY UNIT

虚拟语气与介词

14.1 I couldn't sleep .... very tired. 113
A although I was **B** despite I was **C** despite of being **D** in spite of being

14.2 You should insure your bike .... stolen. 114
A in case it will be **B** if it will be **C** in case it is **D** if it is

14.3 The club is for members only. You .... you're a member. 115
A can't go in if **B** can go in only if **C** can't go in unless
D can go in unless

14.4 We watched TV all evening .... we didn't have anything better to do. 116
A when **B** as **C** while **D** since

14.5 'What's that noise?' 'It sounds .... a baby crying.' 117, 118
A as **B** like **C** as if **D** as though

14.6 They are very kind to me. They treat me .... their own son. 118
A as I am **B** as if I would be **C** as if I am **D** as if I were

14.7 I'll be in Singapore next week. I hope to see some friends of mine .... there. 119
A while I'll be **B** while I'm **C** during my visit **D** during I'm

14.8 Joe is away at the moment. I don't know exactly when he's coming back, but I'm sure he'll be back .... Monday. 120
A by **B** until

介词

15.1 Bye! I'll see you 121
A at Friday morning **B** on Friday morning **C** in Friday morning
D Friday morning

15.2 I'm going away .... the end of January. 122
A at **B** on **C** in

15.3 When we were in Italy, we spent a few days .... Venice. 123, 125
A at **B** to **C** in

15.4 Our apartment is .... the second floor of the building. 124
A at **B** on **C** in **D** to

15.5 I saw Steve .... a conference on Saturday. 125
A at **B** on **C** in **D** to

15.6 When did they .... the hotel? 126
A arrive to **B** arrive at **C** arrive in **D** get to **E** get in

15.7 I'm going .... holiday next week. I'll be away for two weeks. 127
A at **B** on **C** in **D** for

15.8 We travelled .... 6.45 train, which arrived at 8.30. 128
A in the **B** on the **C** by the **D** by

15.9 'Have you read anything .... Ernest Hemingway?' 'No, what sort of books did he write?' 128
A of **B** from **C** by

IF YOU ARE NOT SURE WHICH IS RIGHT | STUDY UNIT

15.10 The accident was my fault, so I had to pay for the damage .... the other car. — 129
A of **B** for **C** to **D** on **E** at

15.11 I like them very much. They have always been very nice .... me. — 130
A of **B** for **C** to **D** with

15.12 I'm not very good .... repairing things. — 131
A at **B** for **C** in **D** about

15.13 I don't understand this sentence. Can you .... ? — 132
A explain to me this word **B** explain me this word
C explain this word to me

15.14 If you're worried about the problem, you should do something .... it. — 133
A for **B** about **C** against **D** with

15.15 'Who is Tom Hart?' 'I have no idea. I've never heard .... him.' — 134
A about **B** from **C** after **D** of

15.16 'What time will you be home?' 'I don't know. It depends .... the traffic.' — 135
A of **B** for **C** from **D** on

15.17 I prefer tea .... coffee. — 136, 59
A to **B** than **C** against **D** from

短语动词

16.1 These shoes are uncomfortable. I'm going to .... — 137
A take off **B** take them off **C** take off them

16.2 They were playing cards, so I .... — 138
A joined in **B** came in **C** got in **D** broke in

16.3 Nobody believed Paul at first, but he .... to be right. — 139
A worked out **B** came out **C** found out **D** turned out

16.4 We can't .... making a decision. We have to decide now. — 140
A put away **B** put over **C** put off **D** put out

16.5 'Have you finished painting the kitchen?' 'Nearly. I'll .... tomorrow.' — 141
A finish it out **B** finish it over **C** finish it off

16.6 You can always rely on Paul. He'll never .... — 142
A put you up **B** let you down **C** take you over **D** see you off

16.7 Children under 16 .... half the population of the city. — 143
A make up **B** put up **C** take up **D** bring up

16.8 I'm surprised to hear that Sue and Paul have .... They seemed very happy together. — 144
A broken up **B** ended up **C** finished up **D** split up

16.9 I parked in a no-parking zone, but I .... it. — 145
A came up with **B** got away with **C** made off with **D** got on with

练习答案

有些练习需要根据自己的实际情况或想法造句，答案中给出了例句。如有可能，可与学习较好的同学核对答案。

UNIT 1

1.1

2 e
3 g
4 a
5 d
6 h
7 b
8 c

1.2

1 What's / What is he studying
Is he enjoying
2 's / is your new job going
it's getting / it is getting
he isn't enjoying / he's not enjoying
he's beginning / he is beginning

1.3

3 I'm not listening / I am not listening
4 She's having / She is having
5 I'm not eating / I am not eating
6 He's learning / He is learning
7 They aren't speaking / They're not speaking / They are not speaking
8 I'm getting / I am getting
9 isn't working / 's not working / is not working
10 I'm looking / I am looking

1.4

2 is changing
3 's getting / is getting
4 is rising
5 is starting

UNIT 2

2.1

2 drink
3 opens
4 causes
5 live
6 take
7 connects

2.2

2 do the banks close
3 don't use
4 does Ricardo come
5 do you do
6 takes … does it take
7 does this word mean
8 doesn't do

2.3

3 rises
4 make
5 don't eat
6 doesn't believe
7 translates
8 don't tell
9 flows

2.4

2 Does your sister play tennis?
3 Which newspaper do you read?
4 What does your brother do?
5 How often do you go to the cinema?
6 Where do your grandparents live?

2.5

2 I promise
3 I insist
4 I apologise
5 I recommend

UNIT 3

3.1

3 错 is trying
4 错 are they talking
5 对
6 错 It's getting / It is getting
7 对
8 错 I'm coming / I am coming
9 错 are you getting
10 错 He always gets
11 对

3.2

3 Everybody's waiting / Everybody is waiting
4 Are you listening
5 Do you listen
6 flows
7 's flowing / is flowing
8 We usually grow … we aren't growing / we're not growing / we are not growing
9 it's improving / it is improving
10 She's staying / She is staying … She always stays
11 I'm starting / I am starting
12 I'm learning / I am learning … 's teaching / is teaching
13 I finish … I'm working / I am working
14 live … do your parents live
15 's looking / is looking … She's staying / She is staying
16 does your brother do … he isn't working / he's not working / he is not working
17 I usually enjoy … I'm not enjoying / I am not enjoying

3.3

2 It's always breaking down.
3 I'm always making the same mistake. / … that mistake.
4 You're always forgetting your glasses.

UNIT 4

4.1

2 I'm using / I am using
3 I need
4 does he want
5 is he looking
6 believes
7 I don't remember / I do not remember 或 I can't remember
8 I'm thinking / I am thinking
9 I think … You don't use
10 consists

4.2

2 What are you doing?
I'm thinking.
3 Who does this umbrella belong to?
4 The dinner smells good.
5 Is anybody sitting there?
6 These gloves don't fit me.

4.3

2 Do you believe
3 对 (I feel *is also correct*)
4 It tastes
5 I think

4.4

2 's being / is being
3 's / is
4 are you being
5 Is he

UNIT 5

5.1

2 She had
3 She walked to work
4 It took her (about) half an hour
5 She started work
6 She didn't have (any) lunch. / … eat (any) lunch.
7 She finished work
8 She was tired when she got home.
9 She cooked
10 She didn't go
11 She went to bed

12 She slept

5.2
2 taught
3 sold
4 fell … hurt
5 threw … caught
6 spent … bought … cost

5.3
2 did you travel / did you go
3 did it take (you)
4 did you stay
5 Was the weather
6 Did you go to / Did you see / Did you visit

5.4
3 didn't disturb
4 left
5 didn't sleep
6 flew
7 didn't cost
8 didn't have
9 were

UNIT 6

6.1
参考答案：
3 I was working.
4 I was in bed asleep.
5 I was getting ready to go out.
6 I was watching TV at home.

6.2
参考答案：
2 was having a shower
3 were driving home
4 was reading the paper
5 was watching it

6.3
1 didn't see … was looking
2 met … were going … was going … had … were waiting / waited
3 was cycling … stepped … was going … managed … didn't hit

6.4
2 were you doing
3 Did you go
4 were you driving … happened
5 took … wasn't looking
6 didn't know
7 saw … was trying
8 was walking … heard … was following … started
9 wanted
10 dropped … was doing … didn't break

UNIT 7

7.1
2 Lisa has broken her leg.
3 The bus fare has gone up.
4 Her English has improved.
5 Dan has grown a beard.
6 The letter has arrived.
7 The temperature has fallen.

7.2
2 been
3 gone
4 gone
5 been

7.3
2 Yes, I've just seen her. / Yes, I have just seen her. 或 Yes, I just saw her.
3 He's already left. / He has already left. 或 He already left.
4 I haven't read it yet. 或 I didn't read it yet.
5 No, she's already seen the film. / No, she has already seen … 或 No, she already saw …
6 Yes, they've just arrived. / Yes, they have just arrived. 或 Yes, they just arrived.
7 We haven't told him yet. 或 We didn't tell him yet.

7.4
2 he's just gone out / he has just gone out 或 he just went out
3 I haven't finished yet 或 I didn't finish yet
4 I've already done it / I have already done it 或 I already did it
5 Have you found a place to live yet? 或 Did you find a place … ?
6 I haven't decided yet 或 I didn't decide yet
7 she's just come back / she has just come back 或 she just came back

UNIT 8

8.1
2 Have you ever been to California?
3 Have you ever run (in) a marathon?
4 Have you ever spoken to a famous person?
5 What's the most beautiful place you've ever visited? / … you have ever visited?

8.2
3 haven't eaten
4 I haven't played (it)
5 I've had / I have had
6 I haven't read
7 I've never been / I haven't been
8 it's happened / it has happened 或 that's happened / that has happened
9 I've never tried / I haven't tried 或 I've never eaten / I haven't eaten
10 's been / has been
11 I've never seen / I haven't seen

8.3
参考答案：
2 I haven't travelled by bus this week.
3 I haven't been to the cinema recently.
4 I haven't read a book for ages.
5 I haven't lost anything today.

8.4
2 Have you played tennis before? No, this is the first time I've played tennis.
3 Have you ridden a horse before? / Have you been on a horse before? No, this is the first time I've ridden a horse. / … I've been on a horse.
4 Have you been to Japan before? No, this is the first time I've been to Japan.

UNIT 9

9.1
2 She's been watching television. / She has been watching television.
3 They've been playing tennis. / They have been playing tennis.
4 He's been running. / He has been running.

9.2
2 Have you been waiting long?
3 What have you been doing?
4 How long have you been working there?
5 How long have you been selling mobile phones?

9.3
2 've been waiting / have been waiting
3 've been learning Spanish / have been learning Spanish
4 She's been working there / She has been working there
5 They've been going there / They have been going there

9.4
2 I've been looking / I have been looking
3 are you looking
4 She's been teaching / She has been teaching
5 I've been thinking / I have been thinking
6 he's working / he is working
7 She's been working / She has been working

UNIT 10

10.1

2 She's been travelling / She has been travelling
She's visited / She has visited
3 He's won / He has won …
He's / He has been playing tennis
4 They've / They have been making (films …)
They've / They have made (five films …)

10.2

2 Have you been waiting long?
3 Have you caught any fish?
4 How many people have you invited?
5 How long have you been teaching?
6 How many books have you written?
How long have you been writing books?
7 How long have you been saving?
How much money have you saved?

10.3

2 Somebody's broken / Somebody has broken
3 Have you been working
4 Have you ever worked
5 has she gone
6 He's appeared / He has appeared
7 I haven't been waiting
8 it's stopped / it has stopped
9 I've lost / I have lost … Have you seen
10 I've been reading / I have been reading … I haven't finished
11 I've read / I have read
12 I've had / I have had

UNIT 11

11.1

3 错 have been married
4 对
5 错 It's been raining / It has been raining
6 错 have you been living 或 have you lived
7 错 has been working
8 对
9 错 I haven't drunk
10 错 have you had

11.2

2 How long have you been teaching English? 或
How long have you taught …
3 How long have you known Katherine?
4 How long has your brother been in Australia?
5 How long have you had that jacket?
6 How long has Joe been working at the airport? 或
How long has Joe worked …
7 How long have you been having guitar lessons?
8 Have you always lived in Chicago?

11.3

3 's been / has been
4 've been waiting / have been waiting
5 've known / have known
6 haven't played
7 's been watching / has been watching
8 haven't watched
9 've had / have had
10 hasn't been
11 've been feeling / have been feeling 或 've felt / have felt
12 's lived / has lived 或
's been living / has been living
13 haven't been
14 've always wanted / have always wanted

UNIT 12

12.1

2 since
3 for
4 for
5 since
6 for
7 since
8 since
9 for

12.2

2 How long has Kate been learning Japanese?
When did Kate start learning Japanese?
3 How long have you known Simon?
When did you first meet Simon? / When did you and Simon first meet?
4 How long have Rebecca and David been married?
When did Rebecca and David get married? / When did Rebecca and David marry?

12.3

3 He has been ill since Sunday.
4 He has been ill for a few days.
5 She got married a year ago.
6 I've had a headache since I woke up.
7 She went to Italy three weeks ago.
8 I've been working in a hotel for six months. 或 I've worked in a hotel for six months.

12.4

2 No, I haven't seen Laura/her for about a month.
3 No, I haven't been to the cinema for a long time.
4 No, I haven't eaten in a restaurant for ages. / No, I haven't been to a restaurant for ages.
6 No, it's about a month since I (last) saw Laura/her. / No, it's been about a month since …
7 No, it's a long time since I (last) went to the cinema. / No, it's been a long time since …
8 No, it's ages since I (last) ate in a restaurant. / No, it's been ages since … 或 … since I went to a restaurant.

UNIT 13

13.1

2 has gone
3 forgot
4 went
5 had
6 has broken

13.2

3 错 did William Shakespeare write
4 对
5 对
6 错 Who invented
7 错 were you born
8 对
9 错 Albert Einstein was … who developed

13.3

3 I've forgotten / I have forgotten
4 arrested
5 it's improved / it has improved
6 I've finished / I have finished (I'**m** finished *is also correct*)
7 I applied
8 It was
9 There's been / There has been
10 He broke 或 He's broken / He has broken … did that happen … He fell

UNIT 14

14.1

3 对
4 错 I bought
5 错 Where were you
6 错 Lucy left school
7 对
8 对
9 对
10 错 When was this book published?

14.2

2 The weather has been cold recently.

3 It was cold last week.
4 I didn't read a newspaper yesterday.
5 I haven't read a newspaper today.
6 Emily has earned a lot of money this year.
7 She didn't earn so much last year.
8 Have you had a holiday recently?

14.3

3 Have you seen … I saw
4 I didn't sleep
5 There were
6 worked … he gave
7 She's lived / She has lived
8 Did you go … it was … was
9 died … I never met
10 I've never met / I have never met
11 I haven't seen
12 have you lived 或 have you been living … did you live … did you live

14.4

参考答案：
2 I haven't bought anything today.
3 I didn't watch TV yesterday.
4 I went out with some friends yesterday evening.
5 I haven't been to the cinema recently.
6 I've read a lot of books recently.

UNIT 15

15.1

2 It had changed a lot.
3 She'd arranged to do something else. / She had arranged …
4 The film had already started.
5 I hadn't seen him for five years.
6 She'd just had breakfast. / She had just had …

15.2

2 I'd never heard it before. / I had never heard …
3 He'd never played (tennis) before. / He had never played …
4 We'd never been there before. / We had never been …

15.3

1 we called
2 there was …
She'd gone / She had gone
3 He'd just come back from / He had just come back from …
He looked
4 got a phone call
He was
He'd sent her / He had sent her …
she'd never replied to them / she had never replied to them

15.4

2 went
3 had gone
4 broke
5 saw … had broken … stopped

UNIT 16

16.1

2 They'd been playing football. / They had been playing …
3 I'd been looking forward to it. / I had been looking forward …
4 She'd been dreaming. / She had been dreaming.
5 He'd been watching a film. / He had been watching …

16.2

2 I'd been waiting for 20 minutes when I realised that I was in the wrong restaurant. 或 … that I had come to the wrong restaurant.
3 At the time the factory closed down, Sarah had been working there for five years.
4 The orchestra had been playing for about ten minutes when a man in the audience started shouting.
5 参考答案：
I'd been walking along the road for about ten minutes when a car suddenly stopped just behind me.

16.3

3 he was walking
4 She'd been running / She had been running
5 They were eating
6 They'd been eating / They had been eating
7 He was looking
8 was waiting … she'd been waiting / she had been waiting
9 I'd had / I had had
10 We'd been travelling / We had been travelling

UNIT 17

17.1

3 I don't have a ladder. / I haven't got a ladder.
4 We didn't have enough time.
5 He didn't have a map.
6 She doesn't have any money. / She hasn't got any money.
7 I don't have enough energy. / I haven't got enough energy.
8 They didn't have a camera.

17.2

2 B
3 A 或 C
4 A 或 C
5 A
6 C

17.3

3 错 he didn't have
4 错 I have 或 I've got
5 对
6 错 I didn't have
7 对 (或 He hasn't got)
8 错 Did you have
9 对

17.4

2 has a break
3 had a party
4 have a look
5 's having / is having a nice time
6 had a chat
7 Did you have trouble
8 had a baby
9 was having a shower
10 Did you have a good flight?

UNIT 18

18.1

2 used to have/ride
3 used to live
4 used to eat/like/love
5 used to be
6 used to take
7 used to be
8 did you use to go

18.2

2–10
- She used to have lots of friends, but she doesn't know many people these days.
- She used to be very lazy, but she works very hard these days.
- She didn't use to like cheese, but she eats lots of cheese now.
- She used to be a hotel receptionist, but she works in a bookshop now.
- She used to play the piano, but she hasn't played the piano for years. / … played it for years.
- She never used to read / She didn't use to read newspapers, but she reads a newspaper every day now.
- She didn't use to drink tea, but she likes it now.
- She used to have a dog, but it died two years ago.
- She used to go to a lot of parties, but she hasn't been to a party for ages.

18.3

参考答案：
3 I used to be a vegetarian, but now I eat meat sometimes.

4 I used to watch TV a lot, but I don't watch it much now.
5 I used to hate getting up early, but now it's no problem.
7 I didn't use to drink coffee, but I drink it every day now.
8 I didn't use to like hot weather, but now I love it.

UNIT 19

19.1
2 How long are you going for?
3 When are you leaving?
4 Are you going alone?
5 Are you travelling by car?
6 Where are you staying?

19.2
2 I'm working late. / I'm working till 9 o'clock.
3 I'm going to the theatre.
4 I'm meeting Julia.

19.3
参考答案：
2 I'm working tomorrow morning.
3 I'm not doing anything tomorrow evening.
4 I'm playing football next Sunday.
5 I'm going to a party this evening.

19.4
3 We're having / We are having
4 finishes
5 I'm not going / I am not going … I'm staying / I am staying
6 Are you doing
7 We're going / We are going … It starts
8 I'm leaving / I am leaving
9 we're meeting / we are meeting
10 does this train get
11 I'm going / I am going … Are you coming
12 does it end
13 I'm not using / I am not using
14 's coming / is coming … She's travelling / She is travelling … arrives

UNIT 20

20.1
2 What are you going to wear?
3 Where are you going to put it?
4 Who are you going to invite?

20.2
2 I'm going to take it back to the shop.
3 I'm not going to accept it.
4 I'm going to phone her tonight.
5 I'm going to complain.

20.3
2 He's going to be late.
3 The boat is going to sink.
4 They're going to run out of petrol.

20.4
2 was going to buy
3 were going to play
4 was going to phone
5 was going to give up
6 were you going to say

UNIT 21

21.1
2 I'll turn / I'll switch / I'll put
3 I'll send
4 I'll do
5 I'll show
6 I'll have
7 I'll stay / I'll wait
8 I'll pay / I'll give
9 I'll try

21.2
2 I'll go to bed.
3 I think I'll walk.
4 I'll eat anything.
5 I don't think I'll go swimming.

21.3
3 I'll meet
4 I'll lend
5 I'm having
6 I won't forget
7 does your train leave
8 won't tell
9 Are you doing
10 Will you come

21.4
2 Shall I buy it?
3 What shall I give/buy/get Helen (for her birthday)?
4 Where shall we go (on holiday)?
5 Shall we go by car or (shall we) walk? / … or (shall we go) on foot?
6 What time shall I come?

UNIT 22

22.1
2 I'm going
3 will get
4 is coming
5 we're going
6 It won't hurt

22.2
2 won't
3 'll / will
4 won't
5 'll / will
6 won't

22.3
2 It will look
3 you'll like / you will like
4 You'll get / You will get
5 people will live
6 we'll meet / we will meet
7 she'll come / she will come
8 it will be

22.4
2 Do you think it will rain?
3 When do you think it will end?
4 How much do you think it will cost?
5 Do you think they'll get married? / … they will get married?
6 What time do you think you'll be back? / … you will be back?
7 What do you think will happen?

22.5
参考答案：
2 I'll be in bed.
3 I'll be at work.
4 I'll probably be at home.
5 I don't know where I'll be this time next year.

UNIT 23

23.1
2 I'll lend
3 I'll get
4 I'm going to wash
5 are you going to paint
6 I'm going to buy
7 I'll show
8 I'll have
9 I'll call
10 He's going to have … he's going to do

23.2
2 I'm going to take … I'll join
3 you'll find ('you're going to find' *is possible*)
4 I'm not going to apply 或 I'm not applying
5 We're going to be late.
6 it's going to fall down
7 I'll take … I'll pick … Kate is going to take 或 Kate is taking

UNIT 24

24.1
2 b 对
3 a 和 c 对
4 b 和 d 对
5 c 和 d 对
6 c 对

24.2
2 We'll have finished
3 we'll be playing
4 I'll be working
5 the meeting will have ended
6 he'll have spent
7 you'll still be doing
8 she'll have travelled
9 I'll be staying
10 Will you be seeing

UNIT 25

25.1
2 she goes
3 you know
4 Will you be … I get
5 there are … I'll call / I will call
6 it's / it is
7 you see … you won't recognise / you will not recognise
8 I'll be / I will be … he gets
9 you need … I'm / I am
10 I'll wait / I will wait … you're / you are

25.2
2 I'll give you my address when I find somewhere to live. 或 … when I've found somewhere to live.
3 I'll come straight back home after I do the shopping. 或 … after I've done the shopping.
4 Let's go home before it gets dark.
5 I won't speak to her until she apologises. 或 … until she has apologised.

25.3
2 you go / you leave
3 you decide 或 you've decided / you have decided
4 you're in Hong Kong / you go to Hong Kong
5 build the new road 或 've built the new road / have built the new road

25.4
2 if
3 When
4 If
5 If
6 when
7 if
8 if

UNIT 26

26.1
3 can
4 be able to
5 been able to
6 can 或 will be able to
7 be able to

26.2
参考答案：
2 I used to be able to run fast.
3 I'd like to be able to play the piano.
4 I've never been able to get up early.

26.3
2 could run
3 can wait
4 couldn't eat
5 can't hear
6 couldn't sleep

26.4
2 was able to finish it
3 were able to find it
4 was able to get away

26.5
4 couldn't
5 managed to
6 could
7 managed to
8 could
9 managed to
10 couldn't

UNIT 27

27.1
2 We could have fish.
3 You could phone (her) now.
4 You could give her a book.
5 We could hang it in the kitchen.

27.2
3 I could kill him!
4 对 (could have *is also possible*)
5 I could stay here all day
6 it could be in the car (may/might *are also possible*)
7 对
8 对 (could borrow *is also possible*)
9 You could fall. (may/might *are also possible*)

27.3
2 could have come/gone
3 could apply
4 could have been
5 could have got/taken
6 could come

27.4
3 couldn't wear
4 couldn't have found
5 couldn't get
6 couldn't have been
7 couldn't have come/gone

UNIT 28

28.1
2 must
3 can't
4 must
5 must
6 can't
7 must
8 must
9 can't

28.2
3 go
4 have taken / have stolen / have moved
5 be
6 have been
7 be looking
8 have been
9 have heard
10 be following

28.3
3 It must have been very expensive.
4 They must have gone away.
5 I must have left it in the restaurant last night.
6 It can't have been easy for her. 或 It couldn't have been easy for her.
7 He must have been waiting for somebody.
8 She can't have understood what I said. 或 She couldn't have understood what I said.
9 I must have forgotten to lock it.
10 My neighbours must have been having a party.
11 The driver can't have seen the red light. 或 The driver couldn't have seen …

UNIT 29

29.1
2 She might be busy.
3 She might be working.
4 She might want to be alone.
5 She might have been ill yesterday.
6 She might have gone home early.
7 She might have had to go home early.
8 She might have been working yesterday.
9 She might not want to see me.
10 She might not be working today.
11 She might not have been feeling well yesterday.

You can use **may** *instead of* **might** *in all these sentences.*

29.2
2 be
3 have been
4 be waiting
5 have arrived / have come / be here

29.3
2 a She might be watching TV.
b She might have gone out.
3 a It might be in the car.
b You might have left it in the restaurant.

4 a He might have gone to bed early.
b He might not have heard the doorbell.
c He might have been in the shower.
You can use **may** *instead of* **might** *in all these sentences.*

29.4
3 might not have received it / might not have got it
4 couldn't have been an accident
5 couldn't have tried
6 might not have been American

UNIT 30

30.1
2 I might buy a Honda.
3 He might come on Saturday.
4 I might hang it in the dining room.
5 She might go to university.
You can use **may** *instead of* **might** *in all these sentences.*

30.2
2 might wake
3 might bite
4 might need
5 might slip
6 might break
You can use **may** *instead of* **might** *in all these sentences.*

30.3
2 might be able to meet
3 might have to work
4 might have to leave
5 might have to sell
6 might be able to fix
You can use **may** *instead of* **might** *in all these sentences.*

30.4
2 I might not go out this evening.
3 We might not be able to get tickets for the game.
4 Sam might not be able to go out with us tonight.
You can use **may** *instead of* **might** *in all these sentences.*

30.5
2 I might as well go
3 We might as well paint the bathroom.
4 We might as well watch it. / … watch the film.
You can use **may** *instead of* **might** *in all these sentences.*

UNIT 31

31.1
3 We had to close
4 She has to leave 或 She'll have to leave / She will have to leave
5 do you have to be
6 I have to go 或 I'll have to go / I will have to go
7 Does he have to travel
8 do you have to go 或 will you have to go
9 did you have to wait
10 had to do

31.2
3 have to make
4 don't have to do
5 had to ask
6 don't have to pay 或 won't have to pay / will not have to pay
7 didn't have to go
8 has to make
9 will have to drive 或 is going to have to drive

31.3
3 对 (have to *is also correct*)
4 He **has to** work.
5 I **had to** work late yesterday evening.
6 对 (have to *is also correct*)
7 She **has had to** wear glasses since she was very young.
For the present perfect (**has had**) *with* **for** *and* **since**, *see Units* ***11–12***.

31.4
3 don't have to
4 mustn't
5 don't have to
6 mustn't
7 doesn't have to
8 mustn't
9 mustn't
10 don't have to

UNIT 32

32.1
2 don't need to
3 must
4 mustn't
5 don't need to
6 needn't
7 must … mustn't
8 needn't … must

32.2
2 needn't come
3 needn't walk
4 needn't ask
5 needn't explain

32.3
2 You needn't have walked home. You could have taken a taxi.
3 You needn't have stayed at a hotel. You could have stayed with us.
4 She needn't have phoned me in the middle of the night. She could have waited until the morning.
5 You needn't have shouted at me. You could have been more patient.
6 You needn't have left without saying anything. You could have said goodbye to me.

32.4
3 You needn't worry / You don't need to worry / You don't have to worry
4 You needn't wait / You don't need to wait / You don't have to wait
5 对 (You needn't keep *is also correct*)
6 I didn't need to go / I didn't have to go
7 对

UNIT 33

33.1
2 You should look for another job.
3 He shouldn't go to bed so late.
4 You should take a photo.
5 She shouldn't use her car so much.
6 He should put some pictures on the walls.

33.2
2 I don't think you should go out. / I think you should stay at home.
3 I think you should apply for it. / … for the job.
4 I don't think the government should increase taxes.

33.3
3 should come
4 should do
5 should have done
6 should have won
7 should win
8 should be
9 should have turned

33.4
3 We should have reserved a table.
4 The shop should be open (now). / The shop should have opened by now. 或 It should …
5 She shouldn't be doing 50. / She shouldn't be driving so fast. / She should be driving more slowly.
6 I should have written down her address. / I should have written her address down. 或 I should have written it down.
7 The driver in front shouldn't have stopped without warning. / … shouldn't have stopped so suddenly.
8 I should have been looking where I was going. / I shouldn't have been

looking behind me.

UNIT 34

34.1

2 I should stay / I stay / I stayed a little longer
3 they should visit / they visit / they visited the museum after lunch
4 we should pay / we pay / we paid the rent by Friday
5 I should go / I go / I went away for a few days

34.2

1 b 正确
c 正确
d 错误
2 a 正确
b 错误
c 正确

34.3

2 should say
3 should worry
4 should leave
5 should ask
6 should listen

34.4

2 If it should rain
3 If there should be any problems
4 If anyone should ask
5 Should there be any problems
6 Should anyone ask (where I'm going)

34.5

2 I should keep
3 I should phone
4 I should get

UNIT 35

35.1

2 You'd better put a plaster on it.
3 We'd better reserve a table.
4 You'd better not go to work (this morning).
5 I'd better pay my phone bill (soon). / I'd better pay it (soon).
6 I'd better not disturb him.

35.2

3 'd better
4 should
5 should
6 'd better
7 should
8 should

35.3

1 b 'd/had
c close/shut
d hadn't
2 a did
b was done
c thought

35.4

2 It's time I had a holiday.
3 It's time the train left.
4 It's time I/we had a party.
5 It's time some changes were made. / It's time the company made some changes.
6 It's time he tried something else.

UNIT 36

36.1

参考答案：
2 I wouldn't like to be a teacher.
3 I'd love to learn to fly a plane.
4 It would be nice to have a big garden.
5 I'd like to go to Mexico.

36.2

2 'd enjoy / would enjoy
3 'd have enjoyed / would have enjoyed
4 would you do
5 'd have stopped / would have stopped
6 would have been
7 'd be / would be
8 'd have passed / would have passed
9 would have

36.3

2 e
3 b
4 f
5 a
6 d

36.4

2 He promised he'd call. / … he would call.
3 You promised you wouldn't tell her.
4 They promised they'd wait (for us). / … they would wait.

36.5

2 wouldn't tell
3 wouldn't speak
4 wouldn't let

36.6

2 would shake
3 would always help
4 would share
5 would always forget

UNIT 37

37.1

2 Can/Could I leave a message (for her)? 或 Can/Could you give her a message?
3 Can/Could you tell me how to get to the station? 或 … the way to the station? 或 … where the station is?
4 Can/Could I try on these trousers? 或 Can/Could I try these (trousers) on?
5 Can I give/offer you a lift?

37.2

3 Do you think you could check these forms (for me)? / … check them (for me)?
4 Do you mind if I leave work early?
5 Do you think you could turn the music down? / … turn it down?
6 Is it OK if I close the window?
7 Do you think I could have a look at your paper? / … at your newspaper?

37.3

2 Can/Could/Would you show me? 或 Do you think you could show me? 或 … do it for me?
3 Would you like to sit down? 或 Would you like a seat? 或 Can I offer you a seat?
4 Can/Could/Would you slow down? 或 Do you think you could … ?
5 Can/Could/May I/we have the bill, please? 或 Do you think I/we could have … ?
6 Would you like to borrow it?

UNIT 38

38.1

2 b
3 a
4 b
5 b
6 a
7 b

38.2

2 bought
3 asked
4 would lose
5 'd be / would be
6 were … stopped
7 gave … 'd have / would have

38.3

2 If he did his driving test now, he'd fail (it) / … he would fail (it).
3 If we stayed at a hotel, it would cost too much.
4 If she left her job, she wouldn't get another one.
5 If we invited Ben (to the party), we'd have to invite his friends too. / … we would have to …
6 If I told him what happened, he wouldn't believe me.

38.4

参考答案：

2 I'd be very angry if somebody broke into my house.
3 If you bought a car, it would cost you a lot to maintain it.
4 I'd be surprised if the economic situation improved.
5 Would you mind if I didn't go out with you tonight?

UNIT 39

39.1

3 I'd help / I would help
4 we lived
5 we'd live / we would live
6 It would taste
7 were/was
8 I wouldn't wait … I'd go / I would go
9 you didn't go
10 there weren't … there wouldn't be

39.2

2 I'd buy it / I would buy it if it weren't/wasn't so expensive.
3 We'd go out / We would go out more often if we could afford it.
4 If I didn't have to work late, I could meet you tomorrow. 或 … I'd meet / I would meet … 或 … I'd be able to meet …
5 We could have lunch outside if it weren't raining / wasn't raining.
6 If I wanted his advice, I'd ask for it / I would ask for it.

39.3

2 I wish I had a computer.
3 I wish Helen were/was here.
4 I wish it weren't/wasn't (so) cold.
5 I wish I didn't live in a big city.
6 I wish I could go to the party.
7 I wish I didn't have to get up early tomorrow.
8 I wish I knew something about cars.
9 I wish I were feeling / was feeling better.

39.4

参考答案：

1 I wish I was at home.
2 I wish I had a big garden.
3 I wish I could tell jokes.
4 I wish I was taller.

UNIT 40

40.1

2 If he'd missed / he had missed (the train), he'd have missed / he would have missed (his flight too).
3 I'd have forgotten / I would have forgotten (if) you hadn't reminded
4 I'd had / I had had (your address), I'd have sent / I would have sent (you an email)
5 we'd have enjoyed / we would have enjoyed (it more if the weather) had been (better)
6 It would have been (quicker if) I'd walked / I had walked
7 I were / I was
8 I'd been / I had been

40.2

2 If the road hadn't been icy, the accident wouldn't have happened.
3 If I'd known / If I had known that Joe had to get up early, I'd have woken / I would have woken him up.
4 If I hadn't lost my phone (或 If I'd had my phone), I'd have called you / I would have called you / I would have been able to call you / I could have called you.
5 If Karen hadn't been wearing a seat belt, she'd have been injured / she would have been injured (in the crash). 或 … she might/could have been injured
6 If you'd had / If you had had breakfast, you wouldn't be hungry now.
7 If I'd had / If I had had enough money, I'd have got / I would have got a taxi.

40.3

2 I wish I'd applied / I wish I had applied for it. 或 … for the job.
3 I wish I'd learned / I wish I had learned to play a musical instrument (when I was younger). 或 I wish I could play … / I wish I was able to play …
4 I wish I hadn't painted it red. 或 … the gate red.
5 I wish I'd brought / I wish I had brought my camera. 或 I wish I had my camera (with me).
6 I wish they'd phoned / I wish they had phoned me first (to say they were coming). 或 I wish I'd known / I wish I had known they were coming.

UNIT 41

41.1

2 hope
3 wish
4 wished
5 hope
6 wish … hope

41.2

2 I wish Jane/she would come. 或 … would hurry up.
3 I wish somebody would give me a job.
4 I wish the/that baby would stop crying.
5 I wish you would buy some new clothes. 或 I wish you would get some new clothes.
6 I wish you wouldn't drive so fast.
7 I wish you wouldn't leave the door open (all the time).
8 I wish people wouldn't drop litter in the street.

41.3

2 对
3 I wish I had more free time.
4 I wish our flat was/were a bit bigger.
5 对
6 对
7 I wish everything wasn't/weren't so expensive.

41.4

3 I knew
4 I'd taken / I had taken
5 I could come
6 I wasn't / I weren't
7 they'd hurry up / they would hurry up
8 we didn't have
9 we could have stayed
10 it wasn't / it weren't
11 he'd decide / he would decide
12 we hadn't gone

UNIT 42

42.1

2 is made
3 was damaged
4 were invited
5 are shown
6 are held
7 was written … was translated
8 were overtaken
9 is surrounded

42.2

2 When was television invented?
3 How are mountains formed?
4 When were antibiotics discovered?
5 What is silver used for?

42.3

3 covers
4 is covered
5 are locked
6 was sent … arrived
7 sank … was rescued
8 died … were brought up

9 grew up
10 was stolen
11 disappeared
12 did Sue resign
13 was Ben fired
14 is owned
15 called … was injured … wasn't needed
16 were these pictures taken … Did you take
17 'm not bothered / am not bothered

42.4

2 All flights were cancelled because of fog.
3 This road isn't used much.
4 I was accused of stealing money.
5 How are languages learned/learnt?
6 We were warned not to go out alone.

UNIT 43

43.1

2 it can't be broken
3 it can be eaten
4 it can't be used
5 it can't be seen
6 it can be carried

43.2

3 be made
4 be spent
5 have been repaired
6 be carried
7 be woken up
8 have been arrested
9 have been caused

43.3

2 The computer is being used at the moment.
3 I didn't realise that our conversation was being recorded.
4 … we found that the game had been cancelled.
5 A new ring road is being built round the city.
6 A new hospital has been built near the airport.

43.4

3 It's been stolen! / It has been stolen!
4 Somebody has taken it. 或 … taken my umbrella.
5 He's been promoted. / He has been promoted.
6 It's being redecorated. / It is being redecorated.
7 It's working again. / It is working again.
It's been repaired. / It has been repaired.

8 The furniture had been moved.
9 He hasn't been seen since then.
10 I haven't seen her for ages.
11 Have you ever been mugged?

UNIT 44

44.1

2 I was asked some difficult questions at the interview.
3 Amy was given a present by her colleagues when she retired.
4 I wasn't told about the meeting.
5 How much will you be paid for your work?
6 I think Tom should have been offered the job.
7 Have you been shown what to do?

44.2

2 being invited
3 being given
4 being knocked down
5 being treated
6 being stuck

44.3

2–6
- Ludwig van Beethoven was born in 1770.
- Galileo was born in 1564.
- Mahatma Gandhi was born in 1869.
- Michael Jackson was born in 1958.
- Martin Luther King was born in 1929.
- Elvis Presley was born in 1935.
- William Shakespeare was born in 1564.
- Leonardo da Vinci was born in 1452.

7 I was born in …

44.4

2 got stung
3 get used
4 got stolen
5 get paid
6 got stopped
7 get damaged
8 get asked

UNIT 45

45.1

2 The weather is expected to be good tomorrow.
3 The thieves are believed to have got in through a window in the roof.
4 Many people are reported to be homeless after the floods.
5 The prisoner is thought to have escaped by climbing over a wall.
6 The man is alleged to have been driving at 110 miles an hour.
7 The building is reported to have been badly damaged by the fire.
8 a The company is said to be losing a lot of money.
b The company is believed to have lost a lot of money last year.
c The company is expected to make a loss this year.

45.2

2 He is supposed to know a lot of famous people.
3 He is supposed to be very rich.
4 He is supposed to have twelve children.
5 He is supposed to have been an actor when he was younger.

45.3

2 You're / You are supposed to be my friend.
3 I'm / I am supposed to be on a diet.
4 It was supposed to be a joke.
5 Or maybe it's / it is supposed to be a flower.
6 You're / You are supposed to be working.

45.4

2 're / are supposed to start
3 was supposed to phone
4 aren't / 're not / are not supposed to block
5 was supposed to depart

UNIT 46

46.1

1 b
2 a
3 a
4 b

46.2

2 Sarah has her car serviced once a year.
3 It cost twelve pounds to have my suit cleaned.
4 The last time I had my eyes tested was two years ago.
5 We've had some new cupboards fitted in the kitchen.
6 We need to get this document translated as soon as possible.

46.3

2 I had it cut.
3 We had them cleaned.
4 He had it built.
5 I had them delivered.

46.4
2 have another key made
3 you had your hair cut
4 Do you have a newspaper delivered
5 we're having / we are having a garage built
6 Have you had the washing machine fixed / Did you have the washing machine fixed
7 have your ears pierced
9 She had her credit cards stolen.
10 We all had our bags searched.

UNIT 47

47.1
2 He said (that) his father wasn't very well.
3 He said (that) Rachel and Mark were getting married next month.
4 He said (that) his sister had had a baby.
5 He said (that) he didn't know what Joe was doing.
6 He said (that) he'd seen / he had seen Helen at a party in June and she'd seemed / she had seemed fine. 或 He said (that) he saw Helen … and she seemed …
7 He said (that) he hadn't seen Amy recently.
8 He said (that) he wasn't enjoying his job very much.
9 He said (that) I could come and stay at his place if I was ever in London.
10 He said (that) his car had been stolen a few days ago.
或 … his car was stolen a few days ago.
11 He said (that) he wanted to go on holiday, but (he) couldn't afford it.
12 He said (that) he'd tell / he would tell Chris he'd seen / he had seen me. 或 … he saw me.

47.2
参考答案：
2 she wasn't coming / she was going somewhere else / she couldn't come
3 they didn't like each other / they didn't get on with each other / they couldn't stand each other
4 he didn't know anyone
5 she would be away / she was going away
6 you were staying at home
7 he couldn't speak / he didn't speak any other languages
8 he'd seen you / he saw you last weekend

UNIT 48

48.1
2 But you said you didn't like fish.
3 But you said you couldn't drive.
4 But you said she had a very well-paid job.
5 But you said you didn't have any brothers or sisters.
6 But you said you'd / you had never been to the United States.
7 But you said you were working tomorrow evening.
8 But you said she was a friend of yours.

48.2

2 Tell	7 tell … said
3 Say	8 tell … say
4 said	9 told
5 told	10 said
6 said	

48.3
2 her to slow down
3 her not to worry
4 asked Tom to give me a hand
或 … to help me
5 asked me to open my bag
6 asked him to get (me) a paper
7 told him to mind his own business
8 asked her to marry him
9 told her not to wait (for me) if I was late

UNIT 49

49.1
2 Were you born there?
3 Are you married?
4 How long have you been married?
5 Have you got (any) children?
或 Do you have (any) children?
6 How old are they?
7 What do you do?
8 What does your wife do?

49.2
3 Who paid it? / Who paid the bill?
4 What happened?
5 What did she/Diane say?
6 Who does it / this book belong to?
7 Who lives in that house? / Who lives there?
8 What did you fall over?
9 What fell off the shelf?
10 What does it / this word mean?
11 Who did you borrow it from? / … borrow the money from?
12 What are you worried about?

49.3
2 How is cheese made?
3 When was the computer invented?
4 Why isn't Sue working today?
5 What time are your friends coming?
6 Why was the trip cancelled?
7 Where was your mother born?
8 Why didn't you come to the party?
9 How did the accident happen?
10 Why doesn't this machine work?

49.4
2 Don't you like him?
3 Isn't it good?
4 Haven't you got any? 或 Don't you have any?

UNIT 50

50.1

2 c	6 c
3 a	7 b
4 b	8 a
5 b	

50.2
2 How far is it to the airport?
3 I wonder how old Tom is.
4 When is Lisa going on holiday?
5 Could you tell me where the post office is?
6 I don't know whether anyone was injured in the accident.
7 Do you know what time you will arrive tomorrow?

50.3
2 He asked me where I'd been. / … where I had been.
3 He asked me how long I'd been back. / … how long I had been back.
4 He asked me what I was doing now.
5 He asked me why I'd come back. / … why I had come back. 或 … why I came back.
6 He asked me where I was living.
7 He asked me if/whether I was glad to be back.
8 He asked me if/whether I had any plans to go away again.
9 He asked me if/whether I could help him find a job.

UNIT 51

51.1
2 doesn't
3 was
4 will
5 am … isn't 或 'm not … is 或 can … can't 或 can't … can 或 am … can't 或 can't … is
6 should
7 won't
8 do
9 didn't
10 would … could … can't

51.2
3 Do you? I don't.
4 Didn't you? I did.
5 Haven't you? I have.
6 Did you? I didn't.

51.3
参考答案：
3 So did I. 或
Did you? What did you watch?
4 Neither will I. 或
Won't you? Where will you be?
5 So do I. 或
Do you? What sort of books do you like?
6 So would I. 或
Would you? Where would you like to live?
7 Neither can I. 或
Can't you? Why not?

51.4
2 I hope so.
3 I expect so.
4 I don't think so.
5 I'm afraid not.
6 I'm afraid so.
7 I suppose so.
8 I hope not.
9 I think so.

UNIT 52

52.1
3 don't you
4 were you
5 does she
6 isn't he
7 hasn't she
8 can't you
9 will they
10 aren't there
11 shall we
12 is it
13 aren't I
14 would you
15 hasn't she
16 should I
17 had he
18 will you

52.2
2 It's (very) expensive, isn't it?
3 The course was great, wasn't it?
4 You've had your hair cut, haven't you? 或
You had your hair cut, didn't you?
5 She has a good voice, hasn't she?
或
She's got / She has got a good voice, hasn't she? 或 She has a good voice, doesn't she?
6 It doesn't look very good, does it?
7 This bridge isn't very safe, is it? 或
… doesn't look very safe, does it?

52.3
2 Joe, you couldn't give me a hand (with this table), could you?
3 Kate, you don't know where Sarah is, do you? 或 … you haven't seen Sarah, have you?
4 Helen, you haven't got a bicycle pump, have you? 或 … you don't have a bicycle pump, do you?
5 Ann, you couldn't take me to the station, could you? 或
… you couldn't give me a lift to the station, could you?
6 Robert, you haven't seen my keys, have you?

UNIT 53

53.1
2 playing tennis
3 driving too fast
4 going swimming
5 breaking the DVD player
6 waiting a few minutes

53.2
2 making
3 listening
4 applying
5 reading
6 living
7 using
8 forgetting
9 paying
10 being
11 trying
12 losing

53.3
2 travelling
3 painting the kitchen
4 turning the music down
5 not interrupting

53.4
参考答案：
2 going out
3 sitting on the floor
4 having a picnic
5 laughing
6 breaking down

UNIT 54

54.1
2 to help him
3 to carry her bag (for her)
4 to meet at 8 o'clock
5 to tell him her name / to give him her name
6 not to tell anyone

54.2
2 to get
3 to live
4 (how) to use
5 to tell
6 say 或 to say

54.3
2 to look
3 walking
4 waiting
5 to finish
6 barking
7 to call
8 having
9 missing
10 to be

54.4
2 Tom appears to be worried about something.
3 You seem to know a lot of people.
4 My English seems to be getting better.
5 That car appears to have broken down.
6 David tends to forget things.
7 They claim to have solved the problem.

54.5
2 what to do
3 how to ride
4 whether to go
5 where to put
6 how to use

UNIT 55

55.1
2 or do you want me to lend you some
3 or would you like me to shut it
4 or would you like me to show you
5 or do you want me to repeat it
6 or do you want me to wait

55.2
2 to stay with them
3 to call Joe.
4 him to be careful
5 her to give him a hand

55.3
2 I didn't expect it to rain.
3 Let him do what he wants.
4 Tim's glasses make him look older.
5 I want you to know the truth.
6 Sarah persuaded me to apply for the job.
7 My lawyer advised me not to say anything to the police.
8 I was warned not to believe everything he says.
9 Having a car enables you to get

around more easily.

55.4

2 to go
3 to do
4 cry
5 to study
6 booking 或 you to book
7 borrow
8 to work
9 think

UNIT 56

56.1

2 driving
3 to go
4 raining
5 to win
6 asking
7 asking
8 to answer
9 causing
10 to do
11 being
12 to climb
13 to tell
14 talking… to see

56.2

2 He remembers going to Paris with his parents when he was eight.
3 He doesn't remember crying on his first day at school.
4 He can remember falling into the river.
5 He can't remember saying he wanted to be a doctor. 或
He can't remember wanting to be a doctor.
6 He doesn't remember being bitten by a dog.

56.3

1 b lending
c to phone / to call
d to say
e leaving/putting
2 a saying
b to say
c wearing / having / taking / putting on
3 a to become
b working
c reading / looking at
4 a losing 或 to lose
b to get / to feel
c crying 或 to cry

UNIT 57

57.1

2 Try turning it the other way.
3 Have you tried restarting it?
4 You could try phoning his office.
5 Have you tried taking an aspirin?

57.2

2 It needs painting.
3 It needs cutting.
4 They need tightening.
5 It needs emptying.

57.3

1 b knocking
c to put
d asking
e to reach
f to concentrate
2 a to go
b looking
c cleaning
d cutting
e to iron …
ironing
3 a overhearing
b get 或 to get
c smiling
d make 或 to make

UNIT 58

58.1

参考答案：
2 I don't mind playing cards.
3 I don't like being alone. 或
… to be alone.
4 I enjoy going to museums.
5 I love cooking. 或 I love to cook.

58.2

2 She likes teaching biology.
3 He likes taking pictures.
或 He likes to take pictures.
4 I didn't like working there.
5 She likes studying medicine.
6 He doesn't like being famous.
7 She doesn't like taking risks.
或 She doesn't like to take risks.
8 I like to know things in advance.

58.3

2 to sit
3 waiting
4 going 或 to go
5 to get
6 being
7 to come / to go
8 living
9 to talk
10 to have / to know / to get / to hear / to be told

58.4

2 I would like / I'd like to have seen the programme.
3 I would hate / I'd hate to have lost my watch.
4 I would love / I'd love to have met your parents.
5 I wouldn't like to have been alone.
6 I would prefer / I'd prefer to have travelled by train.

UNIT 59

59.1

参考答案：
2 I prefer basketball to football.
3 I prefer going to the cinema to watching DVDs at home.
4 I prefer being very busy to having nothing to do.
6 I prefer to go to the cinema rather than watch DVDs at home.
7 I prefer to be very busy rather than have nothing to do.

59.2

3 prefer
4 eat/stay
5 I'd rather (wait) / I'd prefer to (wait)
6 to go
7 rather (think) /
prefer to (think)
8 I'd prefer
9 go
11 I'd prefer to go for a swim rather than play tennis.
12 I'd rather eat at home than go to a restaurant.
13 I'd prefer to think about it for a while rather than decide now.
14 I'd rather listen to some music than watch TV.

59.3

2 (would you rather) I told her
3 would you rather I did it
4 would you rather I phoned her

59.4

2 stayed/remained/waited
3 stay
4 didn't
5 were
6 didn't

UNIT 60

60.1

2 applying for the job
3 remembering names
4 winning the lottery
5 being late
6 eating at home, we went to a restaurant
7 having to queue 或 queuing
8 playing very well

60.2

2 by standing on a chair
3 by turning a key
4 by borrowing too much money
5 by driving too fast
6 by putting some pictures on the walls

60.3
2 paying/settling
3 going
4 using
5 going
6 being/travelling/sitting
7 asking/telling/consulting
8 doing/having
9 turning/going
10 taking

60.4
2 I'm looking forward to seeing her. / … seeing Kate.
3 I'm not looking forward to going to the dentist (tomorrow).
4 She's looking forward to leaving school (next summer).
5 I'm looking forward to playing tennis (tomorrow).

UNIT 61

61.1
1 When Jack started working in this job, he wasn't **used to** driving two hours to work every morning, but after some time he **got used to** it. Now it's no problem for him. He**'s used to driving** two hours every morning. / He **is used to driving** …
2 She **wasn't used to working** nights and it took her a few months to **get used to** it. Now, after a year, it's OK for her. She**'s used to working** nights. / She **is used to working** …

61.2
2 No, I'm used to sleeping on the floor.
3 I'm used to working long hours.
4 Yes, I'm not used to going to bed so late.

61.3
2 They soon got used to her. / … to the/their new teacher.
3 She had to get used to living in a much smaller house.
4 (参考答案) They'll have to get used to the weather. / … to the food. / … to speaking a foreign language.

61.4
2 drink
3 eating
4 having
5 have
6 go
7 be
8 being
9 live … living

UNIT 62

62.1
2 doing
3 coming/going
4 spending/having
5 buying/having
6 seeing
7 watching
8 solving
9 buying/having

62.2
2 of causing
3 from walking （或 stop people walking)
4 for interrupting
5 of using
6 of doing
7 from escaping （或 prevent the prisoner escaping)
8 on telling
9 to eating
10 for being
11 for inviting
12 of (not) wearing

62.3
2 on taking Ann to the station
3 on getting married
4 Sue for coming to see her
5 (to me) for not phoning earlier
6 me of being selfish

UNIT 63

63.1
2 There's no point in working if you don't need money.
3 There's no point in trying to study if you feel tired.
4 There's no point in hurrying if you've got plenty of time.

63.2
2 asking David
3 in going out
4 phoning her/Lisa
5 complaining (about what happened)
6 keeping

63.3
2 remembering people's names
3 getting a job
4 getting a ticket for the game
5 understanding him

63.4
2 reading
3 packing / getting ready
4 watching
5 going/climbing/walking
6 getting/being

63.5
2 went swimming
3 go skiing
4 goes riding
5 gone shopping

UNIT 64

64.1
2 I opened the box to see what was in it.
3 I'm saving money to go to Canada.
4 I need a knife to chop these onions.
5 I'm wearing two sweaters to keep warm.
6 I phoned the police to report the accident.

64.2
2 to read
3 to walk / to go on foot
4 to drink
5 to put / to carry
6 to discuss / to consider / to talk about
7 to go / to travel
8 to talk / to speak
9 to wear / to put on
10 to celebrate
11 to help / to assist

64.3
2 for
3 to
4 to
5 for
6 to
7 for
8 for … to

64.4
2 so that I wouldn't be cold.
3 so that he could contact me. / … would be able to contact me.
4 so that nobody else would hear our conversation. / so that nobody else could hear … / … would be able to hear …
5 so that we can start the meeting on time. / so that we'll be able to start …
6 so that we wouldn't forget anything.
7 so that the car behind me could overtake. / … would be able to overtake.

UNIT 65

65.1
2 This machine is easy to use.
3 The window was very difficult to open.
4 Some words are impossible to translate.

5 A car is expensive to maintain.
6 That chair isn't safe to stand on.

65.2
2 It's an easy mistake to make.
3 It's a nice place to live. 或
… a nice place to live in.
4 It was a good game to watch.

65.3
2 It's careless of you to make the same mistake again and again.
3 It was nice of them to invite me (to stay with them). / It was nice of Dan and Jenny to …
4 It's inconsiderate of them to make so much noise. / It's inconsiderate of the neighbours to …

65.4
2 I'm / I am glad to hear 或
I was glad to hear
3 We were surprised to see
4 Pleased to meet

65.5
2 Paul was the last (person) to arrive.
3 Emily was the only student to pass (the exam). / … the only one to pass (the exam).
4 I was the second customer/person to complain (about the service).
5 Neil Armstrong was the first person/man to walk on the moon.

65.6
2 're/are bound to be
3 's/is sure to forget
4 's/is not likely to rain 或
isn't likely to rain
5 's/is likely to be

UNIT 66

66.1
3 I'm afraid of losing it.
4 I was afraid to tell her.
5 We were afraid of missing our train.
6 We were afraid to look.
7 I was afraid of dropping it.
8 a I was afraid to eat it.
b I was afraid of getting sick.

66.2
2 in starting
3 to read
4 in getting
5 to know
6 in looking

66.3
2 sorry to hear
3 sorry for saying /
sorry about saying / sorry I said
4 sorry to disturb
5 sorry for losing / sorry about losing / sorry I lost

66.4
1 b to leave
c from leaving
2 a to solve
b in solving
3 a of/about going
b to go
c to go
d to going
4 a to buy
b on buying
c to buy
d of buying

UNIT 67

67.1
2 arrive
3 take it / do it
4 it ring
5 him play 或 him playing
6 you lock it / you do it
7 her fall

67.2
2 We saw David and Helen playing tennis.
3 We saw Clare eating in a restaurant. / … having a meal in a restaurant.
4 We heard Bill playing his guitar.
5 We could smell the dinner burning.
6 We saw Linda jogging/running.

67.3
3 tell
4 crying
5 riding
6 say
7 run … climb
8 explode
9 crawling
10 slam
11 sleeping

UNIT 68

68.1
2 Amy was sitting in an armchair reading a book.
3 Sue opened the door carefully trying not to make a noise.
4 Sarah went out saying she would be back in an hour.
5 Lisa was in London for two years working in a bookshop.
6 Anna walked around the town looking at the sights and taking pictures.

68.2
2 I fell asleep watching TV.
3 A friend of mine slipped and fell getting off a bus.
4 I got very wet walking home in the rain.
5 Laura had an accident driving to work yesterday.
6 Two people were overcome by smoke trying to put out the fire.

68.3
2 Having bought our tickets, we went into the theatre.
3 Having had lunch, they continued their journey.
4 Having done the shopping, I went for a cup of coffee.

68.4
2 Thinking they might be hungry, …
3 Being a vegetarian, …
4 Not knowing his email address, …
5 Having travelled a lot, …
6 Not being able to speak the local language, …
7 Having spent nearly all our money, …

UNIT 69

69.1
3 We went to **a** very nice restaurant …
4 对
5 I use **a** toothbrush …
6 … if there's **a** bank near here?
7 … for **an** insurance company …
8 对
9 对
10 … we stayed in **a** big hotel.
11 … I hope we come to **a** petrol station soon.
12 … I have **a** problem.
13 … It's **a** very interesting idea.
14 John has **an** interview for **a** job tomorrow.
15 … It's **a** good game.
16 对
17 Jane was wearing **a** beautiful necklace.

69.2
3 a key
4 a coat
5 sugar
6 a biscuit
7 electricity
8 an interview
9 blood
10 a question
11 a moment
12 a decision

69.3
2 days
3 meat
4 a queue
5 jokes
6 friends
7 people
8 air

9 patience
10 an umbrella
11 languages
12 space

UNIT 70

70.1

2 a a paper
b paper
3 a Light
b a light
4 a time
b a wonderful time
5 a nice room
6 advice
7 nice weather
8 bad luck
9 job
10 journey
11 total chaos
12 some bread
13 doesn't
14 Your hair is … it
15 The damage

70.2

2 information
3 chairs
4 furniture
5 hair
6 progress
7 job
8 work
9 permission
10 advice
11 experience
12 experiences

70.3

2 I'd like some information about places to see in the town.
3 Can you give me (some) advice about which courses to do? / … courses I can do?
4 What time is the news (on)?
5 It's a beautiful view, isn't it?
6 What horrible/awful weather!

UNIT 71

71.1

3 It's a vegetable.
4 It's a game. / It's a board game.
5 They're birds.
6 It's a (tall/high) building.
7 They're planets.
8 It's a flower.
9 They're rivers.
10 They're musical instruments.
12 He was a writer / a poet / a playwright / a dramatist.
13 He was a scientist / a physicist.
14 They were US presidents / American presidents / presidents of the USA.
15 She was an actor / an actress / a film actress / a film star / a movie star.
16 They were singers / musicians.
17 They were painters / artists.

71.2

2 He's a waiter.
3 She's a journalist.
4 He's a surgeon.
5 He's a chef.
6 He's a plumber.
7 She's a tour guide.
8 She's an interpreter.

71.3

4 a
5 an
6 – (You're always asking questions!)
7 a
8 Some
9 – (Do you like staying in hotels?)
10 – (I've got sore feet.)
11 a
12 some
13 a … a
14 – (Those are nice shoes.)
15 some
16 You need **a** visa to visit **some** countries
17 Jane is **a** teacher. Her parents were teachers too.
18 He's **a** liar. He's always telling lies.

UNIT 72

72.1

1 … and **a** magazine. **The** newspaper is in my bag, but I can't remember where I put **the** magazine.
2 I saw **an** accident this morning. **A** car crashed into **a** tree. **The** driver of **the** car wasn't hurt, but **the** car was badly damaged.
3 … **a** blue one and **a** grey one. **The** blue one belongs to my neighbours; I don't know who **the** owner of **the** grey one is.
4 My friends live in **an** old house in **a** small village. There is **a** beautiful garden behind **the** house. I would like to have **a** garden like that.

72.2

1 a a
b the
c the
2 a a
b a
c the
3 a a
b the
c the
4 a an … The
b the
c the
5 a the
b a
c a

72.3

2 **the** dentist
3 **the** door
4 **a** mistake
5 **the** bus station
6 **a** problem
7 **the** post office
8 **the** floor
9 **the** book
10 **a** job in **a** bank
11 **a** small apartment in **the** city centre
12 **a** supermarket at **the** end of **the** street

72.4

参考答案：
2 About once a year.
3 Once or twice a year.
4 50 kilometres an hour.
5 About seven hours a night.
6 Two or three times a week.
7 About two hours a day.
8 About £20 a day.

UNIT 73

73.1

2 **a** nice holiday … **the** best holiday
3 **the** nearest shop … **the** end of this street
4 **a** lovely day … **a** cloud in **the** sky
5 to **the** internet … **the** same problem
6 **the** most expensive hotel … **a** cheaper hotel
7 to travel **in space** … go to **the** moon
8 **a** star … **a** planet … **the** largest planet in **the** solar system

73.2

2 watching TV
3 **the** radio
4 **The** television
5 had dinner
6 **the** same time
7 **the** capital
8 for breakfast
9 **the** ground … **the** sky

73.3

2 **the** same thing
3 **Room 25** is on **the** second floor.
4 **The** moon goes round **the** earth every 27 days. 或
… goes round **Earth** …

5 **a** very hot day … **the** hottest day of **the** year
6 We **had lunch** in **a** nice restaurant by **the** sea.
7 at **the** cinema
8 eat **a** good breakfast
9 on **the** wrong platform
10 **The** next train … **from Platform 3**
11 You'll find **the** information you need at **the** top **of page 15**.

73.4
2 the sea
3 question 8
4 the cinema
5 breakfast
6 the gate
7 Gate 21

UNIT 74

74.1
2 to school
3 at home
4 to work
5 in hospital
6 at university
7 in bed
8 to prison

74.2
2 school
3 the school
4 School
5 … get to and from school
… The school isn't very far.
6 school

74.3
1 c 对
d the university
2 a 对
b the hospital … the hospital
c 对
3 a 对
b 对
c the church
4 a 对
b the prison
c 对

74.4
2 in bed
3 after work
4 in the sea
5 like home
6 go to bed
7 The bed
8 at sea
9 work

UNIT 75

75.1
参考答案：
2–5
- I like cats.
- I don't like zoos.
- I don't mind snow.
- I'm not interested in boxing.

75.2
3 spiders
4 meat
5 the questions
6 the people
7 History
8 lies
9 The hotels
10 The water
11 the grass
12 patience

75.3
2 Apples
3 the apples
4 Women … men
5 tea
6 The vegetables
7 Life
8 holidays ('holidays by the sea' in general)
9 education
10 the people
11 people … aggression
12 All the books
13 the rooms
14 war
15 The First World War
16 films
17 the history of modern art
18 the marriage
19 Most people … marriage … family life … society

UNIT 76

76.1
1 b the cheetah
c the kangaroo (and the rabbit)
2 a the swan
b the penguin
c the owl
3 a the wheel
b the laser
c the telescope
4 a the rupee
b the (Canadian) dollar
c the …

76.2
2 a
3 the
4 a
5 the
6 the
7 a
8 The

76.3
2 the injured
3 the unemployed
4 the sick
5 the rich … the poor

76.4
2 a German Germans
3 a Frenchman/Frenchwoman the French
4 a Russian Russians
5 a Chinese the Chinese
6 a Brazilian Brazilians
7 an Englishman/Englishwoman the English
8 …

UNIT 77

77.1
2 the
3 the … the
4 – (President Kennedy was assassinated in 1963.)
5 the
6 – (I'm looking for Professor Brown.)

77.2
3 对
4 **the** United States
5 **The** south of England … **the** north
6 对
7 **the** Channel
8 **the** Middle East
9 对
10 **the** Swiss Alps
11 **The** UK
12 **The** Seychelles … **the** Indian Ocean
13 对
14 **The** river Volga … **the** Caspian Sea

77.3
2 (in) South America
3 **the** Nile
4 Sweden
5 **the** United States
6 **the** Rockies
7 **the** Mediterranean
8 Australia
9 **the** Pacific
10 **the** Indian Ocean
11 **the** Thames
12 **the** Danube
13 Thailand
14 **the** Panama Canal
15 **the** Amazon

UNIT 78

78.1
2 Turner's in Carter Road
3 **the** Crown (Hotel) in Park Road
4 St Peter's in Market Street
5 **the** City Museum in George Street
6 Blackstone's (Books) in Forest Avenue
7 Mario's (Pizza) in George Street
8 Victoria Park at the end of Market Street

78.2

2 **The** Eiffel Tower
3 Buckingham Palace
4 **The** White House
5 **The** Kremlin
6 Broadway
7 **The** Acropolis
8 Gatwick Airport

78.3

2 Central Park
3 St James's Park
4 The Imperial Hotel … Baker Street
5 Dublin Airport
6 Liverpool University
7 Harrison's
8 the Park Plaza
9 The Statue of Liberty … New York Harbour
10 the Science Museum
11 IBM … British Telecom
12 The Classic
13 the Great Wall
14 The Times
15 Cambridge University Press
16 the College of Art

UNIT 79

79.1

3 shorts
4 a means
5 means
6 some scissors 或 a pair of scissors
7 a series
8 series
9 species

79.2

2 politics
3 economics
4 athletics
5 physics
6 gymnastics
7 electronics

79.3

2 don't
3 want
4 was
5 aren't
6 are
7 wasn't
8 does 或 do
9 they are
10 Do
11 is 或 are
12 enjoy

79.4

3 … wearing black jeans.
4 对
5 … very nice **people**.
6 Ten pounds **isn't** …
7 … buy **some** new **pyjamas**. 或 … buy **a** new **pair of pyjamas**.
8 对 (The committee hasn't *is also correct*)
9 There was **a police officer** / **a policeman** / **a policewoman** …
10 What **are** the police …
11 **These** scissors **aren't** …
12 对

UNIT 80

80.1

3 a job interview
4 (your) holiday pictures
5 milk chocolate
6 a factory inspector
7 a race horse
8 a horse race
9 running shoes
10 a university student
11 (your) exam results
12 the living room carpet
13 an oil company scandal
14 car factory workers
15 a road improvement scheme
16 a New York department store
17 a five-day course
18 a two-part question
19 a thirty-year-old man

80.2

2 seat belt
3 credit card
4 weather forecast
5 newspaper editor
6 shop window
7 room number
8 birthday party
9 truck driver

80.3

2 twenty-pound
3 ten-pound
4 15-minute
5 60 minutes
6 two-hour
7 twelve-storey
8 five days
9 Five-star
10 six years old
11 500-year-old
12 twelve-hour … 24-hour

UNIT 81

81.1

3 your friend's umbrella
4 对
5 Charles's daughter
6 Helen and Dan's son
7 对
8 last Monday's newspaper
9 对
10 对
11 Your children's friends
12 Our neighbours' garden
13 对
14 David's hair
15 Katherine's party
16 对
17 Mike's parents' car
18 对
19 对 (the government's economic policy *is also correct*)

81.2

2 a boy's name
3 children's clothes
4 a girls' school
5 a bird's nest
6 a women's magazine

81.3

2 Last week's storm caused a lot of damage.
3 The town's only cinema has closed down.
4 Britain's weather is very changeable.
5 The region's main industry is tourism.

81.4

2 twenty minutes' walk
3 two weeks' holiday / fourteen days' holiday / a fortnight's holiday
4 an/one hour's sleep

UNIT 82

82.1

2 hurt himself
3 blame herself
4 Put yourself
5 enjoyed themselves
6 burn yourself
7 express myself

82.2

2 me
3 myself
4 us
5 yourself
6 you
7 ourselves
8 them
9 themselves

82.3

2 feel
3 dried myself
4 concentrate
5 defend yourself
6 meeting
7 relax

82.4

2 themselves
3 each other
4 each other
5 themselves
6 each other
7 ourselves
8 each other
9 introduced **ourselves** to **each other**

82.5

2 He cuts it himself.
3 No, I'll tell her myself.
4 Linda told me herself. / Linda herself told me. / Linda did herself.
5 Why can't you phone him yourself? / … do it yourself?

UNIT 83

83.1

2 We met a relative of yours.
3 Jason borrowed a book of mine.
4 Lisa invited some friends of hers to her flat.
5 We had dinner with a neighbour of ours.
6 I went on holiday with two friends of mine.
7 Is that man a friend of yours?
8 I met a friend of Jane's at the party.
9 It's always been an ambition of mine (to travel round the world).

83.2

2 his own opinions
3 her own business
4 our own words
5 its own private beach

83.3

2 your own fault
3 her own ideas
4 your own problems
5 his own decisions

83.4

2 makes her own (clothes)
3 bake/make our own (bread)
4 clean your own (shoes)
5 write their own (songs)

83.5

2 my own
3 myself
4 himself
5 themselves
6 herself
7 their own
8 yourself
9 our own
10 her own

UNIT 84

84.1

3 There's / There is
4 there wasn't
5 Is it … it's / it is
6 Is there
7 there was
8 It isn't / It's not
9 there isn't
10 It was
11 There wasn't
12 Is there … there's / there is
13 there was … It was
14 It was
15 It's / It is … There's / There is

84.2

2 There's / There is a lot of salt in the soup. 或 … too much salt …
3 There was nothing in the box. 或 There wasn't anything in the box.
4 There's / There is a lot of violence in the film. 或 … too much violence …
5 There were a lot of people in the shopping mall. 或 … too many people …
6 There is a lot to do in this town. / There is a lot happening in this town.

84.3

2 There may be
3 there will be / there'll be 或 there are going to be
4 There's going to be / There is going to be
5 There used to be
6 there should be
7 there wouldn't be

84.4

2 对
3 **there** will be an opportunity
4 对
5 **There** must have been a reason.
6 对
7 **There's** sure to be a car park somewhere.
8 对
9 **There** has been no change.
10 **There** used to be a church here
11 **there** would be somebody … but **there** wasn't anybody.
12 对

UNIT 85

85.1

2 some
3 any
4 any … some
5 some
6 some … any
7 any
8 any
9 some
10 any
11 some

85.2

2 somebody/someone
3 anybody/anyone
4 anything
5 something
6 somebody/someone … anybody/anyone
7 something … anybody/anyone
8 Anybody/Anyone
9 anybody/anyone
10 anywhere
11 somewhere
12 anywhere
13 anybody/anyone
14 something
15 Anybody/Anyone
16 anything
17 something
18 anybody/anyone anything

85.3

2 Any day
3 Anything
4 anywhere
5 Any job 或 Anything
6 Any time
7 Anybody/Anyone
8 Any newspaper 或 Any one

UNIT 86

86.1

3 no
4 any
5 None
6 none
7 any
8 No
9 no
10 any
11 none
12 no

86.2

2 Nobody/No-one.
3 None.
4 Nowhere.
5 None.
6 Nothing.
8 I wasn't talking to anybody/anyone.
9 I don't want any sugar.
10 I'm not going anywhere.
11 I didn't get any emails.
12 I didn't pay anything.

86.3

2 nobody/no-one
3 Nowhere
4 anything
5 **Nothing**. I couldn't find **anything** …
6 Nothing
7 anywhere
8 **Nobody/No-one** said **anything**.

86.4

2 nobody
3 anyone
4 Anybody
5 Nothing
6 Anything
7 anything
8 any
9 No-one … anyone

UNIT 87

87.1

3 a lot of salt
4 对
5 It cost a lot
6 对
7 many people 或 a lot of people
8 Mike travels a lot.
9 对
10 a lot of money

87.2

2 He has (got) plenty of money.
3 There's plenty of room.
4 … she still has plenty to learn.
5 There is plenty to see.
6 There are plenty of hotels.

87.3

2 little
3 many
4 much
5 few
6 little
7 many

87.4

3 a few dollars
4 对
5 a little time
6 对
7 only a few words
8 a few months

87.5

2 a little
3 a few
4 few
5 little
6 a little
7 little
8 a few

UNIT 88

88.1

3 –
4 of
5 –
6 –
7 of
8 of
9 – (of *is also correct*)
10 –

88.2

3 of my spare time
4 accidents
5 of the buildings
6 of her friends
7 of the population
8 birds
9 of the players
10 of her opinions
11 European countries
12 (of) my dinner

88.3

参考答案：
2 the time
3 my friends
4 (of) the questions
5 the pictures / the photos / the photographs
6 (of) the money

88.4

2 All of them
3 none of us
4 some of it
5 none of them
6 None of it
7 Some of them
8 all of it

UNIT 89

89.1

2 Neither
3 both
4 Either
5 Neither

89.2

2 either
3 both
4 Neither of
5 **neither** driver … **both** / **both the** / **both of the** cars
6 both / both of

89.3

2 either of them
3 both of them
4 Neither of us
5 neither of them

89.4

3 Both Joe and Sam are on holiday.
4 Neither Joe nor Sam has (got) a car.
5 Brian neither watches TV nor reads newspapers.
6 The movie was both boring and long.
7 That man's name is either Richard or Robert.
8 I have (got) neither the time nor the money to go on holiday.
9 We can leave either today or tomorrow.

89.5

2 either
3 any
4 none
5 any
6 either
7 neither

UNIT 90

90.1

3 Everybody/Everyone
4 Everything
5 all
6 everybody/everyone
7 everything
8 All
9 everybody/everyone
10 All
11 everything/all
12 Everybody/Everyone
13 All
14 everything

90.2

2 The whole team played well.
3 He ate the whole box (of chocolates).
4 They searched the whole house.
5 The whole family play/plays tennis.
6 Ann/She worked the whole day.
7 It rained the whole week.
8 Ann worked all day.
9 It rained all week.

90.3

2 every four hours
3 every four years
4 every five minutes
5 every six months

90.4

2 every day
3 all day
4 The whole building
5 every time
6 all the time
7 all my luggage

UNIT 91

91.1

3 Each
4 Every
5 Each
6 every
7 each
8 every

91.2

3 Every
4 Each
5 every
6 every
7 each
8 every
9 each
10 Every
11 each
12 each

91.3

2 Sonia and I had ten pounds each. / Sonia and I each had ten pounds.
3 Those postcards cost 80 pence each. / Those postcards are 80 pence each.
4 We paid £150 each. / We each paid £150.

91.4

2 everyone
3 every one
4 Everyone
5 every one

UNIT 92

92.1

2 A burglar is someone who breaks into a house to steal things.
3 A customer is someone who buys something from a shop.
4 A shoplifter is someone who steals from a shop.
5 A coward is someone who is not brave.
6 An atheist is someone who doesn't believe in God.
7 A pessimist is someone who expects the worst to happen.
8 A tenant is someone who pays rent to live in a house or apartment.

92.2

2 The waitress who/that served us was impolite and impatient.
3 The building that/which was destroyed in the fire has now been rebuilt.
4 The people who/that were arrested have now been released.
5 The bus that/which goes to the airport runs every half hour.

92.3

2 who/that runs away from home
3 that/which were hanging on the wall
4 that/which cannot be explained
5 who/that stole my wallet
6 that/which gives you the meaning of words
7 who/that invented the telephone
8 that/which can support life

92.4

3 the nearest shop **that/which** sells
4 the driver **who/that** caused
5 对 (the person **who** took *is also correct*)
6 a world **that/which** is changing
7 对 (some things about me **which** were *is also* correct)
8 the horse **that/which** won

UNIT 93

93.1

3 对 (the people **who/that** we met *is also correct*)
4 The people **who/that** work in the office
5 对 (the people **who/that** I work with *is also correct*)
6 对 (the money **that/which** I gave you *is also correct*)
7 the money **that/which** was on the table
8 对 (the worst film **that** you've ever seen *is also correct*)
9 the best thing **that** has ever happened to you

93.2

2 you're wearing 或 that/which you're wearing
3 you're going to see 或 that/which you're going to see
4 I/we wanted to visit 或 that/which I/we wanted to visit
5 I/we invited to the party 或 who/whom/that I/we invited …
6 you had to do 或 that/which you had to do
7 I/we rented 或 that/which I/we rented

93.3

2 the wedding we were invited to
3 the hotel you told me about
4 the job I applied for
5 the concert you went to
6 somebody you can rely on
7 the man you were with

93.4

3 – (that *is also correct*)
4 what
5 that
6 what
7 – (that *is also correct*)
8 what
9 – (that *is also correct*)

UNIT 94

94.1

2 whose wife is an English teacher
3 who owns a restaurant
4 whose ambition is to climb Qomolangma
5 who have just got married
6 whose parents used to work in a circus

94.2

2 where I can get some water
3 (The) factory where I work
4 the hotel where Sue is staying
5 (the) park where I/we play football

94.3

2 where
3 who
4 whose
5 whom
6 where
7 whose
8 whom

94.4

参考答案:
2 The reason I left my job was that the salary was too low.
3 I'll never forget the time I got stuck in a lift.
4 Do you remember the day we first met?
5 The reason they don't have a car is that they don't need one.
6 2003 was the year Amanda got married.

UNIT 95

95.1

3 We often go to visit our friends in Cambridge, which is not far from London.
4 I went to see the doctor, who told me I needed to change my diet.
5 Steven, who/whom I've known for a very long time, is one of my closest friends.
6 Lisa, whose job involves a lot of travelling, is away from home a lot.
7 The new stadium, which can hold 90,000 people, will be finished next month.
8 Alaska, where my brother lives, is the largest state in the USA.
9 Our teacher, whose name I have forgotten, was very kind.

95.2

3 The strike at the factory, which began ten days ago, is now over.
4 I've found the book I was looking for this morning. 或 … the book that/which I was looking for.
5 My car, which I've had for 15 years, has never broken down.
6 Few of the people who/that applied for the job had the necessary qualifications.
7 Amy showed me a picture of her son, who is a police officer.

95.3

2 My office**, which** is on the second floor, is very small.
3 对 (The office **that/which** I'm using … *is also correct*)
4 Mark's father**, who** used to be in the army, now works for a TV company.
5 对 (The doctor **who** examined me … *is also correct*)
6 The sun**, which** is one of millions of stars in the universe**,** provides us with heat and light.

UNIT 96

96.1

2 of which he's very proud
3 with whom we went on holiday
4 to which only members of the family were invited

96.2

2 most of which was useless
3 none of whom was suitable
4 one of which she hardly ever uses
5 half of which he gave to his parents
6 both of whom are lawyers
7 neither of which she replied to
8 only a few of whom I knew
9 (the) sides of which were lined with trees
10 the aim of which is to save money

96.3

2 Jane doesn't have a phone, which makes it difficult to contact her.
3 Alex has passed his exams, which is good news.
4 Our flight was delayed, which meant we had to wait three hours at the airport.
5 Kate offered to let me stay at her house, which was very kind of her.
6 The street I live in is very noisy at night, which makes it difficult to sleep sometimes.
7 Our car has broken down, which means we can't go away tomorrow.

UNIT 97

97.1

2 the man sitting next to me on the plane
3 The taxi taking us to the airport
4 a path leading to the river
5 A factory employing 500 people
6 a brochure containing the information I needed

97.2

2 The gate damaged in the storm
3 Most of the suggestions made at the meeting
4 The paintings stolen from the museum
5 the man arrested by the police

97.3

3 living
4 offering
5 called
6 blown
7 sitting … reading
8 working … studying

97.4

3 There's somebody coming.
4 There were a lot of people travelling.
5 There was nobody else staying there.
6 There was nothing written on it.
7 There's a course beginning next Monday.

UNIT 98

98.1

2 a exhausting
b exhausted
3 a depressing
b depressed
c depressed
4 a exciting
b exciting
c excited

98.2

2 interested
3 exciting
4 embarrassing
5 embarrassed
6 amazed
7 amazing
8 amused
9 terrifying … shocked
10 bored … boring
11 boring … interesting

98.3

2 bored
3 confusing
4 disgusting
5 interested
6 annoyed
7 boring
8 exhausted
9 excited
10 amusing
11 interesting

UNIT 99

99.1

2 an unusual gold ring
3 a beautiful old house
4 black leather gloves
5 an old American film
6 a long thin face
7 big black clouds
8 a lovely sunny day
9 an ugly yellow dress
10 a long wide avenue
11 a lovely little restaurant
12 a little old red car
13 a nice new green sweater
14 a small black metal box
15 a big fat black cat
16 beautiful long black hair
17 an interesting old French painting
18 an enormous red and yellow umbrella

99.2

2 tastes/tasted awful
3 feel fine
4 smell nice
5 look wet
6 sounds/sounded interesting

99.3

2 happy
3 happily
4 violent
5 terrible
6 properly
7 good
8 slow

99.4

3 the last two days
4 the first two weeks of May
5 the next few days
6 the first three questions (in the exam)
7 the next two years
8 the last three days of our holiday

UNIT 100

100.1

2 badly
3 easily
4 patiently
5 unexpectedly
6 regularly
7 perfectly … slowly … clearly

100.2

3 selfishly
4 terribly
5 sudden
6 colourfully
7 colourful
8 badly
9 badly
10 safe

100.3

2 careful
3 continuously
4 happily
5 fluent
6 specially
7 complete
8 perfectly
9 nervous
10 financially 或 completely

100.4

2 seriously ill
3 absolutely enormous
4 slightly damaged
5 unusually quiet
6 completely changed
7 unnecessarily long
8 badly planned

UNIT 101

101.1

2 good
3 well
4 good
5 well
6 well … good
7 well
8 good
9 well

101.2

2 well-known
3 well-kept
4 well-written

5 well-informed
6 well-dressed
7 well-paid

101.3
2 对 5 对
3 对 6 slowly
4 hard

101.4
2 hardly hear
3 hardly slept
4 hardly speak
5 hardly said
6 hardly changed
7 hardly recognised

101.5
2 hardly any
3 hardly anything
4 hardly anybody/anyone
5 hardly ever
6 Hardly anybody/anyone
7 hardly anywhere
8 hardly 或 hardly ever
9 hardly any
10 hardly anything … hardly anywhere

UNIT 102

102.1
4 so
5 so
6 such a
7 so
8 such
9 such a
10 such a
11 so
12 so … such
13 so
14 such a
15 such a

102.2
3 I was so tired (that) I couldn't keep my eyes open.
4 We had such a good time on holiday (that) we didn't want to come home.
5 She speaks English so well (that) you would think it was her native language. 或 She speaks such good English (that) …
6 I've got such a lot to do (that) I don't know where to begin. 或 I've got so much to do (that) …
7 The music was so loud (that) you could hear it from miles away.
8 I had such a big breakfast (that) I didn't eat anything else for the rest of the day.
9 It was such horrible weather (that) we spent the whole day indoors.
10 I was so surprised (that) I didn't know what to say.

102.3
参考答案：
2 a She's so friendly.
b She's such a nice person.
3 a It's so lively.
b It's such an exciting place.
4 a It's so exhausting.
b It's such a difficult job.
5 a I haven't seen you for so long.
b I haven't seen you for such a long time.

UNIT 103

103.1
3 enough money
4 enough milk
5 warm enough
6 enough room
7 well enough
8 enough time
9 big enough
10 enough cups

103.2
2 too busy to talk
3 too late to go
4 warm enough to sit
5 too shy to be
6 enough patience to be
7 too far away to hear
8 enough English to read

103.3
2 This coffee is too hot to drink.
3 The piano was too heavy to move.
4 These apples aren't / are not ripe enough to eat.
5 The situation is too complicated to explain.
6 The wall was too high to climb over.
7 This sofa isn't / is not big enough for three people (to sit on).
8 Some things are too small to see without a microscope.

UNIT 104

104.1
2 quite hungry
3 Quite good
4 quite often
5 quite noisy
6 quite surprised
7 quite late
8 quite old

104.2
2 quite a good voice
3 quite a long way
4 a pretty cold wind
5 quite a lot of traffic
6 a pretty busy day

104.3
参考答案：
2 rather long
3 rather disappointed
4 rather strange
5 rather impatient

104.4
3 more than a little …
4 completely
5 more than a little …
6 more than a little …
7 completely

104.5
2 quite safe
3 quite impossible
4 quite right
5 quite different
6 quite unnecessary
7 quite sure

UNIT 105

105.1
2 stronger
3 smaller
4 more expensive
5 warmer/hotter
6 more interesting / more exciting
7 nearer/closer
8 more difficult / more complicated
9 better
10 worse
11 longer
12 more quietly
13 more often
14 further/farther
15 happier / more cheerful

105.2
3 more serious than
4 thinner
5 bigger
6 more interested
7 more important than
8 simpler / more simple
9 more crowded than
10 more peaceful than
11 more easily
12 higher than

105.3
2 It takes longer by train than by car.
3 I ran further/farther than Dan.
4 Joe did worse than Chris in the test.
5 My friends arrived earlier than I expected.
6 The buses run more often than the trains. 或 The buses run more

frequently than … 或 The buses are more frequent than …
7 We were busier than usual in the office today.

UNIT 106

106.1

2 much bigger
3 much more interesting than
4 a bit cooler
5 far more complicated than
6 a bit more slowly
7 a lot easier
8 slightly older

106.2

2 any sooner / any earlier
3 no higher than
4 any further/farther
5 no worse than

106.3

2 bigger and bigger
3 heavier and heavier
4 more and more nervous
5 worse and worse
6 more and more expensive
7 better and better
8 more and more talkative

106.4

2 the more I liked him 或 the more I got to like him
3 the more profit you (will) make 或 the higher your profit (will be) 或 the bigger your profit (will be)
4 the harder it is to concentrate
5 the more impatient she became

106.5

2 more
3 longer
4 any
5 the
6 older
7 elder 或 older
8 slightly
9 no
10 less … better

UNIT 107

107.1

2 My salary isn't as high as yours.
3 You don't know as much about cars as me. 或 … as I do.
4 We aren't as busy today as we were yesterday. 或 … as yesterday.
5 I don't feel as bad as I did earlier. 或 … as I felt earlier.
6 Our neighbours haven't lived here as long as us. 或 … as we have.
7 I wasn't as nervous (before the interview) as I usually am. 或 … as usual.

107.2

3 The station wasn't as far as I thought.
4 The meal cost less than I expected.
5 I don't go out as much as I used to. 或 … as often as I used to.
6 Karen used to have longer hair.
7 You don't know them as well as me. 或 … as I do.
8 There aren't as many people at this meeting as at the last one.

107.3

2 as well as
3 as long as
4 as soon as
5 as often as
6 as quietly as
7 just as comfortable as
8 just as hard as
9 just as bad as

107.4

2 Your hair is the same colour as mine.
3 I arrived (at) the same time as you.
4 My birthday is (on) the same day as Tom's. 或 My birthday is the same as Tom's.

107.5

2 than him / than he does
3 as me / as I do
4 than us / than we were
5 than her / than she is
6 as them / as they have been

UNIT 108

108.1

2 It's the cheapest restaurant in the town.
3 It was the happiest day of my life.
4 She's the most intelligent student in the class.
5 It's the most valuable painting in the gallery.
6 It's the busiest time of the year.
8 He's one of the richest men in the country.
9 It's one of the biggest castles in Europe.
10 She's one of the best players in the team. (on the team *is also possible*)
11 It was one of the worst experiences of my life.
12 It's one of the most famous universities in the world.

108.2

3 larger
4 the smallest
5 better
6 the worst
7 the most popular
8 … the highest mountain in the world … It is higher than …
9 the tallest
10 more comfortable
11 the quickest
12 quicker
13 the most expensive
14 The oldest 或 The eldest

108.3

2 That's the funniest joke I've ever heard.
3 This is the best coffee I've ever tasted.
4 She's the most generous person I've ever met.
5 That's the furthest/farthest I've ever run.
6 It's the worst mistake I've ever made. 或 It was the worst …
7 Who's the most famous person you've ever met?

UNIT 109

109.1

3 Joe doesn't like football very much.
4 对
5 I ate my breakfast quickly and …
6 … a lot of people to the party?
7 对
8 Did you go to bed late last night?
9 对
10 I met a friend of mine on my way home.

109.2

2 We won the game easily.
3 I closed the door quietly.
4 Tanya speaks German quite well.
5 Sam watches TV all the time.
6 Please don't ask that question again.
7 Does Kevin play football every weekend?
8 I borrowed some money from a friend of mine.

109.3

2 I go to the supermarket every Friday.
3 Why did you come home so late?
4 Sarah takes her children to school every day.
5 I haven't been to the cinema recently.
6 Please write your name at the top of the page.
7 I remembered her name after a few minutes.

8 We walked around the town all morning.
9 I didn't see you at the party on Saturday night.
10 We found some interesting books in the library.
11 Laura left her umbrella in a restaurant last night.
12 They are building a new hotel opposite the park.

UNIT 110

110.1

3 I usually have …
4 对
5 Steve hardly ever gets angry.
6 … and I also went to the bank.
7 Jane always has to hurry …
8 I've never worked / I have never worked …
9 对 (I never have enough time.) I'm always busy. / I am always busy.

110.2

2 Katherine is always very generous.
3 I don't usually have to work on Saturdays.
4 Do you always watch TV in the evenings?
5 … he is also learning Japanese.
6 a We were all on holiday in Spain.
  b We were all staying at the same hotel.
  c We all enjoyed ourselves.
7 a The new hotel is probably very expensive.
  b It probably costs a lot to stay there.
8 a I can probably help you.
  b I probably can't help you.

110.3

2 I usually take
3 I am usually / I'm usually
4 were both born
5 She can also sing
6 usually sleeps
7 I have never spoken / I've never spoken
8 You always have to wait
9 I can only read 或 I can read only
10 We were all … we all fell
11 I always am
12 I will probably be leaving / I'll probably be leaving
13 I probably won't be
14 She is hardly ever / She's hardly ever
15 We are still living / We're still living
16 we would never have met / we'd never have met
17 always says … she never does

UNIT 111

111.1

3 He doesn't write poems any more.
4 He still wants to be a teacher.
5 He isn't / He's not interested in politics any more.
6 He's still single.
7 He doesn't go fishing any more.
8 He doesn't have a beard any more. 或 He hasn't got …

10–12
- He no longer writes poems.
- He is / He's no longer interested in politics.
- He no longer goes fishing.
- He no longer has a beard. 或 He's no longer got a beard.

111.2

2 He hasn't gone yet.
3 They haven't finished (repairing the road) yet.
4 They haven't woken up yet.
5 Hasn't she found a place to live yet?
6 I haven't decided (what to do) yet.
7 It hasn't taken off yet.

111.3

5 I don't want to go out yet.
6 she doesn't work there any more
7 I still have a lot of friends there. 或 I've still got …
8 We've already met.
9 Do you still live in the same place
10 have you already eaten
11 He's not here yet.
12 he still isn't here (he isn't here yet *is also possible*)
13 are you already a member
14 I can still remember it very clearly
15 These trousers don't fit me any more.
16 'Have you finished with the paper yet?' 'No, I'm still reading it.'

UNIT 112

112.1

2 even Lisa
3 not even Amy
4 even Lisa
5 even Kate
6 not even Lisa

112.2

2 We even painted the floor.
3 She's even met the prime minister.
4 You could even hear it / You could even hear the noise from the next street. 或 You could hear it / You could hear the noise even from the next street.
6 I can't even remember her name.
7 There isn't even a cinema.
8 He didn't even tell his wife (where he was going).
9 I don't even know the people next door.

112.3

2 even older
3 even better
4 even more difficult
5 even worse
6 even less

112.4

2 if
3 even if
4 even
5 even though
6 Even
7 even though
8 even if
9 Even though

UNIT 113

113.1

2 Although I had never seen her before
3 although it was quite cold
4 although we don't like them very much
5 Although I didn't speak the language well
6 Although the heating was on
7 although I'd met her twice before
8 although we've known each other a long time

113.2

2 a In spite of (或 Despite)
  b Although
3 a because
  b although
4 a because of
  b in spite of (或 despite)
5 a although
  b because of

参考答案：

6 a he hadn't studied very hard
  b he had studied very hard
7 a I was hungry
  b being hungry / my hunger / the fact (that) I was hungry

113.3

2 In spite of having very little money, they are happy. 或 In spite of the fact (that) they have very little money …

3 Although my foot was injured, I managed to walk home. 或 I managed to walk home although my …
4 I enjoyed the film in spite of the silly story. / … in spite of the story being silly. / … in spite of the fact (that) the story was silly. 或 In spite of … , I enjoyed the film.
5 Despite living in the same street, we hardly ever see each other. 或 Despite the fact (that) we live in … 或 We hardly ever see each other despite …
6 Even though I was only out for five minutes, I got very wet in the rain. 或 I got very wet in the rain even though I was …

113.4
2 It's very windy though.
3 We ate it though.
4 I don't like her husband though.

UNIT 114
114.1
2–5
- Take a map in case you get lost.
- Take an anorak in case it rains.
- Take a camera in case you want to take some pictures.
- Take some water in case you're thirsty. / … in case you are thirsty. 或 … you get thirsty.

114.2
2 I'll say goodbye now in case I don't see you again (before you go).
3 Can you check the list in case we forgot something? 或 … forgot anything?
4 You should back up your files in case there's a problem with your computer. / … there is a problem with your computer.

114.3
2 in case I forgot it.
3 in case they were worried (about me).
4 in case she didn't get the first one. / in case she hadn't got … / in case she hadn't gotten …
5 in case they came to London (one day).

114.4
3 If	7 if
4 if	8 in case
5 in case	9 in case
6 if	

UNIT 115
115.1
2 You won't know what to do unless you listen carefully.
3 I'll never speak to her again unless she apologises to me. 或 Unless she apologises to me, I'll …
4 He won't be able to understand you unless you speak very slowly. 或 Unless you speak very slowly, he …
5 The company will have to close unless business improves soon. 或 Unless business improves soon, the company …

115.2
2 I'm not going (to the party) unless you go too. / … unless you're going too.
3 The dog won't attack you unless you move suddenly.
4 Ben won't speak to you unless you ask him something.
5 The doctor won't see you unless it's an emergency.

115.3
2 unless	7 provided
3 providing	8 Unless
4 as long as	9 unless
5 unless	10 as long as
6 unless	

115.4
参考答案：
2 it's not too hot
3 there isn't too much traffic
4 it isn't raining
5 I'm in a hurry
6 you have something else to do
7 you pay it back next week
8 you take risks

UNIT 116
116.1
2 I listened as she told me her story.
3 I burnt myself as I was taking a hot dish out of the oven.
4 The crowd cheered as the two teams came onto the field.
5 A dog ran out in front of the car as we were driving along the road.

116.2
2 As today is a public holiday, many of the shops are shut.
3 As I didn't want to disturb anybody, I was very quiet.
4 As I don't know what to do, I need some advice.
5 As none of us had a watch, we didn't know what time it was.

116.3
3 because
4 at the same time as
5 at the same time as
6 because
7 because

116.4
3 对
4 when I was in London
5 When I left school
6 对
7 when I was a child

116.5
参考答案：
1 I saw you as you were getting into your car.
2 It started to rain just as we started playing tennis.
3 As I didn't have enough money for a taxi, I had to walk home.
4 Just as I took the picture, somebody walked in front of the camera.

UNIT 117
117.1
3 like her mother
4 people like him
5 对
6 like most of his friends 或 as most of his friends are
7 like talking to the wall
8 对
9 对
10 对
11 like a bomb exploding
12 like a fish

117.2
2 like blocks of ice
3 like a beginner
4 as a tour guide
5 like a theatre
6 as a birthday present
7 like winter
8 like a child

117.3
2 like	11 like
3 as	12 as
4 like	13 as
5 like	14 Like
6 as 或 like	15 as
7 like	16 As
8 as	17 like
9 as	18 as 或 like
10 like 或 such as	

UNIT 118
118.1
2 You look like you've seen a ghost. / … like you saw a ghost.

3 You sound as if you're having a good time.
4 I feel like I've (just) run a marathon. / … like I (just) ran a marathon.

118.2

2 It looks like it's going to rain.
3 It sounds like they're having an argument.
4 It looks like there's been an accident.
5 It looks like we'll have to walk.
6 It sounds like you should see a doctor.

118.3

2 as if he meant what he said
3 as if she's hurt her leg / as if she hurt her leg
4 as if he hadn't eaten for a week
5 as if she was enjoying it
6 as if I'm going to be sick
7 as if she didn't want to come
8 as if I didn't exist

118.4

2 as if I was/were
3 as if she was/were
4 as if it was/were

UNIT 119

119.1

3	during	9	during
4	for	10	for
5	during	11	for
6	for	12	for
7	for	13	during
8	for	14	for

119.2

3	while	9	while
4	While	10	during
5	During	11	while
6	while	12	during
7	during	13	while
8	During	14	while

119.3

参考答案：

3 Nobody came to see me while I was in hospital.
4 Can you wait for me while I make a quick phone call?
5 Most of the students looked bored during the lesson.
6 I was asked a lot of questions during the interview.
7 Don't open the car door while the car is moving.
8 The lights suddenly went out while we were watching TV.
9 It started to rain during the game.
10 It started to rain while we were walking home.
11 What are you going to do while you're on holiday?

UNIT 120

120.1

2 I have to be at the airport by 8.30.
3 Let me know by Saturday whether you can come to the party.
4 Please make sure that you're here by 2 o'clock.
5 If we leave now, we should arrive by lunchtime.

120.2

2 by
3 by
4 until
5 until (5.30) … by (now)
6 by
7 until
8 by
9 by
10 until
11 By
12 by

120.3

参考答案：

3 until I come back
4 by 5 o'clock
5 by next Friday
6 until midnight

120.4

2 By the time I got to the station / By the time I'd got to the station
3 By the time I finished (my work) / By the time I'd finished (my work)
4 By the time the police arrived / By the time the police had arrived
5 By the time we got to the top (of the mountain) / By the time we'd got to the top (of the mountain)

UNIT 121

121.1

2 on
3 in
4 At 或 On
5 on 或 I last saw her Tuesday. *(no preposition)*
6 in
7 in
8 at
9 on 或 There are usually a lot of parties New Year's Eve. *(no preposition)*
10 at
11 in
12 at
13 on
14 in
15 **On** Saturday night 或 Saturday night *(no preposition)* … **at** midnight
16 **at** 5 o'clock **in** the morning
17 **on** 7 January … **in** April
18 at home **on** Tuesday morning 或 at home Tuesday morning *(no preposition)* … **in** the afternoon

121.2

2 at night
3 in the evening
4 on 21 July 1969
5 at the same time
6 in the 1920s
7 in about 20 minutes
8 at the moment
9 in the Middle Ages
10 in 11 seconds
11 **on** Saturdays 或 … works Saturdays *(no preposition)*

121.3

3 a
4 *both*
5 b
6 b
7 *both*
8 a
9 b
10 a

UNIT 122

122.1

2 on time
3 in time
4 on time
5 in time
6 on time
7 in time
8 in time
9 on time

122.2

2 I got home just in time.
3 I stopped him just in time.
4 We got to the cinema just in time for the beginning of the film. / … just in time to see the beginning of the film.

122.3

2 at the end of the month
3 at the end of the course
4 at the end of the race
5 at the end of the interview

122.4

2 In the end she resigned (from her job).
3 In the end I gave up (trying to learn German).

4 In the end we decided not to go (to the party). 或
In the end we didn't go (to the party).

122.5

2 In	6 at
3 at … at	7 in
4 in	8 at
5 in	9 in

UNIT 123

123.1

2 On his arm. 或
On the man's arm.
3 At the traffic lights.
4 a On the door.
b In the door.
5 On the wall.
6 In Paris.
7 a At the gate.
b On the gate.
8 On the beach.

123.2

2 on my guitar
3 at the next petrol station
4 in your coffee
5 on that tree
6 in the mountains
7 on the island
8 at the window

123.3

2 on
3 at
4 on
5 in
6 on
7 at
8 **in** a small village **in** the south-west
9 on
10 in
11 **on** the wall **in** the kitchen
12 at

UNIT 124

124.1

2 On the second floor.
3 At/On the corner.
4 In the corner.
5 At the top of the stairs.
6 In the back of the car.
7 At the front.
8 On the left.
9 In the back row.
10 On a farm.

124.2

2 on the right
3 in the world
4 on the way to work
5 on the west coast
6 in the front row
7 at the back of the class
6 on the back of this card

124.3

2 in	9 in
3 in	10 on
4 at	11 in
5 in	12 on
6 on	13 in
7 At	14 on … on
8 in	

UNIT 125

125.1

2 on a train
3 at a conference
4 in hospital / in the hospital
5 at the hairdresser's
6 on his bike
7 in New York
8 at the Savoy Theatre

125.2

2 in a taxi
3 at the cinema
4 in prison
5 at school
6 at the sports centre
7 in hospital
8 at the airport
9 on the plane
10 in Tokyo

125.3

2 at
3 in
4 at
5 **at/in** a very comfortable hotel … **in** Amsterdam
6 in
7 on
8 at
9 in
10 at
11 in
12 **at** home 或 **be home** *(no preposition)* … **at** work
13 in
14 **in** Birmingham … **at** Birmingham University

UNIT 126

126.1

3 at
4 to
5 to
6 into
7 in
8 to
9 into
10 to
11 at
12 to
13 into
14 to
15 get home *(no preposition)* … going **to** bed
16 returned **to** France … two years **in** Brazil
17 born **in** Chicago … moved **to** New York … lives **in** New York

126.2

参考答案：
2–4
- I've been to Sweden once.
- I've never been to the United States.
- I've been to Paris a few times.

126.3

2 in
3 – (no preposition)
4 at
5 to
6 – (no preposition)

126.4

2 I got on
3 I got out of the car. / … my car.
4 I got off the train.
5 I got into the taxi. 或 I got in the taxi.
6 I got off the plane.

UNIT 127

127.1

2 in cold weather
3 in pencil
4 in love
5 in capital letters
6 in the shade
7 in my opinion

127.2

2 on strike
3 on a tour
4 on TV
5 on purpose
6 on a diet
7 on business
8 on holiday
9 on the phone
10 on the whole

127.3

2 on
3 on
4 at
5 in
6 on
7 in
8 on
9 at

10 at
11 on
12 **In** my opinion … **on** television
13 on
14 on
15 on
16 at
17 on
18 in

UNIT 128

128.1
2 by mistake
3 by hand
4 by credit card
5 by canal

128.2
2 on
3 by
4 **by** car … **on** my bike
5 in
6 on
7 by

128.3
2 travelling **by** bus 或 travelling **on** the bus 或 travelling **on buses**
3 taken **with** a very good camera
4 this music is **by** Beethoven
5 **pay cash** 或 pay **in** cash
6 a mistake **by** one of our players

128.4
参考答案：
3–5
- *Ulysses* is a novel by James Joyce.
- *Yesterday* is a song by Paul McCartney.
- *Guernica* is a painting by Pablo Picasso.

128.5
2 by
3 with
4 by
5 by
6 **by** car … **in** your car
7 **by** the bed **with** a lamp and a clock **on** it

128.6
2 The price has gone up by ten pence.
3 Helen won by two votes.
4 I missed her/Kate by five minutes.

UNIT 129

129.1
2 to the problem
3 with her brother
4 in the cost of living
5 to your question
6 for a new road
7 in 或 to working at home
8 in the number of people without jobs
9 for shoes like these any more
10 between your job and mine

129.2
2 invitation to
3 contact with
4 key to (key for *is also possible*)
5 cause of
6 reply to
7 connection between
8 photographs of
9 reason for
10 damage to

129.3
2 to
3 in
4 of
5 in 或 to
6 for
7 to 或 towards
8 with
9 in
10 to
11 of
12 **for** a rise **in** pay
13 to
14 with

UNIT 130

130.1
2 That was nice of him.
3 That was generous of her.
4 That wasn't very nice of them.
5 That's very kind of you.
6 That isn't very polite of him.
7 That's a bit childish of them.

130.2
2 kind to
3 angry with
4 excited about
5 impressed by / impressed with
6 bored with (bored by *is also possible*)
7 amazed at / amazed by
8 careless of

130.3
2 of
3 to
4 with
5 with (by 或 in *are also possible*)
6 to
7 at/by
8 with
9 about
10 about
11 for
12 about/by/at
13 to
14 of
15 by/with
16 about
17 at/by
18 about
19 **with** us **for** making
20 sorry **for/about** … angry **with**

UNIT 131

131.1
2 similar to
3 afraid of
4 interested in
5 responsible for
6 proud of
7 different from / different to (different than *is also possible*)
8 capable of

131.2
2 of furniture
3 on sport
4 of time
5 at tennis
6 to a Russian / to a Russian man / to a Russian guy
7 of him / of Robert
8 from yours / to yours 或 from your problem / to your problem

131.3
2 for
3 of
4 of
5 in
6 of 或 about
7 of … of
8 on
9 of
10 with
11 of
12 in
13 of
14 of
15 at
16 of
17 on
18 of

131.4
参考答案：
2 I'm hopeless at telling jokes.
3 I'm not very good at maths.
4 I'm pretty good at remembering names.
5 I'm good at sport.

UNIT 132

132.1
2 a

3 b
4 b
5 a
6 a
7 b
8 a
9 b
10 b
11 a
12 b

132.2
3 speak to
4 point (them) at
5 look at
6 listen to
7 throw (stones) at
8 throw (it) to
9 reply to

132.3
2 at
3 at
4 to
5 to
6 at
7 at
8 to
9 at
10 at
11 to

UNIT 133

133.1
2 for
3 for
4 to
5 for
6 about
7 – *(no preposition)*
8 about
9 – *(no preposition)*
10 for
11 for
12 about
13 for
14 for

133.2
2 of
3 about
4 for
5 of
6 for
7 about
8 – *(no preposition)*

133.3
2 looking for
3 looked after
4 looking for
5 look for
6 looks after

133.4
2 wait for
3 talk about
4 asked (the waiter) for
5 applied for
6 do (something) about
7 looks after 或 has looked after
8 left (Boston) for

UNIT 134

134.1
2 hear about
3 heard from
4 heard of
5 hear from
6 hear about
7 heard of

134.2
2 think about
3 think of
4 think of
5 thinking of/about
6 think of
7 thought about
8 think (much) of
9 thinking about/of
10 think of

134.3
2 about
3 to … about
4 of
5 of
6 about … about … about … about
7 of
8 about
9 about/of

134.4
2 complaining about
3 think about
4 warn (you) about
5 heard of
6 dream of
7 reminded (me) about
8 remind (you) of

UNIT 135

135.1
2 for
3 of
4 of
5 – *(no preposition)*
6 for
7 of
8 for
9 of
10 for
11 on

135.2
2 for the misunderstanding
3 her/Jane on winning the tournament
4 him from his enemies
5 of eleven players
6 on bread and eggs
7 me for your problems / your problems on me

135.3
2 paid for
3 accused of
4 depends on
5 live on
6 apologise to
7 suffers from
8 congratulated (him) on

135.4
2 from
3 on
4 – *(no preposition)*
5 from
6 depends how *(no preposition)* 或 depends **on** how
7 on
8 of
9 on

UNIT 136

136.1
2 happened to
3 invited to
4 divided into
5 believe in
6 fill (it) with
7 drove into
8 Concentrate on
9 succeeded in

136.2
2 I prefer small towns to big cities
3 Jane provided me with all the information I needed
4 This morning I spent £70 on a pair of shoes
5 The city is divided into ten districts

136.3
2 to
3 on
4 in
5 to
6 in
7 with
8 into
9 in
10 on
11 – *(no preposition)*
12 into
13 on
14 into
15 with
16 **from** (one language) **into** another

136.4

参考答案：

2 on petrol
3 into a wall
4 to volleyball
5 in seafood
6 into many languages

UNIT 137

137.1

2 sit down
3 flew away
4 get out
5 speak up
6 get by
7 gone up
8 looked round

137.2

2 back at
3 up to
4 forward to
5 away with
6 up at
7 in through

137.3

2 wake me up
3 get it out
4 give them back
5 switch it on
6 take them off

137.4

3 I have to take **them back**
4 We can turn **the television off**
或 We can turn **off the television**
5 I knocked **it over**
6 I don't want to wake **her up**
7 *(example answer)* You should put **your coat on** 或
You should put **on your coat**
8 I was able to put **it out**
9 *(example answer)* they've put **the price(s) up** 或
they've put **up the price(s)**
10 Shall I turn **the light**(s) **on**? 或
Shall I turn **on the light**(s)?

UNIT 138

138.1

2 eats
3 moved
4 drop
5 checked
6 cut
7 plug
8 filling / to fill
9 left
10 dive
11 rub/cross
12 dropped

138.2

2 into
3 in
4 out
5 into
6 out of

138.3

2 dropped out
3 moved in
4 left out
5 joined in
6 eating out 或 to eat out
7 taken in
8 dropped in
9 get out of

138.4

2 Fill them in 或 Fill them out
3 cross it out
4 took me in
5 let us in

UNIT 139

139.1

2 a mistake
3 a candle
4 an order
5 a cigarette / a candle
6 a new product
7 a mess

139.2

2 works out
3 carried out
4 ran out
5 sort out / work out
6 find out
7 tried out
8 pointed out
9 work out
10 went out
11 turned out
12 works out / turns out
13 find out
14 put out

139.3

2 giving out / handing out
3 turned out nice/fine/sunny
4 working out
5 fallen out
6 work out how to use the camera / her new camera

139.4

2 try it out
3 work it out
4 sorted it out / worked it out

UNIT 140

140.1

2 put the heating on
3 put the oven on
4 put the kettle on
5 put a CD on

140.2

2 going on
3 take off
4 switched off / turned off
5 drove off / went off
6 put on
7 set off / be off
8 put off
9 called off
10 put on
11 see (me) off

140.3

2 took off
3 tried on a/the hat 或
tried a/the hat on
4 was called off
5 see him off
6 put them on

UNIT 141

141.1

2 went on / carried on
3 walked on / carried on 或
carried on walking
4 dozed off / dropped off / nodded off
5 go on / carry on / keep on
6 went off
7 keeps on phoning me

141.2

2 went off
3 finish off
4 drive on / carry on
5 ripped off
6 getting on
7 dozed off / dropped off / nodded off
8 told off
9 get on
10 going off
11 keep on
12 get on
13 showing off
14 put off

141.3

2 finish it off
3 were ripped off
4 go off
5 did you get on
6 carried on (playing) / went on (playing)
7 tell them off
8 doesn't get on (well) with

UNIT 142

142.1

2 took them down
3 stand up
4 turned it up
5 put their bags down
6 were blown down / fell down
7 put them up
8 bent down (and) picked them up

142.2

2 turn it down
3 calm him down
4 wrote it down
5 let her down
6 turned it down

142.3

2 calm down
3 slowed down
4 was turned down
5 broken down
6 cut down
7 let down
8 (has) closed down
9 be knocked down （或 be pulled down 或 be torn down)
10 turned down
11 was knocked down
12 broke down

UNIT 143

143.1

2 went up to / walked up to
3 catch up with
4 keep up with

143.2

2 used up
3 washed up
4 grow up
5 turn up / show up
6 gave up
7 taking up
8 give up
9 ended up
10 takes up
11 make up

143.3

3 tidy it up / tidy up
4 fixed it up
5 keep up with
6 was brought up
7 keep it up
8 went up to
9 was made up of
10 set it up / fix it up

UNIT 144

144.1

2 d
3 e
4 c
5 g
6 a
7 b

144.2

2 held up
3 did it up
4 cheer him up

144.3

2 blew up
3 beaten up
4 broken up / split up
5 do up
6 clears up / will clear up
7 mixed up

144.4

2 look it up
3 put up with
4 made it up
5 come up with
6 tear it up
7 saving up for

UNIT 145

145.1

2 blew away
3 put it back
4 walked away
5 threw it back (to her)
6 threw them away

145.2

2 be away / have gone away
3 be back
4 ran away
5 smile back
6 get away
7 Keep away / Keep back

145.3

2 Pay
3 throw
4 gets
5 be
6 look
7 gave
8 get

145.4

2 throw it away
3 take them back
4 pay you back / pay it back
5 gave them away
6 call back / call me back

1

3 I'm getting / I am getting
4 do you do
5 we arrived … it was raining
6 phones … she didn't phone
7 you were thinking … I decided
8 are you looking
9 It doesn't rain
10 rang … I was getting
11 we went … she was preparing … We didn't want … we didn't stay
12 told … he didn't believe … He thought … I was joking

2

2 didn't go
3 is wearing
4 went
5 haven't heard
6 is being
7 wasn't reading
8 didn't have
9 It's beginning
10 got
11 wasn't
12 you've been
13 I've been doing
14 did she go
15 I've been playing
16 do you come
17 since I saw her
18 for 20 years

3

3 are you going
4 Do you watch
5 have you lived / have you been living / have you been
6 Did you have
7 Have you seen
8 was she wearing
9 Have you been waiting / Have you been here
10 does it take
11 Have you ridden / Have you ridden on / Have you been on
12 Have you (ever) been

4

2 've known each other / have known each other 或 've been friends / have been friends
3 I've ever had / I've ever been on / I've had for ages (*etc.*)
4 He went / He went home / He went out / He left
5 I've worn it
6 I was playing
7 been swimming for
8 since I (last) went
9 did you buy / did you get

5

1 got … was already waiting … had arrived
2 was lying … wasn't watching … 'd fallen / had fallen … was snoring … turned … woke
3 'd just gone / had just gone … was reading … heard … got … didn't see … went
4 missed … was standing … realised … 'd left / had left … had … got
5 met … was walking … 'd been / had been … 'd been playing / had been playing … were going … invited … 'd arranged / had arranged … didn't have

6

2 Somebody has taken it.
3 They'd only known / They had only known each other (for) a few weeks.
4 It's been raining / It has been raining all day. 或 It's rained / It has rained all day.
5 I'd been dreaming. / I had been dreaming.
6 I'd had / I had had a big breakfast.
7 They've been going / They have been going there for years.
8 I've had it / I have had it since I got up.
9 He's been training / He has been training very hard for it.

7

1 I haven't seen
2 You look / You're looking
3 are you going
4 are you meeting
5 I'm going
6 Do you often go
7 are you going
8 I'm meeting
9 has been
10 I've been waiting
11 has just started / just started
12 is she getting
13 Does she like
14 she thinks
15 Are you working
16 spoke
17 you were working
18 went
19 I started / I'd started
20 I lost
21 you haven't had
22 I've had
23 have you seen
24 has he been
25 I saw
26 he went
27 He'd been
28 he decided / he'd decided
29 He was really looking forward
30 is he doing
31 I haven't heard
32 he left

8

1 invented
2 it's gone / it has gone
3 had gone … left
4 did you do … Did you go
5 have you had
6 was looking 或 'd been looking / had been looking
7 She's been teaching / She has been teaching
8 I bought … I haven't worn 或 I didn't wear
9 I saw … was … I'd seen / I had seen … I remembered … it was
10 Have you heard … She was … died … She wrote … Have you read
11 does this word mean … I've never seen
12 Did you get … it had already started
13 knocked … was … she'd gone / she had gone … she didn't want
14 He'd never used / He had never used … he didn't know
15 went … She needed 或 She'd needed / She had needed … she'd been sitting / she had been sitting

9

3 used to drive
4 was driving
5 were working
6 used to have
7 was living
8 was playing
9 used to play
10 was wearing

10

2 I'm going to the dentist.
3 No, we're going to hire a car.
4 I'll look after the children.
5 I'm having lunch with Sue.
6 What are you going to have? / What are you having?
7 I'll turn on the light.
8 I'm going to turn on the light.

11

2 I'll come
3 shall we meet
4 starts

5 I'll meet
6 I'm seeing
7 Shall I ask
8 I'll see
9 are going
10 does the film start
11 Are you meeting
12 I'll be

12

1 (2) Are you going to do / Are you doing
(3) it starts
(4) you'll enjoy / you're going to enjoy
(5) it will be / it's going to be
2 (1) you're going
(2) We're going
(3) you have
(4) I'll send
(5) I'll get
(6) I get
3 (1) I'm having / I'm going to have
(2) are coming
(3) they'll have left
(4) they're
(5) I won't be / I will not be
(6) you know
(7) I'll call
4 (1) shall we meet
(2) I'll be waiting
(3) you arrive
(4) I'll be sitting
(5) I'll be wearing
(6) Is Agent 307 coming / Is Agent 307 going to come / Will Agent 307 be coming
(7) Shall I bring
(8) I'll explain / I'm going to explain
(9) I see
(10) I'll try

13

1 I'll have
2 Are you going
3 shall I phone
4 It's going to land
5 it's / it is
6 I'll miss / I'm going to miss … you go / you've gone
7 Shall I give … I give … will you call
8 does it end
9 I'm going … is getting
10 I'll tell … I'm … I won't be
11 I'm going to have / I'm having
12 she apologises
13 we'll be living / we'll live
14 you finish / you've finished

14

2 I've had / I have had
3 I bought 或 I got
4 I'll come / I will come 或 I'll be / I will be
5 I've been / I have been 或 I've eaten / I have eaten
6 I used to play
7 I haven't been waiting 或 I haven't been here
8 I'd been / I had been 或 I was
9 I'm going / I am going
10 I haven't seen 或 I haven't heard from
11 I'll have gone / I will have gone 或 I'll have left / I will have left

15

2 I've been travelling
3 I'm beginning
4 I've seen
5 has been
6 I've met
7 I left
8 I stayed 或 I was staying
9 I'd planned 或 I was planning
10 I ended up
11 I enjoyed
12 I took
13 met
14 I'm staying 或 I'm going to stay 或 I'll be staying 或 I'll stay
15 I continue
16 I'll get
17 I'm
18 I'll let
19 I know
20 I'm staying
21 we're going to visit 或 we're visiting
22 are building 或 have been building
23 it will be
24 I'll be

16

2 A
3 C
4 B 或 C
5 B
6 A 或 C
7 A 或 C
8 C
9 B 或 C
10 A 或 B
11 A
12 C
13 A 或 B
14 B 或 C
15 B

17

2 shouldn't have eaten
3 must have forgotten
4 needn't have gone
5 can't be changed
6 may be watching
7 must have been waiting
8 couldn't have done
9 ought to have been
10 would have helped
11 should have been warned
12 might not have been feeling / might not have felt

18

3 could rain / might rain
4 might have gone / could have gone
5 couldn't go
6 couldn't have seen / can't have seen
7 should get
8 wouldn't recognise / might not recognise
9 must have heard
10 should have turned

19

4 rings
5 you were
6 it's / it is
7 it was / it were
8 it had been
9 you had
10 we hadn't had
11 you'd driven / you had driven 或 you'd been driving / you had been driving
12 I didn't read

20

2 came
3 I'd known / I had known … wouldn't have disturbed
4 They'd be / They would be … told
5 hadn't frightened … wouldn't have attacked
6 wouldn't have got / wouldn't have gotten … I'd had / I had had
7 hadn't been / hadn't got / hadn't gotten … wouldn't have failed 或 would have passed / 'd have passed

21

参考答案：
1 I wasn't feeling so tired
2 I hadn't had so much to do
3 I would have forgotten Jane's birthday
4 I'd take a picture of you
5 I'll take a picture of you
6 you were in trouble
7 you hadn't taken so long to get ready
8 I would have gone to the concert
9 I might have got the job
10 you'd eaten lunch
11 there was less traffic
12 people would go out more

22

3 was cancelled
4 has been repaired
5 is being restored
6 It's believed / It is believed
7 I'd be sacked / I would be sacked
8 It might have been thrown

9 I was taught
10 being arrested / having been arrested 或 I was arrested
11 Have you ever been arrested
12 are reported … have been injured

23

3 've sold / have sold 或 sold
4 's been sold / has been sold 或 was sold
5 are made
6 might be stolen
7 must have been stolen
8 must have taken
9 can be solved
10 should have left
11 is delayed
12 is being built … is expected

24

Castle Fire
2 was discovered
3 was injured
4 be rescued
5 are believed to have been destroyed
6 is not known

Shop robbery
1 was forced
2 being threatened
3 had been stolen
4 was later found
5 had been abandoned
6 has been arrested / was arrested
7 is still being questioned

Road delays
1 is being resurfaced
2 are asked / are being asked / have been asked
3 is expected
4 will be closed / is going to be closed
5 will be diverted / is going to be diverted

Accident
1 was taken
2 was allowed
3 was blocked
4 be diverted
5 have been killed

25

1 I told **her (that) Paul had gone out** and **I didn't know when he'd be back**.
I asked **(her) if/whether she wanted to leave a message**, but she said **(that) she'd try again** later.
2 I had reserved a hotel room, but when I got to the hotel they told **me (that) they had no record of a reservation in my name**.
When I asked **(them) if/whether they had any rooms free anyway**, they said **(that) they were sorry**, but **the hotel was full**.
3 The immigration official asked us **why we were visiting the country**, and we told **him(that) we were on holiday**.
Then he wanted to know **how long we intended to stay** and **where we would be staying during our visit**.
4 She said **(that) she'd phone (us) from the airport when she arrived**. 或 She said **(that) she'll phone (us) from the airport when she arrives**.
No, she said **not to come to the airport**.
She said **(that) she'd take the bus**. 或 She said **(that) she'll take the bus**.
5 He wanted to know **what my job was** and asked **(me) how much I earned**. 或
He wanted to know **what my job is** and asked **(me) how much I earn**.
… so I told **him to mind his own business** and I put the phone down.
6 He said **(that) he'd be at the restaurant at 7.30**.
He said **(that) he knew where the restaurant was**. And I told **him to phone me if there was any problem**.
7 You just said **(that) you weren't hungry**.
But you said **(that) you didn't like bananas**. You told **me not to buy any**.

26

3 changing
4 to change
5 change
6 being
7 saying
8 to call
9 drinking
10 to be
11 to see
12 to be
13 to think … making
14 living … to move
15 to be … playing
16 being stopped … stealing … driving
17 work … pressing

27

3 I don't fancy going out.
4 He tends to forget things.
5 Would you mind helping me? / Do you mind helping me?
6 Everybody seems to have gone out.
7 We're / We are thinking of moving.
8 I was afraid to touch it.
9 He's / He is afraid of being robbed.
10 It's / It is not worth seeing.
11 I'm not used to walking so far.
12 She seems to be enjoying herself.
13 He insisted on showing them to me.
14 I'd rather somebody else did it.

28

3 I've given up reading newspapers.
4 I'd rather not go out tonight / … stay at home tonight.
5 He has trouble sleeping at night.
6 Do you want me to phone you this evening?
7 I came in without anybody/anyone seeing me / … without being seen.
8 I was accused of being a cheat / … of cheating.
9 I'm looking forward to seeing them again.
10 What do you advise me to do?
11 I'd like to have gone out with you last night.
12 I regret not taking your advice / … that I didn't take your advice.

29

2 a foreign country … the language
3 an economist … in the United States … for an investment company
4 I love sport, especially tennis … two or three times a week … not a very good player
5 for dinner … after work … to the cinema
6 When unemployment is … for people to find work … a big problem
7 an accident … going home … taken to hospital / taken to the hospital … I think most accidents … by people driving
8 the name of the hotel … The Ambassador … in Queen Street in the city centre … near the station
9 The older one … a pilot with British Airways … The younger one … at school … he leaves school … go to university … study law

30

2 B
3 C
4 A 或 B
5 C
6 B
7 A 或 C
8 A
9 C
10 B 或 C
11 B

12 A
13 A 或 B
14 B

31

3 It's the most polluted place …
4 I was disappointed that …
5 *OK*
6 Joe works hard, but …
7 … in a large modern building.
8 *OK* (as fast as he can *is also correct*)
9 I missed the last three days …
10 *OK*
11 The weather has been unusually cold …
12 The water in the pool was too dirty to swim in.
13 … to wait such a long time. 或 … to wait so long.
14 *OK*
15 … I got up earlier than usual.

32

2 If
3 when
4 if
5 when
6 if
7 if
8 unless
9 if
10 as long as
11 in case
12 in case
13 if
14 even if
15 Although
16 Although
17 When
18 when

33

2 on
3 **at** 9.30 **on** Tuesday morning
4 at / on
5 on
6 at
7 In
8 at
9 during
10 **on** Friday … **since** then
11 for
12 at
13 **at** the moment … **until** Friday
14 by
15 in

34

1 in
2 by
3 at
4 on
5 in
6 on
7 **to** a party **at** Lisa's house
8 on
9 on
10 to … to
11 **in** Vienna … **at** the age of 35
12 **in** this photo … **on** the left
13 **to** the theatre … **in** the front row
14 **on** the wall … **by** the door / **next to** the door / **beside** the door
15 at
16 on
17 **in** a tower block … **on** the fifteenth floor
18 on
19 by
20 **on** the bus … **by** car
21 on … on
22 in
23 **in** Chicago … **to** Italy
24 to
25 on

35

1 for
2 at
3 to
4 to
5 in
6 with
7 of
8 to
9 of
10 at/by
11 of
12 about

36

1 of
2 after
3 – (no preposition)
4 about
5 to
6 – (no preposition)
7 into
8 of (about *is also possible*)
9 to
10 – (no preposition)
11 on
12 of
13 of
14 – (no preposition)
15 in
16 at (about *is also possible*)
17 on
18 If Alex asks you **for** money
19 I apologised **to** Sarah **for** keeping …
20 I thanked her **for** everything

37

2 h
3 e
4 g
5 a
6 k
7 c
8 j
9 b
10 f
11 i

38

2 D
3 B
4 B
5 A
6 A
7 D
8 C
9 C
10 B
11 A
12 D

39

2 out to
3 up with
4 forward to
5 up with
6 out of
7 on with
8 out with
9 up with
10 back on
11 out about
12 on with

40

3 went off
4 turned up / showed up
5 fill it in / fill it out
6 knocked down / pulled down / torn down
7 sorted out
8 give up
9 dozed off / dropped off / nodded off
10 split up / break up
11 put up with it
12 get by / live on
13 went on
14 put it off

41

2 put
3 moving
4 put
5 done
6 turned / turns
7 find
8 Calm
9 set
10 held
11 left / 've left / have left 或 missed / 've missed / have missed
12 works
13 join
14 works
15 drop / call
16 sort / work
17 **went** off … **woke** me up

现在时与过去时比较

1.1	A
1.2	B
1.3	C
1.4	B, C
1.5	C
1.6	A

现在完成时与一般过去时比较

2.1	B
2.2	C
2.3	A
2.4	C
2.5	A
2.6	B
2.7	A
2.8	D
2.9	A
2.10	A
2.11	C
2.12	A
2.13	C
2.14	C
2.15	D
2.16	C

将来时

3.1	B
3.2	A
3.3	C
3.4	A, C
3.5	B
3.6	C
3.7	A

情态动词

4.1	A, B
4.2	B
4.3	A, C, D
4.4	C
4.5	B
4.6	C, D
4.7	B
4.8	A, C
4.9	B, C
4.10	A, B, D
4.11	A
4.12	D, E
4.13	A

条件句与 wish

5.1	B
5.2	C
5.3	B
5.4	D
5.5	A

被动语态

6.1	C
6.2	B
6.3	D
6.4	A
6.5	A, B
6.6	C
6.7	D

间接引语

7.1	A
7.2	B
7.3	A

疑问句与助动词

8.1	C
8.2	A
8.3	D
8.4	A
8.5	B

动词的 -ing 形式与不定式比较

9.1	A
9.2	B, D
9.3	B
9.4	A
9.5	A
9.6	A
9.7	C
9.8	D
9.9	C
9.10	C
9.11	B
9.12	C, D
9.13	B, D
9.14	B
9.15	A, B
9.16	A
9.17	A
9.18	B, C

冠词与名词

10.1	B
10.2	A
10.3	B, C
10.4	B
10.5	C
10.6	A
10.7	A
10.8	A
10.9	D
10.10	C
10.11	C
10.12	A
10.13	C
10.14	B

代词与限定词

11.1	A
11.2	B
11.3	D
11.4	B
11.5	B
11.6	C
11.7	A, C
11.8	C
11.9	D
11.10	A, C
11.11	B

定语从句

12.1	A, C
12.2	A, B
12.3	C
12.4	B
12.5	D
12.6	B, C

形容词与副词比较

13.1	B
13.2	C
13.3	B, C
13.4	A
13.5	A, D
13.6	B
13.7	B, C
13.8	C
13.9	C
13.10	B, C
13.11	D
13.12	A, B
13.13	B
13.14	D
13.15	D

虚拟语气与介词

14.1	A, D
14.2	C
14.3	B, C
14.4	B, D
14.5	B
14.6	D
14.7	B, C
14.8	A

介词

15.1	B, D
15.2	A
15.3	C
15.4	B
15.5	A
15.6	B, D
15.7	B
15.8	B
15.9	C
15.10	C
15.11	C
15.12	A
15.13	C
15.14	B
15.15	D
15.16	D
15.17	A

短语动词

16.1	B
16.2	A
16.3	D
16.4	C
16.5	C
16.6	B
16.7	A
16.8	A, D
16.9	B

索引

本索引中的数字指单元号而不是页码。